PB-PH

Modern European Languages

Library of Congress Classification
2009

LIBRARY OF CONGRESS

Prepared by the Policy and Standards Division

LIBRARY OF CONGRESS
Cataloging Distribution Service
Washington, D.C.

This edition cumulates all additions and changes to subclasses PB-PH through Weekly List 2009/31, dated August 5, 2009. Additions and changes made subsequent to that date are published in weekly lists posted on the World Wide Web at

<http://www.loc.gov/aba/cataloging/classification/weeklylists/>

and are also available in *Classification Web*, the online Web-based edition of the Library of Congress Classification.

Library of Congress Cataloging-in-Publication Data

Library of Congress.
Library of Congress classification. PB-PH. Modern European languages / prepared by the Policy and Standards Division. — 2009 ed.
p. cm.
"This edition cumulates all additions and changes to subclasses PB-PH through Weekly list 2009/31, dated August 5, 2009. Additions and changes made subsequent to that date are published in weekly lists posted on the World Wide Web ... and are also available in Classification Web, the online Web-based edition of the Library of Congress classification" — T.p. verso.
Includes index.
ISBN: 978-0-8444-9505-7
1. Classification, Library of Congress. 2. Classification—Books—Philology, Modern. 3. Classification—Books—Languages, Modern. I. Library of Congress. Policy and Standards Division. II. Title. III. Title: Modern European languages.
Z696.U5P63 2009 025.4'64—dc22 2009035706

For sale by the Library of Congress Cataloging Distribution Service,
101 Independence Avenue, S.E., Washington, DC 20541-4912.
Product catalog available on the Web at **www.loc.gov/cds**.

PREFACE

Class P: Subclasses PB-PH, *Modern European Languages*, was originally published in 1933 and was reprinted in 1966 with supplementary pages of additions and changes. PG2900-PG3698 (Russian Literature) was published as a separate schedule in 1948 and was reprinted in 1965 with supplementary pages of additions and changes. Beginning with the 1999 edition, the Russian literature numbers were incorporated into the main text. A 2005 edition cumulated all additions and changes that were made during the period 1999- 2005. This 2009 edition cumulates changes made since the 2005 edition was published. It includes all modern European languages as well as all modern European literatures except those classed in PQ, PR, and PT. Individual authors and titles in subclass PG now include Cyrillic characters in addition to the Romanized forms of names. These Cyrillic characters were provided by Lucas Graves, of the staff of the Policy and Standards Division.

In the Library of Congress classification schedules, classification numbers or spans of numbers that appear in parentheses are formerly valid numbers that are now obsolete. Numbers or spans that appear in angle brackets are optional numbers that have never been used at the Library of Congress but are provided for other libraries that wish to use them. In most cases, a parenthesized or angle-bracketed number is accompanied by a "see" reference directing the user to the actual number that the Library of Congress currently uses, or a note explaining Library of Congress practice.

Access to the online version of the full Library of Congress Classification is available on the World Wide Web by subscription to *Classification Web*. Details about ordering and pricing may be obtained from the Cataloging Distribution Service at

<http://www.loc.gov/cds/>

New or revised numbers and captions are added to the L.C. Classification schedules as a result of development proposals made by the cataloging staff of the Library of Congress and cooperating institutions. Upon approval of these proposals by the weekly editorial meeting of the Policy and Standards Division, new classification records are created or existing records are revised in the master classification database. Weekly lists of newly approved or revised classification numbers and captions are posted on the World Wide Web at

<http://www.loc.gov/aba/cataloging/classification/weeklylists/>

Janis Young, cataloging policy specialist in the Policy and Standards Division, is responsible for coordinating the overall intellectual and editorial content of class P and its various subclasses. Kent Griffiths, assistant editor of classification schedules, is responsible for creating new classification records, maintaining the master database, and creating index terms for the captions.

Barbara B. Tillett, Chief
Policy and Standards Division

August 2009

PB1-3029	Modern languages. Celtic languages
PB1-431	Modern languages
PB1001-3029	Celtic languages and literature
PB1101-1200	Goidelic. Gaelic
PB1201-1449	Irish
PB1501-1709	Gaelic (Scottish Gaelic, Erse)
PB1801-1867	Manx
PB1950	Pict
PB2001-3029	Brittanic group
PB2101-2499	Welsh. Cymric
PB2501-2621	Cornish
PB2801-2932	Breton. Armorican
PB3001-3029	Gaulish
PC1-5498	Romance
PC1-400	General
PC601-872	Romanian
PC901-986	Raeto-Romance Including Romansh
PC1001-1977	Italian
PC1981-1984	Sardinian
PC2001-3761	French
PC2700-(3708)	Dialects. Provincialisms
PC2813-(2898)	Old French
PC3201-3366	Provencal (Old)
PC3371-3420.5	Modern patois of South France
PC3420.8-3495	Langue d'oc dialects
PC3721-3761	Slang. Argot
PC3801-3976	Catalan
PC4001-4977	Spanish
PC5001-5498	Portuguese
PD1-(7159)	Germanic
PD1-780	General
PD1001-1350	Old Germanic dialects
PD1101-1211	Gothic
PD1501-(7159)	North Germanic. Scandinavian
PD2201-2393	Old Norse. Old Icelandic and Old Norwegian
PD2401-2446	Modern Icelandic
PD(2501)-2999	Norwegian
PD3001-3929	Danish
PD5001-5929	Swedish

OUTLINE

	Slavic. Baltic. Albanian
	Slavic
	Russian literature
	History and criticism - Continued
PG(3100)-(3155)	Folk literature
	Including texts
PG3199-3299	Collections
PG3199-3205	General
PG(3211)-3219	Translations
PG3223-3229.2	Special periods
PG3230-3238	Poetry
PG3240-3255	Drama
PG3260-3299	Prose
PG3300-3493.96	Individual authors and works
PG3300-3308	Early to 1700
PG3310-3319	18th century
PG3312	Derzhavin
PG3314	Karamzin
PG3316	Lomonosov
PG3318	Sumarokov
PG3320-3447	1800-1870
PG3325-3328	Dostoyevsky
PG3332-3335	Gogol'
PG3340-3359	Pushkin
PG3365-3417	Tolstoi
PG3420-3445	Turgenev
PG3450-3470	1870-1917
PG3452	Andreev
PG3455-3458	Chekhov
PG3462-3465	Gorky
PG3475-3476	1917-1960
PG3477-3490	1961-2000
PG3491.2-3493.96	2001-
PG3500-3505	Provincial, local, etc.
PG3515-3550	Outside the Russian Federation
PG(3651)-(3698)	Special subjects
PG3801-3987	Ukrainian
PG3990	Carpatho-Rusyn
PG4001-5146	Czech
PG5201-5546	Slovak
PG5631-5689	Sorbian (Wendic)
PG6001-7446	Polish
PG7900-7925	Lechitic dialects

OUTLINE

Modern languages. Celtic languages

1-431 Modern languages (Table P-PZ2 modified)

Class here works dealing with all or with several of the languages spoken in western Europe (notably English, French, German)

For groups of European languages and individual European languages see PA1000+ ; PB1001+ ; and subclasses PC-PH

For Asian, African, and other languages see subclasses PJ-PM

Periodicals. Serials

1 English and American

2 French

3 German

4 Italian

5 Other (including polyglot)

Societies

6.A1 International

6.A2-Z English and American

7 French

8 German

9 Italian

10 Other (including polyglot)

11 Congresses

Collections

12 Texts. Sources, etc.

Celtic (General)

1001-1013 Celtic philology (Table P-PZ4a modified)

History of philology

Cf. PB1015 History of the languages

1007 General works

Biography, memoirs, etc.

1009.A2 Collective

1009.A5-Z Individual, A-Z

Subarrange each by Table P-PZ50

1014-1093 Celtic languages (Table P-PZ4b modified)

Add number in table to PB1000

Class here works dealing with all or with several of the Celtic languages specified in PB1100+

1015.5 Proto-Celtic languages

(1017.5) Script (Ogham)

see PB1217

Etymology

1083.5 Dictionaries (exclusively etymological)

Lexicography

For biography of lexicographers see PB1009.A2+

1087 Treatises. Collections

Including periodicals devoted exclusively to lexicography

1089 Dictionaries

For etymological dictionaries see PB1083.5

Celtic (General)
Celtic languages -- Continued
Linguistic geography
1093 General works
(1095) Atlases. Maps
see class G
Celtic literature
History and criticism
Generalities: Periodicals. Societies, etc. see PB1001+
Treatises
1096 General
1097 Special
Texts (Collections)
1098 General
1099 Special
1100 Translations. Adaptations
Goidelic. Gaelic. (Irish, Scottish Gaelic, and Manx)
1101-1113 Philology (Table P-PZ4a modified)
History of philology
Cf. PB1115 History of the language
1107 General works
Biography, memoirs, etc.
1109.A2 Collective
1109.A5-Z Individual, A-Z
Subarrange each by Table P-PZ50
1114-1193 Language (Table P-PZ4b modified)
Add number in table to PB1100
Class here works dealing with the Goidelic languages collectively
Style. Composition. Rhetoric
For study and teaching see PB1111
1175 General works
Etymology
1183.5 Dictionaries (exclusively etymological)
Lexicography
For biography of lexicographers see PB1109.A2+
1187 Treatises. Collections
Including periodicals devoted exclusively to lexicography
1189 Dictionaries
For etymological dictionaries see PB1183.5
Linguistic geography
1193 General works
(1195) Atlases. Maps
see class G
Literature
History and criticism
Generalities: Periodicals, Societies, etc. see PB1101+

Goidelic. Gaelic. (Irish, Scottish Gaelic, and Manx)
Literature
History and criticism -- Continued
Treatises
1196 General
1197 Special
Texts
1198 General
1199 Special
1200 Translations
Irish
1201-1213 Philology (Table P-PZ4a modified)
History of philology
Cf. PB1215 History of the language
1207 General works
Biography, memoirs, etc.
1209.A2 Collective
1209.A5-Z Individual, A-Z
Subarrange each by Table P-PZ50
1214-1299 Language (Table P-PZ4b modified)
Add number in table to PB1200
1217 Script (Ogham, Ogom)
Grammar
1218 Historical
Including Old Irish and Middle Irish
Cf. PB1288.A2+ Old Irish glossaries
1219 Comparative
Style. Composition. Rhetoric
For study and teaching see PB1211
1275 General works
Etymology
1283.5 Dictionaries (exclusively etymological)
Lexicography
For biography of lexicographers see PB1209.A2+
1287 Treatises
Glossaries (Old Irish)
1288.A2-.A4 Collections
1288.A5-Z Particular glossaries, by editor
1289 Dictionaries with definitions in Irish
1291 Dictionaries with definitions in English
1293.A-Z Dictionaries with definitions in other languages. By language, A-Z
Dictionaries exclusively etymological see PB1283.5
1295 Special lists
Linguistic geography. Dialects, etc.
1296.A1 Linguistic geography
Dialects. Provincialisms, etc.

Irish
Language
Linguistic geography. Dialects, etc.
Dialects. Provincialisms, etc. -- Continued
1296.A2-.A29 Periodicals. Collections
1296.A3 Collections of texts, etc.
1296.A5-Z General works. Grammar (General and special)
1297 Dictionaries
(1298.A1) Atlases. Maps
see class G
1298.A5-Z Local. By region, place, etc.
1299 Slang. Argot
Literature
Cf. PR8700+ English literature of Ireland
Generalities: Periodicals. Societies, etc.
see PB1201+
History
1306 General
1307 General special. Minor
1314.A-Z Special topics, A-Z
1314.C45 Christianity
1314.D45 Deirdre (Legendary character)
1314.E48 Education
1314.M87 Music
1314.W65 Women
1317 Biography (Collective)
By period
1321 Old Irish (700-1100)
1322 Middle Irish (1100-1550)
1325 Modern Irish (1550-)
Epic literature (Prose intermingled with poetry)
1327 General
1329 General special
Poetry
1331 General
1333 General special
Prose
1336 General
1337 General special
(1343) Proverbs
see PN6505.C5
Texts
Collections
1345 General. Ancient and modern literature
Early (to 1800)
1347 General works
1351 Selections, etc.

Irish
Literature
Texts
Collections -- Continued
Modern
1353 19th-20th centuries
1354 21st century
By form
Epic literature
1356 General
1357 Special
For special cycles (Ulster cycle; Finn or Ossianic cycle) see PB1397.A+
Poetry
1359 General
1360 Special
Including ballads
Drama
1369 General
1370 Special
Prose
1379 General
1380 Special
Folk literature
see GR153.4+
For proverbs see PN6505.C5
(1382) History and criticism
(1383) Collections of texts
Local
1395.A-Z By region, province, county, etc., A-Z
1396.A-Z By city, A-Z
Outside of Ireland
1396.3 General
1396.4 United States and Canada
1396.5.A-Z Other, A-Z
Individual authors and works
1397.A-Z Cycles and anonymous works to 1800, A-Z
For translations see PB1421+
Acallam na senórach
1397.A3 Text
1397.A33 Criticism
Aided Muichertaig meic Erca
1397.A36 Text
1397.A362 Criticism
Aislinge Meic Conglinne
1397.A37 Text
1397.A372 Criticism

Irish
Literature
Individual authors and works
Cycles and anonymous works to 1800, A-Z -- Continued
Alexander the Great (Romances, etc.)
1397.A4 Text
1397.A42 Criticism
Amra Choluimb Chille
1397.A5 Text
1397.A52 Criticism
Audacht Morainn
1397.A75 Text
1397.A752 Criticism
Auraicept na n-éces
1397.A8 Text
1397.A82 Criticism
Baile in scáil
1397.B34 Text
1397.B342 Criticism
Bás cearbhaill agus farbhlaidhe
1397.B37 Text
1397.B372 Criticism
Book of Fenagh
1397.B6 Text
1397.B62 Criticism
Book of O'Hara
1397.B65 Text
1397.B652 Criticism
British Museum. Mss. [Harleian 5280]
1397.B85 Text
1397.B852 Criticism
Bruiden Da Choca
1397.B86 Text
1397.B862 Criticism
Buile Suibhne Geilt
1397.B87 Text
1397.B872 Criticism
Cáin Adamnáin
1397.C25 Text
1397.C252 Criticism
Caithréim Cellaig
1397.C27 Text
1397.C272 Criticism
Cath Almaine
1397.C32 Text
1397.C322 Criticism
Cath Finntrága

Irish
Literature
Individual authors and works
Cycles and anonymous works to 1800, A-Z
Cath Finntrága -- Continued

1397.C33 Text
1397.C332 Criticism

Coimheasgar na gCuradh

1397.C55 Text
1397.C552 Criticism

Comhairle Mhic Clamha ó Achadh na Muilleann

1397.C553 Text
1397.C5532 Criticism

Comracc Líadaine i Cuirithir

1397.C554 Text
1397.C5542 Criticism

Cormac Mac Airt, King of Ireland, fl. 227-260

1397.C556 Text
1397.C5563 Criticism

Cuchulain. Ulster cycle (General)

Class individual works belonging to the cycle under their respective numbers

1397.C7 Text
1397.C8 Criticism

De chophur in dá muccida

1397.D4 Text
1397.D42 Criticism

Eachtra na gCuradh

1397.E2 Text
1397.E22 Criticism

Eachtra Ridire na Leomhan

1397.E25 Text
1397.E252 Criticism

Echtrae Chonnlai

1397.E27 Text
1397.E272 Criticism

Feis tighe Chónain

1397.F3 Text
1397.F32 Criticism

Fenian or Ossianic cycle (General)

Class individual works belonging to the cycle under their respective numbers

1397.F4 Text
1397.F5 Criticism

Fís Adamnáin

1397.F543 Text
1397.F544 Criticism

Irish
Literature
Individual authors and works
Cycles and anonymous works to 1800, A-Z -- Continued
Fled Dúin na nGéd
1397.F6 Text
1397.F62 Criticism
Geinealach na nDéisi
1397.G45 Text
1397.G452 Criticism
Immram Brain
1397.I6 Text
1397.I62 Criticism
Immram curaig Máele Dúin
1397.I63 Text
1397.I632 Criticism
Immrama
1397.I65 Text
1397.I652 Criticism
King and hermit
1397.K55 Text
1397.K552 Criticism
Lebor Gabála Érenn
1397.L43 Text
1397.L432 Criticism
Longes mac nUsnig
1397.L59 Text
1397.L6 Criticism
Merlin (Allegory)
1397.M38 Text
1397.M382 Criticism
Mesca Ulad
1397.M4 Text
1397.M42 Criticism
Odysseus
1397.O3 Text
1397.O32 Criticism
Oidheadh chloinne hUisneach
1397.O35 Text
1397.O352 Criticism
Pairlement Chloinne Tomáis
1397.P35 Text
1397.P352 Criticism
Prophecy of Berchán
1397.P76 Text
1397.P762 Criticism
Saltair na rann

Irish
Literature
Individual authors and works
Cycles and anonymous works to 1800, A-Z
Saltair na rann -- Continued
1397.S33 Text
1397.S34 Criticism
Scél mucci Mic Dathó
1397.S35 Text
1397.S352 Criticism
Scéla Cano meic Gartnáin
1397.S37 Text
1397.S372 Criticism
Siabhradh Mhic na Míochomhairle
1397.S46 Text
1397.S462 Criticism
Slan seiss, a Brigit co mbúaid
1397.S5 Text
1397.S52 Criticism
Stair Ercuil ocus a bás
1397.S7 Text
1397.S72 Criticism
Táin bó Cúailnge
1397.T3 Text
1397.T33 Criticism
Táin bó Fráich
1397.T34 Text
1397.T35 Criticism
Togail bruidne Da Derga
1397.T65 Text
1397.T652 Criticism
Togail na Tebe
1397.T7 Text
1397.T72 Criticism
Togail Troí
1397.T73 Text
1397.T732 Criticism
Tóraigheacht Taise Taoibhghile
1397.T74 Text
1397.T742 Criticism
Tóruigheacht Dhiarmada agus Ghráinne
1397.T752 Text
1397.T753 Criticism
Ulster cycle see PB1397.C7+
1398.A-Z Individual authors to 1800, A-Z
Subarrange each author by Table P-PZ40
1398.B5 Blaithmaic, Saint, d. ca. 827 (Table P-PZ40)

Irish
Literature
Individual authors and works
Individual authors to 1800, A-Z -- Continued
1398.H3 Haicéad, Pádraigín (Table P-PZ40)
1398.M2 Mac Aingil, Aodh, 1571-1626 (Table P-PZ40)
1398.M275 Mac Cruitín, Aodh Buí, ca. 1680-1755 (Table P-PZ40)
1398.M34 Mac Gearailt, Muiris mac Dáibhí Dhuibh, ca. 1565-ca. 1635 (Table P-PZ40)
1398.N83 Nugent, William, 1550-1625 (Table P-PZ40)
1398.O16 O Braonáin, Mícheál (Table P-PZ40)
1398.O24 O Bruadair, Dáibhí, ca. 1625-1698 (Table P-PZ40)
1398.O26 Ó Caiside, Tomás, fl. 1750 (Table P-PZ40)
1398.O3 O'Connell, Eileen, b. ca. 1743 (Table P-PZ40)
1398.O5 O'Donnell, Manus, d. 1564 (Table P-PZ40)
1398.O57 Ó Longáin, Mícheál Óg. 1766-1837 (Table P-PZ40)
1398.O63 O'Rahilly, Egan, fl. 1670-1724 (Table P-PZ40)
1398.O64 Ó Rathaille, Aodhagán, ca. 1670-ca. 1727 (Table P-PZ40)
1398.O67 O Súilleabháin, Tadhg Gaelach, 1715-1795 (Table P-PZ40)
1399.A-Z Individual authors, 1800-2000, A-Z
Subarrange each author by Table P-PZ40
1399.B46 Bheldon, Riobard, ca. 1835-1914 (Table P-PZ40)
1399.D336 De Bhailis, Colm, 1796-1906 (Table P-PZ40)
1399.H9 Hyde, Douglas, 1860-1949 (Table P-PZ40)
1399.M1396 Mac Bionaid, Art, 1793-1879 (Table P-PZ40)
1399.M162 Mac Giolla Bhrighde, Niall, 1861-1942 (Table P-PZ40)
1399.R3 Raftery, Anthony, 1784-1835 (Table P-PZ40)
1400.A-Z Individual authors, 2001- , A-Z
Subarrange each author by Table P-PZ40
Translations
(1419) From foreign languages into Irish
see the original language
From Irish literature into foreign languages
English
1421 General and miscellaneous (Minor) collections
Including old and modern collections of early literature, to 1800
1423.A-Z Particular cycles or tales, legends, etc., A-Z
e. g.
1423.C8 Cuchulain
1423.T3 Táin bó Cúailnge
1424 Poetry
19th-21st centuries
1427 General
1429 Poetry

Irish
Literature
Translations
From Irish literature into foreign languages
English
19th-21st centuries -- Continued
1431 Prose
(1433) Individual authors
see PB1399+
1441 French
1445 German
1449.A-Z Other. By language, A-Z
Gaelic (Scottish Gaelic, Erse)
1501-1513 Philology (Table P-PZ4a modified)
History of philology
Cf. PB1515 History of the language
1507 General works
Biography, memoirs, etc.
1509.A2 Collective
1509.A5-Z Individual, A-Z
Subarrange each by Table P-PZ50
1514-1599 Language (Table P-PZ4b modified)
Add number in table to PB1500
1517 Script (Ogham, Ogom)
Grammar
1518 Historical
Including Old Scottish Gaelic and Middle Scottish Gaelic
Cf. PB1588.A2+ Old Gaelic glossaries
1519 Comparative
Style. Composition. Rhetoric
For study and teaching see PB1511
1575 General works
Etymology
1583.5 Dictionaries (exclusively etymological)
Lexicography
For biography of lexicographers see PB1509.A2+
1587 Treatises
Glossaries (Old Gaelic)
1588.A2-.A4 Collections
1588.A5-Z Particular glossaries, by editor
1589 Dictionaries with definitions in Scottish Gaelic
1591 Dictionaries with definitions in English
1593.A-Z Dictionaries with definitions in other languages. By language, A-Z
Dictionaries exclusively etymological see PB1583.5
1595 Special lists
Linguistic geography. Dialects, etc.

Gaelic (Scottish Gaelic, Erse)
Language
Linguistic geography. Dialects, etc. -- Continued
1596.A1 Linguistic geography
Dialects. Provincialisms, etc.
1596.A2-.A29 Periodicals. Collections
1596.A3 Collections of texts, etc.
1596.A5-Z General works. Grammar (General and special)
1597 Dictionaries
(1598.A1) Atlases. Maps
see class G
1598.A5-Z Local. By region, place, etc., A-Z
1599 Slang. Argot
Literature
Cf. PR8500+ English literature of Scotland
Generalities: Periodicals. Societies, etc. see PB1501+
History
1605 General
1607 General special
1613 Biography (Collective)
Texts
Collections
1631 General
1632.A-Z Older manuscript collections, A-Z
1632.D4 Book of Deer
1632.L5 Book of Lismore
1633 Selections. Anthologies
1634 Special
For Ossianic ballads see PB1397.F4+
(1645) Folk literature
see GR143+
(1645.8) Proverbs
see PN6505.C4
Local
1646.A-Z By region, province, county, etc., A-Z
1647.A-Z By place, A-Z
1648.A-Z Individual authors and works, A-Z
Subarrange each author by Table P-PZ40
e.g.
1648.B8 Buchanan, Dugald, 1716-1768 (Table P-PZ40)
1648.D5 Donn, Rob, 1714-1778 (Table P-PZ40)
1648.M185 MacCormaig, Iain, 1859 or 60-1947 (Table P-PZ40)
1648.M2 MacDonald, Alexander, ca. 1700-ca. 1780 (Table P-PZ40)
1648.M226 Macdonald, Sìleas, ca. 1660-ca. 1729 (Table P-PZ40)
1648.M3 MacIntyre, Duncan Ban, 1724-1812 (Table P-PZ40)
1648.M3287 Macleod, Mary, fl. 1675-1705 (Table P-PZ40)

Gaelic (Scottish Gaelic, Erse)
Literature
Individual authors and works, A-Z -- Continued
1648.N48 Nic a' Phearsain, Màiri, 1821-1898 (Table P-PZ40)
Translations
(1671) From foreign languages into Gaelic
see the original language
From Gaelic (Scottish-Gaelic) into foreign languages
For translations of the older literature (to ca. 1500 or 1600) prefer PB1421+
1681 English
General and miscellaneous (Minor) collections, including old and modern collections of early literature to 1800
1683.A-Z Particular cycles or tales, legends, etc., A-Z
1684 Poetry
19th-21st centuries
1687 General
1689 Poetry
1691 Prose
(1695) Individual authors
see PB1648
1701 French
1705 German
1709.A-Z Other. By language, A-Z
Manx
1801-1846 Language (Table P-PZ5)
Literature
Cf. PR8450+ English literature
1851 History
1853 Biography (Collective)
Texts
1858 Collections
1860 Translations
(1863) Folk literature
see GR153.M3
(1864) Proverbs
see PN6505.C6
1865.A-Z Local, A-Z
1867.A-Z Individual authors or works, A-Z
Subarrange each author by Table P-PZ40
1950 Pict
Cf. P1088 Pictish (pre-Celtic)
Britannic (Brytonic or Cymric) group (Welsh, Cornish, and Breton)
2001-2029 Language (Table P-PZ6 modified)
(2008) Script
see PB1217

Britannic (Brytonic or Cymric) group (Welsh, Cornish, and Breton) -- Continued
Literature
History and criticism
Generalities: Periodicals. Societies, etc.
see PB2001+
Treatises
2056 General
2057 Special
Texts (Collections)
2058 General
2059 Special
2060 Translations. Adaptations
Welsh. Cymric
2101-2113 Philology (Table P-PZ4a modified)
History of philology
Cf. PB2115 History of the language
2107 General works
Biography, memoirs, etc.
2109.A2 Collective
2109.A5-Z Individual, A-Z
Subarrange each by Table P-PZ50
2114-2199 Language (Table P-PZ4b modified)
Add number in table to PB2100
Grammar
2118 Historical
Including Old Welsh and Middle Welsh
Cf. PB2188.A2+ Old Welsh glossaries
2119 Comparative
Style. Composition. Rhetoric
For study and teaching see PB2111
2175 General works
Etymology
2183.5 Dictionaries (exclusively etymological)
Lexicography
For biography of lexicographers see PB2109.A2+
2187 Treatises
Glossaries (Old Welsh)
2188.A2-.A4 Collections
2188.A5-Z Particular glossaries, by editor
2189 Dictionaries with definitions in Welsh
2191 Dictionaries with definitions in English
2193.A-Z Dictionaries with definitions in other languages. By language, A-Z
Dictionaries exclusively etymological see PB2183.5
2195 Special lists
Linguistic geography. Dialects, etc.

Welsh. Cymric
Language
Linguistic geography. Dialects, etc. -- Continued

2196.A1 Linguistic geography
Dialects. Provincialisms, etc.
2196.A2-.A29 Periodicals. Collections
2196.A3 Collections of texts, etc.
2196.A5-Z General works. Grammar (General and special)
2197 Dictionaries
(2198.A1) Atlases. Maps
see class G
2198.A5-Z Local. By region, place, etc., A-Z
2199 Slang. Argot

Literature
Cf. PR8950+ English literature of Wales
2202 Encyclopedias. Dictionaries
History
2206 General
2207 General special
2207.5 Collected essays
2208 Special topics
Including Eisteddfodd
2217 Biography (Collective)
By period
2221 Early, through 1550/1660
2222 1550/1660-1800
2223 19th-20th centuries
2224 21st century
Poetry
2227 General
2231 Special
2234 Drama
Prose. Prose fiction
2236 General
2237 Special
(2241) Folk literature
see GR149+
Texts
Collections
2245 General
2246 Selections. Anthologies
2248 Poetry
2251 Drama
Prose. Prose fiction
2259 General
2261 General special
Early Welsh to 1550/1600

Welsh. Cymric
Literature
Texts
Early Welsh to 1550/1600 -- Continued
Medieval collections

2271 Compilations

2273.A-Z Particular collections, works and authors, A-Z
Subarrange authors by P-PZ40 unless otherwise indicated
Subarrange individual works by P-PZ43 unless otherwise indicated
For translations of cycles, tales, and legends see PB2361+

2273.A7-.A73 Aneirin (including Book of Aneirin) (Table P-PZ43)

2273.B3-.B33 Black book of Carmarthen (Table P-PZ43)

Book of Aneirin see PB2273.A7+

Book of Taliesin see PB2273.T3+

2273.B7-.B73 Book of the Anchorite (Llyvyr agkyr Llandewivrevi) (Table P-PZ43)

2273.B84-.B843 Breuddwyd Rhonabwy (Table P-PZ43)

2273.C84-.C843 Culhwch and Olwen (Table P-PZ43)

2273.C95 Cynddelw Brydydd Mawr (Table P-PZ40)

2273.D3 Dafydd ap Gwilym, 14th cent. (Table P-PZ40)

2273.D43 Dafydd y Coed (Table P-PZ40)

2273.G75 Gruffudd ap Maredudd ap Dafydd (Table P-PZ40)

2273.H95 Hywel Swrdwal, fl. 1430-1475 (Table P-PZ40)

2273.I38 Ieuan Brydydd Hir, fl. 1440-1470 (Table P-PZ40)

2273.L42 Lewys Môn, ca. 1465-1527 (Table P-PZ40)

2273.L45 Lewys Morgannwg, fl. ca. 1523-1555 (Table P-PZ40)

2273.L53 Llawdden, fl. 1450 (Table P-PZ40)

2273.L63 Llywelyn ap Gutun (Table P-PZ40)

Mabinogion
Cf. PB2273.R4+ Red Book of Hergest
Cf. PB2273.W5+ White Book of Rhydderch

2273.M3 Texts. By date

(2273.M3A-.M3Z) Translations. By language, A-Z
see PB2363.M2; PB2403.M2; PB2423.M2; PB2450

2273.M33 Criticism

2273.O95 Owain ap Llywelyn ab y Moel (Table P-PZ40)

2273.R4-.R43 Red book of Hergest (Llyfr coch o Hergest) (Table P-PZ43)

2273.T3-.T33 Taliesin (Table P-PZ43)
Including Book of Taliesin

2273.T7-.T73 Triads of the Isle of Britain (Trioedd Ynys Prydain) (Table P-PZ43)

Welsh. Cymric
Literature
Texts
Early Welsh to 1550/1600
Medieval collections
Particular collections, works and authors, A-Z -- Continued

White book of Mabinogion see PB2273.W5+
2273.W5-.W53 White book of Rhydderch (Table P-PZ43)
2273.Y95-.Y953 Ywain (Table P-PZ43)
2281 Poetry
2283 Drama
2285 Prose. Prose fiction
Modern Welsh, 1550/1600-
Collections
2287 General
2289 Poetry
2291 Drama
2293 Prose. Prose fiction
Individual authors
2297.A-Z Ca. 1550/1600-1800/1830
Subarrange each author by P-PZ40
2297.G7 Griffiths, Ann Thomas, 1776-1805 (Table P-PZ40)
2297.H56 Hopcyn, Wil, 1700-1741 (Table P-PZ40)
Iolo Morganwg, 1746-1826 see PB2297.W45
2297.L6 Llwyd, Morgan, 1619-1659 (Table P-PZ40)
2297.O8 Owen, Goronwy, 1723-1769? (Table P-PZ40)
Pantycelyn see PB2297.W5
2297.R63 Roberts, Ellis, d. 1789 (Table P-PZ40)
2297.T84 Tudur, Siôn (Table P-PZ40)
2297.W45 Williams, Edward, 1746-1826 (Table P-PZ40)
For English works see PR3765.W535
2297.W5 Williams, William, 1717-1791 (Williams Pantycelyn) (Table P-PZ40)
2297.W57 Williams, William, 1738-1817 (Table P-PZ40)
2297.W8 Wynne, Ellis, 1671-1734 (Table P-PZ40)
2298.A-Z 1800/1830-2000
Subarrange each author by P-PZ40
2298.A56 Ap Iwan, Emrys, 1851-1906 (Table P-PZ40)
2298.C37 Carneddog, 1861-1947 (Table P-PZ40)
2298.C73 Cranogwen, 1839-1916 (Table P-PZ40)
2298.E43 Eifion, Wyn, 1867-1926 (Table P-PZ40)
Hughes, John Gruffydd, 1866-1944 see PB2298.M47
2298.J63 Jones, T. Gwynn, 1871-1949 (Table P-PZ40)
2298.L32 Levi, Thomas, 1825-1916 (Table P-PZ40)
2298.M47 Moelwyn, 1866-1944 (Table P-PZ40)

Welsh. Cymric
Literature
Texts
Modern Welsh, 1550/1600-
Individual authors
1800/1830-2000 -- Continued

2298.O75 Owen, Daniel, 1836-1895 (Table P-PZ40)
2298.P395 Payne, Mary Annes (Table P-PZ40)
2298.R39 Rees, George, 1873-1950 (Table P-PZ40)
2298.R638 Roberts, Samuel, 1800-1885 (Table P-PZ40)
2298.R65 Roberts, William John, 1827-1920 (Table P-PZ40)
2298.T26 Talhaiarn, 1810-1869 (Table P-PZ40)
2299.A-Z 2001-
Subarrange each author by P-PZ40
(2311) Folk literature
see GR149+
(2313) Proverbs
see PN6505.C7
Local
2317.A-Z By region, province, county, etc., A-Z
2319.A-Z By place, A-Z
Translations
(2351) From foreign languages into Welsh
see the original language
From Welsh literature into foreign languages
English
2361 General and miscellaneous (Minor) collections
Including old and modern collections of early literature to 1800
2363.A-Z Particular cycles or tales, legends, etc., A-Z
e.g.
2363.M2A-.M2Z Mabinogion. By translator, A-Z
2369 Poetry
(2373) Individual authors to 1800
see PB2297
19th-21st centuries
2381 General
2383 Poetry
2385 Drama
2387 Prose
(2389) Individual authors
see PB2298+
French
2401 General and miscellaneous (Minor) collections
Including old and modern collections of early literature to 1800

Welsh. Cymric
Literature
Translations
From Welsh literature into foreign languages
French -- Continued
2403.A-Z Particular cycles or tales, legends, etc., A-Z
e.g.
2403.M2A-.M2Z Mabinogion. By translator, A-Z
2405 Poetry
(2409) Individual authors
see PB2297
19th-21st centuries
2411 General
2413 Poetry
2415 Drama
2417 Prose
(2419) Individual authors
see PB2298+
German
2421 General and miscellaneous (Minor) collections
Including old and modern collections of early literature to 1800
2423.A-Z Particular cycles or tales, legends, etc.
e.g.
2423.M2A-.M2Z Mabinogion. By translator, A-Z
2425 Poetry
(2429) Individual authors
see PB2297
19th-21st centuries
2431 General
2433 Poetry
2435 Drama
2437 Prose
(2439) Individual authors
see PB2298+
2450.A-Z Other, A-Z. By language
2499 Curiosa
Cornish
2501-2546 Language (Table P-PZ5)
Literature
Cf. PR8310+ English literature in Cornwall
History
2551 General
2552 Special
Including drama
2554 Biography (Collective)
Texts

Cornish
Literature
Texts -- Continued
Collections
2563 General
Special
2567 Poetry
2569 Drama
2571 Prose
(2573) Proverbs
see PN6505.C37
2577.A-Z Local, A-Z
2591.A-Z Individual authors or works, A-Z
Subarrange each individual author by Table P-PZ40
Subarrange each individual work by Table P-PZ43
Translations
(2611) From foreign languages into Cornish
see the original language
2621.A-Z From Cornish into foreign languages. By language, A-Z
Breton. Armorican
2801-2846 Language (Table P-PZ5 modified)
Lexicography
Dictionaries
2835 Dictionaries with definitions in Breton
2837.A-Z Dictionaries with definitions in French or other languages.
Subarrange by author
Literature
History
2856 General
2858 Special
Including drama
2864 Biography (Collective)
Texts
Collections
2871 General
2873 Selections. Anthologies
2881 To 1800
2883 1800-
2887 Poetry
2889 Drama
2891 Prose
Folk literature
see GR162.A+
(2895) General
(2897) Special
Including Barzas Breiz controversy

Breton. Armorican
Literature
Folk literature -- Continued

(2899) Proverbs
see PN6505.C33

2901.A-Z Local, A-Z

Individual authors and works

2903.A-Z To 1800
Subarrange each individual authors by Table P-PZ40
Subarrange each individual work by Table P-PZ43

2903.N68 Nourry, Pierre, 1743-1804 (Table P-PZ40)

2905.A-Z 1800-
Subarrange each individual author by Table P-PZ40
Subarrange each individual work by Table P-PZ43
e.g.

2905.G84 Guillôme, Joachim, 1797-1857 (Table P-PZ40)

2905.I54 Inisan, Lan, 1826-1891 (Table P-PZ40)

2905.P76 Proux, Prosper, 1811-1873 (Table P-PZ40)

Translations

(2929) From foreign languages into Breton
see the original language

2931-2932 From Breton literature into foreign languages (Table P-PZ30)

Continental Celtic

3000 General works

3001-3029 Gaulish language (Table P-PZ6)
Including the languages of ancient Gaul (General)
Cf. P1072 Ligurian

Celtiberian see P1081

Romance philology and languages
General
Class here works dealing with all or with several of the languages derived from Latin
Philology
Periodicals. Serials
1 English and American
2 French
3 German
4 Italian
5 Other
Societies
6 English and American
7 French
8 German
9 Italian
10 Other
11 Congresses
Collections
(12) Texts. Sources
see PN818+
Monographs. Studies
13 Various authors. Series
14.A-Z Studies in honor of a particular person or institution, A-Z
15 Individual authors
19 Encyclopedias
(20) Atlases. Maps
see class G
Philosophy. Theory. Method
21 General works
23 Relations
History of philology
Cf. PC45+ History of the language
Cf. PC35+ Study and teaching
25 General works
26 General special
By period
27 Earliest. Middle Ages. Renaissance
29 Modern
31.A-Z By region or country, A-Z
Biography, memoirs, etc.
33 Collective
34.A-Z Individual, A-Z
Study and teaching. Research
35 General works
36 General special

General
Philology
Study and teaching. Research -- Continued
By period
For period of history of the languages see PC47+
For period of study, teaching, or research see PC27+
38.A-Z By region or country, A-Z
39.A-Z By school, A-Z
39.5.A-Z By research institute, A-Z
41 General works
43-400 Languages (Table P-PZ2a modified)
Add number in table to PC0
General
53 Compends
Grammar
Treatises
60 Early to 1836
61 Later, 1836-
General works
see PC60+
To 1836
see PC60
1836-
see PC61
Style. Composition. Rhetoric
For study and teaching see PC35+
240 General works
Lexicography
323 General works
Biography of lexicographers see PC33+
Linguistic geography. Dialects, etc.
350 Linguistic geography
Dialects. Provincialisms, etc.
351 Periodicals. Collections
353 Collections of texts, etc.
355 General works
Grammar
361 General
(365) Special
see PC76+
390 Dictionaries
(393) Atlases. Maps
see class G
395.A-Z Local. By region, place, etc., A-Z
400 Slang. Argot
Literature
General see PN801+

General
Literature -- Continued
Particular literatures
French, Italian, Spanish, Portuguese
see PQ1+
Other
see the divisions for Literature in PC800+ PC950+ PC3301+ PC3381+ PC3900+ etc.
Romanian
601-623 Philology (Table P-PZ3a modified)
History of philology
Cf. PC625 History of the language
Biography, memoirs, etc.
617.A2 Collective
617.A5-Z Individual, A-Z
Subarrange each by Table P-PZ50
624-799 Language (Table P-PZ3b modified)
Add number in table to PC600
Style. Composition. Rhetoric
For study and teaching see PC619+
735 General works
Etymology
763 Dictionaries (exclusively etymological)
Lexicography
771 Periodicals. Societies. Serials. Collections (nonserial)
773 General works
Biography of lexicographers see PC617.A2+
773.5 Criticism, etc., of particular dictionaries
Dictionaries
Romanian only
775 General
776 Picture dictionaries
777 Supplementary dictionaries. Dictionaries of new words
778 Dictionaries with definitions in two or more languages, or dictionaries of two or more languages with definitions in Romanian
779 Romanian-English; English-Romanian
781.A-Z Romanian-French [-German, etc.]; French [German, etc.]-Romanian. By language, A-Z
Dictionaries exclusively etymological see PC763
782 Dictionaries of particular periods (other than periods separately specified elsewhere)
Rhyming dictionaries
see PC758
784 Special dictionaries

Romanian
Language
Lexicography
Dictionaries -- Continued
785 Other special lists
Including glossaries, dictionaries of terms and phrases, word frequency lists, reverse indexes, and lists of abbreviations
Linguistic geography. Dialects, etc.
787.A1 Linguistic geography

Dialects. Provincialisms, etc.
787.A2-.A29 Periodicals. Societies. Congresses
787.A3-Z Collections of texts (by editor)
788 Treatises. Monographs. Studies
Grammar
789 General
790 Special
791 Dictionaries
(792) Atlases. Maps
see class G
By region
Daco-Romanian
The Romanian as spoken by the vast majority of the people in the northern part of Romania is called Daco-Romanian, in distinction from the dialects in the southern and western regions
General
see PC1+
794.A-Z Local, A-Z
e.g.
794.B3 Banat
794.B5 Bessarabia
794.B8 Bukovina
794.M6-.M695 Moldavia. Moldova (Table P-PZ16a)
794.T7 Transylvania
794.W3 Wallachia
795 Meglenitian
797-797.95 Macedo-Romanian (Aromanian) (Table P-PZ15a)
798 Istro-Romanian
799 Slang. Argot
Literature
History
800 Periodicals. Societies. Collections
800.3 Study and teaching
Biography of teachers, critics, and historians
800.5 Collective

Romanian
Literature
History
Biography of teachers, critics, and historians -- Continued
800.6.A-Z Individual, A-Z
Subarrange each by Table P-PZ50
801 General works. Compends
802 General special
803 Collected essays
Treatment of special subjects, classes, etc.
803.7.A-Z Subjects, A-Z
803.7.A73 Architecture
803.7.B95 Byron, George Gordon Byron, Baron, 1788-1824
803.7.C68 Country life
803.7.D74 Dreams
803.7.F35 Fantasy
803.7.F65 Folklore
803.7.H85 Humanism
803.7.M54 Military art and science
803.7.N36 Names, Personal
803.7.O74 Orient
803.7.P38 Patriotism
803.7.P47 Persona
803.7.P53 Picaresque, The
803.7.P57 Plagiarism
803.7.R43 Realism
803.7.R65 Romania
803.7.R66 Romanticism
803.7.R95 Russia
803.7.V37 Vasile Lupu, Voivode of Moldavia, 1593-1661
803.7.W37 War of Independence, 1876-1878
803.8.A-Z Classes and ethnic groups, A-Z
803.8.D33 Dacians
803.8.J48 Jews
803.8.W6 Women
804 Biography (Collective)
For teachers, critics, etc. see PC800.5+
For individual authors see PC838.7+
804.3 Criticism
(804.9) Bibliography. Bio-bibliography
see class Z
By period
805 Origins
806 Early to 1800
808 19th and 20th centuries
809 21st century
810 Poetry

Romanian
Literature
History -- Continued
811 Drama
811.8 Prose
812 Fiction
812.2 Other
Folk literature
For general works on and collections of folk literature see GR257+
(814.5) Periodicals. Societies. Serials
History and criticism
(815) General works
(816) Addresses, essays, lectures
(816.2.A-Z) Special topics, A-Z
Collections of texts
(819) General collections
By form
Poetry. Folk songs. Ballads
821 General
821.2.A-Z Individual folk songs, poems, A-Z
821.5 Drama
(822) Proverbs
see PN6505.R7
823 Chapbooks
Folktales. Fairy tales. Legends see GR257+
(824.A-Z) By locality, region, etc., A-Z
(827.A-Z) Translations. By language, A-Z
Individual folktales, fairy tales, legends see GR257+
Collections
829 General
830 Selections. Anthologies
830.5.A-Z Special classes of authors, A-Z
830.5.C5 Child authors
830.7.A-Z Special topics, A-Z
830.7.A7 Armed Forces
830.7.C43 Ceaușescu, Nicolae
830.7.C58 Civilization
830.7.H5 Historical. Patriotic. Political
830.7.H85 Hunting
830.7.I2 Iancu, Avram
830.7.M38 May Day
830.7.M6 Mothers
830.7.O84 Ovidius Naso, Publius
By period
831 Early to ca. 1800

Romanian
Literature
Collections
By period -- Continued
(832) Later, ca. 1800-
see PC829+
Poetry
832.5 Periodicals
833 General
Cf. PC821 Folk poetry and folk songs
834 Selections. Anthologies
834.2 Selections from women poets
834.5.A-Z Special. By form or subject, A-Z
834.5.A78 Art
834.5.A88 Autumn
834.5.B35 Bălcescu, Nicolae, 1819-1852
834.5.C45 Children
834.5.C47 Christian poetry
834.5.C74 Creangă, Ion, 1839-1899
834.5.E65 Epic poetry
Folk poetry see PC821+
834.5.F67 Forests. Trees
834.5.H34 Haiku
834.5.H5 Historical, political, patriotic poetry
834.5.H6 Horia, ca. 1730-1785
834.5.H85 Humorous poetry
834.5.L68 Love
834.5.M6 Mothers
834.5.N37 Nature
834.5.O48 Olt River (Romania)
834.5.P29 Parodies
834.5.P3 Pastoral poetry
834.5.P64 Political prisoners
834.5.P74 Prose poems
834.5.R45 Religious poetry
834.5.S23 Sadoveanu, Mihail, 1880-1961
834.5.S6 Sonnets
Drama
835 General
836 Selections. Anthologies
836.2 Anthologies of plays for children and youth
Prose
837 General
838 Fiction
838.5.A-Z Other, A-Z
838.5.E7 Essays
838.5.L4 Letters

Romanian
Literature
Collections
Prose
Other, A-Z -- Continued
838.5.S27 Satire
838.5.S3 Science fiction
838.5.S69 Spy stories
Individual authors
838.7.A-Z Through 1800
Subarrange each author by Table P-PZ40 unless otherwise specified
838.7.B37-.B373 Barlaam and Joasaph (Table P-PZ43)
838.7.C6-.C63 Codicele Voronețean (Table P-PZ43)
838.7.C67 Costin, Miron, 1633-1691 (Table P-PZ40)
838.7.D5 Dimitrie Cantemir, 1673-1723 (Table P-PZ40)
838.7.D67 Dosoftei, Metropolitan of Moldava, 1624?-1693 (Table P-PZ40)
838.7.M3 Maior, Petru, 1760 or 61-1821 (Table P-PZ40)
838.7.M4-.M43 Mesterul Manole (Table P-PZ43)
838.7.N3 Năsterul, Udriște, 1596 or 7-1659 (Table P-PZ40)
838.7.V33 Văcărescu, Ienăchita, ca. 1740-1797 (Table P-PZ40)
838.7.Z6 Zoba din Vinț, Ioan, 17th cent. (Table P-PZ40)
839.A-Z 1801-1960
Subarrange each author by Table P-PZ40 unless otherwise specified
e. g.
839.A5 Alecsandri, Vasile, 1821-1890 (Table P-PZ40)
839.A55 Alexandrescu, Grigore, 1812-1885 (Table P-PZ40)
839.A57 Anghel, Dimitrie, 1872-1914 (Table P-PZ40)
839.A73 Aricescu, C.D., 1823-1886 (Table P-PZ40)
839.A82 Asachi, Gheorghe, 1788-1869 (Table P-PZ40)
839.B23 Bacalbașa, Anton, 1865-1899 (Table P-PZ40)
839.B27 Banu, Constantin G., 1873-1940 (Table P-PZ40)
839.B33 Barbilian, Dan, 1895-1961 (Table P-PZ40)
Barbu, Ion see PC839.B33
839.B335 Baronzi, George, 1828-1896 (Table P-PZ40)
Bart, Jean, 1874-1933 see PC839.B6
839.B57 Bolintineanu, Dimitrie, 1819?-1872 (Table P-PZ40)
839.B573 Bolliac, Cezar, 1813-1881 (Table P-PZ40)
839.B6 Botez, Eugeniu, 1874-1933 (Table P-PZ40)
839.B633 Botiș-Ciobanu, Maria, 1866-1950 (Table P-PZ40)
839.B68 Brăescu, Gh. (Gheorghe), 1871-1949) (Table P-PZ40)
839.B69 Bratescu-Voinești, Ioan Alexandru, 1868-1946 (Table P-PZ40)
839.B85 Budai-Deleanu, Ion, ca. 1760-1820 (Table P-PZ40)
839.B86 Bujoreanu, Ioan M., 1834-1899 (Table P-PZ40)

Romanian
Literature
Individual authors
1801-1960 -- Continued

839.C33 Caragiale, Ion Luca, 1852-1912 (Table P-PZ40)
839.C43 Chendi, Ilarie, 1871-1913 (Table P-PZ40)
839.C49 Cîpariu, Timotei, 1805-1887 (Table P-PZ40)
839.C515 Cîrlova, Vasile, 1809-1831 (Table P-PZ40)
839.C58 Coșbuc, George, 1866-1918 (Table P-PZ40)
839.C7 Creangă, Ion, 1839-1889 (Table P-PZ40)
839.D33 Davila, Alexandru, 1862-1929 (Table P-PZ40)
839.D4 Delavrancea, Barbu, 1858-1918 (Table P-PZ40)
839.D42 Demetrescu, Traian, 1866-1896 (Table P-PZ40)
839.D46 Depărățeanu, Alexandru, 1834-1865 (Table P-PZ40)
839.D63 Donici, Alexandru, 1806-1866 (Table P-PZ40)
839.E5 Eminescu, Mihail, 1850-1889 (Table P-PZ40)
839.F5 Filimon, Nicolae, 1819-1865 (Table P-PZ40)
Fondane, Benjamin, 1898-1944 see PC839.F84
839.F84 Fundoianu, Benjamin, 1898-1944 (Table P-PZ40)
839.G32 Gane, Nicolae, 1838-1916 (Table P-PZ40)
839.G66 Gorun, Ion, 1863-1929 (Table P-PZ40)
839.G7 Grandea, Grigore Haralamb, 1843-1897 (Table P-PZ40)
839.H3 Hasdeu, Bogdan Petriceicu, 1838-1907 (Table P-PZ40)
839.H4 Heliade-Rădulescu, Ion, 1802-1872 (Table P-PZ40)
839.H56 Hogaș, Calistrat, 1847-1917 (Table P-PZ40)
839.I56 Ionescu, Radu, 1834-1872 (Table P-PZ40)
839.I58 Iorga, Nicolae (Table P-PZ40)
For biography see DR216.9.I5
839.I8 Ispirescu, Petre, 1830-1887 (Table P-PZ40)
839.K48 Khyzhdeu, Aleksandru, 1811-1872 (Table P-PZ40)
839.L26 Lapedatu, Ioan A., 1844-1878 (Table P-PZ40)
839.M23 Macedonski, Alexandru, 1854-1920 (Table P-PZ40)
839.M32 Marian, Simion Florea, 1847-1907 (Table P-PZ40)
839.M47 Micle, Veronica, 1850-1889 (Table P-PZ40)
839.M478 Mille, Constantin, 1861-1927 (Table P-PZ40)
839.M838 Mureșanu, Andrei, 1816-1863 (Table P-PZ40)
839.N25 Nădejde, Sofia, 1856-1946 (Table P-PZ40)
839.N4 Negruzzi, Constantin, 1808-1868 (Table P-PZ40)
839.N42 Negruzzi, Iacob, 1842-1932 (Table P-PZ40)
839.O3 Odobescu, Alexandru Ionescu, 1834-1895 (Table P-PZ40)
839.P27 Pann, Anton, ca. 1797-1854 (Table P-PZ40)
839.P353 Pauleti, Nicolae, 1816 or 17-1848 (Table P-PZ40)
839.P636 Popescu, Spiridon, 1864-1933 (Table P-PZ40)
839.P68 Porumbescu, Iraclie, 1823-1896 (Table P-PZ40)
839.R35 Ralet, Dimitrie, ca. 1816-1858 (Table P-PZ40)

Romanian
Literature
Individual authors
1801-1960 -- Continued
839.R8 Russo, Alexandru, 1819?-1859 (Table P-PZ40)
839.S353 Săvescu, Iuliu Cezar, 1866-1903 (Table P-PZ40)
839.S55 Slavici, Ioan, 1848-1925 (Table P-PZ40)
839.S78 Stere, Constantin, 1865-1936 (Table P-PZ40)
839.T38 Teleor, Dimitrie, 1858-1920 (Table P-PZ40)
839.T385 Teliman, Mihai, 1863-1902 (Table P-PZ40)
839.T5 Theodorian, Canton, 1871- (Table P-PZ40)
839.U7 Urechiă, Vasilie Alexandrescu, 1834-1901 (Table P-PZ40)
839.V2 Văcărescu, Elena, 1868-1947 (Table P-PZ40)
839.V23 Văcărescu, Ianeu, 1792-1863 (Table P-PZ40)
839.V36 Vârnav, Teodor, b. 1801 (Table P-PZ40)
839.V58 Vlahută, Alexandru, 1859-1919 (Table P-PZ40)
839.V85 Vulcan, Iosif, 1841-1907 (Table P-PZ40)
839.V855 Vulcan, Petru, 1869-1932 (Table P-PZ40)
839.V86 Vulcan, Samuil, 1758-1839 (Table P-PZ40)
839.Z3 Zamfirescu, Duiliu, 1858-1922 (Table P-PZ40)
840-840.36 1961-2000 (Table P-PZ29)
840.4-.436 2001- (Table P-PZ29a)
841.A-Z By region, province, or place, A-Z

Under each:

	History
.x	*General*
.x2	*Special*
	Collections
.x3	*General*
.x4	*Special*

Outside of Romania
For individual authors see PC838.7+
843 Moldova (Table P-PZ25 modified)
For individual authors see PC838.7+
844.A-Z Other regions or countries, A-Z
Subarrange each region or country by Table P-PZ26
Translations
From foreign language into Romanian
see the original language
871-872 From Romanian into foreign languages (Table P-PZ30)
890 Dalmatian (Vegliote)
For Serbo-Croatian dialects see PG1+

Raeto-Romance

Also known, in Switzerland, as Rhaeto (Rheto)-Romanic, Romansh, or Ladin, and in Italy, as Ladin or Friulian; Ladin is applied particularly to the dialects of the Engadine, and again, in local usage, to the dialect of a few villages in the Gader Valley in the Tyrol, between Enneberg and Gader Abtei. The principal groups are (1) the dialects of the upper Rhine basin (Vorder and Hinter Rhein, and their confluents) east of the St. Gotthard, and north and west of the Suretta massif and the Septimer and Albula passes, (2) those of the Engadine (Upper and Lower) and the Münster Valley, (3) of the Southern Tyrol, Trentino, etc., and (4) of Friuli, from the Carnic Alps to the Adriatic, and west to east, from the Piave to the Isonzo. The demarcations are broken and irregular, and naturally there are transition and mixed dialects, especially in certain adjoining Italian border districts

Language

901 Periodicals. Societies. Serials

901.5 Congresses

902 Collections (nonserial)

903 Encyclopedias

904 Philosophy. Theory. Method. Relations

History of Raeto-Romance studies

905 General works

Biography, memoirs, etc.

906.A2 Collective

906.A5-Z Individual, A-Z

Subarrange each by Table P-PZ50

907 Study and teaching

908 General works

909 History of the language

Grammar

911 Treatises. Compends (advanced)

913 Textbooks. Readers, etc.

915 Phonology. Phonetics

917 Orthography. Spelling

918 Alphabet

918.9 Morphophonemics

919 Morphology. Inflection. Accidence

921 Parts of speech (Morphology and syntax)

923 Syntax

927 Style. Composition. Rhetoric

For study and teaching see PC907

928 Translating

For special subjects, see the subject in classes B-Z, e.g. T11.5 Technology

929 Prosody. Metrics. Rhythmics

Raeto-Romance
Language -- Continued
930 Lexicology
Etymology
931 General treatises. Dictionaries
932 Semantics
933 Synonyms. Antonyms. Paronyms. Homonyms
933.5 Onomatopoeic words
933.9.A-Z Particular words, A-Z
Lexicography
934 General works
937 Dictionaries
Linguistic geography. Dialects
941 General works
By region
Rhine basin
942.A1 General
942.A3-Z Local, by place A-Z
Engadine. Ladin in Switzerland
General, and Upper Engadine
943.A1 General
943.A3-Z Local, by place A-Z
Lower Engadine
944.A1 General
944.A3-Z Local, by place A-Z
Dolomite Region. Trentino-Alto Adige. Ladin in Italy
945.A1 General
945.A3-Z Local, by place, A-Z
Literature
945.5 History and criticism
945.7 Collections
947-947.95 Friuli (Table P-PZ15a modified)
Literature
947.9.A-Z Individual authors and works, A-Z
Subarrange each author by Table P-PZ40
947.9.B47 Biancone, Girolamo, ca. 1530-ca. 1585 (Table P-PZ40)
947.9.D66 Donato, Giovan Battista, 1534-1604 (Table P-PZ40)
947.9.L56-.L563 Linute (Drama) (Table P-PZ43)
947.9.M45 Merlo, Luis, 1843-1918 (Table P-PZ40)
947.9.O36 Odorlico, da Cividale, fl. 1360-1370 (Table P-PZ40)
947.9.R6 Roja, Antonio, 1875-1943 (Table P-PZ40)
947.9.S8 Stella, Eusebio, 1602-1671 (Table P-PZ40)
947.9.Z67 Zorutti, Pietro, 1792-1867 (Table P-PZ40)
949 Argot. Slang

Raeto-Romance -- Continued
Literature
History
950 Periodicals. Societies. Collections
951 General works
953 Biography (Collective)
Texts (Collections)
955 General
957 Special
959.A-Z Individual authors. Anonymous works. By author or title, A-Z
Subarrange each author by Table P-PZ40 unless otherwise specified
Class here works in all dialects of Raeto-Romance except Friulian
For works in Friulian dialect see PC947.9.A+
Ruffieux, Cyprien, 1859-1940 see PC959.T58
959.T58 Tobi di-j-èlyudzo, 1859-1940 (Table P-PZ40)
Translations
From foreign language into Raeto-Romance
see the original language
985-986 From Raeto-Romance into foreign languages (Table P-PZ30)
Italian
1001-1071 Philology (Table P-PZ1a modified)
History of philology
Cf. PC1075+ History of the language
Biography, memoirs, etc.
1063 Collective
1064.A-Z Individual, A-Z
Subarrange each by Table P-PZ50
Study and teaching. Research
1065 General works
By period
For period of study, teaching, or research see PC1053+
For period of history of the language see PC1077+
General works
1070 Early works to 1700
1071 Later, 1701-
1073-1977 Language (Table P-PZ1b modified)
Add number in table to PC1000
Grammar
Readers
Primers
1114 Early to 1870
1115 Later

Italian
Language -- Continued
Style. Composition. Rhetoric
For study and teaching see PC1065+
1410 General works
Etymology
1580 Dictionaries (exclusively etymological)
1582.A-Z Special elements. By language, A-Z
1582.A3 Foreign elements (General)
Cf. PC1670 Dictionaries
Lexicography
1601 Periodicals. Societies. Serials. Collections (nonserial)
1611 General works
Biography of lexicographers see PC1063+
1617 Criticism, etc., of particular dictionaries
Dictionaries
Italian only
1620 Early to 1800
1800-
1625 General
1628 Minor, abridged, school dictionaries
1629 Picture dictionaries
1630 Supplementary dictionaries. Dictionaries of new words
1635 Polyglot (definitions in two or more languages)
Bilingual
1640 Italian-English; English-Italian
1645.A-Z Other. By language, A-Z
Classify with language less known
Italian-French; French-Italian
1645.F2 To 1850
1645.F3 1851-
Italian-German; German-Italian
1645.G2 To 1850
1645.G3 1851-
Italian-Portuguese; Portuguese-Italian see PC5335.I8
Italian-Spanish; Spanish-Italian
1645.S7 To 1850
1645.S8 1851-
Dictionaries exclusively etymological see PC1580
(1655) Particular authors
see the author (e.g. Dante, PQ4464)
1660 Names
Cf. CS2300+ Personal and family names
Cf. PC1673 Foreign names
1667 Obsolete or archaic words

Italian
Language
Lexicography
Dictionaries -- Continued
Foreign words
1670 General
1673 Names
Special. By language see PC1582.A+
Rhyming dictionaries
see PC1519
Other special lists
1680 Miscellaneous
(1683) By subject
Only subjects not provided for in classes A-N, Q-Z
1689 Dictionaries of terms and phrases
1691 Other
Including word frequency, etc.
1693 Abbreviations (Lists, etc.)
Linguistic geography. Dialects, etc.
1700 Linguistic geography
Dialects. Provincialisms, etc.
For works, biography and criticism of individual Italian authors, regardless of dialect see PQ4265+
1701 Periodicals. Societies. Congresses
For local dialect societies see PC1781+
Collections
1702 Texts. Sources, etc.
1703 Monographs. Studies
1704 Encyclopedias. Dictionaries
(1705) Atlases. Maps
see class G
Philosophy. Theory. Method see PC1711
General works
1711 Treatises
1712 Compends. Outlines, syllabi, etc. Popular
History of dialects
Cf. PC1771+ Old Italian
1713 General
1714 General special
1715 Earliest. Medieval
1716 (16th)-17th century. (17th)-18th century
1718 19th century. 20th century. 21st century
Grammar
1721 General works
1726 Phonology. Phonetics
1736 Morphology. Inflection. Accidence
1746 Syntax

Italian
Language
Linguistic geography. Dialects, etc.
Dialects. Provincialisms, etc.
Grammar -- Continued
1751 Style
1756 Prosody. Metrics. Rhythmics
1761 Etymology
1766 Lexicography
1771-1774 Old Italian (13th-14th centuries) (Table P-PZ14)
By region, province, etc.
1781 Regions (other than named below, or several in combination) (Table P-PZ15)
1784 Judeo-Italian (Table P-PZ15)
Southern dialects
1786 General
1791-1794 Sardinia (Table P-PZ14)
Cf. PC1981+ Sardinian language
(1796-1799) Corsica
see PC1918
1801-1804 Sicily (Table P-PZ14)
1805 Abruzzo. Molise (Table P-PZ15)
1806-1809 Apulia (Table P-PZ14)
1811-1814 Campania (Table P-PZ14)
1815-1818 Calabria (Table P-PZ14)
1819 Basilicata (Lucania) (Table P-PZ15)
Central Italian dialects
1821 General
1825 Latium (Table P-PZ15)
1826 Umbria (Table P-PZ15)
1827 Marches (Table P-PZ15)
(1828) Northern Sardinia (Gallura and Sassari)
see PC1984.Z9
1831-1834 Tuscany (Table P-PZ14)
Northern dialects
1841 General
1845 Trentino-Alto Adige (Table P-PZ15)
Cf. PC945.A1+ Raeto-Romance dialect
1846-1849 Veneto (Table P-PZ14 modified)
Including Northeastern dialects
1849.A-.Z9 Local. By dialect name or place, A-Z
1849.F7 Friuli
Cf. PC947+ Raeto-Romance dialect
(1850) Istria. Dalmation coast
see PC1929
Gallo-Italic dialects
1851 General

Italian
Language
Linguistic geography. Dialects, etc.
Dialects. Provincialisms, etc.
By region, province, etc.
Northern dialects
Gallo-Italic dialects -- Continued
1856-1859 Emilia (Table P-PZ14)
1860 Romagna (Table P-PZ15)
1861-1864 Lombardy (Table P-PZ14)
1866-1869 Piedmont (Table P-PZ14)
1871-1874 Liguria (Table P-PZ14)
(1875) Nice
see PC1916
(1876-1879) Trentino dialects
see PC1845
Italian in foreign parts
1910 General works
1916 France (Table P-PZ15)
1918 Corsica (Table P-PZ15)
1921 Malta (Table P-PZ15)
1926 Switzerland (Table P-PZ15)
1929 Yugoslavia (Table P-PZ15)
Including Istria and the Dalmatian Coast
1931 Africa (Table P-PZ15)
America
1937 North America (Table P-PZ15)
1938 South America (Table P-PZ15)
1943 Asia (Table P-PZ15)
1945 Oceania. Australia (Table P-PZ15)
Slang. Argot
1951 Collections. Studies
Texts
1955 Collections, General
1957 Special
General works
1961 General
1966 Grammatical studies
1969 Miscellaneous
1971 Dictionaries. Lists
Special classes
1974.A-Z Special categories of words, A-Z
1974.F37 Fashion
1974.I58 Invective
1974.S48 Sex. Erotica
1974.T44 Telephone
Special groups of persons

Italian
Language
Linguistic geography. Dialects, etc.
Slang. Argot
Special classes
Special groups of persons -- Continued
1975 Beggars. Gypsies. Tramps. Thieves, etc.
1977.A-Z Others, A-Z
1977.S34 Sailors
1977.S6 Soldiers
1977.S8 Students
1977.U4 Umbrella repairers
1977.Y6 Youth
Literature see PQ4001+
1981-1984 Sardinian (Table P-PZ11 modified)
Cf. PC1791+ Italian language in Sardinia
Literature
1984.A3-.Z5 Individual authors or works
Subarrange individual authors by Table P-PZ40
Subarrange individual works by Table P-PZ43
1984.A368 Antonio Maria, da Esterzili, fra, 1644?-1727 (Table P-PZ40)
1984.A73 Araolla, Gerolamo, ca.1520-ca.1590 (Table P-PZ40)
1984.C39 Cau, Felice, 1867-1908 (Table P-PZ40)
1984.D45 Delogu Ibba, Giovanni, 1664-1738 (Table P-PZ40)
1984.D47 Dessanai, Pascale 1868-1919 (Table P-PZ40)
1984.F34 Falchi Massidda, Anna Maria, 1824-1873 (Table P-PZ40)
1984.M35 Mannu, Francesco Ignazio, 1758-1839 (Table P-PZ40)
1984.M47 Mereu, Peppinu, 1872-1901 (Table P-PZ40)
1984.M65 Montanaru, 1878-1957 (Table P-PZ40)
1984.O66-.O663 Opposizione del vicario di Bulzi (Table P-PZ43)
1984.P87 Purqueddu, Antonio, 1743-1810 (Table P-PZ40)
1984.S59 Spano, Ausonio, 1870-1942 (Table P-PZ40)
French
2001-2071 Philology (Table P-PZ1a modified)
History of philology
Cf. PC2075+ History of the language
Biography, memoirs, etc.
2063 Collective
2064.A-Z Individual, A-Z
Subarrange each by Table P-PZ50
Study and teaching. Research
2065 General works
By period
For period of study, teaching, or research see PC2053+
For period of history of the language see PC2077+
General works

French
Philology
General works -- Continued
2070 Early works to 1700
2071 Later, 1701-
2073-2693 Language (Table P-PZ1b modified)
Add number in table to PC2000
History of the language
By period
2079 (15th)-16th century
Including La deffence et illustration de la langue françoyse
Grammar
Readers
2113 Series
Primers
2114 Early to 1800
2115 Later
Parts of speech (Morphology and syntax)
Verb
2272 Conjugation
Style. Composition. Rhetoric
For study and teaching see PC2065+
2410 General works
Etymology
2580 Dictionaries (exclusively etymological)
2582.A-Z Special elements. By language, A-Z
2582.A3 Foreign elements (General)
Cf. PC2670 Dictionaries
Lexicography
2601 Periodicals. Societies. Serials. Collections (nonserial)
2611 General works
Biography of lexicographers see PC2063+
2617 Criticism, etc., of particular dictionaries
Dictionaries
(2619) Glossaries, etc.
see PC2680
French only
2620 Early to 1800
2625 Later
2628 Minor, abridged, school dictionaries
2629 Picture dictionaries
2630 Supplementary dictionaries. Dictionaries of new words
2635 Polyglot (definitions in two or more languages)
Bilingual
2640 French-English; English-French

French
Language
Lexicography
Dictionaries
Bilingual -- Continued
2645.A-Z Other. By language, A-Z
Classify with less known language
French-German; German-French
2645.G2 Early to 1850
2645.G3 Later
(2645.I8) French-Italian; Italian-French
see PC1645.F2+
French-Portuguese; Portuguese-French see PC5335.F8
(2645.S7) French-Spanish; Spanish-French
see PC4645.F2+
Dictionaries exclusively etymological see PC2580
2650 Dictionaries of particular periods (other than periods separately specified elsewhere)
(2655) Particular authors
see authors, PQ
2660 Dictionaries of names
Cf. CS2300+ Personal and family names
Cf. PC2673 Foreign names
2667 Dictionaries, etc., of obsolete or archaic words
Dictionaries of foreign words
2670 General
2673 Names
Special. By language see PC2582.A+
Rhyming dictionaries
see PC2519
Other special lists
2680 Glossaries
(2683.A-Z) By subject, A-Z
see the subject in classes A-N, Q-Z
2689 Dictionaries of terms and phrases
2691 Word frequency lists
2692 Reverse indexes
2693 Abbreviations, Lists of
Dialects of France
2700 Linguistic geography
Dialects. Provincialisms, etc.
2701 Periodicals. Societies. Congresses
For local dialect societies see PC2921+
Collections
2702 Texts. Sources, etc.

Dialects of France
Dialects. Provincialisms, etc.
Collections -- Continued
2703 Monographs. Collected studies (Several, or individual authors)
(2705) Atlases. Maps
see class G
Philosophy. Theory. Method see PC2711
General works
2711 Treatises
2712 Compends. Outlines, syllabi, etc. Popular
History of dialects
2713 General
2714 General special
(2715) Earliest. Medieval
see PC2813+
2716 (16th)-17th century. (17th)-18th century
2718 19th century. 20th century. 21st century
Grammar
2721 General works
2726 Phonology. Phonetics
2736 Morphology. Inflection. Accidence
2746 Syntax
2751 Style
2756 Prosody. Metrics. Rhythmics
2761 Etymology
2766 Lexicography
Including treatises, dictionaries, glossaries, etc.
By region, province, etc.
Northern France (Langue d'oïl)
General
see PC2701+
Old French
Class individual authors and works of the Old French period with Old French literature PQ1411+ regardless of dialect. For collections of works in a particular dialect, see the dialect
Generalities: Periodicals. Societies, etc.
see PC2001+
2813-2896 Language (Table P-PZ4b modified)
Add number in table to PC2800
2813 Treatises
2814 General special
Etymology
2883.5 Dictionaries (exclusively etymological)
Lexicography
For biography of lexicographers see PC2063+

Dialects of France
By region, province, etc.
Northern France (Langue d'oïl)
Old French
Language
Lexicography -- Continued

2887 Treatises
2888 Ancient glossaries
Dictionaries
2889 Definitions in French
2891 Definitions in English
2893 Definitions in other languages
By author, A-Z
Dictionaries exclusively etymological see PC2883.5
2895 Special
Linguistic geography. Dialects, etc.
(2896.A1) Linguistic geography
see PC2700
2896.A2-.A29 Collections of texts
2896.A5-Z Treatises: Grammar, etc.
(2897) Dictionaries
see PC2889+
(2898.A1) Atlases. Maps
see class G
(2898.A5-Z) Local
see PC2921+
(2901-2908) Early (Modern) French, ca. 1400/1500-1700
see PC2001+
Special French dialects
2921-2928 Ile de France. Paris (dialecte francien) (Table P-PZ12)
2931-2938 Norman (Table P-PZ12)
2941-2948 Anglo-Norman. Anglo-French (Table P-PZ12)
2951-2958 Patois of the West (Table P-PZ12)
Including Bretagne, Manceau, Angevin, Tourangeau
2971-2978 Patois of the Southwest (Table P-PZ12)
Including Poitevin, Angoumoisin, Saintongeais, Aunisien
2981-2988 Central France (Table P-PZ12)
Including Orléanais, Berry (Berrichon), Nivernais, etc.
2991-2998 Patois of the Southeast (Table P-PZ12)
Including Bourbonnais, Morvandeau, Bourguignon, Verdun
3011-3018 Champenois (Table P-PZ12)
3021-3028 Lorrain (Table P-PZ12)
Including Meuse, Vosges, Alsace, Nancy, Toul, Metz (Messin), Longwy
3041-3048 Walloon (Table P-PZ12)
Cf. PC3581 French language in Belgium

Dialects of France
By region, province, etc.
Special French dialects -- Continued
3061-3068 Picard (Table P-PZ12)
Franco-Provençal dialects
Dialects of the Middle Rhône, and of east central France
3081-3088 General (Table P-PZ12 modified)
(3087.A-Z) Local
see PC3091+
3091-3098 Dauphinois (Dept. de l'Isère) (Table P-PZ12)
Cf. PC3461+ Langue d'oc dialects
3101-3108 Lyonnais. Forezien (Table P-PZ12)
3111-3118 Savoisien (Table P-PZ12)
3121-3128 Ain: Bugiste. Bressan (Table P-PZ12)
3131-3138 Franc-Comtois (Table P-PZ12)
3141-3148 French Switzerland (Table P-PZ12)
Cf. PC3661 French language in Switzerland
3149 Italy (Table P-PZ15)
3151-3158 Judeo-French (Table P-PZ12)
3171.A-Z Regions, departments, cities, etc. including various dialects, A-Z
3171.A7 Ardennes
Southern France (Langue d'oc)
Provençal (To 1500)
For works dealing primarily with modern Langue d'oc, in which earlier Provençal is treated in a summary manner merely by way of introduction, see PC3371+
3201-3213 Philology (Table P-PZ4a modified)
History of philology
Cf. PC3215 History of the language
3207 General works
Biography, memoirs, etc.
3209.A2 Collective
3209.A5-Z Individual, A-Z
Subarrange each by Table P-PZ50
(3210) Bibliography. Bio-bibliography
see Z7033.P8
3214-3299 Language (Table P-PZ4b modified)
Add number in table to PC3200
Etymology
3283.5 Dictionaries (exclusively etymological)
Lexicography
For biography of lexicographers see PC3209.A2+
3287 General works
Dictionaries
3289 Dictionaries with definitions in Provençal

Dialects of France
By region, province, etc.
Southern France (Langue d'oc)
Provençal (To 1500)
Language
Lexicography
Dictionaries -- Continued
3290 Dictionaries with definitions in two or more languages, or dictionaries of two or more languages with definitions in Provençal
3291 Dictionaries with definitions in English
3293.A-Z Dictionaries with definitions in other languages. By language, A-Z
Dictionaries exclusively etymological see PC3283.5
3293.2 Dictionaries of particular periods (other than periods separately specified elsewhere)
3295 Other special lists
Linguistic geography. Dialects, etc.
3296 Linguistic geography
Dialects. Provincialisms, etc.
Periodicals. Grammars. Dictionaries
see PC3201+
Texts
see PC3322+
3297.A-Z By region, place, etc., A-Z
(3298) Atlases. Maps
see class G
3299 Slang. Argot
Literature
(3300) Periodicals. Societies. Collections
see PC3201
History
3301 General (Medieval and modern)
3302 General special
3303 Special (not limited to period)
Medieval (to ca. 1500)
3304 General. Troubadours
3305 Contemporary works. "Las vidas dels trobadors," etc.
Cf. PC3330.A+ Individual troubadours
3306 Popular works
3307 Addresses, essays, lectures
3308 Special topics (not A-Z)
3309 Troubadours in foreign countries
3310 Provençal (troubadour) poetry by foreign authors
Special forms

Dialects of France
By region, province, etc.
Southern France (Langue d'oc)
Provençal (To 1500)
Literature
History
Medieval (to ca. 1500)
Special forms -- Continued
Poetry
3315 General. Lyric
3316.A-Z Special (Lyric), A-Z
3316.A6 Alba
3316.P3 Partimen
3316.S5 Sirvente
3316.T4 Tenson
3317 Epic. Narrative
3318 Didactic. Religious
3319 Drama
3320 Prose
3321 Fourteenth and fifteenth centuries
For special forms see PC3315+
Texts
Collections
3322.A1 General
3322.A2 Medieval (Facsimile reproductions or literal editions of manuscripts)
3322.A3 Modern
Readers
see PC3225
Poetry
3322.A4-Z General. Lyric
3323.A-Z Special (Lyric), A-Z
3323.A6 Alba
3323.S5 Sirvente
3323.S57 Songs
3323.S6 Sordello di Goito
3323.T4 Tenson
3324 Epic. Narrative
3325 Didactic (Religious, moral, allegoric-satirical, etc.)
3326 Drama
3327 Prose
Individual authors and works
3328.A-Z Anonymous works, A-Z
Subarrange each work by Table P-PZ43 unless otherwise specified
e.g.

Dialects of France
By region, province, etc.
Southern France (Langue d'oc)
Provençal (To 1500)
Literature
Individual authors and works
Anonymous works, A-Z -- Continued
3328.B55-.B553 Blandin de Cornouaille (Table P-PZ43)
3328.C28-.C283 Canso d'Antioca (Table P-PZ43)
3328.F5-.F53 Flamenca, Roman de (Table P-PZ43)
Girart de Rossillon
Chanson de Geste
3328.G6 Editions. By date
Translations (Modern). By language and date
3328.G6A1 Provençal
3328.G6A2 French
3328.G6A21 English
3328.G6A22 German
3328.G6A23 Other
3328.G6A35 Vita Girardi de Rossillon (12th cent.)
3328.G6A37 Old French translation
Poem of the 14th cent. (Alexandrine verse)
3328.G6A4 Editions
3328.G6A6 Criticism. By date
3328.G6A8-.G6Z3 Criticism (General, and Chanson de geste)
3328.I88-.I883 Istoria Petri et Pauli (Table P-PZ43)
3328.J3-.J33 Jaufre (Provençal romance) (Table P-PZ43)
3328.R65-.R653 Roland à Saragosse (Table P-PZ43)
3328.R68-.R683 Roman d'Arles (Table P-PZ43)
3330.A-Z Troubadours, A-Z
Subarrange each troubadour by Table P-PZ38 unless otherwise specified
3330.A5 Aimeric, de Belenoi, fl. 1217-1242 (Table P-PZ38)
3330.A74 Arnaut Daniel, fl. 1189 (Table P-PZ38)
3330.A745 Arnaut-Guilhem, de Marsan, ca. 1125 -ca. 1185 (Table P-PZ38)
3330.B37 Berenguer de Palazol, d. 1194 (Table P-PZ38)
3330.B38 Berguedà, Guillem de, fl. 1138-1192 (Table P-PZ38)
3330.B4 Bernart de Ventadorn (Table P-PZ38)
3330.B42 Bernart de Venzac (Table P-PZ38)
3330.B45 Bertran de Born (Table P-PZ38)
3330.B78 Brunenc, Uc. fl. 1190-1220 (Table P-PZ38)
3330.B89 Buvalelli, Rambertino, d. 1221 (Table P-PZ38)
3330.C3 Cadenet, 13th cent. (Table P-PZ38)
3330.C37 Castelnou, Raimon de, 13th cent. (Table P-PZ38)
3330.C4 Cercamon, 12th cent. (Table P-PZ38)

Dialects of France
By region, province, etc.
Southern France (Langue d'oc)
Provençal (To 1500)
Literature
Individual authors and works
Troubadours, A-Z -- Continued

3330.C45 Cerverí, de Girona, 13th cent. (Table P-PZ38)
3330.E46 Elias, Cairèl, fl. 1208-1215 (Table P-PZ38)
3330.F43 Febrer, Jaime (Table P-PZ38)
3330.F6 Folquet de Lunel, 1244-ca. 1301 (Table P-PZ38)
3330.F65 Folquet, de Marseille, Bishop of Toulouse, 1160-1231 (Table P-PZ38)
3330.F67 Folquet, de Romans, fl. ca. 1200 (Table P-PZ38)
3330.G32 Garin, lo Brun, 12th cent. (Table P-PZ38)
3330.G34 Gavaudan, fl. 1195-1215 (Table P-PZ38)
3330.G4 Giraut de Borneil, 12th cent. (Table P-PZ38)
3330.G65 Guilhem de la Tor, 13th cent. (Table P-PZ38)
3330.G7 Guillaume IX, Duke of Aquitaine, 1070-1127 (Table P-PZ38)
3330.G8 Guillem Augier Novella, fl. 1185-1235 (Table P-PZ38)
3330.J3 Jaufré Rudel, 12th cent. (Table P-PZ38)
3330.M3 Marcabrun, 12th cent. (Table P-PZ38)
3330.M7 Montaudon, monk of, fl. 1180-1200 (Table P-PZ38)
3330.P36 Paulet, de Marseille, 13th cent. (Table P-PZ38)
3330.P4 Peire Cardinal, fl. 1210-1230 (Table P-PZ38)
3330.P44 Peire d'Auvergne, 12th cent. (Table P-PZ38)
3330.P5 Peire Vidal, fl. 1200 (Table P-PZ38)
3330.R27 Raimbaut, d'Aurenga, 12th cent. (Table P-PZ38)
3330.R28 Raimbaut de Vaqueiras, 12th cent. (Table P-PZ38)
3330.R3 Raimon the Miraval, fl. 1200 (Table P-PZ38)
3330.R33 Raimon Feraut, fl. 1300-1324 (Table P-PZ38)
3330.R34 Raimon Jordan (Table P-PZ38)
3330.R55 Riquier, Guiraut (Table P-PZ38)
3330.R6 Rogier, Peire (Table P-PZ38)
3330.S35 Savaric de Mauléon, fl. 1180-1232 (Table P-PZ38)
3330.S6 Sordello, of Goito, 13th cent. (Table P-PZ38)
3330.U8 Ussel, Gui d', 13th cent. (Table P-PZ38)
3340.A-Z Other, A-Z
Subarrange each author by Table P-PZ38 unless otherwise specified
3340.E7 Ermengau, Matfré, fl. 1288-1322 (Table P-PZ38)

Dialects of France
By region, province, etc.
Southern France (Langue d'oc)
Provençal (To 1500)
Literature
Individual authors and works
Other, A-Z -- Continued
3340.G84 Guillaume, de Tudéle, fl. 1210-1213 (Table P-PZ38)
By region, province, or place
3343 Provence
3344 Languedoc
3345 Auvergnat
3346 Limousin
3347 Gascogne
3348.A-Z Other regions or places of southern France, A-Z
3349 Outside of Southern France
By subject
see the subject in classes A - Z
(3351) Polygraphy (Encyclopedic works)
(3352) Religion
(3353) History. Geography
(3354) Political science. Law
(3355) Language. (Grammar. Poetics)
(3357) Literature
(3359) Other
Including science, medicine
Translations
From foreign language into Provençal
see the original language
3365-3366 From Provençal into foreign languages (Table P-PZ30)
Modern patois of South France. "Langue des Félibres." Langue d'oc
3371-3378 Language (Table P-PZ12)
Literature
History
3381 General
3382 16th-18th centuries
19th-20th centuries
3383 General. Félibrige
3384 General special
3385 Poetry
3386 Drama
3387 Prose. Prose fiction
3388 Miscellaneous
21st century

Dialects of France
By region, province, etc.
Southern France (Langue d'oc)
Modern patois of South France. "Langue des Félibres." Langue d'oc
Literature
History
21st century -- Continued

3389 General
3390.3 Poetry
3390.4 Drama
3390.5 Prose. Prose fiction

Folk literature
see GR162.A+

(3391) History
(3393) Collections of texts (exclusively)

Texts
Collections
3396 Anthologies, etc.
3397 16th-18th centuries
3398 19th-20th centuries
3399 21st century

Individual authors and works
3401.A-Z 16th-18th centuries
Subarrange each author by Table P-PZ40 unless otherwise specified

3401.B55 Blanc, Francois, 1662-1742 (Table P-PZ40)
3401.B58 Blouin, Mathieu, d. ca. 1615 (Table P-PZ40)
3401.B7 Brueys, Claude, 1570 or 1571-ca. 1637 (Table P-PZ40)
3401.C32 Cabanes, Jean de, 1654-1717 (Table P-PZ40)
3401.C36 Casaurang, Jean, ca. 1740-ca. 1810 (Table P-PZ40)
3401.C45 Chabert, Pierre, 17th cent. (Table P-PZ40)
3401.D47 Despourrin, Cyprien, 1698?-1759 (Table P-PZ40)
3401.D86 Du Pré, André, 17th cent. (Table P-PZ40)
3401.F3 Favre, Jean Baptiste Castor, 1727-1783 (Table P-PZ40)
3401.G34 Garros, Pey de, ca. 1525 - ca. 1583 (Table P-PZ40)
3401.G6 Godolin, Pierre, b. 1580 (Table P-PZ40)
3401.L36 Larade, Bertrain, 1581-1630? (Table P-PZ40)
3401.M37 Marin, Michel-Ange, 1697-1767 (Table P-PZ40)
3401.M94-.M943 Le Mystère de Saint Eustache (Table P-PZ43)
3401.R44 Rempnoux, François (Table P-PZ40)
3401.R67 Roudil, Jacques, 1612-1684? (Table P-PZ40)

Dialects of France
By region, province, etc.
Southern France (Langue d'oc)
Modern patois of South France. "Langue des Félibres."
Langue d'oc
Literature
Texts
Individual authors and works
16th-18th centuries -- Continued

3401.S23 Saboly, Nicholas, 1614-1675 (Table P-PZ40)
3401.S35-.S353 Scatabronda (Table P-PZ43)
3401.T76 Tronc, Michel (Table P-PZ40)
3402.A-Z 19th-20th centuries
Subarrange each author by Table P-PZ40 unless otherwise specified
e.g.
3402.A27 Abric, Louvis, 1886-1953 (Table P-PZ40)
3402.A45 André, Marius, 1868-1927 (Table P-PZ40)
3402.A5 Arbaud, Joseph d', 1874-1950 (Table P-PZ40)
3402.A8 Aubanel, Théodore, 1829-1886 (Table P-PZ38)
3402.B4 Bernard, Valère, 1860-1936 (Table P-PZ40)
3402.B52 Bladé, Jean-François, 1827-1900 (Table P-PZ40)
3402.B587 Boissière, Jules, 1863-1897 (Table P-PZ40)
3402.B592 Bonnet, Baptiste, 1844-1925 (Table P-PZ40)
3402.C3 Camelat, Miquèu de, 1871-1962 (Table P-PZ40)
3402.C32 Cabanes, Jean de, 1654-1717 (Table P-PZ40)
3402.C354 Carvin (Table P-PZ40)
3402.C366 Cassan, Denis Casimir, 1810-1883 (Table P-PZ40)
3402.F56 Fourès, Auguste, 1848-1891 (Table P-PZ40)
3402.G43 Gelú, Victor, 1806-1885 (Table P-PZ40)
3402.G7 Gras, Fèlis, 1845-1901 (Table P-PZ40)
3402.J27 Jasmin, 1798-1864 (Table P-PZ40)
3402.L3 Laforêt, 1877-1937 (Table P-PZ40)
3402.L32 Lafosse, Albert (Table P-PZ40)
3402.L43 Legré, Ludovic, 1838-1904 (Table P-PZ40)
3402.M35 Mathieu, Anselme, 1828?-1895 (Table P-PZ40)
3402.M5 Mistral, Frédéric, 1830-1914 (Table P-PZ40)
3402.P4 Perbosc, Antonin, 1861-1944 (Table P-PZ40)
3402.R48 Rieu, Charlain, 1850-1924 (Table P-PZ40)
3402.R56 Roquille, Guillaume, 1804-1860 (Table P-PZ40)
3402.R6 Roumanille, Joseph, 1818-1891 (Table P-PZ40)
3402.T55 Tixier, Victor, 1815-1885 (Table P-PZ40)
3402.V37 Verdié, Meste, 1779-1820 (Table P-PZ40)

Dialects of France
By region, province, etc.
Southern France (Langue d'oc)
Modern patois of South France. "Langue des Félibres."
Langue d'oc
Literature
Texts
Individual authors and works -- Continued
3403.A-Z 21st century
Subarrange each author by Table P-PZ40
Local
For texts prefer PC3428, PC3448, etc.
3411.A-Z By region, province, etc., A-Z
3415.A-Z By place, A-Z
Translations
From foreign languages into Langue d'oc
see the original language
3420.4.A-Z From Langue d'oc into foreign languages. By language, A-Z
Langue d'oc dialects
3420.8 General
By region, province, etc.
Gascon
3421-3428 Language (Table P-PZ12 modified)
3427.A-Z Local. By dialect name or place, A-Z
3427.A5 Agenias
3427.A7 Aran Valley (Spain)
3427.A74 Ariège
3427.B3 Bayonne
3427.C68 Couserans
3427.S24 Salat River Valley
3427.S45 Sentenac d'Oust
(3429) Literature
(3429.2) Texts
see PC3428
Provence
Including the Rhodanien dialects of the Dept. of Bouches-du-Rhône, Marseille, Nice and Menton
3431-3438 Language (Table P-PZ12)
(3439) Literature
Languedoc
3441-3448 Language (Table P-PZ12)
(3449) Literature
Dauphiné
3461-3468 Language (Table P-PZ12)
(3469) Literature
Auvergne

Dialects of France
By region, province, etc.
Southern France (Langue d'oc)
Langue d'oc dialects
By region, province, etc.
Auvergne -- Continued
3471-3478 Language (Table P-PZ12)
(3479) Literature
Limousin
3481-3488 Language (Table P-PZ12)
(3489) Literature
3493.A-Z Other, A-Z
e.g.
3493.C7 Comtat-Venaissin
3495.A-Z Isolated dialects, by region, A-Z
French provincialisms, archaisms, etc.
General, see PC2711+
Dictionaries, see PC2667
Local, see PC2921+
Slang, see PC3721+
French in foreign parts
3551-3558 General (Table P-PZ12 modified)
(3557.A-Z) Local
see PC3561+
3561-3568 Algeria (Table P-PZ12)
3581 Belgium
Cf. PC3041+ Walloon dialect
3601-3646 Canada (Table P-PZ5)
3661 Switzerland
Cf. PC3141+ Franco-Provencal dialects in Switzerland
3680.A-Z Other, A-Z
e.g.
3680.A38 Africa
3680.A47 America
3680.C35 Cameroon
3680.G5 Germany
3680.I5 Indian Ocean islands
3680.I9 Ivory Coast. Côte d'Ivoire
3680.L43 Lebanon
3680.R48 Réunion
3680.R6 Romania
3680.R8 Russia
3680.S45 Senegal
3680.T64 Togo
United States
3680.U6 General

Dialects of France
By region, province, etc.
French in foreign parts
Other, A-Z
United States -- Continued
3680.U7A-.U7Z By state, region, etc., A-Z
(3701-3708) Creole languages
see PM7851+
Slang. Argot. Vulgarisms
3721 Collections. Studies, etc.
Texts
3725 Collections, General
3727 Special
General works
3731 General
3736 Grammatical studies
3739 Miscellaneous
3741 Dictionaries. Lists
Special classes
3744.A-Z Special categories of words, A-Z
3744.E8 Erotic literature
3744.I5 Industrial arts
3744.M65 Money
3744.S9 Swearing
Special groups of persons
3746 Beggars, gypsies, tramps, thieves, prostitutes, etc.
3747.A-Z Other
3747.C45 Children
3747.C6 Clergy
3747.P6 Police
3747.S4 Sailors
3747.S7 Soldiers
3747.S8 Students
3747.W65 Women
3747.Y68 Youth
3761.A-Z Special. Local, A-Z
French literature see PQ1+
Catalan
Philology
3801.A3 Congresses
3801.A4-Z Periodicals. Societies. Serials
Collections
3801.5 Texts. Sources, etc.
Monographs. Studies
3802.A2 Various authors
3802.A5-Z Individual authors
3803 Encyclopedias

Catalan
Philology -- Continued
(3804) Atlases. Maps
see class G
3805 Philosophy. Theory. Method. Relations
History of philology
Cf. PC3815 History of the language
Cf. PC3811 Study and teaching
3807 General works
Biography, memoirs, etc.
3809.A2 Collective
3809.A5-Z Individual, A-Z
Subarrange each by Table P-PZ50
(3810) Bibliography. Bio-bibliography
see Z7033.C37
3811 Study and teaching. Research
3813 General works
3814-3899 Language (Table P-PZ4b modified)
Add number in table to PC3800
3816 Outlines
3817 Popular
Style. Composition. Rhetoric
For study and teaching see PC3811
3875 General works
Etymology
3883.5 Dictionaries (exclusively etymological)
Lexicography
For biography of lexicographers see PC3809.A2+
3887 General works
Dictionaries
3889 Dictionaries with definitions in Catalan
3890 Dictionaries with definitions in two or more languages, or dictionaries of two or more languages with definitions in Catalan
3891 Dictionaries with definitions in English
3893.A-Z Dictionaries with definitions in other languages. By language, A-Z
Dictionaries exclusively etymological see PC3883.5
3893.2 Dictionaries of particular periods (other than periods separately specified elsewhere)
3895 Other special lists
Linguistic geography. Dialects, etc.
3896.A1 Linguistic geography
Dialects, provincialisms, etc.
Periodicals. Grammars. Dictionaries
see PC3801+
Texts see PC3945+

Catalan
Language
Linguistic geography. Dialects, etc.
Dialects, provincialisms, etc. -- Continued
3896.A5-Z General works. Grammar
3897.A-Z By region, place, etc., A-Z
(3898) Atlases. Maps
see class G
3899 Slang. Argot
Literature
Periodicals. Societies. Collections, etc. see PC3801.A4+; PC3801.5+
Biography of teachers, critics, and historians
3900 Collective
3900.5.A-Z Individual, A-Z
Subarrange each by Table P-PZ50
History
3901 General (Medieval, and modern)
3902 General special
3903 Special (not limited to period)
3904 Biography (Collective)
For individual authors see PC3937+
3906 Women authors. Literary relations of women
By period
3909 Medieval, and later, to 1840
3911 1840-
3913 Poetry
3915 Drama
3917 Prose
Texts
Collections
3925 General
3927 Selections. Anthologies
3929 Poetry
3929.5 Drama
Prose. Prose fiction
3930.A1 General
3930.A3-Z Special, A-Z
3930.A54 Animal stories
3930.C46 Christian fiction
3930.C48 Christmas stories
3930.D5 Detective and mystery stories
3930.F35 Fantasy fiction
3930.L4 Letters
3930.O7 Orations
3930.S34 Science fiction
3930.S4 Short stories

Catalan
Literature
Texts -- Continued
Individual authors and works

3937.A-Z To 1840
Subarrange each author by Table P-PZ40 unless otherwise indicated
Subarrange each separate work by Table P-PZ43 unless otherwise indicated

3937.A67 Anyes, Joan Baptista, 1480-1553 (Table P-PZ40)
3937.B34-.B343 Ball del Sant Crist de Salomó (Table P-PZ43)
3937.C3 Canals, Antoni, 1352-1419 (Table P-PZ40)
3937.C36-.C363 Cançoneret de Ripoll (Table P-PZ43)
3937.C37 Carroç Pardo de la Casta, Francesch (Table P-PZ40)
3937.C8-.C83 Curial e Güelfa (Table P-PZ43)
3937.E87 Eura, Agustí, 1684-1763 (Table P-PZ40)
3937.F3-.F33 Famosa comèdia de la gala està en sont punt (Table P-PZ43)
3937.F354 Febrer i Cardona, Antoni, 1761-1841 (Table P-PZ40)
3937.F36 Fenollar, Bernat (Table P-PZ40)
3937.F65 Fontanella, Francesc, 1622-ca. 1700 (Table P-PZ40)
3937.G28 Gaçull, Jaume, ca. 1450-ca. 1515 (Table P-PZ40)
3937.G37 García, Vicente, 1580-1625 (Table P-PZ40)
3937.G73 Gras, Lluis, 15th cent. (Table P-PZ40)
3937.J6 Jordi de Sant Jordi, 15th cent. (Table P-PZ40)
3937.L6 Lull, Ramón, d. 1315 (Table P-PZ40)
3937.M3 March, Auzias, 1397?-1459 (Table P-PZ38)
3937.M34 March, Pere, ca. 1337-1413 (Table P-PZ40)
3937.M4 Martorell, Joanot, d. 1468 (Table P-PZ38)
3937.M42 Mas Casellas i Enric, Josep M. (Josep Maria), 1767-1815 (Table P-PZ40)
3937.M45 Metge, Bernat, ca. 1350-ca. 1410 (Table P-PZ40)
3937.M67 Morlá, Pere Jacint, d. 1656 (Table P-PZ40)
3937.P55 Penya, Pere d'Alcàntara (Table P-PZ40)
3937.P72 Prats, Francesc, 1450?-1503 (Table P-PZ40)
Rector de Vallfogona, 1580-1625 see PC3937.G37
3937.R45 Robreño, Joseph, 1780-1838 (Table P-PZ40)
3937.R6 Roig, Jaime, d. 1478 (Table P-PZ40)
3937.R8 Roís de Corella, Joan, 1433?-1497 (Table P-PZ40)
Sant Jordi, Jordi de, ca. 1400-ca. 1424 see PC3937.J6
3937.S36 Serafí, Pere, ca. 1505-1567 (Table P-PZ40)
3937.S37 Serra i Postius, Pere, 1671-1748 (Table P-PZ40)
3937.S38 Serradell, Bernat (Table P-PZ40)
3937.S44 Simon, Bartomeu, 1734-1817 (Table P-PZ40)
3937.T47 Terrades, Abdó, 1812-1856 (Table P-PZ40)
3937.T52 Tío, Jaime, 1816-1844 (Table P-PZ40)

Catalan
Literature
Texts
Individual authors and works
To 1840 -- Continued

3937.T54 Togores i Zanglada, Joseph, 1767-1831 (Table P-PZ40)
3937.T58 Torrent i Vinyas, Marià, 1779-1823 (Table P-PZ40)
3937.T65 Torroella, Guillem de, 1348-1375 (Table P-PZ40)
3937.T8 Turmeda, Anselm, 1352-1432? (Table P-PZ40)
3937.V49-.V493 Viatge a l'Infern d'en Pere Porter (Table P-PZ43)
3937.V53 Vinyoles, Narcís, 15th cent. (Table P-PZ40)
3941.A-Z 1840-1960

Subarrange each author by Table P-PZ40 unless otherwise indicated

Subarrange each separate work by Table P-PZ43 unless otherwise indicated

e. g.

3941.A47 Aguiló, Tomàs, 1812-1884 (Table P-PZ40)
3941.A5 Aguilo y Fuster, Mariano, 1825-1897 (Table P-PZ40)
3941.A7 Albert y Paradís, Catalina, 1869-1966 (Table P-PZ40)
3941.A712 Alcover, Antoni Maria, 1862-1932 (Table P-PZ40)
3941.A713 Alcover y Maspons, Juan, 1854-1926 (Table P-PZ40)
3941.A7144 Alomar, Gabriel, 1873-1941 (Table P-PZ40)
3941.A71774 Angelon, Manuel, 1831-1889 (Table P-PZ40)
3941.A748 Artís-Gener, Arelí (Table P-PZ40)
3941.B24 Badenes i Dalmau, Francesc, 1858-1917 (Table P-PZ40)
3941.B32 Balaguer, Victor, 1824-1901 (Table P-PZ40)
3941.B365 Bell·lloc, Maria de, 1841-1907 (Table P-PZ40)
3941.B387 Bernat y Baldoví, José, 1810-1864 (Table P-PZ40)
3941.B43 Bertrana, Prudenci, 1867-1941 (Table P-PZ40)
Biel de la Mel, 1873-1941 see PC3941.A7144
3941.B62 Bosch de la Trinxeira, Carles (Table P-PZ40)
3941.B622 Bosch i Sureda, Joan Bartomeu, 1823-1898 (Table P-PZ40)
3941.C364 Casellas y Dou, Raimundo, 1855-1910 (Table P-PZ40)
Catala, Victor, 1869-1966 see PC3941.A7
3941.C6 Corominas, Pedro, 1870-1939 (Table P-PZ40)
3941.C7 Costa y Llobera, Miguel, 1854-1922 (Table P-PZ40)
3941.D49-.D493 Diversió de realistes i desengany de liberals (Table P-PZ43)
Dolç, Miguel, 1912- see PC3941.D6
3941.D6 Dolz, Miguel (Table P-PZ40)
3941.E86 Estadella i Arnó, Josep, 1880-1951 (Table P-PZ40)
3941.G43 Genís i Aguilar, Martí, 1847-1932 (Table P-PZ40)

Catalan
Literature
Texts
Individual authors and works
1840-1960 -- Continued
Gorkiano see PC3941.S344
3941.G84 Guimerá, Angel, 1845-1924 (Table P-PZ40)
3941.J594 Jordà y Puigmoltó, Milagro, 1823-1887 (Table P-PZ40)
3941.L53 Llombart, Constantí, 1848-1893 (Table P-PZ40)
3941.L573 Llorente, Teodoro, 1836-1911 (Table P-PZ40)
3941.M3 Maragall, Juan, 1860-1911 (Table P-PZ40)
Cf. PQ6623.A58 Spanish literature
Maspons i Labros, Pilar, 1841-1907 see PC3941.B365
3941.M65 Morera y Galicia, Magín, 1853-1927 (Table P-PZ40)
3941.O43 Oliver, Joan (Table P-PZ40)
3941.O5 Oller, Narciso, 1846-1930 (Table P-PZ40)
3941.P35-.P353 Els Pastorells (Table P-PZ43)
3941.P53 Pin i Soler, Josep, 1842-1927 (Table P-PZ40)
3941.P623 Pons i Gallarza, Josep Lluis, 1823-1894 (Table P-PZ40)
3941.P625 Pons i Massaveu, Joan, 1850-1918 (Table P-PZ40)
3941.P64 Pous y Pagés, José, 1873-1952 (Table P-PZ40)
Quart, Pere see PC3941.O43
3941.R567 Robert, Robert, 1830-1873 (Table P-PZ40)
3941.R8 Rusiñol, Santiago, 1861-1931 (Table P-PZ40)
3941.R9 Ruyra, Joaquín, 1858-1939 (Table P-PZ40)
3941.S344 Salvat-Papasseit, Joan, 1894-1924 (Table P-PZ40)
Sempronio see PC3941.A748
3941.S6 Soler, Frederico, 1839-1895 (Table P-PZ40)
3941.T48 Thos i Codina, Terenci, 1841-1903 (Table P-PZ40)
3941.T625 Torres Jordi, Pere Antoni, 1844-1901 (Table P-PZ40)
3941.V316 Vallmitjana, Julio (Table P-PZ40)
3941.V34 Vayreda, Maria, 1853-1903 (Table P-PZ40)
3941.V4 Verdaguer, Jacinto, 1845-1902 (Table P-PZ40)
3941.Z35 Zanné, Jerónimo, 1873-1934 (Table P-PZ40)
3942-3942.36 1961-2000 (Table P-PZ29 modified)
3942.13 C
Colomines, Joan, 1922- see PC3942.13.O55
3942.13.O55 Colomines y Puig, Juan, 1922- (Table P-PZ40)
3942.32 V
Vidal, Andreu, 1959- see PC3942.32.I334
3942.32.I334 Vidal i Sastre, Andreu, 1959- (Table P-PZ40)
3942.4-.436 2001- (Table P-PZ29a)
Local
Spain

Catalan
Literature
Local
Spain -- Continued
3945.A-Z By region, province, A-Z
Subarrange each by Table P-PZ26
3946.A-Z By place, A-Z
Subarrange each by Table P-PZ26
Outside of Spain
3947 General
Europe
3948.A2 General
3948.A3-Z By place, A-Z
Subarrange each by Table P-PZ26
America
3949 General
3950 United States and Canada
Spanish America
3951.A2 General
3951.A3-Z By country, region, etc., A-Z
Subarrange each by Table P-PZ26
3952.A-Z By place, A-Z
Subarrange each by Table P-PZ26
3953 Brazil
3955 Other
3975-3976 Translations from Catalan into foreign language (Table P-PZ30)
Spanish
4001-4071 Philology (Table P-PZ1a modified)
Periodicals. Serials
4008 Spanish
Societies
4018 Spanish
History of philology
Cf. PC4075+ History of the language
Biography, memoirs, etc.
4063 Collective
4064.A-Z Individual, A-Z
Subarrange each by Table P-PZ50
Study and teaching. Research
4065 General works
By period
For period of study, teaching, or research see PC4053+
For period of history of the language see PC4077+
General works
4070 Early works to 1700
4071 Later, 1701-

Spanish -- Continued
4073-4977 Language (Table P-PZ1b modified)
Add number in table to PC4000
Grammar
Readers
Primers
4114 Early to 1870
4115 Later
Style. Composition. Rhetoric
For study and teaching see PC4065+
4410 General works
Etymology
4580 Dictionaries (exclusively etymological)
4582.A-Z Special elements. By language, A-Z
4582.A3 Foreign elements (General)
Cf. PC4670 Dictionaries
Lexicography
4601 Periodicals. Societies. Serials. Collections (nonserial)
4611 General works
Biography of lexicographers see PC4063+
4617 Criticism, etc., of particular dictionaries
Dictionaries
Spanish only
4620 Early to 1800
1800-
4625 General
4628 Minor, abridged, school dictionaries
4629 Picture dictionaries
4630 Supplementary dictionaries. Dictionaries of new words
4635 Polyglot (definitions in two or more languages)
Bilingual
4640 Spanish-English; English-Spanish
4645.A-Z Other. By language, A-Z
Classify with language less known
Spanish-French; French-Spanish
4645.F2 To 1850
4645.F3 1851-
Spanish-German; German-Spanish
4645.G2 To 1850
4645.G3 1851-
Spanish-Italian; Italian-Spanish see PC1645.S7+
Spanish-Portuguese; Portuguese-Spanish see PC5335.S8
Dictionaries exclusively etymological see PC4580
4650 Dictionaries of particular periods (other than periods separately specified elsewhere)

Spanish
Language
Lexicography
Dictionaries -- Continued
(4655) Dictionaries of particular authors
see the author in classes PA-PT
4660 Dictionaries of names
Cf. CS2300+ Personal and family names
Cf. PC4673 Foreign names
4667 Dictionaries, etc., of obsolete or archaic words
Dictionaries of foreign words
4670 General
4673 Names
Special. By language see PC4582.A+
Rhyming dictionaries
see PC4519
Other special lists
4680 Glossaries
(4683.A-Z) By subject, A-Z
see the subject in classes A-N, Q-Z
4689 Dictionaries of terms and phrases
4691 Word frequency lists
4692 Reverse indexes
4693 Abbreviations, Lists of
Linguistic geography. Dialects, etc.
4700 Linguistic geography
Dialects. Provincialisms, etc.
4701 Periodicals. Societies. Congresses
For local societies see PC4781+
Collections
4702 Texts. Sources, etc.
4703 Monographs. Studies. By various or individual authors
4704 Encyclopedias
(4705) Atlases. Maps
see class G
General works
4711 Treatises
4712 Compends. Outlines, syllabi, etc. Popular. Minor
History of dialects
4713 General
4714 General special
4715 Earliest. Medieval. Old Spanish
4715.Z5 Vocabularies. Dictionaries
4716 (16th)-17th century. (17th)-18th century
4718 19th century. 20th century. 21st century
Grammar

Spanish
Language
Linguistic geography. Dialects, etc.
Dialects. Provincialisms, etc.
Grammar -- Continued
4721 General works
4726 Phonology. Phonetics
4736 Morphology. Inflection. Accidence
4746 Syntax
4751 Style
4756 Prosody. Metrics. Rhythmics
4761 Etymology
4766 Lexicography
By region, province, etc.
4781-4784 Navarrese-Aragonese (Table P-PZ14)
4786-4789 Asturian (Bable). Oviedo province (Table P-PZ14)
Mirandese dialect see PC5401+
4790 Cantabrian (Montañes) (Table P-PZ15)
4791-4794 Leonese (Table P-PZ14)
4796-4799 Castilian (Table P-PZ14)
4801-4804 Extremeño (Table P-PZ14)
4806-4809 Andalusian (Table P-PZ14)
4811 Aljamia (Spanish written in Arabic characters) (Table P-PZ15)
(4812) Germania, Jerga, Jerigonza
see PC4975
4813-4813.95 Jewish Spanish (Ladino) and Hakétia language and literature (Table P-PZ15a)
4814 Gitano (Table P-PZ15)
4815.A-Z Other, A-Z
e. g.
4815.A6 Alava
4815.M8 Murcia
Provincialisms. Archaisms, etc.
(4816) General
see PC4701+
(4816.22) Dictionaries
see PC4667
(4816.24) Local
see PC4781+
Slang
see PC4951+
Spanish in foreign parts
4816.5 General works
4816.55 Austria (Table P-PZ15)
4816.7 Flanders (Table P-PZ15)
4817 Africa (Table P-PZ15)

Spanish
Language
Linguistic geography. Dialects, etc.
Spanish in foreign parts -- Continued
4821-4824 America (Table P-PZ14 modified)
Cf. PC4826+ Particular countries and states
4822 Hispanicized Indian words in Spanish and Spanish Americanisms in general
4826-4829 United States (Table P-PZ14)
4831-4834 Mexico (Table P-PZ14)
4838 Caribbean Area (Table P-PZ15)
4841-4844 Central America (Table P-PZ14)
4851-4854 West Indies (Table P-PZ14 modified)
4854.A-.Z9 Local. By dialect name or place, A-Z
4854.C8 Cuba
4854.D6 Dominican Republic
4854.H3 Haiti
4854.J3 Jamaica
4854.P8 Puerto Rico
South America
4861 General
4871-4874 Argentina (Table P-PZ14)
4876-4879 Bolivia (Table P-PZ14)
4881-4884 Chile (Table P-PZ14)
4886-4889 Colombia (Table P-PZ14)
4891-4894 Ecuador (Table P-PZ14)
4896-4899 Paraguay (Table P-PZ14)
4901-4904 Peru (Table P-PZ14)
4906-4909 Uruguay (Table P-PZ14)
4911-4914 Venezuela (Table P-PZ14)
Asia
Former Spanish colonies
4921-4924 Philippines (Table P-PZ14)
4941 Other (Table P-PZ15)
(4949) Creole languages
see PM7841+
Slang. Argot
4951 Collections
Texts
4955 Collections. General
4957 Special
General works
4961 General works
4966 Grammatical studies
4969 Miscellaneous
4971 Dictionaries. Lists
Special classes

Spanish
Language
Linguistic geography. Dialects, etc.
Slang. Argot
Special classes -- Continued
4974.A-Z Special categories of words, A-Z
4974.O2 Obscene words
Special groups of persons
4975 Beggars, tramps, thieves, prostitutes, etc.
(4976) Gypsies
see PC4814
4977.A-Z Other, A-Z
4977.G39 Gays
4977.Y68 Youth
Spanish literature see PQ6001+
Portuguese
Philology
5001 Periodicals. Serials
5003 Societies
5009 Congresses
Collections
5012 Texts. Sources
Prefer PQ9122+ PQ9131+
Monographs. Studies
5013 Various authors
5014.A-Z Studies in honor of a particular person or institution, A-Z
5015 Individual authors
5019 Encyclopedias
(5020) Atlases. Maps
see class G
Philosophy. Theory. Method
5021 General works
5023 Relations
History of philology
Cf. PC5035+ Study and teaching
Cf. PC5045+ History of the language
5025 General
5026 General special
By period
5027 Earliest. Middle Ages. Renaissance
5029 Modern
5031.A-Z By region or country, A-Z
(5032) Bibliography. Bio-bibliography
see Z2725
Biography. Memoirs. Correspondence
5033 Collective

Portuguese
Philology
History of philology
Biography. Memoirs. Correspondence -- Continued
5034.A-Z Individual, A-Z
Study and teaching
5035 General
5036 General special
By period
For period of study, teaching, or research see PC5027+
For period of history of the language see PC5047+
5038.A-Z By region or country, A-Z
5039.A-Z By university, college, school, etc., A-Z
5041 General works
Language
5043 Treatises
5044 Relation to other languages
5044.5 Language data processing
5044.7 Language standardization and variation
5044.73 Political aspects
5044.75 Social aspects
5044.8 Spoken language
5044.85 Language acquisition
History of the language
For history of the language in a specific place see PC5371+
5045 General works
By period
5047 Middle Ages. (15th)-16th century
5049 (16th)-18th century
5051 19th-20th century
5052 21st century
5057 Popular. Minor
Grammar
5059 Comparative (Two or more languages)
5061 Historical
General works
5063 To 1800
5064 1800-
5065 General special
Textbooks. Exercises
5065.5 History and criticism
5066 Early to 1851
5067 Later, 1851-1949
5067.3 1950-
5067.5 Self-instructors
5067.7 Audiovisual instructors

Portuguese
Language
Grammar -- Continued
Readers
5067.9 History and criticism
5069 Primary
5071 Advanced (including Intermediate)
Phonetic readers see PC5088
5071.5 Examination questions, etc.
5072.A-Z Manuals for special classes of students, A-Z
For list of Cutter numbers, see Table P-PZ1 120.A+
5073 Conversation. Phrase books
5074.2.A-Z Readers on special subjects, A-Z
For list of Cutter numbers, see Table P-PZ1 127.A+
Textbooks for foreign speakers
5074.3 Theory, methods, etc., for teachers
5074.5 General
5075.A-Z By language, A-Z
Phonology
Including phonemics
5076 General works
Phonetics
5077 General works
5079 Pronunciation
5081 Accent
5081.5 Intonation
Orthography. Spelling
5083 History. General works
5085 Spelling books
5087 Spelling reform
5088 Phonetic readers
Alphabet. Vowels. Consonants, etc.
5089 General works
5091 Vowels
5093 Consonants
5094 Contraction (Hiatus. Elision)
5098 Syllabication
Punctuation see PC5258
5099 Capitalization
5100 Morphophonemics
Morphology. Inflection. Accidence
5101 General
5103 Word formation
Special: Noun, Verb, etc.
see PC5119+
5111 Tables. Paradigms
Parts of speech (Morphology and syntax)

Portuguese
Language
Grammar
Parts of speech (Morphology and syntax) -- Continued
5119 General works
Noun
5121 General works
5125 Gender
5127 Number
5129 Case
Adjective. Adverb. Comparison
5133 General works
5135 Numerals
5137 Article
5141 Pronoun
Verb
5145 General works
5147 Person
5149 Number
5151 Voice
5153 Mood
5159 Tense
5160 Aspects of verbal action
Infinitive and participle
5162 General works
5164 Participle, gerund, etc.
5165.A-Z Special classes of verbs, A-Z
For list of Cutter numbers, see Table P-PZ1 315.A+
5167.A-Z Particular verbs, A-Z
5169 Other. Miscellaneous
Particle
5171 General works
5173 Adverb
5177 Preposition
5181 Conjunction
5187 Interjection
5191.A-Z Other special, A-Z
5191.C54 Clitics
5191.N4 Negatives
Syntax
5201 General
5207 General special
Sentences
5211 General arrangement, etc.
5213 Order of words
5215 Order of clauses
5217 Clauses

Portuguese
Language
Grammar
Syntax
Sentences -- Continued
5225 Other special
5228.A-Z Other aspects, A-Z
For list of Cutter numbers, see Table P-PZ1 398.A+
(5231) Grammatical usage of particular authors
see the author in classes PA-PT

Style. Composition. Rhetoric
For study and teaching see PC5035+
5240 General works
5245 Textbooks
5250 Outlines, questions, exercises, specimens. List of subjects
5252 Discourse analysis
Special parts of rhetoric
5253 Style. Invention, narrative, etc.
5255 Other special. Figures, tropes, allegory, etc.
5256 Choice of words. Vocabulary, etc.
5258 Punctuation
5260 Idioms. Errors. Blunders
Special classes of composition
5263 Essays, lectures, newspaper style, precis writing, report writing, etc.
Letter writing
5265 General works
5267 Specimens. Collections
Translating
For special subjects, see classes B-Z, e.g. T11.5 Technology
5268 General works
5269 Machine translating
Including research
Prosody. Metrics. Rhythmics
5271 History of the science
General works
5274 Early to 1800
5275 1800-
5279 Textbooks
5281 Versification
5283 Rhyme. Rhyming dictionaries
5285.A-Z Special. By form, A-Z
5290.A-Z Special meters, A-Z
5295 Other special
Including epithets

Portuguese
Language
Prosody. Metrics. Rhythmics -- Continued
(5297) Special authors
see the author in classes PA-PT
5298 Rhythm
5299 Rhythm in prose
5299.5 Lexicology
Etymology
5301 Treatises
5303 Names (General)
For personal names see CS2300+ ; for place names, see G104+ (General) or classes D-F for names of specific continents or countries
5305 Dictionaries (exclusively etymological)
5307.A-Z Special elements. By language, A-Z
5307.A3 Foreign elements (General)
Cf. PC5343 Dictionaries
5307.5 Other special
5308 Folk etymology
5310 Semantics
5315 Synonyms. Antonyms. Homonyms
5317 Onomatopoeic words
5319.A-Z Particular words, A-Z
Lexicography
5320 Periodicals. Societies. Serials. Collections (nonserial)
5323 General works
Biography of lexicographers see PC5033+
5323.5 Criticism, etc., of particular dictionaries
Dictionaries
Portuguese only
5325 Early, to ca. 1800
5327 Later, ca. 1800-
5328 Picture dictionaries
5329 Supplementary dictionaries. Dictionaries of new words
5331 Polyglot (Definitions in two or more languages)
Bilingual
5333 Portuguese-English; English-Portuguese
5335.A-Z Other. By language, A-Z
Classify with language less known
5335.F8 Portuguese-French; French-Portuguese
5335.G5 Portuguese-German; German-Portuguese
5335.I8 Portuguese-Italian; Italian-Portuguese
5335.S8 Portuguese-Spanish; Spanish-Portuguese
Dictionaries exclusively etymological see PC5305

Portuguese
Language
Lexicography
Dictionaries -- Continued
5337 Dictionaries of particular periods (other than periods separately specified elsewhere)
(5339) Dictionaries of particular authors
see the author in classes PA-PT
5341 Dictionaries of names
Cf. CS2300+ Genealogy
Cf. PC5344 Foreign words
5342 Dictionaries of obsolete or archaic words
Dictionaries of foreign words
5343 General
5344 Names
Special. By language see PC5307.A+
Other special lists
5345 Miscellaneous
(5346) By subject
See the subject in Classes A-N, Q-Z
5347 Dictionaries of terms and phrases
5348 Other
Including word frequency, etc.
For research on word frequency, etc., in connection with machine translating see PC5269
Linguistic geography
5350 General works
Dialects. Provincialisms, etc.
5351 Periodicals. Societies. Congresses
For local dialect societies see PC5371+
Collections
5353 Texts. Sources, etc.
5354 Monographs. Studies
(5355) Atlases. Maps
see class G
General works
5357 Treatises
5358 General special
5359 History of dialects
5360 Old Portuguese (to 1500)
Grammar
5361 General works
5362 Phonology. Phonetics
5363 Morphology. Inflection. Accidence
5364 Syntax
5365 Etymology

Portuguese
Language
Linguistic geography
Dialects. Provincialisms, etc. -- Continued
5367 Lexicography
By region, province, etc.
Dialects of continental Portugal and Spain
(5371-5374) General
see PC5351+
5376-5379 Entre-Douro-e-Minho ("Interamnense") (Table P-PZ14)
5381-5384 Tras-os-Montes ("Transmontano"). Dialect "Raiano" (of the frontier and of Ermisende in Spain) (Table P-PZ14)
5386-5389 Dialect of Beira ("Beirão") (Table P-PZ14)
Southern dialects
5390 General works
5391-5394 Alemtejo (Table P-PZ14 modified)
5394.A-.Z9 Local. By dialect name or place, A-Z
5394.B3 Barrancos
5394.O6 Olivença (Spain)
5395 Algarve (Table P-PZ15)
5396-5399 Estremadura (Table P-PZ14)
5401-5404 Dialect of Miranda (Mirandese) (Table P-PZ14)
Called codialect by Leite de Vasconcellos in distinction from Portuguese dialects proper
5405 Sendim (Subdialect) (Table P-PZ15)
Called codialect by Leite de Vasconcellos in distinction from Portuguese dialects proper
5407 Guadramil dialect (Table P-PZ15)
Called codialect by Leite de Vasconcellos in distinction from Portuguese dialects proper
5409 Riodonor (Rionor) dialect (Table P-PZ15)
Called codialect by Leite de Vasconcellos in distinction from Portuguese dialects proper
5411-5414 Galician (Gallego) (Table P-PZ14)
Called codialect by Leite de Vasconcellos in distinction from Portuguese dialects proper
5415 Aljamia (Portuguese written in Arabic characters) (Table P-PZ15)
5416-5419 Insular Portuguese (Table P-PZ14)
Including Azores, Madeira
5423 Jewish Portuguese (Table P-PZ15)
Including Amsterdam and The Hague in Netherlands, Hamburg in Germany, etc.
Portuguese in foreign parts
5426 General works

Portuguese
Language
Linguistic geography
Dialects. Provincialisms, etc.
By region, province, etc.
Portuguese in foreign parts -- Continued
5428 Europe (Table P-PZ15)
5431 Africa (Table P-PZ15)
Including Angola, Mozambique
America
South America
5441-5448 Brazil (Table P-PZ12)
5451 Paraguay (Table P-PZ15)
5453 Uruguay (Table P-PZ15)
5455 Argentina (Table P-PZ15)
5461 North America (Table P-PZ15)
Including California, Massachusetts, Rhode Island
5471 Asia (Table P-PZ15)
Including Ceylon, Goa, Coromandel, Macau ("Macaista")
Creole dialects
see PM7846+
5498 Slang. Argot
Portuguese literature see PQ9000+

Germanic philology and languages
General
Class here works dealing collectively with the Germanic languages or the West Germanic languages
Philology
Periodicals
1 American and English
2 French
3 German
4 Dutch
5 Scandinavian
9 Other
10 Annuals. Yearbooks, etc.
Societies
11 American and English
12 French
13 German
14 Dutch
15 Scandinavian
19 Other
21 Congresses
Collections
23 Texts. Sources, etc.
Cf. PN821+ Germanic literatures
Monographs. Studies
25 Various authors. Series
26.A-Z Studies in honor of a particular person or institution, A-Z
27 Individual authors
31 Encyclopedias. Dictionaries
(33) Atlases. Maps
see class G
Philosophy. Theory. Method
35 General works
37 Relations to other sciences
History of philology
51 General
60.A-Z By region or country, A-Z
(62) Bibliography. Bio-bibliography
see Z7036+
Biography. Memoirs. Correspondence
63 Collective
64.A-Z Individual, A-Z
Subarrange each by Table P-PZ50
Study and teaching
65 General
66 General special

General
Philology
Study and teaching -- Continued
68.A-Z By region or country, A-Z
69.A-Z By university, college, etc., A-Z
71 General works
73-780 Languages (Table P-PZ1b modified)
Add table number to PD0
History
76 Proto-Germanic languages
91 Compends
Etymology
580 Dictionaries (exclusively etymological)
582.A-Z Special elements. By language, A-Z
582.A3 Foreign elements (General)
Cf. PD670 Dictionaries
Lexicography
601 Periodicals. Societies. Serials. Collections (nonserial)
611 General works
Biography of lexicographers see PD63+
617 Criticism, etc. of particular dictionaries
Dictionaries
625 General dictionaries
Dictionaries exclusively etymological see PD580
660 Dictionaries of names
667 Dictionaries, etc. of obsolete or archaic words
Dictionaries of foreign words
670 General
673 Names
Special. By language see PD582.A+
Other special lists
680 Glossaries
689 Dictionaries of terms and phrases
691 Word frequency lists
692 Reverse indexes
693 Lists of abbreviations
Linguistic geography. Dialects, etc.
700 Linguistic geography
Dialects. Provincialisms, etc.
(701) Periodicals. Collections
see PD1+
707 Collections of texts, etc.
710 General works
Grammar
see PD99+
770 Dictionaries

General
Languages
Linguistic geography. Dialects, etc.
Dialects. Provincialisms, etc. -- Continued
(777) Atlases. Maps
see class G
780.A-Z Local. By region, place, etc., A-Z
Literature
General see PN821+
Particular literatures see PR1+; PS1+; PT1+
Old Germanic dialects
1001-1029 Prehistoric Germanic ("Urgermanisch") (Table P-PZ6)
Old Germanic dialects
1031-1059 General (Table P-PZ6)
1060 Texts
(1061-1068) West Germanic (Anglo-Saxon, Old Frisian, Old Saxon, Old High German)
see PD1031+
North Germanic see PD1501+
(1071-1099) East Germanic (Gothic, or Gothic and Scandinavian)
see PD1101+ PD1501+
Gothic
1101-1113 Philology (Table P-PZ4a modified)
History of philology
Cf. PD1115 History of the language
1107 General works
Biography, memoirs, etc.
1109.A2 Collective
1109.A5-Z Individual, A-Z
Subarrange each by Table P-PZ50
1114-1186.9 Language (Table P-PZ4b modified)
Add number in table to PD1100
Etymology
1183.5 Dictionaries (exclusively etymological)
Lexicography
For biography of lexicographers see PD1109.A2+
For etymological dictionaries see PD1183.5
1187 General works
1193 Dictionaries. Glossaries, etc.
Literature
1194 History
Collections
(1195) Bible
see BS105+
1196 Other

Old Germanic dialects
Old Germanic dialects
Gothic
Literature -- Continued
1197.A-Z Individual authors or works, A-Z
Subarrange each author by Table P-PZ38
Subarrange each separate work by Table P-PZ43
1211 Crimean Gothic
1270 Vandal
1301 Burgundian
1350 Langobardian
North Germanic. Scandinavian (General)
Philology
Periodicals
1501 English and American
1503 Scandinavian. German. Dutch
1504 Other
Societies
1505 English and American
1506 Scandinavian. German. Dutch
1507 Other
1509 Congresses
Collections
1511 Texts, sources, etc.
Monographs. Studies
1513 Various authors. Series
1514.A-Z Studies in honor of a particular person or institution, A-Z
1515 Individual authors
1519 Encyclopedias. Dictionaries
Philosophy. Theory. Method
1521 General works
1523 Relations
History of philology
Cf. PD1545+ History of the language
Cf. PD1535+ Study and teaching
1525 General
1531.A-Z By region or country, A-Z
(1532) Bibliography. Bio-bibliography
see Z2555
Biography. Memoirs. Correspondence
1533 Collective
1534.A-Z Individual, A-Z
Subarrange each by Table P-PZ50
Study and teaching. Research
1535 General
1538.A-Z By region or country, A-Z

North Germanic. Scandinavian (General)
Philology
Study and teaching. Research -- Continued
1539.A-Z By university, college, etc., A-Z
1539.5.A-Z By research institute, A-Z
1541 General works
1543-1895 Languages (Table P-PZ2a modified)
Add number in table to PD1500
Style. Composition. Rhetoric
For study and teaching see PD1535+
1740 General works
Lexicography
1823 General works
Biography of lexicographers see PD1533+
Linguistic geography. Dialects, etc.
1850 Linguistic geography
Dialects. Provincialisms, etc.
(1851) Periodicals. Collections
see PD1501+
1853 Collections of texts, etc.
1855 General works
(1861-1880) Grammar
see PD1559+
1890 Dictionaries
(1893) Atlases. Maps
see class G
1895.A-.A Local. By region, place, etc., A-Z
Scandinavian literatures see PT7001+
Prehistoric Scandinavian ("Urnordisk"). Runic inscriptions
Including the runic inscriptions of the later (Old Norse) period written in the alphabet of 16 runes and runic inscriptions of non-Scandinavian countries
2001 Treatises (General)
Texts: Runic inscriptions
Collections
2002 General
2003 Anglo-Saxon
2005 Other
2007.A-Z Particular inscriptions and works, A-Z (by locality or title)
Treatises (on Runes)
2013 General
2014 General special. Minor
2017 Script
2093 Dictionaries
Old Norse: Old Icelandic and Old Norwegian
Includes Norrønt maal, Western Norse, ca. 800 to ca. 1550

Old Norse: Old Icelandic and Old Norwegian -- Continued
2201-2223 Philology (Table P-PZ3a modified)
Cf. PD1501+ North Germanic. Scandinavian
History of philology
Cf. PD2225 History of the language
Biography, memoirs, etc.
2217.A2 Collective
2217.A5-Z Individual, A-Z
Subarrange each by Table P-PZ50
2224-2393 Language (Table P-PZ3b modified)
Add number in table to PD2200
Script (Runes)
see PD2002+
Etymology
2363 Dictionaries (exclusively etymological)
Lexicography
2371 Periodicals. Societies. Serials. Collections (nonserial)
2373 Treatises
Biography of lexicographers see PD2217.A2+
2373.5 Criticism, etc., of particular dictionaries
Dictionaries
2376 Icelandic-Scandinavian; Scandinavian-Icelandic
Definitions in Modern Icelandic or Norwegian or Danish or Swedish
2378 Icelandic-Latin; Latin-Icelandic
2379 Icelandic-English; English-Icelandic
2381 Icelandic-German [-Italian, etc.]; German [Italian, etc.] - Icelandic
Do not subarrange by language; subarrange by main entry only
Dictionaries exclusively etymological see PD2363
2384 Names
2385 Other special lists
Including glossaries, dictionaries of terms and phrases, word frequency lists, reverse indexes, and lists of abbreviations
Linguistic geography. Dialects
Cf. PD3771+ Old and Middle Danish dialects
Cf. PD5771+ Old and Middle Swedish dialects
2387 Linguistic geography
Dialects. Provincialisms, etc.
2388 Treatises
(2389) Grammar
see PD2229+
(2392) Atlases. Maps
see class G
2393.A-Z Local. By region, place, etc., A-Z

Old Norse: Old Icelandic and Old Norwegian -- Continued
Icelandic and Old Norse literature see PT7101+
Modern Icelandic (ca. 1550-)
2401-2446 Language (Table P-PZ5 modified)
General works
2408 Treatises (Philology, General)
History of the language
Cf. PD2224+ Old Icelandic and Old Norwegian
2409 General works
Grammar
2419 Morphology. Inflection. Accidence
Lexicography
Dictionaries
2437.A-Z Dictionaries with definitions in English or other languages. By main entry, A-Z
Do not subarrange by language; subarrange by main entry only
Modern Icelandic literature see PT7351+
Other insular Scandinavian languages and dialects
2483 Faroe Islands
For Faroese literature see PT7581+
2485 Shetland Islands ("Norn"; Norrøn")
Cf. PE2331+ English dialects
2487 Orkney Islands
Cf. PE2296+ English dialects
2489 Hebrides
Norwegian
(2501-2550) Old Norwegian
see PD2201+
2571-2578 Middle Norwegian (ca. 1350-ca. 1550) (Table P-PZ12)
2601-2699 Modern Norwegian (Dano-Norwegian. Riksmaal) (Table P-PZ4 modified)
Cf. PD3001+ Danish language
Grammar
Readers
2624 Primary
2625 Intermediate and advanced
Lexicography
2688.A-Z Dictionaries with definitions in Norwegian (Riksmaal)
Dictionaries with definitions in Norwegian (Landsmaal) see PD2988.A+
Other dictionaries
Other Scandinavian languages
2689 Norwegian-Danish; Danish-Norwegian
Norwegian-Icelandic; Icelandic-Norwegian
see PD2376, PD2437

Norwegian
Modern Norwegian (Dano-Norwegian. Riksmaal)
Lexicography
Other dictionaries
Other Scandinavian languages -- Continued
Norwegian-Swedish; Swedish-Norwegian
see PD5632, PD2989
2901-2999 New Norwegian (Landsmaal, Nynorsk) (Table P-PZ4 modified)
Lexicography
2988.A-Z Dictionaries with definitions in Norwegian (Riksmaal or Landsmaal)
Other dictionaries
Other Scandinavian languages
2989 Norwegian-Danish; Danish-Norwegian; Norwegian-Swedish; Swedish-Norwegian
Norwegian-Icelandic; Icelandic-Norwegian
see PD2376, PD2437
Norwegian literature see PT8301+
Danish
3001-3071 Philology (Table P-PZ1a modified)
Periodicals. Serials
3004 Scandinavian
Societies
3014 Scandinavian
(3033) Atlases. Maps
see class G
History of philology
Cf. PD3075+ History of the language
Biography, memoirs, etc.
3063 Collective
3064.A-Z Individual, A-Z
Subarrange each by Table P-PZ50
Bibliography. Bio-bibliography
see Z2575
Study and teaching. Research
3065 General works
By period
For period of study, teaching, or research see PD3053+
For period of history of the language see PD3077+
3073-3929 Language (Table P-PZ1b modified)
Add number in table to PD3000
Grammar
General works
3103 Early to 1870
3105 Later, 1871-

Danish
Language -- Continued
Style. Composition. Rhetoric
For study and teaching see PD3065+
3410 General works
Etymology
3580 Dictionaries (exclusively etymological)
3582.A-Z Special elements. By language, A-Z
3582.A3 Foreign elements (General)
Cf. PD3670 Dictionaries
Lexicography
3601 Periodicals. Societies. Serials. Collections (nonserial)
3611 General works
Biography of lexicographers see PD3063+
3617 Criticism, etc., of particular dictionaries
Dictionaries
Dictionaries with definitions in Danish
3620 Early to 1800
1800-
3625 General
3628 Minor, abridged, school dictionaries
3629 Picture dictionaries
3630 Supplementary dictionaries. Dictionaries of new words
3635 Dictionaries with definitions in two or more languages, or dictionaries of two or more languages with definitions in one language
3640 Dictionaries with definitions in English
3645.A-Z Dictionaries with definitions in other languages. By language, A-Z
Classify with language less known
Danish-Icelandic; Icelandic-Danish
see PD2376, PD2437
Danish-Norwegian (Riksmaal); Norwegian-Danish
see PD2689
Danish-Norwegian (Landsmaal); Norwegian-Danish
see PD2989
Danish-Oriental; Oriental-Danish
see subclasses PJ-PL
Danish-Slavic; Slavic-Danish
see subclass PG
Danish-Swedish; Swedish-Danish
see PD5631
Dictionaries exclusively etymological see PD3580
3650 Dictionaries of particular periods (other than periods separately specified elsewhere)

Danish
Language
Lexicography
Dictionaries -- Continued
(3655) Dictionaries of particular authors
see the author in classes PA-PT
3660 Dictionaries of names
Cf. CS2300+ Personal and family names
Cf. PD3673 Foreign words
3667 Dictionaries, etc. of obsolete or archaic words
Dictionaries of foreign words
3670 General
3673 Names
Special. By language see PD3582.A+
Rhyming dictionaries
see PD3519
Other special lists
3680 Glossaries
(3683) By subject
see the subject in classes A-N, Q-Z
3689 Dictionaries of terms and phrases
3691 Word frequency lists
3692 Reverse indexes
3693 Abbreviations, Lists of
Linguistic geography. Dialects, etc.
3700 Linguistic geography
Dialects. Provincialisms, etc.
3701 Periodicals. Societies. Congresses
For local dialect societies see PD3801+
Collections
3702 Texts. Sources, etc.
3703 Monographs. Studies
3704 Encyclopedias. Dictionaries
(3705) Atlases. Maps
see class G
General works
3711 Treatises
3712 Compends. Popular
History of dialects
3713 General
3714 General special
3715 Earliest. Medieval
3716 (16th-)17th and (17th-)18th centuries
3718 19th century. 20th century. 21st century
Grammar
3721 General works
3726 Phonology. Phonetics

Danish
Language
Linguistic geography. Dialects, etc.
Dialects. Provincialisms, etc.
Grammar -- Continued
3736 Morphology. Inflection. Accidence
3746 Syntax
3751 Style
3756 Prosody. Metrics. Rhythmics
3761 Etymology
3766 Lexicography
3771-3778 Old Danish (Table P-PZ12)
11th to 15th century, including "Middle Danish," ca. 1350-1550
(3781-3788) Early modern Danish, ca. 1400/1550-1700
see PD3073+
By region, province, etc.
3801-3808 Skåne (Scania, Schonen) dialect (Table P-PZ12)
Includes Skåne, Halland, Blekinge
Cf. PD5831+ South Swedish dialects
3811-3818 Insular dialects (Table P-PZ12 modified)
Cf. PD5831+ South Swedish dialects
3817.A-Z Local. By dialect name or place, A-Z
3817.A4 Als
3817.B7 Bornholm
3817.Z5 Zealand (Sjælland)
3821-3828 Jutish (Table P-PZ12)
Dano-Norwegian see PD2601+
3850.2-3895 Danish in foreign parts
Dano-Norwegian see PD2601+
3851 General works
3860 Iceland
3870 Greenland
America
3880 General works
3890 West Indies
3895.A-Z Other, A-Z
Slang. Argot
3901 Collections
Texts
3905 Collections (General)
3907 Special
General works
3911 General
3916 Grammatical studies
3919 Miscellaneous
3921 Dictionaries. Lists

Danish
Language
Linguistic geography. Dialects, etc.
Slang. Argot -- Continued
Special classes
3925 Beggars. Gypsies. Tramps. Thieves, etc.
3927.A-Z Other, A-Z
3929.A-Z Special. Local, A-Z
Danish literature see PT7601+
Swedish
5001-5071 Philology (Table P-PZ1a modified)
Periodicals. Serials
5004 Scandinavian
Societies
5014 Scandinavian
(5033) Atlases. Maps
see class G
History of philology
Cf. PD5075+ History of the language
Biography, memoirs, etc.
5063 Collective
5064.A-Z Individual, A-Z
Subarrange each by Table P-PZ50
Bibliography. Bio-bibliography
see Z2635
Study and teaching. Research
5065 General works
By period
For period of study, teaching, or research see PD5053+
For period of history of the language see PD5077+
5073-5929 Language (Table P-PZ1b modified)
Add number in table to PD5000
Grammar
General works
5103 Early to 1870
5105 Later, 1871-
Style. Composition. Rhetoric
For study and teaching see PD5065+
5410 General works
Etymology
5580 Dictionaries (exclusively etymological)
5582.A-Z Special elements. By language, A-Z
5582.A3 Foreign elements (General)
Cf. PD5670 Dictionaries
Lexicography
5601 Periodicals. Societies. Serials. Collections (nonserial)
5611 General works

PD

Swedish
Language
Lexicography -- Continued
Biography of lexicographers see PD5063+
5617 Criticism, etc., of particular dictionaries
Dictionaries
Dictionaries with definitions in Swedish
5620 Early to 1800
1800-
5625 General
5628 Minor, abridged, school dictionaries
5629 Picture dictionaries
5630 Supplementary dictionaries. Dictionaries of new words
Swedish-Scandinavian
5631 Swedish-Danish; Danish-Swedish
5632 Swedish-Norwegian (Riksmaal); Norwegian-Swedish
(5633) Swedish-Norwegian (Landsmaal); Norwegian-Swedish
see PD2989
(5634) Swedish-Icelandic; Icelandic-Swedish
see PD2376, PD2437
Dictionaries with definitions in two or more languages, or dictionaries of two or more languages with definitions in one language
5635 Trilingual (Definitions in two languages)
For dictionaries including English see PD5640
For dictionaries including Finnish see PH278
5638 Other (Definitions in three or more languages)
5640 Swedish-English; English-Swedish
5645.A-Z Swedish-German [-French, etc.]; German [French, etc.]-Swedish. By language, A-Z
Classify with language less known
Swedish-Oriental; Oriental-Swedish
see subclasses PJ-PL
Swedish-Russian; Russian-Swedish see PG2643.S8
Swedish-Slavic; Slavic-Swedish
see subclass PG
Dictionaries exclusively etymological see PD5580
5650 Dictionaries of particular periods (other than periods separately specified elsewhere)
(5655) Dictionaries of particular authors
see the author in classes PA-PT
5660 Dictionaries of names
Cf. CS2300+ Personal and family names
Cf. PD5673 Foreign words
5667 Dictionaries, etc. of obsolete or archaic words

Swedish
Language
Lexicography
Dictionaries -- Continued
Dictionaries of foreign words
5670 General
5673 Names
Special. By language see PD5582.A+
Rhyming dictionaries
see PD5519
Other special lists
5680 Glossaries
(5683) By subject
see the subject in classes A-N, Q-Z
5688 Dictionaries of terms and phrases
5691 Word frequency lists
5692 Reverse indexes
5693 Abbreviations, Lists of
Linguistic geography. Dialects, etc.
5700 Linguistic geography
Dialects. Provincialisms, etc.
5701 Periodicals. Societies. Congresses
For local dialect societies see PD5801+
Collections
5702 Texts. Sources, etc.
5703 Monographs. Studies
5704 Encyclopedias. Dictionaries
(5705) Atlases. Maps
see class G
General works
5711 Treatises
5712 Compends. Popular
History of dialects
5713 General
5714 General special
5715 Earliest. Medieval
5716 (16th-)17th century. (17th-)18th century
5718 19th century. 20th century. 21st century
Grammar
5721 General works
5726 Phonology. Phonetics
5736 Morphology. Inflection. Accidence
5746 Syntax
5751 Style
5756 Prosody. Metrics. Rhythmics
5761 Etymology
5766 Lexicography

Swedish
Language
Linguistic geography. Dialects, etc.
Dialects. Provincialisms, etc. -- Continued

5771-5778 Old Swedish (Table P-PZ12)
11th to 15th century, including "Middle Swedish," ca. 1350-1550

5781-5788 Early modern Swedish (Table P-PZ12)
ca. 1400/1500 to 1700

By region, province, etc.

5801-5808 East Swedish (Table P-PZ12)
Includes Finland, Estonia

5811-5818 Dialects of the coastal regions (Table P-PZ12 modified)
Includes Angermanland-Gestrikland, Upland, Westmanland

5817.A-Z Local. By dialect name or place, A-Z

5817.N58 Njurunda

5821-5828 Midland Swedish dialects (Table P-PZ12 modified)

5827.A-Z Local. By dialect name or place, A-Z

5827.B6 Bohuslän

5827.F7 Fryksdal

5827.J4 Jemtland

5827.O3 Öland. Dalecarlia (Dalarna)

5827.O4 Östergötland

5827.S6 Småland

5827.S76 Stockholm

5827.V25 Värmland

5827.V3 Västergötland

5831-5838 South Swedish dialects (Table P-PZ12 modified)
Cf. PD3801+ Skåne dialect
Cf. PD3811+ Insular Danish dialects

5837.A-Z Local. By dialect name or place, A-Z

5837.B4 Blekinge

5837.B7 Bornholm

5837.H2 Halland

5837.H35 Hälsingland

5837.J6 Jönköping

5837.K35 Kalmar

5837.K7 Kristianstad

5837.L34 Landskrona

5837.S3 Scania. Skåne. Schonen

5841-5848 Gotland (Table P-PZ12)
Includes Forngutnisk (Altgutnisch)
Cf. PD5771+

5851-5858 North Swedish dialects (Table P-PZ12 modified)

5857.A-Z Local. By dialect name or place, A-Z

Swedish
Language
Linguistic geography. Dialects, etc.
Dialects. Provincialisms, etc.
By region, province, etc.
North Swedish dialects
Local. By dialect name or place, A-Z -- Continued

5857.A78 Arvidsjaur
5857.B87 Burträsk
5857.H47 Herjedal
5857.H63 Hössjö
5857.N67 Norrland
5857.O48 Overkalix
5857.V37 Västerbotten
5857.V54 Vilhelmina

Swedish in foreign parts
5861 Russia
5862 Finland
5871 America

Argot. Slang
5901 Collections
Texts
5905 Collections (General)
5907 Special
General works
5911 General
5916 Grammatical studies
5919 Miscellaneous
5921 Dictionaries. Lists
Special classes
5924.A-Z Special categories of words, A-Z
5924.O38 Obscene words
Special groups of persons
5925 Beggars, gypsies, tramps, thieves, etc.
5927.A-Z Other, A-Z
5927.M4 Metal workers
5927.M5 Miners
5927.N37 Narcotic addicts
5927.S6 Soldiers
5929.A-Z Special. Local, A-Z

Swedish literature see PT9201+

<6000-7159> Scandinavian dialects, Modern

To avoid segregation of kindred material some libraries may prefer the subjoined classification of Scandinavian dialects on a linguistic basis. Here may also be classified works on local dialects restricted to the pre-reformation period. If these numbers are used, apply Tables P-PZ8, P-PZ14, or P-PZ15 as appropriate

General

<6000> Linguistic geography

Dialects. Provincialisms, etc.

<6001> Periodicals. Societies. Congresses

For local dialect societies see the place

Collections

<6002> Texts. Sources, etc.

<6003> Monographs. Studies

<6004> Encyclopedias. Dictionaries

General works

<6011> Treatises

<6012> Compends. Popular

History of dialects

<6013> General

<6014> General special

<6015> Earliest. Medieval

<6016> (16th-)17th century. (17th-)18th century

<6018> 19th century. 20th century. 21st century

Grammar

<6021> General works

<6026> Phonology. Phonetics

<6036> Morphology. Inflection. Accidence

<6046> Syntax

<6051> Style

<6056> Prosody. Metrics. Rhythmics

<6061> Etymology

<6066> Lexicography

<7000-7009> Icelandic

see PD2401+

<7031> Faroe Islands

see PD2483

<7035> Shetland Islands ("Norn"; Norrøn)

see PD2485

<7041> Orkney Islands

see PD2487

<7045> Hebrides

see PD2489

<7051-7059> West Scandinavian (Western Norway)

see PD2601+ (especially PD2696+) and also PD2900+ (especially PD2996+)

Scandinavian dialects, Modern -- Continued

<7061-7069> North Scandinavian

<7071-7074> Eastern Norway

see PD2601+ (especially PD2696+) and also PD2900+ (especially PD2996+)

<7075-7078> North Swedish

see PD5851+

<7081-7084> East Swedish (Estonia, Finland)

see PD5801+

<7091-7099> Gotland (Gutniska)

see PD5841+

<7101-7109> Middle Scandinavian

see PD5821+

<7121-7129> South Scandinavian

<7131-7134> South Swedish

see PD5831+

<7141-7144> Danish Islands

see PD3801+

<7151-7159> Jutish

Includes Jutland (Jylland), Schleswig

see PD3821+

English philology and language
Philology
Class here general works devoted to English studies in the wider sense, i.e. comprising both language and literature
For works restricted to the modern English language see PE1001+
For works dealing with literature exclusively or principally see subclass PR
Periodicals. Serials
1 American and English
2 French
3 German
9 Other
10 Annuals. Yearbooks, etc.
Societies
11 American and English
12 French
13 German
19 Other
23 Congresses
Collections
25 Monographs. Studies (Various authors)
26.A-Z Studies in honor of a particular person or institution, A-Z
27 Individual authors
31 Encyclopedias
32 Computer network resources
Including the Internet
(33) Atlases. Maps
see class G
Philosophy. Theory. Method
35 General works
37 Relations
History of philology
Cf. PE65+ Study and teaching
Cf. PE1075+ History of modern English
51 General works
By period
54 Middle Ages
55 Renaissance
Modern
57 General works
58 19th-20th centuries
59 21st century
60.A-Z By region or country, A-Z
Biography, memoirs, etc.
63 Collective

Philology
History of philology
Biography, memoirs, etc. -- Continued
64.A-Z Individual, A-Z
Subarrange each by Table P-PZ50
Bibliography see Z2015.A1+
Study and teaching. Research
65 General works
66 General special
By period
For period of study, teaching, or research see PE54+
For period of history of the language see PE1077+
68.A-Z By region or country, A-Z
69.A-Z By university, college, etc., A-Z
71 General works
Anglo-Saxon. Old English
ca. 600-1150
101-123 Philology (Table P-PZ3a modified)
History of philology
Cf. PE125 History of the language
Biography, memoirs, etc.
117.A2 Collective
117.A5-Z Individual, A-Z
Subarrange each by Table P-PZ50
Language
124 General. Relation to other languages
125 History
128 Script
Cf. PD2003 Runic inscriptions
Grammar
129 Early works to 1800
131 Later, 1801-
135 Elementary. Introductory
137 Readers. Chrestomathies
Phonology
140 General
141 Phonetics
144 Pronunciation
145 Orthography and spelling
Alphabet
151 General works
153 Vowels
154 Diphthongs
155 Consonants
157 Particular letters
158 Syllabication
Morphology. Inflection. Accidence

Anglo-Saxon. Old English
Language
Grammar
Morphology. Inflection. Accidence -- Continued
159 General works
161 Word formation, derivation, etc.
Noun. Verb, etc. see PE170+
162 Inflection
169 Tables. Paradigms
Parts of speech (Morphology and syntax)
170 General
Noun
171 General works
173 Gender. Number
175 Case
Adjective. Adverb. Comparison
177 General works
179 Numerals
181 Article
183 Pronoun
Verb
185 General
187 Person
188 Number
189 Voice
191 Mood
195 Tense
195.5 Aspects of verbal action
196 Infinitive and participle
Including gerund
197 Other special
Particle
201 General works
203 Adverb
205 Preposition
206 Postposition
207 Conjunction
209 Interjection
211.A-Z Other special, A-Z
211.N4 Negatives
Syntax
213 General
Sentences
219 General arrangment, etc.
221 Order of words
223 Order of clauses
225 Other special

Anglo-Saxon. Old English
Language
Grammar -- Continued
229.A-Z Other aspects, A-Z
For list of Cutter numbers, see Table P-PZ1 398.A+
231.A-Z Usage of particular authors, or works, A-Z
Cf. PR1509+ Anglo-Saxon literature
Style. Composition. Rhetoric
235 General
241 Special
250 Translating
Prosody. Metrics. Rhythmics
253 General
257 Versification
258 Rhyme. Rhyming dictionaries
259.A-Z Special forms, meters, etc., A-Z
260 Rhythm. Rhythm in prose
260.5 Lexicology
Etymology
261 Treatises
262 Names (General)
For personal names see CS2300+ ; for place names, see G104+ (General) or classes D-F for names of specific continents or countries
263 Dictionaries (exclusively etymological)
264.A-Z Special elements. By language, A-Z
264.A3 Foreign elements (General)
265 Semantics
267 Synonyms. Antonyms. Paronyms. Homonyms
268 Onomatopoeic words
269.A-Z Particular words, A-Z
Lexicography
271 Periodicals. Societies. Serials. Collections (nonserial)
273 General works
Biography of lexicographers see PE117.A2+
273.5 Criticism, etc., of particular dictionaries
Glossaries
274.A5 Collections
274.A6-Z Individual
Dictionaries
275 Early to 1800
In whatever language defined or edited
Later, 1800-
279 Anglo-Saxon and English
281.A-Z Other. By language, A-Z
285.A-Z Special subjects, A-Z
Linguistic geography. Dialects

Anglo-Saxon. Old English
Language
Linguistic geography. Dialects -- Continued
287 General
288 General special
(290) West Saxon
see PE101+
Northumbrian
291 General works
292 Grammar
293 Dictionaries. Glossaries
294 Texts
Mercian
296 Texts
297 Other
Kentish
298 Texts
299 Other
(401-408) Late Anglo-Saxon ("Semi-Saxon"; "Transition Old English," ca. 1050-1150)
see PE101+
(451-458) Early Middle English ("Old English"; ca. 1150 to 1250 or to 1350/70)
see PE501+
Anglo-Saxon literature
see subclass PR
Middle English
ca. 1150 to ca. 1500
501-523 Philology (Table P-PZ3a modified)
History of philology
Cf. PE525 History of the language
Biography, memoirs, etc.
517.A2 Collective
517.A5-Z Individual, A-Z
Subarrange each by Table P-PZ50
Language
524 General. Relation to other languages
524.7 Language standardization and variation
525 History
528 Script
Cf. PD2003 Runic inscriptions
Grammar
529 Early works to 1800
531 Later, 1801-
535 Elementary. Introductory
537 Readers
539 Conversation. Phrase books

	Middle English
	Language
	Grammar -- Continued
	Textbooks for foreign speakers
539.3	General
539.5.A-Z	By language, A-Z
	Cf. PE551+ Alphabet
	Phonology
	Including phonemics
540	General works
541	Phonetics
543	Pronunciation
545	Orthography. Spelling
	Alphabet
551	General works
553	Vowels
554	Diphthongs
555	Consonants
556	Contraction (Hiatus. Elision)
557	Particular letters
	Morphology. Inflection. Accidence
559	General works
561	Word formation, derivation, etc.
	Noun. Verb, etc. see PE570+
569	Tables. Paradigms
	Parts of speech (Morphology and syntax)
570	General works
	Noun
571	General works
573	Gender. Number
575	Case
577	Adjective. Adverb. Comparison
581	Article
583	Pronoun
	Verb
585	General
597	Special
	Particle
601	General works
603	Adverb
605	Preposition
606	Postposition
607	Conjunction
609	Interjection
611.A-Z	Other special, A-Z
611.N4	Negatives
	Syntax

Middle English
Language
Grammar
Syntax -- Continued
613 General
Sentences
619 General works
621 Order of words
625 Other special
631.A-Z Usage of particular authors or works, A-Z
For literary authors or works see the author or work in PR1803+
Style. Composition. Rhetoric
635 General
641 Special
Prosody. Metrics. Rhythmics
653 General
657 Versification
658 Rhyme. Rhymning dictionaries
659.A-Z Special forms, meters, etc., A-Z
659.A6 Alliteration
660 Rhythm. Rhythm in prose
660.5 Lexicology
Etymology
661 Treatises
662 Names (General)
For personal names see CS2300+ ; for place names, see G104+ (General) or classes D-F for names of specific continents or countries
663 Dictionaries (exclusively etymological)
664.A-Z Special elements. By language, A-Z
664.A3 Foreign elements (General)
664.3 Other special
664.5 Folk etymology
665 Semantics
667 Synonyms. Antonyms. Paronyms. Homonyms
668 Onomatopoeic words
669.A-Z Particular words, A-Z
Lexicography
673 General works
Biography of lexicographers see PE517.A2+
Glossaries
674.A5 Collections
674.A6-Z Individual
Dictionaries
For dictionaries exclusively etymological see PE663

Middle English
Language
Lexicography
Dictionaries -- Continued
675 Early to 1800
In whatever language defined or edited
Later, 1800-
679 English
681.A-Z Other. By language, A-Z
685.A-Z Special subjects, A-Z
Linguistic geography. Dialects, etc.
687 Linguistic geography
Dialects
688 Collections of texts. By editor
General works. Grammar
(689) Treatises. Monographs. Studies
see PE529+
(691) Dictionaries
see PE675+
(692) Atlases. Maps
see class G
(693) Local. By region, place, etc.
see PE1771+
Literature
see subclass PR
Early Modern English
ca. 1450/1500-1700
Generalities: Periodicals, etc.
see PE1+
Language
(814) General
see PE1073, PE1075, PE1077+
(815) History
see PE1073, PE1075, PE1077+
Grammar
Treatises
821 General works
823 Elementary. Introductory
For contemporaneous textbooks see PE1109
825 Readers
828 Phonology
For specific topics in phonology see PE1135+
839 Morphology. Inflection. Accidence
For specific topics in morphology see PE1175+
871 Syntax
For specific topics in syntax see PE1365+

Early Modern English
Language
Grammar -- Continued
873.A-Z Particular authors or works, A-Z
For literary authors or works see the author or work, e.g. Shakespeare, PR3075+
877 Style. Composition. Rhetoric
881 Prosody. Metrics. Rhythmics
(883) Etymology
see PE1571+
Lexicography
For biography of lexicographers see PE63+
887 Treatises
Dictionaries. Glossaries, etc.
891 General
Special
(892) Authors
see the author
(893) Names
see PE1660
895 Other
896 Linguistic geography. Dialects, etc.
For local see PE1771+
Modern English
ca. 1500-
Philology see PE1+
Language
1001 Periodicals
1010 Annuals. Yearbooks
1011 Societies
Study and teaching
For works on the study and teaching of the English language in English-speaking countries at the elementary or secondary levels, see LB1576 and LB1631 respectively
1065 General
1066 General special
For teaching foreigners see PE1128+
1067 Audio-visual instruction
1068.A-Z By region or country, A-Z
For textbooks, grammars, readers, etc., for foreign students see PE1128+
For theory, methods, etc., manuals for teachers see PE1128.A2
1069.A-Z By school, A-Z
1072 General works. Collected essays
Including external history: extension, distribution, etc.
Cf. PE1700 Linguistic geography

Modern English
Language -- Continued
1073 General special
Including relation to other languages; English as the universal language
"Basic English"
1073.5.A1-.Z8 General works
1073.5.Z9 Texts. Examples
1074 Pamphlets, etc.
1074.5 Language data processing
Cf. PE1499 Machine translating
1074.7 Language standardization and variation
1074.75 Social aspects
1074.8 Spoken language
1074.85 Language acquisition
History (Internal)
Including development of the language from a linguistic, psychological, cultural point of view
Cf. PE1101 Historical gammar
1075 General works
1075.5 Texts. Examples
Special periods
1077 Middle Ages
1079 (15th-)16th century
1081 (16th-)17th century
1083 (17th-)18th century
1085 19th century
1087 20th century
1088 21st century
By region
see PE1700+
1091 Compends
1093 Outlines
1095 Popular
Grammar
1097 Theory. Terminology, etc.
1098 History
Comprehensive works. Compends
1099 Comparative
1101 Historical
Descriptive
1103 Early to 1870
1105 Later, 1871-1949
1106 1950-
Textbooks. Exercises
1108 History and criticism
1109 Early (before 1870)

PE

Modern English
Language
Grammar
Textbooks. Exercises -- Continued
1111 Later, 1870-1949
1112 1950-
1112.3 Self-instruction
1112.5 Programmed instruction
1112.7 Audiovisual instruction
1113 Outlines. Syllabi
1114 Quizzes. Examination questions, etc.
Manuals for special classes of students
1115 Commercial
For general manuals and forms see HF5726
For rhetoric or style see PE1479.B87
1116.A-116.Z Other, A-Z
1116.A3 Accountants
1116.B34 Bank employees
1116.C57 Christian students
1116.F55 Flight attendants
1116.J6 Journalists
1116.L24 Landscaping industry employees
1116.L3 Law reporters
1116.M44 Medical personnel
1116.N8 Nurses
1116.P6 Police
1116.R47 Restaurant and hotel personnel
1116.S42 Secretaries
1116.S7 Soldiers
(1116.T4) Technical
see T11
1116.T68 Tourism industry employees
Readers
Series
1117.A1 Early (before 1870)
1117.A2-Z Later, 1870-
McGuffey readers
1117.M23 History and criticism
1117.M235.A-Z Selections, by editor, A-Z
1117.M24-.M2855 Editions
1118 Hornbooks
Primers. Primary grade readers
1119.A1 Early (before 1870)
New England primer
1119.A1N39-.A1N399 Editions before 1727 (None extant so far as known)
Editions of 1727

Modern English
Language
Grammar
Readers
Primers. Primary grade readers
Early (before 1870)
New England primer
Editions of 1727 -- Continued

1119.A1N4 Original (earliest extant)
1119.A1N43 Ford's facsimile, 1897
1119.A1N44 Ford's facsimile, 1899
1119.A1N5 date Editions after 1727
1119.A1N501-.A1N700 History and criticism, by author, alphabetically
1119.A2-Z Later, 1870-
For series see PE1117.A1+
1119.A3 History and criticism
Intermediate and advanced (through high school)
1120 Early (before 1870)
1121 Later, 1870-
1121.3 History and criticism
1122 College readers (General)
For readers for rhetorical analysis see PE1417
Readers for special classes of students
Religious
Catholic
1123 General works
1123.A2 History and criticism
Other Christian
1124.A1 General
1124.A2-Z By denomination, A-Z
1125 Jewish readers
1125.5.A-1125.Z Other religious groups, A-Z
1125.5.B5 Black Muslims
1125.5.M8 Muslims
1126.A-Z Other classes, A-Z
1126.A4 Adults
1126.A44 Africans
(1126.B8) British readers
see PE1117+
(1126.C3) Canadian readers
see PE1117+
1126.D4 Disabilities, Children with
Cf. HV1701 Apparatus for the blind
Cf. HV2469.E5 Textbooks for the deaf
Cf. LC4620 Reading instruction for children with mental disabilities

Modern English
Language
Grammar
Readers
Readers for special classes of students
Other classes, A-Z -- Continued

(1126.F4) Female readers
see PE1117+
Foreign students see PE1128+
(1126.N4) New England
see PE1117+
1126.N43 New literates
1126.S6 Soldiers
1127.A-Z Readers on special subjects, A-Z
1127.A29 Adventure
1127.A4 Aeronautics
African Americans see PE1127.B55
1127.A6 Animals
1127.A7 Art
1127.A8 Athletics
1127.A9 Autobiography
1127.B3 Baseball
1127.B5 Bible
1127.B53 Biography
1127.B54 Biology
1127.B55 Blacks. African Americans
1127.B6 Boxing
1127.B86 Business
1127.C47 China
1127.C5 Chronology
1127.C53 City and town life
Civics see PE1127.H4+
1127.C55 Cloth
1127.C87 Curiosities and wonders
1127.D72 Drama
Economics see PE1127.G4
1127.E37 Education
1127.E44 Electronic data processing
Ethics see PE1127.R4
1127.F3 Fairy tales. Mythology, folklore, etc.
1127.F35 Family
1127.G4 Geography. Economics. Industries, etc.
1127.G45 Ghosts
History. Civics. Patriotic readers
1127.H4 General
United States history
1127.H5 General works

Modern English
Language
Grammar
Readers
Readers on special subjects, A-Z
History. Civics. "Patriotic" readers
United States history -- Continued

1127.H6A-.H6W States, A-W
1127.H75A-.H75Z Other countries, A-Z
1127.H8 World War I
1127.H83 Hockey
1127.H85 Holidays
1127.H88 Home economics
1127.I5 Indians
Industries see PE1127.G4
1127.I58 Inventions
1127.J35 Jamaica
1127.L47 Linguistics
Literature
(1127.L5) General
see PE1117+
1127.L6 Special authors
Special genres
see PE1127.D72, etc.
1127.M3 Mathematics
1127.M34 Mauritius
1127.M4 Medicine
1127.M47 Mexican Americans
1127.M5 Minorities
Morals see PE1127.R4
(1127.M8) Music
see class M
Nature see PE1127.S3
1127.N3 Naval science
Negroes see PE1127.B55
Patriotism see PE1127.H4+
1127.P45 Performing arts. Theater
1127.P47 Petroleum
1127.P55 Physics
1127.P57 Poetry
1127.P6 Popular culture
1127.P7 Printing
1127.R34 Radio
1127.R4 Religion. Morals. Ethics, etc.
1127.R6 Rodeos
1127.S27 Scandinavia
1127.S28 Schools

Modern English
Language
Grammar
Readers
Readers on special subjects, A-Z -- Continued

1127.S3 Science. Nature readers
Includes elementary, "first" science readers only
For advanced works see Q209
For nature study see QH53
1127.S33 Science fiction
1127.S4 Sex role
1127.S45 Short stories
1127.S5 Skis and skiing
1127.S6 Social sciences. Social history
1127.S8 Sports
1127.S9 Submarine diving
1127.T37 Technology
1127.T45 Tennis
Theater see PE1127.P45
1127.T68 Tourist trade
1127.V5 Violence
1127.W3 War
1127.W58 Women
Wonders and curiosities see PE1127.C87
1127.W65 Work
Textbooks: Grammars. Readers, etc., for foreign students
1128.A2 Theory, methods, etc. Manuals for teachers
1128.A3-Z General
Class here only general textbooks for foreign speakers; for specific subjects, see the subject, e.g. PE1137, Pronunciation; PE1439, Paragraph writing; etc.
1128.Z9 Catalogs of audiovisual materials
1128.3 Computer-assisted instruction
By language
1129.A-Z European languages, A-Z
1129.A4 Afrikaans
1129.A45 Albanian
1129.D8 Dutch
1129.E8 Estonian
1129.F5 Finnish
1129.F7 French
1129.G3 German
1129.G7 Greek
1129.H8 Hungarian
1129.I7 Italian
1129.L3 Latvian

Modern English
Language
Grammar
Readers
Textbooks: Grammars. Readers, etc., for foreign students
By language
European languages, A-Z -- Continued

1129.L5 Lithuanian
1129.N66 Norwegian
1129.P8 Portuguese
1129.R8 Romanian
Scandinavian
1129.S2 Danish. Norwegian
1129.S3 Swedish
Slavic
1129.S4 Russian
1129.S5 Czech
1129.S6 Polish
1129.S71 Bulgarian
1129.S73 Serbo-Croatian
Ruthenian see PE1129.S775
1129.S76 Slovak
1129.S77 Slovenian
1129.S775 Ukrainian
1129.S78 Wendic. Sorbian
1129.S8 Spanish
1129.W4 Welsh
Yiddish see PE1130.H55
1130.A-Z Asian languages, A-Z
Including Semitic languages
For languages of the Philippines and East Indies see PE1130.5.A+
1130.A2 General
1130.A5 Amharic
Annamese see PE1130.V5
1130.A8 Arabic
1130.A9 Armenian
1130.A97 Azerbaijani
1130.B8 Burmese
1130.C4 Chinese
1130.H5 Hebrew
1130.H55 Yiddish
1130.H66 Hmong
Indic
1130.I8 Indic (General)
1130.I82 Bengali

Modern English
Language
Grammar
Readers
Textbooks: Grammars. Readers, etc., for foreign students
By language
Asian languages, A-Z
Indic -- Continued

1130.I83 Gujarati
1130.I84 Hindi
1130.I843 Kannada
1130.I845 Nepali
1130.I85 Panjabi
1130.I86 Sinhalese
1130.I87 Tamil
1130.J3 Japanese
1130.K45 Khmer
1130.K6 Korean
1130.L3 Lao
Malayan see PE1130.5.M2
1130.M6 Mongolian
1130.P4 Persian
1130.T27 Tajik
1130.T45 Thai
1130.T8 Turkish
1130.T82 Turkmen
1130.V5 Vietnamese
1130.3.A-Z African languages, A-Z
1130.3.A2 African (General)
Afrikaans see PE1129.A4
Amharic see PE1130.A5
1130.3.H3 Hausa
1130.3.I33 Igbo
Malagasy see PE1130.5.M17
1130.3.N67 Northern Sotho
1130.3.S56 Somali
1130.3.T54 Tigrinya
1130.3.T76 Tsonga
1130.3.V46 Venda
1130.3.Z8 Zulu
1130.5.A-Z Other languages (Oceanic, American Indian, Artificial, etc.), A-Z
American Indian and Eskimo
1130.5.A5 General
1130.5.A53 Dakota
1130.5.A55 Hopi

Modern English
Language
Grammar
Readers
Textbooks: Grammars. Readers, etc., for foreign students
By language
Other languages (Oceanic, American Indian, Artificial, etc.), A-Z
American Indian and Eskimo -- Continued

1130.5.A554 Inupiaq
1130.5.A56 Laguna
1130.5.A57 Navajo
1130.5.A58 Sioux
1130.5.A59 Taos
1130.5.A95 Australian (Aboriginal)
1130.5.C4 Chamorro
1130.5.H4 Hawaiian
1130.5.I8 Indonesian
1130.5.M17 Malagasy
1130.5.M2 Malayan
1130.5.M26 Maori
1130.5.P5 Philippine
1131 Conversation. Phrase books
Phonology
1133 General works
1135 Phonetics
Pronunciation
1137 General works
1137.A2 Early works to 1870
1139 Accent
1139.5 Intonation
1139.7 Prosodic analysis
Orthography. Spelling
1141 History
General works
1142 Early to 1800
1143 Later
Spelling books
1144 Early to 1860
1145 1860-1949
1145.2 1950-
1145.4 Programmed instruction
1146 Alphabetical lists
Spelling reform
1147 Periodicals. Societies. Collections
History

Modern English
Language
Grammar
Phonology
Orthography. Spelling
Spelling reform
History -- Continued
1148 General works
1149 Collections of opinions
Treatises
1150.A2 Early to 1870
1150.A3-Z Later
1151 Spelling systems, alphabets; by name of author, or system
1152 Texts in phonetic spelling; readers, etc.
e. g.
Bibles
1152.B6 Whole Bibles
1152.B61 Selections
Old Testament
1152.B62 General works
1152.B63 Special parts
New Testament
1152.B65 General works
1152.B66 Selections
1152.B67 Special parts
1152.B68 Paraphrases
1153 Dictionaries
Alphabet
Includes treatises on the script of the English language, also elementary works on the script and pronunciation of the sounds represented in the alphabet.
1155 General
1156 Transliteration
1157 Vowels
1158 Diphthongs
1159 Consonants
1161 Contraction (Hiatus. Elision)
1165 Particular letters
1168 Syllabication
1170 Morphophonemics
Morphology. Inflection. Accidence
1171 General works
1175 Word formation. Derivation. Suffixes, etc.
(1181) Noun. Declension
see PE1201+

Modern English
Language
Grammar
Morphology. Inflection. Accidence -- Continued
(1186) Adjective. Adverb
see PE1241 , PE1325
(1196) Verb. Conjugation
see PE1271+
1197 Tables. Paradigms
Parts of speech (Morphology and syntax)
1199 General works
Noun
1201 General
1205 General special (Classes, etc.)
1211 Gender
1216 Number
1221 Case
1241 Adjective
1246 Numerals
1251 Article
1261 Pronoun
Verb
1271 General works
1273 Conjugation
1276 Person
1280 Number
1285 Voice
1290 Mood
1301 Tense
1306 Aspect
1311 Infinitive. Participle
1313 Gerund. Participle, etc.
1315.A-Z Special classes of verbs, A-Z
1315.A8 Auxiliary
1315.I5 Impersonal
Intransitive see PE1315.T72
1315.I6 Irregular
1315.M6 Modal
1315.P5 Phrasal
1315.T72 Transitive/Intransitive
1317.A-Z Particular verbs, A-Z
1319 Other. Miscellaneous
Particle
1321 General works
Adverb
1325 General works
1326 Adverbials

Modern English
Language
Grammar
Parts of speech (Morphology and syntax)
Particle -- Continued
1335 Preposition
1345 Conjunction
1355 Interjection
1359.A-Z Other special, A-Z
1359.N44 Negatives
Syntax
1361 General
1365 Outlines
Cf. PE1113 Grammar outlines
1369 General special
Sentence
1375 General
1380 Special
Including concord of subject and predicative verb
1385 Classes of sentences; clauses and phrases
1390 Order of words
1395 Other special
1398.A-Z Other aspects, A-Z
1398.A52 Anaphora
1398.D45 Deixis
(1400) Grammatical usage of particular authors or works
see the author or work
Rhetoric. Style. Composition
Oratory. Elocution. Oral English see PE1431; PN4001+
Oral English (Elementary) see PE1111
Theory. Philosophy
1402 Early works to 1870
1403 Later
Study and teaching
1404 General works
1405.A-Z By region or country, A-Z (English-speaking countries)
(1406) By school
Treatises. Compends. Textbooks
Cf. PN171.4+ Literature (General)
Cf. PN3355+ Prose
1407 Early to 1860
Later
1408 English
1409 Other
1409.5 Programmed instruction
1411 Outlines. Quizzes. Rules, etc.
1413 Exercises and specimens

Modern English
Language
Rhetoric. Style. Composition -- Continued

1415 Lists of subjects. Outline topics
1417 Readers for rhetorical analysis, etc.
Prefer PE1117+ for readers below the college level
(1419.A-Z) Particular authors, A-Z
see the author in subclasses PR or PS
1421 Style
Cf. PN203 Literature (General)
1422 Discourse analysis
Special elements and kinds of style
1423 Invention
1425 Narration
1427 Description
1429 Exposition
1431 Argumentation (and debate)
Cf. PN4177+ Oratory
1433 Analysis
1435 Brief
Special parts of discourse
1439 Paragraph
1441 Sentence
1442 Phrases
1443 Words, syllables, etc.
Figures and tropes
Cf. PN227+ Literature (General)
1445.A2 General
1445.A5-Z Special, A-Z
1445.M4 Metaphor
1445.P3 Parallelism
1445.S5 Simile
1445.U54 Understatement
1447 Epithets
Cf. PN229 Literature (General)
1449 Choice of words. Vocabulary, etc.
Punctuation and capitalization
1450.A2 Early to 1860
1450.A3-Z 1860-
Idioms. Errors. Usage
1460 General works
1464 Dictionaries
Special classes of composition
(1470) Fiction. Novels. Stories
see PN3355+
1471 Essays
1473 Lectures

PE

Modern English
Language
Rhetoric. Style. Composition
Special classes of composition -- Continued
1475 Scientific papers
Cf. T11+ Technical writing
1477 Précis writing
1478 Report writing
General works only; special subjects, see Classes A-N, Q-Z
Cf. LB2369 Preparation of college research papers, book reports, etc.
1479.A-Z Other, A-Z
1479.A76 Art
1479.A88 Autobiography
1479.B87 Business
For general works on business correspondence see HF5720.2+
For grammar manuals see PE1115
1479.C7 Criticism
1479.E35 Economics
1479.L3 Law
1479.N28 Nature
1479.N3 Naval
1479.S62 Social sciences
Letter-writing. Epistolography
1481 Early works to 1860
Later
1483 General works
(1483.2) Business
see HF5721+
(1483.3) Diplomatic
see JX1677
(1483.5) Etiquette
see BJ2100+
(1483.6) Love letters
see HQ801.3
(1483.7) Military
see UB160+
Textbooks
1485 General works
(1487) Catholic
(1489) English and German
Manuals for immigrants, etc. in other languages see PE1129.A+
Specimens
1495 Early works to 1860

Modern English
Language
Rhetoric. Style. Composition
Special classes of composition
Letter-writing. Epistolography
Specimens -- Continued
1497 Later works
Translating
For special subjects, see Classes B-Z, e.g. T11.5, Technology
1498 General works
1498.2.A-Z Special languages, A-Z
1498.2.A93 Azerbaijani
1498.2.C55 Chinese
1498.2.D37 Danish
1498.2.E88 Estonian
1498.2.F74 French
1498.2.G34 Galician
1498.2.G46 Georgian
1498.2.G47 German
1498.2.H42 Hebrew
1498.2.H56 Hindi
1498.2.I73 Italian
1498.2.J36 Japanese
1498.2.L36 Latvian
1498.2.P67 Portuguese
1498.2.R65 Romanian
1498.2.R87 Russian
1498.2.S56 Slovenian
1498.2.S65 Spanish
1498.2.V53 Vietnamese
1499 Machine translation
Including research
1500 Transcription
Prosody. Metrics. Rhythmics
1501 History of metrical studies
Treatises (Theory and history)
1504 Early works to 1800
1505 Later
1509 Textbooks. Compends
1511 Specimens. Exercises
1515 Blank verse (Heroic verse)
1517 Rhyme
1519 Rhyming dictionaries
1521.A-Z Special, by form, A-Z
1521.B35 Ballads
1521.E6 Epic

Modern English
Language
Prosody. Metrics. Rhythmics
Special, by form, A-Z -- Continued

1521.H3 Haiku
1521.S7 Sonnet
1531.A-Z Special meters, A-Z
1531.F73 Free verse
1531.I24 Iambic pentameter
1531.I25 Iambic tetrameter
1541 Other special
(1551) Special authors
see the author
1559 Rhythm
1561 Rhythm in prose

Lexicology. Etymology
1571 Treatises
1574 Popular works
Textbooks
1575 Early to 1870
1576 Later
Names
1578.A2 General
(1578.A5-Z) Personal
see CS2500+
(1579) Geographical
see classes DA, E and F
Dictionaries (Exclusively etymological)
1580.A2 Early works to 1800
1580.A3-Z 1800-
Special elements: Foreign words, etc.
Cf. PE1670 Foreign word dictionaries
1582.A3 General
1582.A5-Z Special. By language, A-Z
1583 Other special
1584 Folk etymology
1585 Semantics
Synonyms. Antonyms
1591.A2 Early works to 1870
1591.A3-Z 1870-
1595 Homonyms
1596 Eponyms
1597 Onomatopoeic words
1598 Metonyms
1599.A-Z Particular words, A-Z
1599.C65 Condom
1599.D36 Damn

Modern English
Language
Lexicology. Etymology
Particular words, A-Z -- Continued

1599.D4 Death
1599.D43 Decadence
1599.D8 Duty
1599.E9 Experiment
1599.F83 Fuck
1599.G4 Get
1599.H65 Homo
1599.I7 Irony
1599.L4 Leisure
1599.L68 Love
1599.O94 Over
1599.P45 People
1599.R34 Race
1599.S29 Say
1599.S59 Shyster
1599.S67 Spade
1599.S93 Sweet
1599.T75 Tribe
1599.W54 Will

Lexicography
1601 Collections
1611 General works. History. Treatises
(1615) Biography of lexicographers
see PE63+
1617.A-Z Criticism of particular dictionaries. (By author or title of dictionary, A-Z)
Dictionaries
English only
1620 Early to 1800
1625 Later
1628 Minor abridged dictionaries
1628.5 Juvenile, school dictionaries
1629 Picture dictionaries
1630 Supplementary (New words, neologisms, etc.)
Cf. PE1670 Foreign word dictionaries
Interlingual
1635 Polyglot (definitions or equivalents in two or more languages
1635.A2 Early to 1800
(1645) Bilingual
Classify with language less known
(1645.F8) English-French and French-English
see PC2640

PE

Modern English
Language
Lexicography
Dictionaries
Interlingual
Bilingual -- Continued

(1645.G5) English-German and German-English
see PF3640

(1645.R8) English-Russian and Russian-English
see PG2640

Etymological (for dictionaries exclusively etymological)
see PE1580.A2+

1650 Particular periods (of Modern English)
Cf. PE275+ Old English
Cf. PE675+ Middle English

(1655) Particular authors or works
see the author or work in subclasses PR or PS

1660 Names
Cf. CS2500+

1667 Obsolete or archaic words

Local provincialisms
see PE1700+

Foreign words
Cf. PE1582.A3+ Etymology

1670 General

1670.A2 Early to 1800

1673 Names

(1675) Special, by language
see PE1582

Special lists. Glossaries. Vocabularies

1680 General works

1680.A2 Early to 1850

1683 By subjects (not provided for in classes A-N, Q-Z)

1689 Terms and phrases

1691 Other
Includes word frequency, etc.
For research on word frequency, etc., in connection with machine translating see PE1499

1692 Reverse indexes

1693 Lists of abbreviations, acronyms, etc.

Linguistic geography. Dialects, etc.
For general works on Middle English dialects see PE687+
For general works on early modern English dialects see PE896

1700 Linguistic geography

Dialects. Provincialisms, etc.

Linguistic geography. Dialects, etc.
Dialects. Provincialisms, etc. -- Continued
1701 Periodicals. Societies. Congresses
For local dialect societies see PE1801+
Collections
1702.A1-.A29 Texts. Sources. Specimens, etc.
1702.A5-Z Monographs. Studies
1704 Encyclopedias. Dictionaries
(1705) Atlases. Maps
see class G
(1706-1710) Study and teaching. History of study and teaching
see PE65+ PE1065+
General works
1711 Treatises
1712 Compends. Popular. Minor
History of dialects
1713 General
1714 General special
1715 Earliest. Medieval
Cf. PE125 Anglo-Saxon language
Cf. PE287+ Anglo-Saxon dialects
Cf. PE525 Middle English
Cf. PE687+ Middle English dialects
1716 (16th-)17th and (17th-)18th centuries
1718 19th century. 20th century. 21st century
Grammar
1721 General works
1726 Phonology. Phonetics
1736 Morphology. Inflection. Accidence
1746 Syntax
1751 Style
1756 Prosody
1761 Etymology
1766 Lexicography
1771 Regions comprising (parts of) several counties
Dialects of England and Wales
1801-1804 Anglesea (Table P-PZ14)
1806-1809 Bedfordshire (Table P-PZ14)
1811-1814 Berkshire (Table P-PZ14)
1816-1819 Brecknockshire (Table P-PZ14)
1821-1824 Buckinghamshire (Table P-PZ14)
1826-1829 Cambridgeshire (Table P-PZ14)
1831-1834 Cardiganshire (Table P-PZ14)
1836-1839 Camarthenshire (Table P-PZ14)
1841-1844 Carnarvonshire (Table P-PZ14)
1846-1849 Cheshire (Table P-PZ14)
1851-1854 Cornwall (Table P-PZ14)

PE

Linguistic geography. Dialects, etc.
Dialects of England and Wales -- Continued

1856-1859	Cumberland (Table P-PZ14)
1861-1864	Denbighshire (Table P-PZ14)
1866-1869	Derbyshire (Table P-PZ14)
1871-1874	Devonshire (Table P-PZ14)
1876-1879	Dorsetshire (Table P-PZ14)
1881-1884	Durham (Table P-PZ14)
1886-1889	East Anglia (Table P-PZ14)
1891-1894	Essex (Table P-PZ14)
1896-1899	Flintshire (Table P-PZ14)
1901-1904	Glamorganshire (Table P-PZ14)
1906-1909	Gloucestershire (Table P-PZ14)
1911-1914	Hampshire (Table P-PZ14)
1916-1919	Herefordshire (Table P-PZ14)
1921-1924	Hertfordshire (Table P-PZ14)
1926-1929	Huntingdonshire (Table P-PZ14)
1931-1934	Isle of Man (Table P-PZ14)
1936-1939	Isle of Wight (Table P-PZ14)
1941-1944	Kent (Table P-PZ14)
1946-1949	Lancashire (Table P-PZ14)
1951-1954	Leicestershire (Table P-PZ14)
1956-1959	Lincolnshire (Table P-PZ14)
1961-1964	London (Table P-PZ14)
1966-1969	Merionethshire (Table P-PZ14)
1971-1974	Middlesex (Table P-PZ14)
1976-1979	Monmouthshire (Table P-PZ14)
1981-1984	Montgomeryshire (Table P-PZ14)
1986-1989	Norfolk (Table P-PZ14)
1991-1994	Northamptonshire (Table P-PZ14)
1996-1999	Northumberland (Table P-PZ14)
2001-2004	Nottinghamshire (Table P-PZ14)
2006-2009	Oxfordshire (Table P-PZ14)
2011-2014	Pembrokeshire (Table P-PZ14)
2016-2019	Radnorshire (Table P-PZ14)
2021-2024	Rutlandshire (Table P-PZ14)
2026-2029	Shropshire (Table P-PZ14)
2031-2034	Somersetshire (Table P-PZ14)
2036-2039	Southampton (Table P-PZ14)
2041-2044	Staffordshire (Table P-PZ14)
2046-2049	Suffolk (Table P-PZ14)
2051-2054	Surrey (Table P-PZ14)
2056-2059	Sussex (Table P-PZ14)
2061-2064	Warwickshire (Table P-PZ14)
2066-2069	Westmoreland (Table P-PZ14)
2071-2074	Wiltshire (Table P-PZ14)
2076-2079	Worcestershire (Table P-PZ14)

Linguistic geography. Dialects, etc.
Dialects of England and Wales -- Continued
2081-2084 Yorkshire (Table P-PZ14)
2091-2094 Dialects of the Channel Islands (Table P-PZ14)
Cf. PC2937 Norman French dialects
2101-2108 Dialects of Scotland (Table P-PZ12 modified)
(2107.A-Z) Local
see PE2121+
2111-2118 Early Scotch (Scots) to ca. 1650 (Table P-PZ12)
2121.A-Z Regions, A-Z
2121.M5 Midland
2121.N6 Northern
2121.N7 Northeastern
2121.N8 Northwestern
2121.S7 Southern
2121.S8 Southeastern
2121.S9 Southwestern
2121.W4 Western
2151-2154 Aberdeen (Table P-PZ14)
2156-2159 Angus (Table P-PZ14)
2161-2164 Argyll (Table P-PZ14)
2166-2169 Ayr (Table P-PZ14)
2171-2174 Banff (Table P-PZ14)
2176-2179 Berwyk (Table P-PZ14)
2181-2184 Buchan (Table P-PZ14)
2186-2189 Bute (Table P-PZ14)
2191-2194 Caithness (Table P-PZ14)
2196-2199 Clackmannan (Table P-PZ14)
2201-2204 Clydesdale (Table P-PZ14)
2206-2209 Cromarty (Table P-PZ14)
2211-2214 Dumbarton (Table P-PZ14)
2216-2219 Dumfries (Table P-PZ14)
2221-2224 Edinburgh (Table P-PZ14)
2226-2229 Elgin (Table P-PZ14)
2231-2234 Fife (Table P-PZ14)
2236-2239 Forfar (Table P-PZ14)
2241-2244 Galloway (Table P-PZ14)
2246-2249 Haddington (Table P-PZ14)
2251-2254 Inverness (Table P-PZ14)
2256-2259 Kincardine (Table P-PZ14)
2261-2264 Kinross (Table P-PZ14)
2266-2269 Kirkcudbright (Table P-PZ14)
2271-2274 Lanark (Table P-PZ14)
2276-2279 Linlithgow (Table P-PZ14)
2281-2284 Lothian (Table P-PZ14)
2286-2289 Moray (Table P-PZ14)
2291-2294 Nairn (Table P-PZ14)

Linguistic geography. Dialects, etc.
Dialects of Scotland -- Continued

2296-2299 Orkney Islands (Table P-PZ14)
Cf. PD2487 Scandinavian dialects
2301-2304 Peebles (Table P-PZ14)
2306-2309 Perth (Table P-PZ14)
2311-2314 Renfrew (Table P-PZ14)
2316-2319 Ross (Table P-PZ14)
2321-2324 Roxburgh (Table P-PZ14)
2326-2329 Selkirk (Table P-PZ14)
2331-2334 Shetland Islands (Table P-PZ14)
Cf. PD2485 Scandinavian dialects
(2336-2339) South Scotland
see PE2121.S7
2341-2344 Stirling (Table P-PZ14)
2346-2349 Sutherland (Table P-PZ14)
2351-2354 Tweeddale (Table P-PZ14)
(2356-2359) West Scotland
see PE2121.W4
2361-2364 Wigtown (Table P-PZ14)
2401-2408 Dialects of Ireland (Table P-PZ12 modified)
(2407.A-Z) Local
see PE2411+
2411 Regions
2431-2434 Antrim (Table P-PZ14)
2436-2439 Armagh (Table P-PZ14)
2441-2444 Carlow (Table P-PZ14)
2446-2449 Cavan (Table P-PZ14)
2451-2454 Clare (Table P-PZ14)
2456-2459 Connaught (Table P-PZ14)
2461-2464 Cork (Table P-PZ14)
2466-2469 Donegal (Table P-PZ14)
2471-2474 Down (Table P-PZ14)
2476-2479 Dublin (Table P-PZ14)
2481-2484 Fermanagh (Table P-PZ14)
2486-2489 Galway (Table P-PZ14)
2491-2494 Kerry (Table P-PZ14)
2496-2499 Kildare (Table P-PZ14)
2501-2504 Kilkenny (Table P-PZ14)
2506-2509 King's County. Offaly (Table P-PZ14)
Laois see PE2561+
2511-2514 Leinster (Table P-PZ14)
2516-2519 Limerick (Table P-PZ14)
2526-2529 Londonderry (Table P-PZ14)
2531-2534 Longford (Table P-PZ14)
2536-2539 Louth (Table P-PZ14)
2541-2544 Mayo (Table P-PZ14)

Linguistic geography. Dialects, etc.
Dialects of Ireland -- Continued
2546-2549 Meath (Table P-PZ14)
2551-2554 Monaghan (Table P-PZ14)
2556-2559 Munster (Table P-PZ14)
Offaly see PE2506+
2561-2564 Queen's County. Laois (Table P-PZ14)
2566-2569 Roscommon (Table P-PZ14)
2571-2574 Sligo (Table P-PZ14)
2576-2579 Tipperary (Table P-PZ14)
2581-2584 Tyrone (Table P-PZ14)
2586-2589 Ulster (Table P-PZ14)
2591-2594 Waterford (Table P-PZ14)
2596-2599 Westmeath (Table P-PZ14)
2601-2604 Wexford (Table P-PZ14)
2606-2609 Wicklow (Table P-PZ14)
English outside of the British Isles
2751 General
2801-3102 United States (and America general) (Table P-PZ5 modified)
Lexicography
Dictionaries
(2837.A-Z) Dictionaries with definitions in other languages
see the other language, e.g. PC2640 French
Linguistic geography. Dialects, etc.
Dialects, provincialisms, etc.
(2845.A5-Z) Local
see PE2901+
Special regions
Prefer classification by ethnic group
2901-2908 New England (Table P-PZ12)
2911-2918 Middle Atlantic States (Table P-PZ12)
2921-2928 South (Table P-PZ12)
2931-2938 North Central States. Middle West (Table P-PZ12)
2941-2948 Northwest (Table P-PZ12)
2961-2968 Southwest (Table P-PZ12)
2970.A-Z Other regions, A-Z
2970.A6 Appalachia
2970.E2 East
2970.E23 Eastern Shore (Maryland and Virginia)
2970.G85 Gulf States
2970.O9 Ozark Mountain region
2970.W4 West
3101.A-.W Particular states, A-W
3102.A-Z Ethnic groups, A-Z
3102.C45 Chinese Americans
3102.F54 Finnish Americans

PE

Linguistic geography. Dialects, etc.
English outside of the British Isles
United States (and America general)
Ethnic groups, A-Z -- Continued
3102.I55 Indians
3102.I8 Italian Americans
3102.M4 Mexican Americans
Negroes. African Americans
3102.N4 Collections
3102.N42 General. History
3102.N43 Grammar
3102.N44 Exercises, phrase books, etc.
3102.N45 Etymology
3102.N46 Dictionaries. Wordlists
3102.N47.A-Z Local, A-Z
3102.N48 Texts
3102.P45 Pennsylvania Dutch
3102.P8 Puerto Ricans
3102.S86 Swedish Americans
3201-3246 Canada. British America (Table P-PZ5)
Central America
3270 General works
3272 Honduras (Table P-PZ15)
3301-3305 West Indies (Table P-PZ9)
Cf. PM7871+ English-based creole languages
British West Indies
3310 General works
3311 Bahamas (Table P-PZ15)
3312 Bermudas (Table P-PZ15)
3312.5 British Virgin Islands (Table P-PZ15)
3313 Jamaica (Table P-PZ15)
Leeward Islands
3314 General works
3315.A-Z Individual islands, A-Z
Subarrange each by Table P-PZ16a
3316 Tobago (Table P-PZ15)
3317 Trinidad (Table P-PZ15)
Windward Islands
3318 General works
3319.A-Z Individual islands, A-Z
3319.G84-.G8495 Grenada (Table P-PZ16a)
3319.M435-.M43595 Martinique (Table P-PZ16a)
Virgin Islands of the United States
3321 General works
3322 Saint Croix (Table P-PZ15)
3323 Saint John (Table P-PZ15)
3324 Saint Thomas (Table P-PZ15)

Linguistic geography. Dialects, etc.
English outside of the British Isles -- Continued

3330.A-Z Other islands in the Atlantic, A-Z
3330.S2-.S295 Saint Helena (Table P-PZ16a)
3330.T7-.T795 Tristan da Cunha (Table P-PZ16a)
South America
3370 General works
3370.2 Argentina (Table P-PZ15)
3372 Guyana (Table P-PZ15)
Africa
3401 General works
North Africa
3411 General
3412.A-Z Local, A-Z
3412.A5-.A595 Algeria (Table P-PZ16a)
3412.E4-.E495 Egypt (Table P-PZ16a)
3412.L4-.L495 Libya (Table P-PZ16a)
3412.M5-.M595 Morocco (Table P-PZ16a)
3412.S83-.S8395 Sudan (Table P-PZ16a)
3412.T8-.T895 Tunisia (Table P-PZ16a)
Central Africa
3421 General
3422.A-Z Local, A-Z
Subarrange each by Table P-PZ16a
(3422.Z34) Zambia
see PE3452.Z33
East Africa
3431 General
3432.A-Z Local, A-Z
Subarrange each by Table P-PZ16a
West Africa
3441 General
3442.A-Z Local, A-Z
Benin see PE3442.D3+
3442.C3-.C395 Cameroon (Table P-PZ16a)
Côte d'Ivoire see PE3442.I8+
3442.D3-.D395 Dahomey. Benin (Table P-PZ16a)
3442.G5-.G595 Ghana (Table P-PZ16a)
3442.I8-.I895 Ivory Coast (Table P-PZ16a)
3442.L5-.L595 Liberia (Table P-PZ16a)
3442.M4-.M495 Mauritania (Table P-PZ16a)
3442.N5-.N595 Nigeria (Table P-PZ16a)
3442.S4-.S495 Senegal (Table P-PZ16a)
3442.T6-.T695 Togo (Table P-PZ16a)
Southern Africa
3451 General works
3452.A-Z Local, A-Z

Linguistic geography. Dialects, etc.
English outside of the British Isles
Africa
Southern Africa
Local, A-Z -- Continued
3452.B55-.B5595 Botswana (Table P-PZ16a)
3452.L5-.L595 Lesotho (Table P-PZ16a)
3452.M33-.M3395 Malawi (Table P-PZ16a)
3452.N3-.N395 Namibia (Table P-PZ16a)
3452.S6-.S695 South Africa (Table P-PZ16a)
3452.S78-.S7895 Swaziland (Table P-PZ16a)
3452.Z33-.Z3395 Zambia (Table P-PZ16a)
3452.Z55-.Z5595 Zimbabwe (Table P-PZ16a)
Islands of the Indian Ocean
3471 General works
3472.A-Z Individual islands, A-Z
3472.M37-.M3795 Mauritius (Table P-PZ16a)
Asia
3501 General
3502.A-Z By region or country, A-Z
(3502.A83) Asia, Southeastern
see PE3502.S65
3502.C35-.C3595 Cambodia (Table P-PZ16a)
3502.C54-.C5495 China (Table P-PZ16a)
3502.I6-.I695 India (Table P-PZ16a)
3502.K6-.K695 Korea. South Korea (Table P-PZ16a)
3502.M3-.M395 Malaysia (Table P-PZ16a)
3502.N42 Near East
3502.P5-.P595 Philippines (Table P-PZ16a)
3502.S5-.S595 Singapore (Table P-PZ16a)
3502.S64 South Asia
3502.S65 Southeast Asia
3502.S74-.S7495 Sri Lanka (Table P-PZ16a)
Oceania
3600 General
3601 Australia (Table P-PZ15)
Hawaii see PE3101.A+
3602 New Zealand (Table P-PZ15)
Pitcairn see PM7895.P5+
Slang. Argot. Vulgarisms
3701 Collections
Texts
3705 Collections, General
3707 Individual
3711 General works
3715 Grammatical studies
3719 Miscellaneous

Linguistic geography. Dialects, etc.
Slang. Argot. Vulgarisms -- Continued
3721 Dictionaries. Lists
Special classes
3724 Special categories of words
3724.H85 Human physiology
3724.O3 Obscene words
3724.R4 Reduplicated words
3724.R5 Rhyming slang
3724.S85 Swear words
Special groups of persons
3726 Beggars, gypsies, tramps, thieves, etc.
3727.A-Z Other, A-Z
3727.A35 Air pilots
African Americans see PE3727.N4
3727.B43 Beat generation
Blacks see PE3727.N4
3727.B76 Brokers
3727.C6 Cowboys
3727.F35 Family
3727.G39 Gay men
3727.G87 Gurus
3727.H5 Highway transport workers
3727.L3 Labor. Working class
3727.L8 Lumbermen
3727.M54 Miners
3727.N3 Narcotic addicts
3727.N4 Negroes. African Americans. Blacks
3727.P4 Petroleum workers
3727.P74 Prisoners
3727.R3 Railroad workers
3727.S3 Sailors
3727.S7 Soldiers
3727.S8 Students
3727.T43 Teenagers
3727.U64 Upper class
Working class see PE3727.L3
3727.Y68 Youth
3729.A-Z Special. By country, A-Z
English literature see PR1+
American literature see PS1+

West Germanic philology and languages
Dutch
1-71 Philology (Table P-PZ1a modified)
Periodicals. Serials
4 Dutch and Scandinavian
Societies
14 Dutch and Scandinavian
(33) Atlases. Maps
see class G
History of philology
Cf. PF75+ History of the language
Biography, memoirs, etc.
63 Collective
64.A-Z Individual, A-Z
Subarrange each by Table P-PZ50
Bibliography. Bio-bibliography
see Z2445
Study and teaching. Research
65 General works
By period
For period of study, teaching, or research see PF53+
For period of history of the language see PF77+
73-979 Language (Table P-PZ1b modified)
Add number in table to PF0
(97) Script
see PF153
Style. Composition. Rhetoric
For study and teaching see PF65+
410 General works
Etymology
580 Dictionaries (exclusively etymological)
582.A-Z Special elements. By language, A-Z
582.A3 Foreign elements (General)
Cf. PF670 Dictionaries
Lexicography
601 Collections
611 General works. History. Treatises
(615) Biography of lexicographers
see PF63+
617.A-Z Criticism of particular dictionaries (by author, or title of dictionary, A-Z)
Dictionaries
Dutch only
620 Early to 1850
625 Later, 1851-
628 Minor, abridged, school dictionaries
629 Picture dictionaries

Dutch
Language
Lexicography
Dictionaries
Dutch only -- Continued
630 Supplementary (New words. Neologisms, etc.)
Interlingual
635 Polyglot (definitions in two or more languages)
Bilingual
Classify with language less known
640 Dutch-English; English-Dutch
640.A2 Early works to 1850
645.A-Z Dictionaries with definitions in other languages. By language, A-Z
645.F5 Dutch-French; French-Dutch
645.G5 Dutch-German; German-Dutch
Dutch-Slavic; Slavic-Dutch
see subclass PG
Dictionaries exclusively etymological see PF580
650 Particular periods (of Modern Dutch)
(655) Particular authors or works
see the author or work in PT
660 Names
For personal and family names see CS2520+
Cf. PF673 Foreign words
667 Obsolete or archaic words
Local provincialisms see PF781+
Foreign words
670 General
673 Names
Special. By language see PF582.A+
Rhyming dictionaries
see PF519
Other special lists
680 Miscellaneous
(683) By subject
see the subject in Classes A-N, Q-Z
689 Dictionaries of terms and phrases
691 Other
Including word frequency, etc.
693 Abbreviations, Lists of
Linguistic geography. Dialects, etc.
700 Linguistic geography
Dialects. Provincialisms, etc.
Cf. PF1414+ Friesian
Cf. PF5701+ Westphalian
Cf. PF5706+ Northern Westphalian

Dutch
Language
Linguistic geography. Dialects, etc.
Dialects. Provincialisms, etc. -- Continued

701 Periodicals. Societies. Congresses
For local dialect societies see PF781+
Collections
702 Texts. Sources. Specimens etc.
703 Monographs. Studies
704 Encyclopedias. Dictionaries
(705) Atlases. Maps
see class G
General works
711 Treatises
712 Compends. Popular. Minor
History of dialects
713 General
714 General special
715 Earliest. Medieval
716 (16th-) 17th and (17th-) 18th centuries
718 19th century. 20th century. 21st century
Grammar
721 General works
726 Phonology. Phonetics
736 Morphology. Inflection. Accidence
746 Syntax
751 Style
756 Prosody. Metrics. Rhythmics
761 Etymology
766 Lexicography
771-778 Early Dutch to ca. 1550 (Table P-PZ12)
Including "Old Low Franconian," ca. 800 to 1200, and Middle Dutch, ca. 1200 to 1550
Low Franconian
781 General works
By region or province
791-794 Friesland (Table P-PZ14)
Including Stadsfries
795-798 North Holland. South Holland (Table P-PZ14)
801-804 North Brabant (Netherlands). Antwerp (Belgium : Province). Vlaams-Brabant (Belgium) (Table P-PZ14)
805-809 Zeeland (Table P-PZ14)
821-828 West Flanders. Nord (France : Dept.) (Table P-PZ12)
Cf. PF5640 Low Franconian dialects of German
831-838 East Flanders (Table P-PZ12)

Dutch
Language
Linguistic geography. Dialects, etc.
Dialects. Provincialisms, etc.
Low Franconian
By region or province -- Continued
841-844 Limburg (Netherlands). Limburg (Belgium) (Table P-PZ14)
851-854 Low Saxon (Table P-PZ14)
Dutch in foreign parts
859 General works
861-864 Africa. Afrikaans (Table P-PZ14)
871-874 Transvaal and Orange River Colony (Table P-PZ14)
881-884 Cape Colony (Table P-PZ14)
Afrikaans literature see PT6500+
891 America
Asia
901 General works
911 Dutch East Indies
913.A-Z Other regions or countries, A-Z
(921) Creole Dutch
see PM7861+
Argot. Slang. Vulgarisms
951 Collections
Texts
955 Collections (General)
957 Special
General works
961 General works
966 Grammatical studies
969 Miscellaneous
971 Dictionaries. Lists
Special classes
975 Beggars. Gypsies. Tramps. Thieves, etc.
977.A-Z Other, A-Z
977.N63 Nobility
977.S77 Students
977.Y6 Youth
979.A-Z Special. Local, A-Z
Dutch literature see PT5001+
<1001-1184.22> Flemish
The numbers below <PF1001-PF1184> are no longer used by the Library of Congress. Works on Dutch as spoken in Belgium are classified with the Dutch language
see PF1+
<1001-1023> Philology (Table P-PZ3a modified)

PF

Flemish
Philology -- Continued
History of philology
Cf. PF1025 History of the language
Biography, memoirs, etc.
<1017.A2> Collective
<1017.A5-Z> Individual, A-Z
Subarrange each by Table P-PZ50
Language
<1024> General. Relation to other languages
<1024.7> Language standardization and variation
<1025> History
Grammar
<1033> General works. Compends (Advanced). Historical. Comparative. Descriptive
<1035> Textbooks. Exercises
Readers. Chrestomathies
<1036> Primary
<1037> Intermediate. Advanced
<1039> Conversation. Phrase books
Phonology
<1040> General works
Phonetics
<1041> General works
<1043> Pronunciation
<1049> Orthography. Spelling
<1051> Alphabet. Vowels, consonants, etc.
Morphology. Inflection. Accidence
<1059> General
(1061-1067) Noun. Verb, etc.
see PF1070+
<1069> Tables. Paradigms
Parts of speech (Morphology and syntax)
<1070> General works
<1071> Noun
<1077> Adjective. Adverb. Comparison
<1083> Pronoun
Verb
<1085> General
<1097> Special
<1101> Particle
Syntax
<1113> General
<1125> Special
Style. Composition. Rhetoric
<1135> General works
<1145> Idioms. Errors. Blunders

Flemish
Language
Style. Composition. Rhetoric -- Continued
<1149> Letter writing
<1153> Prosody. Metrics. Rhythmics
Etymology
<1161> Treatises
<1163> Dictionaries (exclusively etymological)
<1164> Foreign elements
<1165> Semantics
<1167> Synonyms. Antonyms. Homonyms
Lexicography
<1173> General works
Biography of lexicographers see PF1017.A2+
Dictionaries
<1175> Flemish (including Flemish-Dutch)
<1178> Polyglot
<1179> Flemish-English; English-Flemish
<1181.A-Z> Dictionaries with definitions in other languages, A-Z
<1184> Special dictionaries
Linguistic geography. Dialects, etc. see PF700+
Flemish literature see PT6000+
Frisian language
Comprises Old Frisian to ca. 1500, East Frisian of Wangeroog and Saterland (Oldenburg), North Frisian (west coast of Schleswig, Halligan Islands, Helgoland, Sylt, Amrum and Föhr), and West Frisian (province of Friesland, and islands of Schiermonnikoog, and Terschelling)
For works confined strictly to a local dialect see PF1497
Cf. PF791+ Friesland dialects of Dutch
Cf. PF5641+ East Friesian (Low German)
1401-1413 Philology (Table P-PZ4a modified)
1402.A2-Z Collections (nonserial)
For texts, sources, specimens, etc. see PF1513
History of philology
Cf. PF1415 History of the language
1407 General works
Biography, memoirs, etc.
1409.A2 Collective
1409.A5-Z Individual, A-Z
Subarrange each by Table P-PZ50
1414-1486.9 Language (Table P-PZ4b modified)
Add number in table to PF1400
(1414) General works
see PF1415
1415 Treatises (including History of language)
1416 Outlines

Friesian language
Language -- Continued
1417 Popular
Style. Composition. Rhetoric
For study and teaching see PF1411
1475 General works
Etymology
1483.5 Dictionaries (exclusively etymological)
Lexicography
For biography of lexicographers see PF1409.A2+
1487 General works
1493 Dictionaries
For etymological dictionaries see PF1483.5
Linguistic geography. Dialects
1496 General. General special
(1496.Z5) Collections of texts
see PF1513
Treatises. Grammar, etc.
see PF1421+
Dictionaries see PF1493
(1497.A1) Atlases. Maps
see class G
1497.A5-Z Local. (By region, island, etc.)
e. g.
1497.N7 North Frisian
1497.W4 West Frisian
Literature
History
Treatises
1501 General
1502 Special
1513 Collections
1524-1525 Translations from Frisian into foreign languages (Table P-PZ30)
1531.A-Z Individual authors or works, A-Z
Subarrange each author by Table P-PZ40
Subarrange each separate work by Table P-PZ43
e.g.
1531.D5 Dijkstra, Waling Gerrits, 1821-1914 (Table P-PZ40)
1531.J3 Japiks, Gijsbert, 1602-1666 (Table P-PZ40)
1531.K5 Kiestra, Douwe Hermans, 1899-1970 (Table P-PZ40)
1531.T76 Troelstra, Pieter Jelles, 1860-1930 (Table P-PZ40)
1541.A-Z Local, A-Z
German

German -- Continued
3001-3071 Philology (Table P-PZ1a modified)
Class here works devoted entirely or prevailingly to German philology and language; for Germanic (Teutonic) philology, see PD1+ PD1001+
Periodicals. Serials
3004 Dutch. Scandinavian
Societies
3014 Dutch. Scandinavian
(3033) Atlases. Maps
see class G
History of philology
Cf. PF3075+ History of the language
Biography, memoirs, etc.
3063 Collective
3064.A-Z Individual, A-Z
Subarrange each by Table P-PZ50
Bibliography. Bio-bibliography
see Z2235
Study and teaching. Research
3065 General works
By period
For period of study, teaching, or research see PF3053+
For period of history of the language see PF3077+
3073-3693 Language (Table P-PZ1b modified)
Add number in table to PF3000
Script
see PF3153+
Grammar
Readers. Chrestomathies
Primers and primary grade
3114 Early (to 1870)
3115 Later, 1871-
Intermediate. Advanced
3116 Early (to 1870)
3117 Later, 1871-
3120.A-Z Manuals for special classes of students, A-Z
3120.A75 Art historians
3120.C5 Chemists
3120.C7 Commercial
Cf. HF5719 Business report writing
Cf. HF5721 Business correspondence
3120.L5 Librarians
3120.M4 Medical personnel
3120.M87 Musicians
3120.P6 Police
3120.S3 Scientific personnel

PF

German
Language
Grammar
Manuals for special classes of students, A-Z -- Continued
3120.S7 Soldiers
3120.T45 Theologians
Orthography. Spelling
Spelling books. Rules. Exercises
3144 Early to 1850
Later, 1851-
3145 General works
Official rules
3145.A2 German Empire
3145.A3 Prussia
3145.A31 Baden
3145.A33 Bavaria
3145.A35 Hesse
3145.A37 Saxony
3145.A39 Württemberg
3145.A4 Austria
3145.A5 Switzerland
3145.A6-Z Other. By author
3147 Special topics
Includes use of capitals
Alphabet
Including script
3156 Mutation (Umlaut)
Syntax
Sentences
(3380) Order of words
see PF3390
3385 Classes of sentences. Clauses and phrases
3390 Order of words
Style. Composition. Rhetoric
For study and teaching see PF3065+
3410 General works
3425 Exercises and specimens
3430 List of subjects. Outline topics
(3432) Readers for rhetorical analysis
see PF3117, PF3127
Etymology
3580 Dictionaries (exclusively etymological)
3582.A-Z Special elements. By language, A-Z
3582.A3 Foreign elements (General)
Cf. PF3670 Dictionaries
Lexicography
3601 Collections

German
Language
Lexicography -- Continued
3611 General works. History. Treatises
(3615) Biography of lexicographers
see PF3063+
3617.A-Z Criticism of particular dictionaries (by author, or title of dictionary, A-Z)
Dictionaries
German only
3620 Early to 1850
3625 Later, 1851-
3628 Minor, abridged, school dictionaries
3630 Supplementary (New words. Neologisms, etc.)
Interlingual
3635 Polyglot (definitions in two or more languages)
Bilingual
Classify with language less known
German-English; English-German
3640 General works
3640.A2 Early works to 1850
German-Dutch; Dutch-German see PF645.G5
German-French; French-German see PC2645.G2+
German-Italian; Italian-German see PC1645.G2+
German-Portuguese; Portuguese-German see PC5335.G5
German-Spanish; Spanish-German see PC4645.G2+
Dictionaries exclusively etymological see PF3580
3650 Particular periods (of Modern German)
Cf. PF3975+ Old High German
Cf. PF4325+ Middle High German
Cf. PF4591+ Early modern German
(3655) Particular authors or works
see the author or work in PT
3660 Names
Cf. CS2300+ Genealogy
Cf. PF3673 Foreign names
3667 Obsolete or archaic words
Local provincialisms
see PF5071+
Foreign words
3670 General
3673 Names
Special. By language see PF3582.A+
Rhyming dictionaries
see PF3519

German
Language
Lexicography
Dictionaries -- Continued
Special lists. Terms and phrases
3680 Miscellaneous
(3683.A-Z) By subject, A-Z
see the subject in classes A-N, Q-Z
3689 Dictionaries of terms and phrases
3691 Other
Including word frequency, etc.
3693 Abbreviations, Lists of
Old High German
(3801-3823) Philology
see PF3001+
Language
3824 General works
3824.5 General special
3825 History
Grammar
3831 Historical. Comparative. Descriptive
3835 Elementary. Introductory
3837 Readers. Chrestomathies
3838.A-Z Special dialects, A-Z
3838.A5 Alemannic
3838.B3 Bavarian
3838.C6 Cologne
3838.F7 Franconian
3840 Phonology
3845 Orthography. Spelling
Alphabet
3851 General works
3853 Vowels. Consonants, etc.
Morphology. Inflection. Accidence
3859 General works
3861 Word formation. Derivation. Suffixes, etc.
Noun. Verb, etc. see PF3870+
3869 Tables. Paradigms
Parts of speech (Morphology and syntax)
3870 General works
3871 Noun
3877 Adjective. Adverb. Comparison
3883 Pronoun
Verb
3885 General
3887 Special
3901 Particle

German
Old High German
Language
Grammar -- Continued
Syntax
3913 General
3925 Special
(3931.A-Z) Usage of particular authors and works, A-Z
3953 Prosody. Metrics. Rhythmics
Etymology
3961 General works
3963.A-Z Foreign elements, by language, A-Z
3965 Semantics
3969.A-Z Particular words, A-Z
Lexicography
3973 General works
3974 Glossaries
Dictionaries
3975 General works
3976 Special: Names, etc.
3977.A-Z Special dialects, A-Z
Literature
History see PT183
Collections
3985 General
3986 Minor
3986.3 Concordances, dictionaries, indexes, etc.
Translations
3986.5.A1 Modern German, by date
3986.5.A3-Z By language, A-Z
Individual works and authors
3987 A-N
3987.B56-.B563 Bischöfliches Priesterseminar zu Trier. Bibliothek. Manuscript. RIII.13, fol. 102-114 (Table P-PZ43)
3987.D8-.D83 Düsseldorf. Landes-und-Stadtbibliothek. Heine-Archiv. MSS. (F1) (Table P-PZ43)
3987.G46-.G463 Georgslied (Table P-PZ43)
3987.G56-.G563 Glossae Salomonis (Table P-PZ43)
3987.H5-.H7 Hildebrandslied (Table P-PZ42a)
3987.I8 Isidorus, Saint, Bp. of Seville, d. 636. De fide Catholica (Old High German translation)
Class here criticism of Old High German texts
3987.M47-.M473 Merseburger Zauberspruche (Table P-PZ43)
3987.M55-.M553 Murbacher Hymnen (Table P-PZ43)
3987.M6-.M8 Muspilli (Table P-PZ42a)
Notker III Labeo, Teutonicus, d. 1022
Collected and selected works

German
Old High German
Literature
Individual works and authors
Notker III Labeo, Teutonicus, d. 1022
Collected and selected works -- Continued
3988.A1 General collections. By date
Latin
see PA
Latin-German
Aristoteles
Categoriae
3988.A2 Texts. By date
3988.A2A-.A2Z Criticism
De interpretatione
3988.A25 Texts. By date
3988.A25A-.A25Z Criticism
Bible. O.T. Psalms
3988.A3 Texts. By date
3988.A3A-.A3Z Criticism
Bible. O.T. Psalms (Vienna manuscript)
3988.A4 Texts. By date
3988.A4A-.A4Z Criticism
Boethius. De consolatione philosophiae
3988.A5 Texts. By date
3988.A5A-.A5Z Criticism
De musica
In German only; based upon Boethius. De musica
3988.A6 Texts. By date
3988.A6A-.A6Z Criticism
Martianus Capella. De nuptiis philologiae et Mercurii
3988.A7 Texts. By date
3988.A7A-.A7Z Criticism
3988.A8-.Z3 Biography. Criticism
3988.Z4 Language
3988.Z5 Glossaries
Otfrid, of Weissenburg, 9th cent.
Evangeliorum liber (Krist)
3989.A1 Editions. By date
Translations
3989.A2 Modern German
3989.A3-.A39 Other. By language and date
3989.A4-.Z3 Biography. Criticism
3989.Z4 Language. Metrics, etc.
3989.Z5 Glossaries. By date
3991 O-Z

German
Old High German
Literature
Individual works and authors
O-Z -- Continued

3991.P37-.P373 Pariser (Altdeutsche) Gespräche (Table P-PZ43)
3991.R37 Ratpert, d. ca. 890 (Table P-PZ38)
3991.S23-.S25 Saint-Mihiel (France). Bibliothèque municipale. Manuscript. 25 (Table P-PZ42a)
3991.S46-.S48 Severus, Sulpicius. Vita S. Martini Episcopi (Table P-PZ42a)
3991.S7-.S72 St. Pauler Lukasglossen (Table P-PZ43a)
3991.T22 Tatian. Diatessaron (Old High German translation)
Class here criticism of Old High German texts
3991.T42-.T43 Tegernseer Vergilglossen (Table P-PZ43a)
3991.T72-.T723 Treves. Stadtbibliothek. MSS. (1093/1694) (Table P-PZ43)
3991.U53-.U54 Universitätsbibliothek Kiel. Manuscript. Cod. MS. K.B. 145 (Table P-PZ43a)

Old Saxon
to ca. 1100 A.D.
Language
3992.A1-.A5 Collections
3994 General works. Grammar
3995 Metrics
3996 Etymology. Dictionaries. Glossaries
Literature
3997.A1 Collections of texts
3997.A5-Z General works
Individual works and authors
Genesis (Old Saxon poem)
3998.A2 Texts, by date
3998.A5-Z Criticism
Heliand
3999.A2 Editions, by date
Translations
3999.A31 Modern German
3999.A32 English
3999.A33 French
3999.A34-.A39 Other languages
4000 Criticism. Language, etc.
4000.Z5 Dictionaries. Glossaries
4010.A-Z Other, A-Z
4010.C6 Colmjon, Gerben (Table P-PZ40)

Middle High German
1050/1100-ca. 1500 A.D.
Generalities: Periodicals, etc. see PF3001+

German
Middle High German -- Continued
4043-4349 Language (Table P-PZ2a modified)
Add number in table to PF4000
Grammar
Textbooks
4066 Early to 1870
4067 1870-2000
4067.3 2001-
Readers
4069 Primers. Intermediate and advanced readers
(4071) Intermediate and advanced readers
see PF4069
Morphology. Inflection. Accidence
4101 General works
4103 Word formation. Derivation. Suffixes, etc.
Style. Composition. Rhetoric
Special parts of rhetoric
4255 Other special. Figures, tropes, allegory, etc.
Including "Geblümter Stil"
Lexicography
Biography of lexicographers see PF3063+
Dictionaries
4333 Dictionaries with definitions in English
Other special lists
4348 Word frequency lists
4348.5 Reverse indexes
(4350) Linguistic geography
see PF5000
Dialects. Provincialisms, etc.
see PF5001+
Early Modern German
(1400/1500-ca. 1700)
Philology
(4501-4513) Generalities: Periodicals, etc.
see PF3001+
Language
4514 General
(4515) History
see PF3079+
Grammar
(4519) Contemporaneous
see PF3103, PF3109
4521 Historical. Comparative. Descriptive
4523 Elementary. Introductory
4525 Readers. Chrestomathies
4528 Phonology. Phonetics

German
Early Modern German
Language
Grammar -- Continued
Orthography and spelling see PF3141+
Morphology. Inflection. Accidence
4539 General works
Special
see PF3175+
Syntax
4571 General works
Special
see PF3365+
(4573) Usage of special authors or works
see the author or work in subclass PT
4577 Style. Composition. Rhetoric
4581 Prosody. Metrics. Rhythmics
Etymology. Semantics, etc.
see PF3571+
Lexicography
4587 Treatises
Dictionaries. Glossaries, etc.
4591 General
4595.A-Z Special, A-Z
(4596) Linguistic geography. Dialects, etc.
see PF5000+ , PF5016
Linguistic geography. Dialects, etc.
5000 Linguistic geography
Dialects. Provincialisms, etc.
5001 Periodicals. Societies. Congresses
For local societies see PF5071; PF5101+
Collections
5002 Texts. Sources. Specimens, etc.
Monographs. Studies
5003.A1-.A29 Several authors
5003.A3-Z Individual authors
5004 Encyclopedias. Dictionaries
(5005) Atlases. Maps
see class G
General works
5011 Treatises
5012 Compends. Outlines, syllabi, etc. Popular. Minor
History of dialects
5013 General
5014 General special
Earliest. Medieval
Old High German see PF3801+

German
Linguistic geography. Dialects, etc.
Dialects. Provincialisms, etc.
History of dialects
Earliest. Medieval -- Continued
Middle High German see PF4042.2+
Old Saxon see PF3992+
5016 (16th-)17th, and (17th-)18th centuries
5018 19th century. 20th century. 21st century
Grammar
5021 General works
5026 Phonology. Phonetics
5036 Morphology. Inflection. Accidence
5046 Syntax
5051 Style
5056 Prosody. Metrics. Rhythmics
5061 Etymology
5066 Lexicography
5071 Regions (other than PF5101-5844)
High German Dialects
Upper German
5101-5108 General (Table P-PZ12 modified)
(5107.A-Z) Local
see PF5131+
Old High German see PF3801+
Middle High German see PF4042.2+
Alemannic dialects
5121-5128 General (Table P-PZ12 modified)
(5127.A-Z) Local
see PF5131+
(5129) Old Alemannic
see PF3838.A5
Swiss
5131-5138 General (Table P-PZ12 modified)
(5137.A-Z) Local
see PF5141+
Particular dialects
5141-5144 Aargau (Table P-PZ14)
5146-5149 Appenzell (Table P-PZ14)
5151-5154 Basel (Table P-PZ14)
5156-5159 Bern (Table P-PZ14)
5161-5164 Freiburg (Fribourg) (Table P-PZ14)
Gallen see PF5181+
5166-5169 Glarus (Table P-PZ14)
5171-5174 Graubünden (Grisons) (Table P-PZ14)
5176-5179 Luzern (Lucerne) (Table P-PZ14)
5181-5184 Sankt Gallen (Saint Gall) (Table P-PZ14)

German
Linguistic geography. Dialects, etc.
Dialects. Provincialisms, etc.
High German Dialects
Upper German
Alemannic dialects
Swiss
Particular dialects -- Continued
5186-5189 Schaffhausen (Table P-PZ14)
5191-5194 Schwyz (Table P-PZ14)
5196-5199 Solothurn (Table P-PZ14)
5201-5204 Tessin (Ticino) (Table P-PZ14)
5206-5209 Thurgau (Table P-PZ14)
5211-5214 Unterwalden (Table P-PZ14)
5216-5219 Uri (Table P-PZ14)
5226-5229 Wallis (Valais) (Table P-PZ14)
5231-5234 Zürich (Table P-PZ14)
5236-5239 Zug (Table P-PZ14)
Alsatian
Including Alemannic dialects in Baden
5241-5248 General (Table P-PZ12)
5261-5264 Breisgau (Table P-PZ14)
5271-5274 Northwestern Italy (Table P-PZ14)
Swabian
5281-5288 General (Table P-PZ12)
5291-5294 Swabian in West Prussia (Table P-PZ14)
5296-5299 Vorarlberg and Liechtenstein (Table P-PZ14)
Bavarian-Austrian
5301-5308 General (Table P-PZ12 modified)
(5307.A-Z) Local
see PF5311+
(5309) Old Bavarian
see PF3838.B3
5311-5318 Bavarian (General) (Table P-PZ12)
Austrian
5321-5324 General (Table P-PZ14 modified)
(5324.A-.Z9) Local
see PF5326+
5326-5329 Austria, Upper (Table P-PZ14)
5331-5334 Austria, Lower (Table P-PZ14)
5336-5339 Vienna (Table P-PZ14)
Bohemia see PF5396+; PF5506+; PF5541+
5341-5344 Carinthia (Table P-PZ14)
5346-5349 Salzburg (Table P-PZ14)
5351-5354 Styria (Table P-PZ14)
Transylvania see PF5496+
5356-5359 Tyrol. Northern Tyrol (Table P-PZ14)

German
Linguistic geography. Dialects, etc.
Dialects. Provincialisms, etc.
High German Dialects
Upper German
Bavarian-Austrian
Austrian -- Continued
5361-5364 Northeastern Italy. Southern Tyrol (Table P-PZ14 modified)
5364.A-.Z9 Local. By dialect name or place, A-Z
5364.C3 Carnic Alps
5364.F4 Fersina Valley
5364.F7 Friaul
5364.L8 Luserna
5364.P87 Pusteria Valley (Pustertal)
Cimbrian
Carnic Alps see PF5364.C3
5364.S4 Sette Comuni (Sieben Gemeinden)
Including Tredici Comuni
5364.T7 Tredici Comuni (Dreizehn Gemeinden)
5365 Tyrol in Moravia
Isolated dialects of the former Austria-Hungary ("Sprachinseln")
5370 General works
5374 Slovenia (Table P-PZ15)
5375 Hungary (Table P-PZ15)
5377 Banat (Table P-PZ15)
5379 Bukovina (Table P-PZ15)
5380.A-Z Other, A-Z
Dialects of the Upper Palatinate (Ober Pfalz) and Western Bohemia
5381-5384 General (Table P-PZ14)
5396-5399 Bavarian dialect in Bohemia (Table P-PZ14)
Upper Franconian, South (Southern Rheno-) Franconian, East Franconian
see PF5411+
Middle German (Central German; Midland German)
Including works restricted to West Middle German
For East Middle German see PF5506+
5401-5408 General (Table P-PZ12 modified)
(5407.A-Z) Local
see PF5411+
Franconian
Cf. PF3838.F7 Old High German
Cf. PF5640 Low German
5411-5414 General (Table P-PZ14 modified)

German
Linguistic geography. Dialects, etc.
Dialects. Provincialisms, etc.
High German Dialects
Middle German (Central German; Midland German)
Franconian
General -- Continued
(5414.A-.Z9) Local
see PF5416+
5416-5419 Upper and East Franconian (Table P-PZ14)
5421-5424 Henneberg (Table P-PZ14)
Rheno-Franconian
5426-5429 General (Table P-PZ14)
5431-5434 Palatinate dialects, including Eastern Lorraine (Table P-PZ14)
For Palatinate dialects in Russia see PF5876
Pennsylvania German see PF5931+
5441-5444 Hessian (Southern and Upper Hessian) and Nassauan (Table P-PZ14)
5451-5454 Hessian (Lower) (Table P-PZ14)
Middle (Moselle) Franconian
5461-5464 General (Table P-PZ14 modified)
(5464.A-.Z9) Local
see PF5466+
5466-5469 Siegerland (Table P-PZ14)
5471-5474 Sayn (Table P-PZ14)
5476-5479 Westerwald (Table P-PZ14)
5481-5484 Moselle Valley, Saarlouis to Koblenz (Table P-PZ14)
5486-5489 Eifel (Table P-PZ14)
5491-5494 Luxemburg (Table P-PZ14)
5496-5499 Transylvania (Table P-PZ14)
5501-5504 Ripuarian Franconian (Southern). (Cologne-Aachen) (Table P-PZ14)
For Ripuarian Franconian (Northern) see PF5640
Cf. PF5637.C7 Cologne (Low German)
East Middle German
5506-5509 General (Table P-PZ14 modified)
(5509.A-.Z9) Local
see PF5511+
Thuringian-Upper Saxon
5511-5514 General (Table P-PZ14 modified)
(5514.A-.Z9) Local
see PF5516+
5516-5519 Thuringian (Table P-PZ14)
5521-5524 Osterland dialect (Table P-PZ14)
5531-5534 Meissen dialect (Table P-PZ14)

German
Linguistic geography. Dialects, etc.
Dialects. Provincialisms, etc.
High German Dialects
East Middle German
Thuringian-Upper Saxon -- Continued
5536 Anhalt
5541-5544 Erzgebirge and northern Bohemia (Table P-PZ14)
Cf. PF5396+ Bavarian dialect in Bohemia
Lusatian-Silesian
Including Lower Silesian
5551-5554 General (Table P-PZ14 modified)
(5554.A-.Z9) Local
see PF5556+
5556-5559 Lusatian (Table P-PZ14)
Silesian (Dialects of the Sudetic mountains)
5561-5564 General (Table P-PZ14 modified)
(5564.A-.Z9) Local
see PF5566+
5566-5569 Austrian Silesian (Table P-PZ14)
Including the German dialects in Moravia and Iglau
5571-5574 Riesengebirge and Glatz (Table P-PZ14)
5576-5579 Silesian in Ermland (East Prussia) (Table P-PZ14)
5581-5584 Silesian in northern Hungary (Table P-PZ14)
Low German
5601-5629 General works (Table P-PZ6 modified)
Dialects
(5628.A-Z) Special dialects
see PF5631+
Old Saxon see PF3992+
5631-5638 Middle Low German (Table P-PZ12 modified)
5637.A-Z Local. By dialect name or place, A-Z
5637.C7 Cologne
5638 Texts
For editions of texts without grammatical treatises, prefer PT4846
5640 Low Franconian (Northern Ripuarian) (Table P-PZ15)
Low Saxon
Generalities: Periodicals. Societies, etc. see PF5601+
Northern Low Saxon
5641-5644 East Friesian (Table P-PZ14)
Not a dialect of the Frisian language, but of the German region known as Ostfriesland
5645 Jeverland
5646 Oldenburg

German
Linguistic geography. Dialects, etc.
Dialects. Provincialisms, etc.
Low German
Low Saxon
Northern Low Saxon -- Continued

5647 Osnabrück
5648 Lower Weser Valley
5649 Bremen
5650 Brunswick
5651 Stade
5652 Hanover
5653 Lüneburg-Uelzen
5654 Lingen
5655 Hamburg (Table P-PZ15)
5656-5659 Schleswig-Holstein (Table P-PZ14)
Including works confined to Schleswig
5660 Ditmarsch (Table P-PZ15)
5661 Eiderstedt
5664 Anglian
5666-5669 Holstein (Table P-PZ14)
5672 Probstei, or Propstei
5674 Wagrian, including Lübeck
5677 Lauenburg
5681-5684 Mecklenburg, Hither-Pomerania, including Ruegen (Table P-PZ14)
5686-5689 Ems River Valley. Emsland (Table P-PZ14)

Westphalian
Cf. PF841+ Limburg dialects of Dutch
Cf. PF851+ Low Saxon in the Netherlands

5701-5704 General (Table P-PZ14 modified)
(5704.A-.Z9) Local
see PF5706+
5706-5709 Westphalian, Northern (Table P-PZ14)
5741-5744 Westphalian, Southern (Table P-PZ14)
5751 Lippe
5755 Ravensberg
5758 Waldeck
5771-5774 Eastphalian (Table P-PZ14)

Eastern Low Saxon

5781-5784 General (Table P-PZ14 modified)
(5784.A-.Z9) Local
see PF5786+
5786-5789 Brandenburg (Table P-PZ14)
5796-5799 Middle Pomeranian (Table P-PZ14)
Including Stettin and surrounding country

PF

German
Linguistic geography. Dialects, etc.
Dialects. Provincialisms, etc.
Low German
Low Saxon
Eastern Low Saxon -- Continued
5811-5814 Farther Pomeranian; Pomerellen; Netze valley (Table P-PZ14)
5821-5824 West Prussia (Table P-PZ14)
Including works on both West and East Prussia
5831-5834 East Prussia (Table P-PZ14)
5841-5844 Baltic Provinces (Table P-PZ14)
5851-5854 Lower Saxony (Table P-PZ14)
Including Peine and surrounding country
German in foreign parts
5861 General works
5871 Austria-Hungary
For dialects see PF5321+
5872 Belgium
5873 Denmark
Italy (Northeastern Italy. Southern Tyrol) see PF5361+
Italy (Northwestern Italy) see PF5271+
5876 Russia
Cf. PF5841+ Baltic Provinces
5881 Switzerland
For dialects see PF5141+
5891.A-Z Africa. By country, A-Z
5901.A-Z Asia. By country, A-Z
America
5921 General works
North America
5924 General works
5925 United States
5931-5938 Pennsylvania German (Table P-PZ12)
5938.5.A-Z Other U.S. regions or states, A-Z
5939 Canada
5941.A-Z South America. By country, A-Z
5951 Australia
Argot. Slang
5971 Collections
Texts
5975 Collections. General
5977 Separate
General works
5981 General works
5986 Grammatical studies
5989 Miscellaneous

German
Linguistic geography. Dialects, etc.
Argot. Slang -- Continued
5991 Dictionaries. Lists
Special classes
5995 Beggars. Gypsies. Tramps. Thieves, etc.
5997.A-Z Others, A-Z
5997.S6 Soldiers
5997.S8 Students
5997.Y6 Youth
5999.A-Z Special. Local, A-Z

Slavic. Baltic. Albanian
Slavic philology and languages
General
Philology
1 Periodicals. Serials
6 Societies
11 Congresses
Collections
Monographs. Studies
13 Various authors. Series
14.A-Z Studies in honor of a particular person or institution, A-Z
15 Individual authors
19 Encyclopedias. Dictionaries
(20) Atlases. Maps
see class G
Philosophy. Theory. Method
21 General works
23 Relations
History of philology
Cf. PG35+ Study and teaching
Cf. PG45+ History of the language
25 General
By period
27 Earliest. Middle Ages. Renaissance
29 Modern
31.A-Z By region or country, A-Z
Biography. Memoirs. Correspondence
33 Collective
34.A-Z Individual, A-Z
Subarrange each by Table P-PZ50
e.g.
34.C5 Chyz͡hevs'kyĭ, Dmytro, 1894- (Table P-PZ50)
34.C9 Cyril, Saint, Apostle of the Slavs, ca. 827-869 (Table P-PZ50)
Tschižewskij, Dimitirij, 1894-1977 see PG34.C5
Study and teaching
35 General
36 General special
38.A-Z By region or country, A-Z
39.A-Z By university, institution, etc., A-Z
41 General works
43-400 Languages (Table P-PZ2a modified)
Add number in table to PG0
Class here works dealing with all or with several of the Slavic languages
Cf. PG401+ Special groups

PG

Slavic philology and languages
General
Languages -- Continued
General
History of the language
46 Proto-Slavic language (Table P-PZ15)
53 Compends
54 Collected essays
(58) Script
see PG89+
Grammar
Readers
69 Primary grade readers. Intermediate and advanced readers
(71) Intermediate and advanced readers
see PG69
Alphabet
Including script
91 Glagolitic
92 Cyrillic
93 Vowels
94 Diphthongs
95 Consonants
Style. Composition. Rhetoric
For study and teaching see PG35+
240 General works
(299.5) Lexicology
see PG319.5
319.5 Lexicology
Lexicography
323 General works
Biography of lexicographers see PG33+
Linguistic geography. Dialects, etc.
350 Linguistic geography
Dialects. Provincialisms, etc.
351 Periodicals. Collections
355 General works
Grammar
361 General
365 Special
390 Dictionaries
(393) Atlases. Maps
see class G
400 Slang. Argot
Special groups
401-429 Eastern Slavic (General) (Table P-PZ6)
Including Russian, Ukrainian and Belarusian

Slavic philology and languages
General
Special groups -- Continued
Southern Slavic (General)
Including Bulgarian, Macedonian, Serbo-Croatian, Slovenian
431 Periodicals. Societies. Serials. Collections (nonserial)
432 Congresses
433 History of philology
435 Study and teaching
436 General works
437 History
Script see PG89+
Grammar
438 Comparative. Historical. Descriptive
439 Elementary. Introductory
441 Phonology. Phonetics
442 Transliteration
443 Morphology. Inflection. Accidence
444 Parts of speech
445 Syntax
447 Style. Composition. Rhetoric
448 Translating
449 Prosody. Metrics. Rhythmics
450 Lexicology
451 Etymology
Lexicography
453 Treatises
455 Dictionaries
459 Linguistic geography. Dialects
Prefer PG350+
471-499 Western Slavic (General) (Table P-PZ6)
Including Czech, Slovak, Upper and Lower Sorbian (Wendic), and the Lechitic languages (Polish, Polabian, Kashubian and Slovincian)
Slavic literature (General)
500 Periodicals. Societies. Serials
500.3 Congresses
500.4 Encyclopedias. Dictionaries
500.6.A-Z Biography of critics, historians, etc., A-Z
History
501 General works. Compends
502 General special. Minor
502.5 Relation to other literatures
503.A-Z Special topics, A-Z
503.A35 Aesthetics
503.A6 Apollonius of Tyre

Slavic literature (General)
History
Special topics, A-Z -- Continued
503.B3 Baroque literature
503.B52 Bible
503.B8 Bulgaria
503.C93 Cycles
503.D5 Dnieper River
503.E54 Enlightenment
503.F65 Fools and jesters
503.H64 Home
503.K67 Kosovo, Battle of, 1389
503.P6 Postmodernism (Literature)
503.P7 Pride
503.R44 Religion
503.S37 Satire
503.S63 Space and time
503.W3 War
503.W64 Women
504 Biography (Collective)
504.5 Women authors. Literary relations of women
504.6.A-Z Other special classes of authors, A-Z
504.6.O77 Orthodox Eastern authors
(504.9) Bibliography. Bio-bibliography
see Z7041+
505 Origins
To 1800
506 General works
506.5.A-Z Special topics, A-Z
506.5.A87 Autobiography
506.5.C46 Christian literature
19th and 20th centuries
507 General works
509.A-Z Special topics, A-Z
509.A93 Avant-garde
509.B84 Bulgaria
509.C58 Civilization
509.E96 Expressionism
509.F37 Fasts and feasts
509.F64 Folklore and literature
509.L52 Liberty
Literature and politics see PG509.P64
509.M6 Modernism
509.M87 Myth. Mythology
Mythology see PG509.M87
509.N33 Nationalism
509.N35 Nature

	Slavic literature (General)
	History
	19th and 20th centuries
	Special topics, A-Z -- Continued
509.P64	Politics and literature
509.P65	Popular literature
509.P75	Psychology
509.R4	Realism
509.R44	Religion
509.R6	Romanticism
509.R87	Russia
509.S6	Social aspects
509.S64	Space
509.T56	Tito, Josip Broz, 1892-1980
509.W67	World War II
	21st century
509.2	General works
509.4.A-Z	Special topics, A-Z
510	Poetry
	Drama
511	General works
511.5.A-Z	Special types of drama, A-Z
511.5.R33	Radio plays
512	Other
	Folk literature
	For general works on and collections of folk literature see GR138
	History
(513)	General works
513.4.A-Z	Special forms, A-Z
513.4.C45	Christmas carols
513.4.E64	Epic poetry
513.4.F64	Folk poetry
513.4.L35	Laments
(514)	Collections of texts (exclusively)
(518.A-Z)	Translations. By language, A-Z
519	Juvenile literature (General)
	For special genres, see the genre
	Collections
520	General
521	Poetry
522	Drama
523	Other
551-552	Translations from Slavic literatures into foreign languages (Table P-PZ30)
	Special groups

Slavic literature (General)
Special groups -- Continued
Southern Slavic literature. Yugoslav literature
Including the literature of Yugoslavia, and of Yugoslavia and Bulgaria combined
For Bulgarian see PG1000+
For Macedonian see PG1180+
For Serbian, Croatian, and Bosnian see PG1400+
For Slovenian see PG1900+

560	Periodicals. Societies. Serials
	History
561	General works
562	General special
562.5	Relation to other literatures
563.A-Z	Special topics, A-Z
563.K67	Kosovo, Battle of, 1389
563.R4	Realism
564	Biography (Collective)
565	Origins
566	Through 1800
	19th and 20th centuries
567	General works
569.A-Z	Special topics, A-Z
569.E96	Expressionism
569.F64	Folklore and literature
569.J48	Jews
569.M95	Mysticism
569.N33	Nationalism
569.P64	Politics and literature
569.P67	Postmodernism
569.R4	Realism
569.R65	Romanticism
569.S6	Social aspects
569.S94	Symbolism
569.T56	Tito, Josip Broz, 1892-1980
569.U76	Utopias
569.W67	World War II
	21st century
569.2	General works
569.4.A-Z	Special topics, A-Z
570	Poetry
	Drama
571	General works
571.5.A-Z	Special types of drama, A-Z
571.5.R33	Radio plays
572	Other

Slavic literature (General)
Special groups
Southern Slavic literature. Yugoslav literature -- Continued
Folk literature
For general works on and collections of folk literature see GR250+
History
(573) General works
573.4.A-Z Special forms, A-Z
573.4.E64 Epic poetry
(574) Collections of texts
(578.A-Z) Translations. By language, A-Z
579 Juvenile literature (General)
For special genres, see the genre
Collections
580 General
581 Poetry
582 Drama
583 Other
584-585 Translations from Southern Slavic literature into foreign languages (Table P-PZ30)
Other (Eastern Slavic, Western Slavic)
see PG500+
Church Slavic
Including Old Church Slavic (Old Bulgarian, Palaeo-Slovenian)
Class here works dealing with Church Slavic in general as well as those restricted to Old Church Slavic
For works treating Church Slavic as represented in local variants or national recensions see PG698.A5+
601-699 Philology. Language (Table P-PZ4 modified)
(617.5) Script
see PG637
Grammar
637 Alphabet. Script
Including vowels, consonants, etc.
(673) Grammatical usage of particular authors or works
see PG705
Linguistic geography. Dialects, etc.
Dialects, provincialisms, etc.
(697) Dictionaries
see PG693
698.A5-Z Local. By region, place, etc., A-Z
e.g.
698.B8 Bulgaria
698.M27 Macedonia
698.R6 Romania
698.R87 Russia

Church Slavic -- Continued
Literature
For works that are more significant for the general development of the national literatures than for Church Slavic literature, see the national literature
Periodicals. Societies. Collections, etc.
see PG601+
700.15 Congresses
700.2 Encyclopedias. Dictionaries
700.3 Study and teaching
700.6.A-Z Biography of critics, historians, etc., A-Z
Subarrange each by Table P-PZ50
History
701 General works
701.2 General special
701.3 Addresses, essays, lectures
701.4.A-Z Relation to other literatures, A-Z
701.45 Translations into Church Slavic (as a subject)
701.6.A-Z Special topics, A-Z
701.6.A64 Apocalyptic literature
701.6.A66 Apocryphal books
701.6.B53 Bible
702 Biography of authors (Collective)
By period
702.2 Through 1100
702.3 1101-
702.4 Poetry
702.5 Drama
702.6 Other
Collections
703 General
704 Poetry
704.5 Drama
704.6 Other
705.A-Z Individual authors or works, A-Z
Subarrange individual works by Table P-PZ43 unless otherwise specified
Subarrange each author by Table P-PZ40 unless otherwise specified
Class here literary works in Church Slavic and linguistic and literary criticism of Church Slavic translations from foreign languages. For topical works in Church Slavic, such as religion or history, and for discussions of the topical content of such works, see the subject in classes A - Z
705.A27-.A273 Alexander the Great (Romance). Александрия (Table P-PZ43)
705.A29-.A3 Alphabet prayer. Азбучна молитва (Table P-PZ43a)

Church Slavic
Literature
Individual authors or works, A-Z -- Continued

705.A55-.A553 Antiochus, monk of Palestine, 7th cent. Pandekt. Антиох. Пандект (Table P-PZ43)

705.A7-.A73 Arkhangel′skoe evangelie. Архангельское евангелие (Table P-PZ43)

705.A74-.A743 Asemanievoto evangelie (Codex Assemanianus). Асеманиевото евангелие (Table P-PZ43)

705.A8-.A83 Athos (Monasteries). Zograph. Mss. (Table P-PZ43)

705.B34-.B35 Banishko evangelie. Банишко евангелие (Table P-PZ43a)

705.B36-.B37 Bašćanska ploča. Башчанска плоча (Table P-PZ43a)

705.C5 Chernorizets Khrabŭr. Черноризец Храбър (Table P-PZ40)

705.C57-.C573 Cosmas, Indicopleustes, fl. 6th cent. Christianikē topographia. Κοσμᾶς Ἰνδικοπλεύστης. Χριστιανική τοπογραφία. Козьма Индикоплов. Книга нарицаема (Table P-PZ43)

705.C6 Cosmas, Presbyter, 10th cent. Презвитер Козма (Table P-PZ40)

705.C95 Cyril, Saint, Apostle of the Slavs, ca. 827-869. Кирилл (Table P-PZ40)

For general biography and criticism see BX4700.C9

For Cyril's philological work see PG34.C9

705.D4-.D42 Dečani (Monastery). Mss. Codex 88 (Table P-PZ43a)

705.D55 Dimitriĭ, Saint, Metropolitan of Rostov, 1651-1709. Димитрий Ростовский (Table P-PZ40)

705.E37 Efrem, 14th cent. Ефрем (Table P-PZ40)

705.E62-.E63 Ephraem, Syrus, Saint, 303-373. Paraenesis. Ефрем Сирин. Паренесис (Table P-PZ43a)

705.E64 Epifaniĭ Premudryĭ, Monk, 15th cent. Епифаний Премудрый (Table P-PZ40)

705.E86-.E87 Evangelie Kokhno. Евангелие Кохно (Table P-PZ43a)

705.E88-.E883 Evangelium Bucovinense (Table P-PZ43)

705.E885-.E8853 Evangelium Cyrillicum Gothoburgense (Table P-PZ43)

705.E89 Evtimiĭ, Tŭrnovski, Patriarch of Bulgaria, ca. 1327-ca. 1401. Евтимий Търновски (Table P-PZ40)

For general biography and criticism see BX659

Freising fragments see PG1917.B7+

705.F6-.F7 Frycz Modrzewski, Andrzej, ca. 1503-ca. 1572. De Republica emendanda. Church Slavic (Table P-PZ43a)

705.G54-.G543 Glagolita Clozianus (Table P-PZ43)

Church Slavic
Literature
Individual authors or works, A-Z -- Continued

705.G73-.G74 Gregory I, Pope, ca. 540-604. Dialogi. Liber 3-4. Church Slavic. Григорий I, папа римский (Григорий Великий, Григорий Двоеслов). Патерик римский (Table P-PZ43a)

705.H55-.H553 Hludov parimejnik. Хлудов паримејник (Table P-PZ43)

705.H83-.H833 Hvalov zbornik. Хвалов зборник (Table P-PZ43)

705.I43-.I433 Il′ina kniga. Ильина книга (Table P-PZ43)

705.I6 Ĭoan, Exarch of Bulgaria, 10th cent. Йоан Екзарх Български (Table P-PZ40)

705.I76-.I763 Istoricheskai͡a palei͡a. Историческая палея (Table P-PZ43)

705.I82-.I823 Ivan Aleksandroviiat sbornik. Иван Александровият сборник (Table P-PZ43)

705.I87-.I873 Izbornik Svi͡atoslava 1073 g. Изборник Святослава 1073 г. (Table P-PZ43)

705.J44 Jefimija, Monahinja, 1346 or 7?-1405? Монахиња Јефимија (Table P-PZ40)

705.J67-.J673 Josephus, Flavius. De bello Judaico. Иосиф Флавий. Повесть о пленении Иерусалима (Повесть о разорении Иерусалима) (Table P-PZ43)

705.K35 Kantakuzin, Dimitŭr, b. ca. 1435. Димитър Кантакузин (Table P-PZ40)

705.K52-.K523 Kievskie listki (Kiev fragments). Киевские листки (Table P-PZ43)

705.K54 Kiprian, Saint, Metropolitan of Kiev and All Rus, ca. 1333-1406. Киприан, митрополит киевский и всея Руси (Table P-PZ40)

705.K57 Kliment, Ohridski, d. 916. Климент Охридски (Table P-PZ40)

Kokhno Evangelie see PG705.E86+

705.K65 Konstantin, Filozof, 14th/15th cent. Константин Филозоф (Table P-PZ40)

705.K68 Kožičić, Šimun, ca. 1460-1536 (Table P-PZ40)

Kozma, Presbyter, 10th cent. see PG705.C6

705.L3-.L33 Lavrashevskoe Evangelie. Лаврашевское Евангелие (Table P-PZ43)

705.L43-.L44 Lietuvos Mokslų akademija. Biblioteka. Manuscript. F19-233 (15) (Table P-PZ43a)

705.L56-.L57 Ljuština, Vikentije, 1761-1805. Grammatika italianskai͡a. Викентие Лустина. Грамматіка италіанская (Table P-PZ43a)

705.L83 Luchkaĭ, Mikhail, 1789-1843. Михаил Лучкай (Table P-PZ40)

705.N32 Naum, Ohridski, d. 910. Наум Охридски (Table P-PZ40)

Church Slavic
Literature
Individual authors or works, A-Z -- Continued

705.N36 Neagoe Basarab, Voivode of Wallachia, 1482?-1521 (Table P-PZ40)

705.N4 Nestor, annalist, ca. 1056-1113. Нестор (Table P-PZ40)
Cf. PG3300.L43+ Chronicle of Nestor (so-called). Повесть временных лет

705.N42-.N423 New York missal (Table P-PZ43)

705.N48 Nikifor, Metropolitan of Kiev, d. 1121. Никифор (Table P-PZ40)

705.N49 Nikon, Chernogorets, d. 1088. Никон Черногорец (Table P-PZ40)

705.N5 Nikon, Patriarch of Moscow and of Russia, 1605-1681. Никон, патриарх московский и всея Руси (Table P-PZ40)

705.N67-.N673 Norovski psaltir. Норовски псалтир (Table P-PZ43)

705.O87-.O873 Ostromirovo Evangelie. Остромирово Евангелие (Table P-PZ43)

705.P3 Pakhomiĭ Logofet, monk, 15th cent. Пахомий Логофет (Table P-PZ40)

705.P38 Pavlovich, Parteniĭ, 1700-1760. Партений Павлович (Table P-PZ40)

705.P43-.P433 Peresopnyt͡sʹke i͡evanheli͡ie. Пересопницьке євангеліє (Table P-PZ43)

705.P45 Philippos, Monotropos, fl. 1100 (Table P-PZ40)

705.P46-.P463 Physiologus. Славянский физиолог (Table P-PZ43)

705.P65-.P653 Pomelnicul Mânăstirei Bistrița (Table P-PZ43)

705.P67-.P673 Pomęnnik ūsopshykh. ПомѦнникъ □сопшыхъ (Table P-PZ43)

Povestʹ o Zosime i Savvatii. Повесть о Зосиме и Савватии see PG705.Z44+

705.R35-.R353 Razvod istarski. Развод истарски (Table P-PZ43)

705.S23-.S24 Saint Catherine (Monastery: Mount Sinai). Manuscript. Slavic no. 49 (Table P-PZ43a)

705.S33-.S333 Savvina kniga. Саввина книга (Table P-PZ43)

705.S48-.S483 Sevasti͡ianovi͡iat sbornik. Севастияновият сборник (Table P-PZ43)

705.S56-.S563 Sinaĭskiĭ paterik. Синайский патерик (Table P-PZ43)

705.S66-.S663 Stanislavov prolog. Станиславов пролог (Table P-PZ43)

705.S69 Stavrovet͡sʹkyĭ, Kyrylo, d. 1646. Кирило Ставровецький (Table P-PZ40)

705.S94-.S943 Suprasŭlski sbornik (Codex Suprasliensis). Супрасълски сборник (Table P-PZ43)

705.S96-.S963 Svi͡ete Tikhiĭ. Свѣте Тихий (Table P-PZ43)

705.T4 Theophylactus, Archbishop of Ochrida, ca. 1050-ca. 1108. Теофилакт Охридски (Table P-PZ40)

Church Slavic
Literature
Individual authors or works, A-Z -- Continued
705.T53-.T533 Tikveški zbornik. Тиквешки зборник (Table P-PZ43)
705.T66-.T663 Tristan (Romance). Повест о Триштану и Ижоти (Table P-PZ43)
705.T7-.T73 Troy (Romance) (Table P-PZ43)
705.T8 T͡Samblak, Grigoriĭ, ca. 1364-1420. Григорий Цамблак (Table P-PZ40)
705.T84-.T843 T͡Sŭrkolezhki apostol. Църколежки апостол (Table P-PZ43)
705.U87-.U873 Uspenskiĭ sbornik. Успенский сборник (Table P-PZ43)
705.V52 Vid, Omišljanin (Table P-PZ40)
705.V53-.V54 Vienna fragments (Table P-PZ43a)
705.V64 Vladislav, Gramatik, fl. 1456-1480. Владислав Граматик (Table P-PZ40)
705.W4-.W43 Wenceslaus, Saint, Duke of Bohemia, ca. 907-929. Legend (Table P-PZ43)
705.Z34-.Z343 Zagrebski sbornik ot 1469. Загребски сборник от 1469 (Table P-PZ43)
705.Z44-.Z443 Zhitie i chudesa prepodobnykh Zosimy i Savvatii͡a solovet͡skikh chudotvort͡sev. Житие и чудеса преподобных Зосимы и Савватия соловецких чудотворцев (Table P-PZ43)
705.Z48-.Z483 ZHytomyrs′ke i͡evanheliie͡. Житомирське євангеліє (Table P-PZ43)
706.A-Z Local. By region, place, etc., A-Z
Subarrange each by Table P-PZ26
e.g.
706.B9-.B92 Bulgaria (Table P-PZ26)
715-716 Translations into foreign languages (Table P-PZ30)
Bulgarian Church Slavic (Middle Bulgarian)
ca. 1100-ca. 1400
(771-799) Language
see PG698.B8
Literature
see PG706.B9+
Bulgarian
801-823 Philology (Table P-PZ3a modified)
History of philology
Cf. PG825 History of the language
815 General works
Biography, memoirs, etc.
817.A2 Collective
817.A5-Z Individual, A-Z
Subarrange each by Table P-PZ50

Bulgarian -- Continued

824-999 Language (Table P-PZ3b modified)

Add number in table to PG800

(828) Script

see PG89+

Grammar

831 General works

833 Historical grammar

Readers

837 Primers. Primary grade readers

Readers on special subjects

see PG839.15

Readers for special classes of students

see PG838.5

838.A-Z Intermediate and advanced readers

Subarrange by main entry

838.5.A-Z Manuals for special classes of students, A-Z

838.5.T43 Technical students

Style. Composition. Rhetoric

For study and teaching see PG819+

935 General works

Etymology

963 Dictionaries (exclusively etymological)

974 Lexicography

For biography of lexicographers see PG817.A2+

Dictionaries

Bulgarian only

975 General

976 Picture dictionaries

977 Supplementary dictionaries. Dictionaries of new words

978 Polyglot (three or more languages)

Cf. PG2635 Russian first

979 Bulgarian-English; English-Bulgarian

981.A-Z Bulgarian-French [-German, etc]; French [German, etc.]-Bulgarian, A-Z

982.A-Z Bulgarian-Slavic, A-Z

982.C9 Czech

982.P6 Polish

982.R9 Russian

Serbo-Croatian (Serbian, Croatian, Bosnian) see PG1378

982.S5 Slovak

982.S6 Slovenian

982.U4 Ukrainian

Bulgarian-Oriental; Oriental-Bulgarian

see subclasses PJ-PL

Dictionaries exclusively etymological see PG963

Bulgarian
Language
Dictionaries -- Continued
983 Dictionaries of names
Cf. CS2300+ Genealogy
Rhyming dictionaries
see PG958
984 Special. Technical, etc.
985 Other special lists
Including glossaries, dictionaries of terms and phrases, word frequency lists, reverse indexes, and lists of abbreviations
Linguistic geography. Dialects, etc.
987 Linguistic geography
Dialects. Provincialisms, etc.
988 Treatises. Monographs. Studies
989 Grammar
991 Dictionaries
(992) Atlases. Maps
see class G
993.A-Z Special, by region, A-Z
Slang. Argot
995 Collections
996 General works
997 Dictionaries. Lists
997.5 Texts
998.A-Z Special topics, A-Z
For list of Cutter numbers, see Table P-PZ2 421.A+
999.A-Z Special local, A-Z
Literature
1000 Periodicals. Societies. Serials
1000.15 Congresses
Collections
1000.17 Series. Monographs by various authors
1000.18 Individual authors (Collected works, studies, etc.)
1000.2 Encyclopedias. Dictionaries
1000.25 History of Bulgarian literary history and criticism
1000.3 Study and teaching
Biography of critics, historians, etc.
1000.5 Collective
1000.52.A-Z Individual, A-Z
Subarrange each by Table P-PZ50
History
General works. Compends
1001 General works
1002 General special
1003 Collected essays

PG

Bulgarian
Literature
History -- Continued

1003.2.A-Z Relation to other literatures, A-Z
1003.3 Translations (as a subject)
1003.5.A-Z Treatment of special topics and subjects, A-Z
1003.5.C46 Clothing and dress
1003.5.I43 Identity (Psychology)
1003.5.M95 Mythology
1003.5.S47 Serbia
1004 Biography of authors (Collective)
1004.5.A-Z Special classes of authors, A-Z
1004.5.J48 Jews
1004.5.L32 Laboring class. Working class
1004.5.W65 Women
(1004.9) Bibliography
see Z2898.L5
1005 Origins
Cf. PG701+ Church Slavic literature
Through 1800
Cf. PG701+ Church Slavic literature
1006 General works
1006.2.A-Z Special topics, A-Z
1006.2.D35 Damaskini
19th and 20th centuries
1008 General works
1008.2.A-Z Special topics, A-Z
1008.2.A44 Aliens
1008.2.A76 Artists
1008.2.B52 Bible
1008.2.B85 Bulgaria
1008.2.C3 Characters and characteristics
1008.2.C37 Christianity
1008.2.C55 Clothing and dress
1008.2.C6 Communism. Communists
1008.2.C94 Czech Republic
1008.2.D75 Drinking of alcoholic beverages
1008.2.E73 Erotic literature
1008.2.E74 Ethics
1008.2.E94 Expressionism
1008.2.F35 Fantastic literature
1008.2.F65 Folklore and literature
1008.2.H47 Heroes
1008.2.H57 History in literature
1008.2.I36 Icons
1008.2.I45 Ilindensko-preobrazhensko Uprising, 1903
1008.2.M63 Modernism

Bulgarian
Literature
History
19th and 20th centuries
Special topics, A-Z -- Continued

1008.2.P35 Parody
1008.2.P37 Patriotism
1008.2.P63 Politics
1008.2.P65 Popular literature
1008.2.P67 Populism
1008.2.P78 Psychoanalysis and literature
1008.2.R43 Realism
1008.2.R85 Russia
1008.2.R86 Russian Revolution, 1917-1921
1008.2.R87 Russo-Turkish War, 1877-1878
1008.2.S27 Satire
1008.2.S4 September Uprising, 1923
1008.2.S6 Socialist realism
1008.2.S94 Symbolism
1008.2.U6 Uprising, 1876
1008.2.W35 War
1008.2.W67 World War II

21st century
1009 General works
1009.2.A-Z Special topics, A-Z

Poetry
1010 General works
1010.2.A-Z Special topics, A-Z
1010.2.C55 Children's poetry
1010.2.L68 Love
1010.2.M63 Modernism
1010.2.M94 Myth
1010.2.N37 Nature
1010.2.N48 New words
1010.2.P37 Pastoral poetry
1010.2.P55 Philosophy
1010.2.P6 Political poetry
1010.2.R44 Religious poetry
1010.2.R48 Revolutionary poetry
1010.2.S85 Suicide
1010.2.S95 Symbolism
1010.2.W67 World War II

Drama
1011 General works
1011.2.A-Z Special types or topics, A-Z
1011.2.C45 Children's plays
1011.2.C64 Comedy

Bulgarian
Literature
History
Drama
Special types or topics, A-Z -- Continued
1011.2.H47 Heroes
1011.2.M94 Myth
1011.2.N37 Nationalism
1011.2.P65 Political plays
1011.2.T7 Translating and translations
Prose
1012 General works
Fiction
1012.2 General works
1012.3.A-Z Special types of fiction, A-Z
1012.3.C45 Children's stories
1012.3.D48 Detective and mystery stories
1012.3.F34 Fantastic fiction
1012.3.F57 First person narrative
1012.3.H57 Historical fiction
1012.3.P78 Psychological fiction
1012.3.S45 Short stories
1012.4 Other
1012.45.A-Z Special topics, A-Z
1012.45.A56 Anti-fascist movements
1012.45.A88 Autobiography
1012.45.S63 Social realism
1012.45.T7 Travel
1012.45.W38 Water mills
Local see PG1041+
Folk literature
For general works on and collections of folk literature see GR253
(1012.5) Periodicals. Societies. Serials
For special genres, see the genre
History and criticism
(1013) General works
Folk songs and poetry
1013.3 General works
1013.5.A-Z Special forms or topics, A-Z
1013.5.E6 Epic poetry
1013.5.H5 Historical poetry
Collections of texts
(1013.8) General
By form
Folk songs and poetry. Ballads
1014 General

Bulgarian
Literature
Folk literature
Collections of texts
By form
Folk songs and poetry. Ballads -- Continued

1015.A-Z Special forms and topics, A-Z
1015.E6 Epic poetry
1015.H5 Historical poetry
1015.O3 Occupations
1015.R4 Religious poetry
1015.W67 World War II
1016 Drama
Fables, proverbs, riddles, etc.
see subclass PN
Tales, legends, etc. see GR253
(1017.A-Z) By locality, region, etc., A-Z
(1018.A-Z) Translations. By language, A-Z
1019 Juvenile literature (General)
For special genres, see the genre
Collections
1020 General
1020.3.A-Z Special classes of authors, A-Z
1020.3.C48 Children
1020.3.P45 Physicians
1020.3.P68 Postal employees
1020.3.Y68 Youth
1020.4.A-Z Special topics, A-Z
1020.4.A6 April Uprising, 1876
1020.4.A7 Army
1020.4.B8 Bulgaria
1020.4.C5 Children
1020.4.C97 Cyril, Apostle of the Slavs, Saint, ca. 827-869
1020.4.D5 Dimitrov, Georgi, 1882-1949
1020.4.K5 Khisarya
1020.4.L5 Liquor problem
1020.4.M32 Macedonia
1020.4.M5 Miners
1020.4.M53 Ministry of Transport troops
1020.4.M66 Moscow
1020.4.R45 Rhodope Mountains
1020.4.R86 Russian Revolution, 1917-1921
1020.4.R87 Russo-Turkish War, 1877-1878
1020.4.S4 September Uprising, 1923
1020.4.S55 Silistrenski okrŭg
1020.4.S72 Stalin, Joseph, 1879-1953
1020.4.T7 Transport workers

Bulgarian
Literature
Collections
Special topics, A-Z -- Continued

1020.4.T85 Tŭrgovishtki okrŭg
1020.4.V45 Veliko Tŭrnovo
1020.4.W37 War
1020.4.W65 Women
1020.4.Y68 Youth

By period

1020.5 Early through 1800
1020.6 19th century
1020.7 20th century
1020.8 21st century

Poetry

1021 General
1021.15.A-Z Special classes of authors, A-Z
1021.15.C45 Children

By form

1021.2 Ballads
For folk songs see PG1014
1021.3.A-Z Other, A-Z
1021.3.C45 Children's poetry
1021.3.H34 Haiku
1021.3.S65 Sonnets
1021.4.A-Z Special topics, A-Z
1021.4.B68 Botev, Khristo, 1848-1876
1021.4.B85 Bulgaria
1021.4.D42 Death
1021.4.D45 Debeli͡anov, Dimcho, 1887-1916
1021.4.D65 Don Quixote
1021.4.L3 Labor poetry
1021.4.L48 Levski, Vasil Ivanov, 1837-1873
1021.4.L68 Love poetry
1021.4.M3 Macedonia
1021.4.P35 Paradise
1021.4.P37 Patriotic poetry
1021.4.P6 Political poetry
1021.4.R32 Rain
1021.4.R4 Revolutionary poetry
1021.4.R8 Russia
1021.4.R9 Russian Revolution, 1917-1921
1021.4.S4 Sea
1021.4.S45 September Uprising, 1923
1021.4.S64 Sofia (Bulgaria)
(1021.4.S65) Sonnets
see PG1021.3.S65

Bulgarian
Literature
Collections
Poetry
Special topics, A-Z -- Continued
1021.4.S85 Symbolism
1021.4.W6 Women
Drama
1022 General works
1022.5.A-Z Special types or topics, A-Z
1022.5.A45 Amateur plays
Prose
1022.9 General works
1023 Fiction
1024 Other
Individual authors or works
Early through 1800
Cf. PG705.A+ Church Slavic literature
1035.A1A-.A1Z Anonymous works. By title, A-Z
1035.A1T55 Tikhonravovskiĭ damaskin. Тихонравовский дамаскин
1035.A2-Z Individual authors, A-Z
Subarrange each author by Table P-PZ40
1035.P85 Puncho, pop, b. 1744 or 5. Поп Пунчо (Table P-PZ40)
1801-1960
1036.A-Z Anonymous works. By title, A-Z
1036.Z57-.Z573 Zlatogradski sbornik. Златоградски сборник (Table P-PZ43)
1037.A-Z Individual authors, A-Z
Subarrange each author by Table P-PZ40 unless otherwise indicated
Beinsa Duno. Беинса Дуно see PG1037.D85
1037.B58 Blŭskov, Ilii͡a Rashkov, 1839-1913. Илия Рашков Блъсков (Table P-PZ40)
1037.B6-.B62 Botev, Khristo, 1848-1876. Христо Ботев (Table P-PZ44)
1037.C5 Chintulov, Dobri, 1822-1886. Добри Чинтулов (Table P-PZ40)
1037.D47 Dilovski, Dimitŭr, 1895-1925. Димитър Диловски (Table P-PZ40)
1037.D63 Dobroplodni, Sava Il. (Sava Iliev), 1820-1894. Сава Илиев Доброплодни (Table P-PZ40)
Drumev, Vasil, pseud. Васил Друмев see PG1037.K56
1037.D85 Dŭnov, Petŭr, 1864-1944. Петър Дънов (Table P-PZ40)

Bulgarian
Literature
Individual authors or works
1801-1960
Individual authors, A-Z -- Continued

1037.E4 Elin Pelin, 1877-1949. Елин Пелин (Table P-PZ40)

1037.G46 Ginchev, T͡Sani, 1835-1894. Цани Гинчев (Table P-PZ40)

1037.I55 Ĭoakim Kŭrchovski, monakh, ca. 1750-ca. 1820. Йоаким Кърчовски (Table P-PZ40)

1037.K3-.K32 Karavelov, L͡iuben, 1834-1879. Любен Каравелов (Table P-PZ44)

1037.K5434 Kirkov, Georgi, 1867-1919. Георги Кирков (Table P-PZ40)

1037.K56 Kliment, Metropolitan, 1840-1901. Климент Търновски (Table P-PZ40)

1037.K58-.K582 Konstantinov, Aleko, 1863-1897. Алеко Константинов (Table P-PZ44)

1037.K67 Kozlev, Nikola D., 1824-1902. Никола Димов Козлев (Table P-PZ40)

Kŭrchovski, Ĭoakim, ca. 1750-ca. 1820 see PG1037.I55

1037.M2818 Manev, Todor Sŭbev, 1902- . Тодор Събев Манев (Table P-PZ40)

1037.N36 Neofit, Archimandrite, ca. 1780-1848. Неофит Бозвели (Table P-PZ40)

1037.O37 Ogn͡ianovich, Konstantin, 1798-1858. Константин Огнянович (Table P-PZ40)

1037.P346 Peev, Todor, 1842-1904. Тодор Пеев (Table P-PZ40)

Rum͡iant͡sev, Sergeĭ. Сергей Румянцев see PG1037.D47

1037.S52-.S5212 Slaveĭkov, Pencho P., 1866-1912. Пенчо Петков Славейков (Table P-PZ44a)

1037.S522-.S5222 Slaveĭkov, Petko Rachev, 1827-1886. Петко Рачев Славейков (Table P-PZ44)

1037.S56-.S562 Sofroniĭ, Vrachanski, Bishop of Vrat͡sa, 1739-1813. Софроний Врачански (Table P-PZ44)
For Sofroniĭ as a bishop see BX659

1037.S657 Stamatov, Georgi Porfiriev, 1869-1942. Георги Порфириев Стаматов (Table P-PZ40)

1037.S6778 Sto͡ian, Chicho. Чичо Стоян (Table P-PZ40)

Sto͡ianov, Dimitŭr. Димитър Стоянов see PG1037.E4

1037.S73 Sto͡ianov, Zakhari, 1850-1889. Захари Стоянов (Table P-PZ40)

Bulgarian
Literature
Individual authors or works
1801-1960
Individual authors, A-Z -- Continued

1037.S75-.S752 Strashimirov, Anton, 1872-1937. Антон Страшимиров (Table P-PZ44)

1037.T743 TSerkovski, TSanko, 1869-1926. Цанко Церковски (Table P-PZ40)

1037.V3-.V32 Vazov, Ivan Minchov, 1850-1921. Иван Минчов Вазов (Table P-PZ44)

1037.V35 Velichkov, Konstantin, 1855-1907. Константин Величков (Table P-PZ40)

1037.V37 Veliksin, Dimitŭr, 1834-1896. Димитър Великсин (Table P-PZ40)

1037.V56 Vlaĭkov, Todor G., 1865-1943. Тодор Генчов Влайков (Table P-PZ40)

1037.V6 Voĭnikov, Dobri, 1833-1878. Добри Войников (Table P-PZ40)

1037.Z47 Zhinzifov, Raĭko, 1839-1877. Райко Жинзифов (Table P-PZ40)

Zidarov, Kamen, 1902- . Камен Зидаров see PG1037.M2818

1961-2000

1038 Anonymous works. By title, A-Z

1038.1 A

The author number is determined by the second letter of the name

Subarrange each author by Table P-PZ40

1038.12 B

The author number is determined by the second letter of the name

Subarrange each author by Table P-PZ40

1038.13 C

The author number is determined by the second letter of the name

Subarrange each author by Table P-PZ40

1038.14 D

The author number is determined by the second letter of the name

Subarrange each author by Table P-PZ40

Dimitrov, Dimitŭr, 1947- . Димитър Димитров see PG1038.21.O823

1038.15 E

The author number is determined by the second letter of the name

Subarrange each author by Table P-PZ40

PG

Bulgarian
Literature
Individual authors or works
1961-2000 -- Continued

1038.16 F
The author number is determined by the second letter of the name
Subarrange each author by Table P-PZ40

1038.17 G
The author number is determined by the second letter of the name
Subarrange each author by Table P-PZ40

1038.18 H
The author number is determined by the second letter of the name
Subarrange each author by Table P-PZ40

1038.19 I
The author number is determined by the second letter of the name
Subarrange each author by Table P-PZ40

1038.2 J
The author number is determined by the second letter of the name
Subarrange each author by Table P-PZ40

1038.21 K
The author number is determined by the second letter of the name
Subarrange each author by Table P-PZ40

1038.21.O823 Kostov, Kaloi͡an, 1947- . Калоян Костов (Table P-PZ40)

1038.22 L
The author number is determined by the second letter of the name
Subarrange each author by Table P-PZ40

1038.23 M
The author number is determined by the second letter of the name
Subarrange each author by Table P-PZ40

1038.24 N
The author number is determined by the second letter of the name
Subarrange each author by Table P-PZ40

1038.25 O
The author number is determined by the second letter of the name
Subarrange each author by Table P-PZ40

Bulgarian
Literature
Individual authors or works
1961-2000 -- Continued

1038.26 P
The author number is determined by the second letter of the name
Subarrange each author by Table P-PZ40

1038.27 Q
The author number is determined by the second letter of the name
Subarrange each author by Table P-PZ40

1038.28 R
The author number is determined by the second letter of the name
Subarrange each author by Table P-PZ40

1038.29 S
The author number is determined by the second letter of the name
Subarrange each author by Table P-PZ40

1038.3 T
The author number is determined by the second letter of the name
Subarrange each author by Table P-PZ40

1038.31 U
The author number is determined by the second letter of the name
Subarrange each author by Table P-PZ40

1038.32 V
The author number is determined by the second letter of the name
Subarrange each author by Table P-PZ40

1038.33 W
The author number is determined by the second letter of the name
Subarrange each author by Table P-PZ40

1038.34 X
The author number is determined by the second letter of the name
Subarrange each author by Table P-PZ40

1038.35 Y
The author number is determined by the second letter of the name
Subarrange each author by Table P-PZ40

Bulgarian
Literature
Individual authors or works
1961-2000 -- Continued
1038.36 Z
The author number is determined by the second letter of the name
Subarrange each author by Table P-PZ40
1039-1039.36 2001- (Table P-PZ29)
Local
For works, biography, and criticism of individual local authors, including those outside Bulgaria, see PG1037+
By region, province, etc., A-Z
History
1041 General
1042.A-Z Individual regions, provinces, etc., A-Z
Collections
1043 General
1044.A-Z Individual regions, provinces, etc., A-Z
1044.5.A-Z By city, A-Z
Outside of Bulgaria
Balkan Peninsula
History
1045 General
1046.A-Z Individual regions, countries, etc., A-Z
Collections
1047 General
1048.A-Z Individual regions, countries, etc., A-Z
1070 Other countries
1145-1146 Translations from Bulgarian literature into foreign languages (Table P-PZ30)
Macedonian
Philology. Language
1151 Periodicals. Societies. Collections
1153 History of philology
Biography of philologists
1153.5 Collective
1153.52.A-Z Individual, A-Z
Subarrange each by Table P-PZ50
1155 Study and teaching
General works
1156 General works
1157 History of the language
Grammar
1158 General works
1159 Textbooks
Including textbooks for foreign students

	Macedonian
	Philology. Language
	Grammar -- Continued
1160	Readers
1165	Phonology
1166	Orthography and spelling. Alphabet
1167	Morphology. Parts of speech
1168	Syntax
1169	Style. Composition. Rhetoric
1170	Prosody. Metrics. Rhythmics
1170.5	Lexicology
	Etymology
1171	General works
	Foreign elements
1171.5	General works
1171.52.A-Z	By language, A-Z
1172	Eponyms
	Lexicography
1173	Dictionaries with definitions in Macedonian
1174	Dictionaries with definitions in two or more languages, or dictionaries of two or more languages with definitions in Macedonian
1175.A-Z	Dictionaries with definitions in English and other languages. By language, A-Z
1176	Special dictionaries Including etymological, foreign words, etc.
	Linguistic geography. Dialects
1177	General works
1178.A-Z	Local. By region, place, etc., A-Z
1179	Slang. Argot
	Literature
1180	Periodicals. Societies. Collections
1180.2	Encyclopedias. Dictionaries
1180.3	Study and teaching
	Biography of critics, historians, etc.
1180.5	Collective
1180.52.A-Z	Individual, A-Z Subarrange each by Table P-PZ50
	History
1181	General works
1181.2	General special
1181.3	Collected essays
1181.5	Relation to other literatures, A-Z
1182	Biography of authors (Collective)
1182.9.A-Z	Special classes of authors, A-Z
1182.9.W65	Women
	By period

PG

	Macedonian
	Literature
	History
	By period -- Continued
1183	Origins. Through 1800
	19th-20th centuries
1184	General works
1184.2.A-Z	Special topics, A-Z
1184.2.L53	Liberty
1184.2.M64	Modernism
1184.2.P7	Profiteering
1184.2.S64	Socialist realism
1184.2.T87	Turks. Turkey
1184.2.U67	Uprising of 1903
	21st century
1184.3	General works
1184.4.A-Z	Special topics, A-Z
1185	Poetry
1186	Drama
1187	Other
	Folk literature
	For general works on and collections of folk literature see GR250.5.M33
	History and criticism
(1188)	General works
1188.5.A-Z	Special forms, A-Z
1188.5.B34	Ballads
1188.5.F65	Folk drama
1188.5.F67	Folk poetry
(1189)	Collections of texts
(1189.5.A-Z)	By locality, region, etc., A-Z
(1190.A-Z)	Translations. By language, A-Z
1190.5	Juvenile literature (General)
	For special genres, see the genre
	Collections
1191	General
	Poetry
1192	General
1192.5.A-Z	By subject, A-Z
1192.5.S55	Skopje (Macedonia)
1192.5.T56	Tito, Josip Broz, 1892-1980
1192.5.W65	Women
1193	Drama
1194	Other
	Individual authors and works

Macedonian
Literature
Individual authors and works, A-Z -- Continued
1195.A-Z Through 1970, A-Z
Subarrange individual authors by Table P-PZ40
Subarrange individual works by Table P-PZ43
1195.C38 Cepenkov, Marko K., 1829-1920. Марко Костов Цепенков (Table P-PZ40)
1195.H33 Hadži Konstantinov-Džinot, Jordan, ca. 1820-1882. Јордан Хаџи Константинов-Џинот (Table P-PZ40)
1195.K7 Krčovski, Joakim. Јоаким Крчовски (Table P-PZ40)
1195.M53 Miladinov, Konstantin, 1830-1862. Константин Миладинов (Table P-PZ40)
1195.P78 Pulevski, Ǵorǵi, 1838-1895. Ѓорѓи Пулевски (Table P-PZ40)
1195.P8 Pŭrlichev, Grigor St., 1830-1893. Григор Ставрев Пърличев (Григор Прличев) (Table P-PZ40)
For editions and criticism of Pŭrlichev's Greek works see PA5610.P8
Racin, Kočo, 1909-1943. Кочо Рацин see PG1195.S57
1195.S57 Solev, Kosta Apostolov, 1909-1943. Коста Апостолов Солев (Table P-PZ40)
1195.V43-.V433 Veda Slovena. Веда Словена (Table P-PZ43)
1195.V64 Vojnicalija, Milan, 1874-1939. Милан Војницалија (Table P-PZ40)
1196-1196.36 1971- (Table P-PZ29)
Local
For works, biography, and criticism of individual local authors, including those outside Macedonia see PG1195+
1197.A-Z By region, place, etc., A-Z
1197.5 Outside of Macedonian linguistic area
Translations
From foreign literature into Macedonian
see the foreign literature
1198-1199 From Macedonian into foreign languages (Table P-PZ30)
Serbo-Croatian
Including works on Serbian, Croatian, or Bosnian as individual languages
1201-1223 Philology (Table P-PZ3a modified)
History of philology
Cf. PG1225 History of the language
Biography, memoirs, etc.
1217.A2 Collective
1217.A5-Z Individual, A-Z
Subarrange each by Table P-PZ50
Language

Serbo-Croatian
Language -- Continued
1224 General. Relation to other languages
1224.5 Language data processing
1224.7 Language standardization and variation
1224.73 Political aspects
1224.75 Social aspects
1224.8 Spoken language
1224.85 Language acquisition
1225 History
1226 Outlines
1227 Popular
1228 Script
Grammar
No distinction is made here between Serbian, Croatian, or Bosnian except in the case of elementary books (grammars, exercises, readers, conversation and phrase books) professing in their titles to teach one of these languages. Elementary books using the term "Serbo-Croatian" are classified with the Serbian books.
1229 General works. Historical. Comparative. Descriptive
Elementary. Textbooks
1231 Serbian
1232 Croatian
1232.5 Bosnian
Readers
For phonetic readers see PG1250
Serbian
1233 Primary
1234 Intermediate and advanced
Croatian
1236 Primary
1237 Intermediate and advanced
1237.3 Bosnian
Conversation. Phrase books
1238 Serbian
1239 Croatian
1239.3 Bosnian
Textbooks for foreign speakers
1239.5.A1 General works
1239.5.A2-Z By language
Phonology
Including phonemics
Cf. PG1251+ Alphabet
1240 General works
Phonetics
1241 General works

Serbo-Croatian
Language
Grammar
Phonology
Phonetics -- Continued
1242 Palatalization
1243 Pronunciation
1244 Accent
1244.3 Clitics
1244.5 Intonation
1244.7 Prosodic analysis
1244.9 Phonetics of the sentence (Sandhi)
Orthography. Spelling
1245 History. General works
1247 Spelling books
1249 Spelling reform
1250 Phonetic readers
Alphabet
1251 General works
1252 Transliteration
1253 Vowels
1254 Diphthongs
1255 Consonants
1256 Contraction (Hiatus. Elision)
1257 Particular letters
1258 Syllabication
Punctuation see PG1343
1258.5 Capitalization
1258.9 Morphophonemics
Morphology
1259 General works
1261 Word formation. Derivation. Suffixes, etc.
1262 Inflection
Noun. Verb, etc. see PG1270+
1269 Tables. Paradigms
Parts of speech (Morphology and syntax)
1270 General works
Noun
1271 General works
1273 Gender. Number
1275 Case
Adjective. Adverb. Comparison
1277 General works
1279 Numerals
1283 Pronoun
Verb
1285 General works

Serbo-Croatian
Language
Grammar
Parts of speech (Morphology and syntax)
Verb -- Continued
1287 Person
1288 Number
1289 Voice
1291 Mood
1295 Tense
1295.5 Aspects of verbal action
1296 Infinitive and participle
Including gerund
1297.A-Z Special classes of verbs, A-Z
1298.A-Z Particular verbs, A-Z
1299 Other. Miscellaneous
Particle
1301 General works
1303 Adverb
1305 Preposition
1307 Conjunction
1309 Interjection
1311.A-Z Other special, A-Z
1311.C54 Clitics
1311.N4 Negatives
Syntax
1313 General works
Sentences
1319 General arrangement, etc.
1321 Order of words
1323 Order of clauses
1325 Clauses
1327 Other special
1329.A-Z Other aspects, A-Z
1329.A35 Agreement
Style. Composition. Rhetoric
For study and teaching see PG1219+
1335 General works
1337 Textbooks
1339 Outlines, questions, exercises and specimens. List of subjects
(1340.A-Z) Special authors, A-Z
see the author in PG1418+ and PG1618+
1340.5 Discourse analysis
Special parts of rhetoric
1341 Style. Invention, narration, etc. Figures, tropes, allegory, etc.

Serbo-Croatian
Language
Style. Composition. Rhetoric
Special parts of rhetoric -- Continued
1342 Choice of words. Vocabulary, etc.
1343 Punctuation
1345 Idioms. Errors. Blunders
Special classes of composition
1347 Essays, lectures, newspaper style, precis writing, report writing, etc.
Letter writing
1349 General works
1349.5 Specimens. Collections
Translating
For special subjects, see classes B-Z, e.g. T11.5 Technology
1350 General works
1350.5 Machine translating
Including research
Prosody. Metrics. Rhythmics
1351 History of the science
General works
1352 Early to 1800
1353 1800-
1355 Textbooks
1357 Versification
1358 Rhyme. Rhyming dictionaries
1359.A-Z Special forms, meters, etc., A-Z
1360 Rhythm. Rhythm in prose
1360.5 Lexicology
Etymology
1361 Treatises
1361.5 Popular works
1362 Names (General)
For personal names see CS2300+ ; for place names, see G104+ (General) or classes D-F for names of specific continents or countries
1363 Dictionaries (exclusively etymological)
1364.A-Z Special elements. By language, A-Z
1364.A3 Foreign elements (General)
Cf. PG1384 Dictionaries
1364.3 Other special
1364.5 Folk etymology
1365 Semantics
1367 Synonyms. Antonyms. Paronyms. Homonyms
1368 Onomatopoeic words
1369.A-Z Particular words, A-Z
Lexicography

Serbo-Croatian
Language
Lexicography -- Continued
1371 Periodicals. Societies. Serials. Collections (nonserial)
1373 General works
Biography of lexicographers see PG1217.A2+
1373.5 Criticism, etc., of particular dictionaries
Dictionaries
1374 Serbo-Croatian only
Including dictionaries from Serbian to Croatian or Bosnian, from Croatian to Serbian or Bosnian, and from Bosnian to Serbian or Croatian
Interlingual
Classify with language less known
1375 Polyglot
1376 Serbian-English [-German, etc.]; English [German, etc.] -Serbian
Class here dictionaries professing to be Serbian (or Serbo-Croatian) with equivalents in any of the non-Slavic languages of Europe
1377 Croatian-English [-German, etc.]; English [German, etc.] -Croatian
Class here dictionaries professing to be Croatian with equivalents in any of the non-Slavic languages of Europe
1377.5 Bosnian-English [-German, etc.]; English [German, etc.] -Bosnian
Class here dictionaries professing to be Bosnian with equivalents in any of the non-Slavic languages of Europe
1378 Serbo-Croatian (Serbian, Croatian, or Bosnian)-Slavic
Class here dictionaries with equivalents in other Slavic languages
For Slovenian see PG1893.S4
For Ukrainian see PG3893.S4
(1379) Serbo-Croatian-Oriental
see subclasses PJ-PL
1384 Dictionaries of foreign words
For words from a specific language see PG1364.A+
Dictionaries exclusively etymological see PG1363
1385 Other special lists
Including glossaries, dictionaries of terms and phrases, word frequency lists, reverse indexes, and lists of abbreviations
Dialects
1387.A2-.A29 Periodicals. Collections

Serbo-Croatian
Language
Dialects -- Continued
1387.A3-Z Collections of texts, etc.
1388 General works
1389 Grammar
1391 Dictionaries
(1392) Atlases. Maps
see class G
1392.3 Old Serbo-Croatian (Table P-PZ15)
1392.5 Aljamia (Serbo-Croatian written in Arabic characters by Muslims in Bosnia and Hercegovina)
1393 Štokavian (Table P-PZ15)
1394 Čakavian (Table P-PZ15)
1395-1395.95 Kajkavian (Table P-PZ15a)
1396.A-Z Other dialects. By region, A-Z
1399 Slang. Argot
Serbo-Croatian literature
Class here: (1) Serbo-Croatian literature in general, i.e. treatises on, and editions of, both Serbian and Croatian literary works (or Serbian, Croatian, and Bosnian works). (2) Serbian literature proper
Libraries preferring to keep Serbian literature apart may use PG1500+
Libraries preferring to keep Serbian, Croatian, and Bosnian literature together may ignore PG1500+ PG1600+ PG1700+
For works limited to Croatian literature see PG1600+
For works limited to Bosnian literature see PG1700+
Cf. PG560+ Yugoslav literature
History
1400 Periodicals. Societies. Serials
1400.15 Congresses
Collected works (nonserial)
1400.17 Several authors
1400.18 Individual authors
1400.2 Encyclopedias. Dictionaries
1400.3 Study and teaching
Biography of critics, historians, etc.
1400.59 Collective
1400.6.A-Z Individual, A-Z
Subarrange each by Table P-PZ50
1401 General works
1402 General special
1402.5.A-Z Relation to other literatures, A-Z
1403 Addresses, essays, lectures
1404 Biography (Collective)
1404.9.A-Z Special classes of authors, A-Z

Serbo-Croatian literature
History
Special classes of authors, A-Z -- Continued
1404.9.J48 Jews
1404.9.P74 Prisoners
1404.9.W65 Women
1405 Origins
Cf. PG701+ Church Slavic literature
1406 Through 1800
Cf. PG701+ Church Slavic literature
19th and 20th centuries
1408 General works
1408.2.A-Z Special topics, A-Z
1408.2.A93 Avant-garde
1408.2.B44 Belgrade
1408.2.E94 Expressionism
1408.2.F35 Fantastic literature
1408.2.F87 Futurism
1408.2.G73 Greek influence
1408.2.H57 History
1408.2.I34 Ideology
1408.2.I47 Impressionism
1408.2.L38 Law
1408.2.L62 Local color
1408.2.M63 Modernism
1408.2.N37 Nationalism
1408.2.O75 Oriental influences
1408.2.P63 Politics
1408.2.P65 Popular literature
1408.2.R43 Realism
1408.2.R64 Romanticism
1408.2.S87 Surrealism
1408.2.S95 Symbolism
21st century
1409 General works
1409.2.A-Z Special topics, A-Z
Poetry
1410 General works
1410.5.A-Z Special topics, A-Z
1410.5.A93 Avant-garde
1410.5.E43 Elegiac poetry
1410.5.E65 Erotic poetry
1410.5.G63 God
1410.5.M46 Metalanguage
1410.5.R65 Romanticism
1410.5.S95 Surrealism
Drama

Serbo-Croatian literature
History
Drama -- Continued
1411 General works
1411.5.A-Z Special types of drama, A-Z
1411.5.H57 Historical drama
1411.5.R33 Radio plays
1411.5.V45 Verse drama
Prose
1412 General works
Fiction
1412.2 General works
1412.3.A-Z Special types of fiction, A-Z
1412.3.F57 First person narrative
1412.3.H57 Historical fiction
1412.3.S35 Science fiction
1412.3.S45 Short stories
1412.5 Other
1412.6.A-Z Special topics, A-Z
1412.6.M63 Modernism
1412.6.P66 Postmodernism
1412.6.R43 Realism
1412.6.S87 Surrealism
1412.6.T72 The Tragic
1412.6.U86 Utopias
1412.6.V35 Vampires
1412.6.W64 World War I
1412.7 Juvenile literature
For special genres, see the genre
Collections
1413 General
1413.3.A-1413.Z Special classes of authors, A-Z
1413.3.C48 Children
1413.5.A-Z Special topics, A-Z
1413.5.D75 Drinking customs
1413.5.F57 Fishers
1413.5.K68 Kosovo, Battle of, 1389
1413.5.M68 Mountains
1413.5.P37 Paris (France)
1413.5.W65 World War II
Poetry
1414 General
1414.2.A-Z Special classes of authors, A-Z
1414.2.S64 Soldiers
1414.3.A-Z Special types of poetry, A-Z
1414.3.E95 Experimental poetry
1414.3.H35 Haiku

Serbo-Croatian literature
Collections
Poetry
Special types of poetry, A-Z -- Continued

1414.3.S65 Sonnets
1414.5.A-Z Special topics, A-Z
1414.5.A76 Armenia
1414.5.D43 Death
1414.5.D45 Decani (Monastery)
1414.5.K35 Karadžić, Vuk Stefanović, 1787-1864
1414.5.K66 Kosovo Civil War, 1998-1999
1414.5.K72 Krajina (Croatia : Region)
1414.5.L67 Love poetry
1414.5.M68 Mothers
1414.5.P36 Patriotic poetry
1414.5.P65 Popović, Jovan Sterija, 1806-1856
1414.5.R44 Religious poetry
1414.5.R48 Revolutionary poetry
1414.5.S38 Sava, Saint, 1169-1237
1414.5.T58 Tito, Josip Broz, 1892-1980
1414.5.Y84 Yugoslav War, 1991-1995, in literature

Drama

1415 General works
1415.5.A-Z Special types or topics, A-Z
1415.5.R23 Radio plays
1416 Other

Local

For local divisions limited to Croatian literature see PG1640+

For local divisions limited to Bosnian literature see PG1747.A+

1417.A-Z By region, province, etc., A-Z

e. g.

(1417.B6) Bosnia and Hercegovina

see PG1700+

1417.5.A-Z By city, A-Z

Individual authors and works

Including authors whose Serbian or Croatian nationality cannot be determined, or who do not wish to be identified as either Serbian or Croatian

1418.A-Z To 1960, A-Z

Subarrange each author by Table P-PZ40 unless otherwise indicated

1418.A1A-.A1Z Anonymous works. By title, A-Z
1418.B34 Bašagić, Safvet-beg, 1870-1934. Сафвет-бег Башагић (Table P-PZ40)

Serbo-Croatian literature
Individual authors and works
To 1960, A-Z -- Continued

1418.D35 Davičo, Hajim S., 1854-1916. Хајим С. Давичо (Table P-PZ40)

1418.D6755 Đorđević, Vladan, 1844-1930. Владан Ђорђевић (Table P-PZ40)

1418.D676 Đorđević Prizrenac, Manojlo, 1851-1896. Манојло Ђорђевић Призренац (Table P-PZ40)

1418.D77 Dučić, Jovan, 1871-1943. Јован Дучић (Table P-PZ40)

1418.D817 Đurđević, Svetislav, 1860-1891. Светислав Ђурђевић (Table P-PZ40)

1418.G614 Golubović, Mihailo, 1872-1936. Михајло Голубовић (Table P-PZ40)

1418.H3 Hadži Ruvim, 1752-1804. Хаџи Рувим (Table P-PZ40)

1418.H33 Hadžić, Osman Nuri, 1869-1937. Осман Нури Хаџић (Table P-PZ40)
For Osman-Aziz see PG1418.O76

1418.I27 Ibrovac, Milun T., 1852-1917. Милун Т. Ибровац (Table P-PZ40)

1418.I4 Ignjatović, Jakov, 1822-1889. Јаков Игњатовић (Table P-PZ40)

1418.I48 Ilić, Jovan, 1824-1901. Јован Илић (Table P-PZ40)

1418.I5 Ilić, Vojislav, 1860-1894. Војислав Илић (Table P-PZ40)

1418.J33 Jakšić, Đura, 1832-1878. Ђура Јакшић (Table P-PZ40)

1418.J339 Janković, Emanuilo, 1758-1792. Емануило Јанковић (Table P-PZ40)

1418.J6 Jovanović Zmaj, Jovan, 1833-1904. Јован Јовановић Змај (Table P-PZ40)

1418.K648 Kostić, Laza, 1841-1910. Лаза Костић (Table P-PZ40)
For his German works see PT2621.O846

1418.K6482 Kostić, Tadija P., 1863-1927. Тадија П. Костић (Table P-PZ40)

1418.L353 Lazarević, Laza K., 1851-1890. Лаза К. Лазаревић (Table P-PZ40)

1418.L5 Ljubiša, Stjepan Mitrov, 1824-1878. Стјепан Митров Љубиша (Table P-PZ40)

1418.M294 Martinović, Savo Matov, 1806-1896. Саво Матов Мартиновић (Table P-PZ40)

1418.M3 Matavulj, Simo, 1852-1908. Симо Матавуљ (Table P-PZ40)

1418.M515 Milićević, Ivan A., 1868-1950. Иван А. Милићевић (Table P-PZ40)
For Osman-Aziz see PG1418.O76

1418.M527 Miljanov, Marko, 1833-1901. Марко Миљанов (Table P-PZ40)

PG

Serbo-Croatian literature
Individual authors and works
To 1960, A-Z -- Continued

1418.M86 Mušicki, Lukijan, 1777-1837. Лукијан Мушицки (Table P-PZ40)
1418.N38 Nenadić, Ivan Antun, 1723-1784. Иван Антун Ненадић (Table P-PZ40)
1418.N4 Nenadović, Ljubomir, 1826-1895. Љубомир Ненадовић (Table P-PZ40)
1418.N525 Nikolić, Atanasije, 1803-1882. Атанасије Николић (Table P-PZ40)
1418.N68 Novaković, Stojan, 1842-1915. Стојан Новаковић (Table P-PZ40)
1418.N69 Nović, Joksim, 1806-1868. Јоксим Новић (Table P-PZ40)
1418.N8 Nušić, Branislav Đ., 1864-1938. Бранислав Ђ. Нушић (Table P-PZ40)
1418.O18 Obradović, Dositej, 1739-1811. Доситеј Обрадовић (Table P-PZ40)
1418.O35 Ogni͡anovich, Konstantin, 1798-1858. Константин Огнянович (Table P-PZ40)
1418.O7 Orfelin, Zaharija, 1726-1785. Захарија Орфелин (Table P-PZ40)
1418.O76 Osman-Aziz. Осман-Азиз (Table P-PZ40)
For Hadžić, Osman Nuri see PG1418.H33
For Miličević, Ivan A. see PG1418.M515
1418.P39 Peter I, Prince-Bishop of Montenegro, 1747-1830. Петар I Петровић Његош (Table P-PZ40)
1418.P4 Peter II, Prince-Bishop of Montenegro, 1813-1851. Петар II Петровић Његош (Table P-PZ40)
1418.P62 Popović, Jovan Sterija, 1806-1856. Јован Стерија Поповић (Table P-PZ40)
1418.P65 Popović, Zarija R., 1856-1934. Зарија Р. Поповић (Table P-PZ40)
1418.P77 Protić Sokoljanin, Petar, 1827-1854. Петар Протић Сокољанин (Table P-PZ40)
1418.R3 Radičević, Branko, 1824-1853. Бранко Радичевић (Table P-PZ40)
1418.R48 Reljković, Matija Antun, 1732-1798. Матија Антун Рељковић (Table P-PZ40)
1418.S7 Sremac, Stevan, 1855-1906. Стеван Сремац (Table P-PZ40)
1418.S898 Stefanović, Stefan, ca. 1805-ca. 1827. Стефан Стефановић (Table P-PZ40)
1418.S9 Stefanović, Svetislav, 1874-1944. Светислав Стефановић (Table P-PZ40)

Serbo-Croatian literature
Individual authors and works
To 1960, A-Z -- Continued

1418.S953 Stojadinović Srpkinja, Milica, 1830-1878. Милица Стојадиновић Српкиња (Table P-PZ40)

1418.S96 Subotić, Jovan, 1817-1886. Јован Суботић (Table P-PZ40)

1418.S98 Sulejmanpašić-Despotović, Omer-beg, b. 1870. Омер-бег Сулејманпашић-Деспотовић (Table P-PZ40)

1418.T73 Trifković, Kosta, 1843-1875. Коста Трифковић (Table P-PZ40)

1418.V4 Veselinović, Janko M., 1862-1905. Јанко М. Веселиновић (Table P-PZ40)

1418.V53 Vidaković, Milovan, 1780-1841. Милован Видаковић (Table P-PZ40)

1418.V59 Višnjić, Filip, 1767-1834. Филип Вишњић (Table P-PZ40)

1418.V896 Vuličević, Ljudevit, 1839-1916. Људевит Вуличевић (Table P-PZ40)

1419-1419.36 1961-2000 (Table P-PZ29 modified)

1419.14 D

Davidović, Stojanka Grozdanov see PG1419.17.R69

1419.17 G

1419.17.R69 Grozdanov Davidović, Stojanka. Стојанка Грозданов Давидовић (Table P-PZ40)

1419.18 H

1419.18.E74 Herman-Sekulić, Maja. Маја Херман-Секулић (Table P-PZ40)

1419.2 J

1419.2.E9 Jevtović, Danica Lala-, 1930- . Даница Лала-Јевтовић (Table P-PZ40)

1419.22 L

Lala-Jevtović, Danica, 1930- see PG1419.2.E9

1419.29 S

Sekulić, Maja Herman- see PG1419.18.E74

1420-1420.36 2001- (Table P-PZ29)

Folk literature

For general works on and collections of folk literature, see subclass GR

History and criticism

(1450) Periodicals. Societies. Serials

(1451) General works

(1452) General special

By form

Folk songs and poetry

1455.A-Z Special forms, A-Z

1455.B34 Ballads

Serbo-Croatian literature
Folk literature
History and criticism
By form
Folk songs and poetry
Special forms, A-Z -- Continued
1455.E65 Epic poetry
1455.L35 Laments
Collections of texts
(1463) General
By form
Folk songs and poetry. Ballads
1464 General
1464.2.A-Z Special forms and topics, A-Z
1464.2.A85 Athos (Greece)
1464.2.E65 Epic poetry
1464.2.M37 Marko, Prince of Serbia, 1335?-1394
1464.2.N54 Nikolić Pivljanin, Bajo, 1635-1685
1464.3 Drama
Fables, proverbs, riddles see PN1+
Tales, legends, etc.
see GR
(1464.5.A-Z) By locality, region, etc., A-Z
Translations
see subclass GR
Translations
1465 English
1466.A-Z Other. By language, A-Z
Serbian literature
<1500-1518> History. Collections
see PG1400+
<1530-1546> Folk literature
see PG1450+
Local
For the works, biography, and criticism of individual local authors, except North American, see PG1418+
<1551.A-Z> By region, province, etc.
see PG1417
<1555.A-Z> By city
see PG1417.5
Outside of former Yugoslavia
General
1557 History
1558 Collections
United States and Canada
1560 History
1561 Collections

Serbo-Croatian literature
Serbian literature
Local
Outside of former Yugoslavia
United States and Canada -- Continued

1562.A-Z Individual authors, A-Z
Subarrange each author by Table P-PZ40

1570 Latin America

1580.A-Z Other, A-Z

1595-1596 Translations from Serbian into foreign languages (Table P-PZ30)
For individual authors or works see PG1418+

Croatian literature
History

1600 Periodicals. Societies. Serials

1600.15 Congresses

Collected works (nonserial)

1600.17 Several authors

1600.18 Individual authors

1600.2 Encyclopedias. Dictionaries

1600.3 Study and teaching

Biography of critics, historians, etc.

1600.59 Collective

1600.6.A-Z Individual, A-Z
Subarrange each by Table P-PZ50

1601 General works

1602 General special

1602.5.A-Z Relation to other literatures, A-Z

1603 Addresses, essays, lectures

1604 Biography (Collective)

1604.9.A-Z Special classes of authors, A-Z

1604.9.P74 Prisoners

1604.9.W65 Women

1605 Origins

1606 Through 1800

19th and 20th centuries

1608 General works

1608.2.A-Z Special topics, A-Z

1608.2.A93 Avant-garde

1608.2.F35 Fantastic literature

1608.2.G47 German influences

1608.2.G73 Greek influence

1608.2.H57 History

1608.2.I34 Ideology

1608.2.L62 Local color

1608.2.M63 Modernism

1608.2.O75 Oriental influences

Serbo-Croatian literature
Croatian literature
History
19th and 20th centuries
Special topics, A-Z -- Continued

1608.2.P63 Politics
1608.2.P65 Popular literature
1608.2.P67 Postmodernism
1608.2.R43 Realism
1608.2.R45 Religion
1608.2.R64 Romanticism
1608.2.S95 Symbolism
1608.2.W55 Winds

21st century
1609 General works
1609.2.A-Z Special topics, A-Z

Poetry
1610 General works
1610.5.A-Z Special topics, A-Z
1610.5.A93 Avant-garde
1610.5.E43 Elegiac poetry
1610.5.M46 Metalanguage
1610.5.S95 Surrealism

Drama
1611 General works
1611.5.A-Z Special types of drama, A-Z
1611.5.R33 Radio plays
1611.5.V45 Verse drama

Prose
1612 General works
Fiction
1612.2 General works
1612.3.A-Z Special types of fiction, A-Z
1612.3.A87 Autobiographical
1612.3.H57 Historical
1612.3.S45 Short stories
1612.5 Other
1612.6.A-Z Special topics, A-Z
1612.6.I34 Identity (Psychology)
1612.6.M63 Modernism
1612.6.T72 Tragic, The
1612.6.T8 Travel
1612.6.U86 Utopias

1612.7 Juvenile literature (General)
For special genres, see the genre

Collections
1613 General works

Serbo-Croatian literature
Croatian literature
Collections -- Continued

1613.3.A-Z	Special classes of authors, A-Z
1613.3.C48	Children
1613.5.A-Z	Special topics, A-Z
1613.5.C67	Country life
1613.5.I87	Istria (Croatia and Slovenia)
1613.5.K68	Kosovo, Battle of, 1389
1613.5.W65	World War II
	Poetry
1614	General works
1614.3.A-Z	Special forms, A-Z
1614.3.E64	Epic poetry
1614.3.H34	Haiku
1614.3.S65	Sonnets
1614.5.A-Z	By subject, A-Z
1614.5.K35	Karadžić, Vuk Stefanović, 1787-1864
1614.5.L67	Love poetry
1614.5.P65	Popović, Jovan Sterija, 1806-1856
1614.5.R48	Revolutionary poetry
1614.5.S43	Sea poetry
1614.5.T58	Tito, Josip Broz, 1892-1980
1614.5.U37	Ujević, Tin, 1891-1955
	Drama
1615	General works
1615.5.A-Z	Special types or topics, A-Z
1615.5.C55	Christian drama
1615.5.R23	Radio plays
1616	Other
	Individual authors
1618.A-Z	Through 1960, A-Z Subarrange each author by Table P-PZ40 unless otherwise specified Cf. PG1658.A+ Dalmatian authors
1618.A1A-.A1Z	Anonymous works. By title, A-Z
1618.B23	Babić, Ferdinand, 1827-1894 (Table P-PZ40)
1618.B28	Badalić, Hugo, 1851-1900 (Table P-PZ40)
1618.B56	Bogović, Mirko, 1816-1893 (Table P-PZ40)
1618.B58	Bošković, Anica, 1714-1804 (Table P-PZ40)
	Bošnjak, Slavoljub, 1818-1857 see PG1618.J75
1618.B68	Brezovački, Tito, 1757-1805 (Table P-PZ40)
1618.C55	Ciraki, Franjo, 1847-1912 (Table P-PZ40)
1618.D32	Đalski, Ksaver Šandor, 1854-1935 (Table P-PZ40)
1618.D63	Došen, Vid, b. 1720 (Table P-PZ40)
1618.D76	Dukić, Ante, 1867-1952 (Table P-PZ40)
1618.F46	Fiamin, Ivan, 1833-1890 (Table P-PZ40)

Serbo-Croatian literature
Croatian literature
Individual authors
Through 1960, A-Z -- Continued

1618.F47 Filipović, Ivan, 1823-1895 (Table P-PZ40)
1618.F74 Freudenreich, Josip, 1827-1881 (Table P-PZ40)
1618.G28 Gaj, Ljudevit, 1809-1872 (Table P-PZ40)
For general works on Gaj's life and works see DR1578.G34
1618.I57 Ilijašević, Stjepan, 1814-1903 (Table P-PZ40)
1618.I65 Inhof, Bartol, 1866-1945 (Table P-PZ40)
1618.J24 Jarnević, Dragojla, 1812-1875 (Table P-PZ40)
1618.J6 Jorgovanić, Rikard, 1853-1880 (Table P-PZ40)
1618.J75 Jukić, Ivan Frano, 1818-1857 (Table P-PZ40)
Jurić Zagorka, Marija, 1879-1957 see PG1618.Z3
1618.J79 Jurković, Janko, 1827-1889 (Table P-PZ40)
1618.J85 Juzbašić, Ferdo, 1866-1905 (Table P-PZ40)
1618.K25 Kačić Miošić, Andrija, 1704?-1760 (Table P-PZ40)
1618.K265 Kanižlić, Antun, 1699-1777 (Table P-PZ40)
1618.K275 Katančić, Matija Petar, 1750-1825 (Table P-PZ40)
1618.K5736 Korajac, Vilim, 1839-1899 (Table P-PZ40)
1618.K619 Kovačić, Ante, 1854-1869 (Table P-PZ40)
1618.K6198 Kozarac, Ivan, 1885-1910 (Table P-PZ40)
1618.K67 Kranjčević, Silvije Strahimir, 1865-1908 (Table P-PZ40)
1618.K8 Kukuljević Sakcinski, Ivan, 1816-1889 (Table P-PZ40)
1618.L4 Leskovar, Janko, 1861-1949 (Table P-PZ40)
1618.L57 Lorković, Blaž, 1839-1892 (Table P-PZ40)
1618.L62 Lovrenčić, Jakob, 1787-1842 (Table P-PZ40)
1618.L82 Lucić, Hanibal, 1485-1553 (Table P-PZ40)
1618.L85 Lunaček, Vladimir, 1873-1927 (Table P-PZ40)
1618.M217 Magjer, Rudolfo Franjin, 1884-1954 (Table P-PZ40)
1618.M29 Marković, Franjo, 1845-1914 (Table P-PZ40)
1618.M33 Martić, Grga, 1822-1905 (Table P-PZ40)
1618.M35 Matoš, Antun Gustav, 1873-1914 (Table P-PZ40)
1618.M36 Mayer, Milutin, 1874-1958 (Table P-PZ40)
1618.M379 Mažuranić, Fran, 1859-1928 (Table P-PZ40)
1618.M38 Mažuranić, Ivan, 1814-1890 (Table P-PZ40)
1618.M563 Miloradić, Mate, 1850-1928 (Table P-PZ40)
1618.N39 Nedić, Martin, 1810-1895 (Table P-PZ40)
1618.N64 Novak, Vjenceslav, 1859-1905 (Table P-PZ40)
1618.O72 Oriovčanin, Luka Ilić, d. 1878 (Table P-PZ40)
1618.P47 Plevnik, Ivan Dobravec, 1873-1959 (Table P-PZ40)
1618.P7 Preradović, Petar, 1818-1872 (Table P-PZ40)
1618.R38 Reljković, Josip Stjepan, 1754-1801 (Table P-PZ40)
1618.S25 Šarić, Ivan, 1871-1960 (Table P-PZ40)
1618.S32 Šenoa, August, 1838-1881 (Table P-PZ40)
1618.T6 Tomić, Josip Eugen, 1843-1906 (Table P-PZ40)

Serbo-Croatian literature
Croatian literature
Individual authors
Through 1960, A-Z -- Continued

1618.T63 Tommaseo, Niccolò, 1802-1874 (Table P-PZ40)
1618.T64 Tordinac, Nikola, 1858-1888 (Table P-PZ40)
1618.T75 Truhelka, Jagoda, 1864-1957 (Table P-PZ40)
1618.T78 Tucić, Srđan, 1873-1940 (Table P-PZ40)
1618.V37 Velikanović, Iso, 1869-1940 (Table P-PZ40)
1618.V6 Vojnović, Ivo, 1857-1929 (Table P-PZ40)
1618.V67 Vramec, Antun, 1538-1587 (Table P-PZ40)
1618.V7 Vraz, Stanko, 1810-1851 (Table P-PZ40)
1618.Z3 Zagorka, 1879-1957 (Table P-PZ40)
1619-1619.36 1961-2000 (Table P-PZ29)
1620-1620.36 2001- (Table P-PZ29)

Folk literature

For general works on and collections of folk literature, see GR

(1630) History and criticism

Collections of texts

(1635) General
1636 Poetry
(1637) Other
(1638.A-Z) By locality, region, etc., A-Z
(1639.A-Z) Translations. By language, A-Z

Local

For works, biography, and criticism of individual local authors, except North American and Dalmatian see PG1618+

By region, province, etc.
Dalmatia. Dubrovnik (Ragusa)
History

1640 Periodicals. Societies. Serials
1641 General works
1642 General special
1643 Addresses, essays, lectures
1644 Biography (Collective)
1645 Origins
1646 Through 1800
1648 19th and 20th centuries
1649 21st century
1650 Poetry
1651 Drama
1652 Prose. Prose fiction
1652.5 Other
1652.7 Juvenile literature

For special genres, see the genre

Collections

Serbo-Croatian literature
Croatian literature
Local
By region, province, etc.
Dalmatia. Dubrovnik (Ragusa)
Collections -- Continued
1653 General works
1654 Poetry
1655 Drama
1656 Other
1658.A-Z Individual authors, A-Z
Subarrange each author by Table P-PZ40 unless otherwise specified
Class here only pre-19th century authors
For 19th-21st century authors see PG1618+
1658.A1A-.A1Z Anonymous works. By title, A-Z
1658.A1V93 Vučistrah
1658.A75 Armolušić Šibenčanin, Jakov, ca. 1575-1649 (Table P-PZ40)
1658.B37 Baraković, Juraj, 1548-1628 (Table P-PZ40)
1658.B8 Bunić Vučić, Ivan, 1592-1658 (Table P-PZ40)
Čavčić, Nikola Vetranović see PG1658.V46
1658.D7 Držić, Marin, ca. 1508-1567 (Table P-PZ40)
1658.D8 Đurđević, Ignjat, 1675-1737 (Table P-PZ40)
1658.G73 Grabovac, Filip, 1697 or 8-1749 (Table P-PZ40)
1658.G8 Gundulić, Ivan, 1588-1638 (Table P-PZ40)
1658.K28 Kanavelović, Petar, 1637-1719 (Table P-PZ40)
1658.K32 Kašić, Bartol, 1575-1650 (Table P-PZ40)
1658.M26 Marulić, Marko, 1450-1524 (Table P-PZ40)
1658.P32 Palmotić Gjonorić, Jaketa, 1623-1980 (Table P-PZ40)
1658.R35 Ranjina, Dinko, 1536-1607 (Table P-PZ40)
1658.S78 Stulli, Vlaho, 1768-1843 (Table P-PZ40)
1658.V46 Vetranović, Mavro, 1482-1576 (Table P-PZ40)
1658.V56 Vitezović, Pavao Ritter, 1652-1713 (Table P-PZ40)
1661.A-Z Other, A-Z
1665.A-Z By city, A-Z
Outside of Croatia
General
1677 History
1678 Collections
United States and Canada
1680 History
1681 Collections
1682.A-Z Individual authors, A-Z
Subarrange each author by Table P-PZ40 unless otherwise specified

Serbo-Croatian literature
Croatian literature
Local
Outside of Croatia -- Continued
1685 Latin America
1690.A-Z Other, A-Z
Bosnia and Hercegovina see PG1700+
1695-1696 Translations from Croatian into foreign languages (Table P-PZ30)
For individual authors or works see PG1618+
Bosnian literature
Class here literature of Bosnia written in Serbian, Croatian, and/ or Bosnian languages and literature written in the Bosnian language
History
1700 Periodicals. Societies. Serials
1702 Congresses
1705 Encyclopedias. Dictionaries
1708 Study and teaching
1710 General works
1715 Biography (Collective)
1716.A-Z Special classes of authors, A-Z
1716.M87 Muslims
1716.W66 Women
By period
1717 To 1900
1718 20th century
1719 21st century
1720 Poetry
1725 Drama
1728 Prose. Prose fiction
Folk literature
For general works on and collections of folk literature see GR252
History and criticism
General works see GR252
1729 Folk poetry. Folk songs
Collections
General collections see GR252
1729.5 Folk poetry. Folk songs
Collections
1730 General
1732.A-Z Special classes of authors, A-Z
1732.M87 Muslims
1732.W66 Women
By period
1734 To 1900

Serbo-Croatian literature
Bosnian literature
Collections
By period -- Continued
1735 20th century
1736 21st century
1737 Poetry
1740 Drama
1742 Prose. Prose fiction
1745.A-Z Individual authors, A-Z
For authors who identify themselves as Serbian or Croatian see PG1418+ or PG1618+
1747.A-Z Local. By place, A-Z
Subarrange each by Table P-PZ26
1749.A-Z Translations into foreign languages. By language, A-Z
Slovenian
1801-1813 Philology (Table P-PZ4a modified)
History of philology
Cf. PG1815 History of the language
1807 General works
Biography, memoirs, etc.
1809.A2 Collective
1809.A5-Z Individual, A-Z
Subarrange each by Table P-PZ50
1814-1899 Language (Table P-PZ4b modified)
Add number in table to PG1800
Style. Composition. Rhetoric
For study and teaching see PG1811
1875 General works
Etymology
1883.5 Dictionaries (exclusively etymological)
Lexicography
For biography of lexicographers see PG1809.A2+
1887 Treatises
Dictionaries
1888 Slovenian only
Interlingual
Classify with language less known
1889 Polyglot
Cf. PG2635 Russian first
1891 Slovenian-English; English-Slovenian
1892 Slovenian-French [German, etc.]
1893 Slovenian-Slavic
(1893.B8) Bulgarian
see PG982.S6
1893.C9 Czech
1893.R8 Russian

Slovenian
Language
Lexicography
Dictionaries
Interlingual
Slovenian-Slavic -- Continued
1893.S4 Serbo-Croatian (Serbian, Croatian, or Bosnian)
(1894) Oriental languages
see subclasses PJ-PL
1895 Other special lists
For etymological dictionaries see PG1883.5
Linguistic geography. Dialects, etc.
1896.A1 Linguistic geography
Dialects, provincialisms, etc.
1896.A2-.A29 Periodicals. Collections
1896.A3 Collections of texts. Specimens, etc.
1896.A5-Z General works. Grammar
1897 Dictionaries
1898.A-Z Local. By region, place, A-Z
1899 Slang. Argot
Literature
History
1900.A1-.A5 Periodicals. Societies. Serials
1900.A52 Encyclopedias. Dictionaries
1900.A53 Study and teaching
1900.A56A-.A56Z Biography of critics, historians, etc., A-Z
1900.A6-Z General works
1901 General special
1901.5 Addresses, essays, lectures
1901.7.A-Z Relation to other countries, A-Z
1902 Biography (Collective)
1902.2.A-Z Special classes of authors, A-Z
1902.2.H54 High school students
By period
1902.3 Origins. Through 1800
19th-20th centuries
1902.4 General works
1902.42.A-Z Special topics, A-Z
1902.42.B53 Bible
1902.42.C48 Christianity
1902.42.M63 Modernism
1902.42.P64 Popular literature
1902.42.P67 Postmodernism
1902.42.S95 Symbolism
1902.42.T85 Turgenev, Ivan Sergeevich, 1818-1883
21st century
1902.5 General works

Slovenian
Literature
History
By period
21st century -- Continued
1902.52.A-Z Special topics, A-Z
Poetry
1903 General works
1903.5.A-Z Special topics, A-Z
1903.5.C55 Cinquains
1903.5.D4 Death
1903.5.H34 Haiku
1903.5.M63 Modernism
1903.5.R44 Religion
Drama
1904 General works
1904.5.A-Z Special topics, A-Z
1904.5.I58 Intellectuals
1904.5.M95 Myth. Mythology
Mythology see PG1904.5.M95
1904.5.W65 World War II
Prose. Fiction
1905 General works
1905.5.A-Z Special topics, A-Z
1905.5.H57 Historical fiction
1905.5.P68 Postmodernism
1905.5.T73 Travel
1905.5.W37 War stories
1906 Other
Folk literature
For general works on and collections of folk literature see GR258.7
(1908) History and criticism
Collections
(1910) General
1910.2 Folk songs and poetry
(1910.5.A-Z) By locality, region, etc., A-Z
(1911.A-Z) Translations. By language, A-Z
1912 Juvenile literature (General)
For special genres, see the genre
Collections
1913 General
1913.3.A-Z Special classes of authors, A-Z
1913.3.A34 Aged. Older people
1913.3.C45 Children
Older people see PG1913.3.A34
1913.5.A-Z By subject, A-Z

Slovenian
Literature
Collections
By subject, A-Z -- Continued
1913.5.C63 Coal mines and miners
1913.5.M37 Maribor (Slovenia)
1914 Poetry
1914.5 Drama
1915 Prose. Fiction
1916 Other
Individual authors and works
1917.A-Z To 1800, A-Z
Subarrange each author by Table P-PZ40 unless otherwise specified
1917.B7-.B73 Brižinski spomeniki. Freisinger Denkmäler (Table P-PZ43)
1917.L53 Linhart, Anton Tomaž, 1756-1795 (Table P-PZ40)
1917.S85-.S853 Stiški rokopis (Table P-PZ43)
1917.V62 Vodnik, Valentin, 1758-1819 (Table P-PZ40)
1917.V64 Volkmer, Leopold, 1741-1816 (Table P-PZ40)
1918.A-Z 1800-1960, A-Z
Subarrange each author by Table P-PZ40 unless otherwise indicated
e.g.
1918.D4 Detela, Fran (Table P-PZ40)
1918.F5 Finžgar, Franc Saleški, 1871-1962 (Table P-PZ40)
1918.G7 Gregorčič, Simon, 1844-1906 (Table P-PZ40)
1918.J25 Jaklič, Fran, 1868-1937 (Table P-PZ40)
1918.J4 Janko, Simon, 1835-1869 (Table P-PZ40)
1918.J9 Jurčič, Josip, 1844-1881 (Table P-PZ40)
1918.K4 Kersnik, Janko, 1852-1897 (Table P-PZ40)
1918.K8 Kuhar, Lovro (Table P-PZ40)
1918.L4 Levstik, Fran, 1831-1887 (Table P-PZ40)
1918.M38 Mencinger, Janez, 1838-1912 (Table P-PZ40)
1918.M5 Mlakar, Janko, 1874-1953 (Table P-PZ40)
1918.P7 Prešeren, France, 1800-1849 (Table P-PZ40)
Prežihov Voranc see PG1918.K8
1918.S69 Stare, Josip, 1842-1907 (Table P-PZ40)
1918.S7 Stritar, Josip, 1836-1923 (Table P-PZ40)
1918.T38 Tavčar, Ivan, 1851-1923 (Table P-PZ40)
1918.T55 Tomšić, Ivan (Table P-PZ40)
1918.T74 Trinko, Ivan, 1863-1954 (Table P-PZ40)
1918.V79 Vrhovec, Ivan, 1853-1902 (Table P-PZ40)
1919-1919.36 1961-2000 (Table P-PZ29 modified)
1919.1 A
Arih, Rok, 1920- see PG1919.14.R8
1919.14 D

Slovenian
Literature
Individual authors and works
1961-2000
D -- Continued
1919.14.R8 Druškovič, Drago, 1920- (Table P-PZ40)
1919.21 K
1919.21.R55 Kronski, Aaron (Table P-PZ40)
1919.28 R
Rebolj, Tomo see PG1919.21.R55
1920-1920.36 2001- (Table P-PZ29)
Local
For works, biography, and criticism of individual local authors, except North American see PG1917+
1921.A-Z By region, province, etc., A-Z
1925.A-Z By city, A-Z
Outside of Slovenia
General
1927 History
1928 Collections
United States and Canada
1930 History
1931 Collections
1932.A-Z Individual authors, A-Z
Subarrange each author by Table P-PZ40
1940 Latin America
1945 Other
1961-1962 Translations from Slovenian into foreign languages (Table P-PZ30)
For individual authors or works see PG1917+
Russian
2001-2071 Philology (Table P-PZ1a modified)
Periodicals. Serials
2003 Russian and other Slavic languages
Societies
2013 Russian and other Slavic languages
(2033) Atlases. Maps
see class G
History of philology
Cf. PG2075+ History of the language
Biography, memoirs, etc.
2063 Collective
2064.A-Z Individual, A-Z
Subarrange each by Table P-PZ50
Bibliography. Bio-bibliography
see Z2505
Study and teaching. Research

Russian
Philology
Study and teaching. Research -- Continued
2065 General works
By period
For period of study, teaching, or research see PG2053+
For period of history of the language see PG2077+
2067 Teaching of foreign students (General)
2073-2599 Language (Table P-PZ1b modified)
Add number in table to PG2000
2091 Compends
2096 Script
Cf. PG89+ Slavic alphabet
2097 Grammatical theory and terminology
Grammar
General works
2103 Early to 1800
2105 1800-1949
2106 1950-
2120.A-Z Manuals for special classes of students, A-Z
2120.C5 Chemists
2120.C6 Commercial
2120.F58 Fishers
2120.H85 Humanities students
2120.J6 Journalists
2120.L38 Law students. Lawyers
2120.M37 Mathematicians
2120.M44 Medical personnel
2120.S3 Scientists
2120.S7 Soldiers
2120.T4 Technical
2120.T6 Tourists
Syntax
Sentences
2375 General
2380 General special
2390 Order of words
Style. Composition. Rhetoric
For study and teaching see PG2065+
2410 General works
Etymology
2580 Dictionaries (exclusively etymological)
2582.A-Z Special elements. By language, A-Z
2582.A3 Foreign elements (General)
Cf. PG2670 Dictionaries
Lexicography
2601 Periodicals. Societies. Serials. Collections (nonserial)

Russian
Language
Lexicography -- Continued

2611 General works

Biography of lexicographers see PG2063+

2617 Criticism, etc., of particular dictionaries

Dictionaries

Russian only

2620 Early to 1800

1800-

2625 General works

2628 Minor, abridged, school dictionaries

2629 Picture dictionaries

2630 Supplementary dictionaries. Dictionaries of new words

2635 Polyglot

Three or more languages arranged in columns, Russian coming first

Bilingual

Classify with language less known

(2637) Russian-Greek (Ancient)

see PA445

Russian-Greek (Modern) see PA1139.A+

Russian-Latin see PA2365.A+

(2638) Russian-Celtic

see subclass PB

Russian-Germanic

2640 English

2643.A-Z Other. By language, A-Z

2643.D3 Danish

2643.D8 Dutch

2643.G5 German

2643.N6 Norwegian

2643.S8 Swedish

2645.A-Z Russian-Romance. By language, A-Z

2645.C36 Catalan

2645.F5 French

2645.I7 Italian

2645.P7 Portuguese

(2645.R7) Romanian

see PC781

2645.S7 Spanish

(2647.A-Z) Russian-Slavic. By language, A-Z

(2647.A2) Polyglot

see PG2635

(2647.B6) Bohemian (Czech)

see PG4647.R8

Russian
Language
Lexicography
Dictionaries
Bilingual
Russian-Slavic. By language, A-Z -- Continued
(2647.B8) Bulgarian
see PG982.R9
(2647.L3) Latvian
see PG8982
(2647.P7) Polish
see PG6647
(2647.S3) Serbo-Croatian
see PG1378
(2647.S5) Slovak
see PG5382
(2647.S7) Slovenian
see PG1893.R8
(2647.U7) Ukrainian (Ruthenian)
see PG3893.R8
(2649.A-Z) Russian-Other European languages. By language, A-Z
(2649.B3) Basque
see PH5177
(2649.E7) Estonian
see PH625
(2649.F5) Finnish
see PH282
(2649.H7) Hungarian
see PH2647
(2649.L3) Lappish. Sami
see PH725
(2651) Russian-Caucasian
see subclass PK
(2653) Russian-Oriental
see subclasses PJ-PL
(2654) Russian-American (Aboriginal) languages
see subclass PM
Special dictionaries
Dictionaries exclusively etymological see PG2580
(2655) Dictionaries of particular authors
see the author in classes PA-PT
2660 Dictionaries of names
Cf. CS2300+ Personal and family names
Cf. PG2673 Foreign names
2667 Dictionaries, etc., of obsolete or archaic words
Dictionaries of foreign words

Russian
Language
Lexicography
Dictionaries
Special dictionaries
Dictionaries of foreign words -- Continued
2670 General
2673 Names
Special. By language see PG2582.A+
Rhyming dictionaries
see PG2519
Special lists
2680 Miscellaneous
(2683.A-Z) By subject
see the subject in classes A-N, Q-Z
2689 Dictionaries of terms and phrases
2691 Other special
2693 Abbreviations, Lists of
Linguistic geography. Dialects, etc.
2700 Linguistic geography
Dialects. Provincialisms, etc.
2701 Periodicals. Societies. Collections
2707 Collections of texts. Specimens, etc.
2711 General works
Grammar
2713 General works
2715 Phonology. Phonetics
2717 Morphology. Inflection. Accidence
2731 Syntax
2733 Other
2735 Dictionaries
(2737) Atlases. Maps
see class G
2738 Northern dialects (Table P-PZ15 modified)
Local
see PG2750.A+
2738.5 Southern dialects (Table P-PZ15 modified)
Local
see PG2750.A+
Old Russian
2739-2743 General and early to 1300 (Table P-PZ9)
2744-2748 1301-1700 (Table P-PZ9)
2750.A-Z Local. By region, place, etc., A-Z
2751 Russian language outside of Russia
2752 Slang. Argot
Russian Church Slavic see PG698.R87
Little Russian see PG3801+

Russian
Language
Linguistic geography. Dialects. Provincialisms, etc. -- Continued
(2801-2826) Great Russian
see PG2701+
Russian literature
see PG2900+
Belarusian
Philology. Language
2830 Periodicals. Societies. Serials
2830.2 Congresses
2830.25 Collections (nonserial)
2830.27 Computer network resources
Including the Internet
2830.3 History of philology
Biography of philologists
2830.4 Collective
2830.42.A-Z Individual, A-Z
Subarrange each by Table P-PZ50
2830.5 Study and teaching
2832 General works
2832.15 Political aspects
2832.2 History of the language
Grammar
2833 General works
2833.4 Textbooks. Exercises
2833.5 Readers
2833.7 Conversation. Phrase books
2833.8 Phonology
2833.9 Orthography and spelling
2833.92 Alphabet
2833.923 Parts of speech
2833.928 Style. Composition. Rhetoric
2833.93 Prosody. Metrics. Rhythmics
2833.95 Etymology
2833.96 Lexicology
2833.98 Lexicography
2834 Dictionaries
Dialects
2834.1 General works
2834.12.A-Z Special. By name or place, A-Z
Literature
2834.17 Study and teaching
Biography of critics, historians, etc.
2834.18 Collective

	Belarusian
	Literature
	Biography of critics, historians, etc. -- Continued
2834.182.A-Z	Individual, A-Z
	Subarrange each by Table P-PZ50
	History
2834.2	General works
2834.25	Addresses, essays, lectures
2834.27.A-Z	Relations to other literatures, A-Z
2834.28.A-Z	Special topics, A-Z
2834.28.A85	Authorship, Disputed
2834.28.A87	Autobiography
2834.28.N36	Nature
2834.28.R65	Romanticism
2834.3	Biography (Collective)
	By period
2834.32	Origins. Early through 1800
	19th century
2834.33	General works
2834.332.A-Z	Special topics, A-Z
2834.332.A74	Archival resources
2834.332.C65	Cosmology
	20th century
2834.335	General works
2834.336.A-Z	Special topics, A-Z
2834.336.M98	Myth
2834.336.N38	Nationalism
2834.336.N38	Pripet Marshes (Belarus and Ukraine)
2834.336.W67	World War, 1939-1945
	21st century
2834.34	General works
2834.342.A-Z	Special topics, A-Z
	Poetry
2834.35	General works
2834.36.A-Z	Special types or topics, A-Z
2834.36.B34	Ballads
2834.36.E97	Experimental poetry
2834.37	Drama
2834.38	Other
	Collections
2834.4	General
2834.45.A-Z	Special topics, A-Z
2834.45.W46	Western Dvina River Region
2834.5	Poetry
2834.6	Drama
	Prose
2834.632	General

Belarusian
Literature
Collections
Prose -- Continued
Fiction
2834.633 General
By period
2834.634 19th-20th centuries
2834.635 21st century
2834.636.A-Z Special topics or types, A-Z
2834.636.D48 Detective and mystery stories
2834.65 Other
Folk literature see GR203.4+
(2834.7) History and criticism
(2834.8) Collections of texts
(2834.82.A-Z) By region, province, etc., A-Z
2834.85 Juvenile literature (General)
For special genres, see the genre
Individual authors and works
Through 1960
2835.A1A-.A1Z Anonymous works. By title, A-Z
2835.A1A65 Apovests′ pra Tryshchana. Аповесць пра Трышчана
2835.A2-Z Individual authors, A-Z
Subarrange each author by Table P-PZ40 unless otherwise specified
2835.B24 Bahrym, Paŭli͡uk, 1813-ca. 1891. Паўлюк Багрым (Table P-PZ40)
2835.B25 Bahushėvich, Frantsishak Kazimiravich, 1840-1900. Францішак Казіміравіч Багушэвіч (Table P-PZ40)
2835.C3 Charot, M. (Mikhas′), 1896-1938. Міхась Чарот (Table P-PZ40)
2835.D8 Dunin-Martsinkevich, Vintsėnt. Вінцэнт Дунін-Марцінкевіч (Table P-PZ40)
Hlybinny, Uladzimer. Уладзімер Глыбінны see PG2835.S52
Kolas, I͡Akub, 1882-1956. Якуб Колас see PG2835.M49
Kudel′ka, Mikhail Semёnovich, 1896-1938. Михаил Семёнович Куделька see PG2835.C3
Kudzel′ka, Mikhas′ Si͡ami͡onavich, 1896-1938. Міхась Сямёнавіч Кудзелька see PG2835.C3
Kupala, I͡Anka. Янка Купала see PG2835.L85
2835.L7 Luchyna, I͡Anka, 1851-1897. Янка Лучына (Table P-PZ40)

Belarusian
Literature
Individual authors and works
Through 1960
Individual authors, A-Z -- Continued
2835.L85 Lut͡sevich, Ivan Dominikovich, 1882-1942. Иван Доминикович Луцевич (Іван Дамінікавіч Луцэвіч) (Table P-PZ38)
2835.M49 Mit͡skevich, Konstantin Mikhaĭlovich, 1882-1956. Константин Михайлович Мицкевич (Канстанцін Міхайлавіч Міцкевіч) (Table P-PZ40)
2835.M78 Mryĭ, Andrėĭ, 1893-1943. Андрэй Мрый (Table P-PZ40)
Neslukhoŭski, Ivan Li͡utsyi͡anavich, 1851-1897. Іван Лютсыянавіч Неслухоўскі see PG2835.L7
Shashalevich, Andrėĭ Antonavich, 1893-1943. Андрэй Антонавіч Шашалевіч see PG2835.M78
2835.S52 Si͡adura, Uladzimir. Уладзімір Сядура (Table P-PZ40)
2835.2.A-Z 1961-2000, A-Z
Subarrange each author by Table P-PZ40 unless otherwise indicated
2835.3.A-Z 2001- , A-Z
Subarrange each author by Table P-PZ40 unless otherwise indicated
Local
For works, biography, and criticism of individual local authors, including those outside White Russia, see PG2835+
2836.A-Z By province, government, etc., A-Z
Outside Belarus
General
2838 History
2839 Collections
2840.A-Z By region or country, A-Z
2845-2846 Translations from White Russian into foreign languages (Table P-PZ30)
Russian literature
Literary history and criticism
Periodicals
2900.A1 Polyglot
2900.A3-Z Russian
2901 Other languages
(2910-2911) Yearbooks
see PG2900+
Societies
2920 Russian

Russian literature
Literary history and criticism
Societies -- Continued
2921 Other
2925 Congresses
Collections. Monographs. Studies, papers, essays, etc.
2930 Several authors. Series
2932 Several authors. Occasional or minor works. Collections in honor of an individual or institution, A-Z. "Festschriften"
2933 Individual authors. Collected works
2940 Encyclopedias. Dictionaries
(2942) Theory and principles of the study of Russian literature
see PG2945
(2943) History of Russian literary history and criticism
see PG2949
2944 Philosophy. Psychology. Aesthetics
Including national characteristics in literature
Study and teaching
2945 General works. Treatises, compends, etc.
2946.A-Z By region or country, A-Z
2946.5.A-Z By school or college, A-Z
2947 Biography of teachers, critics, and historians
2947.A2 Collective
2947.A3-Z Individual, A-Z
Subarrange each by Table P-PZ50
e.g.
2947.B5 Belinskiĭ, Vissarion Grigor′evich, 1811-1848. Виссарион Григорьевич Белинский (Table P-PZ50)
2947.C3 Chernyshevskiĭ, Nikolaĭ Gavrilovich, 1828-1889. Николай Гаврилович Чернышевский (Table P-PZ50)
2947.D6 Dobroli͡ubov, Nikolaĭ Aleksandrovich, 1836-1861. Николай Александрович Добролюбов (Table P-PZ50)
2947.F5 Flekser, Akim L′vovich, 1863-1926. Аким Львович Флексер (Table P-PZ50)
2947.I8 Ivanov, Razumnik Vasil′evich, 1878-1946. Разумник Васильевич Иванов (Table P-PZ50)
2947.M5 Mikhaĭlovskiĭ, Nikolaĭ Konstantinovich, 1842-1904. Николай Константинович Михайловский (Table P-PZ50)
2947.O8 Ovsi͡aniko-Kulikovskiĭ, Dmitriĭ Nikolaevich, 1853-1920. Дмитрий Николаевич Овсянико-Куликовский (Table P-PZ50)

Russian literature
Literary history and criticism
Biography of teachers, critics, and historians
Individual, A-Z -- Continued
2947.P5 Pisarev, Dmitriĭ Ivanovich, 1840-1868. Дмитрий Иванович Писарев (Table P-PZ50)
2947.R6 Rozanov, Vasiliĭ Vasil′evich, 1856-1919. Василий Васильевич Розанов (Table P-PZ50)
2947.S6 Solov′ev Evgeniĭ Andreevich, 1863-1905. Евгений Андрэвич Соловьев (Table P-PZ50)
Volynskiĭ, A. L., 1863-1926. А.Л. Волынский see PG2947.F5
Criticism of Russian literature
2948 Treatises. Theory. Canons
2949 History
General works. History of Russian literature
Western languages
2950 Russian
For translations into other Western languages see PG2951+
2950.A2 Early works to 1900
2951 English
2952 French
2953 German
2954 Italian
2955 Scandinavian
2956 Spanish
2957 Other (not A-Z)
2959 Other languages (not A-Z)
2970 Outlines. Syllabi. Tables. Charts. Questions and answers
2973 Addresses, essays, pamphlets, etc.
For collected essays see PG2930+
Special aspects and topics
Competition, prizes, etc.
2973.8 General works
2974.A-Z Individual competitions, prizes, etc., A-Z
2974.L58 Literaturnai͡a premii͡a Aleksandra Solzhenit͡syna. Литературная премия Александра Солженицына
2974.P8 Pushkin Prize. Пушкинская премия
2975 Relations to history, civilization, culture, etc.
2976 Relations to art, music, etc.
Relations to other countries and their literatures
2980 General
Special periods
2980.5 Ancient

Russian literature
Literary history and criticism
Special aspects and topics
Relations to pother countries and their literatures
Special periods

2981.A-Z Modern, by country or language, A-Z
Class here works dealing with the influence of foreign authors on Russian literature if written chiefly in the interest of Russian literature
e.g.

2981.F5 France
2981.G3 Germany
2981.G7 Great Britain
2981.P6 Poland
2981.S7 Spain

2982 Russian literature by foreign authors (as subject)
Class here general works only
For individual authors see PG3301+ ; PG3549

2983 Foreign literature by Russian authors (as subject)
Class here general works only
For literature by Russian authors in a specific language see the literature of that language, e.g. subclass PQ for French, subclass PT for German, etc.

2984 Translation of other literatures into Russian (as subject)
2985 Translation of Russian literature (as subject)

2986 Other special aspects (not A-Z)
Cf. PG3030+ History of special relations, movements and currents in Russian literature

2987.A-Z Treatment of special subjects, A-Z
Class here works not limited to or identified with one period or form of literature

2987.B53 Bible
2987.C37 Card games
2987.C63 Cockroaches
2987.C68 Country life
2987.D42 Death
2987.D45 Demonology
2987.D68 Doubles
2987.E56 Ekphrasis
2987.E76 Erotic literature
2987.E83 Eschatology
2987.E85 Ethics
2987.F35 Fantasy
2987.F37 Fasts and feasts
2987.F43 Fear
2987.F74 French Revolution, 1789-1799
2987.F78 Frustration

Russian literature
Literary history and criticism
Special aspects and topics
Treatment of special subjects, A-Z -- Continued

2987.G66 Good and evil
Heroes see PG2989.H4
2987.I46 Icons
2987.I48 Individuality
2987.I5 Insanity
2987.I74 Islam
2987.K84 Kulikovo, Battle of, 1380. Куликовская битва
2987.L38 Laughter
2987.L5 Life change events
2987.L6 Loneliness
2987.M35 Mathematics
2987.M37 Medicine
2987.M4 Melancholy
2987.M45 Metaphor
2987.M9 Mythology
2987.N24 Names, Personal
2987.N27 Nationalism
2987.N3 Nature
2987.P27 Parody
2987.P3 Patriotism
2987.P56 Plots
2987.P58 Politics
2987.R37 Realism
2987.R38 Regret
2987.R4 Religion
2987.R56 Ritual. Rites and ceremonies
2987.R64 Romanticism
2987.S28 Satire
2987.S3 Science
2987.S4 Sea
2987.S58 Social change
2987.S6 Social life. Social conditions. Social ideals, etc.
2987.S73 Steppes
2987.S78 Sublime
2987.S8 Supernatural
2987.T47 Terrorism
2987.W3 War
2987.W55 Wine
2988.A-Z Treatment of special cities, countries, races, etc., A-Z
2988.A4 Albania
2988.A7 Armenia
2988.A75 Asia
2988.B34 Balashov Region

Russian literature
Literary history and criticism
Special aspects and topics
Treatment of special cities, countries, races, etc., A-Z -- Continued

2988.B45 Belarus
2988.C3 Caucasus
2988.C45 Chechen-Ingush A.S.S.R
2988.C5 Chuvashia
2988.C66 Cossacks
2988.C75 Crimea
2988.D3 Daghestan
2988.F3 Finland
2988.F7 France
2988.G4 Germans
2988.I53 India
2988.J4 Jews
2988.K36 Kazakhstan
2988.K53 Kiev (Ukraine)
2988.K64 Komi
2988.L37 Latvia
2988.L4 Leningrad
2988.M67 Moscow
2988.N68 Novgorod
2988.R65 Rome
2988.R8 Russia, Northern
2988.R94 Rzhev (Russia)
2988.S3 Sakhalin
2988.S67 Soviet Far East
2988.U6 United States
2988.V44 Venice (Italy)
2988.W4 West Turkestan
2989.A-Z Treatment of special classes, A-Z
2989.C6 Children
2989.C8 Criminals
2989.H4 Heroes
2989.P4 Peasants
2989.P7 Priests
2989.W6 Women
2990.A-Z Treatment of special persons and characters, A-Z
2990.C64 Don Quixote
2990.G46 George, Saint, d. 303
2990.J47 Jesus Christ
2990.L94 Lzhedmitriĭ I, Czar of Russia, d. 1606. Лжедмитрий I
2990.P84 Pugachev, Emelʹi͡an Ivanovich. Емельян Иванович Пугачев
2990.S34 Salauat I͡Ulaev. Салауат Юлаев (Салават Юлаев)

Russian literature
Literary history and criticism -- Continued
Biography of Russian authors (Collective)
Cf. PG2947 Biography of teachers, critics, and historians

2991 General works
By period
2991.2 Early through 1800
2991.3 19th century
2991.4 20th century
2991.5 21st century
2993 Memoirs. Letters
2994 Relations to women. Love, marriage, etc.
Cf. PG2997 Women authors
2995 Iconography: Portraits, monuments, etc.
2996 Literary landmarks. Homes and haunts of authors
2997 Women authors (General). Literary relations of women
Women authors (Individual)
see PG3301+ ; PG3549
2998.A-Z Special groups of authors, by race, profession, etc.
2998.C6 Clergy
2998.D5 Dissenters
2998.E95 Exiles
2998.J4 Jewish authors
2998.P4 Peasants
2998.P6 Physicians
History, by period
Early to 1700
3001 Works in Russian
3002 Works in English
3003 Works in French
3004 Works in German
3005 Works in other languages (not A-Z)
3005.5.A-Z Special topics and subjects, A-Z
3005.5.A34 Adaptations
3005.5.A4 Alexius, Saint. Алексей, человек Божий
3005.5.A85 Atheism
3005.5.B37 Baroque literature
3005.5.B6 Bohemia
3005.5.B67 Boris, kni͡az′ rostovskiĭ, Saint, d. 1015. Борис, князь ростовский
3005.5.C47 Characters
3005.5.C53 Classical influences
3005.5.C9 Cyprus
3005.5.D35 Death
3005.5.D4 Demonology. Devil
Epilogues see PG3005.5.P76

Russian literature
Literary history and criticism
History, by period
Early to 1700
Special topics and subjects, A-Z

3005.5.F6 Folklore and Russian literature
3005.5.F87 Future life
3005.5.H3 Hagiography
3005.5.L38 Laughter
3005.5.P56 Plots
3005.5.P76 Prologues and epilogues
3005.5.S2 Satire
3005.5.S95 Symbolism of numbers
3005.5.T73 Travel writing. Travel
3005.5.W3 War

18th century

3006 Works in Russian
3007 Works in English
3008 Works in French
3009 Works in German
3010 Works in other languages (not A-Z)
3010.5.A-Z Special topics and subjects, A-Z
3010.5.C44 China
3010.5.C53 Classicism
3010.5.E54 Enlightenment
3010.5.F74 Freemasonry
3010.5.H56 Historicism
3010.5.M6 Moscow
3010.5.P3 Patriotism
3010.5.P47 Personality
3010.5.P7 Pseudo-classicism
3010.5.R4 Realism
3010.5.R44 Religion
3010.5.R87 Russkai͡a pravoslavnai͡a t͡serkov′. Русская православная церковь
3010.5.S34 Satire
3010.5.S4 Sentimentalism
3010.5.S45 Serfdom
3010.5.S79 Style
3010.5.U85 Utopias
3010.5.V42 Vladimir, Grand Duke of Kiev, ca. 956-1015. Владимир Святославич, великий князь киевский

19th century (1800/1820-1900/1917)

3011 Works in Russian
3012 Works in English
3013 Works in French

Russian literature
Literary history and criticism
History, by period
19th century (1800/1820-1900/1917) -- Continued

3014 Works in German
3015 Works in other languages (not A-Z)
3015.5.A-Z Special topics and subjects, A-Z
3015.5.A56 Antisemitism
3015.5.A64 Aphorisms and apothegms
3015.5.A73 Art and literature
3015.5.A8 Authorship
3015.5.A95 Azerbaijan
3015.5.B37 Bashkortostan
3015.5.B52 Bible
3015.5.B66 Books and reading
3015.5.B8 Bulgaria
Calendars, Literary see PG3015.5.L5
3015.5.C3 Caucasus
3015.5.C5 Characters
3015.5.C55 Children
3015.5.C56 China
3015.5.C62 Conflict
3015.5.C65 Consciousness
3015.5.C66 Conservatism
3015.5.C9 Cycles
3015.5.D3 Daghestan
3015.5.D37 Decembrists
3015.5.D47 Devil
3015.5.D54 Digression
3015.5.D82 Dueling
3015.5.D9 Dystopias
3015.5.E74 Ethics
3015.5.E84 Ethnic relations
3015.5.F57 Flowers
3015.5.F65 Folklore and literature
3015.5.G35 Gambling
3015.5.G56 Gnosticism
3015.5.H34 Hagiography and literature
3015.5.H85 Human beings
3015.5.I76 Irony
3015.5.J49 Jews
3015.5.J68 Journalism and literature
3015.5.K3 Karelia
3015.5.L3 Law
3015.5.L5 Literary calendars
3015.5.L68 Love. Lovesickness
3015.5.M37 Masks

Russian literature
Literary history and criticism
History, by period
19th century (1800/1820-1900/1917)
Special topics and subjects, A-Z -- Continued

3015.5.M44 Memory
3015.5.M45 Mental illness
Morality and morals see PG3015.5.E74
3015.5.M95 Mythology. Myth
Myths see PG3015.5.M95
3015.5.N25 Names
3015.5.N32 Napoleonic Wars, 1800-1815
3015.5.N34 National characteristics
3015.5.N46 Nietzsche, Friedrich Wilhelm, 1844-1900
3015.5.N5 Nihilism
3015.5.O33 Occultism
3015.5.O57 Ontology
3015.5.P27 Parody
3015.5.P3 Patriotism
3015.5.P47 Personality
3015.5.P55 Plots
3015.5.P58 Poor. Poverty
3015.5.P6 Populism
Poverty see PG3015.5.P58
3015.5.P73 Psychoanalysis and literature
3015.5.P75 Psychology, Pathological
3015.5.R4 Realism
3015.5.R45 Religion
3015.5.R48 Revolutions
3015.5.R6 Romanticism
3015.5.S3 Satire
3015.5.S36 Schopenhauer, Arthur, 1788-1860
3015.5.S43 Sea
3015.5.S52 Shakespeare, William
3015.5.S53 Slavophilism
3015.5.S6 Social problems
3015.5.S63 Socialism
3015.5.S67 Space and time
3015.5.S83 Style
3015.5.S87 Supernatural
3015.5.S9 Symbolism
3015.5.T3 Tales
3015.5.T73 Travel
3015.5.U53 Underground literature
3015.5.U55 United States
3015.5.W6 Women
3015.5.Z44 Zemstvos. Земства

Russian literature
Literary history and criticism
History, by period -- Continued
20th century

3016 Works in Russian
3017 Works in English
3018 Works in French
3019 Works in German
3020 Works in other languages (not A-Z)
3020.5.A-Z Special topics and subjects, A-Z
3020.5.A27 Absurd (Philosophy)
3020.5.A75 Armenia
3020.5.C5 Characters
3020.5.C57 Comic, The
3020.5.D43 Decadence
3020.5.D79 Drugs
3020.5.E84 Eschatology
3020.5.E94 Expressionism
3020.5.F36 Fantasy
3020.5.F64 Folklore
3020.5.F8 Futurism
3020.5.G74 Greece
3020.5.H65 Home
3020.5.H84 Human beings
3020.5.I43 Identity (Philosophical concept)
3020.5.I74 Islam
3020.5.J68 Journalism
3020.5.L52 Liberalism
3020.5.M44 Mental illness
3020.5.M47 Metamorphosis
3020.5.M6 Modernism
3020.5.M67 Moscow (Russia)
3020.5.O33 Occultism
3020.5.P56 Plots
3020.5.R4 Realism
3020.5.S45 Self
3020.5.S65 Soviet Union
3020.5.S73 Space and time
3020.5.U54 United States
3020.5.V58 Visual literature

Revolutionary epoch. Soviet literature

3021 Works in Russian
3022 Works in English
3023 Works in French
3024 Works in German
3025 Works in other languages (not A-Z)
3026.A-Z Special topics and subjects, A-Z

Russian literature
Literary history and criticism
History, by period
20th century
Revolutionary epoch. Soviet literature
Special topics and subjects, A-Z -- Continued

3026.A4 Animals
3026.A77 Artists. Art
3026.A83 Asia
3026.A94 Autobiography
Avant-garde literature see PG3026.E98
3026.C45 Censorship
3026.C5 Characters
3026.C6 Communism. Communists
3026.C64 Concentration camps
3026.C65 Conflict (Psychology)
3026.C7 Country life
3026.E76 Eroticism
3026.E95 Europe
3026.E98 Experimental literature. Avant-garde literature
Far East, Soviet see PG3026.S68
3026.F3 Farm life
3026.F46 Flight
3026.F6 Formalism
3026.H4 Heroes
3026.H57 History
3026.I9 Ivan IV, Czar of Russia. Иван IV (Иоанн Васильевич)
3026.J48 Jews
3026.K3 Kazakhstan
3026.L3 Labor. Working class
3026.L4 Lenin, Vladimir Il′ich. Владимир Ильич Ленин
3026.L47 Levyĭ front iskusstv. Левый фронт искусств
3026.L68 Love
3026.M37 Masculinity. Men
3026.M5 Minorities
3026.M6 Literature and morals
3026.N38 Nature
3026.N6 Nobel Prize
3026.O24 Obėriu. Обэриу
3026.P33 Parody
3026.P35 Patriotism
3026.P64 Politics
3026.P67 Postmodernism
3026.P79 Psychoanalysis and literature
3026.P87 Pushkin, Aleksandr Sergeevich. Александр Сергеевич Пушкин

Russian literature
Literary history and criticism
History, by period
20th century
Revolutionary epoch. Soviet literature
Special topics and subjects, A-Z -- Continued

3026.R4 Realism
3026.R44 Religion
3026.R49 Revolution, 1917-1921
3026.R5 Revolutionaries
3026.R58 Romanticism
Russian Far East see PG3026.S68
3026.S3 Satire
3026.S34 Scholars
3026.S348 Science. Technology
3026.S43 Sea
3026.S45 Serapion Brotherhood. Серапионовы братья
3026.S47 Sex
3026.S53 Siberia
3026.S58 Socialist realism
3026.S6 Soldiers
3026.S67 Soviet Central Asia
3026.S68 Soviet Far East. Russian Far East
3026.S83 Stalingrad, Battle of, 1942-1943. Сталинградская битва
3026.S9 Style
Technology see PG3026.S348
3026.U5 Underground literature
3026.U8 Utopias
3026.V5 Vietnam War, 1961-1975
3026.V54 Violence
3026.W3 War
3026.W6 Women
Working class see PG3026.L3
3026.Y4 Yerevan
3026.Y67 Youth

21st century
Including 21st century and Post-Soviet 20th century combined
3027 General works
3027.5.A-Z Special topics and subjects, A-Z
3027.5.A58 Antisemitism
3027.5.P67 Postmodernism

History, by region, province, etc. see PG3500+

Russian literature
Literary history and criticism -- Continued
History of special relations, movements and currents in Russian literature
If limited to or identified with one period or form of literature, prefer the period or form
Cf. PG2973.8+ Special aspects or topics

3030 Realism. Naturalism
3031 Romanticism
3035.A-Z Other special, A-Z
3035.C4 Classicism
For Classical literature (Greek and Roman) in relation to Russian literature see PG2980.5
3035.F6 Folklore and Russian literature
3035.G7 Greek church (Influence on Russian literature)
3035.H8 Humanism
3035.I3 Idealism
3035.P3 Patriotism
(3035.S4) Serapion Brotherhood
see PG3026.S45

Special forms of literature
Poetry
3041 General works. Treatises, compends, etc.
3043 Addresses, essays, pamphlets, etc.
By period
3046 16th-18th centuries
3051 19th century
3056 20th century
3057 21st century
Special kinds of poetry
Popular poetry, folk songs see PG3103+
3060 Epic and narrative poetry
3063 Lyric poetry
3064.A-Z Other, A-Z
3064.B3 Ballads
Cf. PG3103+ Folk songs
3064.C45 Children's poetry
3064.D5 Didactic poetry
3064.E94 Experimental poetry
3064.F32 Fables
3064.F73 Free verse
3064.H57 Historical poetry
3064.O34 Odes
3064.P74 Prose poems
3064.P76 Protest poetry
3064.S6 Songs
3064.S63 Sonnets

Russian literature
Literary history and criticism
Special forms of literature
Poetry -- Continued

3065.A-Z Special topics and subjects, A-Z
3065.A24 Acmeism
3065.A3 Adaptations
3065.A7 Armenia
3065.A94 Azerbaijan
3065.B52 Bible
3065.C68 Cosmology
3065.D43 Death
3065.E76 Erotic poetry
Film and video adaptations see PG3065.A3
3065.F8 Futurism
3065.G43 Geographical perception
3065.G46 Georgian S.S.R. Georgia (Republic)
3065.I42 Imagism
3065.I47 Imperatorskiĭ TSarskosel′skiĭ lit͡seĭ
3065.I72 Italy
3065.K67 Koran. Qur'ān
3065.L33 Labor. Working class
Landscape see PG3065.N3
3065.L45 Lenin, Vladimir Il′ich. Владимир Ильич Ленин
3065.L46 Leningrad. Saint Petersburg
3065.L6 Love
3065.M5 Military
3065.M67 Moscow
3065.M87 Music
3065.M95 Myth
3065.N3 Nature. Landscape
3065.P37 Patriotism
3065.P65 Polish question
3065.P79 Psychology
3065.P87 Pushkin (Russia). TSarskoe Selo (Russia)
Qur'ān see PG3065.K67
3065.R4 Religion
Cf. PG3104.7 Folk songs
3065.R45 Revolutionary poetry
Saint Petersburg see PG3065.L46
3065.S28 Satire
3065.S3 Science
3065.S5 Siberia
3065.S63 Space travel
3065.S75 Switzerland
3065.S8 Symbolism
3065.T7 Translations (as subject)

Russian literature
Literary history and criticism
Special forms of literature
Poetry
Special topics and subjects, A-Z -- Continued
TSarskoe Selo (Russia) see PG3065.P87
Video and film adaptations see PG3065.A3
3065.W37 War
Working class see PG3065.L33
3065.W67 World War II
Drama
For history and study of the Russian stage see PN2720+
3071 General works. Treatises, compends, etc.
3073 Addresses, essays, pamphlets, etc.
3074.A-Z Special topics and subjects, A-Z
3074.L46 Lenin, Vladimir Il′ich. Владимир Ильич Ленин
3074.M63 Modernism
3074.P4 Peasants
3074.S47 Setting (Literature)
By period
3076 16th-18th centuries
Including mysteries, miracle plays, school drama, etc.
3081 19th century
3086 20th century
3087 21st century
3089.A-Z Special types of drama, A-Z
3089.C6 Comedy
3089.F6 Folk drama. Popular drama
3089.H5 Historical drama
3089.I5 Interludes
3089.M44 Melodrama
For melodrama in music, see subclass ML
3089.O54 One-act plays
3089.P6 Political drama
3089.R4 Religious drama
Cf. PG3076 Mysteries, miracle plays
3089.T7 Tragedy
Prose
3091 General works. Treatises, compends, etc.
3091.5 Addresses, essays, pamphlets, etc.
3091.9.A-Z Special topics, A-Z
3091.9.A33 Adaptations
3091.9.A76 Artists
3091.9.A93 Autobiography
3091.9.B56 Biography
3091.9.E25 Ecology. Human ecology

Russian literature
Literary history and criticism
Special forms of literature
Prose
Special topics, A-Z -- Continued

3091.9.F6 Folklore
Human ecology see PG3091.9.E25
3091.9.T73 Travel
3091.9.W65 Women
By period
3092 Early to 1800
3093 19th century
3094 20th century
3094.5 21st century
Prose fiction
Technique see PN3355+
3095 General works. Treatises, compends, etc.
3096.A-Z Special topics and subjects, A-Z
3096.A65 Apocalypse
3096.B53 Bible
3096.C66 Communication
3096.C68 Country life
3096.D45 Demonology. Devil
3096.D73 Dreams
3096.E9 Existentialism
3096.F57 First person narrative
3096.G76 Grotesque
3096.H65 Home
3096.I57 Impressionism
3096.I6 Individualism
3096.L35 Landscape
3096.M35 Manners and customs
3096.M42 Melancholy
3096.M45 Men
3096.M95 Myth. Mythology
3096.N38 Nature
3096.N5 Nihilism
3096.O35 Object (Philosophy)
3096.P55 Philosophy
3096.P65 Populism
3096.R4 Realism
3096.R48 Revolutions
3096.R63 Rogues and vagabonds
3096.S45 Sentimentalism
3096.S6 Social conditions
3096.S64 Soldiers
3096.S96 Symbolism

Russian literature
Literary history and criticism
Special forms of literature
Prose
Prose fiction
Special topics and subjects, A-Z -- Continued
3096.T43 Teachers
3096.U94 Utopias
3096.W6 Women
3096.W67 World War II
3096.Y68 Youth
Special kinds of fiction
3097 Short story
3098.A-Z Other, A-Z
3098.C48 Children's stories
3098.C5 Christmas stories
3098.D46 Detective and mystery stories
3098.F34 Fantastic fiction
3098.F6 Folk novels
3098.F73 Frame-stories
3098.H5 Historical fiction
3098.H67 Horror tales
3098.L68 Love stories
3098.P5 Picaresque fiction
3098.S5 Science fiction
3098.S7 Social romances
By period
3098.2 Early through 1800
3098.3 19th century
3098.4 20th century
3098.5 21st century
3099.A-Z Other prose forms, A-Z
3099.D5 Dialogues
3099.E7 Essays
3099.F3 Fables
3099.F48 Feuilletons
3099.L4 Letters
3099.O7 Oratory
3099.W5 Wit and humor
Folk literature
For general works on and collections of folk literature see GR202+
History and criticism
(3100) Periodicals. Societies. Collections
(3101) Treatises. Compends
(3102) Addresses, essays, pamphlets, etc.
Special forms

PG

Russian literature
Literary history and criticism
Special forms of literature
Folk literature
History and criticism
Special forms -- Continued
Popular poetry. Folk songs. Ballads
3103 General works
Special types
Byliny (Epic songs, heroic ballads, sagas). Былины
Including the Vladimir or Kiev Cycle, the Novgorod Cycle, and the Moscow or Imperial Cycle
3104 General works
3104.2.A-Z Special topics or subjects, A-Z
3104.2.F3 Fantasy
3104.2.I6 Il'i͡a Muromet͡s (Ilya saga). Илья Муромец
3104.2.P68 Potyk, Mikhaĭlo (Legendary character). Михайло Потык
Historical songs and ballads
3104.3 General works
3104.4.A-Z Special topics or subjects, A-Z
3104.4.P75 Protest poetry
3104.4.P83 Pugachev, Emel'i͡an Ivanovich. Pugachev's Rebellion. Емельян Иванович Пугачев
3104.4.R4 Revolutionary poetry
Ceremonial songs for holidays, festivals, etc.
3104.5 General works
3104.6.A-Z Special kinds, A-Z
Betrothal songs see PG3104.6.M3
Burial songs see PG3104.6.F8
3104.6.C5 Christmas songs and carols. Koli͡ada. Коляда
3104.6.E3 Easter songs
3104.6.F8 Funeral songs. Funeral laments
3104.6.H3 Harvest songs
3104.6.M3 Marriage songs
3104.6.M5 Midsummer day songs
3104.7 Religious verses, songs, and ballads
3104.8.A-Z By groups or classes of persons, A-Z
3104.8.B5 Beggar songs
3104.8.L3 Laboring class. Working class
3104.8.M56 Minstrels
3104.8.P75 Prisoners' songs
3104.8.R6 Robber songs
3104.9.A-Z Other, A-Z

Russian literature
Literary history and criticism
Special forms of literature
Folk literature
History and criticism
Special forms
Popular poetry. Folk songs. Ballads
Special types
Other, A-Z -- Continued
3104.9.C5 Chastushki. Частушки
3104.9.I5 Incantations
3104.9.L85 Lullabies
3104.9.P7 Proverbs
3104.9.R5 Riddles
3104.9.S4 Skaz. Сказ
Folk drama see PG3089.F6
(3105) Folk tales. Fairy tales. Legends. Charms
Collections of texts
(3110) General
By form
Popular poetry. Folk songs. Ballads
3113 General collections
Special types
Byliny. Былины
3114 General collections
3114.2.A-Z Individual ballads or sagas, A-Z
Historical songs and ballads
3114.3 General collections
3114.4.A-Z Individual songs or ballads, A-Z
Ceremonial songs for holidays, festivals, etc.
3114.5 General collections
3114.6.A-Z Special kinds, A-Z
3114.7 Religious verses, songs, and ballads
3114.8.A-Z By groups or classes of persons, A-Z
3114.8.C47 Children's poetry
3114.9.A-Z Other, A-Z
3114.9.B94 Bylichki. Былички
3114.9.C5 Chastushki. Частушки
3114.9.I5 Incantations
(3114.9.L3) Laments
(3114.9.P7) Proverbs
see PN6505.S5
(3114.9.R5) Riddles
see PN6377.R9
Folk drama
Collections see PG3255.F6
Individual plays see PG3300+

PG

Russian literature
Literary history and criticism
Special forms of literature
Folk literature
Collections of texts (exclusively)
By form -- Continued
Folk tales. Fairy tales. Legends. Charms
(3115) General
(3117.A-Z) Individual tales, A-Z
(3129.A-Z) By region, locality, etc., A-Z
Translations
General collections
(3130) English
(3131) French
(3132) German
(3135.A-Z) Other languages, A-Z
Popular poetry. Folk songs. Ballads
3140 English
3141 French
3142 German
3145.A-Z Other languages, A-Z
Other special
(3150) English
(3151) French
(3152) German
(3155.A-Z) Other languages, A-Z
3190 Juvenile literature (General)
For special genres, see the genre
Collections of Russian literature
3199 Periodicals. Societies. Serial collections
General collections
3200.A2 Published before 1800
3200.A3-Z Published 1800-
3201 Selections. Anthologies
3203.A-Z Special classes of authors, A-Z
3203.C45 Children
3203.J48 Jewish authors
3203.S64 Soldiers
3203.W64 Women
3205.A-Z Special topics, A-Z
3205.A7 Armed Forces
3205.A94 Azerbaijan
3205.B3 Baikal Lake region
3205.B35 Bashkortostan
Belarus see PG3205.B95
3205.B64 Books
Including book collecting and book collectors

Russian literature
Collections of Russian literature
Special topics, A-Z -- Continued

3205.B73 Bread
3205.B95 Byelorussian S.S.R. Belarus
(3205.C5) Children's writings
see PG3203.C45
3205.C7 Crimea
3205.D6 Don River Valley
3205.E37 Easter
3205.E75 Erotic literature
3205.E8 Estonia
3205.F34 Feodosii͡a (Ukraine)
Gays see PG3205.H65
3205.G46 Georgian S.S.R. Georgia (Republic)
3205.H65 Homosexuality. Gays
3205.H8 Hunting stories
3205.I24 I͡Akutskai͡a A.S.S.R. Yakutia. Sakha
3205.J4 Jews. Judaism
3205.K3 Karelia
3205.K84 Kulikovo, Battle of, 1380. Куликовская битва
3205.L5 Lipet͡sk (Russia)
3205.M27 Manors
3205.M3 Marii A.S.S.R. Mari El
3205.M5 Miners
3205.M57 Money
3205.M6 Mothers
3205.N35 Nature
3205.N6 Novgorod
3205.O3 Odessa
3205.P74 Psychology
3205.R4 Religion
3205.R45 Revolutionaries
3205.R8 Russia
3205.R86 Russo-Turkish War, 1877-1878
3205.S35 Saint Petersburg
Sakha (Russia) see PG3205.I24
3205.S56 Simferopol′ (Ukraine)
3205.S64 Smolensk
3205.S8 Stalingrad. Volgograd
3205.S9 Symbolism
3205.V54 Vikings
Volgograd see PG3205.S8
3205.W3 War
3205.W6 Women
3205.W7 Work
Yakutia. see PG3205.I24

Russian literature
Collections of Russian literature -- Continued
(3211) Translations from foreign literatures into Russian
see PA-PT
(3211.A2) Several literatures
see PN6065.R9
(3211.A5-Z) Special literatures by language, A-Z
Translations of Russian literature
3212 Polyglot
3213 English
3214 French
3215 German
3216 Italian
3217 Spanish
3219.A-Z Other languages, A-Z
By period
For translations see PG3212+
3223 Early to 1700
3225 18th century
3226 19th century
20th century. Soviet literature
3227 General works
3227.5 Selections. Anthologies
3228.A-Z By subject, A-Z
3228.A24 Abkhazians
3228.A3 Aesthetics
3228.A47 Amur River Valley
3228.A5 Andersen, Hans Christian
3228.A54 Angara River Valley
3228.A718 Arkhangel′skai͡a oblast′ and region
3228.A72 Armed Forces
3228.A73 Armenia
3228.A88 Atommash. Атоммаш
3228.A9 Authors and authorship
3228.B3 Baikal-Amur Railroad. Байкало-Амурская магистраль
3228.B68 Boundaries of Russia
3228.C47 Children, Vagrant
3228.C48 Chile
3228.C49 Chuvash (Turkic people)
3228.C53 Citizenship. Civics
3228.C69 Creative ability
3228.C72 Crimea
3228.D59 Donets Basin
3228.D6 Donet͡s′k (Ukraine)
3228.E75 Erotic literature
3228.E94 Experimental literature

Russian literature
  Collections of Russian literature
    By period
      20th century. Soviet literature
        By subject, A-Z -- Continued

3228.F67 Forests and forestry
3228.H64 Holocaust, Jewish (1939-1945)
3228.H8 Hunting
3228.I76 Iron mines and mining
3228.I82 Italy
3228.K38 Kazakh S.S.R. Kazakhstan
Komsomol see PG3228.V8
3228.K8 Kuban region
3228.K83 Kuĭbyshev. Samara
3228.K85 Kursk, Battle of, 1943
3228.L37 Lenin, Vladimir Il′ich. Владимир Ильич Ленин
3228.L68 Love
3228.M5 Miners
3228.M6 Moscow
3228.O54 Oil industries
3228.P4 Peace
3228.P75 Prisoners
3228.P8 Psychology
3228.R48 Revolutions
3228.R9 Russia
Samara (Russia) see PG3228.K83
3228.S84 Steel industry and trade
3228.S88 Subways
3228.U52 Underground literature
3228.U54 United States
3228.U93 Uzbek S.S.R. Uzbekistan
3228.V65 Volga River and Valley
3228.V8 Vsesoi͡uznyĭ leninskiĭ kommunisticheskiĭ soi͡uz molodezhi. Всесоюзный ленинский коммунистический союз молодежи
3228.W3 War
3228.W5 Women
3228.W6 Women in war
3228.W7 Work

21st century
3229 General works
3229.2.A-Z By subject, A-Z

Poetry
General collections
3230.A2 Published before 1800
3230.A3-Z Published 1800-
3230.5 Selections. Anthologies

PG

	Russian literature
	Collections of Russian literature
	Poetry -- Continued
3230.7.A-Z	Special classes of authors, A-Z
3230.7.C45	Children
3230.7.C64	College students
3230.7.P64	Political prisoners
3230.7.R63	Rock musicians
3230.7.S28	Scientists
3230.7.W65	Women
	By period
3231	Early to 1800
3232	19th century
3233	20th century
3233.5	21st century
	By form
	Folk songs, ballads, etc. see PG3113+
3234.A-Z	Other forms, A-Z
3234.C45	Children's poetry
3234.E65	Epitaphs
3234.F74	Free verse
3234.H34	Haiku
3234.L84	Lullabies
3234.L9	Lyric poetry
3234.N37	Narrative poetry
3234.S6	Sonnets
3235.A-Z	Special topics, A-Z
3235.A37	Agricultural laborers
3235.A39	Akhmatova, Anna Andreevna, 1889-1966. Анна Андреевна Ахматова
3235.A43	Alexander III. Александр III
3235.A45	Altai Mountains Region
3235.A6	Arctic regions
3235.A65	Armenian massacres
3235.A67	Armenia
3235.A7	Army
3235.A84	Asia
3235.A88	Atheism
3235.B32	Babi Yar Massacre, Ukraine, 1941. Бабий Яр
3235.B47	Beslan Massacre, Beslan, Russia, 2004
3235.B53	Bible
3235.C37	Caucasus
3235.C4	Chechni͡a
3235.C43	Chess
(3235.C45)	Children's writings see PG3230.7.C45

Russian literature
Collections of Russian literature
Poetry
Special topics, A-Z -- Continued

(3235.C57) College verse
see PG3230.7.C64
3235.C6 Communism
Crimea (Ukraine) see PG3235.K79
3235.C75 Crimean War, 1853-1856. Крымская война
3235.C8 Cuba
3235.D4 Decembrists
3235.E26 Ecology
3235.E74 Erotic poetry
3235.E84 Esenin, Sergeĭ Aleksandrovich, 1895-1925. Сергей Александрович Есенин
3235.F67 Forced repatriation
3235.F8 Futuristic poetry
3235.G46 Georgia (Republic)
3235.G63 Goethe, Johann Wolfgang von, 1749-1832
3235.G85 Gumilev, N. (Nikolai), 1886-1921. Николай Степанович Гумилев
3235.H5 History
3235.I73 Iran
3235.J4 Jews
3235.K17 K.R. (Konstantin Romanov), Grand Duke of Russia, 1858-1915. К.Р. (Константин Романов)
3235.K34 Kaliningrad (Kaliningradskai͡a oblastʹ, Russia)
3235.K36 Kama River Region
3235.K49 Khlebnikov, Velimir, 1885-1922. Велимир Хлебников
3235.K6 Kola Peninsula
3235.K73 Krasnokamsk (Russia)
3235.K79 Krymskai͡a oblastʹ (Ukraine). Crimea (Ukraine)
3235.L4 Labor poetry
3235.L42 Latvia
3235.L45 Lenin, Vladimir Ilʹich, 1870-1924. Владимир Ильич Ленин
3235.L47 Leningrad. Saint Petersburg
3235.L48 Lermontov, Mikhail I͡Urʹevich, 1814-1841. Михаил Юрьевич Лермонтов
3235.L5 Liberty
3235.L6 Love
3235.M5 Mickiewicz, Adam, 1798-1855
3235.M6 Moscow
3235.M68 Mothers
3235.N27 Names, Personal
3235.N3 Napoleon I
3235.N35 Nature

Russian literature
Collections of Russian literature
Poetry
Special topics, A-Z -- Continued

3235.N68 Novosibirsk (Russia)
3235.P14 Palestine
3235.P17 Parachute troops
3235.P2 Parodies
3235.P23 Pasternak, Boris Leonidovich, 1890-1960. Борис Леонидович Пастернак
3235.P25 Pastoral poetry
3235.P3 Patriotic poems
3235.P4 Peace
3235.P45 Perm′ (Russia)
3235.P6 Poland
3235.P65 Police
3235.P67 Political poetry
3235.P8 Pushkin, Aleksandr Sergeevich. Александр Сергеевич Пушкин
3235.P83 Pushkin (Russia). T͡Sarskoe Selo (Russia)
3235.R32 Rachmaninoff, Sergei, 1873-1943. Сергей Рахманинов
3235.R35 Religious poetry
3235.R4 Revolutionary songs
Russian history see PG3235.H5
3235.S3 Sailors' songs
Saint Petersburg see PG3235.L47
3235.S35 Satire
3235.S5 Siberia
3235.S7 Soldiers' songs
3235.S8 Stalin, Joseph. Иосиф Сталин
3235.S85 Student songs
3235.S89 Suvorov, Aleksandr Vasil′evich, kni͡azʹ Italiĭskiĭ, 1730-1800. Александр Васильевич Суворов, князь Италийский
3235.T73 Translating and interpreting
3235.T75 Trees
T͡Sarskoe Selo (Russia) see PG3235.P83
3235.T86 Turkic peoples
3235.V64 Voloshin, Maksimilian Aleksandrovich, 1877-1932. Максимилиан Александрович Волошин
3235.V8 Vsesoi͡uznyĭ leninskiĭ kommunisticheskiĭ soi͡uz molodezhi. Всесоюзный ленинский коммунистический союз молодежи
3235.W36 War poetry
(3235.W6) Women's writings
see PG3230.7.W65

Russian literature
Collections of Russian literature
Poetry -- Continued
(3236) Translations of foreign poetry into Russian
see PA-PT
(3236.A2) Several languages
see PN6107
(3236.A5-Z) Special languages, A-Z
Translations of Russian poetry
3237.A2 Polyglot
3237.E5 English
3237.F5 French
3237.G5 German
3237.I5 Italian
3237.S5 Spanish
3238.A-Z Other languages, A-Z
Drama
General collections
3240.A2 Published before 1800
3240.A3-Z Published 1800-
3240.5 Selected plays. Anthologies
By period
3241 Early to 1800
For individual miracle plays, mysteries, moralities
see PG3300.A+
3241.2 19th century
3242 20th century
(3242.2) Plays in typewritten form
3242.5 21st century
(3243) Translations of foreign drama into Russian
see PA - PT
(3243.A2) Several languages
see PN6118
(3243.A5-Z) Special languages
Translations of Russian drama
3244 Polyglot
3245 English
3246 French
3247 German
3248 Italian
3249 Spanish
3250.A-Z Other languages, A-Z
Special types of drama
3252 Tragedy
3253 Comedy
3255.A-Z Other special types, A-Z
3255.A42 Amateur theatricals

Russian literature
Collections of Russian literature
Drama
Special types of drama
Other special types, A-Z -- Continued
3255.C45 Children's plays
3255.F6 Folk drama. Popular drama
3255.H5 Historical drama
3255.P6 Political plays
3255.R4 Religious drama
Prose
General collections
3260.A2 Published before 1800
3260.A3-Z Published 1800-
3260.5 Selections. Anthologies
By period
3261 Early to 1600
3262 17th-18th centuries
3263 19th-20th centuries
3263.5 21st century
(3264) Translations into Russian
see subclasses PA-PT
(3264.A2) Several languages
see PN6065
(3264.A5-Z) Special languages, A-Z
Translations from Russian
3265 Polyglot
3266 English
3267 French
3268 German
3269.A-Z Other languages, A-Z
Prose fiction
General collections
3270.A2 Published before 1800
3270.A3-Z Published 1800-
3270.5 Selections. Anthologies
By period
3271 Early to 1600
3272 17th-18th centuries
3273 19th-20th centuries
3273.5 21st century
(3274) Translations into Russian
see subclasses PA-PT
(3274.A2) Several languages
see PN6120.7
(3274.A5-Z) Special languages, A-Z
Translations from Russian

Russian literature
Collections of Russian literature
Prose
Prose fiction
Translations from Russian -- Continued
3275 Polyglot
3276 English
3277 French
3278 German
3279.A-Z Other languages, A-Z
Short stories
General collections
3280.A2 Published before 1800
3280.A3-Z Published 1800-
3280.5 Selections. Anthologies
By period
3281 Early to 1600
3282 17th-18th centuries
3283 19th-20th centuries
3283.5 21st century
(3284) Translations into Russian
see subclasses PA-PT
(3284.A2) Several languages
see PN6120.7
(3284.A5-Z) Special languages, A-Z
Translations from Russian
3285 Polyglot
3286 English
3287 French
3288 German
3289.A-Z Other languages, A-Z
Other prose forms
3291 Oratory
3292 Letters
3293 Essays
3295 Wit and humor
3299.A-Z Other, A-Z
3299.F4 Feuilletons
Individual authors and works, Early to 1700
Subarrange individual authors by Table P-PZ40 unless otherwise specified
Subarrange individual works by Table P-PZ43 unless otherwise specified
Including certain early writings in the fields of religion, history, travel, biography, etc.

Russian literature
Individual authors and works, Early to 1700 -- Continued

3300.A-Z Anonymous works, A-Z
Including literary tales and romances, poems, plays (miracle plays, mysteries, moralities, etc.), historical and military narratives of literary interest, translations of anonymous works into Russian, etc.
For individual folk tales see subclass GR
For individual folk songs or ballads see PG3114+

3300.A4-.A43 Alexander the Great (Romances, etc.) (Table P-PZ43)
Annals see PG3300.L4+
3300.A6-.A63 Apollonius of Tyre (Table P-PZ43)
3300.B37-.B373 Barlaam and Joasaph. Повесть о Варлааме и Иоасафе (Table P-PZ43)
3300.B48-.B483 Beseda ot͡sa s synom o zhenskoĭ zlobe. Беседа отца с сыном о женской злобе (Table P-PZ43)
3300.B5-.B53 Beuve de Hanstone (Bova Korolevich). Бова Королевич (Table P-PZ43)
Chronicles see PG3300.L4+
3300.D5-.D53 Digenes Acritas (Byzantine epic poem) (Devgenievo dei͡anie). Девгениево деяние (Table P-PZ43)
Cf. PA5310.D5 Byzantine literature
Digenis Akritas see PG3300.D5+
3300.D6-.D63 Domostroĭ. Домострой (Table P-PZ43)
A composite work erroneously ascribed to Pope (priest) Sylvester (16th century) who probably contributed several chapters only
3300.I7-.I73 Istorii͡a o rossiĭskom dvori͡anine, Frole Skobeeve. История о российском дворянине, Фроле Скобееве (Table P-PZ43)
3300.I75-.I753 Istorii͡a o Vasilie Koroleviche Zlatovlasom. История о Василие Королевиче Златовласом (Table P-PZ43)
Letopisi (Chronicles). Летописи
Prefer DK except for literary and philological aspects
3300.L4A2 Texts. By date
3300.L4A3 Selected chronicles. Selections. By date
3300.L4A4-.L4Z Translations. By language
3300.L42 Criticism
Special chronicles
Chronicle of Nestor (so-called). Повесть временных лет
Beginnings of Russia to 1110
Also known as the Primitive chronicle
3300.L43A2 Texts. By date
3300.L43A3 Selections. By date
3300.L43A4-.L43Z Translations. By language
3300.L44 Criticism

Russian literature
Individual authors and works, Early to 1700
Anonymous works, A-Z
Letopisi (Chronicles). Летописи
Special chronicles -- Continued
Chronicle of Kiev. Киевская летопись
1110-1200

3300.L45A2 Texts. By date
3300.L45A3 Selections. By date
3300.L45A4-.L45Z Translations. By language
3300.L46 Criticism

Volhynian chronicle. Галицко-Волынская летопись
1201-1292

3300.L47A2 Texts. By date
3300.L47A3 Selections. By date
3300.L47A4-.L47Z Translations. By language
3300.L48 Criticism

Chronicles of Novgorod. Новгородская летопись
1016-1716

3300.L5A2 Texts. By date
3300.L5A3 Selected chronicles. Selections. By date
3300.L5A4A-.L5Z Translations. By language
3300.L52 Special chronicles, A-Z
3300.L53 Criticism

Chronicle of Suzdal. Суздальская летопись
Known also as the Chronicle of the North

3300.L54A2 Texts. By date
3300.L54A3 Selections. By date
3300.L54A4-.L54Z Translations. By language
3300.L55 Criticism

Annals of Pskov. Псковские летописи

3300.L56A2 Texts. By date
3300.L56A3 Selections. By date
3300.L56A4-.L56Z Translations. By language
3300.L57 Criticism
3300.L58A-.L58Z Other, A-Z
3300.L58I6 Ipat′evskai͡a letopis′. Ипатьевская летопись
3300.L58N54 Nikonovskai͡a letopis′. Никоновская летопись
3300.P4-.P43 Physiologus. Физиолог (Table P-PZ43)
3300.P56-.P563 Povest′ o Dovmonte. Повесть о Довмонте (Table P-PZ43)
3300.P63-.P633 Povest′ o Gore-Zlochastii. Повесть о Горе-Злочастии (Table P-PZ43)
3300.P67-.P673 Povest′ o kupt͡se Basarge. Повесть о купце Басарге (Table P-PZ43)
3300.P675-.P6753 Povest′ o Luke Kolochskom. Повесть о Луке Колочском (Table P-PZ43)

Russian literature
Individual authors and works, Early to 1700
Anonymous works, A-Z -- Continued

3300.P679-.P68 Povest′ o Mitia͡e. Повесть о Митяе (Table P-PZ43a)
3300.P689-.P69 Povest′ o Petre, t͡sareviche ordynskom. Повесть о Петре, царевиче ордынском (Table P-PZ43a)
3300.P692-.P6923 Povest′ o Petre i Fevronii. Повесть о Петре и Февронии (Table P-PZ43)
3300.P694-.P6943 Povest′ o pobedakh Moskovskogo gosudarstva. Повесть о победах Московского государства (Table P-PZ43)
3300.P7-.P713 Povest′ o Savve Grudt͡syne. Повесть о Савве Грудцыне (Table P-PZ43a)
3300.P73-.P733 Povest′ o Solovet͡skom vosstanii. Повесть о Соловецком восстании (Table P-PZ43)
3300.P74-.P743 Povest′ o sude Shemia͡ki. Повесть о суде Шемяки (Table P-PZ43)
3300.P765-.P7653 Povest′ o svia͡tom blagovernom velikom knia͡ze Mikhaile I͡Aroslaviche tverskom. Повесть о святом благоверном великом князе Михаиле Ярославиче тверском (Table P-PZ43)
3300.P77-.P773 Povest′ o t͡sare Aggee. Повесть о царе Аггее (Table P-PZ43)
Povest′ o Varlaame i Ioasafe. Повесть о Варлааме и Иоасафе see PG3300.B37+
3300.P78-.P783 Povest′ o Tverskom Otroche monastyre. Повесть о Тверском Отроче монастыре (Table P-PZ43)
3300.P79-.P793 Povest′ o Vasilii koroleviche Zlatovlasom. Повесть о Василии королевиче Златовласом (Table P-PZ43)
3300.P82-.P823 Povest′ o Zosime i Savvatii. Повесть о Зосиме и Савватии (Table P-PZ43)
3300.P83-.P833 Prolog (Moscow, Russia). Пролог (Table P-PZ43)
3300.R85-.R853 Rukopisanie Magnusha. Рукописание Магнуша (Table P-PZ43)
3300.S28-.S283 Shchit very. Щит веры (Table P-PZ43)
3300.S32-.S323 Skazanie o Borise i Glebe. Сказание о Борисе и Глебе (Table P-PZ43)
3300.S326-.S3263 Skazanie o knia͡ze Mikhaile Chernigovskom i o ego boi͡arine Feodore. Сказание о князе Михаиле Черниговском и о его боярине Феодоре (Table P-PZ43)
3300.S35-.S353 Skazanie o Mamaevom poboishche. Сказание о Мамаевом побоище (Table P-PZ43)
3300.S38-.S383 Skazanii͡a o t͡sare Solomone. Сказания о царе Соломоне (Table P-PZ43)
3300.S4-.S43 Skazka o Eruslane Lazareviche. Сказка о Еруслане Лазаревиче (Table P-PZ43)

Russian literature
Individual authors and works, Early to 1700
Anonymous works, A-Z -- Continued

3300.S45-.S453 Slovo Adama vo ade k Lazari͡u. Слово Адама во аде к Лазарю (Table P-PZ43)

3300.S53-.S533 Slovo o dvenadt͡sati snakh Shakhaishi. Слово о двенадцати снах Шахаиши (Table P-PZ43)

3300.S58-.S583 Slovo o pogibeli Rusky͡ia zemli. Слово о погибели Рускыя земли (Table P-PZ43)

3300.S6-.S63 Slovo o polku Igoreve. Слово о полку Игореве (Table P-PZ43)

3300.S7-.S73 Stikh o Golubinoĭ knige. Стих о Голубиной книге (Table P-PZ43)

3300.T7-.T73 Troy (Romances, etc.) (Table P-PZ43)

3300.Z3-.Z33 Zadonshchina. Задонщина (Table P-PZ43)

3300.Z5-.Z53 Zhalostnai͡a komedii͡a ob Adame i Eve. Жалостная комедия об Адаме и Еве (Table P-PZ43)

3300.Z55-.Z553 Zhitie Aleksandra Nevskogo. Житие Александра Невского (Table P-PZ43)

3301.A-Z Individual authors, A-C

3301.A2 Adashev, Alekseĭ Fedorovich, d. 1560. Алексей Федорович Адашев (Table P-PZ40)

3301.A25 Afanasiĭ, Archbishop of Kholmogory, 1641-1702. Афанасий Холмогорский (Алексей Артемьевич Любимов) (Table P-PZ40)

3301.A3 Agrefeniĭ, archimandrite, fl. ca. 1400. Агрефений (Table P-PZ40 modified)

3301.A3A61-.A3Z458 Separate works. By title

3301.A3K5 Khozhdenie vo svi͡atui͡u zemli͡u. Хождение во святую землю

3301.A4 Aleksandr, deacon, fl. 1393. Александр (Table P-PZ40 modified)

3301.A4A61-.A4Z458 Separate works. By title

3301.A4P8 Puteshestvie v T͡Sar′grad. Путешествие в Царьград

3301.A45 Alekseĭ Mikhaĭlovich, Czar of Russia, 1629-1676. Алексей Михайлович (Table P-PZ40)
For historical works and biography see subclass DK

3301.A85 Avvakum Petrovich, protopope, d. 1682. Аввакум Петрович (Table P-PZ40)
For his memoirs see BX605.A8

Baranovich, Lazar. Лазар Баранович see PG3304.L3

Chernorizet͡s Iakov. Иаков Черноризец see PG3303.I2

Cyprian, Saint, Metropolitan of Kiev, ca. 1333-1406. Киприан, митрополит киевский и всея Руси see PG705.K54

Collected works see BX480

Hagiographical writings see BX394

Russian literature
Individual authors and works, Early to 1700
Individual authors, A-C
Cyprian, Saint, Metropolitan of Kiev, ca. 1333-1406. Киприан, митрополит киевский и всея Руси -- Continued
Biography see BX395.A+

3302.A-Z Individual authors, D-F

3302.D3 Daniil, Metropolitan of Moscow, 1492-1547. Даниил, митрополит московский и всея Руси (Table P-PZ40)
Prefer BX480 , BX513, etc. for collected works, sermons, etc
Prefer BX597 for biography

3302.D4 Daniil Zatochnik, fl. 13th cent. Даниил Заточник (Table P-PZ40 modified)

3302.D4A61-.D4Z458 Separate works. By title
Molenie. Моление see PG3302.D4S6

3302.D4S6 Slovo. Слово

3302.D5 Dimitriĭ, Saint, Metropolitan of Rostov, 1651-1709. Димитрий Ростовский (Table P-PZ40 modified)
For religious works and biography see BL-BX

3302.D5A61-.D5Z458 Separate works. By title

3302.D5C4 Chet′i-Minei. Четьи-Минеи
Prefer BX393

3302.D5E7 Ėsfir′ i Agasfer. Эсфирь и Агасфер

3302.D5G7 Greshnik kai͡ushchiĭsi͡a. Грешник кающийся

3302.D5R6 Rozhdestvenskai͡a drama. Рождественская драма

3302.D5U7 Uspenskai͡a drama. Успенская драма

3302.D5V6 Voskresenie Khristovo. Воскресение Христово

Epifaniĭ Premudryĭ, d. 1420 see PG705.E64
Lives of Saint Sergiĭ Radonezhskiĭ and Saint Stefan Perskiĭ see BX597.A+

3302.F4 Feodosiĭ Pecherskiĭ, d. 1074. Феодосий Печерский (Table P-PZ40)
Abbot of Pecherskai͡a lavra (Печерская лавра), 1062-1074

3302.F65 Fotiĭ, Metropolitan of Kiev, d. 1431. Фотий, митрополит киевский и всея Руси (Table P-PZ40)
Prefer BX480 , BX597, etc. for religious works and biography

3303.A-Z Individual authors, G-I

3303.G4 Gennadiĭ, Archbishop of Novgorod and Pskov, d. 1505. Геннадий Новгородский (Table P-PZ40)
Known also as Gonozov or Gonzov (Гонозов, Гонзов)

Russian literature
Individual authors and works, Early to 1700
Individual authors, G-I -- Continued

3303.G5 Glazatyĭ, Ioann, 16th cent. Иоанн Глазатый (Table P-PZ40)
For his Istorii͡a o Kazanskom t͡sarstve (История о Казанском царстве) see DK511.T17

3303.G6 Goli͡atovskiĭ, Ioannikiĭ, d. 1688. Иоанникий Голятовский (Table P-PZ40)

Gonozov (Гонозов) see PG3303.G4

Gonzov (Гонзов) see PG3303.G4

Grigoriĭ T͡Samblak, Metropolitan of Kiev, b. ca. 1364. Григорий Цамблак see PG705.T8

3303.I2 Iakov Chernorizet͡s, monk, 11th cent. Иаков Черноризец (Table P-PZ40)

I͡Avorskiĭ, Stefan. Стефан Яворский see PG3307.S75

3303.I3 Ignatiĭ Smol'ni͡anin, hierodeacon, d. 1405. Игнатий Смольнянин (Table P-PZ40 modified)

3303.I3A61-.I3Z458 Separate works. By title

3303.I3K5 Khozhdenie. Хождение

3303.I4 Ilarion, Metropolitan of Kiev, fl. 1051-1054. Иларион Киевский (Table P-PZ40)
In general prefer BL-BX for his religious writings and biography

3303.I5 Ioakim, Patriarch of Moscow, 1620-1690. Патриарх Иоаким (Table P-PZ40)

Ioann IV Groznyĭ. Иоанн IV Грозный see PG3303.I8

3303.I55 Ioann, Metropolitan of Kiev, d. ca. 1088? Иоанн, митрополит киевский (Table P-PZ40)

3303.I6 Iosif Volot͡skiĭ, 1440?-1515. Иосиф Волоцкий (Table P-PZ40)
For religious works and biography, prefer BX

3303.I8 Ivan IV, Czar of Russia, 1530-1584. Иван IV (Иоанн Васильевич) (Table P-PZ40)
For his life and reign see DK106

3304.A-Z Individual authors, K-L

3304.K3 Katyrev-Rostovskiĭ, Ivan Mikhaĭlovich, kni͡az', d. 1640. Иван Михайлович Катырев-Ростовский (Table P-PZ40)

Kiprian, Saint, Metropolitan of Kiev see PG705.K54

3304.K5 Kirill, Bishop of Rostov, d. 1230. Кирилл, епископ ростовский (Table P-PZ40)
Prefer BX480 , BX597 for life and works

Russian literature
Individual authors and works, Early to 1700
Individual authors, K-L -- Continued

3304.K55 Kirill I, Metropolitan of Kiev, d. 1233. Кирилл I, митрополит киевский (Table P-PZ40)
Known also as Kirill Filosof (Кирилл Философ)
Prefer BX513 for sermons
Prefer BX597 for biography

3304.K57 Kirill II, Metropolitan of Kiev, d. 1280. Кирилл II, митрополит киевский (Table P-PZ40)
Prefer BX480 , BX513 , BX597, etc. for religious writings and biography

3304.K6 Kirill, Saint, Bishop of Turov, 12th cent. Кирилл Туровский (Table P-PZ40)
Prefer BX513 for sermons
Prefer BX597 for biography

3304.K63 Kirill Belozerskiĭ, 1337-1427. Кирилл Белозерский (Table P-PZ40)
Prefer BX480, BX513, BX597, etc. for religious works and biography

3304.K7 Križanić, Juraj, 1618-1683. Юрий Крижанич (Table P-PZ40)
Croatian author

3304.K8 Kurbskiĭ, Andreĭ Mikhaĭlovich, kni͡azʹ, d. 1583. Андрей Михайлович Курбский (Table P-PZ40)
Prefer DK for his historical writings and epistles

3304.L3 Lazar Baranovich, Archbishop of Chernigov, 1620-1693. Лазар Баранович (Table P-PZ40)
Prefer BX480, BX513, etc. for religious works; BX597 for biography

3304.L5 Lev, Metropolitan of Kiev, d. 1008. Лев, митрополит киевский (Table P-PZ40)
Known also as Leontiĭ, Leon, Leont (Леонтий, Леон, Леонт)

3304.L8 Luka Zhidi͡ata, Bishop of Novgorod, d. 1061? Лука Жидята (Table P-PZ40)
Variant form: Luka Zhiri͡ata (Лука Жирята)
Prefer BX513, BX597, etc. for life and works

3305 Individual authors, M-O

3305.M25 Makariĭ, Saint, Metropolitan of Moscow and All Russia, 1482-1563. Макарий, митрополит московский и всея Руси (Table P-PZ40)
For religious works and biography, prefer BX

Maksim Grek. Максим Грек (Μάχιμος ὁ Γραικός) see PG3305.M3

3305.M28 Matfeĭ, Bishop of Zaraisk. Матфей, епископ зарайский (Table P-PZ40)

Russian literature
Individual authors and works, Early to 1700
Individual authors, M-O -- Continued

3305.M3 Maximus, the Greek, 1480-1556. Максим Грек (Μάξιμος ὁ Γραικός) (Table P-PZ40)
Prefer DK32 for works on the social life and customs of Russia
Cf. B785.M298+ Philosophy
Cf. BX395.M37 Orthodox Church biography

3305.M4 Medvedev, Silʹvestr, 1641-1691. Сильвестр Медведев
Secular name: Semën Medvedev (Семён Медведев)762 P-PZ40

Mikhaĭlovich, Alekseĭ. Алексей Михайлович see PG3301.A45

Mnikh, Iakov see PG3303.I2

Mogila, Petr. Петр Могила see PG3306.P5

Monomakh, Vladimir. Владимир Мономах see PG3308.V55

Nestor, annalist, 1056-1115?. Нестор see PG705.N4

3305.N5 Nikifor, Metropolitan of Kiev and all Russia, fl. 1104-1121. Никифор, митрополит киевский и всея Руси (Table P-PZ40)
Prefer BL-BX for religious writings

3305.N6 Nil Sorskiĭ, 1433-1508. Нил Сорский (Table P-PZ40)

3306 Individual authors, P-R

3306.P3 Palit͡syn, Avraamiĭ, d. 1625. Авраамий Палицын (Table P-PZ40)
Original name: Averkiĭ Ivanovich Palit͡syn (Аверкий Иванович Палицын)
Prefer DK112, Russian history

3306.P5 Petr, Metropolitan of Kiev, 1596-1647. Петр Могила (Table P-PZ40)
Prefer BX480, BX597, etc. for religious writings and biography

3306.P6 Polikarp, Archimandrite, 13th cent. Поликарп, архимандрит (Table P-PZ40)

Polot͡skiĭ, Simeon. Симеон Полоцкий see PG3307.S5

3306.P7 Pozni͡akov, Vasiliĭ, fl. 1558-1561. Василий Позняков (Table P-PZ40 modified)

3306.P7A61-.P7Z458 Separate works. By title

3306.P7K5 Khozhdenie. Хождение

3307 Individual authors, S-T

Sanin, Ivan Ivanovich. Иван Иванович Санин see PG3303.I6

Russian literature
Individual authors and works, Early to 1700
Individual authors, S-T -- Continued

3307.S4 Serapion, Saint, Bishop of Vladimir, d. 1275. Серапион Владимирский (Table P-PZ40)
For religious works and biography, prefer BX

Sil′vestr Medvedev. Сильвестр Медведев see PG3305.M4

3307.S5 Simeon Polot͡skiĭ, 1629-1680. Симеон Полоцкий (Table P-PZ40 modified)
Prefer BL-BX for sermons and other religious writings

3307.S5A61-.S5Z458 Separate works. By title

3307.S5K6 Komedii͡a o Navukhodonosore t͡sare o tele zlate i o triekh otrot͡sekh v peshchi ne sozhzhennykh. Комедия о Навуходоносоре царе, о теле злате и о триех отроцех в пещи не сожженных

3307.S5K65 Komedii͡a pritchi o Bludnem syne. Комедия притчи о Блуднем сыне

3307.S5R5 Rifmologion. Sbornik stikhotvoreniĭ. Рифмологион. Сборник стихотворений

3307.S5V4 Vertograd mnogot͡svetnyĭ. Sbornik stikhotvoreniĭ. Вертоград многоцветный. Сборник стихотворений

3307.S55 Simon, Saint, Bishop of Vladimir and Suzdal, d. 1226. Симон, епископ владимирский и суздальский (Table P-PZ40)
Began compilation of Kievo-pecherskiĭ paterik (Киево-печерский патерик)

3307.S75 Stefan I͡Avorskiĭ, 1658-1722. Стефан Яворский (Table P-PZ40)
For his sermons see BX513

3307.S8 Stefan Novgorodet͡s, fl. ca. 1350. Стефан Новгородец (Table P-PZ40)

Theodosius of the Caves. Феодосий Печерский see PG3302.F4

Theodosius Pechersky. Феодосий Печерский see PG3302.F4

3307.T5 Timofeev, Ivan, 17th cent. Иван Тимофеев (Table P-PZ40)

Tuptalenko, Daniil Savvich. Даниил Саввич Тупталенко see PG3302.D5

Tuptalo, Daniil Savvich. Даниил Саввич Туптало see PG3302.D5

3308 Individual authors, U-Z

Russian literature
Individual authors and works, Early to 1700
Individual authors, U-Z -- Continued

3308.V35 Vasiliĭ, Saint, Archbishop of Novgorod and Pskov, d. 1352. Василий, архиепископ новгородский и псковский (Table P-PZ40)
For religious works and biography, prefer BX

3308.V55 Vladimir Vsevolodovich, Grand Duke of Kiev, 1053-1125. Владимир Всеволодович (Владимир Мономах) (Table P-PZ40)

Zhidi͡ata, Luka. Лука Жидята see PG3304.L8

3308.Z5 Zinoviĭ Otenskiĭ, d. 1568. Зиновий Отенский (Table P-PZ40)

3308.Z6 Zosima, inok, fl. 1414-1422. Зосима, инок (Table P-PZ40)

Individual authors and works, 18th century
Subarrange individual authors by Table P-PZ40 unless otherwise specified
Subarrange individual works by Table P-PZ43 unless otherwise specified

3310.A-Z Anonymous works, A-Z

3310.K7-.K73 Krivonos domosed stradalet͡s modnoĭ. Кривонос домосед страдалец модной (Table P-PZ43)

3311 Individual authors, A - Derzhavin

3311.A3 Ablesimov, Aleksandr Onisimovich, 1742-1783. Александр Онисимович Аблесимов (Table P-PZ40)

Azazesov, Azazes. Азазес Азазесов see PG3311.A3

3311.B3 Barkov, Ivan Semenovich, 1732-1768. Иван Семенович Барков (Table P-PZ40)
Variant patronymic: Stepanovich (Степанович)

Barskiĭ, Vasiliĭ. Василий Барский see PG3313.G7

3311.B37 Barsov, Anton Alekseevich, 1730-1791. Антон Алексеевич Барсов (Table P-PZ40)

3311.B6 Bogdanovich, Ippolit Ḟedorovich, 1744-1802? Ипполит Ѳедорович (Федорович) Богданович (Table P-PZ40 modified)

3311.B6A61-.B6Z458 Separate works. By title

3311.B6B5 Blazhenstvo narodov (Poem). Блаженство народов

3311.B6D6 Dobromysl (Novel). Добромысл

3311.B6D8 Dushen′ka (Novel). Душенька

3311.B6G5 Gimn na brakosochetanie (Poem). Гимн на бракосочетание

3311.B6R3 Radost′ Dushen′ki (Comedy). Радость Душеньки

3311.B6R8 Russkie poslovit͡sy (Proverbs). Русские пословицы

3311.B6S4 Sel′skiĭ prazdnik (Prose). Сельский праздник

3311.B6S65 Slavi͡ane (Drama). Славяне

3311.B6S8 Suguboe blazhenstvo (Poem). Сугубое блаженство

Russian literature
Individual authors and works, 18th century
Individual authors, A - Derzhavin -- Continued

3311.B65 Bolotov, Andreĭ Timofeevich, 1738-1833. Андрей Тимофеевич Болотов (Table P-PZ40)

3311.B7 Boltin, Ivan Nikitich, 1735-1792. Иван Никитич Болтин (Table P-PZ40)

3311.B8 Buslaev, Petr, fl. 1730-1760. Петр Буслаев (Table P-PZ40)

Buturlina, Anna Sergeevna. Анна Сергеевна Бутурлина see PG3319.Z5

Cantemir, Antioche Dmitriévich, prince see PG3313.K3

Catherine II, Empress of Russia, 1729-1796. Екатерина II

For historical works, see DK, DL

For literary works written in French see PQ1960

3311.C3 Collected literary works. By date

3311.C3A2-.C3A59 Translations (Collected or selected). By language, alphabetically

3311.C3A7-.C3Z4 Separate works

3311.C3B9 Byli i nebylit͡sy, ili, Grazhdanskoe uchenie. Были и небылицы, или, Гражданское учение

3311.C3G5 Glupoe pristrastie k poslovit͡sam. Глупое пристрастие к пословицам

3311.C3G6 Gore-bogatyr′ Kosometovich (Tale). Горе-богатырь Косометович

3311.C3G7 Gospozha Vestnikova s sem′eĭu (Comedy). Госпожа Вестникова с семьею

3311.C3I5 Imeniny gospozhi Vorchalkinoĭ (Comedy). Именины госпожи Ворчалкиной

3311.C3I9 Iz zhizni Ri͡urika (Comedy). Из жизни Рюрика

3311.C3L7 L′stet͡s i obol′shchennye. Льстец и обольщенные

3311.C3N4 Ne mozhet byt′ zlo bez dobra. Не может быть зло без добра

3311.C3N45 Nedorazumenii͡a (Comedy). Недоразумения

3311.C3N5 Nevesta nevidimka (Comedy). Невеста невидимка

3311.C3O2 O, vremi͡a! (Comedy). О, время!

3311.C3O3 Obmanshchik (Comedy). Обманщик

3311.C3O4 Obol′shchennyĭ (Comedy). Обольщенный

3311.C3P4 Peredni͡ai͡a znatnogo boi͡arina (Comedy). Передняя знатного боярина

3311.C3R4 Rasstroennai͡a sem′i͡a ostorozhkami i podozrenii͡ami (Comedy). Расстроенная семья осторожками и подозрениями

3311.C3S3 Shaman sibirskiĭ (Comedy). Шаман сибирский

3311.C3S37 Skazka o t͡sareviche Fevee. Сказка о царевиче Февее

Russian literature
Individual authors and works, 18th century
Individual authors, A - Derzhavin
Catherine II, Empress of Russia, 1729-1796. Екатерина II
Separate works -- Continued

3311.C3S4 Skazka o t͡sareviche Khlore. Сказка о царевиче Хлоре

3311.C3T3 Taĭna protivo nelepogo obshchestva. Тайна противо нелепого общества

3311.C3V6 Vot kakovo imet′ korzinu i bel′e (Comedy). Вот каково иметь корзину и белье

Biography, memoirs, letters see DK170

3311.C3Z5-.C3Z99 Criticism

Chemnitzer, Ivan Ivanovich see PG3315.K4

3311.C5 Chulkov, Mikhail Dmitrievich, 1740-1793. Михаил Дмитриевич Чулков (Table P-PZ40)

Danilov, Kirill. Кирилл Данилов see PG3311.D3

3311.D3 Danilov, Kirsha, 18th cent. Кирша Данилов (Table P-PZ40)

3311.D35 Danilov, Mikhail Vasil′evich, 1722-1790? Михаил Васильевич Данилов (Table P-PZ40)
Prefer DK for his historical works and memoirs

3312 Derzhavin, Gavriil Romanovich, 1743-1816. Гавриил Романович Державин (Table P-PZ39 modified)

3312.A61-.Z48 Separate works. By title

3312.A8-.A83 Atabalibo, ili, Razrushenie peruanskoĭ imperii (Tragedy). Атабалибо, или, Разрушение перуанской империи (Table P-PZ43)

Batmendiĭ (Opera). Батмендий see ML50

3312.B4-.B43 Blagodarnost′ Felit͡se. Благодарность Фелице (Table P-PZ43)

3312.D6-.D63 Dobryni͡a (Drama). Добрыня (Table P-PZ43)

Durochka umnee umnykh (Comic opera). Дурочка умнее умных see ML50.2

3312.E8-.E83 Evpraksii͡a (Tragedy). Евпраксия (Table P-PZ43)

Groznyĭ, ili, Pokorenie Kazani (Opera). Грозный, или, Покорение Казани see ML50

3312.I7-.I73 Irod i Mariamna (Tragedy). Ирод и Мариамна (Table P-PZ43)

3312.I9-.I93 Izobrazhenie Felit͡sy. Изображение Фелицы (Table P-PZ43)

3312.N3-.N33 Na smert′ kni͡azi͡a Meshcherskogo. На смерть князя Мещерского (Table P-PZ43)

3312.O2-.O23 Oda Bog. Ода Бог (Table P-PZ43)

3312.O3-.O33 Oda uspokoennoe neverie. Ода успокоенное неверие (Table P-PZ43)

PG

Russian literature
Individual authors and works, 18th century
Derzhavin, Gavriil Romanovich, 1743-1816. Гавриил Романович Державин
Separate works. By title -- Continued

3312.P6-.P63 Pozharskiĭ, ili, Osvobozhdenie Moskvy (Spectacle). Пожарский, или, Освобождение Москвы (Table P-PZ43)

Rudokopy (Opera). Рудокопы see ML50

3312.T5-.T53 Temnyĭ (Tragedy). Темный (Table P-PZ43)

3312.V5-.V53 Videnie Murzy. Видение Мурзы (Table P-PZ43)

3313 Individual authors, Derzhavin - Karamzin

3313.D5 Dmitriev-Mamonov, Fedor Ivanovich, 1728-ca 1790. Федор Иванович Дмитриев-Мамонов (Table P-PZ40)

Dolgorukova, Ekaterina Alekseevna. Екатерина Алексеевна Долгорукова see PG3317.M5

3313.D6 Dolgorukova, Natal'i͡a Borisovna (Sheremeteva), kni͡aginі͡a, 1714-1771. Наталья Борисовна (Шереметева) Долгорукова (Table P-PZ40)
Prefer DK150.8.D6 for her memoirs

3313.D7 Domashnev, Sergeĭ Gerasimovich, 1743-1795. Сергей Герасимович Домашнев (Table P-PZ40)

Dvori͡anin Filosof. Дворянин Философ see PG3313.D5

3313.E3 Efim'ev, Dmitriĭ Vladimirovich, 1768-1804. Дмитрий Владимирович Ефимьев (Table P-PZ40)

Ekaterina II see PG3311.C3+

3313.E35 El'chaninov, Bogdan Egorovich, 1744-1769. Богдан Егорович Ельчанинов (Table P-PZ40)

3313.E4 Ėmin, Fedor Aleksandrovich, 1735?-1770. Федор Александрович Эмин (Table P-PZ40)

3313.F4 Feofan, Archbishop of Novgorod, 1681-1736. Феофан, архиепископ новгородский (Table P-PZ40)

Filosof Dvori͡anin, pseud. Философ Дворянин see PG3313.D5

3313.F6 Fonvizin, Denis Ivanovich, 1745-1792. Денис Иванович Фонвизин (Table P-PZ40 modified)

3313.F6A61-.F6Z458 Separate works. By title

3313.F6B7 Brigadir (Comedy). Бригадир

3313.F6C4 Chortik na drozhkakh (Comic poem). Чортик на дрожках

3313.F6D6 Dobryĭ nastavnik (Comedy). Добрый наставник

3313.F6E6 Ėpigramma na Kni͡azhnina. Эпиграмма на Княжнина

3313.F6K2 K umu moemu (Poem). К уму моему

3313.F6K3 Kalisfen, grecheskai͡a povest'. Калисфен, греческая повесть

3313.F6K6 Korion (Comedy). Корион

Russian literature
Individual authors and works, 18th century
Individual authors, Derzhavin - Karamzin
Fonvizin, Denis Ivanovich, 1745-1792. Денис Иванович Фонвизин
Separate works. By title -- Continued

3313.F6L5 Lisit͡sa-koznodeĭ (Fable). Лисица-козноде́й
3313.F6N4 Nedorosl′ (Comedy). Недоросль
3313.F6O2 Obmanchivai͡a naruzhnost′ (Comedy). Обманчивая наружность
3313.F6P6 Poslanie k slugam moim (Poem). Послание к слугам моим
3313.F6V8 Vybor guvernera (Comedy). Выбор гувернера
3313.F7 Fonvizin, Pavel Ivanovich, 1744-1803. Павел Иванович Фонвизин (Table P-PZ40)
3313.G6 Golit͡syn, Alekseĭ Ivanovich, kni͡az′, 1765-1807. Алексей Иванович Голицын (Table P-PZ40)
3313.G65 Gorchakov, Dmitriĭ Petrovich, kni͡az′, 1758-1824. Дмитрий Петрович Горчаков (Table P-PZ40)
3313.G7 Grigorovich-Barskiĭ, Vasiliĭ, 1702?-1747. Василий Григорович-Барский (Table P-PZ40)

Gzh***. Гж***
see PG3317.M65, PG3317.M66

3313.I5 Il′inskiĭ, Nikolaĭ Stepanovich, 1761-1846. Николай Степанович Ильинский (Table P-PZ40)

K., V. see PG3315.K6

3313.K2 Kain, Ivan Osipov, b. 1718. Иван Осипов Каин (Table P-PZ40)
"Van′ka Kain (Ванька Каин)"

Kamarov, Matveĭ. Матвей Камаров see PG3315.K64

3313.K25 Kamenev, Gavriil Petrovich, 1772-1803. Гавриил Петрович Каменев (Table P-PZ40)

Kamenskai͡a, Aleksandra Fedotovna. Александра Федотовна Каменская see PG3317.R9

3313.K3 Kantemir, Antiokh Dmitrievich, kni͡az′, 1709-1744. Антиох Дмитриевич Кантемир (Table P-PZ40 modified)
3313.K3A16 Collected satires. By date
3313.K3A61-.K3Z458 Separate works
3313.K3B3 Basni (Fables). Басни
3313.K3E6 Ėpigrammy. Эпиграммы
3313.K3F5 Filaret i Evgeniĭ, na zavist′ i gordost′ dvori͡an zlonravnykh (Satire). Филарет и Евгений, на зависть и гордость дворян злонравных
3313.K3K4 K Feofanu, arkhiepiskopu novgorodskomu, o razlichii straseĭ chelovecheskikh (Satire). К Феофану, архиепископу новгородскому, о различии страстей человеческих

PG

Russian literature
Individual authors and works, 18th century
Individual authors, Derzhavin - Karamzin
Kantemir, Antiokh Dmitrievich, kni͡az′, 1709-1744. Антиох Дмитриевич Кантемир
Separate works -- Continued

3313.K3K5 K kni͡azi͡u Nikite I͡Ur′evichu Trubet͡skomu o vospitanii (Satire). К князю Никите Юрьевичу Трубецкому о воспитании

3313.K3K6 K Muze svoeĭ, o opasnosti satiricheskikh sochineniĭ (Satire). К Музе своей, о опасности сатирических сочинений

3313.K3K7 K solnt͡su. Na sostoi͡anie sveta sego (Satire). К солнцу. На состояние света сего

3313.K3K8 K umu svoemu, na khuli͡ashchikh uchenie (Satire). К уму своему, на хулящих учение

3313.K3N3 Na besstydnui͡u nakhal′chivost′ (Satire). На бесстыдную нахальчивость

3313.K3O2 O istinnom blazhenstve (Satire). О истинном блаженстве

3313.K3P4 Petrida (Poem). Петрида

3313.K3S3 Satir i Perierg, na chelovecheskie zlonravii͡a voobshche (Satire). Сатир и Периерг, на человеческие злонравия вообще

3313.K4 Kapnist, Vasiliĭ Vasil′evich, graf, 1757-1823. Василий Васильевич Капнист (Table P-PZ40 modified)

3313.K4A61-.K4Z458 Separate works. By title

3313.K4A8 Antigona (Tragedy). Антигона

3313.K4E6 Ėpigrammy. Эпиграммы

3313.K4I2 I͡Abeda (Comedy). Ябеда

3313.K4O3-.K59 Ody. Оды

3313.K4O3 Collected. By date

3313.K4O32-.K4O39 Series or special groups of odes

3313.K4O33 Ody anakreonticheskie. Оды анакреонтические

3313.K4O34 Ody dukhovnye. Оды духовные

3313.K4O35 Ody ėlegicheskie. Оды элегические

3313.K4O36 Ody gorat͡sianskie. Оды горацианские
Translations and imitations

3313.K4O37 Ody nravouchitel′nye. Оды нравоучительные

3313.K4O38 Ody torzhestvennye. Оды торжественные

3313.K4O4-.K4O49 Special odes
Arrange alphabetically

3313.K4O44 Oda na istreblenie v Rossii zvani͡a raba, Ekaterinoi͡u Vtoroi͡u v 15 den′ fevrali͡a 1786 goda. Ода на истребление в России званя раба, Екатериною Второю в 15 день февраля 1786 года

Russian literature
Individual authors and works, 18th century
Individual authors, Derzhavin - Karamzin
Kapnist, Vasiliĭ Vasil′evich, graf, 1757-1823. Василий Васильевич Капнист
Separate works. By title
Ody. Оды
Special odes -- Continued

3313.K4O47 Oda na rabstvo. Ода на рабство
3313.K4O5-.K4O59 Criticism
3313.K4P6 Poslanii͡a (Poems). Послания
3313.K4S3 Satira. Сатира
3313.K4S5 Sganarev, ili, Mnimai͡a nevernost′ (Comedy). Сганарев, или, Мнимая неверность
For translation into Russian poetry of Molière's Sganarelle; ou, Le cocu imaginaire see PQ1840.S3+

3314 Karamzin, Nikolaĭ Mikhaĭlovich, 1766-1826. Николай Михайлович Карамзин
3314.A1 Collected works. By date
3314.A16 Collected essays, miscellaneous, etc. By date
3314.A17 Collected poems. By date
3314.A18 Collected translations. By date
From foreign literatures into Russian
For separate works, see the special literatures, PA-PT
3314.A2-.A59 Translations (Collected or selected). By language, alphabetically
From Russian into foreign literatures
3314.A6 Selections. By date
3314.A7-.Z4 Separate works
3314.A8-.A83 Arkadskoĭ pami͡atnik (Drama). Аркадской памятник (Table P-PZ43)
3314.B4-.B43 Bednai͡a Liza (Story). Бедная Лиза (Table P-PZ43)
3314.C5-.C53 Chuvstvitel′nyĭ i kholodnyĭ (Story). Чувствительный и холодный (Table P-PZ43)
3314.D3-.D33 Darovanii͡a (Poem). Дарования (Table P-PZ43)
3314.F7-.F73 Frol Silin, blagodetel′noĭ chelovek (Tale). Фрол Силин, благодетельной человек (Table P-PZ43)
3314.I4-.I43 Il′i͡a Muromet͡s, bogatyrskai͡a skazka (Poem). Илья Муромец, богатырская сказка (Table P-PZ43)
Istorii͡a gosudarstva rossiĭskogo. История государства российского see DK71
3314.I8-.I83 Iulii͡a (Story). Иулия (Table P-PZ43)
3314.M3-.M33 Marfa Posadnit͡sa, ili, Pokorenie Novagoroda (Story). Марфа Посадница, или, Покорение Новагорода (Table P-PZ43)

Russian literature
Individual authors and works, 18th century
Karamzin, Nikolaĭ Mikhaĭlovich, 1766-1826. Николай Михайлович Карамзин
Separate works -- Continued

3314.M9-.M93 Mysli ob uedinenii (Essay). Мысли об уединении (Table P-PZ43)

3314.N3-.N33 Natal′i͡a, boi͡arskai͡a doch′ (Story). Наталья, боярская дочь (Table P-PZ43)

3314.N4-.N43 Nezhnost′ druzhby v nizkom sostoi͡anii (Essay). Нежность дружбы в низком состоянии (Table P-PZ43)

3314.O2-.O23 O li͡ubvi k otechestvu i narodnoĭ gordosti (Essay). О любви к отечеству и народной гордости (Table P-PZ43)

3314.O3-.O33 O schastliveĭshem vremeni zhizni (Essay). О счастливейшем времени жизни (Table P-PZ43)

3314.O4-.O43 Oda na sluchaĭ prisi͡agi moskovskikh zhiteleĭ ego imperatorskomu velichestvu Pavlu Pervomu, samoderzht͡su vserossiĭskomu. Ода на случай присяги московских жителей его императорскому величеству Павлу Первому, самодержцу всероссийскому (Table P-PZ43)

3314.O7-.O73 Ostrov Borngol′m (Story). Остров Борнгольм (Table P-PZ43)

3314.O8-.O83 Osvobozhdenie Evropy i slava Aleksandra I (Poem). Освобождение Европы и слава Александра I (Table P-PZ43)

3314.P48-.P483 Pis′ma russkogo puteshestvennika. Письма русского путешественника (Table P-PZ43)

3314.P5-.P53 Pis′mo sel′skogo zhiteli͡a (Essay). Письмо сельского жителя (Table P-PZ43)

3314.P6-.P63 Poslanie k zhenshchinam (Poem). Послание к женщинам (Table P-PZ43)

3314.P7-.P73 Prekrasnai͡a t͡sarevna i schastlivyĭ karla (Tale). Прекрасная царевна и счастливый карла (Table P-PZ43)

3314.P75-.P753 Proteĭ (Poem). Протей (Table P-PZ43)

3314.R4-.R43 Razgovor o schastii. Разговор о счастии (Table P-PZ43)

3314.R9-.R93 Ryt͡sar′ nashego vremeni (Story). Рыцарь нашего времени (Table P-PZ43)

3314.S5-.S53 Sierra Morena (Story). Сиерра Морена (Table P-PZ43)

3314.S6-.S63 Sofii͡a (Unfinished drama). София (Table P-PZ43)

3314.T8-.T83 T͡Svetok na grob moego Agatona (Essay). Цветок на гроб моего Агатона (Table P-PZ43)

Russian literature
Individual authors and works, 18th century
Karamzin, Nikolaĭ Mikhaĭlovich, 1766-1826. Николай Михайлович Карамзин
Separate works -- Continued
Zapiski o drevneĭ i novoĭ Rossii. Записки о древней и новой России see DK71
Biography and criticism
3314.Z5 Autobiographical writings, journals, etc. By date
Letters
3314.Z6A1 Collections. By date
3314.Z6A2A-.A2Z Individual correspondents. By correspondent, A-Z
3314.Z7 General treatises. Life and works
Cf. DK38.7.K35 Russian historians
3314.Z8 Criticism
3314.Z9 Special topics and subjects, A-Z
3314.Z9H57 History
3314.Z9P6 Political and social views
3314.Z9R4 Religion and ethics
Social views see PG3314.Z9P6
3314.Z9S4 Sentimentalism
3315 Individual authors, Karamzin - Lomonosov
3315.K3 Karin, Fedor Grigor′evich, ca. 1740-ca. 1800. Федор Григорьевич Карин (Table P-PZ40)
3315.K4 Khemnit͡ser, Ivan Ivanovich, 1745-1784. Иван Иванович Хемницер (Table P-PZ40 modified)
3315.K4A61-.K4Z458 Separate works. By title
3315.K4B2 Basni i skazki. Басни и сказки
3315.K4B22-.K4B59 Separate fables and tales
Arrange alphabetically by title
3315.K4B27 Dva soseda. Два соседа
3315.K4B34 Koshcheĭ. Кощей
3315.K4B42 Metafizik. Метафизик
3315.K4B55 Skvoret͡s i kukushka. Скворец и кукушка
3315.K4O3 Oda na pobedu pri Zhurzhe. Ода на победу при Журже
3315.K4S3 Satira I (Poem). Сатира I
3315.K4S4 Satira II (Poem). Сатира II
3315.K45 Kheraskov, Mikhail Matveevich, 1733-1807. Михаил Матвеевич Херасков (Table P-PZ40 modified)
3315.K45A61-.K45Z458 Separate works. By title
Anakreonticheskie ody. Анакреонтические оды see PG3315.K45N6
3315.K45B3 Bakharii͡ana, ili, Neizvestnyĭ (Novel in verse). Бахарияна, или, Неизвестный
3315.K45B4 Basni nravouchitel′nye. Басни нравоучительные

Russian literature
Individual authors and works, 18th century
Individual authors, Karamzin - Lomonosov
Kheraskov, Mikhail Matveevich, 1733-1807. Михаил Матвеевич Херасков
Separate works. By title -- Continued

3315.K45B5 Bezbozhnik, iroicheskai͡a komedii͡a. Безбожник, ироическая комедия
3315.K45B6 Borislav (Tragedy). Борислав
3315.K45C4 Chesmenskiĭ boĭ (Poem). Чесменский бой
3315.K45D7 Drug neschastnykh, sleznai͡a drama. Друг несчастных, слезная драма
3315.K45F5 Filosoficheskie ody ili pesni. Философические оды или песни
3315.K45G6 Gonimye, sleznai͡a drama. Гонимые, слезная драма
3315.K45I3 Idolopoklonniki, ili, Gorislava (Tragedy). Идолопоклонники, или, Горислава
3315.K45K3 Kadm i Garmonii͡a (Novel in prose). Кадм и Гармония
3315.K45K5 Khram slavy (Poem). Храм славы
3315.K45M3 Martezii͡a i Falestra (Tragedy). Мартезия и Фалестра
3315.K45N4 Nenavistnik (Comedy). Ненавистник
3315.K45N6 Novye ody. Новые оды
3315.K45N8 Numa, ili, Prot͡svetai͡ushchiĭ Rim (Novel). Нума, или, Процветающий Рим
3315.K45O3 Oda ego imperatorskomu velichestvu, velikomu gosudari͡u Aleksandru Pavlovichu samoderzht͡su vserossiĭskomu, na vseradostnoe ego na prestol vstuplenie. Ода его императорскому величеству, великому государю Александру Павловичу самодержцу всероссийскому, на всерадостное его на престол вступление

Ody nravouchitelʹnye. Оды нравоучительные see PG3315.K45F5

3315.K45O75 Osvobozhdennai͡a Moskva (Tragedy). Освобожденная Москва
3315.K45P5 Piligrimmy, ili, Iskateli schastii͡a (Novel in verse). Пилигриммы, или, Искатели счастия
3315.K45P53 Plamena (Tragedy). Пламена
3315.K45P55 Plody nauk (Poem). Плоды наук
3315.K45P6 Poėt. Поэт
3315.K45P65 Polidor, syn Kadma i Garmonii (Novel). Полидор, сын Кадма и Гармонии
3315.K45R4 Razdelennai͡a Rossii͡a, ili, Zareida i Rostislav (Tragedy). Разделенная Россия, или, Зареида и Ростислав
3315.K45R6 Rossii͡ada (Epic poem). Россияда

Russian literature
Individual authors and works, 18th century
Individual authors, Karamzin - Lomonosov
Kheraskov, Mikhail Matveevich, 1733-1807. Михаил Матвеевич Херасков
Separate works. By title -- Continued

3315.K45S3 Schastlivaia Rossiia, ili, Dvadtsatipiatiletniĭ iubileĭ (Prolog). Счастливая Россия, или, Двадцатипятилетний юбилей
3315.K45S4 Selim i Selima (Poem). Селим и Селима
3315.K45T7 TSar′, ili, Spasennyĭ Novgorod (Novel in verse). Царь, или, Спасенный Новгород
3315.K45U8 Uteshenie greshnykh (Poems). Утешение грешных
3315.K45V4 Venetsianskaia monakhinia (Tragedy). Венецианская монахиня
3315.K45V55 Vladimir vozrozhdennyĭ (Poem). Владимир возрожденный
Zareida i Rostislav. Зареида и Ростислав see PG3315.K45R4
3315.K45Z4 Zolotoĭ prut (Story). Золотой прут
3315.K453 Kheraskova, Elizaveta Vasil′evna (Neronova), 1737-1809. Елизавета Васильевна (Неронова) Хераскова (Table P-PZ40)
3315.K46 Khovanskiĭ, Grigoriĭ Aleksandrovich, kniaz′, 1767-1796. Григорий Александрович Хованский (Table P-PZ40)
3315.K465 Khrapovitskiĭ, Mikhail Vasil′evich, 1758-1819 Михаил Васильевич Храповицкий (Table P-PZ40)
Kirsha Danilov. Кирша Данилов see PG3311.D3
3315.K468 Kliucharev, Fedor Petrovich, 1751-1822. Федор Петрович Ключарев (Table P-PZ40)
3315.K47 Klushin, Aleksandr Ivanovich, 1763-1804. Александр Иванович Клушин (Table P-PZ40 modified)
3315.K47A61-.K47Z458 Separate works. By title
3315.K47K5 Khudo byt′ blizorukimi (Comedy). Худо быть близорукими
3315.K47O3 Oda na pozhalovanie ordena sv. Apostola Andreia, ego siiat. grafu Iv. Pavl. Kutaisovu. Ода на пожалование ордена св. Апостола Андрея, его сият. графу Ив. Павл. Кутаисову
3315.K47S55 Smekh i gore (Comedy). Смех и горе
3315.K47S75 Stikhi na pribytie I. Aleksandra iz Moskvy v Peterburg. Стихи на прибытие И. Александра из Москвы в Петербург
3315.K47U7 Usluzhlivyĭ (Comedy). Услужливый

Russian literature
Individual authors and works, 18th century
Individual authors, Karamzin - Lomonosov
Klushin, Aleksandr Ivanovich, 1763-1804. Александр Иванович Клушин
Separate works. By title -- Continued

3315.K47V4 Verterovy chuvstvovanii͡a, ili, Neschastnyĭ M. (Maslov). Вертеровы чувствования, или Несчастный М. (Маслов)

3315.K5 Kni͡azhnin, I͡Akov Borisovich, 1742-1791. Яков Борисович Княжнин (Table P-PZ40 modified)

3315.K5A61-.K5Z458 Separate works. By title

3315.K5B3 Basni. Басни

3315.K5B31-.K5B39 Separate fables

Arrange alphabetically by title

3315.K5B35 Merkuriĭ i Apollon. Меркурий и Аполлон

3315.K5B36 Morždvereĭ. Мор зверей

3315.K5C4 Chudaki (Comedy). Чудаки

3315.K5D5 Didona (Tragedy). Дидона

3315.K5K4 Khvastun (Comedy). Хвастун

3315.K5N5 Neudachnyĭ primiritel′, ili, Bez obedu domoĭ poedu (Comedy). Неудачный примиритель, или, Без обеду домой поеду

3315.K5O3 Oda na brakosochetanie vel. kni͡azi͡a Pavla Petrovicha s vel. kn. Nataliei͡u Alekseevnoi͡u. Ода на бракосочетание вел. князя Павла Петровича с вел. кн. Наталиею Алексеевною

3315.K5O7 Orfeĭ (Melodrama). Орфей

3315.K5P6 Poslanie (Poems). Послание

3315.K5R6 Rosslav (Tragedy). Росслав

3315.K5S4 Skazki. Сказки

3315.K5S41-.K5S49 Separate tales

Arrange alphabetically by title

3315.K5S46 Popugaĭ. Попугай

3315.K5S48 Sud′i͡a i vor. Судья и вор

3315.K5S49 Volosochesatel′ sochinitel′. Волосочесатель сочинитель

3315.K5S6 Sofonisba (Tragedy). Софонисба

3315.K5T5 Titovo miloserdie (Tragedy). Титово милосердие

3315.K5T7 Traur, ili, Uteshennai͡a vdova (Comedy). Траур, или, Утешенная вдова

3315.K5V3 Vadim Novgorodskiĭ (Tragedy). Вадим Новгородский

3315.K5V5 Vladimir i I͡Aropolk (Tragedy). Владимир и Ярополк

3315.K5V6 Vladisan (Tragedy). Владисан

Kni͡azhnina, Ekaterina Aleksandrovna. Екатерина Александровна Княжнина see PG3319.S4

Russian literature
Individual authors and works, 18th century
Individual authors, Karamzin - Lomonosov -- Continued

3315.K53 Kokoshkin, Ivan Alekseevich, 1765-1835? Иван Алексеевич Кокошкин (Table P-PZ40)

3315.K55 Kolmakov, Alekseĭ Vasil′evich, d. 1804. Алексей Васильевич Колмаков (Table P-PZ40)

3315.K6 Kolychev, Vasiliĭ Petrovich, 1736-1797. Василий Петрович Колычев (Table P-PZ40 modified)

3315.K6A61-.K6Z458 Separate works. By title

3315.K6B5 Bedstvo, proizvedennoe strast′i͡u, ili, Sal′viniĭ i Adel′son (Tragedy). Бедство, произведенное страстью, или, Сальвиний и Адельсон

3315.K6D8 Dvori͡ani͡ushcheĭsi͡a kupet͡s (Comedy). Дворянющейся купец

3315.K6R3 Razvratnost′, ispravli͡aemai͡a blagomysliem (Comedy). Развратность, исправляемая благомыслием

3315.K6T7 Trudy uedineni͡i͡a (Poems). Труды уединения

3315.K64 Komarov, Matveĭ, fl. 1770-1800. Матвей Комаров (Table P-PZ40)

3315.K65 Kondratovich, Kir′i͡ak Andreevich, 1703-ca. 1790. Кирьяк Андреевич Кондратович (Table P-PZ40)

3315.K67 Kop′ev, A. (Aleksi͡eĭ), 1767-1846. Алексѣй Копьевъ (Алексей Копьев) (Table P-PZ40)

3315.K7 Kostrov, Ermil Ivanovich, ca. 1750-1796. Ермил Иванович Костров (Table P-PZ40 modified)

3315.K7A61-.K7Z458 Separate works. By title

3315.K7B6 Blagodarstvennai͡a pesn′ I. Ekaterine II, chitannai͡a v torzh. sobranii M. univ-ta. Благодарственная песнь И. Екатерине II, читанная в торж. собрании М. унив-та

3315.K7O3 Ody. Оды

3315.K7O31-.K7O39 Separate odes

Arrange alphabetically by title

3315.K7O36 Oda na den′ rozhdeni͡i͡a imp. Ekateriny II, 1781. Ода на день рождения Имп. Екатерины II, 1781

3315.K7P6 Poėma Ėl′vir

3315.K7S7 Stikhi na konchinu grafa F.G. Orlova. Стихи на кончину графа Ф.Г. Орлова

3315.K7T3 Taktika Vol′tera. Тактика Вольтера

3315.K75 Kotel′nit͡skiĭ, Aleksandr, fl. 1790-1810. Александр Котельницкий (Table P-PZ40 modified)

3315.K75A61-.K75Z458 Separate works. By title

Russian literature
Individual authors and works, 18th century
Individual authors, Karamzin - Lomonosov
Kotel′nit͡skiĭ, Aleksandr, fl. 1790-1810. Александр Котельницкий
Separate works. By title. By title -- Continued

3315.K75E5 Ėneida (Parody). Энеида
Books 5 and 6 only
Collaborated with Nikolaĭ Petrovich Osipov PG3317.O7E5

Pokhishchenie Prozerpiny. Похищение Прозерпины see PG3315.L6P6

3315.K75P65 Pokhval′nai͡a pesn′ Imp. Pavlu I. Похвальная песнь Имп. Павлу I.

3315.K75S8 Stikhi gr. N.P. Sheremetevu. Стихи гр. Н.П. Шереметеву

3315.K8 Kozel′skiĭ, Fedor I͡Akovlevich, b. 1734. Федор Яковлевич Козельский (Table P-PZ40)

3315.K83 Kozel′skiĭ, I͡Akov Pavlovich, b. 1735. Яков Павлович Козельский (Table P-PZ40)

Kozodavlev, Osip Petrovich. Осип Петрович Козодавлев see PG3337.K658

3315.K9 Kurganov, Nikolaĭ Gavrilovich, 1725 or 6-1796. Николай Гаврилович Курганов (Table P-PZ40)

3315.L4 Leont′ev, Nikolaĭ Vasil′evich, d. 1824. Николай Васильевич Леонтьев (Table P-PZ40)

3315.L5 Lifanov, Evgraf, fl. 1790-1800. Евграф Лифанов (Table P-PZ40)

3315.L6 Li͡ut͡senko, Efim Petrovich, 1776-1854. Ефим Петрович Люценко (Table P-PZ40 modified)

3315.L6A61-.L6Z458 Separate works. By title

3315.L6P6 Pokhishchenie Prozerpiny (Poem). Похищение Прозерпины
Aleksandr Kotel′nit͡skiĭ, joint author

3316 Lomonosov, Mikhail Vasil′evich, 1711-1765. Михаил Васильевич Ломоносов

3316.A1 Collected works. By date

3316.A15 Selected works. By date

3316.A17 Collected poems. By date

3316.A2-.A59 Translations (Collected or selected). By language, alphabetically

3316.A6 Selections. By date

3316.A7-.Z4 Separate works
For scientific writings on physics, chemistry, physical geography, etc., see QC, QD, GB, etc.
For technical writings on metallurgy, glass manufacture, etc., see TN, TP, etc.

Russian literature
Individual authors and works, 18th century
Lomonosov, Mikhail Vasil′evich, 1711-1765. Михаил Васильевич Ломоносов
Separate works -- Continued
3316.D4-.D43 Demofont (Tragedy). Демофонт (Table P-PZ43)
Ody. Оды
3316.O3 Collected. By date
Spiritual, panegyrical, etc.
Cf. PG3316.P7+ Psalmy
Odes to Elizabeth, Empress of Russia
Cf. DK161 Works on life and reign of Elizabeth
3316.O36 Collected
3316.O38 Separate odes
Arrange by date
Separate odes
Other than those in PG3316.O38 or PG3316.P8
3316.O4F4 Oda Fenelona. Ода Фенелона
3316.O4N7 Oda na vosshestvie na prestol Imperatora Petra III. Ода на восшествие на престол Императора Петра III
3316.O4N8 Oda na vosshestvie na prestol Imperatrit͡sy Ekateriny II. Ода на восшествие на престол Императрицы Екатерины II
3316.O4N9 Oda na vzi͡atie Khotina. Ода на взятие Хотина
3316.O4V9 Oda, vybranna͡ia iz Iova. Ода, выбранная из Иова
3316.P4-.P43 Petr Velikiĭ, geroichesk͡aia poėma. Петр Великий, героическая поэма (Table P-PZ43)
3316.P5-.P53 Pis′mo o pol′ze stekla (Poem). Письмо о пользе стекла (Table P-PZ43)
3316.P6-.P63 Polidor (Idyl). Полидор (Table P-PZ43)
Psalmy. Псалмы
Paraphrased psalms
3316.P7 Collected. By date
3316.P8-.P89 Separate psalms
Arrange by number of psalm
Rossiĭsk͡aia grammatika. Российская грамматика see PG2103
3316.T3-.T33 Tamira i Selim (Tragedy). Тамира и Селим (Table P-PZ43)
Biography and criticism
3316.Z5 Letters
3316.Z6 General treatises. Life and works
3316.Z7 Criticism
3317 Individual authors, Lomonosov - Sumarokov
3317.L6 Lopukhin, Ivan Vladimirovich, 1756-1816. Иван Владимирович Лопухин (Table P-PZ40 modified)

Russian literature
Individual authors and works, 18th century
Individual authors, Lomonosov - Sumarokov
Lopukhin, Ivan Vladimirovich, 1756-1816. Иван Владимирович Лопухин -- Continued

3317.L6A61-.L6Z458 Separate works. By title
3317.L6P6 Podrazhanie nekotorym pesni͡am Davidovym (in verse). Подражание некоторым песням Давидовым
3317.L6T6 Torzhestvo pravosudii͡a i dobrodeteli, ili, Dobryĭ sud'i͡a (Drama). Торжество правосудия и добродетели, или, Добрый судья
3317.L7 Lukin, Vladimir Ignat'evich, 1737-1794. Владимир Игнатьевич Лукин (Table P-PZ40)
3317.L75 L'vov, Nikolaĭ Aleksandrovich, 1751-1803. Николай Александрович Львов (Table P-PZ40)
3317.L8 L'vov, Pavel I͡Ur'evich, 1770-1825. Павел Юрьевич Львов (Table P-PZ40 modified)
3317.L8A61-.L8Z458 Separate works. By title
3317.L8A64 Aleksandr i I͡Ulii͡a, istinnai͡a povest'. Александр и Юлия, истинная повесть
3317.L8R6 Rossiĭskai͡a Pamela, ili, Istorii͡a Marii, dobrodetel'noĭ poseli͡anki (Novel). Российская Памела, или, История Марии, добродетельной поселянки
3317.L8R7 Roza i Li͡ubim, sel'skai͡a povest'. Роза и Любим, сельская повесть
3317.M3 Maĭkov, Vasiliĭ Ivanovich, 1728-1778. Василий Иванович Майков (Table P-PZ40 modified)
3317.M3A61-.M3Z458 Separate works. By title
3317.M3A75 Agriopa (Tragedy). Агриопа
3317.M3A8 Arkas (Eclogue). Аркас
3317.M3D4 Derevenskiĭ prazdnik, ili, Uvenchannai͡a dobrodetel' (Pastoral drama). Деревенский праздник, или, Увенчанная добродетель
3317.M3E5 Eliseĭ, ili, Razdrazhennyĭ Vakkh (Poem). Елисей, или, Раздраженный Вакх
3317.M3F4 Femist i Ieronima (Tragedy). Фемист и Иеронима
3317.M3I5 Igrok Lombera (Poem). Игрок Ломбера
Meropa (Tragedy). Меропа see PQ2077.M5+
3317.M3N7 Nravouchitel'nye basni. Нравоучительные басни
Ody. Оды
3317.M3O3 Collected. By date
Odes to Catherine II, Empress of Russia
3317.M3O32 Collected. By date
3317.M3O33 Separate. By date

Russian literature
Individual authors and works, 18th century
Individual authors, Lomonosov - Sumarokov
Maĭkov, Vasiliĭ Ivanovich, 1728-1778. Василий Иванович Майков
Separate works. By title
Ody. Оды -- Continued

3317.M3O34-.M3O49 Separate odes
Arrange alphabetically by title
Other than those in PG3317.M3O33

3317.M3O4 Oda o suete mira, pisannai͡a k Aleksandru Petrovichu Sumarokovu. Ода о суете мира, писанная к Александру Петровичу Сумарокову

3317.M3O7 Osvobozhdennai͡a Moskva (Poem). Освобожденная Москва

Pigmalion; ili, Sila li͡ubvi (Drama). Пигмалион, или, Сила любви see PQ2040.P9

Prevrashchenii͡a, pervye chetyre knigi. Превращения, первые четыре книги see PA6528.A+

3317.M3P8 Psalmy. Псалмы
Paraphrased psalms

3317.M3S8 Sud Paridov (Song). Суд Паридов

3317.M3T6 Torzhestvui͡ushchiĭ Parnass (Prolog). Торжествующий Парнасс

3317.M3V6 Voennai͡a nauka (Poem). Военная наука

Makentin, Khariton. Харитон Макентин see PG3313.K3

3317.M34 Maksimovich-Ambodik, Nestor, 1744-1812. Нестор Максимович-Амбодик (Table P-PZ40)

3317.M4 Matinskiĭ, Mikhail, 1750-1820. Михаил Матинский (Table P-PZ40)

3317.M45 Matveev, Filiter, fl. 1790-1800. Филитер Матвеев (Table P-PZ40 modified)

3317.M45A61-.M45Z458 Separate works. By title

3317.M45D6 Dobrodetel′nai͡a prestupnit͡sa, ili, Prestupnik ot li͡ubvi (Drama). Добродетельная преступница, или, Преступник от любви

3317.M45E8 Evgenii͡a Mikhaĭlovna (Tale). Евгения Михайловна

Melet͡skiĭ, I͡Uriĭ Aleksandrovich Neledinskiĭ see PG3317.N4

3317.M5 Men′shikova, Ekaterina Alekseevna (Dolgorukova) kni͡aginia, 1747-1791. Екатерина Алексеевна (Долгорукова) Меньшикова (Table P-PZ40)

Russian literature
Individual authors and works, 18th century
Individual authors, Lomonosov - Sumarokov -- Continued

3317.M65 Moskvina, Elizaveta Osipovna. Елизавета Осиповна Москвина (Table P-PZ40)
Pseudonym: Gzh*** (Гж***)

3317.M66 Moskvina, Mariīa Osipovna. Мария Осиповна Москвина (Table P-PZ40)
Pseudonym: Gzh*** (Гж***)

3317.M8 Murav′ev, Mikhail Nikitich, 1757-1807. Михаил Никитич Муравьев (Table P-PZ40 modified)

3317.M8A61-.M8Z458 Separate works. By title

3317.M8B3 Basni (in verse). Басни

3317.M8E5 Ėmilievy pis′ma. Эмилиевы письма
Continuation of Obitatel′ predmestīa, PG3317.M8O2

3317.M8O2 Obitatel′ predmestīa. Обитатель предместья
Continued by Ėmilievy pis′ma PG3317.M8E5

Ody. Оды

3317.M8O3 Collected

3317.M8O32-.M8O39 Separate odes
Arrange alphabetically

3317.M8P5 Pis′ma k molodomu cheloveku. Письма к молодому

3317.M8P6 Povest′ Oskol′d. Повесть Оскольд

3317.M8R3 Razgovor mertvykh. Разговор мертвых

3317.M8V6 Voennaīa pesn′. Военная песнь

3317.M9 Murzina, Aleksandra Petrovna, fl. 1790-1800. Александра Петровна Мурзина (Table P-PZ40)

3317.N2 Naryshkin, Semen Vasil′evich, 1731?-1807. Семен Васильевич Нарышкин (Table P-PZ40)

3317.N3 Natal′īa Alekseevna, Grand Duchess of Russia, 1673-1716. Наталья Алексеевна (Table P-PZ40)

3317.N4 Neledinskii-Meletskiĭ, Īuriĭ Aleksandrovich, 1752-1828. Юрий Александрович Нелединский-Мелецкий (Table P-PZ40)

Neronova, Elizaveta Vasil′evna. Елизавета Васильевна Неронова see PG3315.K453

3317.N5 Nikolev, Nikolaĭ Petrovich, 1758-1815. Николай Петрович Николев (Table P-PZ40 modified)

3317.N5A61-.N5Z458 Separate works. By title

3317.N5B3 Basni. Басни

Feniks (Opera). Феникс see ML50.2

3317.N5I7 Ispytannoe postoīanstvo (Comedy). Испытанное постоянство

3317.N5M6 Molitvy (Prayers in verse). Молитвы

3317.N5O3-.O59 Ody. Оды

3317.N5O3 Collected

Russian literature
Individual authors and works, 18th century
Individual authors, Lomonosov - Sumarokov
Nikolev, Nikolai Petrovich, 1758-1815. Николай Петрович Николев
Separate works. By title
Ody. Оды
Collected -- Continued
3317.N5O33 Psalmy. Псалмы
Paraphrased psalms
Odes to Catherine II, Empress of Russia
3317.N5O35 Collected
3317.N5O36 Separate odes
Arrange by date
3317.N5O4-.N5O59 Separate odes
Arrange alphabetically
Except those classified in PG3317.N5O36
3317.N5P3 Pal′mira (Tragedy). Пальмира
3317.N5P6 Popytka ne shutka, ili, Udachnyĭ opyt (Comedy). Попытка не шутка, или, Удачный опыт
3317.N5P65 Poslanie (Poems). Послание
3317.N5P7 Prikashchik (One-act play). Прикащик
Psalmy. Псалмы see PG3317.N5O33
3317.N5R6 Rozana i Li͡ubim (Drama). Розана и Любим
3317.N5S3 Samoli͡ubivyĭ stikhotvoret͡s (Comedy). Самолюбивый стихотворец
3317.N5S4 Satiry (Poems). Сатиры
3317.N5S6 Sorena i Zamir (Tragedy). Сорена и Замир
3317.N5Z4 Zloumnyĭ (Comedy). Злоумный
3317.N6 Novikov, Nikolaĭ Ivanovich, 1774-1818. Николай Иванович Новиков (Table P-PZ40)
3317.O7 Osipov, Nikolaĭ Petrovich, 1751-1799. Николай Петрович Осипов (Table P-PZ40 modified)
3317.O7A61-.O7Z458 Separate works. By title
3317.O7E5 Ėneida (Parody). Энеида
Cf. PG3315.K75E5 Collaborator: Aleksandr Kotel′nit͡skiĭ
3317.P3 Perepechin, Aleksandr Ivanovich, fl. 1760-1800. Александр Иванович Перепечин (Table P-PZ40)
3317.P35 Peter I, Emperor of Russia, 1672-1725. Петр I Алексеевич (Петр Великий) (Table P-PZ40)
Prefer DK for life, letters, journals, etc.
3317.P39 Petrov, Aleksandr Andreevich, d. 1793. Александр Андреевич Петров (Table P-PZ40)
3317.P4 Petrov, Vasiliĭ Petrovich, 1736-1799. Василий Петрович Петров (Table P-PZ40 modified)
3317.P4A61-.P4Z458 Separate works. By title

Russian literature
Individual authors and works, 18th century
Individual authors, Lomonosov - Sumarokov
Petrov, Vasilii Petrovich, 1736-1799. Василий Петрович Петров
Separate works. By title

3317.P4N5 Na novye uchrezhdenii͡a dli͡a upravlenii͡a guberniĭ, satira na shvedskogo koroli͡a Gustava III, 1788. На новые учреждения для управления губерний, сатира на шведского короля Густава III, 1788

3317.P4N8 Na torzhestvo mira 1793 goda. На торжество мира 1793 года

3317.P4O3 Oda Ekaterine II, samoderzhit͡se vserossiĭskoĭ na prisoedinenie Pol′skikh oblasteĭ k Rossii, 1793 goda. Ода Екатерине II, самодержице всероссийской на присоединение Польских областей к России, 1793 года

3317.P4P4 Pis′mo Imperatrit͡se Ekaterine II (in verse). Письмо Императрице Екатерине II

3317.P4P5 Plach i uteshenie Rossii, k Imperatoru Pavlu Pervomu (in verse). Плач и утешение России, к Императору Павлу Первому

3317.P4P7 Prikli͡uchenii͡a Gustava III, koroli͡a shvedskogo, 1788 goda. Приключения Густава III, короля шведского, 1788 года

3317.P5 Plavil′shchikov, Petr Alekseevich, 1760-1812. Петр Алексеевич Плавильщиков (Table P-PZ40 modified)

3317.P5A61-.P5Z458 Separate works. By title

3317.P5B3 Barskiĭ prostupok (Drama). Барский проступок

3317.P5B6 Bobyl′ (Comedy). Бобыль

3317.P5B7 Brat′i͡a Svoeladovy, ili, Neudacha luchshe udachi (Comedy). Братья Своеладовы, или, Неудача лучше удачи

3317.P5C5 Chistoserdechie (Comedy). Чистосердечие

3317.P5D7 Druzhestvo (Tragedy). Дружество

3317.P5E7 Ermak, pokoritel′ Sibiri (Tragedy). Ермак, покоритель Сибири

3317.P5G7 Graf Val′tron, ili, Voinskai͡a podchinennost′ (Drama). Граф Вальтрон, или, Воинская подчиненность

3317.P5L4 Lensa, ili, Dikie v Amerike (Drama). Ленса, или, Дикие в Америке

3317.P5M4 Mel′nik i sbitenshchik--soperniki (Comedy). Мельник и сбитенщик--соперники

3317.P5P3 Parik (Comedy). Парик

3317.P5R5 Ri͡urik (Tragedy). Рюрик

Russian literature
Individual authors and works, 18th century
Individual authors, Lomonosov - Sumarokov
Plavil′shchikov, Petr Alekseevich, 1760-1812. Петр Алексеевич Плавильщиков
Separate works. By title -- Continued

3317.P5S4 Sgovor Kuteĭkina (Comedy). Сговор Кутейкина
3317.P5S45 Sibiri͡ak (Comedy). Сибиряк
3317.P5S5 Sidelet͡s (Comedy). Сиделец
3317.P5T3 Takhmas-Kulykhan (Tragedy). Тахмас-Кулыхан
3317.P54 Podshivalov, Vasiliĭ Sergeevich, 1765-1813. Василий Сергеевич Подшивалов (Table P-PZ40)
3317.P6 Popov, Anton Ivanovich, 1748-1788. Антон Иванович Попов (Table P-PZ40)
3317.P63 Popov, Ivan Vasil′evich, fl. 1790-1810. Иван Васильевич Попов (Table P-PZ40)
3317.P66 Popov, Mikhail Vasil′evich, d. ca. 1790. Михаил Васильевич Попов (Table P-PZ40)
3317.P67 Popov, Petr, fl. 1760-1770. Петр Попов (Table P-PZ40)
3317.P68 Popovskiĭ, Nikolaĭ Nikitich, 1730?-1760. Николай Никитич Поповский (Table P-PZ40)
3317.P69 Poroshin, Semen Andreevich, 1741-1769. Семен Андреевич Порошин (Table P-PZ40)
3317.P7 Pososhkov, Ivan Tikhonovich, 1652?-1726. Иван Тихонович Посошков (Table P-PZ40)
Prefer H for his writings on economic subjects.
3317.P73 Pospelova, Marii͡a Alekseevna, 1780-1805. Мария Алексеевна Поспелова (Table P-PZ40)
3317.P75 Potemkin, Pavel Sergeevich, graf, 1743-1796. Павел Сергеевич Потемкин (Table P-PZ40)
Prokopovich, Eleazar. Элеазар Прокопович see PG3313.F4
Prokopovich, Feofan. Феофан Прокопович see PG3313.F4
3317.P85 Prokudin-Gorskiĭ, Mikhail Ivanovich, 18th cent. Михаил Иванович Прокудин-Горский (Table P-PZ40)
3317.P88 Protopopov, Vasiliĭ Mikhaĭlovich, d. 1810. Василий Михайлович Протопопов (Table P-PZ40)
3317.R3 Radishchev, Aleksandr Nikolaevich, 1749-1802. Александр Николаевич Радищев (Table P-PZ40 modified)
3317.R3A61-.R3Z458 Separate works. By title
3317.R3B6 Bova, povest′ bogatyrskai͡a (Poem). Бова, повесть богатырская
3317.R3O3 O cheloveke, o ego smertnosti i bezsmertii. О человеке, о его смертности и безсмертии
3317.R3P5 Pesn′ istoricheskai͡a. Песнь историческая

Russian literature
Individual authors and works, 18th century
Individual authors, Lomonosov - Sumarokov
Radishchev, Aleksandr Nikolaevich, 1749-1802. Александр Николаевич Радищев
Separate works. By title -- Continued
Puteshestvie iz Peterburga v Moskvu. Путешествие из Петербурга в Москву
see HN525

3317.R3V6 Vol′nost′, oda. Вольность, ода

3317.R8 Ruban, Vasiliĭ Grigor′evich, 1742-1795. Василий Григорьевич Рубан (Table P-PZ40)

3317.R9 Rzhevskai͡a, Aleksandra Fedotovna (Kamenskai͡a), 1740-1769. Александра Федотовна (Каменская) Ржевская (Table P-PZ40)

3317.R92 Rzhevskiĭ, Alekseĭ Andreevich, 1737-1804. Алексей Андреевич Ржевский (Table P-PZ40)

3317.S3 Sankovskiĭ, Vasiliĭ Demʹi͡anovich, b. 1741. Василий Демьянович Санковский (Table P-PZ40)

3317.S4 Shcherbatov, Mikhail Mikhaĭlovich, kni͡az′, 1733-1790. Михаил Михайлович Щербатов (Table P-PZ40)
Prefer DK for his history of Russia

3317.S5 Sheremetev, Boris Petrovich, graf, 1652-1719. Борис Петрович Шереметев (Table P-PZ40)
For books of travel and military history, see D

Sheremeteva, Natalʹi͡a Borisovna. Наталья Борисовна Шереметева see PG3313.D6

3317.S56 Skovoroda, Hryhoriĭ Savych, 1722-1794. Григорий Саввич Сковорода (Григорій Савич Сковорода) (Table P-PZ40)
For general biography and criticism see B4218.S47+
For Skovoroda's Ukrainian literary works see PG3948.S532

3317.S67 Strakhov, Nikolaĭ Ivanovich, fl. 1780-1810. Николай Иванович Страхов (Table P-PZ40)

3317.S7 Struĭskiĭ, Nikolaĭ Eremeevich, d. 1796. Николай Еремеевич Струйский (Table P-PZ40)

3317.S8 Sudovshchikov, Nikolaĭ Rodionovich, 18th-19th cent. Николай Родионович Судовщиков (Table P-PZ40 modified)

3317.S8A61-.S8Z458 Separate works. By title

3317.S8N4 Ne znaesh′, ne revnuĭ, a znaesh′, tak molchat′ (Comedy). Не знаешь, не ревнуй, а знаешь, так молчать

3317.S8N5 Neslykhannoe divo, ili, Chestnyĭ sekretar′ (Comedy). Неслыханное диво, или, Честный секретарь

3317.S8O6 Opyt iskusstva (Comedy). Опыт искусства

Russian literature
Individual authors and works, 18th century -- Continued

3318 Sumarokov, Aleksandr Petrovich, 1718-1777. Александр Петрович Сумароков
3318.A1 Collected works. By date
3318.A17 Collected poems. By date
3318.A19 Collected plays. By date
3318.A2-.A59 Translations (Collected or selected). By language, alphabetically
3318.A6 Selections. By date
3318.A7-.Z4 Separate works
Alʹt͡sesta (Opera). Альцеста see ML50.2
3318.A8-.A83 Artistona (Tragedy). Артистона (Table P-PZ43)
3318.C5-.C53 Chudovishchi (Comedy). Чудовищи (Table P-PZ43)
3318.D5-.D53 Dimitriĭ Samozvanet͡s (Tragedy). Димитрий Самозванец (Table P-PZ43)
3318.E35-.E353 Ėklogi. Эклоги (Table P-PZ43)
3318.E4-.E43 Ėlegii. Элегии (Table P-PZ43)
3318.E5-.E53 Ėpigrammy. Эпиграммы (Table P-PZ43)
3318.E6-.E63 Ėpistoly (in verse). Эпистолы (Table P-PZ43)
3318.E7-.E73 Ėpitafii. Эпитафии (Table P-PZ43)
3318.G3-.G33 Gamlet (Tragedy). Гамлет (Table P-PZ43)
3318.I2-.I23 I͡Adovityĭ (Comedy). Ядовитый (Table P-PZ43)
3318.I25-.I253 I͡Aropolk i Dimiza (Tragedy). Ярополк и Димиза (Table P-PZ43)
3318.I3-.I33 Idillii. Идиллии (Table P-PZ43)
3318.K4-.K43 Khorev (Tragedy). Хорев (Table P-PZ43)
3318.K5-.K53 Khory. Хоры (Table P-PZ43)
3318.L5-.L53 Likhoimet͡s (Comedy). Лихоимец (Table P-PZ43)
3318.L55-.L553 Li͡ubovnye gadatelʹnye knizhki (Drama). Любовные гадательные книжки (Table P-PZ43)
3318.M3-.M33 Madrigaly. Мадригалы (Table P-PZ43)
3318.M35-.M353 Matʹ sovmestnit͡sa docheri (Comedy). Мать совместница дочери (Table P-PZ43)
3318.M6-.M63 Mnenie vo snovidenii o frant͡suzskikh tragedii͡akh. Мнение во сновидении о французских трагедиях (Table P-PZ43)
3318.M8-.M83 Mstislav (Tragedy). Мстислав (Table P-PZ43)
3318.N3-33318.N33 Nart͡siss (Comedy). Нарцисс (Table P-PZ43)
3318.N6-.N63 Novye lavry (Prolog). Новые лавры (Table P-PZ43)
3318.O3-.O33 Ody. Оды (Table P-PZ43)
3318.O6-.O63 Opekun (Comedy). Опекун (Table P-PZ43)
3318.P4-.P43 Pesni. Песни (Table P-PZ43)
3318.P6-.P63 Pribezhishche dobrodeteli (Ballet). Прибежище добродетели (Table P-PZ43)
3318.P65-.P653 Pridanoe obmanom (Comedy). Приданое обманом (Table P-PZ43)

Russian literature
Individual authors and works, 18th century
Sumarokov, Aleksandr Petrovich, 1718-1777. Александр Петрович Сумароков
Separate works -- Continued

3318.P7-.P73	Pritchi. Притчи (Table P-PZ43)
3318.P75-.P753	Psalmy. Псалмы (Table P-PZ43)
3318.P8-.P83	Pustai͡a ssora (Comedy). Пустая ссора (Table P-PZ43)
3318.P85-.P853	Pustynnik (Drama). Пустынник (Table P-PZ43)
3318.R6-.R63	Rogonoset͡s po voobrazhenii͡u (Comedy). Рогоносец по воображению (Table P-PZ43)
3318.S3-.S33	Satiry. Сатиры (Table P-PZ43)
3318.S4-.S43	Semira (Tragedy). Семира (Table P-PZ43)
3318.S5-.S53	Sinav i Truvor (Tragedy). Синав и Трувор (Table P-PZ43)
3318.S6-.S63	Sonety. Сонеты (Table P-PZ43)
3318.S7-.S73	Stansy. Стансы (Table P-PZ43)
3318.T6-.T63	Tresotinius (Comedy). Тресотиниус (Table P-PZ43)
3318.T7-.T73	Tri brata sovmestniki (Comedy). Три брата совместники (Table P-PZ43)
3318.V8-.V83	Vysheslav (Tragedy). Вышеслав (Table P-PZ43)
3318.V9-.V93	Vzdorshchit͡sa (Comedy). Вздорщица (Table P-PZ43)
3318.Z3-.Z33	Zagadki. Загадки (Table P-PZ43)
	Biography and criticism
	Letters
3318.Z6	Collected. By date
3318.Z7	Individual correspondents, A-Z
3318.Z8	General treatises. Life and works
3318.Z9	Criticism
3319	Individual authors, Sumarokov - Z
	Sumarokov, Pankratiĭ Platonovich. Панкратий Платонович Сумароков see PG3361.S82
3319.S4	Sumarokova, Ekaterina Aleksandrovna, 18th cent. Екатерина Александровна Сумарокова (Table P-PZ40)
3319.S5	Sushkov, Mikhail Vasil′evich, 1705-ca. 1792. Михаил Васильевич Сушков (Table P-PZ40)
3319.T5	Tin′kov, Aleksandr, 18th cent. Александр Тиньков (Table P-PZ40)
3319.T55	Titov, Nikolaĭ Sergeevich, d. 1776. Николай Сергеевич Титов (Table P-PZ40)
3319.T7	Tred′i͡akovskiĭ, Vasiliĭ Kirillovich, 1703-1769. Василий Кириллович Тредьяковский (Table P-PZ40 modified)
3319.T7A61-.T7Z458	Separate works. By title For Tred′i͡akovskiĭ's translations of other authors see the author in PA-PQ

Russian literature
Individual authors and works, 18th century
Individual authors, Sumarokov - Z
Tred'īakovskiĭ, Vasiliĭ Kirillovich, 1703-1769. Василий Кириллович Тредьяковский
Separate works. By title -- Continued

3319.T7D4 Deidamīa (Tragedy). Деидамия

3319.T7E5 Ėlegīa o smerti Petra Velikogo. Элегия о смерти Петра Великого

(3319.T7E9) Ėzopovy basni. Эзоповы басни
see PA3855

3319.T7I3 Īazon (Drama). Язон

Ody. Оды
Collected odes

3319.T7O3 General. By date

3319.T7O33 Ody bozhestvennye. Оды божественные
Including paraphrases of psalms, Isaiah's prophecies, etc.

3319.T7O34 Ody pokhval'nye. Оды похвальные

3319.T7O35-.T7O49 Separate odes
Alphabetically, by title, e.g.

3319.T7O48 Veshnee teplo. Вешнее тепло

Psalmy. Псалмы see PG3319.T7O33

3319.T7T48 Tilemakhida. Тилемахида

3319.T7T5 Tit, Vespasianov syn (Drama). Тит, Веспасианов сын

3319.U7 Urusova, Ekaterina Sergeevna knīazhna, b. 1747. Екатерина Сергеевна Урусова (Table P-PZ40)

V.K. В.К. see PG3315.K6

Van'ka Kain. Ванька Каин see PG3313.K2

Vasiliĭ Barskiĭ (Grigorovich-Barskiĭ). Василий Барский (Григорович-Барский) see PG3313.G7

Vasiliĭ Kievskiĭ. Василий Киевский see PG3313.G7

3319.V4 Verevkin, Mikhail Ivanovich, 1732-1795. Михаил Иванович Веревкин (Table P-PZ40 modified)

3319.V4A61-.V4Z458 Separate works. By title

3319.V4A8 Astreīa (Comedy). Астрея
Not preserved

3319.V4I5 Imeninniki (Comedy). Именинники

3319.V4N3 Na nasheĭ ulitse prazdnik (Comedy). На нашей улице праздник
Not preserved

3319.V4T3 Tak i dolzhno (Comedy). Так и должно

3319.V4T6 Toch' v toch' (Comedy). Точь в точь

3319.V5 Vinogradov, Ivan Ivanovich, d. 1801? Иван Иванович Виноградов (Table P-PZ40)

Vizin, Denis Ivanovich von see PG3313.F6

Russian literature
Individual authors and works, 18th century
Individual authors, Sumarokov - Z -- Continued
Von Vizin, Denis Ivanovich see PG3313.F6
3319.Z5 Zhukova, Anna Sergeevna (Buturlina), d. 1799. Анна Сергеевна (Бутурлина) Жукова (Table P-PZ40)
3319.Z6 Zolotnit͡skiĭ, Vladimir Trofimovich, b. 1741. Владимир Трофимович Золотницкий (Table P-PZ40)
Individual authors and works, 1800-1870
Subarrange each author by Table P-PZ40 unless otherwise specified
3320 Anonymous works (Table P-PZ28 modified)
3320.A1A-.A1Z Works without any indication of author, either by symbol or initial. By title, A-Z
3320.A1A33 Adelʹ. Адель
3320.A1A53 Angliĭskiĭ tabor. Английский табор
3320.A1D85 Dvadt͡satʹ tysi͡ach pridanogo. Двадцать тысяч приданого
3320.A1D87 Dvori͡anskie vybory. Дворянские выборы
3320.A1G67 Grafini͡a Roslavleva. Графиня Рославлева
3320.A1K27 Kak li͡ubi͡at zhenshchiny? Как любят женщины?
3320.A1K28 Kak vyigryvai͡ut dvesti tysi͡ach! Как выигрываяут двести тысяч!
3320.A1K65 Kondrashka Bulavin, buntovshchik, byvshiĭ v t͡sarstvovanii Imperatora Petra I. Кондрашка Булавин, бунтовщик, бывший в царствовании Императора Петра I
3320.A1K8 Kupecheskiĭ synok. Купеческий сынок
3320.A1M57 Mirskai͡a skhodka. Мирская сходка
3320.A1P47 Pevet͡s sredi russkikh voĭnov vozvrativshikhsi͡a v otechestvo v 1816m godu. Певец среди русских войнов возвратившихся в отечество в 1816м году
3320.A1P54 Pi͡esnʹ o prepodobnom Aleksi͡ie, chelovi͡eki͡e Bozhīem. Пѣснь о преподобномъ Алексіѣ, человѣкѣ Божіемъ
3320.A1P87 Puteshestvīe v Troit͡skui͡u Sergievu lavru. Путешествіе в Троицкую Сергиеву лавру
3320.A1R47 Retirada bolʹshoĭ frant͡suzskoĭ armii. Ретирада большой французской армии
3320.A1S43 Shumskiĭ. Шумский
3320.A1S46 Shutka. Шутка
3320.A1S83 Svekrovʹ i teshcha. Свекровь и теща
3320.A1S9 Syn aktrisy. Сын актрисы
3320.A1T67 Torzhestvennai͡a poėma Kievli͡anina. Торжественная поэма Киевлянина
3320.A1T7 Tri povesti. Три повести

Russian literature
Individual authors and works, 1800-1870
Anonymous works
Works without any indication of author, either by symbol or initial. By title, A-Z -- Continued

3320.A1U3 Uchitel′skai͡a vnuchka, ili, Pochemu̇ znat′, chego ne znaesh′? Учительская внучка, или, Почему знать, чего не знаешь?

3320.A1V19 V sem′e ne bez uroda. В семье не без урода

3320.A1Z34 Zapiski moskvicha. Записки москвича

3320.A1Z38 Zaverbovannyĭ gusar, ili, Nagrada synovneĭ li͡ubvi. Завербованный гусар, или, Награда сыновней любви

3321 Individual authors, A - Dostoyevsky

Adamantov, В. Б. Адамантов see PG3321.A63

3321.A3 Afanas′ev-Chuzhbinskiĭ, Aleksandr Stepanovich, 1817-1875. Александр Степанович Афанасьев-Чужбинский (Table P-PZ40 modified)

3321.A3A61-.A3Z458 Separate works. By title

3321.A3B3 Babushka. Бабушка

3321.A3B8 Burbon. Бурбон

3321.A3C5 Chinovnik. Чиновник

3321.A3D6 Dominikant͡sy. Доминиканцы

3321.A3D8 Duėlisty. Дуэлисты

3321.A3F3 Fani͡a. Фаня

3321.A3G6 Gorod Smurov. Город Смуров

3321.A3I85 Iz kornetskoĭ zhizni. Из корнетской жизни

3321.A3I9 Iz vospominaniĭ okhotnika. Из воспоминаний охотника

3321.A3K6 Konokrady. Конокрады

3321.A3M3 Maskaradnyĭ sirota. Маскарадный сирота

3321.A3M4 Mel′nit͡sa bliz′ sela Voroshilova. Мельница близь села Ворошилова

3321.A3M6 Monshery. Моншеры

Ocherki proshlogo. Очерки прошлого

3321.A3O2 Collected and selected. By date

Separate sketches, by title see PG3321.A3A61+

3321.A3O3 Odin iz mnogikh. Один из многих

3321.A3P4 Peterburgskie igroki (Novel). Петербургские игроки

3321.A3P5 Plastuny. Пластуны

(3321.A3P6) Poezdka v i͡uzhnui͡u Rossii͡u. Поездка в южную Россию
see DK509

3321.A3P65 Praporshchik Saf′i͡anchikov. Прапорщик Сафьянчиков

Provint͡sial′nye ocherki. Провинциальные очерки

3321.A3P7 Collected and selected. By date

Russian literature
Individual authors and works, 1800-1870
Individual authors, A - Dostoyevsky
Afanas′ev-Chuzhbinskiĭ, Aleksandr Stepanovich, 1817-1875. Александр Степанович Афанасьев-Чужбинский
Separate works. By title
Provint͡sial′nye ocherki. Провинциальные очерки -- Continued
Separate sketches, by title see PG3321.A3A61+

3321.A3P75 Provint͡sial′nyĭ lev. Провинциальный лев
3321.A3P9 Pylkai͡a natura. Пылкая натура
3321.A3R4 Remontery prezhnego vremeni. Ремонтеры прежнего времени
3321.A3R8 Russkiĭ soldat (Story in verse). Русский солдат
3321.A3R9 Ryt͡sari zelenogo poli͡a. Рыцари зеленого поля
3321.A3S3 Samodury. Самодуры
3321.A3S5 Shkola svetskikh prilichiĭ. Школа светских приличий
3321.A3S6 Sosedka. Соседка
3321.A3S8 Stoi͡anka v Dymogare (Don-Zhuan). Стоянка в Дымогаре (Дон-Жуан)
3321.A3V2 V sadu. В саду
3321.A3Z3 Zabytai͡a istorii͡a. Забытая история
3321.A33 Agafi, Aleksandr Dmitrievich, fl. 1810-1820. Александр Дмитриевич Агафи (Table P-PZ40)
3321.A4 Akhlopkov, Sergeĭ, fl. 1840-1850. Сергей Ахлопков (Table P-PZ40)
3321.A43 Akilov, P.G. П.Г. Акилов (Table P-PZ40)
3321.A45 Aksakov, Ivan Sergeevich, 1823-1886. Иван Сергеевич Аксаков (Table P-PZ40 modified)
3321.A45A61-.A45Z458 Separate works. By title
3321.A45B7 Brodi͡aga. Бродяга
3321.A45Z3 Zhizn′ chinovnika (Mystery). Жизнь чиновника
3321.A45Z4 Zimnii͡ai͡a doroga. Зимняя дорога
3321.A47 Aksakov, Konstantin Sergeevich, 1817-1860. Константин Сергеевич Аксаков (Table P-PZ40)

Aksakov, Sergeĭ Timofeevich, 1791-1859. Сергей Тимофеевич Аксаков
3321.A5 Collected works. By date
3321.A5A17 Collected poems. By date
3321.A5A2-.A5A59 Translations (Collected or selected). By language, alphabetically
3321.A5A7-.A5Z4 Separate works
3321.A5A75 Alen′koĭ t͡svetochek. Аленькой цветочек

Biografii͡a M.N. Zagoskina. Биография М.Н. Загоскина see PG3447.Z2

Russian literature
Individual authors and works, 1800-1870
Individual authors, A - Dostoyevsky
Aksakov, Sergeĭ Timofeevich, 1791-1859. Сергей Тимофеевич Аксаков
Separate works -- Continued

3321.A5B8 Buran. Буран
3321.A5N3 Natasha. Наташа
Unfinished work
(3321.A5R3) Rasskazy i vospominanii͡a okhotnika o raznykh okhotakh. Рассказы и воспоминания охотника о разных охотах
see SK324
Semeĭnai͡a khronika. Семейная хроника see PG3321.A5Z535
(3321.A5Z3) Zapiski ob uzhen′e ryby. Записки об уженье рыбы
see SH633
(3321.A5Z33) Zapiski ruzheĭnogo okhotnika Orenburgskoĭ gubernii. Записки ружейного охотника Оренбургской губернии
see SK316
3321.A5Z5-.A5Z99 Biography and criticism
3321.A5Z5 Vospominanii͡a. Воспоминания
3321.A5Z52 Detskie gody Bagrova-vnuka. Детские годы Багрова-внука
3321.A5Z53 Literaturnye i teatral′nye vospominanii͡a. Литературные и театральные воспоминания
3321.A5Z535 Semeĭnai͡a khronika. Семейная хроника
Vospominanii͡a o D.B. Mertvago. Воспоминания о Д.Б. Мертваго see DK190.6.A+
Vospominanii͡a ob Aleksandre Semenoviche Shishkove. Воспоминания об Александре Семеновиче Шишкове see PG3361.S45
Znakomstvo s Gogolem. Знакомство с Гоголем see PG3335.A6+
3321.A5Z54-.A5Z59 Letters
3321.A5Z6-.A5Z99 General treatises. Life and works
3321.A52 Alad′in, Egor Vasil′evich, 1796-1860. Егор Васильевич Аладьин (Table P-PZ40)
Aleksandrov, pseud. Александров see PG3330.D8+
Aleksandrov, Aleksandr Andreevich, pseud. Александр Андреевич Александров see PG3330.D8+
3321.A53 Aleksandrov, Mikhail Nikolaevich, 1806-1833. Михаил Николаевич Александров (Table P-PZ40)
3321.A58 Alfer′ev, Vasiliĭ Petrovich, 1823-1854. Василий Петрович Алферьев (Table P-PZ40)

Russian literature
Individual authors and works, 1800-1870
Individual authors, A - Dostoyevsky -- Continued

3321.A6 Alipanov, Egor Ipat′evich, 1800-1860. Егор Ипатьевич Алипанов (Table P-PZ40)

3321.A63 Almazov, Boris Nikolaevich, 1827-1876. Борис Николаевич Алмазов (Table P-PZ40 modified)

3321.A63A61-.A63Z458 Separate works. By title

3321.A63B5 Beskorystnyĭ reformator (Poem). Бескорыстный реформатор

3321.A63D5 Dissonansy (Poems). Диссонансы

3321.A63G7 Graf Alarkos (Poem). Граф Аларкос

3321.A63I7 Ispoved′ damy (Poem). Исповедь дамы

3321.A63I8 Istina (Tale in verse). Истина

3321.A63K3 Katen′ka (Story). Катенька

3321.A63P6 Poslanie k chinovniku-liberalu ot mirnogo obyvateli͡a (Fantasy). Послание к чиновнику-либералу от мирного обывателя

3321.A63R6 Roland. Роланд

Andreev, pseud. Андреев see PG3321.C6

3321.A64 Anikita, hieromonach, 1783-1837. Аникита (Table P-PZ40)

3321.A65 Annenkov, Nikolaĭ Epafroditovich, 1805-1826. Николай Епафродитович Анненков (Table P-PZ40)

3321.A67 Annenkov, Pavel Vasil′evich, 1813-1887. Павел Васильевич Анненков (Table P-PZ40)

3321.A7 Annenkova, Varvara Nikolaevna, b. 1795. Варвара Николаевна Анненкова (Table P-PZ40)

Apekhtina, Aleksandra Andreevna. Александра Андреевна Апехтина see PG3330.F8

3321.A74 Arapov, P.N. (Pimen Nikolaevich), 1796-1861. Пимен Николаевич Арапов (Table P-PZ40)

3321.A75 Arbuzov, Nikolaĭ Aleksandrovich, d. 1868. Николай Александрович Арбузов (Table P-PZ40)

3321.A77 Aristov, S.I., fl. 1810-1815. С.И. Аристов (Table P-PZ40)

3321.A785 Artemiĭ, Araratskiĭ, 1774-1831? Араратский Артемий (Table P-PZ40)

3321.A8 Ashik, Anton Baltazarovich, 1802-1854. Антон Балтазарович Ашик (Table P-PZ40)

3321.A83 Askochenskiĭ, Viktor Ipat′evich, 1813-1879. Виктор Ипатьевич Аскоченский (Table P-PZ40)

3321.A834 Askol′dov, fl. 1849. Аскольдов (Table P-PZ40)

3321.A85 Atreshkov, Pavliniĭ, fl. 1830-1840. Павлиний Атрешков (Table P-PZ40)

3321.A9 Avdeev, Mikhail Vasil′evich, 1821-1876. Михаил Васильевич Авдеев (Table P-PZ40 modified)

Russian literature
Individual authors and works, 1800-1870
Individual authors, A - Dostoyevsky
Avdeev, Mikhail Vasil′evich, 1821-1876. Михаил Васильевич Авдеев -- Continued

3321.A9A61-.A9Z458 Separate works. By title
3321.A9D4 Derevenskiĭ vizit (Sketch). Деревенский визит
3321.A9D6 Dorozhnye zametki. Дорожные заметки
3321.A9G6 Gory (Tale). Горы
3321.A9I3 I͡Asnye dni (Idyl). Ясные дни
Ivanov. Иванов see PG3321.A9T47+
3321.A9M3 Magdalina (Story). Магдалина
3321.A9M4 Meshchanskai͡a semʹi͡a (Comedy). Мещанская семья
3321.A9M5 Mezh dvukh ogneĭ (Novel). Меж двух огней
3321.A9N3 Na doroge (Tale). На дороге
3321.A9N9 Nyneshni͡ai͡a li͡ubov′ (Story). Нынешняя любовь
3321.A9O4 Ognennyĭ zmeĭ (Tale). Огненный змей
3321.A9P4 Perepiska dvukh baryshen′ (Story). Переписка двух барышень
3321.A9P45 Pestren′kai͡a zhizn′ (Story). Пестренькая жизнь
3321.A9P6 Podvodnyĭ kamen′ (Novel). Подводный камень
3321.A9P65 Pori͡adochnyĭ chelovek (Story). Порядочный человек
3321.A9P67 Prilichnai͡a partii͡a (Story). Приличная партия
3321.A9S8 Sukhai͡a li͡ubov′ (Story). Сухая любовь
3321.A9T3 Tamarin (Novel). Тамарин
3321.A9T4-.A9T43 Varen′ka. Варенька
3321.A9T44-.A9T46 Tetrad′ iz zapisok Tamarina. Тетрадь из записок Тамарина
3321.A9T47-.A9T49 Ivanov. Иванов
Tetrad′ iz zapisok Tamarina. Тетрадь из записок Тамарина see PG3321.A9T44+
3321.A9V3 V sorokovykh godakh (Story). В сороковых годах
Varen′ka. Варенька see PG3321.A9T4+
Zapiski Tamarina. Записки Тамарина see PG3321.A9T3
3321.A93 Avorazh, N., fl. 1840-1850. Н. Аворaж (Table P-PZ40)
3321.B2 Babikov, Konstantin Ivanovich, 1841-1873. Константин Иванович Бабиков (Table P-PZ40 modified)
3321.B2A61-.B2Z458 Separate works. By title
3321.B2G5 Glukhai͡a uli͡tsa (Novel). Глухая улица
3321.B2L8 Lukavyĭ poputal (Tale). Лукавый попутал
3321.B2P4 Pervye slezy (Tale). Первые слезы
3321.B2P6 Porvannye struny (Story). Порванные струны
3321.B2S5 Shtabs-kapitan Bubent͡sov i devit͡sa Plisova (Tale). Штабс-капитан Бубенцов и девица Плисова
3321.B2T5 Tish′ da glad′ (Stories and tales). Тишь да гладь
3321.B2Z3 Zakholust′e (Story). Захолустье

PG

Russian literature
Individual authors and works, 1800-1870
Individual authors, A - Dostoyevsky -- Continued

3321.B25 Bagenskiĭ, Aleksandr, fl. 1850-1870. Александр Багенский (Table P-PZ40)

Baĭdarov, Vadim. Вадим Байдаров see PG3321.B87

3321.B27 Bakhtin, Ivan Ivanovich, 1756-1818. Иван Иванович Бахтин (Table P-PZ40)

Balakirev, Ivan. Иван Балакирев see PG3337.P6

3321.B28 Bantysh-Kamenskiĭ, D.N. (Dmitriĭ Nikolaevich), 1788-1850. Дмитрій Николаевичъ Бантышъ-Каменскій (Table P-PZ40)

Baranova, Anna Ivanovna. Анна Ивановна Баранова see PG3361.S87

3321.B3 Baratynskiĭ, Evgeniĭ Abramovich, 1800-1844. Евгений Абрамович Баратынский (Table P-PZ40 modified)

3321.B3A61-.B3Z458 Separate works. By title

3321.B3B3 Bal. Бал

3321.B3E4 Ėda, finli͡andskai͡a povestʹ. Эда, финляндская повесть

3321.B3N3 Nalozhnit͡sa. Наложница

3321.B3P5 Piry, opisatelʹnai͡a poema. Пиры, описательная поема

3321.B3S8 Sumerki. Сумерки

Baron Brambeus. Барон Брамбеус see PG3361.S33

3321.B33 Bashkatov, Alekseĭ Vasilʹevich, fl. 1830-1840. Алексей Васильевич Башкатов (Table P-PZ40)

3321.B35 Bashmakov, Ivan Ivanovich, d. 1865. Иван Иванович Башмаков (Table P-PZ40 modified)

3321.B35A61-.B35Z458 Separate works. By title
For his juvenile works see PZ62

3321.B35B6 Boi͡aryshni͡a nesmei͡ana. Боярышня несмеяна

3321.B35B7 Brichka, ili, Obratnyĭ putʹ s Parnasa. Бричка, или, Обратный путь с Парнаса

3321.B35C4 Chudak, ili, Chelovek, kakikh malo (Novel). Чудак, или, Человек, каких мало

3321.B35M4 Mezhdudelʹe. Междуделье

3321.B35P7 Prikli͡ucheni͡ia s moimi znakomymi. Приключения с моими знакомыми

3321.B35R8 Russkie narodnye rasskazy. Русские народные рассказы

3321.B35R85 Russkie pesni. Русские песни

3321.B35S4 Semeĭnye prikli͡ucheni͡ia zhivotnykh. Семейные приключения животных

3321.B35S5 Seroe gore. Серое горе

3321.B35S55 Skazka russkai͡a. Сказка русская

3321.B35S6 Soldat I͡Ashka. Солдат Яшка

Russian literature
Individual authors and works, 1800-1870
Individual authors, A - Dostoyevsky
Bashmakov, Ivan Ivanovich, d. 1865. Иван Иванович Башмаков
Separate works. By title -- Continued

3321.B35V5 Vetka. Ветка
3321.B35Z45 Zvezdochka. Звездочка
3321.B36 Bashut͡skiĭ, Aleksandr Pavlovich, 1801-1876. Александр Павлович Башуцкий (Table P-PZ40)
3321.B37 Batalin, Aleksandr Efimovich, fl. 1830-1840. Александр Ефимович Баталин (Table P-PZ40)
3321.B38 Baten′kov, Gavriil Stepanovich, 1793-1863. Гавриил Степанович Батеньков (Table P-PZ40)
3321.B4 Bati͡ushkov, Konstantin Nikolaevich, 1787-1855. Константин Николаевич Батюшков (Table P-PZ40)
3321.B414 Bazarov, 1840-1895. Базаров (Table P-PZ40)
3321.B415 Bazhanov, Vasiliĭ Vasil′evich, fl. 1850-1860. Василий Васильевич Бажанов (Table P-PZ40)
3321.B416 Bazhenov, Nikolaĭ Kirillovich, 1804-1848. Николай Кириллович Баженов (Table P-PZ40)
3321.B418 Bazilevich, Nikolaĭ, fl. 1840. Николай Базилевич (Table P-PZ40)
3321.B42 Bedni͡akov, Vasiliĭ Patrikievich, fl. 1860-1870. Василий Патрикиевич Бедняков (Table P-PZ40)

Bedri͡aga, Marii͡a Evgrafovna (Izvekova). Мария Евграфовна (Извекова) Бедряга see PG3337.I95

3321.B424 Begichev, Dmitriĭ Nikitich, 1786-1855. Дмитрий Никитич Бегичев (Table P-PZ40)
3321.B43 Belinskiĭ, Vissarion Grigor′evich, 1811-1848. Виссарион Григорьевич Белинский (Table P-PZ40)
Chiefly a literary critic and historian
Cf. PG2947.B5 Biography

Belosel′skai͡a-Belozerskai͡a, Zinaida Aleksandrovna. Зинаида Александровна Белосельская-Белозерская see PG3447.V6

3321.B435 Benediktov, Vladimir Grigor′evich, 1807-1873. Владимир Григорьевич Бенедиктов (Table P-PZ40)

Berendeev, Evstafiĭ. Евстафий Берендеев see PG3361.T25

3321.B436 Berezaĭskiĭ, Vasiliĭ Semenovich, 1762-1821. Василий Семенович Березайский (Table P-PZ40)
3321.B438 Berg, Nikolaĭ Vasil′evich, 1824-1884. Николай Васильевич Берг (Table P-PZ40)

Bernet, Evstafiĭ. Евстафий Бернет see PG3447.Z43

3321.B44 Beshent͡sov, A., fl. 1850-1880. А. Бешенцов (Table P-PZ40)

Russian literature
Individual authors and works, 1800-1870
Individual authors, A - Dostoyevsky -- Continued

3321.B45 Bestuzhev, Aleksandr Aleksandrovich, 1797-1837. Александр Александрович Бестужев (Table P-PZ40 modified)

3321.B45A61-.B45Z458 Separate works. By title

3321.B45A75 Ammalat-Bek. Аммалат-Бек

3321.B45A8 Andreĭ, kni͡az′ perei͡aslavskiĭ. Андрей, князь переяславский

3321.B45F7 Fregat Nadezhda. Фрегат Надежда

3321.B45I7 Ispytanie. Испытание

3321.B45I9 Izmennik. Изменник

3321.B45K7 Krasnoe pokryvalo. Красное покрывало

3321.B45L3 Latnik. Латник

3321.B45L4 Leĭtenant Belozor. Лейтенант Белозор

3321.B45M4 Mest′. Месть

3321.B45M6 Morekhod Nikitin. Мореход Никитин

3321.B45M8 Mulla Nur. Мулла Нур

3321.B45N3 Naezdy. Наезды

3321.B45O5 On byl ubit. Он был убит

3321.B45P5 Pis′mo k dokturu Ėrmanu. Письмо к доктуру Эрману

3321.B45P6 Poezdka v Revel′. Поездка в Ревель

3321.B45P7 Proshchanie s Kaspiem. Прощание с Каспием

3321.B45P8 Put′ do goroda Kuby. Путь до города Кубы

3321.B45R3 Rasskaz ofit͡sera, byvshogo v plenu u gort͡sev. Рассказ офицера, бывшого в плену у горцев

3321.B45R4 Revel′skiĭ turnir. Ревельский турнир

3321.B45R6 Roman i Ol′ga. Роман и Ольга

3321.B45S7 Strashnoe gadan′e. Страшное гаданье

3321.B45V4 Vecher na bivuake. Вечер на бивуаке

3321.B45V42 Vtoroĭ vecher na bivuake. Второй вечер на бивуаке

3321.B45V5 Vecher na kavkazskikh vodakh v 1824 godu. Вечер на кавказских водах в 1824 году

3321.B45Z3 Zamok Ėĭzen. Замок Эйзен

3321.B45Z4 Zamok Neĭgauzen. Замок Нейгаузен

3321.B46 Bestuzhev, Nikolaĭ Aleksandrovich, 1791-1855. Николай Александрович Бестужев (Table P-PZ40)

3321.B47 Bestuzhev-Ri͡umin, Mikhail Alekseevich, ca. 1802-1832. Михаил Алексеевич Бестужев-Рюмин (Table P-PZ40)

Bezborodko, Grigoriĭ Aleksandrovich Kushelev-. Григорий Александрович Кушелев-Безбородко see PG3337.K88

Russian literature
Individual authors and works, 1800-1870
Individual authors, A - Dostoyevsky -- Continued

3321.B49 Bezdarnyĭ, Petr, fl. 1830-1840. Петр Бездарный (Table P-PZ40)

Bez′erov, pseud. Безьеров see PG3337.L15

Bezglasnyĭ, V. B. Безгласный see PG3337.O3

Bibikova, A.I. А.И. Бибикова see PG3337.L793

3321.B53 Bibikova, Elisaveta Andreevna, fl. 1840-1850. Елисавета Андреевна Бибикова (Table P-PZ40)

3321.B54 Bibikova, Sof′i͡a, fl. 1860-1870. Софья Бибикова (Table P-PZ40)

3321.B543 Bi͡eli͡tsyn, S. C. Бѣлицынъ (Table P-PZ40)

Blagonravov, Ėrast. Эраст Благонравов see PG3321.A63

3321.B55 Blagoveshchenskiĭ, Nikolaĭ Aleksandrovich, 1837-1889. Николай Александрович Благовещенский (Table P-PZ40 modified)

3321.B55A61-.B55Z458 Separate works. By title

3321.B55A8 Afon. Афон

3321.B55B7 Brodi͡agi-stranniki. Бродяги-странники

3321.B55N4 Nevinnye zabavy. Невинные забавы

3321.B55P4 Pechal′nye vstrechi. Печальные встречи

3321.B55P45 Pered rassvetom (Novel). Перед рассветом

3321.B55P5 Pis′ma mizantropa. Письма мизантропа

3321.B55S8 Strannit͡sa. Странница

3321.B56 Bludov, Dmitriĭ Nikolaevich, graf, 1785-1864. Дмитрий Николаевич Блудов (Table P-PZ40)

3321.B58 Boborykin, Nikolaĭ Nikolaevich, ca. 1812-1888. Николай Николаевич Боборыкин (Table P-PZ40)

3321.B6 Bobrov, Semen Sergeevich, ca. 1767-1810. Семен Сергеевич Бобров (Table P-PZ40)

3321.B62 Bobylev, Nikolaĭ, fl. 1830-1860. Николай Бобылев (Table P-PZ40)

3321.B63 Bocharov, Ivan Petrovich, d. 1892. Иван Петрович Бочаров (Table P-PZ40)

Bogrov, Grigoriĭ Isaakovich. Григорий Исаакович Богров see PG3453.B643

Bogucharov, I. И. Богучаров see PG3337.K64

Bolkhovitinov, Evfimiĭ Alekseevich. Евфимий Алексеевич Болховитинов see PG3330.E8

Boratynskiĭ, Evgeniĭ Abramovich. Евгений Абрамович Боратынский see PG3321.B3

3321.B66 Borispolet͡s, Timofeĭ Nikiforovich, d. 1849. Тимофей Никифорович Борисполец (Table P-PZ40)

Russian literature
Individual authors and works, 1800-1870
Individual authors, A - Dostoyevsky -- Continued

3321.B67 Borodin, Andreĭ Nikolaevich, 1813-1865. Андрей Николаевич Бородин (Table P-PZ40)

3321.B7 Borozdna, Ivan Petrovich, 1803-1858. Иван Петрович Бороздна (Table P-PZ40)

Borshov, V. B. Боршов see PG3361.T6

3321.B72 Botvinovskiĭ, Kiril, fl. 1840-1850. Кирил Ботвиновский (Table P-PZ40)

3321.B73 Braĭkevich, Dmitriĭ, fl. 1830-1840. Дмитрий Брайкевич (Table P-PZ40)

3321.B74 Braĭkevich, V. I., d. 1822. В.И. Брайкевич (Table P-PZ40)

Brambeus, Baron. Барон Брамбеус see PG3361.S33

3321.B75 Brankevich, Mikhail Stepanovich, d. 1812. Михаил Степанович Бранкевич (Table P-PZ40)

3321.B76 Brant, Leopol′d Vasil′evich, fl. 1840-1850. Леопольд Васильевич Брант (Table P-PZ40)

Bri͡anska͡ia, Avdot′i͡a I͡Akovlevna. Авдотья Яковлевна Брянская see PG3337.P24

3321.B78 Bruskov, N. fl. 1855-1865. Н. Брусков (Table P-PZ40)

3321.B79 Bukharskiĭ, Andreĭ Ivanovich, b. 1767. Андрей Иванович Бухарский (Table P-PZ40)

3321.B8 Bulgarin, Faddeĭ Venediktovich, 1789-1859. Фаддей Венедиктович Булгарин (Table P-PZ40 modified)

3321.B8A61-.B8Z458 Separate works. By title

3321.B8B4 Bednyĭ Makar, ili, Kto za pravdu geroĭ, tot istyĭ geroĭ (Story). Бедный Макар, или, Кто за правду герой, тот истый герой

3321.B8B5 Begstvo Stanislava Leshchinskogo iz Dant͡siga (Story). Бегство Станислава Лещинского из Данцига

3321.B8C5 Chelovek i mysl′ (Fable). Человек и мысль

3321.B8D5 Dmitriĭ Samozvanet͡s (Novel). Дмитрий Самозванец

3321.B8E8 Ėsterka (Story). Эстерка

3321.B8F5 Filosofskiĭ kamen′, ili, Gde schast′e (Story). Философский камень, или, Где счастье

3321.B8G7 Grom Bozhiĭ (Tale). Гром Божий

3321.B8I2 I͡Ad. Cherty iz chastnoĭ zhizni. Яд. Черты из частной жизни

3321.B8I3 I͡Anychar, ili, Zhertva mezhdousobii͡a. Янычар, или, Жертва междоусобия

3321.B8I8 Ivan Vyzhigin (Novel). Иван Выжигин

Continued by Petr Ivanovich Vyzhigin, PG3321.B8P5

3321.B8K6 Komary. Vsi͡aka͡ia vsi͡achina. Комары. Всякая всячина

Russian literature
Individual authors and works, 1800-1870
Individual authors, A - Dostoyevsky
Bulgarin, Faddeĭ Venediktovich, 1789-1859. Фаддей Венедиктович Булгарин
Separate works. By title -- Continued

3321.B8L4 Leokaliia, ili, Zhertva neobdumannogo braka (Story). Леокалия, или, Жертва необдуманного брака
3321.B8M3 Mazepa (Story). Мазепа
3321.B8O5 Omar i Prosveshchenie. Омар и Просвещение
3321.B8P3 Padenie Vendena (Story). Падение Вендена
3321.B8P4 Pervaia liubov'. Первая любовь
3321.B8P5 Petr Ivanovich Vyzhigin (Novel). Петр Иванович Выжигин
Sequel to Ivan Vyzhigin, PG3321.B8I8
3321.B8R3 Razdel nasledstva (Story). Раздел наследства
3321.B8S5 Slaviane, ili, Osvobozhdenie Arkony (Story). Славяне, или, Освобождение Арконы
3321.B8V3 Vakan i sovest' (Story). Вакан и совесть

Bułharyn, Tadeusz see PG3321.B8

3321.B83 Bunina, Anna Petrovna, 1774-1828. Анна Петровна Бунина (Table P-PZ40)

Bur'ianov, Viktor. Виктор Бурьянов see PG3321.B87

3321.B85 Burinskiĭ, Zakhar Alekseevich, 1780-1808. Захар Алексеевич Буринский (Table P-PZ40)
3321.B87 Burnashev, Vladimir Petrovich, 1809-1888. Владимир Петрович Бурнашев (Table P-PZ40)
3321.B89 Butkov, Iakov Petrovich, d. 1856. Яков Петрович Бутков (Table P-PZ40)
3321.B9 Butovskiĭ, Leonid, fl. 1860-1870. Леонид Бутовский (Table P-PZ40)
3321.B93 Butyrskiĭ, Nikita Ivanovich, 1783-1848. Никита Иванович Бутырский (Table P-PZ40)
3321.B95 Bystroglazov, A., fl. 1830-1840. А. Быстроглазов (Table P-PZ40)

Bystroglazova, Mariia Antonovna. Мария Антоновна Быстроглазова see PG3337.K638
Bystroretskiĭ, M. M. Быстрорецкий see PG3337.M24
Bystroretskiĭ, Makariĭ. Макарий Быстрорецкий see PG3337.M24

3321.C2 Chaadaev, Petr Iakovlevich, 1796-1856. Петр Яковлевич Чаадаев (Table P-PZ40)
3321.C3 Chebotarev, D., fl. 1855-1865. Д. Чеботарев (Table P-PZ40)
3321.C32 Chebyshev-Dmitriev, Aleksandr Pavlovich, 1834-1877. Александр Павлович Чебышев-Дмитриев (Table P-PZ40)

Russian literature
Individual authors and works, 1800-1870
Individual authors, A - Dostoyevsky -- Continued

3321.C4 Cherni͡avskiĭ, Nikolaĭ Ivanovich, ca. 1840-1871. Николай Иванович Чернявский (Table P-PZ40)
Pseudonym: Literaturnyĭ medium (Литературный медиум)

Chernova, Nadezhda Andreevna (Durova). Надежда Андреевна (Дурова) Чернова see PG3330.D8+

3321.C45 Chernyshev, Fedor Sergeevich, 1805-1869. Федор Сергеевич Чернышев (Table P-PZ40)

3321.C5 Chernyshev, Ivan Egorovich, 1833-1863. Иван Егорович Чернышев (Table P-PZ40 modified)

3321.C5A61-.C5Z458 Separate works. By title

3321.C5A8 Aktrisa (Novel). Актриса
Sequel to Ugolki teatral′nogo mira, PG3321.C5U3

3321.C5B4 Benefisnye khlopoty (Scene). Бенефисные хлопоты

3321.C5D3 Dachnyĭ rasskaz. Дачный рассказ

3321.C5I7 Isporchenna͡ia zhizn′ (Comedy). Испорченная жизнь

3321.C5N4 Ne v den′gakh schast′e (Comedy). Не в деньгах счастье

3321.C5O8 Ote͡ts semeĭstva (Drama). Отец семейства

Peterburgskie aktrisy. Петербургские актрисы see PG3321.C5A8

3321.C5P7 Primadonna (Scenes). Примадонна

3321.C5U3 Ugolki teatral′nogo mira (Novel). Уголки театрального мира
Continued by Aktrisa, PG3321.C5A8

3321.C5Z42 Zhenikh iz dolgovogo otdeleni͡ia (Comedy). Жених из долгового отделения

3321.C6 Chernyshevskiĭ, Nikolaĭ Gavrilovich, 1828-1889. Николай Гаврилович Чернышевский (Table P-PZ40 modified)
For Chernyshevskiĭ as a literary critic see PG2947.C3

3321.C6A61-.C6Z458 Separate works. By title

Chto delat′? (Novel). Что делать?

3321.C6C4 Editions. By date

Translations

3321.C6C5 English. By date

3321.C6C52 French. By date

3321.C6C53 German. By date

3321.C6C54 Hungarian. By date

3321.C6C55 Italian. By date

3321.C6C56 Romanian. By date

3321.C6C57 Spanish. By date

3321.C6C58-.C6C59 Other, by language (alphabetically)

3321.C6C6 Criticism

3321.C6D6 Dnevnik Levi͡tskogo (Novel). Дневник Левицкого

Russian literature
Individual authors and works, 1800-1870
Individual authors, A - Dostoyevsky
Chernyshevskiĭ, Nikolaĭ Gavrilovich, 1828-1889. Николай Гаврилович Чернышевский
Separate works. By title -- Continued
3321.C6G5 Gimn Deve Neba. Гимн Деве Неба
3321.C6P7 Prolog (Novel). Пролог
3321.C6P72 Prolog k prologu. Пролог к прологу
Variant title: Prolog prologa (Пролог пролога)
3321.C6T5 T͡i͡uremnye rasskazy. Тюремные рассказы
3321.C62 Chizhov, P., fl. 1830-1840. П. Чижов (Table P-PZ40)
3321.C8 Churylkin, Kir͡i͡ushka, fl. 1850-1860. Кирюшка Чурылкин (Table P-PZ40)
Chuzhbinskiĭ, A.S. А.С. Чужбинский see PG3321.A3
3321.D2 Dal′, Vladimir Ivanovich, 1801-1872. Владимир Иванович Даль (Table P-PZ40 modified)
3321.D2A61-.D2Z458 Separate works. By title
3321.D2B9 Byli i nebyl͡it͡sy. Были и небылицы
3321.D2G6 Gofmanska͡i͡a kapl͡i͡a (Story). Гофманская капля
3321.D2K3 Kartiny russkogo byta. Картины русского быта
3321.D2K5 Khmel′, son i ͡i͡av′. Хмель, сон и явь
3321.D2K6 Kolbasniki i borodachi (Tale). Колбасники и бородачи
Lezgine͡t͡s Assan. Лезгинец Ассан see PG3321.D2R4
3321.D2M3 Matrosskie dosugi. Матросские досуги
3321.D2N4 Nebyvaloe v bylom, ili, Byloe v nebyvalom (Story). Небывалое в былом, или, Былое в небывалом
3321.D2O8 Ote͡t͡s s synom (Story). Отец с сыном
3321.D2P3 Pavel Alekseevich Igrivyĭ (Story). Павел Алексеевич Игривый
3321.D2P6 Pokhozhdeni͡i͡a Khristiana Khristianovicha Viol′damura, i ego Arsheta (Novel). Похождения Христиана Христиановича Виольдамура, и его Аршета
Poslovi͡t͡sy russkogo naroda. Пословицы русского народа see PN6505.S5
3321.D2P7 Priemysh (Tale). Приемыш
3321.D2R3 Rasplokh (Tale). Расплох
3321.D2R4 Rasskaz lezgin͡t͡sa Asana o pokhozhdeni͡i͡akh svoikh. Рассказ лезгинца Асана о похождениях своих
3321.D2R8 Russkie skazki. Русские сказки
3321.D2S3 Saveliĭ Grab, ili, Dvoĭnik (Tale). Савелий Граб, или, Двойник
3321.D2S6 Soldatskie dosugi. Солдатские досуги

Russian literature
Individual authors and works, 1800-1870
Individual authors, A - Dostoyevsky
Dal′, Vladimir Ivanovich, 1801-1872. Владимир Иванович Даль
Separate works. By title -- Continued

3321.D2V3 Vakkh Sidorov Chaĭkin (Story). Вакх Сидоров Чайкин

3321.D25 Danilevskiĭ, Grigoriĭ Petrovich, 1829-1890. Григорий Петрович Данилевский (Table P-PZ40 modified)

3321.D25A61-.D25Z458 Separate works. By title

825 god (Vosem′sot dvadt͡sat′ pi͡atyĭ god). 825 год (Восемьсот двадцать пятый год) see PG3321.D25V7

3321.D25B3 Babushkin raĭ (Tale). Бабушкин рай

3321.D25B5 Beglye v Novorossii (Novel). Беглые в Новороссии

3321.D25C5 Chernyĭ god (Pugachevshchina) (Novel). Черный год (Пугачевщина)

3321.D25C55 Chetyre vremeni goda ukrainskoĭ okhoty. Четыре времени года украинской охоты

3321.D25C6 Chumaki. Чумаки

3321.D25D4 Devi͡atyĭ val (Novel). Девятый вал

3321.D25E4 Ekaterina Velikai͡a na Dnepre (Tale). Екатерина Великая на Днепре

3321.D25F4 Fenichka (Tale). Феничка

3321.D25G8 Gvai͡a-lir, ili, Meksikanskie nochi (Tale in verse). Гвая-лир, или, Мексиканские ночи

3321.D25I5 Imeniny prababushki (Tale). Именины прабабушки

3321.D25I7 Istoricheskie rasskazy. Исторические рассказы

3321.D25I9 Iz Ukraïny (Stories and tales). Из Украйны

3321.D25K3 Kamenka (Tale). Каменка

3321.D25K4 Kazaki i stepi. Казаки и степи

3321.D25K6 Kni͡azhna Tarakanova (Novel). Княжна Тараканова

3321.D25K7 Krymskie stikhotvorenii͡a. Крымские стихотворения

3321.D25L4 Leĭb-kampanet͡s (Tale). Лейб-кампанец

3321.D25M5 Mirovich (Novel). Мирович

3321.D25N3 Na Indii͡u pri Petre I (Novel). На Индию при Петре I

3321.D25N4 Ne vytant͡sovalos′ (Story). Не вытанцовалось

3321.D25N6 Novye mesta (Novel). Новые места

3321.D25P2 Pami͡ati prababushki (Tale). Памяти прабабушки

3321.D25P3 Pensil′vant͡sy i karolint͡sy (Tale). Пенсильванцы и каролинцы

3321.D25P4 Pervai͡a iskra. Первая искра

3321.D25P5 Pesni͡a bandurista. Песня бандуриста

3321.D25P6 Potemkin na Dunae (Novel). Потемкин на Дунае

3321.D25R3 Rasskaz prababushki. Рассказ прабабушки

Russian literature
Individual authors and works, 1800-1870
Individual authors, A - Dostoyevsky
Danilevskiĭ, Grigoriĭ Petrovich, 1829-1890. Григорий Петрович Данилевский
Separate works. By title -- Continued

3321.D25S4 Selo Sorokopanovka. Село Сорокопановка
3321.D25S45 Semeĭnai͡a starina (Tales). Семейная старина
For individual tales see the title in PG3321.D25A61+ PG3321.D25B3, Babushkin raĭ
3321.D25S5 Slobozhane. Malorossiĭskie rasskazy. Слобожане. Малороссийские рассказы
3321.D25S6 Sozhzhennai͡a Moskva (Novel). Сожженная Москва
3321.D25S7 Starobubnov bor. Старобубнов бор
3321.D25S8 Stepnye skazki (Tales chiefly in verse). Степные сказки
3321.D25S85 Strelochnik (Tale). Стрелочник
3321.D25S9 Svi͡atochnye vechera (Tale). Святочные вечера
3321.D25T7 T͡Sar′ Alekseĭ s sokolom (Tale). Царь Алексей с соколом
3321.D25T75 T͡Sarevich Alekseĭ (Story). Царевич Алексей
(3321.D25T8) T͡Simbelin (Drama). Цимбелин
see PR2786
3321.D25U4 Ukrainskie skazki (Tales in verse). Украинские сказки
3321.D25U5 Umanskai͡a rezni͡a (Story). Уманская резня
3321.D25V6 Voli͡a (Beglye vorotilis′). Воля (Беглые воротились)
3321.D25V7 Vosem′sot dvadt͡sat′ pi͡atyĭ god (825 god). Восемьсот двадцать пятый год (825 год)
(3321.D25Z4) Zhizn′ i smert′ Koroli͡a Richarda Tret′ego. Жизнь и смерть Короля Ричарда Третьего
see PR2786
3321.D28 Dankov, Iv., fl. 1840-1850. Ив. Данков (Table P-PZ40)
3321.D3 Davydov, Denis Vasil′evich, 1784-1839. Денис Васильевич Давыдов (Table P-PZ40)
3321.D33 Davydov, Dmitriĭ, fl. 1850-1860. Дмитрий Давыдов (Table P-PZ40)
Debi͡utant, pseud. Дебютант see PG3447.Z53
3321.D35 Delari͡u, Mikhail Danilovich, 1811-1868. Михаил Данилович Деларю (Table P-PZ40)
3321.D36 Delaver′n′, Aleksandr. Александр Делаверьнь (Table P-PZ40)
Delibi͡urader, pseud. Делибюрадер see PG3337.O95
3321.D37 Delit͡syn, Gavriil, fl. 1860-1870. Гавриил Делицын (Table P-PZ40)
3321.D4 Del′vig, Anton Antonovich, baron, 1798-1831. Антон Антонович Дельвиг (Table P-PZ40 modified)

	Russian literature
	Individual authors and works, 1800-1870
	Individual authors, A - Dostoyevsky
	Delʹvig, Anton Antonovich, baron, 1798-1831. Антон Антонович Дельвиг -- Continued
3321.D4A61-.D4Z458	Separate works. By title
3321.D4D8	Dva lit͡seĭskie stikhotvorenii͡a. Два лицейские стихотворения
3321.D4P6	Poslanie k Karelinoĭ (Poem). Послание к Карелиной
3321.D42	Dementʹev, E., fl. 1846-1854. Е. Дементьев (Table P-PZ40)
3321.D43	Dementʹev, Vasiliĭ A., fl. 1850-1860. Василий А. Дементьев (Table P-PZ40)
3321.D45	Demidov, M., fl. 1830-1840. М. Демидов (Table P-PZ40)
3321.D46	Dershau, Fedor Karlovich, fl. 1840-1850. Федор Карлович Дершау (Table P-PZ40)
	Derzhavin, Gavriil Romanovich. Гавриил Романович Державин see PG3312
3321.D48	De-Vitt, Nikolaĭ, fl. 1860-1872. Николай Де-Витт (Table P-PZ40)
3321.D5	Dʹi͡achenko, Viktor Antonovich, 1818-1876. Виктор Антонович Дьяченко (Table P-PZ40 modified)
3321.D5A61-.D5Z458	Separate works. By title
3321.D5B5	Blesti͡ashchai͡a karʹera (Drama). Блестящая карьера
3321.D5B6	Boleznennai͡a strastʹ (Drama). Болезненная страсть
3321.D5G5	Gimnazistka (Drama). Гимназистка
3321.D5G8	Guverner (Comedy). Гувернер
3321.D5I5	Institutka (Drama). Институтка
3321.D5K3	Kara Bozhii͡a (Drama). Кара Божия
3321.D5N4	Ne pervyĭ, ne posledniĭ (Comedy). Не первый, не последний
3321.D5N5	Nerovni͡a (Drama). Неровня
3321.D5N6	Novoe vremi͡a i starye nravy (Drama). Новое время и старые нравы
3321.D5N7	Novyĭ sud (Drama). Новый суд
3321.D5N9	Nyneshni͡ai͡a li͡ubovʹ (Drama). Нынешняя любовь
3321.D5P4	Peterburgskie korshuny (Drama). Петербургские коршуны
3321.D5P6	Podvig grazhdanki (Drama). Подвиг гражданки
3321.D5P7	Prakticheskiĭ gospodin (Drama). Практический господин
3321.D5P75	Pri͡amai͡a dusha (Drama). Прямая душа
3321.D5P8	Probnyĭ kamenʹ (Drama). Пробный камень
3321.D5S4	Semeĭnye porogi (Drama). Семейные пороги
3321.D5S5	Skrytoe prestuplenie (Drama). Скрытое преступление

Russian literature
Individual authors and works, 1800-1870
Individual authors, A - Dostoyevsky
D'i͡achenko, Viktor Antonovich, 1818-1876. Виктор Антонович Дьяченко
Separate works. By title -- Continued

3321.D5S6 Sovremennai͡a baryshni͡a (Drama). Современная барышня
3321.D5S8 Svetskie shirmy (Drama). Светские ширмы
3321.D5V4 Vecher dokladnogo dni͡a (Drama). Вечер докладного дня
3321.D5Z2 Zakinutye teneta (Drama). Закинутые тенета
3321.D5Z3 Zakonnai͡a zhena (Drama). Законная жена
3321.D5Z4 Zhertva za zhertvu (Drama). Жертва за жертву
3321.D515 D'i͡achkov, Semen Dmitrievich, fl. 1830-1840. Семен Дмитриевич Дьячков (Table P-PZ40)
3321.D52 Dmitrevskiĭ, Mikhail, fl. 1800-1810. Михаил Дмитревский (Table P-PZ40)
Dmitriev, Aleksandr Pavlovich Chebyshev-. Александр Павлович Чебышев-Дмитриев see PG3321.C32
Dmitriev, Ivan Ivanovich, 1760-1837. Иван Иванович Дмитриев
3321.D53 Collected works. By date
3321.D53A17 Collected poems. By date
3321.D53A61-.D53Z458 Separate works. By title
3321.D53C5 Chuzhoĭ tolk (Satire). Чужой толк
3321.D53E7 Ermak (Ode). Ермак
3321.D53G6 Golubok (Song). Голубок
3321.D53I2 I moi bezdelki (Poems). И мои безделки
3321.D53K2 K Volge (Ode). К Волге
3321.D53M6 Modnai͡a zhena (Tale). Модная жена
3321.D53P7 Prichudnit͡sa (Tale). Причудница
3321.D53V6 Vozdushnye bashni (Tale). Воздушные башни
3321.D53Z5-.D53Z99 Biography and criticism
3321.D53Z5 Vzgli͡ad na moi͡u zhizn'. Взгляд на мою жизнь
3321.D54 Dmitriev, Mikhail Aleksandrovich, 1796-1866. Михаил Александрович Дмитриев (Table P-PZ40 modified)
3321.D54A61-.D54Z458 Separate works. By title
3321.D54E4 Ekaterina II (Poem). Екатерина II
3321.D54E6 Ėpigrammy. Эпиграммы
3321.D54L5 Li͡ut͡siferov prazdnik (Poem). Люциферов праздник
3321.D54M6 Moskovskie ėlegii (Poems). Московские элегии
3321.D54P6 Poslednïai͡a ieremiada Nikolaevskoĭ ėpokhi (Poem). Последняя иеремиада Николаевской эпохи

Russian literature
Individual authors and works, 1800-1870
Individual authors, A - Dostoyevsky -- Continued

3321.D55 Dmitriev, Nikolaĭ Dmitrievich, 1824 or 5-1874. Николай Дмитриевич Дмитриев (Table P-PZ40 modified)
3321.D55A61-.D55Z458 Separate works. By title
3321.D55D5 Dikai͡a (Tale). Дикая
3321.D55L4 Lesnye golosa (Tale). Лесные голоса
3321.D55L5 Lesnye start͡sy (Tale). Лесные старцы
3321.D55N3 Ne zabud′ (Story). Не забудь
3321.D55N4 Nechistai͡a sila (Story). Нечистая сила
3321.D55N5 Nedalekoe proshloe (Stories and tales). Недалекое прошлое
3321.D55P6 Pod berezami (Story). Под березами
3321.D55S5 Slezy i grezy (Tale). Слезы и грезы
3321.D55V6 Voda (Story). Вода
3321.D57 Dobrokhotov, Feofil, fl. 1830-1840. Феофил Доброхотов (Table P-PZ40)
3321.D573 Dobroli͡ubov, Nikolaĭ Aleksandrovich, 1836-1861. Николай Александрович Добролюбов (Table P-PZ40)
For Dobroli͡ubov as a literary critic see PG2947.D6
3321.D58 Dolgorukoĭ, Aleksandr Ivanovich, kni͡az′, 1794-1868. Александр Иванович Долгорукой (Table P-PZ40)
Variant of surname: Dolgorukov (Долгоруков)
3321.D59 Dolgorukoĭ, Dimitriĭ Ivanovich, kni͡az′, 1797-1867. Димитрий Иванович Долгорукой (Table P-PZ40)
Variant of surname: Dolgorukov (Долгоруков)
3321.D6 Dolgorukoĭ, Ivan Mikhaĭlovich, kni͡az′, 1764-1823. Иван Михайлович Долгорукой (Table P-PZ40 modified)
Variant of surname: Dolgorukov (Долгоруков)
3321.D6A61-.D6Z458 Separate works. By title
3321.D6B9 Bytie serdt͡sa moego (Poems). Бытие сердца моего
3321.D6D8 Durylom (Comedy). Дурылом
3321.D6N4 Nevinnost′ (Ode). Невинность
3321.D6O8 Otchai͡anie bez pechali (Comedy). Отчаяние без печали
3321.D6R3 Rassuzhdenie o sud′be (Ode). Рассуждение о судьбе
3321.D6S8 Sumerki moeĭ zhizni (Poems). Сумерки моей жизни
3321.D7 Dolinskiĭ, Aleksandr, fl. 1830-1840. Александр Долинский (Table P-PZ40)
Dostoevskiĭ, Fedor Mikhaĭlovich, 1821-1881. Федор Михайлович Достоевский see PG3325+
Dostoyevsky, Fyodor, 1821-1881. Федор Михайлович Достоевский

	Russian literature
	Individual authors and works, 1800-1870
	Dostoyevsky, Fyodor, 1821-1881. Федор Михайлович Достоевский -- Continued
3325.A1	Collected works. By date
3325.A16	Collected essays, miscellanies, etc. By title
3325.A16D6	Dnevnik pisateli͡a. Дневник писателя. By date Cf. PG3325.K7+ Krotkai͡a
3325.A2	Selected works. Selections. By date
3325.A3-Z	Separate works For translations see PG3326+
3325.B4-.B43	Bednye li͡udi (Novel). Бедные люди (Table PG2)
3325.B5-.B53	Belye nochi (Novel). Белые ночи (Table PG2)
3325.B6-.B63	Besy (Novel). Бесы (Table PG2)
3325.B7-.B73	Brat′i͡a Karamazovy (Novel). Братья Карамазовы (Table PG2)
3325.C4-.C43	Chestnyĭ vor (Tale). Честный вор (Table PG2) Published also under title: Rasskazy byvalogo cheloveka
3325.C5-.C53	Chuzhai͡a zhena (Tale). Чужая жена (Table PG2)
3325.C6-.C63	Chuzhai͡a zhena i muzh pod krovat′i͡u (Tale). Чужая жена и муж под кроватью (Table PG2) In 1865, "Chuzhai͡a zhena" was combined with "Revnivyĭ muzh" to form this work
3325.D5-.D53	Di͡adi͡ushkin son (Novel). Дядюшкин сон (Table PG2)
3325.D8-.D83	Dvoĭnik (Narrative poem). Двойник (Table PG2)
3325.E4-.E43	Elka i svad′ba (Tale). Елка и свадьба (Table PG2)
3325.G6-.G63	Gospodin Prokharchin (Story). Господин Прохарчин (Table PG2)
3325.I3-.I33	Idiot (Novel). Идиот (Table PG2)
3325.I4-.I43	Igrok (Novel). Игрок (Table PG2)
3325.K5-.K53	Khozi͡aĭka (Story). Хозяйка (Table PG2)
3325.K6-.K63	Krokodil (Tale). Крокодил (Table PG2)
3325.K7-.K73	Krotkai͡a. Кроткая (Table PG2) A tale from "Dnevnik pisateli͡a," PG3325.A16D6
3325.M3-.M33	Mal′chik u Khrista na elke (Tale). Мальчик у Христа на елке (Table PG2)
3325.M4-.M43	Malen′kiĭ geroĭ (Tale). Маленький герой (Table PG2)
3325.M8-.M83	Muzhik Mareĭ (Tale). Мужик Марей (Table PG2)
3325.N3-.N33	Na evropeĭskie sobytii͡a v 1854 godu (Poem). На европейские события в 1854 году (Table PG2)
3325.N4-.N43	Netochka Nezvanova (Novel). Неточка Незванова (Table PG2)
3325.P5-.P53	Podrostok (Novel). Подросток (Table PG2)
3325.P6-.P63	Polzunkov (Tale). Ползунков (Table PG2)
3325.P7-.P73	Prestuplenie i nakazanie (Novel). Преступление и наказание (Table PG2)

Russian literature
Individual authors and works, 1800-1870
Dostoyevsky, Fyodor, 1821-1881. Федор Михайлович Достоевский
Separate works -- Continued
Rasskazy byvalogo cheloveka. Рассказы бывалого человека see PG3325.C4+

3325.R4-.R43 Revnivyĭ muzh. Ревнивый муж (Table PG2)
In 1865 combined with "Chuzhai͡a zhenai͡a" under the title "Chuzhai͡a zhena i muzh pod krovatʹi͡u, PG3325.C6

3325.R6-.R63 Roman v devi͡ati pisʹmakh (Tale). Роман в девяти письмах (Table PG2)

3325.S4-.S43 Selo Stepanchikovo i ego obitateli (Story). Село Степанчиково и его обитатели (Table PG2)

3325.S5-.S53 Skvernyĭ anekdot (Tale). Скверный анекдот (Table PG2)

3325.S6-.S63 Slaboe serdt͡se (Story). Слабое сердце (Table PG2)

3325.S7-.S73 Stoletni͡ai͡a (Tale). Столетняя (Table PG2)

3325.U5-.U53 Unizhennye i oskorblennye (Novel). Униженные и оскорбленные (Table PG2)

3325.V5-.V53 Vechnyĭ muzh (Tale). Вечный муж (Table PG2)

3325.Z3-.Z33 Zapiski iz mertvogo doma (Novel). Записки из мертвого дома (Table PG2)

3325.Z4-.Z43 Zapiski iz podpolʹi͡a (Tale). Записки из подполья (Table PG2)

Translations
For translations of letters see PG3328.A3+
English

3326.A1 Collected works. By date

3326.A15 Collected novels and tales

3326.A16 Collected essays, miscellanies, etc. By translator or editor

3326.A2 Selected works. Selections. By date

3326.A3-Z Separate works. By Russian title, A-Z
Subarrange by date
e. g.

3326.B4 Bednye li͡udi (Poor folk). Бедные люди

3326.B7 Bratʹi͡a Karamazovy (The brothers Karamazov). Братья Карамазовы

3326.B8 Dramatization

3326.D8 Dvoĭnik (The double). Двойник

3326.I3 Idiot (The idiot). Идиот

3326.I4 Igrok (The gambler). Игрок

3326.P7 Prestuplenie i nakazanie (Crime and punishment). Преступление и наказание

3326.Z3 Zapiski iz mertvogo doma (House of the dead). Записки из мертвого дома

Russian literature
Individual authors and works, 1800-1870
Dostoyevsky, Fyodor, 1821-1881. Федор Михайлович Достоевский
Translations -- Continued

3327.A-Z Other languages, A-Z
Subarrange each language by Table PG1
e.g.
3327.F5 French (Table PG1)
3327.G5 German (Table PG1)
3327.I5 Italian (Table PG1)
3327.P5 Polish (Table PG1)
3327.S5 Spanish (Table PG1)
3327.9 Illustrations
Biography and criticism
3328.A09 Dictionaries
3328.A1-.A19 Autobiography. Journals
Dnevnik pisateli͡a. Дневник писателя see PG3325.A16D6
Letters
3328.A2 Collected. By editor
3328.A3-.A4 Translations
3328.A3 English. By translator or editor
3328.A4 Other languages, A-Z
3328.A5 Individual correspondents, A-Z
e. g.
3328.A5D5 Dostoevskai͡a, Anna Grigor′evna (Snitkina). Анна Григорьевна (Сниткина) Достоевская
Dostoeyevsky's second wife
3328.A5D53 English translations
3328.A6-.Z4 General treatises. Life and works
Including memoirs and diaries by members of his family
3328.D6 Dostoevskai͡a, Anna Grigor′evna (Snitkina). Анна Григорьевна (Сниткина) Достоевская
3328.Z43 Love and marriage. Relations to women
3328.Z44 Homes and haunts. Local associations
Including Siberian exile
3328.Z5 Iconography. Museums. Exhibitions
Criticism
3328.Z6 General works
3328.Z7 Special topics, A-Z
3328.Z7A3 Aesthetics
3328.Z7A77 Art. Arts
3328.Z7A84 Asia
3328.Z7C47 Characters (General)
3328.Z7C5 Children
3328.Z7D48 Demonology. Devil

Russian literature
Individual authors and works, 1800-1870
Dostoyevsky, Fyodor, 1821-1881. Федор Михайлович Достоевский
Biography and criticism
Criticism
Special topics, A-Z -- Continued

3328.Z7E4 Education
3328.Z7E53 Elijah (Biblical prophet)
3328.Z7E56 Emotions
3328.Z7E9 Evil
3328.Z7F37 Fate
3328.Z7F56 Film adaptations
3328.Z7F64 Folklore
3328.Z7G73 Great Britain
3328.Z7H47 Heroes. Heroines
Heroines see PG3328.Z7H47
3328.Z7H64 Holy fools
3328.Z7H85 Humor
3328.Z7J4 Jews
3328.Z7L26 Language. Style
3328.Z7L3 Law
3328.Z7M87 Music
3328.Z7M9 Myth
3328.Z7N5 Nihilism
3328.Z7P5 Philosophy
3328.Z7P59 Poetics
3328.Z7P6 Political and social views
3328.Z7P795 Psychology. Psychiatry
3328.Z7R38 Realism
3328.Z7R39 Redemption
3328.Z7R4 Religion and ethics
3328.Z7S35 Saint Petersburg (Russia)
3328.Z7S49 Sex
3328.Z7S52 Shame
3328.Z7S83 Stage history and presentation
Style see PG3328.Z7L26
3328.Z7S88 Suicide
3328.Z7T43 Technique
3328.Z7W65 Women
3330 Individual authors, Dostoyevsky - F
3330.D5 Dreĭgarfen, M., fl. 1840-1850. М. Дрейгарфен (Table P-PZ40)
3330.D6 Driīanskiĭ, E. Ė. (Egor Ėduardovich), fl. 1850-1860. Егор Эдуардович Дриянский (Table P-PZ40 modified)
3330.D6A61-.D6Z458 Separate works. By title
3330.D6A75 Amazonka. Амазонка

Russian literature
Individual authors and works, 1800-1870
Individual authors, Dostoyevsky - F
Drii͡anskiĭ, E. Ė. (Egor Ėduardovich), fl. 1850-1860. Егор Эдуардович Дриянский
Separate works. By title -- Continued

3330.D6A8 Anton Antonovich (Novel). Антон Антонович
3330.D6B6 Bog ne vydast--svin'i͡a ne s"est (Comedy). Бог не выдаст--свинья не съест
3330.D6K5 Komedii͡a v komedii (Comedy). Комедия в комедии
3330.D6K6 Konfetka (Biografii͡a Luki Lukicha). Конфетка (Биография Луки Лукича)
3330.D6K8 Kvartet (Story). Квартет
3330.D6L5 Likhoĭ sosed (Story). Лихой сосед
3330.D6P7 Priton; ne byl', a pravda. Притон; не быль, а правда
3330.D6T8 Tuz (Novel). Туз
3330.D6Z3 Zapiski melkotravchatogo (Novel). Записки мелкотравчатого
3330.D7 Druzhinin, Aleksandr Vasil'evich, 1824-1864. Александр Васильевич Дружинин (Table P-PZ40 modified)
3330.D7A61-.D7Z458 Separate works. By title
3330.D7D4 Derevenskiĭ rasskaz. Деревенский рассказ
3330.D7D7 Dramy iz obydennoĭ, preimushchestvenno stolichnoĭ zhizni. Драмы из обыденной, преимущественно столичной жизни
3330.D7D73 Razdum'e artista. Раздумье артиста
3330.D7D76 Opasnye sosedi. Опасные соседи
3330.D7D8 Dve vstrechi (Tale). Две встречи
3330.D7F7 Freĭleĭn Vil'gel'mina. Фрейлейн Вильгельмина
3330.D7I7 Istorii͡a odnoĭ kartinki. История одной картинки
3330.D7L4 Legenda o kislykh vodakh (Story). Легенда о кислых водах
3330.D7L6 Lola Montes (Tale). Лола Монтес
3330.D7M3 Mademoiselle Jeannette (Tale)
3330.D7N4 Ne vsi͡akomu slukhu ver' (Comedy). Не всякому слуху верь
3330.D7O2 Obruchennye (Story). Обрученные
Opasnye sosedi see PG3330.D7D76
3330.D7P3 Pashen'ka (Story). Пашенька
3330.D7P4 Peterburgskai͡a idillii͡a (Story). Петербургская идиллия
3330.D7P45 Petergofskiĭ fontan (Story). Петергофский фонтан
3330.D7P5 Pevit͡sa (Tale). Певица
3330.D7P6 Polin'ka Saks (Story). Полинька Сакс
Razdum'e artista see PG3330.D7D73
3330.D7R3 Rasskaz Aleksei͡a Dmitricha. Рассказ Алексея Дмитрича

Russian literature
Individual authors and works, 1800-1870
Individual authors, Dostoyevsky - F
Druzhinin, Aleksandr Vasil′evich, 1824-1864. Александр Васильевич Дружинин
Separate works. By title -- Continued
3330.D7S3 Sentimental′noe puteshestvie Ivana Chernoknizhnikova po Peterburgskim dacham. Сентиментальное путешествие Ивана Чернокнижникова по Петербургским дачам
3330.D7S5 Sharlotta Sh--t͡s. Шарлотта Ш--ц
3330.D7Z3 Zakat soln͡tsa (Tale). Закат солнца
3330.D7Z4 Zhi͡uli (Novel). Жюли
Durova, Nadezhda Andreevna, 1783-1866. Надежда Андреевна Дурова
3330.D8 Collected works. By date
3330.D8A6 Selected works. Selections. By date
3330.D8A7-.D8Z4 Separate works
3330.D8E4 Elena, T--ska͡ia krasavit͡sa (Tale). Елена, Т--ская красавица
3330.D8G6 God zhizni v Peterburge, ili, Nevygody tret′ego poseshcheni͡ia. Год жизни в Петербурге, или, Невыгоды третьего посещения
3330.D8G7 Graf Mavrit͡skiĭ (Story). Граф Маврицкий
3330.D8G8 Gudishki (Novel). Гудишки
3330.D8I3 I͡Archuk. Sobaka-dukhovidet͡s. Ярчук. Собака-духовидец
3330.D8K5 Klad. Клад
3330.D8O4 Ol′ga. Ольга
3330.D8P3 Pavil′on (Story). Павильон
3330.D8S4 Sernyĭ kli͡uch. Cheremisska͡ia povest′. Серный ключ. Черемисская повесть
3330.D8U3 Ugol. Угол
(3330.D8Z5-.D8Z99) Biography, autobiography
see DK190.6.D8
3330.D9 Dzhunkovskiĭ, Stepan Semenovich, 1762-1839. Степан Семенович Джунковский (Table P-PZ40)
3330.E3 Efremov, K.P., fl. 1850-1870. К.П. Ефремов (Table P-PZ40)
3330.E4 Efremov, Luka, fl. 1850-1860. Лука Ефремов (Table P-PZ40)
Egorov, Ivan. Иван Егоров see PG3321.C5
Ėks, pseud. Экс see PG3321.C32
3330.E5 Elagin, Vladimir Nikolaevich, 1831-1863. Владимир Николаевич Елагин (Table P-PZ40)
3330.E6 Ėngel′gardt, Sof′i͡a Vladimirovna, 1828- . Софья Владимировна Энгельгардт (Table P-PZ40)

Russian literature
Individual authors and works, 1800-1870
Individual authors, Dostoyevsky - F -- Continued

3330.E7 Ershov, Petr Pavlovich, 1815-1869. Петр Павлович Ершов (Table P-PZ40)

3330.E8 Evgeniĭ, metropolitan of Kiev, 1767-1837. Евгений, митрополит киевский (Table P-PZ40)

Fadeeva, Elena Andreevna. Елена Андреевна Фадеева see PG3331.G3

Fan-Dim, F. Ф. Фан-Дим see PG3337.K58

3330.F3 Fateev, Andreĭ Mikhaĭlovich, 1814-1865. Андрей Михайлович Фатеев (Table P-PZ40)

3330.F35 Fedorov, Boris Mikhaĭlovich, 1794-1875. Борис Михайлович Федоров (Table P-PZ40)

3330.F4 Fedorov, Pavel Stepanovich, 1803-1879. Павел Степанович Федоров (Table P-PZ40)

3330.F44 Fedorov, Vasiliĭ Mikhaĭlovich, fl. 1800-1830. Василий Михайлович Федоров (Table P-PZ40)

3330.F47 Fedorovich, Ivan Andreevich, 1811-1870. Иван Андреевич Федорович (Table P-PZ40)

3330.F475 Fedorovich, N. H. Федорович (Table P-PZ40)

3330.F485 Feonov, V.T. (Vasiliĭ Tikhonovich), 1792?-1835. Василий Тихонович Феонов (Table P-PZ40)

Feopempt Misailov. Феопемпт Мисаилов see PG3337.L15

Fet, A. A. Фет see PG3361.S4

3330.F5 Filimonov, Vladimir Sergeevich, 1787-1858. Владимир Сергеевич Филимонов (Table P-PZ40)

Foeth, A. see PG3361.S4

3330.F6 Fomin, Nikolaĭ Il′ich, fl. 1825-1845. Николай Ильич Фомин (Table P-PZ40)

Fon-Lizander, D. (Dmitriĭ), 1824-1894. Дмитрий Фон-Лизандер see PG3337.L68

3330.F8 Fuks, Aleksandra Andreevna (Apekhtina), 1805-1853. Александра Андреевна (Апехтина) Фукс (Table P-PZ40)

3330.F9 Furman, Petr Romanovich, 1809-1856. Петр Романович Фурман (Table P-PZ40)

3331 Individual authors, G - Gogol′

3331.G2 Gagarin, Grigoriĭ Ivanovich, kni͡az′, 1782-1837. Григорий Иванович Гагарин (Table P-PZ40)

3331.G23 Galakhov, Alekseĭ Dmitrievich, 1807-1892. Алексей Дмитриевич Галахов (Table P-PZ40)

3331.G25 Galinkovskiĭ, I͡Akov Andreevich, 1777-1815. Яков Андреевич Галинковский (Table P-PZ40)

Galka, Ieremii͡a. Иеремия Галка see PG3337.K64

Russian literature
Individual authors and works, 1800-1870
Individual authors, G - Gogol′ -- Continued

3331.G27 Gamalei͡a, Semen Ivanovich, 1743-1822. Семен Иванович Гамалея (Table P-PZ40)

3331.G3 Gan, Elena Andreevna (Fadeeva), 1814-1842. Елена Андреевна (Фадеева) Ган (Table P-PZ40)

Garaĭnov, Afanasiĭ Vasil′evich. Афанасий Васильевич Гарайнов see PG3337.G63

Gari͡aĭnov, Afanasiĭ Vasil′evich. Афанасий Васильевич Гаряйнов see PG3337.G63

3331.G35 Gendre, Nikolaĭ Pavlovich, 1818-1895. Николай Павлович Жандр (Table P-PZ40)

3331.G4 Gensler, I.S., fl. 1860-1870. И.С. Генслер (Table P-PZ40)

3331.G45 Georgievskiĭ, Ivan Sergeevich, ca. 1793-1818 Иван Сергеевич Георгиевский (Table P-PZ40)

3331.G5 Gerbel′, Nikolaĭ Vasil′evich, 1827-1883. Николай Васильевич Гербель (Table P-PZ40)

Germogen Trekhzvezdochkin. Гермоген Трехзвездочкин see PG3337.M25

Gert͡sen, Aleksandr Ivanovich. Александр Иванович Герцен see PG3337.H4

3331.G53 Giat͡sintov, A.K., fl. 1860-1870. А.К. Гиацинтов (Table P-PZ40)

3331.G55 Glibov, Leonid, fl. 1860-1875. Леонид Глибов (Table P-PZ40)

3331.G58 Glinka, Avdot′i͡a Pavlovna (Golenishcheva-Kutuzova), 1795-1863. Авдотья Павловна (Голенищева-Кутузова) Глинка (Table P-PZ40)

3331.G6 Glinka, Fedor Nikolaevich, 1786-1880. Федор Николаевич Глинка (Table P-PZ40)

3331.G7 Glinka, Sergeĭ Nikolaevich, 1775-1847. Сергей Николаевич Глинка (Table P-PZ40)

3331.G8 Gnedich, Nikolaĭ Ivanovich, 1784-1833. Николай Иванович Гнедич (Table P-PZ40)

Gogol′, Nikolaĭ Vasil′evich, 1809-1852. Николай Васильевич Гоголь

3332.A1 Collected works. By date

3332.A15 Collected novels and tales

3332.A19 Collected plays

3332.A6 Selections

3332.A61-Z Separate works

For translations see PG3333+

3332.A7-.A73 Arabeski. Арабески (Table PG2)

For separate stories, essays, etc., see the title in PG3332.A61+

Russian literature
Individual authors and works, 1800-1870
Gogolʹ, Nikolaĭ Vasilʹevich, 1809-1852. Николай Васильевич Гоголь
Separate works -- Continued
Bisavri͡uk. Бисаврюк see PG3332.V3+
3332.I5-.I53 Igroki (Dramatic piece). Игроки (Table PG2)
3332.I8-.I83 Ivan Fedorovich Shponʹka i ego tetushka (Story). Иван Федорович Шпонька и его тетушка (Table PG2)
3332.K6-.K63 Koli͡aska (Story). Коляска (Table PG2)
3332.L3-.L33 Lakeĭskai͡a (Dramatic piece). Лакейская (Table PG2)
3332.M3-.M33 Maĭskai͡a nochʹ, ili, Utoplennit͡sa (Story). Майская ночь, или, Утопленница (Table PG2)
3332.M4-.M43 Mertvye dushi (Novel). Мертвые души (Table PG2)
3332.M5-.M53 Mirgorod (Stories). Миргород (Table PG2)
For separate stories see the title in PG3332.A61+
3332.N4-.N43 Nevskiĭ prospekt (Story). Невский проспект (Table PG2)
3332.N5-.N53 Nochʹ pered Rozhdestvom (Story). Ночь перед Рождеством (Table PG2)
3332.N6-.N63 Nos (Story). Нос (Table PG2)
3332.O7-.O73 Ostranit͡sa (Story). Остраница (Table PG2)
3332.P4-.P43 Peterburgskie povesti. Петербургские повести (Table PG2)
Pokhozhdenii͡a Chichikova. Похождения Чичикова see PG3332.M4+
3332.P6-.P63 Portret (Story). Портрет (Table PG2)
3332.P65-.P653 Povestʹ o kapitane Kopeĭkine. Повесть о капитане Копейкине (Table PG2)
3332.P7-.P73 Povestʹ o tom, kak possorilsi͡a Ivan Ivanovich s Ivanom Nikiforovichem. Повесть о том, как поссорился Иван Иванович с Иваном Никифоровичем (Table PG2)
3332.P75-.P753 Propavshai͡a gramota (Story). Пропавшая грамота (Table PG2)
3332.R4-.R43 Revizor (Comedy). Ревизор (Table PG2)
3332.R5-.R53 Rim (Story). Рим (Table PG2)
3332.S5-.S53 Shinelʹ (Story). Шинель (Table PG2)
3332.S6-.S63 Sorochinskai͡a i͡armarka (Story). Сорочинская ярмарка (Table PG2)
3332.S7-.S73 Starosvetskie pomeshchiki (Story). Старосветские помещики (Table PG2)
3332.S8-.S83 Strashnai͡a mestʹ (Story). Страшная месть (Table PG2)
3332.T3-.T33 Taras Bulʹba (Story). Тарас Бульба (Table PG2)
3332.T5-.T53 Ti͡azhba (Dramatic piece). Тяжба (Table PG2)

Russian literature
Individual authors and works, 1800-1870
Gogol′, Nikolaĭ Vasil′evich, 1809-1852. Николай Васильевич Гоголь
Separate works -- Continued

3332.U8-.U83 Utro delovogo cheloveka (Dramatic piece). Утро делового человека (Table PG2)
3332.V3-.V33 Vecher nakanune Ivana Kupala (Story). Вечер накануне Ивана Купала (Table PG2)
3332.V4-.V43 Vechera na khutore bliz Dikan′ki (Stories). Вечера на хуторе близ Диканьки (Table PG2)
For separate stories see the title in PG3332.A61+
3332.V5-.V53 Vii (Story). Вии (Table PG2)
3332.V6-.V63 Vladimir 3-ĭ stepeni (Comedy). Владимир 3-й степени (Table PG2)
3332.V9-.V93 Vybrannye mesta iz perepiski s druz′i͡ami. Выбранные места из переписки с друзьями (Table PG2)
3332.Z2-.Z23 Zakoldovannoe mesto (Story). Заколдованное место (Table PG2)
3332.Z3-.Z33 Zapiski sumasshedshogo (Story). Записки сумасшедшого (Table PG2)
3332.Z4-.Z43 Zhenit′ba (Comedy). Женитьба (Table PG2)
Translations
For translations of letters see PG3335.A4+
3333 English
3333.A1 Collected works. By date
3333.A15 Collected novels and tales. By date
3333.A19 Collected plays. By date
3333.A6 Selections. By date
3333.A61-Z Separate works. By Russian title, A-Z
Subarrange by date
e. g.
3333.M4 Mertvye dushi (Dead souls). Мертвые души
3333.R4 Revizor (The inspector general). Ревизор
3333.T3 Taras Bul′ba. Тарас Бульба
3334.A-Z Other languages, A-Z
Subarrange each by Table PG1
e.g.
3334.F5 French (Table PG1)
3334.G5 German (Table PG1)
3334.I5 Italian (Table PG1)
3334.S5 Spanish (Table PG1)
3334.9 Illustrations
Biography and criticism
3335.A1 Anniversaries, celebrations, etc.
3335.A15 Autobiography
3335.A2 Journals. Diaries. Memoirs

Russian literature
Individual authors and works, 1800-1870
Gogol′, Nikolaĭ Vasil′evich, 1809-1852. Николай Васильевич Гоголь
Biography and criticism -- Continued
Letters

3335.A3	Collected. By date
	Translations. By translator or editor
3335.A4	English
3335.A45A-.A45Z	Other languages, A-Z
3335.A5A-.A5Z	Individual correspondents
3335.A6-.Z6	General treatises. Life and works
3335.Z65	Homes and haunts. Local associations
3335.Z7	Iconography. Museums. Exhibitions
	Criticism
3335.Z8	General works
3335.Z9A-.Z9Z	Special topics, A-Z
3335.Z9A37	Aesthetics
3335.Z9C43	Characters
3335.Z9E83	Ethics
3335.Z9F6	Food
3335.Z9H85	Humanism
3335.Z9H86	Humor
3335.Z9M87	Music
3335.Z9N38	National characteristics
3335.Z9P45	Philosophy
3335.Z9R4	Religion
3335.Z9S72	Stage history and presentation
3337	Individual authors, Gogol′ - Pushkin
3337.G2	Golishev, Nikolaĭ, fl. 1840-1850. Николай Голишев (Table P-PZ40)
3337.G25	Golit͡syn, Mikhail Grigor′evich, kni͡az′, 1813-1870. Михаил Григорьевич Голицын (Table P-PZ40)
3337.G3	Golit͡syn, Sergeĭ Vladimirovich, kni͡az′, 1828-1859? Сергей Владимирович Голицын (Table P-PZ40)
3337.G35	Golit͡synskiĭ, A.P., fl. 1860-1870. А.П. Голицынский (Table P-PZ40)
	Golovacheva-Panaeva, Avdot′i͡a I͡Akovlevna (Bri͡anskai͡a). Авдотья Яковлевна (Брянская) Головачева-Панаева see PG3337.P24
3337.G4	Golovin, Ivan Gavrilovich, b. 1816. Иван Гаврилович Головин (Table P-PZ40)
3337.G5	Golubin, Ippolit, fl. 1840-1850. Ипполит Голубин (Table P-PZ40)
3337.G6	Goncharov, Ivan Aleksandrovich, 1812-1891. Иван Александрович Гончаров (Table P-PZ40 modified)
3337.G6A61-.G6Z458	Separate works. By title

PG

Russian literature
Individual authors and works, 1800-1870
Individual authors, Gogol′ - Pushkin
Goncharov, Ivan Aleksandrovich, 1812-1891. Иван Александрович Гончаров
Separate works. By title -- Continued

(3337.G6F7) Fregat Pallada. Ocherki puteshestvii͡a. Фрегат Паллада. Очерки путешествия
see G490

3337.G6I8 Ivan Savich Podzhabrin (Sketch). Иван Савич Поджабрин

3337.G6O12 Oblomov (Novel). Обломов

3337.G6O14 Son Oblomova (Episode). Сон Обломова

3337.G6O18 Obryv (Novel). Обрыв

3337.G6O2 Obyknovenna͡ia istorii͡a (Novel). Обыкновенная история

3337.G6S5 Slugi starogo veka (Sketches). Слуги старого века

3337.G6S6 I. Valentin. Валентин

3337.G6S7 II. Anton. Антон

3337.G6S8 III. Stepan s sem′eĭ. Степан с семьей

3337.G6S9 IV. Matveĭ. Матвей

Son Oblomova. Сон Обломова see PG3337.G6O14

3337.G62 Gorbunov, Ivan Fedorovich, 1831-1895. Иван Федорович Горбунов (Table P-PZ40)

Gorchakov, Dimitriĭ Petrovich. Димитрий Петрович Горчаков see PG3313.G65

3337.G63 Gori͡ainov, Afanasiĭ Vasil′evich, 1819 or 20-1877. Афанасий Васильевич Горяинов (Table P-PZ40)

3337.G635 Gorodchaninov, Grigoriĭ Nikolaevich, 1772-1852. Григорий Николаевич Городчанинов (Table P-PZ40)

Gorokhov, Nik. Ник. Горохов see PG3337.L5+

3337.G64 Gorskiĭ, Petr, fl. 1860-1870. Петр Горский (Table P-PZ40)

Govorilin. Говорилин see PG3337.K79

3337.G65 Gradt͡sev, Aleksandr, fl. 1840-1850. Александр Градцев (Table P-PZ40)

3337.G66 Grammatin, Nikolaĭ Fedorovich, 1786-1827. Николай Федорович Грамматин (Table P-PZ40)

Grebenka, Evgeniĭ Pavlovich. Евгений Павлович Гребенка see PG3337.H7

3337.G67 Grech, Nikolaĭ Ivanovich, 1787-1867. Николай Иванович Греч (Table P-PZ40)

3337.G68 Grekov, Nikolaĭ Perfil′evich, 1810-1866. Николай Перфильевич Греков (Table P-PZ40)

3337.G69 Gren, Aleksandr Evgenievich, fl. 1830-1840. Александр Евгениевич Грен

Russian literature
Individual authors and works, 1800-1870
Individual authors, Gogolʹ - Pushkin -- Continued

3337.G7 Griboedov, Aleksandr Sergeevich, 1795-1829. Александр Сергеевич Грибоедов (Table P-PZ40 modified)

3337.G7A61-.G7Z458 Separate works. By title

1812 god. 1812 год see PG3337.G7T9

3337.G7D5 Dialog polovet͡skikh muzheĭ (Fragment). Диалог половецких мужей

3337.G7G6 Gore ot uma (Comedy). Горе от ума

3337.G7G7 Gruzinskai͡a nochʹ (Fragment of tragedy). Грузинская ночь

3337.G7M6 Molodye suprugi (Comedy). Молодые супруги

3337.G7P7 Pritvornai͡a nevernostʹ (Comedy). Притворная неверность

3337.G7P8 Proba intermedii. Проба интермедии

3337.G7P9 Prolog Fausta (Drama). Пролог Фауста

3337.G7S8 Student (Drama). Студент

3337.G7S9 Svoi͡a semʹi͡a (Fragment of comedy). Своя семья

3337.G7T9 Tysi͡acha vosemʹsot dvenadt͡satyĭ god (1812 god) (Fragment of comedy). Тысяча восемьсот двенадцатый год (1812 год)

Grigorenko, Grigoriĭ. Григорий Григоренко see PG3337.K88

3337.G72 Grigorʹev, Apollon Aleksandrovich, 1822-1864. Аполлон Александрович Григорьев (Table P-PZ40)

3337.G75 Grigorʹev, Petr Ivanovich, 1806-1871? Петр Иванович Григорьев (Table P-PZ40)

3337.G77 Grigorovich, Dmitriĭ Vasilʹevich, 1822-1899. Дмитрий Васильевич Григорович (Table P-PZ40)

Grit͡sko-Grigorenko. Грицко-Григоренко see PG3337.K88

3337.G79 Grum-Grzhimaĭlo, Kondratiĭ Ivanovich, 1794-1874. Кондратій Ивановичъ Грумъ-Гржимайло (Table P-PZ40)

3337.G8 Gruzinov, Iosif, fl. 1840-1850. Иосиф Грузинов (Table P-PZ40)

3337.G83 Gruzint͡sov, Aleksandr. Александр Грузинцов (Table P-PZ40)

3337.G87 Guber, Ėduard Ivanovich, 1814-1847. Эдуард Иванович Губер (Table P-PZ40)

3337.G89 Gumilevskiĭ, Aleksandr Vasilʹevich, 1830-1869. Александр Васильевич Гумилевский (Table P-PZ40)

Gusʹ, pseud. Гусь see PG3447.Z53

PG

Russian literature
Individual authors and works, 1800-1870
Individual authors, Gogol′ - Pushkin -- Continued

Gusi͡atnikova, Evgenii͡a Petrovna. Евгения Петровна Гусятникова see PG3337.M23

Hert͡sen, Aleksandr Ivanovich. Александр Иванович Герцен see PG3337.H4

3337.H4 Hertzen, Aleksandr Ivanovich, 1812-1870. Александр Иванович Герцен

For political, socialistic writings, etc. see subclasses DK, HX, etc.

Collected works see AC65

3337.H4A15 Collected tales

3337.H4A6 Selected works. Selections. By date

3337.H4A7-.H4Z4 Separate works

Doktor Krupov. Доктор Крупов see PG3337.H4I9

3337.H4D6 Dolg prezhde vsego (Tale). Долг прежде всего

3337.H4I9 Iz sochinenīĭ doktora Krupova (Story). Из сочинений доктора Крупова

Iz zapisok odnogo molodogo cheloveka. Из записок одного молодого человека see PG3337.H4Z3

3337.H4K8 Kto vinovat? (Novel). Кто виноват?

3337.H4M5 Mimoezdom (Tale, fragment). Мимоездом

3337.H4P5 Pis′ma iz "Avenue Marigny" (Tale). Письма из "Avenue Marigny"

3337.H4P6 Povrezhdennyĭ (Tale). Поврежденный

3337.H4S6 Soroka-vorovka (Tale). Сорока-воровка

3337.H4Z3 Zapiski odnogo molodogo cheloveka (Tale). Записки одного молодого человека

3337.H4Z5-.H4Z99 Biography and criticism

Class here biography and criticism of Hertzen as an author

For general biography, memoirs, letters, etc. see DK209.6.H4

Herzen, Aleksandr Ivanovich. Александр Иванович Герцен see PG3337.H4

3337.H7 Hrebinka, I͡Evgen, 1812-1848. Євген Павлович Гребінка (Евгений Павлович Гребенка) (Table P-PZ40)

For Hrebinka's Ukrainian works, as well as general biography and criticism see PG3948.H694

3337.I2 I͡Akovlev, Alekseĭ Semenovich, 1773-1817. Алексей Семенович Яковлев (Table P-PZ40)

3337.I23 I͡Akovlev, Pavel Luk′i͡anovich, 1789-1817. Павел Лукьянович Яковлев (Table P-PZ40)

3337.I27 I͡Akubovich, Luk′i͡an Andreevich, 1805-1839. Лукьян Андреевич Якубович (Table P-PZ40)

Russian literature
Individual authors and works, 1800-1870
Individual authors, Gogol′ - Pushkin -- Continued

3337.I3 I͡Akushkin, Pavel Ivanovich, 1820-1872. Павел Иванович Якушкин (Table P-PZ40)

I͡Anish, Karolina Karlovna. Каролина Карловна Яниш see PG3337.P35

3337.I34 I͡Apanko-Molotov, E.I. Е.И. Япанко-Молотов (Table P-PZ40)

I͡Aroslavt͡sev, Andreĭ Konstantinovich. Андрей Константинович Ярославцев see PG3337.I37

3337.I37 I͡Aroslavt͡sov, Andreĭ Konstantinovich, 1815-1884. Андрей Константинович Ярославцов (Table P-PZ40)

3337.I4 I͡Azykov, Nikolaĭ Mikhaĭlovich, 1803-1846. Николай Михайлович Языков (Table P-PZ40 modified)

3337.I4A61-.I4Z458 Separate works (including poems). By title

3337.I4K2 K Reĭnu (Poem). К Рейну

3337.I4K3 Kambi (Poem). Камби

3337.I4L5 Lipy (Story in verse). Липы

3337.I4O7 Otrok Vi͡achko (Drama in verse). Отрок Вячко

3337.I4S7 Strannyĭ sluchaĭ (Dramatic piece in verse). Странный случай

3337.I4T7 Trigorskoe (Poem). Тригорское

3337.I4V6 Vodopad (Poem). Водопад

3337.I4Z3 Zemletri͡asen′e (Poem). Землетрясенье

3337.I4Z4 Zhar-ptit͡sa (Dramatic tale in verse). Жар-птица

3337.I43 Īevlev, A. A. Іевлевъ (Table P-PZ40)

3337.I45 Ignat′ev, Ruf Gavrilovich, 1819-1886. Руф Гаврилович Игнатьев (Table P-PZ40)

3337.I5 Il′in, Nikolaĭ Ivanovich, 1773-1823. Николай Иванович Ильин (Table P-PZ40)

Il′inskiĭ, Nikolaĭ Stepanovich. Николай Степанович Ильинский see PG3313.I5

3337.I55 Illichevskiĭ, Alekseĭ Dem′i͡anovich, 1798-1837. Алексей Демьянович Илличевский (Table P-PZ40)

3337.I6 Iovskiĭ, Petr Alekseevich, fl. 1820-1840. Петр Алексеевич Иовский (Table P-PZ40)

3337.I64 Irtyshev, Mikhail. Михаил Иртышев (Table P-PZ40)

Iskander, 1812-1870. Искандер see PG3337.H4

3337.I65 I͡Ur′ev, Sergeĭ Andreevich, 1821-1888. Сергей Андреевич Юрьев (Table P-PZ40)

I͡Ur′eva, Devit͡sa, pseud. Девица Юрьева see PG3337.K62

I͡Ushkova, Anna Petrovna. Анна Петровна Юшкова see PG3447.Z58

Russian literature
Individual authors and works, 1800-1870
Individual authors, Gogol′ - Pushkin

3337.I67 I͡Uzefovich, M.V. (Mikhail Vladimīrovich), 1802-1889. Михаилъ Владимiровичъ Юзефовичъ (Table P-PZ40)

3337.I7 Ivanchin-Pisarev, Nikolaĭ Dmitrievich, 1795-1849. Николай Дмитриевич Иванчин-Писарев (Table P-PZ40)

3337.I75 Ivanit͡skiĭ, Aleksandr Ivanovich, 1812-1850. Александр Иванович Иваницкий (Table P-PZ40)

3337.I8 Ivanov, Fedor Fedorovich, 1777-1816. Федор Федорович Иванов (Table P-PZ40)

3337.I82 Ivanov, I. (Ivan). Иван Иванов (Table P-PZ40)

3337.I83 Ivanov, N., fl. 1860-1870. Н. Иванов (Table P-PZ40)

Ivanov-Zheludkov, V.I. В.И. Иванов-Желудков see PG3337.K34

3337.I85 Izmaĭlov, Aleksandr Efimovich, 1779-1831. Александр Ефимович Измайлов (Table P-PZ40)

3337.I9 Izmaĭlov, Vladimir Vasil′evich, 1773-1830. Владимир Васильевич Измайлов (Table P-PZ40)

3337.I95 Izvekova, Marii͡a Evgrafovna, 1794-1830. Мария Евграфовна Извекова (Table P-PZ40)

3337.K15 Kalaĭdovich, Konstantin Fedorovich, 1792-1832. Константин Федорович Калайдович (Table P-PZ40)

3337.K16 Kalambiĭ. Каламбій (Table P-PZ40)

3337.K18 Kalashnikov, Ivan Timofeevich, 1797-1863. Иван Тимофеевич Калашников (Table P-PZ40)

3337.K2 Kamenskai͡a, Marii͡a Fedorovna (Tolstai͡a), 1817-1898. Мария Федоровна (Толстая) Каменская (Table P-PZ40)

3337.K22 Kamenskiĭ, Pavel Pavlovich, 1840-1870. Павел Павлович Каменский (Table P-PZ40)

3337.K23 Kandaurov, Vasiliĭ Alekseevich, 1830-1888. Василий Алексеевич Кандауров (Table P-PZ40)

Kapnist, Vasiliĭ Vasil′evich. Василий Васильевич Капнист see PG3313.K4

3337.K24 Karabanov, Petr Matveevich, 1764-1829. Петр Матвеевич Карабанов (Table P-PZ40)

3337.K25 Karamzin, Aleksandr Nikolaevich, 1816-1888. Александр Николаевич Карамзин (Table P-PZ40)

Karamzin, Nikolaĭ Mikhaĭlovich. Николай Михайлович Карамзин see PG3314

3337.K26 Karatygin, Petr Andreevich, 1805-1879. Петр Андреевич Каратыгин (Table P-PZ40)

3337.K27 Karelin, Il′i͡a, fl. 1830-1850. Илья Карелин (Table P-PZ40)

Russian literature
Individual authors and works, 1800-1870
Individual authors, Gogol′ - Pushkin -- Continued

Kartavt͡sev, Ivan Afanas′evich. Иван Афанасьевич Картавцев see PG3337.K28

3337.K28 Kartavt͡sov, Ivan Afanas′evich, fl. 1830-1840. Иван Афанасьевич Картавцов (Table P-PZ40)

Kas′i͡anov, Kas′i͡an. Касьян Касьянов see PG3321.B87

3337.K3 Katenin, Pavel Aleksandrovich, 1792-1853. Павел Александрович Катенин (Table P-PZ40)

3337.K32 Katkov, Mikhail Nikiforovich, 1818-1887. Михаил Никифорович Катков (Table P-PZ40)

Kavalerist-devit͡sa, pseud. Кавалерист-девица see PG3330.D8+

3337.K34 Kel′siev, Vasiliĭ Ivanovich, 1835-1872. Василий Иванович Кельсиев (Table P-PZ40)

3337.K36 Kern, Anna Petrovna (Poltorat͡skai͡a), 1800-1879 Анна Петровна (Полторацкая) Керн (Table P-PZ40)

Khamar-Dabanov. Хамар-Дабанов see PG3337.L2

3337.K37 Khli͡udzinskiĭ, Viktor. Виктор Хлюдзинский (Table P-PZ40)

3337.K38 Khmel′nit͡skiĭ, Nikolaĭ Ivanovich, 1789-1845. Николай Иванович Хмельницкий (Table P-PZ40)

3337.K4 Khomi͡akov, Alekseĭ Stepanovich, 1804-1860. Алексей Степанович Хомяков (Table P-PZ40)

3337.K42 Khvoshchinskai͡a, Nadezhda Dmitrievna, 1825-1889. Надежда Дмитриевна Хвощинская (Table P-PZ40)

Khvoshchinskai͡a, Sof′i͡a Dmitrievna, 1828-1865. Софья Дмитриевна Хвощинская see PG3447.V47

3337.K44 Khvostov, Dmitriĭ Ivanovich, graf, 1757-1835. Дмитрий Иванович Хвостов (Table P-PZ40)

3337.K45 Khvostova, Ekaterina Aleksandrovna (Sushkova), 1812-1868. Екатерина Александровна (Сушкова) Хвостова (Table P-PZ40)

3337.K47 Kicheev, Petr Grigor′evich, fl. 1860-1870. Петр Григорьевич Кичеев (Table P-PZ40)

3337.K48 Kireevskiĭ, Ivan Vasil′evich, 1806-1856. Иван Васильевич Киреевский (Table P-PZ40)

3337.K49 Kireevskiĭ, Petr Vasil′evich, 1808-1856. Петр Васильевич Киреевский (Table P-PZ40)

3337.K5 Ki͡ukhel′beker, Vil′gel′m Karlovich, 1797-1846. Вильгельм Карлович Кюхельбекер (Table P-PZ40)

3337.K52 Klassen, Egor Ivanovich, d. 1862. Егор Иванович Классен (Table P-PZ40)

3337.K53 Kli͡ushnikov, Ivan Petrovich, 1811-1895. Иван Петрович Клюшников (Table P-PZ40)

Russian literature
Individual authors and works, 1800-1870
Individual authors, Gogol′ - Pushkin -- Continued

3337.K534 Kni͡azhnin, A. (Aleksandr), 1771-1829. Александр Княжнин (Table P-PZ40)

Kobi͡akova, A. A. Кобякова see PG3361.S787

Kochka-Sokhrana, V. B. Кочка-Сохрана see PG3321.A83

Kokhanovska͡ia, N. H. Кохановская see PG3361.S67

3337.K55 Kokorev, Ivan Timofeevich, 1826-1853. Иван Тимофеевич Кокорев (Table P-PZ40)

3337.K56 Kokoshkin, Fedor Fedorovich, 1773-1838. Федор Федорович Кокошкин (Table P-PZ40)

Kokoshkin, Ivan Alekseevich. Иван Алексеевич Кокошкин see PG3315.K53

Kolechkin, Antip Antipovich. Антип Антипович Колечкин see PG3321.D46

3337.K57 Kolenkovskiĭ, Aleksandr, fl. 1840-1850. Александр Коленковский

3337.K58 Kologrivova, Elizaveta Vasil′evna, 1809-1884. Елизавета Васильевна Кологривова (Table P-PZ40)

Kolomenskiĭ Starozhil. Коломенский Старожил see PG3337.K635

3337.K587 Kolosov, M. M. Колосов (Table P-PZ40)

3337.K59 Kolosov, Vasiliĭ Mikhaĭlovich, fl. 1800-1820. Василий Михайлович Колосов (Table P-PZ40)

Kol′t͡sov, Alekseĭ Vasil′evich, 1809-1842. Алексей Васильевич Кольцов

3337.K6 Collected works (Collected poems and poems and prose). By date

3337.K6A11-.K6A14 Selected works. By title (alphabetically)

3337.K6A15-.K6A19 Selections. By title (alphabetically)

3337.K6A2-.K6A59 Translations (Collected or selected). By language, alphabetically

3337.K6A7-.K6Z4 Separate poems

e. g.

3337.K6C5 Chto ty spish′, muzhichok. Что ты спишь, мужичок

3337.K6D8 Duma sokola. Дума сокола

3337.K6K6 Kosar′. Косарь

3337.K6K67 Krest′i͡anska͡ia pirushka. Крестьянская пирушка

3337.K6L4 Les (Chto dremuchiĭ les, prizadumals͡ia?). Лес (Что дремучий лес, призадумался?)

3337.K6N4 Ne shumi ty rozh′. Не шуми ты рожь

3337.K6P3 Pesn͡ia (Akh zachem men͡ia siloĭ vydali). Песня (Ах зачем меня силой выдали)

Russian literature
Individual authors and works, 1800-1870
Individual authors, Gogol′ - Pushkin
Kol′t͡sov, Alekseĭ Vasil′evich, 1809-1842. Алексей Васильевич Кольцов
Separate poems -- Continued

3337.K6P5 Pesni͡a Likhacha Kudri͡avicha. Песня Лихача Кудрявича
3337.K6P6 Pesni͡a pakhari͡a. Песня пахаря
3337.K6P7 Pora li͡ubvi. Пора любви
3337.K6R3 Razmyshlenie poseli͡anina. Размышление поселянина
3337.K6S8 Stârai͡a pesni͡a. Старая песня
3337.K6U7 Urozhaĭ. Урожай
3337.K6Z5-.K6Z99 Biography and criticism
Letters
3337.K6Z52 Collected. By date
3337.K6Z53-.K6Z59 Individual correspondents (alphabetically)
3337.K6Z6-.K6Z99 General treatises. Life and works
3337.K615 Komarov, Andreĭ, fl. 1860-1870. Андрей Комаров (Table P-PZ40)
3337.K617 Kondaraki, V. Kh. (Vasiliĭ Khristoforovich), 19th cent. Василій Христофоровичъ Кондараки (Table P-PZ40)
3337.K618 Koni, Fedor Alekseevich, 1809-1879. Федор Алексеевич Кони (Table P-PZ40)
3337.K62 Koni, Irina Semenovna (I͡Ur′eva), 1811-1891. Ирина Семеновна (Юрьева) Кони (Table P-PZ40)
3337.K6215 Kononov, A., fl. 1850-1860. А. Кононов (Table P-PZ40)
3337.K622 Konshin, Nikolaĭ Mikhaĭlovich, 1793-1859. Николай Михайлович Коншин (Table P-PZ40)
3337.K625 Koptev, Alekseĭ Alekseevich, 19th cent. Алексей Алексеевич Коптев (Table P-PZ40)
3337.K628 Koptev, Dmitriĭ Ivanovich, 1820-1867. Дмитрий Иванович Коптев (Table P-PZ40)
3337.K629 Korbelet͡skiĭ, Fedor Ivanovich, fl. 1790-1820. Федор Иванович Корбелецкий (Table P-PZ40)
3337.K63 Korf, Fedor Andreevich, baron, 1808-1839. Федор Андреевич Корф (Table P-PZ40)
3337.K632 Korf, Fedor Fedorovich, baron, 1803-1853. Федор Федорович Корф (Table P-PZ40)
3337.K635 Korsakov, Petr Aleksandrovich, 1790-1844. Петр Александрович Корсаков (Table P-PZ40)
3337.K638 Korsini, Marii͡a Antonovna (Bystroglazova), 1815-1859. Мария Антоновна (Быстроглазова) Корсини (Table P-PZ40)

Russian literature
Individual authors and works, 1800-1870
Individual authors, Gogolʹ - Pushkin -- Continued

3337.K64 Kostomarov, Nikolaĭ Ivanovich, 1817-1885. Николай Иванович Костомаров (Table P-PZ40)

Kotelʹnit͡skiĭ, Aleksandr. Александр Котельницкий see PG3315.K75

3337.K643 Kotli͡arevskiĭ, Ivan Petrovich, 1769-1838. Иван Петрович Котляревский (Table P-PZ40)

3337.K646 Kovalevskiĭ, Egor Petrovich, 1811-1868. Егор Петрович Ковалевский (Table P-PZ40)

3337.K648 Kovalevskiĭ, Nikolaĭ, fl. 1840-1870. Николай Ковалевский (Table P-PZ40)

3337.K65 Kovalevskiĭ, Pavel Mikhaĭlovich, 1823-1907. Павел Михайлович Ковалевский (Table P-PZ40)

3337.K654 Kozlov, Ivan Ivanovich, 1779-1840. Иван Иванович Козлов (Table P-PZ40)

3337.K656 Kozlov, Vasiliĭ Ivanovich, 1792-1825. Василий Иванович Козлов (Table P-PZ40)

3337.K658 Kozodavlev, Osip Petrovich, 1754-1819. Осип Петрович Козодавлев (Table P-PZ40)

3337.K66 Krasnit͡skiĭ, Viktor, fl. 1850-1860. Виктор Красницкий (Table P-PZ40)

3337.K663 Krasnopolʹskiĭ, Nikolaĭ Stepanovich. Николай Степанович Краснопольский (Table P-PZ40)

Krasnorogskiĭ, pseud. . Красногорский see PG3363

3337.K665 Krasov, Vasiliĭ Ivanovich, 1810-1855. Василий Иванович Красов (Table P-PZ40)

Krestovskiĭ, N. H. Крестовский see PG3337.K8

Krestovskiĭ, V. B. Крестовский see PG3337.K42

3337.K67 Krichevskai͡a, Li͡ubovʹ I͡Akovlevna, fl. 1820-1830. Любовь Яковлевна Кричевская (Table P-PZ40)

Krinit͡skiĭ, pseud. Криницкий see PG3447.V112

Kri͡udener, Varvara-I͡Uliana, 1764-1824 see PG3337.K683

Kri͡udener, Varvara-I͡Ulii͡a, 1764-1824 see PG3337.K683

3337.K675 Kri͡ukova, Olʹga Petrovna, 1817-1885. Ольга Петровна Крюкова (Table P-PZ40)

3337.K678 Kri͡ukovskiĭ, Matveĭ Vasilʹevich, 1781-1811. Матвей Васильевич Крюковский (Table P-PZ40)

3337.K68 Krolʹ, Nikolaĭ Ivanovich, 1823-1871. Николай Иванович Кроль (Table P-PZ40)

3337.K682 Krotkov, Ivan Vasilʹevich, fl. 1850-1860. Иван Васильевич Кротков (Table P-PZ40)

3337.K683 Krüdener, Barbara Juliane, Freifrau von, 1764-1824. Варвара-Юлиана Крюденер (Варвара-Юлия Крюденер) (Table P-PZ40)

Russian literature
Individual authors and works, 1800-1870
Individual authors, Gogol′ - Pushkin -- Continued

3337.K684 Kruglikov, Ivan, fl. 1850-1860. Иван Кругликов (Table P-PZ40)
3337.K686 Kruglopolev, N.N., fl. 1850-1860. Н.Н. Круглополев (Table P-PZ40)
3337.K688 Krutogorov, Antoniĭ, fl, 1860-1870. Антоний Крутогоров (Table P-PZ40)
3337.K689 Krylov, A. A. Крылов (Table P-PZ40)
3337.K69 Krylov, Aleksandr Abramovich, 1798-1829. Александр Абрамович Крылов (Table P-PZ40)
3337.K7 Krylov, Ivan Andreevich, 1768-1844. Иван Андреевич Крылов (Table P-PZ40 modified)
3337.K7A61-.K7Z458 Separate works. By title
Basni (Fables). Басни
3337.K7B3 Collected. By date
3337.K7B32 Selected fables. By date
3337.K7B33-.K7B39 Translations (Collected or selected)
Alphabetically by language
3337.K7B4-.K7B79 Special fables (alphabetically)
e. g.
3337.K7B45 Dem′i͡anova ukha. Демьянова уха
3337.K7B47 Fortuna i nishchiĭ. Фортуна и нищий
3337.K7B5 Kot i povar. Кот и повар
3337.K7B53 Krest′i͡anin i smert′. Крестьянин и смерть
3337.K7B57 Lzhet͡s. Лжец
3337.K7B6 Martyshka i ochki. Мартышка и очки
3337.K7B65 Pustynnik i medved′. Пустынник и медведь
3337.K7B68 Shchuka i kot. Щука и кот
3337.K7B7 Slon i Mos′ka. Слон и Моська
3337.K7B73 Trishkin kaftan. Тришкин кафтан
3337.K7B75 Volk i zhuravl′. Волк и журавль
3337.K7B78 Zerkalo i obez′i͡ana. Зеркало и обезьяна
3337.K7B8 Beshenai͡a sem′i͡a (Comic opera). Бешеная семья
3337.K7F5 Filomela (Tragedy). Филомела
3337.K7K3 Kaib (Story). Каиб
3337.K7L4 Lenti͡aĭ (Comedy). Лентяй
3337.K7M6 Modnai͡a lavka (Comedy). Модная лавка
3337.K7P5 Pirog (Comedy). Пирог
Podshchipa. Подщипа see PG3337.K7T7
3337.K7P7 Prokazniki (Comedy). Проказники
3337.K7S6 Sochinitel′ v prikhozheĭ (Comedy). Сочинитель в прихожей
3337.K7T5 Ti͡ufi͡ak (Novel). Тюфяк
3337.K7T7 Trumf (Tragedy). Трумф
3337.K7U7 Urok dochkam (Comedy). Урок дочкам

Russian literature
Individual authors and works, 1800-1870
Individual authors, Gogol′ - Pushkin -- Continued

3337.K72 Krylov, Ivan Zakharovich, 1816-1869. Иван Захарович Крылов (Table P-PZ40)

Kube, Elena Ivanovna. Елена Ивановна Кубе see PG3447.V38

3337.K727 Kublit͡skiĭ, M. (Mikhail), 1821-1875. Михаилъ Кублицкій (Table P-PZ40)

Kuchina, Tat′i͡ana Petrovna. Татьяна Петровна Кучина see PG3337.P27

3337.K73 Kudri͡avt͡sev, Petr Nikolaevich, 1816-1858. Петр Николаевич Кудрявцев (Table P-PZ40)

3337.K74 Kugushev, Grigoriĭ Vasil′evich, kni͡az′ 1824-1871. Григорий Васильевич Кугушев (Table P-PZ40)

3337.K75 Kugushev, Nikolaĭ Mikhaĭlovich, kni͡az′, fl. 1800-1810. Николай Михайлович Кугушев (Table P-PZ40)

3337.K76 Kukol′nik, Nestor Vasil′evich, 1809-1868. Нестор Васильевич Кукольник (Table P-PZ40)

3337.K77 Kukol′nik, Pavel Vasil′evich, 1795-1884. Павел Васильевич Кукольник (Table P-PZ40)

3337.K78 Kul′chinskiĭ, Aleksandr I͡Akovlevich, 1815-1845. Александр Яковлевич Кульчинский (Table P-PZ40)

3337.K79 Kul′chit͡skiĭ, M.T., d. 1846. M.T. Кульчицкий (Table P-PZ40)

3337.K8 Kulikov, Nikolaĭ Ivanovich, 1815-1891. Николай Иванович Куликов (Table P-PZ40)

3337.K82 Kul′man, Elizaveta Borisovna, 1808-1825. Елизавета Борисовна Кульман (Table P-PZ40)

3337.K83 Kulzhinskiĭ, Ivan Grigor′evich, 1803-1884. Иван Григорьевич Кулжинский (Table P-PZ40)

3337.K84 Kurakin, N.I., fl. 1860-1880. Н.И. Куракин (Table P-PZ40)

3337.K85 Kurochkin, Nikolaĭ Stepanovich, 1830-1884. Николай Степанович Курочкин (Table P-PZ40)

3337.K86 Kurochkin, Vasiliĭ Stepanovich, 1831-1875. Василий Степанович Курочкин (Table P-PZ40)

3337.K88 Kushelev-Bezborodko, Grigoriĭ Aleksandrovich, graf, 1832-1870. Григорий Александрович Кушелев-Безбородко (Table P-PZ40)

3337.K89 Kushnerev, Ivan Nikolaevich, 1827-1896. Иван Николаевич Кушнерев (Table P-PZ40)

3337.K895 Kutorga, Mikhail Semenovich, 1809-1886. Михаил Семенович Куторга (Table P-PZ40)

3337.K9 Kuzhba, Nikolaĭ Il′ich, fl. 1860-1880. Николай Ильич Кужба (Table P-PZ40)

Russian literature
Individual authors and works, 1800-1870
Individual authors, Gogolʹ - Pushkin -- Continued

3337.K92 Kuzʹmich, Aleksandr Petrovich, fl. 1840-1850. Александр Петрович Кузьмич (Table P-PZ40)
3337.K93 Kuzmichev, Fedot Semenovich, 1809-1860? Федот Семенович Кузмичев (Table P-PZ40)
3337.K95 Kvitka, Grigoriĭ Fedorovich, 1778-1843. Григорий Федорович Квитка (Table P-PZ40)
3337.L15 Labzin, Aleksandr Fedorovich, 1766-1825. Александр Федорович Лабзин (Table P-PZ40)
3337.L2 Lachinova, Ekaterina Petrovna, fl. 1840-1850. Екатерина Петровна Лачинова (Table P-PZ40)
3337.L23 Lapin, Vasiliĭ Innokentʹevich, 1823-1886. Василий Иннокентьевич Лапин (Table P-PZ40)
3337.L25 Lavrov, N., fl. 1830-1840. Н. Лавров (Table P-PZ40)
3337.L28 Lazhechnikov, Ivan Ivanovich, 1792-1869. Иван Иванович Лажечников (Table P-PZ40)
3337.L29 Leĭn, A. A. Лейн (Table P-PZ40)
3337.L3 Lenskiĭ, Dmitriĭ Timofeevich, 1805-1860. Дмитрий Тимофеевич Ленский (Table P-PZ40)
3337.L35 Leonard, Pavel St., fl. 1860-1880. Павел Ст. Леонард (Table P-PZ40)
Leontʹev, Konstantin Nikolaevich. Константин Николаевич Леонтьев see PG3467.L4
3337.L37 Leontʹev, N.I. Н.И. Леонтьев (Table P-PZ40)
Lermontov, Mikhail I͡Urʹevich, 1814-1841. Михаил Юрьевич Лермонтов
3337.L4 Collected works. By date
3337.L4A15 Collected novels and tales. By date
3337.L4A17 Collected poems. By date
3337.L4A19 Collected plays. By date
Translations (Collected or selected)
3337.L4A2-.L4A29 English. By translator, if given, or date
3337.L4A3-.L4A39 French. By translator, if given, or date
3337.L4A4-.L4A49 German. By translator, if given, or date
3337.L4A5-.L4A59 Other. By language
3337.L4A6 Selections. Quotations
3337.L4A61-.L4Z458 Separate works. By title
3337.L4A75 Angel smerti (Poem). Ангел смерти
3337.L4A8 Ashik-Kerib (Tale). Ашик-Кериб
3337.L4A85 Aul Bastundzhi (Poem). Аул Бастунджи
3337.L4A9 Azrail (Poem). Азраил
3337.L4B3 Ballady. Баллады
3337.L4B4 Beglet͡s (Legend in verse). Беглец
Bėla. Бэла see PG3337.L4G42
3337.L4B5 Boi͡arin Orsha (Poem). Боярин Орша

Russian literature
Individual authors and works, 1800-1870
Individual authors, Gogol′ - Pushkin
Lermontov, Mikhail I͡Ur′evich, 1814-1841. Михаил Юрьевич Лермонтов
Separate works. By title -- Continued

3337.L4B6 Borodino (Ballad). Бородино
3337.L4D4 Demon (Story in verse). Демон
3337.L4D8 Dva brata (Drama). Два брата
3337.L4D9 Dzhulio (Poem). Джулио
Fatalist. Фаталист see PG3337.L4G47
3337.L4G4 Geroĭ nashego vremeni (Novel). Герой нашего времени
3337.L4G42 Bėla. Бэла
3337.L4G43 Maksim Maksimych. Максим Максимыч
3337.L4G44 Zhurnal Pechorina. Журнал Печорина
3337.L4G45 Taman′. Тамань
3337.L4G46 Kni͡azhna Meri. Княжна Мери
3337.L4G47 Fatalist. Фаталист
3337.L4G6 Goshpital′ (Tales in verse). Гошпиталь
3337.L4I7 Ispant͡sy (Tragedy). Испанцы
3337.L4I8 Ispoved′ (Poem). Исповедь
3337.L4I9 Ismail-Beĭ (Story in verse). Исмаил-Бей
3337.L4K2 Kally (Story in verse). Каллы
3337.L4K3 Kaznacheĭsha (Poem). Казначейша
3337.L4K4 Khadzhi-Abrek (Poem). Хаджи-Абрек
3337.L4K5 Kni͡agini͡a Ligovskai͡a (Novel). Княгиня Лиговская
Kni͡azhna Meri. Княжна Мери see PG3337.L4G46
3337.L4K6 Korsar (Poem). Корсар
3337.L4L4 Legendy. Легенды
3337.L4L5 Litvinka (Poem). Литвинка
Li͡udi i strasti. Люди и страсти see PG3337.L4M4
Maksim Maksimych. Максим Максимыч see PG3337.L4G43
3337.L4M3 Maskarad (Drama). Маскарад
3337.L4M4 Menschen und Leidenschaften (Drama)
Title in Russian: Li͡udi i strasti (Люди и страсти)
3337.L4M6 Mongo (Poem). Монго
3337.L4M8 Mt͡syri (Poem). Мцыри
3337.L4N3 Na smert′ Pushkina (Poem). На смерть Пушкина
3337.L4P4 Pesni͡a pro t͡sari͡a Ivana Vasil′evicha. Песня про царя Ивана Васильевича
3337.L4P5 Petergofskiĭ prazdnik (Poem). Петергофский праздник
3337.L4P6 Posledniĭ syn vol′nosti (Story in verse). Последний сын вольности
3337.L4P75 Povest′ bez zaglavii͡a. Повесть без заглавия

Russian literature
Individual authors and works, 1800-1870
Individual authors, Gogol′ - Pushkin
Lermontov, Mikhail I͡Ur′evich, 1814-1841. Михаил Юрьевич Лермонтов
Separate works. By title -- Continued

3337.L4S3	Sashka (Poem). Сашка
3337.L4S8	Strannyĭ chelovek (Drama). Странный человек
	Taman′. Тамань see PG3337.L4G45
	Tambovskai͡a kaznacheĭsha. Тамбовская казначейша see PG3337.L4K3
3337.L4U4	Ulansha (Poem). Уланша
3337.L4V3	Vadim (Story). Вадим
3337.L4V4	Valerik (Poem). Валерик
	Zhurnal Pechorina. Журнал Печорина see PG3337.L4G44
	Biography and criticism
3337.L42A1-.L42A19	Periodicals. Societies. Collections
3337.L42A2-.L42A3	Dictionaries, indexes, etc.
3337.L42A5-.L42Z	General treatises. Life and works
3337.L43	Homes and haunts
3337.L44	Anniversaries and celebrations
3337.L45	Iconography. Museums. Exhibitions
	Criticism and interpretation
3337.L46	General works
3337.L47	Special topics, A-Z
3337.L47C38	Caucasus
3337.L47C48	Characters
3337.L47I54	Influence
3337.L47K83	Kuban River Region
3337.L47P45	Philosophy
3337.L47P74	Prose
3337.L47R7	Romanticism
3337.L48	Language. Style
3337.L49	Translations (as subject)
	Leskov, Nikolaĭ Semenovich, 1831-1895. Николай Семенович Лесков
3337.L5	Collected works. By date
3337.L5A12	Selected works. By date
	Translations (Collected or selected)
3337.L5A2-.L5A29	English. By translator, if given, or date
3337.L5A3-.L5A39	French. By translator, if given, or date
3337.L5A4-.L5A49	German. By translator, if given, or date
3337.L5A5-.L5A59	Other. By language
3337.L5A6	Selections. By date
3337.L5A61-.L5Z458	Separate works. By title
3337.L5A8	Amur z lapotochkakh (Novel). Амур з лапоточках

PG

Russian literature
Individual authors and works, 1800-1870
Individual authors, Gogol′ - Pushkin
Leskov, Nikolaĭ Semenovich, 1831-1895. Николай Семенович Лесков
Separate works. By title -- Continued

3337.L5A85 Antuka (Tale). Антука
3337.L5A9 Askalonskiĭ zlodeĭ. Аскалонский злодей
3337.L5B4 Belyĭ orel (Story). Белый орел
3337.L5C2 Chai͡ushchie dvizhenii͡a vody (Romantic chronicle). Чающие движения воды
3337.L5C3 Chas voli Bozh′eĭ (Tale). Час воли Божьей
3337.L5C4 Chelobitnai͡a (Poem). Челобитная
3337.L5C5 Chelovek na chasakh. Человек на часах
3337.L5C6 Chertogon (Tale). Чертогон
3337.L5C7 Chortovy kukly (Novel). Чортовы куклы
3337.L5D8 Dukh gospozhi Zhanlis (Tale). Дух госпожи Жанлис
3337.L5F5 Figura (Tale). Фигура
3337.L5G6 Gora (Novel). Гора
3337.L5G7 Grabezh (Tale). Грабеж
3337.L5I2 I͡Azvitel′nyĭ (Tale). Язвительный
3337.L5I5 Improvizatory. Импровизаторы
3337.L5I7 Istorii͡a odnogo umopomeshatel′stva (Tale). История одного умопомешательства
3337.L5K5 Khristos v gosti͡akh u muzhika (Tale). Христос в гостях у мужика
3337.L5K6 Kotin Doilet͡s o Platonida (Story). Котин Доилец о Платонида
3337.L5L4 Ledi Makbet Mt͡senskogo uezda (Sketch). Леди Макбет Мценского уезда
3337.L5L43 Legendarnye kharaktery. Легендарные характеры
3337.L5L45 Levsha (Legend). Левша
3337.L5M4 Melochi arkhiereĭskoĭ zhizni. Мелочи архиерейской жизни
For separate stories see the title in PG3337.L5A61+
3337.L5M6 Monasheskie ostrova na Ladozhskom ozere. Монашеские острова на Ладожском озере
3337.L5M7 Morskoĭ kapitan s sukhoĭ Nedny (Tale). Морской капитан с сухой Недны
Na krai͡u sveta. На краю света see PG3337.L5R92
3337.L5N2 Na nozhakh (Novel). На ножах
3337.L5N3 Nekreshchennyĭ pop (Tale). Некрещенный поп
3337.L5N4 Nekuda (Novel). Некуда
3337.L5N5 Nesmertel′nyĭ Golovan (Tale). Несмертельный Голован
3337.L5N6 Nevinnyĭ Prudent͡siĭ (Story). Невинный Пруденций
3337.L5N7 Nezametnyĭ sled (Novel). Незаметный след

Russian literature
Individual authors and works, 1800-1870
Individual authors, Gogol′ - Pushkin
Leskov, Nikolaĭ Semenovich, 1831-1895. Николай Семенович Лесков
Separate works. By title -- Continued

3337.L5O2 Oboĭdennye (Novel). Обойденные
3337.L5O3 Ocharovannyĭ strannik (Tale). Очарованный странник
3337.L5O4 Odnodum (Tale). Однодум
3337.L5O8 Ostrovit͡iane (Novel). Островитяне
3337.L5O9 Ov͡tsebyk (Tale). Овцебык
3337.L5P3 Pavlin (Tale). Павлин
3337.L5P5 Polunoshchniki (Sketch). Полунощники
3337.L5P6 Poslednee prividenie Inzhenernogo zamka (Tale). Последнее привидение Инженерного замка
3337.L5P65 Povest′ o bogougodnom drovokole. Повесть о богоугодном дровоколе
3337.L5P7 Pravedniki (Tales). Праведники
For separate tales see the title in PG3337.L5A61+
3337.L5P8 Prekrasna͡ia Aza (Legend). Прекрасная Аза
3337.L5P9 Pustopl͡iasy (Tale). Пустоплясы
3337.L5R2 Raĭskiĭ zmeĭ (Story). Райский змей
3337.L5R25 Rakushanskiĭ melamed (Tale). Ракушанский меламед
3337.L5R3 Rasskazy kstati. Рассказы кстати
For separate tales see the title in PG3337.L5A61+
3337.L5R4 Rastochitel′ (Drama). Расточитель
3337.L5R5 Razboĭnik (Tale). Разбойник
3337.L5R7 Rozhdestvenska͡ia noch′ v vagone (Story). Рождественская ночь в вагоне
3337.L5R8 Russka͡ia rozn′. Русская рознь
For separate sketches and tales see the title in PG3337.L5A61+
3337.L5R9 Russkie bogonos͡tsy. Русские богоносцы
3337.L5R92 Na kra͡iu sveta (Tale). На краю света
3337.L5R93 Vladychnyĭ sud (Tale). Владычный суд
3337.L5R95 Russkiĭ demokrat v Pol′she. Русский демократ в Польше
3337.L5S3 Sheramur (Tale). Шерамур
3337.L5S4 Shtopal′shchik (Sketch). Штопальщик
Skaz o tul′skom kosom Levshe i o stal′noĭ blokhe. Сказ о тульском косом Левше и о стальной блохе see PG3337.L5S45
3337.L5S45 Skazanie o Fedore-Khristianine i o druge ego Abrame-Zhidovine. Сказание о Федоре-Христианине и о друге его Абраме-Жидовине

Russian literature
Individual authors and works, 1800-1870
Individual authors, Gogolʹ - Pushkin
Leskov, Nikolaĭ Semenovich, 1831-1895. Николай Семенович Лесков
Separate works. By title -- Continued
3337.L5S5 Skomorokh Pamfalon (Legend). Скоморох Памфалон
3337.L5S55 Smekh i gore. Смех и горе
3337.L5S6 Sobori͡ane. Stargorodskai͡a khronika. Соборяне. Старгородская хроника
3337.L5S7 Sokoliĭ perelet (Novel). Соколий перелет
3337.L5S75 Sovestnyĭ Danila (Legend). Совестный Данила
Stalʹnai͡a blokha. Стальная блоха see PG3337.L5S45
3337.L5S8 Starye gody v sele Plodomasove (Sketch). Старые годы в селе Плодомасове
3337.L5S9 Svi͡atochnye rasskazy. Святочные рассказы
For separate tales see the title in PG3337.L5A61+
3337.L5T8 Tupeĭnyĭ khudozhnik (Tale). Тупейный художник
3337.L5U5 Umershee soslovie (Tale). Умершее сословие
3337.L5V2 V tarantase (Tale). В тарантасе
3337.L5V3 Vdokhnovennye brodi͡agi (Tales). Вдохновенные бродяги
3337.L5V4 Velikosvetskiĭ raskol. Великосветский раскол
Vladychnyĭ sud. Владычный суд see PG3337.L5R93
3337.L5V6 Voitelʹnit͡sa (Sketch). Воительница
3337.L5Z2 Za vorotami t͡iurʹmy (Tale). За воротами тюрьмы
3337.L5Z22 Zagadochnyĭ chelovek (Episode). Загадочный человек
3337.L5Z24 Zai͡achiĭ remiz. Заячий ремиз
3337.L5Z26 Zakhudalyĭ rod (Chronicle). Захудалый род
3337.L5Z28 Zapechatlennyĭ angel (Tale). Запечатленный ангел
3337.L5Z3 Zheleznai͡a voli͡a (Tale). Железная воля
3337.L5Z32 Zhidovskai͡a kuvyrkalegii͡a (Story). Жидовская кувыркалегия
3337.L5Z4 Zverʹ (Tale). Зверь
3337.L5Z5-.L5Z99 Biography and criticism
3337.L55 Levitov, Aleksandr Ivanovich, 1835-1877. Александр Иванович Левитов (Table P-PZ40)
3337.L57 Levshin, Vasiliĭ Alekseevich, 1746-1826. Василий Алексеевич Левшин (Table P-PZ40)
Li͡eskov, Nikolaĭ Semenovich. Николай Семеновичъ Лѣсковъ see PG3337.L5+
3337.L6 Likhachev, Egor Filippovich, b. 1807. Егор Филиппович Лихачев (Table P-PZ40)

Russian literature
Individual authors and works, 1800-1870
Individual authors, Gogol′ - Pushkin -- Continued

3337.L62 Likhachev, V︠i︡acheslav, fl. 1850-1860. Вячеслав Лихачев (Table P-PZ40)

3337.L64 Lisit︠s︡yna, Marii︠a︡, fl. 1820-1840. Мария Лисицына (Table P-PZ40)

3337.L66 Livanov, Fedor Vasil′evich, fl. 1860-1880. Федор Васильевич Ливанов (Table P-PZ40)

Livenskiĭ, N. H. Ливенский see PG3337.M44

3337.L68 Lizander, Dmitriĭ Karlovich fon, 1824-1894. Дмитрий Карлович фон Лизандер (Table P-PZ40)

3337.L7 Lobanov, Mikhail Evstaf′evich, 1787-1846. Михаил Евстафьевич Лобанов (Table P-PZ40)

3337.L73 Lobysevich, Petr, fl. 1790-1820. Петр Лобысевич (Table P-PZ40)

Lodyzhenska︠i︡a, Elizaveta Aleksandrovna (Sushkova). Елизавета Александровна (Сушкова) Лодыженская see PG3447.V115

3337.L78 Lomachevskiĭ, A.I., fl. 1830-1850. А.И. Ломачевский (Table P-PZ40)

Lopukhin, Ivan Vladimirovich. Иван Владимирович Лопухин see PG3317.L6

Luganskiĭ, Kazak, pseud. Казак Луганский see PG3321.D2

Luganskiĭ, Vladimir, pseud. Владимир Луганский see PG3321.D2

3337.L79 Lukin, G.G. (Grigoriĭ Grigor′evich). Григорій Григорьевичъ Лукинъ (Table P-PZ40)

3337.L793 Lunskiĭ, Evgeniĭ. Евгений Лунский (Table P-PZ40)

3337.L8 Lutkovskiĭ, Nikolaĭ Petrovich, fl. 1820-1840. Николай Петрович Лутковский (Table P-PZ40)

3337.L85 L′vov, Fedor Petrovich, 1766-1836. Федор Петрович Львов (Table P-PZ40)

3337.L9 L′vov, Nikolaĭ Mikhaĭlovich, 1821-1872. Николай Михайлович Львов (Table P-PZ40)

L′vov, Pavel I︠U︡r′evich. Павел Юрьевич Львов see PG3317.L8

L′vova, Mar′i︠a︡ Fedorovna. Марья Федоровна Львова see PG3360.R63

3337.M16 Magnit︠s︡kiĭ, Mikhail Leont′evich, 1778-1844. Михаил Леонтьевич Магницкий (Table P-PZ40)

3337.M18 Maĭkov, Apollon Aleksandrovich, 1761-1838. Аполлон Александрович Майков (Table P-PZ40)

3337.M2 Maĭkov, Apollon Nikolaevich, 1821-1897. Аполлон Николаевич Майков (Table P-PZ40)

Russian literature
Individual authors and works, 1800-1870
Individual authors, Gogol′ - Pushkin -- Continued

3337.M22 Maĭkov, Mikhail Aleksandrovich, fl. 1820-1840. Михаил Александрович Майков (Table P-PZ40)

3337.M23 Maĭkova, Evgenii͡a Petrovna (Gusi͡atnikova), 1803-1880. Евгения Петровна (Гусятникова) Майкова (Table P-PZ40)

3337.M24 Makarov, Mikhail Nikolaevich, 1789-1847. Михаил Николаевич Макаров (Table P-PZ40)

3337.M25 Makarov, Nikolaĭ Petrovich, 1810-1890. Николай Петрович Макаров (Table P-PZ40)

3337.M26 Makarov, Petr Ivanovich, 1765-1804. Петр Иванович Макаров (Table P-PZ40)

3337.M264 Makarova, Sofʹi͡a, 1834-1887. Софья Макарова (Table P-PZ40)

3337.M27 Makashin, Semen Akimovich, 1827-ca. 1862. Семен Акимович Макашин (Table P-PZ40)

3337.M28 Maksheeva, Varvara Dmitrievna, fl. 1830-1840. Варвара Дмитриевна Макшеева (Table P-PZ40)

3337.M287 Maksimov, G.M. (Gavriil Mikhaĭlovich), d. 1882. Гавріилъ Михайловичъ Максимовъ (Table P-PZ40)

3337.M29 Maksimov, Mikhail, fl. 1820-1850. Михаил Максимов (Table P-PZ40)

3337.M3 Maksimov, Sergeĭ Vasil′evich, 1831-1901. Сергей Васильевич Максимов (Table P-PZ40)

3337.M32 Marchenko, Anastasii͡a I͡Akovlevna, 1830-1880. Анастасия Яковлевна Марченко (Table P-PZ40)

3337.M33 Marin, Sergeĭ Nikiforovich, 1775-1813. Сергей Никифорович Марин (Table P-PZ40)

3337.M35 Markov, Alekseĭ Ivanovich, 1794-1869. Алексей Иванович Марков (Table P-PZ40)

3337.M36 Markov, Mikhail Aleksandrovich, 1810-1876. Михаил Александрович Марков (Table P-PZ40)

Marlinskiĭ, A. A. Марлинский see PG3321.B45

3337.M38 Masal′skiĭ, Konstantin Petrovich, 1802-1861. Константин Петрович Масальский (Table P-PZ40)

3337.M39 Mashkov, Petr Alekseevich, fl. 1830-1850. Петр Алексеевич Машков (Table P-PZ40)

Matinskiĭ, Mikhail. Михаил Матинский see PG3317.M4

3337.M4 Meĭ, Lev Aleksandrovich, 1822-1862. Лев Александрович Мей (Table P-PZ40)

3337.M42 Meĭsner, Alekseĭ I͡Akovlevich, 1807-1882. Алексей Яковлевич Мейснер (Table P-PZ40)

3337.M44 Mel′gunov, Nikolaĭ Aleksandrovich, 1804-1867. Николай Александрович Мельгунов (Table P-PZ40)

Russian literature
Individual authors and works, 1800-1870
Individual authors, Gogol′ - Pushkin -- Continued

3337.M45 Mel′nikov, Pavel Ivanovich, 1819-1883. Павел Иванович Мельников (Table P-PZ40)

3337.M46 Men′shikov, P.N., fl. 1840-1870. П.Н. Меньшиков (Table P-PZ40)

3337.M48 Merzli͡akov, Alekseĭ Fedorovich, 1778-1830. Алексей Федорович Мерзляков (Table P-PZ40)

3337.M49 Mezhakov, Pavel Aleksandrovich, 1786-1860. Павел Александрович Межаков (Table P-PZ40)

3337.M5 Mi͡atlev, Ivan Petrovich, 1796-1844. Иван Петрович Мятлев (Table P-PZ40)

3337.M52 Mikhaĭlov, Mikhail Larionovich, 1826-1865. Михаил Ларионович Михайлов (Table P-PZ40)

3337.M53 Mikhalovskiĭ, Dmitriĭ Lavrent′evich, 1828-1905. Дмитрий Лаврентьевич Михаловский (Table P-PZ40)

Miklashevich, Varvara Semenovna. Варвара Семеновна Миклашевич see PG3337.P84

3337.M54 Mili͡ukov, Aleksandr Petrovich, 1817-1897. Александр Петрович Милюков (Table P-PZ40)

3337.M545 Miliūs, F. Ф. Милiусъ (Table P-PZ40)

3337.M547 Mil′ki͡eev, E., fl. 1840-1850. Е. Милькѣевъ (Table P-PZ40)

3337.M55 Miller, Fedor Bogdanovich, 1818-1881. Федор Богданович Миллер (Table P-PZ40)

3337.M56 Milonov, Mikhail Vasil′evich, 1792-1821. Михаил Васильевич Милонов (Table P-PZ40)

3337.M57 Min, Dmitriĭ Egorovich, 1818-1885. Дмитрий Егорович Мин (Table P-PZ40)

3337.M58 Minaev, Dmitriĭ Ivanovich, 1808-1876. Дмитрий Иванович Минаев (Table P-PZ40)

3337.M59 Miroshevskiĭ, Vasiliĭ, fl. 1830-1850. Василий Мирошевский (Table P-PZ40)

Misailov, Feopempt. Феопемпт Мисаилов see PG3337.L15

3337.M6 Moller, Egor Aleksandrovich, 1812-1879. Егор Александрович Моллер (Table P-PZ40)

3337.M7 Mordovt͡seva, Anna Nikanorovna (Zaletaeva), 1823-1885. Анна Никаноровна (Залетаева) Мордовцева (Table P-PZ40)

3337.M8 Murav′ev, Andreĭ Nikolaevich, 1806-1874. Андрей Николаевич Муравьев (Table P-PZ40)

3337.M85 Murav′ev, Nikolaĭ Nazarovich, 1775-1845. Николай Назарович Муравьев (Table P-PZ40)

3337.M9 Murav′ev-Apostol, Ivan Matveevich, 1765-1851. Иван Матвеевич Муравьев-Апостол (Table P-PZ40)

Russian literature
Individual authors and works, 1800-1870
Individual authors, Gogol′ - Pushkin -- Continued

3337.M94 Myl′nikov, Aleksandr. Александр Мыльников (Table P-PZ40)

N., Ol′ga. Ольга Н. see PG3330.E6

3337.N15 Nadezhdin, Nikolaĭ Ivanovich, 1804-1856. Николай Иванович Надеждин (Table P-PZ40)

3337.N2 Nakhimov, Akim Nikolaevich, 1782-1814. Аким Николаевич Нахимов (Table P-PZ40)

3337.N3 Narezhnyĭ, Vasiliĭ Trofimovich, 1780-1825. Василий Трофимович Нарежный (Table P-PZ40)

Narskai͡a, E. E. Нарская see PG3361.S363

3337.N32 Naumova, Anna Aleksandrovna, d. 1862. Анна Александровна Наумова (Table P-PZ40)

3337.N35 Nebol′sin, Pavel Ivanovich, 1817-1893. Павел Иванович Небольсин (Table P-PZ40)

Neĭtral′nyĭ, Sergeĭ. Сергей Нейтральный see PG3337.P57

3337.N4 Nekrasov, Nikolaĭ Alekseevich, 1821-1877. Николай Алексеевич Некрасов (Table P-PZ40 modified)

3337.N4A61-.N4Z458 Separate works. By title

3337.N4A8 Akter (Farce-vaudeville). Актер

3337.N4B2 Baba-I͡Aga kosti͡anai͡a noga (Tale in verse). Баба-Яга костяная нога

3337.N4B3 Balet (Poem). Балет

Bednost′ i chest′. Бедность и честь see PG3337.N4M39

3337.N4D4 Dedushka (Poem). Дедушка

3337.N4D45 Dedushka Mazaĭ i zai͡tsy (Poem). Дедушка Мазай и зайцы

3337.N4D5 Detstvo (Poem). Детство

3337.N4F4 Feoklist Onufrich Bob (Vaudeville). Феоклист Онуфрич Боб

3337.N4G3 Gazetnai͡a (Poem). Газетная

3337.N4G4 Geroi vremeni (Tragicomedy). Герои времени

3337.N4G6 Gore starogo Nauma (Poem). Горе старого Наума

3337.N4I8 I͡Unost′ Lomonosova (Dramatic fantasy). Юность Ломоносова

3337.N4K3 Kak ubit′ vecher (Drama). Как убить вечер

3337.N4K4 Kamennoe serdt͡se (Story). Каменное сердце

3337.N4K6 Komu na Rusi zhit′ khorosho (Poem). Кому на Руси жить хорошо

3337.N4K7 Korobeĭniki (Poem). Коробейники

3337.N4K8 Kuznet͡s (Poem). Кузнец

3337.N4M3 Makar Osipovich Sluchaĭnyĭ (Tale). Макар Осипович Случайный

Russian literature
Individual authors and works, 1800-1870
Individual authors, Gogol′ - Pushkin
Nekrasov, Nikolaĭ Alekseevich, 1821-1877. Николай Алексеевич Некрасов
Separate works. By title -- Continued

3337.N4M35 Masha (Poem). Маша
3337.N4M37 Mat′ (Poem). Мать
3337.N4M39 Materinskoe blagoslovenie, ili, Bednost′ i chest′ (Drama). Материнское благословение, или, Бедность и честь
3337.N4M4 Mechty i zvuki (Poems). Мечты и звуки
3337.N4M45 Medvezh′i͡a okhota (Dramatic piece in verse). Медвежья охота
3337.N4M47 Mertvoe ozero (Novel). Мертвое озеро
3337.N4M6 Moroz, krasnyĭ-nos (Poem). Мороз, красный-нос
3337.N4N3 Na Volge (Poem). На Волге
3337.N4N4 Neobyknovennyĭ zavtrak (Tale). Необыкновенный завтрак
3337.N4N5 Neszhatai͡a polosa (Poem). Несжатая полоса
3337.N4N6 Novoizobretennai͡a kraska Derlinga (Tale). Новоизобретенная краска Дерлинга
3337.N4N7 Novyĭ god (Poem). Новый год
3337.N4O2 O pogode (Poem). О погоде
3337.N4O4 Ogorodnik (Poem). Огородник
3337.N4O6 Opytnai͡a zhenshchina (Tale). Опытная женщина
3337.N4O7 Osennii͡a skuka (Dramatic piece). Осенняя скука
3337.N4P4 Pesni o svobodnom slove. Песни о свободном слове
3337.N4P45 Peterburgskie ugly (Tale). Петербургские углы
3337.N4P5 Peterburgskiĭ rostovshchik (Vaudeville). Петербургский ростовщик
3337.N4P55 Pevit͡sa (Story). Певица
3337.N4P57 Poėt i grazhdanin (Dialog in verse). Поэт и гражданин
3337.N4P6 Poslednie pesni. Последние песни
3337.N4P65 Potonuvshie (Tale). Потонувшие
3337.N4P7 Povest′ o bednom Klime. Повесть о бедном Климе
3337.N4P75 Psovai͡a okhota (Poem). Псовая охота
3337.N4P8 Russkie zhenshchiny (Poems). Русские женщины
3337.N4S3 Sasha (Poem). Саша
3337.N4S6 Sonichka (Sketch). Соничка
3337.N4S7 Sovremenniki (Poems). Современники
3337.N4S8 Sud (Story in verse). Суд
3337.N4T6 Tonkiĭ chelovek (Tale). Тонкий человек
3337.N4T7 Tri strany sveta (Novel). Три страны света
3337.N4U8 Utro v redakt͡sii (Vaudeville). Утро в редакции

Russian literature
Individual authors and works, 1800-1870
Individual authors, Gogol′ - Pushkin
Nekrasov, Nikolaĭ Alekseevich, 1821-1877. Николай Алексеевич Некрасов
Separate works. By title -- Continued

3337.N4V6 Vlas (Poem). Влас

3337.N4Z3 Zheleznai͡a doroga (Poem). Железная дорога

3337.N4Z35 Zhizn′ i pokhozhdenii͡a Kir′i͡akova (Tale). Жизнь и похождения Кирьякова

3337.N4Z4 Zhizn′ i pokhozhdenii͡a Tikhona Trosnikova (Tale). Жизнь и похождения Тихона Тросникова

Nekrassov, Nicholas see PG3337.N4

Neledinskiĭ-Melet͡skiĭ, I͡Uriĭ Aleksandrovich. Юрий Александрович Нелединский-Мелецкий see PG3317.N4

3337.N47 Nesterov, P., fl.1850-1860. П. Нестеров (Table P-PZ40)

Nestroev, A. A. Нестроев see PG3337.K73

3337.N5 Nevedomskiĭ, Nikolaĭ Vasil′evich, 1791-1853. Николай Васильевич Неведомский (Table P-PZ40)

3337.N53 Nevel′skiĭ, Vladimir, fl. 1860-1870. Владимир Невельский (Table P-PZ40)

3337.N58 Nevzorov, Maksim Ivanovich, 1762-1827. Максим Иванович Невзоров (Table P-PZ40)

Nezamaĭ, V. B. Незамай see PG3321.A83

3337.N6 Nikitenko, Aleksandr Vasil′evich, 1804 or 5-1877. Александр Васильевич Никитенко (Table P-PZ40)

3337.N65 Nikitin, Aleksandr, fl. 1830-1840. Александр Никитин (Table P-PZ40)

3337.N68 Nikitin, Andreĭ Afanas′evich, d. 1859. Андрей Афанасьевич Никитин (Table P-PZ40)

3337.N7 Nikitin, Ivan Savvich, 1824-1861. Иван Саввич Никитин (Table P-PZ40)

Nikolev, Nikolaĭ Petrovich. Николай Петрович Николев see PG3317.N5

Novinskai͡a, A. A. Новинская see PG3337.P33

3337.O2 Obodovskiĭ, Platon Grigor′evich, 1803-1864. Платон Григорьевич Ободовский (Table P-PZ40)

3337.O25 Odoevskiĭ, Aleksandr Ivanovich, kni͡az′, 1803-1839. Александр Иванович Одоевский (Table P-PZ40)

3337.O3 Odoevskiĭ, Vladimir Fedorovich, kni͡az′, 1803-1869. Владимир Федорович Одоевский (Table P-PZ40)

3337.O35 Ofrosimov, Mikhail Aleksandrovich, 1797-1868. Михаил Александрович Офросимов (Table P-PZ40)

3337.O4 Ogarev, Nikolaĭ Platonovich, 1813-1877. Николай Платонович Огарев (Table P-PZ40)

Russian literature
Individual authors and works, 1800-1870
Individual authors, Gogolʹ - Pushkin -- Continued

3337.O5 Orlov, Aleksandr Anfimovich, 1791-1840. Александр Анфимович Орлов (Table P-PZ40)

3337.O55 Orlov, Vasiliĭ Ivanovich, 1792-1860. Василий Иванович Орлов (Table P-PZ40)

Osnovʹi͡anenko. Основьяненко see PG3337.K95

3337.O6 Osnovskiĭ, Nil Andreevich, d. 1871. Нил Андреевич Основский (Table P-PZ40)

Ostenek, Aleksandr Khristoforovich. Александр Христофорович Остенек see PG3447.V87

3337.O7 Ostolopov, Nikolaĭ Fedorovich, 1782-1833. Николай Федорович Остолопов (Table P-PZ40)

Ostrovskiĭ, Aleksandr Nikolaevich, 1823-1886. Александр Николаевич Островский see PG3337.O8+

Ostrovsky, Aleksandr Nikolaevich, 1823-1886. Александр Николаевич Островский

3337.O8 Collected works. By date

3337.O8A12 Selected works. By date

Translations of Ostrovsky's works (Collected or selected)

3337.O8A2-.O8A29 English. By translator, if given, or date

3337.O8A3-.O8A39 French. By translator, if given, or date

3337.O8A4-.O8A49 German. By translator, if given, or date

3337.O8A5-.O8A59 Other. By language

3337.O8A6 Translations by Ostrovsky from foreign languages. By date

For separate works or collected works from one foreign language, see the original language

3337.O8A7-.O8Z4 Separate works. By title

3337.O8B3 Bednai͡a nevesta (Comedy). Бедная невеста

3337.O8B35 Bednostʹ ne porok (Comedy). Бедность не порок

3337.O8B4 Beshenye denʹgi (Comedy). Бешеные деньги

3337.O8B45 Bespridannit͡sa (Drama). Бесприданница

3337.O8B5 Bez viny vinovatye (Drama). Без вины виноватые

3337.O8B55 Blazhʹ (Comedy). Блажь

Joint author: P.M. Nevezhin (Петр Михайлович Невежин)

3337.O8B6 Bogatye nevesty (Comedy). Богатые невесты

3337.O8D4 Dikarka (Comedy). Дикарка

Joint author: N. I͡A. Solovʹev (Николай Яковлевич Соловьев)

3337.O8D5 Dmitriĭ Samozvanet͡s i Vasiliĭ Shuĭskiĭ (Drama). Дмитрий Самозванец и Василий Шуйский

3337.O8D555 Dobryĭ barin (Dramatic scene). Добрый барин

PG

Russian literature
Individual authors and works, 1800-1870
Individual authors, Gogol′ - Pushkin
Ostrovsky, Aleksandr Nikolaevich, 1823-1886.
Александр Николаевич Островский
Separate works. By title -- Continued

3337.O8D6 Dokhodnoe mesto (Comedy). Доходное место
3337.O8G6 Gori͡achee serdt͡se (Comedy). Горячее сердце
3337.O8G65 Grekh da beda na kogo ne zhivet (Drama). Грех да беда на кого не живет
3337.O8G7 Groza (Drama). Гроза
3337.O8K5 Komik XVII stoleti͡ia (Comedy). Комик XVII столетия
3337.O8K6 Koz′ma Zakhar′ich Minin, Sukhoruk (Drama). Козьма Захарьич Минин, Сухорук
Edition of 1921 published under the title: Kos′ma Minin, ili, Kak okonchilas′ smuta (Косьма Минин, или, Как окончилась смута)
3337.O8K8 Krasavet͡s-muzhchina (Comedy). Красавец-мужчина
3337.O8L4 Les (Comedy). Лес
3337.O8N2 Na boĭkom meste (Comedy). На бойком месте
3337.O8N25 Na vsi͡akogo mudret͡sa dovol′no prostoty (Comedy). На всякого мудреца довольно простоты
3337.O8N3 Ne bylo ni grosha, da vdrug altyn (Comedy). Не было ни гроша, да вдруг алтын
3337.O8N35 Ne ot mira sego (Dramatic scene). Не от мира сего
3337.O8N4 Ne soshlis′ kharakterami! (Dramatic piece). Не сошлись характерами!
3337.O8N45 Ne tak zhivi, kak khochetsi͡a (Drama). Не так живи, как хочется
3337.O8N5 Ne v svoi sani ne sadis′ (Comedy). Не в свои сани не садись
3337.O8N55 Ne vse kotu masli͡anit͡sa (Dramatic scenes). Не все коту масляница
3337.O8N6 Nevol′nit͡sy (Comedy). Невольницы
3337.O8P6 Posledni͡ai͡a zhertva (Comedy). Последняя жертва
3337.O8P65 Pozdni͡ai͡a li͡ubov′ (Dramatic scene). Поздняя любовь
3337.O8P7 Pravda khorosho, a schast′e luchshe (Comedy). Правда хорошо, а счастье лучше
3337.O8P8 Prazdnichnyĭ son - do obeda (Dramatic piece). Праздничный сон - до обеда
3337.O8P9 Puchina (Dramatic scenes). Пучина
3337.O8S2 Schastlivyĭ den′ (Drama). Счастливый день
Joint author: N. I͡A Solov′ev (Николай Яковлевич Соловьев)
3337.O8S3 Semeĭnai͡a kartina (Drama). Семейная картина
3337.O8S4 Serdt͡se ne kamen′ (Comedy). Сердце не камень
3337.O8S5 Shutniki (Dramatic piece). Шутники

Russian literature
Individual authors and works, 1800-1870
Individual authors, Gogol′ - Pushkin
Ostrovsky, Aleksandr Nikolaevich, 1823-1886. Александр Николаевич Островский
Separate works. By title -- Continued

3337.O8S6 Snegurochka (Drama). Снегурочка
3337.O8S7 Staryĭ drug luchshe novykh dvukh (Dramatic piece). Старый друг лучше новых двух
3337.O8S75 Svetit da ne greet (Drama). Светит да не греет
Joint author: N. I͡A. Solov′ev (Николай Яковлевич Соловьев)
3337.O8S8 Svoi li͡udi - sochtems͡ia! (Comedy). Свои люди - сочтемся!
3337.O8S9 Svoi sobaki gryzuts͡ia, chuzha͡ia ne pristavaĭ (Dramatic piece). Свои собаки грызутся, чужая не приставай
3337.O8T3 Talanty i poklonniki (Comedy). Таланты и поклонники
3337.O8T5 T͡iazhelye dni (Dramatic scenes). Тяжелые дни
3337.O8T7 Trudovoĭ khleb (Comedy). Трудовой хлеб
3337.O8T8 Tushino (Drama). Тушино
3337.O8U8 Utro molodogo cheloveka (Dramatic scenes). Утро молодого человека
3337.O8V2 V chuzhom piru pokhmel′e (Comedy). В чужом пиру похмелье
3337.O8V3 Vasilisa Melent′eva (Drama). Василиса Мелентьева
3337.O8V5 Voevoda (Comedy). Воевода
3337.O8V6 Volki i ov͡tsy (Comedy). Волки и овцы
3337.O8V7 Vospitanni͡tsa (Comedy). Воспитанница
3337.O8Z3 Zachem poĭdesh′, to i naĭdesh′ (Dramatic piece). Зачем пойдешь, то и найдешь
3337.O8Z4 Zhenit′ba Belugina (Comedy). Женитьба Белугина
Joint author: N. I͡A. Solov′ev (Николай Яковлевич Соловьев)

Biography and criticism
3337.O8Z52 Journals
Letters
3337.O8Z53 Collected. By date
3337.O8Z54-.O8Z59 Individual correspondents (alphabetically)
3337.O8Z6-.O8Z99 General treatises. Life and works
3337.O83 Ostrozhnikov, S.B., d. 1892. С.Б. Острожников (Table P-PZ40)
3337.O9 Ozerov, Vladislav Aleksandrovich, 1769-1816. Владислав Александрович Озеров (Table P-PZ40)
3337.O95 Oznobishin, Dmitriĭ Petrovich, 1804-1877. Дмитрий Петрович Ознобишин (Table P-PZ40)

Russian literature
Individual authors and works, 1800-1870
Individual authors, Gogol′ - Pushkin -- Continued

3337.P15 Pakatskiĭ, Gavriil Abramovich, 1756-ca. 1840. Гавриил Абрамович Пакатский (Table P-PZ40)

3337.P18 Palit͡syn, Aleksandr Aleksandrovich, ca. 1750-1816. Александр Александрович Палицын (Table P-PZ40)

3337.P2 Panaev, Ivan Ivanovich, 1812-1862. Иван Иванович Панаев (Table P-PZ40)

3337.P22 Panaev, Vladimir Ivanovich, 1792-1859. Владимир Иванович Панаев (Table P-PZ40)

3337.P24 Panaeva, Avdot′i͡a I͡Akovlevna (Bri͡anskai͡a). Авдотья Яковлевна (Брянская) Панаева (Table P-PZ40)
Variant of forename: Evdokii͡a (Евдокия)

Panaeva-Golovacheva, Avdot′i͡a I͡Akovlevna (Bri͡anskai͡a). Авдотья Яковлевна (Брянская) Панаева-Головачева see PG3337.P24

3337.P27 Passek, Tat′i͡ana Petrovna (Kuchina), 1810-1889. Татьяна Петровна (Кучина) Пассек (Table P-PZ40)

3337.P28 Passek, Vadim Vasil′evich, 1807-1842. Вадим Васильевич Пассек (Table P-PZ40)

3337.P29 Pavlov, A.A., fl. 1830-1840. А.А. Павлов (Table P-PZ40)

3337.P3 Pavlov, Nikolaĭ Filippovich, 1805-1864. Николай Филиппович Павлов (Table P-PZ40)

3337.P33 Pavlova, Anna Vasil′evna, 1852-1877. Анна Васильевна Павлова (Table P-PZ40)

3337.P35 Pavlova, Karolina Karlovna (I͡Anish), 1807-1893. Каролина Карловна (Яниш) Павлова (Table P-PZ40)

3337.P37 Pavlova, Ol′ga Petrovna, fl. 1850-1890. Ольга Петровна Павлова (Table P-PZ40)

3337.P39 Pecherin, V. S. (Vladimir Sergeevich), 1807-1885. Владимир Сергеевич Печерин (Table P-PZ40)

Pecherskiĭ, Andreĭ. Андрей Печерский see PG3337.M45

3337.P4 Perevoshchikov, Vasiliĭ Matveevich, 1785-1851. Василий Матвеевич Перевощиков (Table P-PZ40)

3337.P42 Perovskiĭ, Alekseĭ Alekseevich, 1787-1836. Алексей Алексеевич Перовский (Table P-PZ40)

3337.P44 Pert͡sov, Ėrast Petrovich, 1804-1873. Эраст Петрович Перцов (Table P-PZ40)

3337.P46 Petrov, M.A., fl 1850-1870. М.А. Петров (Table P-PZ40)

3337.P48 Pisarev, Aleksandr Ivanovich, 1803-1828. Александр Иванович Писарев (Table P-PZ40)

Pisarev, Nikolaĭ Dmitrievich Ivanchin-. Николай Дмитриевич Иванчин-Писарев see PG3337.I7

Russian literature
Individual authors and works, 1800-1870
Individual authors, Gogol′ - Pushkin -- Continued

3337.P5 Pisemskiĭ, Alekseĭ Feofilaktovich, 1820-1881. Алексей Феофилактович Писемский (Table P-PZ40 modified)
3337.P5A61-.P5Z458 Separate works. By title
3337.P5B3 Bat′ka (Story). Батька
3337.P5B55 Bogatyĭ zhenikh (Novel). Богатый жених
3337.P5B6 Boi͡arshchina (Novel). Боярщина
3337.P5B65 Boĭt͡sy i vyzhidateli (Drama). Бойцы и выжидатели
Brak po strasti. Брак по страсти see PG3337.P5S5
3337.P5B9 Byvye sokoly (Tragedy). Бывые соколы
3337.P5F3 Fanfaron (Tale). Фанфарон
3337.P5F5 Finansovyĭ geniĭ (Comedy). Финансовый гений
3337.P5G6 Gor′kai͡a sud′bina (Drama). Горькая судьбина
3337.P5I5 Intershchik (Tale). Интерщик
3337.P5I6 Iona T͡Sinik (Tale). Иона Циник
3337.P5I7 Ipokhondrik (Comedy). Ипохондрик
3337.P5K5 Khishchniki (Comedy). Хищники
3337.P5K6 Komik (Tale). Комик
3337.P5L4 Leshiĭ (Tale). Леший
3337.P5L5 Li͡udi sorokovykh godov (Novel). Люди сороковых годов
3337.P5M2 M-r Batmanov (Sketch). М-р Батманов
3337.P5M3 Masony (Novel). Масоны
3337.P5M4 Materi-sopernit͡sy (Tragedy). Матери-соперницы
3337.P5M5 Meshchane (Novel). Мещане
3337.P5M6 Miloslavskie i Naryshkiny (Tragedy). Милославские и Нарышкины
3337.P5N5 Nina (Tale). Нина
3337.P5O3 Ocherki iz krest′i͡anskogo byta. Очерки из крестьянского быта
For separate sketches see the title in PG3337.P5A61+
3337.P5P3 Pasha Vikhrov (Tale). Паша Вихров
3337.P5P4 Pitershchik (Tale). Питерщик
3337.P5P5 Plotnich′i͡a artel′ (Tale). Плотничья артель
3337.P5P6 Podkopy (Comedy). Подкопы
3337.P5P65 Poruchik Gladkov (Tragedy). Поручик Гладков
3337.P5P7 Prosveshchennoe vremi͡a (Tragedy). Просвещенное время
3337.P5P8 Pten͡tsy poslednego sleta (Tragedy). Птенцы последнего слета
3337.P5P9 Putevye ocherki. Путевые очерки
3337.P5R3 Razdel (Comedy). Раздел
3337.P5R8 Russkie lguny (Sketches). Русские лгуны
3337.P5S3 Samouprav͡tsy (Tragedy). Самоуправцы

Russian literature
Individual authors and works, 1800-1870
Individual authors, Gogolʹ - Pushkin
Pisemskiĭ, Alekseĭ Feofilaktovich, 1820-1881. Алексей Феофилактович Писемский
Separate works. By title -- Continued

3337.P5S4 Semeĭnyĭ omut (Drama). Семейный омут

3337.P5S5 Sergeĭ Petrovich Khozarov i Mari Stupit͡syna (Story). Сергей Петрович Хозаров и Мари Ступицына
Alternative title: Brak po strasti (Брак по страсти)

3337.P5S7 Stari͡a baryni͡a (Tale). Старая барыня

3337.P5S8 Starcheskiĭ grekh (Story). Старческий грех

3337.P5T5 Ti͡ufi͡ak (Story). Тюфяк

3337.P5T9 Tysi͡acha dush (Novel). Тысяча душ

3337.P5V2 V vodovorote (Novel). В водовороте

3337.P5V3 Vaal (Drama). Ваал

3337.P5V4 Veteran i novobranet͡s (Dramatic piece). Ветеран и новобранец

3337.P5V6 Vinovata-li ona? Виновата-ли она?

3337.P5V9 Vzbalamuchennoe more (Novel). Взбаламученное море

Plavilʹshchikov, Petr Alekseevich. Петр Алексеевич Плавильщиков see PG3317.P5

3337.P54 Pleshcheev, Alekseĭ Nikolaevich, 1825-1893. Алексей Николаевич Плещеев (Table P-PZ40)

3337.P55 Pletnev, Petr Aleksandrovich, 1792-1865. Петр Александрович Плетнев (Table P-PZ40)

3337.P56 Pnin, Ivan Petrovich, 1773-1805. Иван Петрович Пнин (Table P-PZ40)

3337.P57 Pobedonost͡sev, Sergeĭ Petrovich, 1816- . Сергей Петрович Победоносцев (Table P-PZ40)

3337.P58 Podolinskiĭ, Andreĭ Ivanovich, 1806-1886. Андрей Иванович Подолинский (Table P-PZ40)

Podshivalov, Vasiliĭ Sergeevich. Василий Сергеевич Подшивалов see PG3317.P54

3337.P59 Pogodin, Mikhail Petrovich, 1800-1875. Михаил Петрович Погодин (Table P-PZ40)

Pogorelʹskiĭ, Antoniĭ. Антоний Погорельский see PG3337.P42

3337.P593 Pogoskiĭ, Aleksandr Fomich, 1815-1874. Александр Фомич Погоский (Table P-PZ40)
Surname also written "Pogosskiĭ" (Погосский)

3337.P595 Polevoĭ, Ksenofont Alekseevich, 1801-1867. Ксенофонт Алексеевич Полевой (Table P-PZ40)

3337.P6 Polevoĭ, Nikolaĭ Alekseevich, 1796-1846. Николай Алексеевич Полевой (Table P-PZ40)

Russian literature
Individual authors and works, 1800-1870
Individual authors, Gogol′ - Pushkin -- Continued
Polevoĭ, Petr Nikolaevich. Петр Николаевич Полевой see PG3470.P39
3337.P7 Polezhaev, Aleksandr Ivanovich, 1805-1838. Александр Иванович Полежаев (Table P-PZ40)
3337.P72 Polonskiĭ, I͡Akov Petrovich, 1819-1898. Яков Петрович Полонский (Table P-PZ40)
3337.P724 Polozov, Nikolaĭ, fl. 1850-1860. Николай Полозов (Table P-PZ40)
3337.P726 Polozova, Kleopatra, fl. 1830-1840. Клеопатра Полозова (Table P-PZ40)
Poltorat͡skai͡a, Anna Petrovna. Анна Петровна Полторацкая see PG3337.K36
3337.P73 Pomi͡alovskiĭ, Nikolaĭ Gerasimovich, 1835-1863. Николай Герасимович Помяловский (Table P-PZ40)
Popov, Ivan Vasil′evich. Иван Васильевич Попов see PG3317.P63
3337.P732 Popov, Nikolaĭ, fl. 1860-1870. Николай Попов (Table P-PZ40)
3337.P733 Popov, Vasiliĭ Petrovich, 1828-1886. Василий Петрович Попов (Table P-PZ40)
3337.P735 Poroshin, Viktor Stepanovich, 1811-1868. Виктор Степанович Порошин (Table P-PZ40)
Pospelova, Marii͡a Alekseevna. Мария Алексеевна Поспелова see PG3317.P73
3337.P737 Potanin, Gavriil Nikitich, fl. 1860-1870. Гавриил Никитич Потанин (Table P-PZ40)
3337.P738 Potapov, Vasiliĭ F., fl. 1845-1855. Василий Ф. Потапов (Table P-PZ40)
3337.P8 Potekhin, Alekseĭ Antipovich, 1829-1908. Алексей Антипович Потехин (Table P-PZ40)
3337.P82 Potekhin, Nikolaĭ Antipovich, 1834-1896. Николай Антипович Потехин (Table P-PZ40)
3337.P83 Prakudin-Gorskiĭ, E. E. Пракудин-Горский (Table P-PZ40)
Preobrazhenskiĭ, Pr. Пр. Преображенский see PG3337.K85
3337.P84 Privalovskiĭ, I͡Uriĭ, 1786-1846. Юрій Приваловскій (Table P-PZ40)
3337.P85 Prokopovich, Nikolaĭ I͡Akovlevich, 1810-1857. Николай Яковлевич Прокопович (Table P-PZ40)
Protopopov, Aleksandr Pavlovich. Александр Павлович Протопопов see PG3361.S54
3337.P87 Protopopov, Pavel Ivanovich, 1771-1820. Павел Иванович Протопопов (Table P-PZ40)

PG

Russian literature
Individual authors and works, 1800-1870
Individual authors, Gogolʹ - Pushkin -- Continued

3337.P9 Prutkov, Kozʹma. Козьма Прутков (Table P-PZ40)
Collective pseudonym for: Alekseĭ Konstantinovich Tolstoĭ, PG3363; Alekseĭ Mikhaĭlovich Zhemchuzhnikov, PG3447.Z37; and Vladimir Mikhaĭlovich Zhemchuzhnikov, PG3447.Z38

Przecławski, Józef, 1799-1879 see PG3337.P93

3337.P93 Przhet͡slavskiĭ, Osip Antonovich, 1799-1879. Осип Антонович Пржецлавский (Table P-PZ40)

3337.P95 Puchkova, Ekaterina Naumovna, 1792-1867. Екатерина Наумовна Пучкова (Table P-PZ40)

Pushkin, Aleksandr Sergeevich, 1799-1837. Александр Сергеевич Пушкин

3340.A1 Collected works. By date

3340.A15 Collected novels and tales. By date
For Skazki see PG3343.S5+
Cf. PG3343.P65+ Povesti Belkina

3340.A17 Collected poems. By date

3340.A19 Collected plays. By date

3340.A3-Z Selected works. By editor

3341 Selections. Anthologies. By editor

Translations see PG3347+

3343.A-Z Separate works, A-Z
For translations see PG3347+

3343.A5-.A53 Andzhelo (Story in verse). Анджело (Table PG2)

3343.A7-.A73 Arap Petra Velikogo (Novel). Арап Петра Великого (Table PG2)

3343.B3-.B33 Bakhchisaraĭskiĭ fontan (Poem). Бахчисарайский фонтан (Table PG2)

3343.B4-.B43 Baryshni͡a krestʹi͡anka (Story). Барышня крестьянка (Table PG2)

Boris Godunov (Drama). Борис Годунов

3343.B6 Texts. By date

3343.B64 Criticism

3343.B7-.B73 Bratʹi͡a razboĭniki (Poem). Братья разбойники (Table PG2)

3343.C45-.C453 Chernai͡a shalʹ. Черная шаль (Table PG2)

3343.D6-.D63 Domik v Kolomne (Tale in verse). Домик в Коломне (Table PG2)

3343.D8-.D83 Dubrovskiĭ (Story). Дубровский (Table PG2)

3343.E3-.E33 Egipetskie nochi (Story). Египетские ночи (Table PG2)

3343.E8-.E83 Evgeniĭ Onegin (Novel in verse). Евгений Онегин (Table PG2)

3343.G3-.G33 Galub (Poem). Галуб (Table PG2)

3343.G4-.G43 Gavriiliada (Poem). Гавриилиада (Table PG2)

Russian literature
Individual authors and works, 1800-1870
Pushkin, Aleksandr Sergeevich, 1799-1837. Александр Сергеевич Пушкин
Separate works, A-Z -- Continued

3343.G7-.G73 Graf Nulin (Tale in verse). Граф Нулин (Table PG2)
3343.G8-.G83 Grobovshchik (Story). Гробовщик (Table PG2)
3343.I3-.I33 I͡A pami͡atnik sebe vozdvig nerukotvornyĭ. Я памятник себе воздвиг нерукотворный (Table PG2)
Istorii͡a Pugachevskogo bunta. История Пугачевского бунта see DK183
3343.I7-.I73 Istorii͡a sela Gorokhina (Story). История села Горохина (Table PG2)
3343.K27-.K273 Kamennyĭ gostʹ (Drama). Каменный гость (Table PG2)
3343.K3-.K33 Kapitanskai͡a dochka (Novel). Капитанская дочка (Table PG2)
3343.K35-.K353 Kavkazskiĭ plennik (Poem). Кавказский пленник (Table PG2)
3343.K5-.K53 Kirdzhali (Story). Кирджали (Table PG2)
3343.M4-.M43 Mednyĭ vsadnik (Story in verse). Медный всадник (Table PG2)
3343.M5-.M53 Metelʹ (Story). Метель (Table PG2)
3343.M6-.M63 Mot͡sart i Salʹeri (Drama). Моцарт и Сальери (Table PG2)
3343.P4-.P43 Pesni zapadnykh slavi͡an. Песни западных славян (Table PG2)
3343.P5-.P53 Pikovai͡a dama (Story). Пиковая дама (Table PG2)
3343.P55-.P553 Pir vo vremi͡a chumy (Drama). Пир во время чумы (Table PG2)
3343.P6-.P63 Poltava (Poem). Полтава (Table PG2)
3343.P65-.P653 Povesti pokoĭnogo Ivana Petrovicha Belkina. Повести покойного Ивана Петровича Белкина (Table PG2)
For separate stories see the title in PG3343
3343.P7-.P73 Predislovie (Story). Предисловие (Table PG2)
3343.R6-.R63 Rodoslovnai͡a moego geroi͡a (Poem). Родословная моего героя (Table PG2)
3343.R65-.R653 Roslavlev (Story). Рославлев (Table PG2)
3343.R8-.R83 Rusalka (Drama). Русалка (Table PG2)
3343.R85-.R853 Ruslan i Li͡udmila (Poem). Руслан и Людмила (Table PG2)
Skazki. Сказки
3343.S5 Collected
Separate tales
3343.S52M4 O mertvoĭ t͡sarevne i o semi bogatyri͡akh. О мертвой царевне и о семи богатырях

PG

Russian literature
Individual authors and works, 1800-1870
Pushkin, Aleksandr Sergeevich, 1799-1837. Александр Сергеевич Пушкин
Separate works
Skazki. Сказки
Separate tales -- Continued

3343.S52P6 O pope i rabotnike ego Balde. О попе и работнике его Балде
3343.S52R9 O rybake i rybke. О рыбаке и рыбке
3343.S52T7 O t͡sare Saltane. О царе Салтане
3343.S52Z6 O zolotom petushke. О золотом петушке
3343.S53A-.S53Z Other, A-Z
3343.S53B6 Bova. Бова
3343.S53K3 Kak vesennei͡u teploĭ poroi͡u. Как весеннею теплой порою
3343.S53S8 Svat Ivan. Сват Иван
3343.S6-.S63 Skupoĭ ry͡tsar′ (Drama). Скупой рыцарь (Table PG2)
3343.S7-.S73 Stant͡sionnyĭ smotritel′ (Story). Станционный смотритель (Table PG2)
3343.S8-.S83 St͡seny iz ry͡tsarskikh vremen (Story). Сцены из рыцарских времен (Table PG2)
3343.T67-.T673 TSar′ Nikita i sorok ego docheреĭ (Poem). Царь Никита и сорок его дочерей (Table PG2)
3343.T7-.T73 TSygane. Цыгане (Table PG2)
3343.V66-.V663 Vospominanie. Воспоминание (Table PG2)
3343.V8-.V83 Vystrel (Story). Выстрел (Table PG2)
3344 Doubtful or spurious works
Correspondence
3345.A1 Collections. By date
3345.A3A-.A3Z Translations. By language, A-Z, and date
3345.A5-Z Individual correspondents
Translations
For translations of letters see PG3345.A3A+
English
3347.A1 Collected works
3347.A15 Collected novels and tales
3347.A17 Collected poetry
3347.A19 Collected plays
3347.A2 Selections. Anthologies
3347.A3-.Z4 Separate works. By Russian title, A-Z
e. g.
3347.B6 Boris Godunov. Борис Годунов
3347.E8 Evgeniĭ Onegin. Евгений Онегин
(3347.Z5) Correspondence
see PG3345.A3A+
3348.F5 French (Table PG1)

Russian literature
Individual authors and works, 1800-1870
Pushkin, Aleksandr Sergeevich, 1799-1837. Александр Сергеевич Пушкин
Translations -- Continued

3348.G5 German (Table PG1)
3348.G7 Greek, Modern (Table PG1)
3348.I5 Italian (Table PG1)
3348.S5 Spanish (Table PG1)
3349.A-Z Other languages, A-Z
Subarrange each by Table PG1
3350 Biography and criticism
3350.A1 Periodicals and societies
Bibliography see Z8718
3350.A3 Dictionaries, indexes, etc.
3350.A4 Collected works
Cf. PG3352 Anniversaries
3350.A5 Autobiography. Journals. Memoirs
3350.A51-.Z7 General treatises. Life and works
3350.Z8 Essays, addresses, etc.
3350.5.A-Z Biographical details, A-Z
3350.5.D4 Death
3350.5.J68 Journeys (General)
For journeys to specific places see PG3351.5
3350.5.L37 Last years
3350.5.M6 Moldavian exile
3350.7 Family. Ancestry. Descendants
3350.8 Relations with women
3351 Relations to contemporaries
3351.5 Homes and haunts. Local associations
Correspondence see PG3345.A+
3352 Anniversaries. Celebrations
For collected papers see PG3350.A4
3353 Memorials. Testimonials to his genius
3354 Iconography. Museums. Exhibitions
3355 Authorship
3355.2 Autographs
3355.3.A-Z Influence of special authors or works, A-Z
e. g.
3355.3.S5 Slovo o polku Igoreve. Слово о полку Игореве
Criticism and interpretation
History of the study, appreciation, and influence of Pushkin
3355.5 General and in Russia
3355.7.A-Z In countries other than Russia, A-Z
e. g.
3355.7.F7 France

Russian literature
Individual authors and works, 1800-1870
Pushkin, Aleksandr Sergeevich, 1799-1837. Александр Сергеевич Пушкин
Biography and criticism
Criticism and interpretation
History of the study, appreciation, and influence of Pushkin
In countries other than Russia, A-Z -- Continued

3355.7.Y8 Yugoslavia
3356 General works
For criticism of separate works see PG3343.A+
3357 Relation to the drama and stage
3358.A-Z Special topics, A-Z
3358.A58 Antiquities. Archaeology
Archaeology see PG3358.A58
3358.B3 Ballet
3358.B66 Book arts and sciences
3358.C3 Caucasus
3358.C45 Censorship
3358.C66 Contradiction
3358.C7 Pushkin as critic
3358.D43 Death
3358.D7 Dreams
3358.E43 Elegiac poetry
Ethics see PG3358.R4
3358.F38 Faust
3358.F5 Fictional works
3358.F53 Film and video adaptations
3358.F57 Folk poetry
3358.F6 Folklore
3358.F8 Freemasonry
3358.F84 French literature
3358.G45 Gems
3358.G47 Germany
3358.G74 Greek War of Independence, 1821-1829
3358.H45 History
3358.I53 Influence
3358.K34 Kalmykia
3358.K5 Kirghizistan
Kyrgyzstan see PG3358.K5
3358.L3 Latin literature
3358.L6 Love
3358.M37 Marvelous, The
3358.M45 Mental illness
3358.M84 Muses
3358.M86 Music

Russian literature
Individual authors and works, 1800-1870
Pushkin, Aleksandr Sergeevich, 1799-1837. Александр Сергеевич Пушкин
Biography and criticism
Criticism and interpretation
Special topics, A-Z -- Continued

3358.N38 Navy. Naval history
3358.N4 Near East
3358.O74 Orient
3358.P3 Patriotism
3358.P35 Peter I, the Great, 1672-1725
3358.P5 Philosophy
3358.P64 Poland
Political views see PG3358.S6
3358.P67 Psychology
3358.R33 Race awareness
3358.R37 Realism
3358.R4 Religion and ethics
3358.R6 Romanticism
3358.S34 Science
3358.S5 Siberia
3358.S6 Social and political views
Video adaptations see PG3358.F53
3359 Language. Style
3360 Individual authors, Pushkin - R
3360.P6 Pushkin, Vasiliĭ L′vovich, 1770-1830. Василий Львович Пушкин (Table P-PZ40)
R--v, Zeneida, pseud. Зенеида Р--в see PG3331.G3
3360.R14 Rabinovich, Osip Aaronovich, 1818-1869. Осип Ааронович Рабинович (Table P-PZ40)
3360.R17 Raevskiĭ, Andreĭ Fedoseevich, d. 1822. Андрей Федосеевич Раевский (Table P-PZ40)
3360.R2 Raevskiĭ, Vladimir Fedoseevich, 1795-1872. Владимир Федосеевич Раевский (Table P-PZ40)
3360.R25 Raich, Semen Egorovich, 1792-1855. Семен Егорович Раич (Table P-PZ40)
Raĭskiĭ, Semen. Семен Райский see PG3361.T25
Rastopchina, Evdokiia Petrovna. Евдокия Петровна Растопчина see PG3360.R6
Rastovskaia, Mariia Fedorovna. Мария Федоровна Растовская see PG3360.R63
3360.R3 Razin, Alekseĭ Egorovich, 1823-1875. Алексей Егорович Разин (Table P-PZ40)
3360.R4 Reshetnikov, Fedor Mikhaĭlovich, 1841-1871. Федор Михайлович Решетников (Table P-PZ40)

Russian literature
Individual authors and works, 1800-1870
Individual authors, Pushkin - R -- Continued

3360.R45 Ri͡abinin, Petr P., fl. 1830-1840. Петр П. Рябинин (Table P-PZ40)

3360.R5 Ri͡abinin, Trofim Grigor′evich, 1791-1885. Трофим Григорьевич Рябинин (Table P-PZ40)

3360.R53 Rodislavskiĭ, Vladimir Ivanovich, 1828-1885. Владимир Иванович Родиславский (Table P-PZ40)

Rodzi͡anko, Adelaida Alekseevna (Zubova). Аделаида Алексеевна (Зубова) Родзянко see PG3447.Z87

3360.R55 Rogashinskiĭ, Ivan, fl. 1860-1870. Иван Рогашинский (Table P-PZ40)

3360.R57 Romanovich, Vasiliĭ, fl. 1830-1840. Василий Романович (Table P-PZ40)

Rosen, Egor Fedorovich, baron see PG3360.R7

Rosenheim, Mikhail Pavlovich see PG3360.R74

Rosset, Aleksandra Osipovna. Александра Осиповна Россет see PG3361.S62

Rostislav, pseud. Ростислав see PG3364.T5

3360.R58 Rostopchin, Fedor Vasil′evich, graf, 1763-1826. Федор Васильевич Ростопчин (Table P-PZ40)

Cf. DK190.6.R6 Russian history

3360.R6 Rostopchina, Evdokii͡a Petrovna (Sushkova), grafini͡a, 1811-1858. Евдокия Петровна (Сушкова) Ростопчина (Table P-PZ40)

3360.R63 Rostovskai͡a, Mar′i͡a Fedorovna (L′vova), d. 1872. Марья Федоровна (Львова) Ростовская (Table P-PZ40)

Chiefly a writer of books for children

3360.R65 Rostovt͡sev, I͡Akov Ivanovich, 1803-1860. Яков Иванович Ростовцев (Table P-PZ40)

3360.R7 Rozen, Egor Fedorovich, baron, 1800-1860. Егор Федорович Розен (Table P-PZ40)

3360.R74 Rozengeĭm, Mikhail Pavlovich, 1820-1887. Михаил Павлович Розенгейм (Table P-PZ40)

3360.R76 Rudykovskiĭ, Andreĭ Petrovich, 1796-1874. Андрей Петрович Рудыковский (Table P-PZ40)

3360.R77 Russov, Stepan Vasil′evich, 1768?-1842. Степан Васильевич Руссов (Table P-PZ40)

3360.R8 Ryleev, Kondratiĭ Fedorovich, 1795-1826. Кондратий Федорович Рылеев (Table P-PZ40)

3360.R9 Ryndovskiĭ, Fedor, fl. 1830-1840. Федор Рындовский (Table P-PZ40)

3361 Individual authors, S - Tolstoĭ

Salias de Turnemir, Elizaveta Vasil′evna (Sukhovo-Kobylina), grafini͡a. Елизавета Васильевна (Сухово-Кобылина) Салиас де Турнемир see PG3418.T75

Russian literature
Individual authors and works, 1800-1870
Individual authors, S - Tolstoĭ -- Continued

3361.S3 Saltykov, Mikhail Evgrafovich, 1826-1889. Михаил Евграфович Салтыков (Table P-PZ40 modified)

3361.S3A61-.S3Z458 Separate works. By title

3361.S3B5 Blagonamerennye rechi (Sketches). Благонамеренные речи
For separate sketches see the title in PG3361.S3A61+

3361.S3B8 Bylye vremena (Tales). Былые времена
For separate tales see the title in PG3361.S3A61+

3361.S3C4 Chizhikovo gore (Tale). Чижиково горе

3361.S3C5 Chudinov (Sketch). Чудинов

3361.S3D4 Den′ v pomeshchich′eĭ usad′be (Tale). День в помещичьей усадьбе

3361.S3D5 Deti Moskvy (Tale). Дети Москвы

3361.S3D6 Dnevnik provint͡siala v Peterburge (Sketches). Дневник провинциала в Петербурге
For separate sketches see the title in PG3361.S3A61+

3361.S3D8 Dvori͡anskai͡a khandra (Tale). Дворянская хандра

3361.S3G6 Gospoda Golovlevy (Novel). Господа Головлевы

3361.S3G65 I͡Udushka (Drama based on the novel). Юдушка

3361.S3G7 Gospoda Tashkentt͡sy (Satire). Господа Ташкентцы

3361.S3G8 Gubernskie ocherki. Губернские очерки
For separate sketches see the title in PG3361.S3A61+

3361.S3I7 Istorii͡a odnogo goroda (Satire). История одного города

3361.S3I8 Itogi. Итоги

I͡Ubileĭ zemlepasht͡sa. Юбилей землепашца see PG3361.S3S6

I͡Udushka. Юдушка see PG3361.S3G65

3361.S3K3 Kak vysekli deĭstvitel′nogo statskogo sovetnika, ili, Tashkentt͡sy, obrativshiesi͡a vnutr′ (Tale). Как высекли действительного статского советника, или, Ташкентцы, обратившиеся внутрь

3361.S3K4 Karas′-idealist (Tale). Карась-идеалист

3361.S3K5 Koni͡aga (Tale). Коняга

3361.S3K6 Konon (Tale). Конон

3361.S3K7 Kruglyĭ god (Sketch). Круглый год

3361.S3M4 Melochi zhizni (Sketches). Мелочи жизни
For separate sketches see the title in PG3361.S3A61+

3361.S3M5 Misha i Vani͡a (Tale). Миша и Ваня

3361.S3N3 Nedokonchennye besedy. Недоконченные беседы

3361.S3N4 Nepochtitel′nyĭ Koronat (Sketch). Непочтительный Коронат

3361.S3N5 Nevinnye rasskazy. Невинные рассказы
For separate tales see the title in PG3361.S3A61+

Russian literature
Individual authors and works, 1800-1870
Individual authors, S - Tolstoĭ
Saltykov, Mikhail Evgrafovich, 1826-1889. Михаил Евграфович Салтыков
Separate works. By title -- Continued

3361.S3O8 Otet͡s i syn (Tale). Отец и сын
3361.S3P3 Palach (Tale). Палач
3361.S3P4 Pis′ma k teten′ke (Satire). Письма к тетеньке
3361.S3P5 Pis′ma o provint͡sii. Письма о провинции
3361.S3P55 Pokhorony (Tale). Похороны
3361.S3P6 Pompadury i pompadurshi (Satire). Помпадуры и помпадурши
3361.S3P63 Portnoĭ Grishka (Sketch). Портной Гришка
3361.S3P65 Poshekhonskai͡a starina (Novel). Пошехонская старина
3361.S3P66 Poshekhonskie rasskazy. Пошехонские рассказы
For separate tales see the title in PG3361.S3A61+
3361.S3P68 Povest′ o tom, kak muzhik dvukh generalov prokormil (Tale). Повесть о том, как мужик двух генералов
3361.S3P7 Premudryĭ piskar (Tale). Премудрый пискар
3361.S3P73 Prevrashchenie (Tale). Превращение
3361.S3P75 Priznaki vremeni. Признаки времени
3361.S3P8 Proshlye vremena (Tale). Прошлые времена
Also published under the title: Rasskaz pod″i͡achego
Rasskaz pod″i͡achego. Рассказ подъячего see PG3361.S3P8
3361.S3R3 Razveseloe zhit′e (Tale). Развеселое житье
3361.S3S2 Satir skitalet͡s (Tale). Сатир скиталец
3361.S3S3 Sbornik. Сборник
For separate tales, sketches, etc., see the title in PG3361.S3A61+
3361.S3S4 Skazki. Сказки
3361.S3S5 Smert′ Pazukhina (Comedy). Смерть Пазухина
3361.S3S6 Son v letni͡ui͡u noch′ (Tale). Сон в летнюю ночь
Also published under the title: I͡Ubileĭ zemlepasht͡sa
3361.S3S65 Sovremennai͡a idillii͡a. Современная идиллия
3361.S3S7 Starcheskoe gore, ili, Nepredvidennye posledstvii͡a zabluzhdenii͡a uma (Tale). Старческое горе, или, Непредвиденные последствия заблуждения ума
3361.S3S8 Stolp (Tale). Столп
Tashkent͡sy, obrativshiesi͡a vnutr′. Ташкентцы, обратившиеся внутрь see PG3361.S3K3
3361.S3T4 Teten′ka Anfisa Porfir′evna (Tale). Тетенька Анфиса Порфирьевна

Russian literature
Individual authors and works, 1800-1870
Individual authors, S - Tolstoĭ
Saltykov, Mikhail Evgrafovich, 1826-1889. Михаил Евграфович Салтыков
Separate works. By title -- Continued

3361.S3U3 Ubezhishche Monrepo (Satire). Убежище Монрепо

3361.S3V2 V srede umerennosti i akkuratnosti (Sketches). В среде умеренности и аккуратности

3361.S3V3 Van′ka-Kain (Tale). Ванька-Каин

3361.S3Z3 Za rubezhom (Satire). За рубежом

3361.S315 Samarin, Ivan Vasil′evich, d. 1882. Иван Васильевич Самарин (Table P-PZ40)

3361.S32 Samsonov, Lev Nikolaevich, d. 1882. Лев Николаевич Самсонов (Table P-PZ40)

3361.S325 Sandunov, Nikolaĭ Nikolaevich, 1769?-1832. Николай Николаевич Сандунов (Table P-PZ40)

3361.S326 Sandunov, Sila Nikolaevich, 1761-1813? Сила Николаевич Сандунов (Table P-PZ40)

3361.S33 Sękowski, Józef, 1800-1858 (Table P-PZ40)

3361.S334 Selivanov, Il′i͡a Vasil′evich, d. 1882. Илья Васильевич Селиванов (Table P-PZ40)

3361.S336 Selivanov, Vasiliĭ Vasil′evich, 1813-1875. Василий Васильевич Селиванов (Table P-PZ40)

Senkovskiĭ, Osip Ivanovich. Осип Иванович Сенковский see PG3361.S33

3361.S34 Sentimer, Elizaveta, fl. 1850-1870. Елизавета Сентимер (Table P-PZ40)

3361.S3435 Sergeev, Alekseĭ. Алексей Сергеев (Table P-PZ40)

3361.S345 Shakhova, Elizaveta Nikitishna, 1831-1899. Елизавета Никитишна Шахова (Table P-PZ40)

3361.S347 Shakhovskai͡a, Ekaterina Aleksandrovna, kni͡azhna, fl. 1830-1840. Екатерина Александровна Шаховская (Table P-PZ40)

3361.S35 Shakhovskoĭ, Aleksandr Aleksandrovich, kni͡az′, 1777-1846. Александр Александрович Шаховской (Table P-PZ40)

3361.S36 Shalikov, Petr Ivanovich, kni͡az′, 1768-1852. Петр Иванович Шаликов (Table P-PZ40)

3361.S363 Shalikova, Natal′i͡a Petrovna, kni͡azhna, 1815-1878. Наталья Петровна Шаликова (Table P-PZ40)

Shardin, A. A. Шардин see PG3361.S795

3361.S367 Sharzhinskiĭ, Alekseĭ V., fl. 1860-1870. Алексей В. Шаржинский (Table P-PZ40)

3361.S37 Shatrov, Nikolaĭ Mikhaĭlovich, 1765-1841. Николай Михайлович Шатров (Table P-PZ40)

Shch, N., pseud. Н.Щ. see PG3361.S39

Russian literature
Individual authors and works, 1800-1870
Individual authors, S - Tolstoĭ -- Continued

Shchedrin, N. H. Щедрин see PG3361.S3

3361.S375 Shcheglov, Fedor, fl. 1820-1830. Федор Щеглов (Table P-PZ40)

3361.S377 Shchepkin, Mikhail Semenovich, 1788-1863. Михаил Семенович Щепкин (Table P-PZ40)
For Shchepkin as an actor see PN2720+

3361.S38 Shcherbina, Nikolaĭ Fedorovich, 1821-1869. Николай Федорович Щербина (Table P-PZ40)

3361.S39 Shchukin, Nikolaĭ Semenovich, fl. 1830-1840. Николай Семенович Щукин (Table P-PZ40)

3361.S4 Shenshin, Afanasiĭ Afanas′evich, 1820-1892. Афанасий Афанасьевич Шеншин (Table P-PZ40 modified)

3361.S4A61-.S4Z458 Separate works. By title

3361.S4B8 Buri͡a (Poem). Буря

3361.S4D5 Di͡adi͡ushka i dvoi͡urodnyĭ brate͡ts (Story). Дядюшка и двоюродный братец

3361.S4I9 Iz derevni (Sketches). Из деревни

3361.S4K3 Kaktus (Tale). Кактус

3361.S4K4 Kalenik (Tale). Каленик

3361.S4L3 Lastochki (Poem). Ласточки

3361.S4N4 Ne te (Tale). Не те

3361.S4S5 Shopot (Poem). Шопот

3361.S4V4 Vechera i nochi (Poem). Вечера и ночи

3361.S4V5 Vechernie ogni (Poems). Вечерние огни

Sherere, pseud. Шерере see PG3337.K85

3361.S42 Shevchenko, Taras, 1814-1861. Тарас Шевченко (Table P-PZ40)
For Shevchenko as a painter see ND699.S48
For biography and Ukrainian works see PG3948.S5+

3361.S43 Shevyrev, Stepan Petrovich, 1806-1864. Степан Петрович Шевырев (Table P-PZ40)

3361.S44 Shirinskiĭ-Shikhmatov, Platon Aleksandrovich, kni͡az′, 1790-1853. Платон Александрович Ширинский-Шихматов (Table P-PZ40)

Shirinskiĭ-Shikhmatov, Sergeĭ Aleksandrovich, kni͡az′. Сергей Александрович Ширинский-Шихматов see PG3321.A64

3361.S45 Shishkov, Aleksandr Semenovich, 1754-1841. Александр Семенович Шишков (Table P-PZ40)

3361.S46 Shkli͡arevskiĭ, Pavel, 1806-1830. Павел Шкляревский (Table P-PZ40)

3361.S47 Shpilevskiĭ, Pavel Mikhaĭlovich, 1827-1861. Павел Михайлович Шпилевский (Table P-PZ40)

Russian literature
Individual authors and works, 1800-1870
Individual authors, S - Tolstoĭ -- Continued

3361.S48 Shteven, Ivan Petrovich, fl. 1830-1850. Иван Петрович Штевен (Table P-PZ40)

3361.S49 Shumakher, Petr Vasil′evich, 1817-1891. Петр Васильевич Шумахер (Table P-PZ40)

3361.S5 Skal′kovskiĭ, Apollon Aleksandrovich, 1808-1897. Аполлон Александрович Скальковский (Table P-PZ40)

Skavronskiĭ, A. A. Скавронский see PG3321.D25

Skavronskiĭ, N. H. Скавронский see PG3447.U6

Skimnin, pseud. Скимнин see PG3337.L85

3361.S52 Skobelev, Ivan Nikitich, 1778-1849. Иван Никитич Скобелев (Table P-PZ40)

Skorbnyĭ poėt. Скорбный поэт see PG3447.Z53

Skorpionov, Efim. Ефим Скорпионов see PG3337.K85

3361.S54 Slavin, Aleksandr Pavlovich, 1814-1867. Александр Павлович Славин (Table P-PZ40)

3361.S55 Slavutinskiĭ, Stepan Timofeevich, 1825-1884. Степан Тимофеевич Славутинский (Table P-PZ40)

3361.S57 Slept͡sov, Vasiliĭ Alekseevich, 1836-1878. Василий Алексеевич Слепцов (Table P-PZ40)

3361.S58 Slepushkin, Fedor Nikiforovich, 1783-1848. Федор Никифорович Слепушкин (Table P-PZ40)

3361.S6 Smirnov, N.E., fl. 1860-1870. Н.Е. Смирнов (Table P-PZ40)

3361.S62 Smirnova, Aleksandra Osipovna (Rosset), 1809-1882. Александра Осиповна (Россет) Смирнова (Table P-PZ40)

3361.S63 Smirnova, Anna, fl. 1850-1860. Анна Смирнова (Table P-PZ40)

3361.S64 Smirnovskiĭ, Platon, fl. 1830-1860. Платон Смирновский (Table P-PZ40)

3361.S65 Sobolev, Aleksandr, fl. 1810-1820. Александр Соболев (Table P-PZ40)

3361.S66 Sobolevskiĭ, Sergeĭ Aleksandrovich, 1803-1870. Сергей Александрович Соболевский (Table P-PZ40)

3361.S67 Sokhanskai͡a, Nadezhda Stepanovna, 1825-1884. Надежда Степановна Соханская (Table P-PZ40)

3361.S678 Sokolov, N. H. Соколов (Table P-PZ40)

3361.S68 Sokolov, N. S., fl. 1830-1850. Н.С. Соколов (Table P-PZ40)

3361.S685 Sokolovskiĭ, Nikolaĭ Mikhaĭlovich, 1835- . Николай Михайлович Соколовский (Table P-PZ40)

3361.S69 Sokolovskiĭ, Vladimir Ignat′evich, 1808-1839. Владимир Игнатьевич Соколовский (Table P-PZ40)

Russian literature
Individual authors and works, 1800-1870
Individual authors, S - Tolstoĭ -- Continued

3361.S7 Sollogub, Vladimir Aleksandrovich, graf, 1814-1882. Владимир Александрович Соллогуб (Table P-PZ40 modified)

3361.S7A61-.S7Z458 Separate works. By title

30 avgusta 1756 g. (Comedy). 30 августа 1756 г. see PG3361.S7T8

3361.S7A8 Aptekarsha (Story). Аптекарша

3361.S7B3 Bal (Story). Бал

3361.S7B4 Beda ot nezhnogo serdt͡sa (Comedy-vaudeville). Беда от нежного сердца

3361.S7B6 Bolʹshoĭ svet (Story). Большой свет

3361.S7B8 Bukety, ili, Peterburgskoe t͡svetobesie (Farce). Букеты, или, Петербургское цветобесие

3361.S7C5 Chinovnik (Comedy). Чиновник

3361.S7D3 Dagerrotip, ili, Znakomye vse lit͡sa (Farce-vaudeville). Дагерротип, или, Знакомые все лица

3361.S7D8 Dve minuty (Story). Две минуты

3361.S7G6 Gorbun, ili, Vybor nevesty (Vaudeville). Горбун, или, Выбор невесты

3361.S7I2 I͡Amshchik, ili, Shalostʹ gusarskogo ofit͡sera (Dramatic portrait). Ямщик, или, Шалость гусарского офицера

3361.S7I8 Istorii͡a dvukh kalosh. История двух калош

3361.S7K6 Kni͡aginі͡a (Story). Княгиня

3361.S7L4 Lev (Tale). Лев

3361.S7M3 Masterskai͡a russkogo zhivopist͡sa (Vaudeville). Мастерская русского живописца

3361.S7M4 Medvedʹ. Медведь

3361.S7M45 Mestnichestvo (Drama). Местничество

3361.S7M5 Met͡senat (Farce). Меценат

3361.S7M6 Modnye, peterburgskie lechenii͡a (Farce-vaudeville). Модные, петербургские лечения

3361.S7M8 Mylʹnye puzyri (Vaudeville). Мыльные пузыри

3361.S7N5 Nigilist (Poem). Нигилист

3361.S7N6 Nochʹ pered svadʹboĭ (Farce). Ночь перед свадьбой

3361.S7N7 Nochʹ v dukhane (Dramatic sketch). Ночь в духане

3361.S7P7 Prikli͡uchenie na zheleznoĭ doroge. Приключение на железной дороге

3361.S7R3 Razocharovannye (Comedy). Разочарованные

3361.S7R6 Rossii͡a pered vragami (Ode). Россия перед врагами

3361.S7S6 Sobachka (Tale). Собачка

Russian literature
Individual authors and works, 1800-1870
Individual authors, S - Tolstoĭ
Sollogub, Vladimir Aleksandrovich, graf, 1814-1882. Владимир Александрович Соллогуб
Separate works. By title -- Continued

3361.S7S65 Sotrudniki, ili, Chuzhim dobrom ne nazhivesh'si͡a. Сотрудники, или, Чужим добром не наживешься
3361.S7S7 Starushka (Story). Старушка
3361.S7S8 Sud istorii (Dramatic poem in verse). Суд истории
3361.S7T3 Tarantas. Тарантас
3361.S7T7 Tridt͡sat′ (Poems). Тридцать
3361.S7T8 Tridt͡satoe avgusta 1756 g. (Comedy). Тридцатое августа 1756 г.
3361.S7V4 Vchera i segodni͡a (Literaturnyĭ sbornik). Вчера и сегодня
3361.S7V6 Vospitannit͡sa (Story). Воспитанница
3361.S714 Somov, Orest, 1793-1833. Орест Сомов (Table P-PZ40)
3361.S715 Spasovich, Vladimir Danilovich, 1829-1906. Владимир Данилович Спасович (Table P-PZ40)
3361.S72 Stakhovich, Mikhail Aleksandrovich, 1819-1858. Михаил Александрович Стахович (Table P-PZ40)
3361.S73 Stamati, K.K., fl. 1850-1860. К.К. Стамати (Table P-PZ40)
3361.S74 Stanevich, Evstafiĭ Ivanovich, 1775-1835. Евстафий Иванович Станевич (Table P-PZ40)
Stanit͡skiĭ, N. H. Станицкий see PG3337.P24
3361.S743 Stankevich, Aleksandr Vladimirovich, 1821- . Александр Владимирович Станкевич (Table P-PZ40)
3361.S745 Stankevich, Nikolaĭ Vladimirovich, 1813-1840. Николай Владимирович Станкевич (Table P-PZ40)
3361.S747 Starodubskiĭ, Vladimir, fl. 1860-1870. Владимир Стародубский (Table P-PZ40)
Starozhil kolomenskiĭ. Старожил коломенский see PG3337.K635
Staryĭ transformist. Старый трансформист see PG3321.C6
Stebnit͡skiĭ, M. M. Стебницкий see PG3337.L5+
3361.S75 Stepanov, Aleksandr Petrovich, 1781-1837. Александр Петрович Степанов (Table P-PZ40)
3361.S76 Stepanov, Petr Ivanovich, 1812-1876. Петр Иванович Степанов (Table P-PZ40)
3361.S765 Stepanovskai͡a, Vera, fl. 1860-1870. Вера Степановская (Table P-PZ40)
Sto-odin, pseud. Сто-один see PG3331.G23

Russian literature
Individual authors and works, 1800-1870
Individual authors, S - Tolstoĭ -- Continued

3361.S768 Stolypin, Nikolaĭ Alekseevich. Николай Алексеевич Столыпин (Table P-PZ40)

3361.S77 Stopanovskiĭ, Mikhail Mikhaĭlovich, 1830-1877. Михаил Михайлович Стопановский (Table P-PZ40)

Strakhov, Nikolaĭ Ivanovich. Николай Иванович Страхов see PG3317.S67

3361.S775 Strakhov, Nikolaĭ Nikolaevich, 1828-1896. Николай Николаевич Страхов (Table P-PZ40)

3361.S78 Strugovshchikov, Aleksandr Nikolaevich, 1808-1878. Александр Николаевич Струговщиков (Table P-PZ40)

3361.S783 Struĭskiĭ, Dmitriĭ I͡Ur'evich, 1806-1856. Дмитрий Юрьевич Струйский (Table P-PZ40)

3361.S787 Studzinska͡ia, A.P., fl. 1850-1870. А.П. Студзинская (Table P-PZ40)

Sudovshchikov, Nikolaĭ Rodionovich. Николай Родионович Судовщиков see PG3317.S8

3361.S79 Sukhanov, Mikhail Dmitrievich, 1801?-1843. Михаил Дмитриевич Суханов (Table P-PZ40)

3361.S795 Sukhonin, Petr Petrovich, 1821-1884. Петр Петрович Сухонин (Table P-PZ40)

3361.S8 Sukhovo-Kobylin, Aleksandr Vasil'evich, 1817-1903. Александр Васильевич Сухово-Кобылин (Table P-PZ40)

Sukhovo-Kobylina, Elizaveta Vasil'evna. Елизавета Васильевна Сухово-Кобылина see PG3418.T75

3361.S82 Sumarokov, Pankratiĭ Platonovich, 1763-1814. Панкратий Платонович Сумароков (Table P-PZ40)

3361.S83 Sumarokov, Pavel Ivanovich, d. 1846. Павел Иванович Сумароков (Table P-PZ40)

3361.S84 Sushkov, Dmitriĭ Petrovich, d. 1877. Дмитрий Петрович Сушков (Table P-PZ40)

3361.S85 Sushkov, Nikolaĭ Vasil'evich, 1796-1871. Николай Васильевич Сушков (Table P-PZ40)

Sushkova, Ekaterina Aleksandrovna. Екатерина Александровна Сушкова see PG3337.K45

Sushkova, Elizaveta Aleksandrovna. Елизавета Александровна Сушкова see PG3447.V115

Sushkova, Evdoki͡ia Petrovna. Евдокия Петровна Сушкова see PG3360.R6

3361.S87 Suvorina, Anna Ivanovna (Baranova), 1840-1874. Анна Ивановна (Баранова) Суворина (Table P-PZ40)

Sverchok, pseud. Сверчок see PG3340+

3361.S88 Svi͡atogoret͡s, d. 1853. Святогорец (Table P-PZ40)

Russian literature
Individual authors and works, 1800-1870
Individual authors, S - Tolstoĭ -- Continued

3361.S9 Svin'in, Pavel Petrovich, 1788-1839. Павел Петрович Свиньин (Table P-PZ40)
3361.T2 Tairov, V.S. В.С. Таиров (Table P-PZ40)
Tal't͡sev, pseud. Тальцев see PG3447.Z87
3361.T25 Tarnovskiĭ, Konstantin Avgustovich, 1826-1892. Константин Августович Тарновский (Table P-PZ40)
Temrizov, A. A. Темризов see PG3337.M32
3361.T3 Tepli͡akov, Viktor Grigor'evich, 1804-1842. Виктор Григорьевич Тепляков (Table P-PZ40)
3361.T4 Teplova, Nadezhda Sergeevna, 1814-1848. Надежда Сергеевна Теплова (Table P-PZ40)
Teri͡ukhina, Nadezhda Sergeevna. Надежда Сергеевна Терюхина see PG3361.T4
3361.T42 Terskoĭ, Konstantin. Константин Терской (Table P-PZ40)
3361.T43 Timofeev, Alekseĭ Vasil'evich, 1812-1883. Алексей Васильевич Тимофеев (Table P-PZ40)
3361.T44 Titov, I. И. Титов (Table P-PZ40)
3361.T45 Titova, Elizaveta Ivanovna, 1780- . Елизавета Ивановна Титова (Table P-PZ40)
Ti͡utchev, Fedor Ivanovich, 1803-1873. Федор Иванович Тютчев
3361.T5 Collected works (Collected poems, and poems and prose). By date
3361.T5A12 Selections. Anthologies. By date
Translations
From the author's works in Russian (Collected or selected)
3361.T5A2-.T5A29 English. By translator, if given, or date
3361.T5A3-.T5A39 French. By translator, if given, or date
3361.T5A4-.T5A49 German. By translator, if given, or date
3361.T5A5-.T5A59 Other. By language
3361.T5A6 From foreign literatures into Russian (Collected or selected). By date
For separate works or collected works from one foreign language, see the original language
3361.T5A7-.T5Z3 Separate poems
e. g.
3361.T5D4 Den' i noch'. День и ночь
3361.T5I8 Ital'i͡anskai͡a villa. Итальянская вилла
3361.T5N3 Na vzi͡atie Varshavy. На взятие Варшавы
3361.T5N4 Ne to, chto mnite vy, priroda. Не то, что мните вы, природа
3361.T5O2 O, veshchai͡a dusha moi͡a. О, вещая душа моя

	Russian literature
	Individual authors and works, 1800-1870
	Individual authors, S - Tolstoĭ
	Tiutchev, Fedor Ivanovich, 1803-1873. Федор Иванович Тютчев
	Separate poems -- Continued
3361.T5O7	Osenniĭ vecher. Осенний вечер
3361.T5S5	Silentium
3361.T5S6	Son na more. Сон на море
3361.T5S8	Sumerki. Сумерки
3361.T5Z4-.T5Z49	Poems in French
3361.T5Z4	Collected. By date
3361.T5Z42-.T5Z49	Separate poems (alphabetically)
3361.T5Z492-.T5Z99	Biography and criticism
	Bibliography see Z8882.7
3361.T5Z5	Reminiscences. Journals
	Letters
3361.T5Z53	Collected. By date
3361.T5Z54-.T5Z59	Individual correspondents (alphabetically)
3361.T5Z6-.T5Z99	General treatises. Life and works
3361.T6	Tolbin, Vasiliĭ Vasil′evich, 1821-1869. Василий Васильевич Толбин (Table P-PZ40)
3361.T67	Toliverova, A. N. (Aleksandra Nikolaevna), 1864-1918. Александра Николаевна Толиверова (Table P-PZ40)
3361.T7	Toll, Feliks Gustavovich, 1823-1867. Феликс Густавович Толл (Table P-PZ40)
	Tolstaia, Mariia Fedorovna. Мария Федоровна Толстая see PG3337.K2
3363	Tolstoĭ, Alekseĭ Konstantinovich, graf, 1817-1875. Алексей Константинович Толстой Cf. PG3337.P9 Koz′ma Prutkov, collective pseudonym
3363.A1	Collected works. By date
3363.A15	Collected novels and tales. By date
3363.A17	Collected poems. By date
3363.A19	Collected plays. By date
	Translations (Collected or selected)
3363.A2-.A29	English. By translator, if given, or date
3363.A3-.A39	French. By translator, if given, or date
3363.A4-.A49	German. By translator, if given, or date
3363.A5-.A59	Other. By language
3363.A6	Selections
3363.A7-.Z4	Separate works
3363.A75-.A753	Alkhimik (Poem). Алхимик (Table P-PZ43)
3363.A8-.A83	Amena (Story). Амена (Table P-PZ43)
3363.A85-.A853	Artemiĭ Semenovich Bervenkovskiĭ (Story). Артемий Семенович Бервенковский (Table P-PZ43)

Russian literature
Individual authors and works, 1800-1870
Tolstoĭ, Alekseĭ Konstantinovich, graf, 1817-1875. Алексей Константинович Толстой
Separate works -- Continued

3363.B3-.B33 Ballady. Баллады (Table P-PZ43)
3363.B4A-.B4Z Separate ballads, A-Z
3363.B4V3 Vasiliĭ Shibanov. Василий Шибанов
3363.D6-.D63 Don-Zhuan (Dramatic poem). Дон-Жуан (Table P-PZ43)
3363.D7-.D73 Drakon (Story in verse). Дракон (Table P-PZ43)
3363.D8-.D83 Dva dni͡a v Kirgizskoĭ stepi (Story). Два дня в Киргизской степи (Table P-PZ43)
3363.G7-.G73 Greshni͡tsa (Poem). Грешница (Table P-PZ43)
3363.I6-.I63 Ioann Damaskin (Poem). Иоанн Дамаскин (Table P-PZ43)
3363.K5-.K53 Kni͡az′ Serebri͡anyĭ (Novel). Князь Серебряный (Table P-PZ43)
3363.P4-.P43 Pesni͡a o Potoke-bogatyre. Песня о Потоке-богатыре (Table P-PZ43)
3363.P6-.P63 Portret (Story in verse). Портрет (Table P-PZ43)
3363.P7-.P73 Posadnik (Drama). Посадник (Table P-PZ43)
Prepodobnyĭ Ioann Damaskin. Преподобный Иоанн Дамаскин see PG3363.I6+
3363.R8-.R83 Russkai͡a istorii͡a ot Gostomysla s IX po XIX v. (Poem). Русская история от Гостомысла с IX по XIX в. (Table P-PZ43)
3363.S4-.S43 Sem′i͡a Burdalaka (Tale). Семья Бурдалака (Table P-PZ43)
3363.S5-.S53 Smert′ Ioanna Groznago (Tragedy). Смерть Иоанна Грознаго (Table P-PZ43)
3363.T7-.T73 T͡Sar′ Boris (Tragedy). Царь Борис (Table P-PZ43)
3363.T8-.T83 T͡Sar′ Feodor Ioannovich (Tragedy). Царь Феодор Иоаннович (Table P-PZ43)
3363.U6-.U63 Upyr′ (Story). Упырь (Table P-PZ43)
Biography and criticism
3363.Z5 Autobiography
Letters
3363.Z6 Collected. By date
3363.Z7 Individual correspondents, A-Z
3363.Z8 General treatises. Life and works
3363.Z9 Criticism
3364 Individual authors, Tolstoĭ, A. - Tolstoĭ, L.
3364.T5 Tolstoĭ, Feofil Matveevich, 1809-1881. Феофил Матвеевич Толстой (Table P-PZ40)
Tolstoĭ, Lev Nikolaevich, graf, 1828-1910 (Tolstoy, Leo). Лев Николаевич Толстой

Russian literature
Individual authors and works, 1800-1870
Tolstoĭ, Lev Nikolaevich, graf, 1828-1910 (Tolstoy, Leo). Лев Николаевич Толстой -- Continued

3365.A1 Collected works. By date
3365.A12 Posthumous works. By date
3365.A15 Collected and selected novels, stories, etc. By date
Cf. PG3365.D5+ Detstvo, Otrochestvo, I͡Unost′
3365.A17 Collected essays. By date
3365.A19 Collected plays. By date
3365.A2 Selections. By editor
3365.A3-.Z5 Separate works
For works on special subjects, see the subject
For juvenile works see PZ63, PZ64.2, etc.
For translations see PG3366+
3365.A4-.A43 Al′bert (Tale). Альберт (Table PG2)
3365.A6-.A63 Anna Karenina (Novel). Анна Каренина (Table PG2)
3365.A7-.A73 Assiriĭskiĭ t͡sar′ Assarkhadon (Tale). Ассирийский царь Ассархадон (Table PG2)
Bab′i͡a doli͡a. Бабья доля see PG3368.B2+
3365.C5-.C53 Chem li͡udi zhivy (Tale). Чем люди живы (Table PG2)
3365.C6-.C63 Chto-zhe delat′? (Tale). Что-же делать? (Table PG2)
3365.D4-.D43 Dekabristy (Fragment of novel). Декабристы (Table PG2)
Detstvo. Otrochestvo. I͡Unost′ (Three novels). Детство. Отрочество. Юность
3365.D5 Texts of trilogy. By date
3365.D52-.D523 Detstvo. Детство (Table PG2)
3365.D55-.D553 Otrochestvo. Отрочество (Table PG2)
3365.D57-.D573 I͡Unost′. Юность (Table PG2)
3365.D58 Criticism of trilogy
3365.D6-.D63 D′i͡avol (Tale). Дьявол (Table PG2)
3365.D8-.D83 Dva gusara (Story). Два гусара (Table PG2)
3365.D85-.D853 Dva sputnika (Tale). Два спутника (Table PG2)
3365.D9-.D93 Dva starika (Tale). Два старика (Table PG2)
3365.F3-.F33 Fal′shivyĭ kupon (Tale). Фальшивый купон (Table PG2)
3365.F7-.F73 Fransuaza (Tale). Франсуаза (Table PG2)
3365.G4-.G43 Gde li͡ubov′ tam i Bog (Tale). Где любовь там и Бог (Table PG2)
3365.I2-.I23 I svet vo t′me svetit (Drama). И свет во тьме светит (Table PG2)
3365.I3-.I33 I͡Agody (Tale). Ягоды (Table PG2)
I͡Unost′ (Novel). Юность see PG3365.D57+
Iz zapisok kni͡azi͡a D. Nekhli͡udova. Из записок князя Д. Нехлюдова see PG3365.L5+

Russian literature
Individual authors and works, 1800-1870
Tolstoĭ, Lev Nikolaevich, graf, 1828-1910 (Tolstoy, Leo). Лев Николаевич Толстой
Separate works -- Continued

3365.K2-.K23 Kai͡ushchiĭsi͡a greshnik (Legend). Кающийся грешник (Table PG2)
3365.K25-.K253 Kamni (Tale). Камни (Table PG2)
3365.K3-.K33 Karma (Tale). Карма (Table PG2)
3365.K35-.K353 Kavkazskiĭ plennik (Tale). Кавказский пленник (Table PG2)
3365.K4-.K43 Kazaki (Novel). Казаки (Table PG2)
3365.K5-.K53 Khadzhi-Murat (Tale). Хаджи-Мурат (Table PG2)
3365.K55-.K553 Khodite v svete, poka est′ svet (Story). Ходите в свете, пока есть свет (Table PG2)
3365.K6-.K63 Kholstomer (Tale). Холстомер (Table PG2)
3365.K65-.K653 Khozi͡ain i rabotnik (Tale). Хозяин и работник (Table PG2)
3365.K7-.K73 Kreĭt͡serova sonata (Novel). Крейцерова соната (Table PG2)
3365.K8-.K83 Krestnik (Legend). Крестник (Table PG2)
3365.L5-.L53 Li͡ut͡sern (Tale). Люцерн (Table PG2)
3365.M4-.M43 Metel′ (Tale). Метель (Table PG2)
3365.M5-.M53 Mnogo-li cheloveku zemli nuzhno? (Legend). Много-ли человеку земли нужно? (Table PG2)
3365.M6-.M63 Molitva (Tale). Молитва (Table PG2)
3365.N3-.N33 Nabeg (Tale). Набег (Table PG2)
3365.N4-.N43 Narodnye rasskazy. Народные рассказы (Table PG2)
For separate tales see the title in PG3365.A3+
3365.N5-.N53 Nikolaĭ Palkin (Tale). Николай Палкин (Table PG2)
3365.O7-.O73 Ot neĭ vse kachestva (Comedy). От ней все качества (Table PG2)
3365.O8-.O83 Ot͡et͡s Sergiĭ (Tale). Отец Сергий (Table PG2)
Otrochestvo (Novel). Отрочество see PG3365.D55+
3365.P4-.P43 Pervyĭ vinokur (Comedy). Первый винокур (Table PG2)
3365.P5-.P53 Plody prosveshcheni͡ia (Comedy). Плоды просвещения (Table PG2)
3365.P6-.P63 Polikushka (Story). Поликушка (Table PG2)
3365.P7-.P73 Posle bala (Tale). После бала (Table PG2)
3365.R8-.R83 Rubka lesa (Tale). Рубка леса (Table PG2)
3365.S3-.S33 Semeĭnoe schast′e (Novel). Семейное счастье (Table PG2)
3365.S4 Sevastopol′skie rasskazy. Севастопольские рассказы
3365.S42 Sevastopol′ v dekabre (1854). Севастополь в декабре
3365.S45 Sevastopol′ v mae (1855). Севастополь в мае

Russian literature
Individual authors and works, 1800-1870
Tolstoĭ, Lev Nikolaevich, graf, 1828-1910 (Tolstoy, Leo). Лев Николаевич Толстой
Separate works
Sevastopolʹskie rasskazy. Севастопольские рассказы -- Continued

3365.S47 Sevastopolʹ v avguste (1855). Севастополь в августе

3365.S49-.S493 Skazka o pustom barabane. Сказка о пустом барабане (Table PG2)

3365.S5-.S53 Skazka ob Ivane durake. Сказка об Иване дураке (Table PG2)

3365.S6-.S63 Smertʹ Ivana Ilʹicha (Story). Смерть Ивана Ильича (Table PG2)

3365.S7-.S73 Sorok let (Legend). Сорок лет (Table PG2)

3365.S8-.S83 Suratskai͡a kofeĭnai͡a (Tale). Суратская кофейная (Table PG2)

3365.S9-.S93 Svechka (Tale). Свечка (Table PG2)

3365.T6-.T63 Trebovanii͡a li͡ubvi (Tale). Требования любви (Table PG2)

3365.T65-.T653 Tri pritchi (Tale). Три притчи (Table PG2)

3365.T7-.T73 Tri smerti (Tale). Три смерти (Table PG2)

3365.T75-.T753 Tri start͡sa (Tale). Три старца (Table PG2)

3365.T8-.T83 Tri syna (Tale). Три сына (Table PG2)

3365.T85-.T853 Tri voprosa (Tale). Три вопроса (Table PG2)

3365.T9-.T93 Trud, smertʹ i boleznʹ (Legend). Труд, смерть и болезнь (Table PG2)

3365.U6-.U63 Upustishʹ ogonʹ ne potushishʹ (Tale). Упустишь огонь не потушишь (Table PG2)

3365.U8-.U83 Utro pomeshchika (Story). Утро помещика (Table PG2)

3365.V5-.V53 Vlastʹ tʹmy, ili, Kogotok uvi͡az, vseĭ ptichke propastʹ (Drama). Власть тьмы, или, Коготок увяз, всей птичке пропасть (Table PG2)

Voĭna i mir (Novel). Война и мир

3365.V6 Texts. By date

3365.V62 Selections. By date

3365.V65 Criticism

3365.V7-.V73 Voskresenʹe. Воскресенье (Table PG2)

3365.V8-.V83 Vstrecha v otri͡ade s moskovskim znakomym (Tale). Встреча в отряде с московским знакомым (Table PG2)

3365.Z2-.Z23 Za chto? (Tale). За что? (Table PG2)

3365.Z3-.Z33 Zapiski markera (Story). Записки маркера (Table PG2)

3365.Z4-.Z43 Zerno s kurinoe i͡ait͡so (Legend). Зерно с куриное яйцо (Table PG2)

Russian literature
Individual authors and works, 1800-1870
Tolstoĭ, Lev Nikolaevich, graf, 1828-1910 (Tolstoy, Leo). Лев Николаевич Толстой
Separate works -- Continued

3365.Z5-.Z53 Zhivoĭ trup (Drama). Живой труп (Table PG2)
3365.Z8 Imitations. Paraphrases. Adaptations
Translations
For translations of journals, diaries, and memoirs see PG3377.A5+
For translations of letters see PG3379.A2A+
English
3366.A1 Collected works. By date
3366.A12 Posthumous works. By date
3366.A13 Selections. By translator
3366.A15 Collected novels and stories. By translator or editor
3366.A17 Collected essays. By date
3366.A18 Collected poems. By date
3366.A19 Collected plays. By date
3366.A3-Z Separate works. By Russian title, A-Z
e. g.
3366.I2 I svet vo t′me svetit (The light that shines in darkness). И свет во тьме светит
3366.P5 Plody prosveshchenii͡a (Fruits of enlightenment). Плоды просвещения
3366.S3 Semeĭnoe schast′e (Family happiness). Семейное счастье
3366.V5 Vlast′ t′my (Power of darkness). Власть тьмы
3366.V6 Voĭna i mir (War and peace). Война и мир
3366.Z5 Zhivoĭ trup (The living corpse). Живой труп
3367.A-Z Other languages, A-Z
Subarrange each by Table PG1
e.g.
3367.D3 Danish (Table PG1)
3367.F5 French (Table PG1)
3367.G5 German (Table PG1)
3367.G7 Greek, Modern (Table PG1)
3367.I5 Italian (Table PG1)
3367.N6 Norwegian (Table PG1)
3367.S5 Spanish (Table PG1)
3368 Works edited by Tolstoĭ
e. g.
3368.B2-.B2Z Bab′i͡a doli͡a. Бабья доля (My life, as told by the peasant Anis′i͡a (Anissia)(Анисья))
3368.B2 Russian texts. By date
3368.B2A-.B2Z Translations. By language
Biography and criticism

Russian literature
Individual authors and works, 1800-1870
Tolstoĭ, Lev Nikolaevich, graf, 1828-1910 (Tolstoy, Leo). Лев Николаевич Толстой
Biography and criticism -- Continued
Bibliography see Z8883.8
3370 Periodicals and societies
3371 Dictionaries, indexes, etc.
3375 Autobiography
3377 Journals. Diaries. Memoirs
3377.A5-.Z4 Translations. By language and translator
3379 Correspondence
3379.A1 General
3379.A2A-.A2Z Translations. By language
3379.A3-Z Individual correspondents
e. g.
3379.O2 Obolenskai͡a, Marii͡a L′vovna, kni͡aginii͡a (Tolstoĭ's daughter). Мария Львовна Оболенская
3379.T5 Tolstai͡a, Aleksandra Andreevna, grafinii͡a (Tolstoĭ's cousin). Александра Андреевна Толстая
3385 General treatises. Life and works
Including memoirs by members of his family
e. g.
3385.T5 Tolstai͡a, Aleksandra L′vovna, grafinii͡a (Tolstoĭ's daughter). Александра Львовна Толстая
3385.T6 Tolstai͡a, Sof′i͡a Andreevna (Bers), grafinii͡a (Tolstoĭ's wife). Софья Андреевна (Берс) Толстая
3385.T7 Tolstoĭ, Il′i͡a L′vovich, graf (Tolstoĭ's son). Илья Львович Толстой
3385.T8 Tolstoĭ, Lev L′vovich, graf (Tolstoĭ's son). Лев Львович Толстой
3386 Essays, pamphlets, etc.
3387 Early life. Education
3388 Love and marriage. Relations to women
3390 Biography of Tolstoĭ's wife, Grafinia Sof′ia Andreevna Tolstaia (Софья Андреевна (Берс) Толстая)
Cf. PG3385.T6 Memoirs and diaries
3395 Later life. Death
3400 Relations to contemporaries
3401 Homes and haunts. Local associations
3403 Anniversaries. Celebrations
3405 Memorials. Testimonials to his genius
3407 Museums. Exhibitions
3408 Iconography. Portraits. Monuments
3409 Authorship. Sources, associates, followers, etc.
Criticism and interpretation

Russian literature
Individual authors and works, 1800-1870
Tolstoĭ, Lev Nikolaevich, graf, 1828-1910 (Tolstoy, Leo).
Лев Николаевич Толстой
Biography and criticism
Criticism and interpretation -- Continued
History of the study, appreciation, and influence of Tolstoĭ

3409.5 General, and in Russia
3409.7.A-Z In countries other than Russia, A-Z
e. g.
3409.7.F7 France
3410 General works
3411 Essays, pamphlets, etc.
Criticism of separate works see PG3365.A3+
Characters
3412 General
Special
3413 Women
Individual
see the special work in PG3365.A3+
3414.A-Z Other, A-Z
3415.A-Z Treatment and knowledge of special subjects, A-Z
3415.A3 Aesthetics
3415.A7 Art
3415.A8 Authorship
3415.B65 Books and reading
3415.C37 Caucasus
3415.C48 Chess
3415.C5 China
3415.C7 Crime and criminals
3415.C8 Culture
3415.D42 Death
3415.E2 The East
3415.E3 Economics (Money, property, etc.)
3415.E4 Education
3415.E8 Ethics
3415.F54 Film adaptations
3415.G74 Great Britain
3415.H5 History
3415.L3 Law
3415.M43 Medicine
3415.M45 Mental health
3415.M85 Music
3415.P4 Peace and war
3415.P5 Philosophy
3415.P55 Pleasure

Russian literature
Individual authors and works, 1800-1870
Tolstoĭ, Lev Nikolaevich, graf, 1828-1910 (Tolstoy, Leo). Лев Николаевич Толстой
Biography and criticism
Criticism and interpretation
Treatment and knowledge of special subjects, A-Z -- Continued

3415.P58 Poland
3415.P6 Political problems
Reading see PG3415.B65
3415.R4 Religion
3415.R87 Rural conditions
3415.S3 Science
3415.S53 Shakespeare, William, 1564-1616
3415.S6 Social problems
War see PG3415.P4
3415.5 Language. Style
3416 Dramatic presentations of Tolstoĭ's plays
3417.A-Z Special, A-Z
e. g.
3417.Z5 Zhivoĭ trup. Живой труп
3418 Individual authors, Tolstoĭ, L. - Turgenev
3418.T3 Tolstoĭ, Mikhail Vladimirovich, graf, 1812-1896. Михаил Владимирович Толстой (Table P-PZ40)
Tolstoy, Leo, graf, 1828-1910 see PG3365+
Trekhzvezdochkin, Germogen. Гермоген Трехзвездочкин see PG3337.M25
Trilunnyĭ, pseud. Трилунный see PG3361.S783
T͡Siprinus, pseud. Ципринус see PG3337.P93
3418.T4 T͡Sitovich, Nikolaĭ Dmitrievich, fl. 1830-1840. Николай Дмитриевич Цитович (Table P-PZ40)
3418.T5 T͡Syganov, Nikolaĭ Grigor'evich, 1797-1831. Николай Григорьевич Цыганов (Table P-PZ40)
3418.T6 Tumanov, Aleksandr, 19th cent. Александр Туманов (Table P-PZ40)
3418.T7 Tumanskiĭ, Vasiliĭ Ivanovich, 1800-1860. Василий Иванович Туманский (Table P-PZ40)
3418.T75 Tur, Evgenii͡a. Евгения Тур (Table P-PZ40)
3418.T8 Turbin, Sergeĭ Ivanovich, 1821-1884. Сергей Иванович Турбин (Table P-PZ40)
Turgenev, Ivan Sergeevich, 1818-1883. Иван Сергеевич Тургенев
3420.A1 Collected works. By date
3420.A13 Selected works. By editor
3420.A15 Collected novels and tales. By date
3420.A17 Collected poems. By date

Russian literature
Individual authors and works, 1800-1870
Turgenev, Ivan Sergeevich, 1818-1883. Иван Сергеевич Тургенев -- Continued

3420.A19 Collected plays. By date
3420.A2 Selections. By editor
3420.A3-Z Separate works
For translations see PG3421+
3420.A5-.A53 Andreĭ (Poem). Андрей (Table PG2)
3420.A6-.A63 Andreĭ Kolosov (Story). Андрей Колосов (Table PG2)
Annouchka see PG3420.A7+
Anuchka see PG3420.A7+
3420.A7-.A73 Asi͡a (Story). Ася (Table PG2)
3420.B4-.B43 Bezdenezh′e (Dramatic scenes). Безденежье (Table PG2)
3420.B5-.B53 Bezhin lug (Sketch). Бежин луг (Table PG2)
3420.B6-.B63 Biri͡uk (Sketch). Бирюк (Table PG2)
3420.B7-.B73 Bretter (Story). Бреттер (Table PG2)
3420.B8-.B83 Brigadir (Tale). Бригадир (Table PG2)
3420.B9-.B93 Burmistr (Sketch). Бурмистр (Table PG2)
3420.C4-.C43 Chasy (Tale). Часы (Table PG2)
3420.C5-.C53 Chertopkhanov i Nedopi͡uskin (Sketch). Чертопханов и Недопюскин (Table PG2)
3420.C6-.C63 Chuzhoĭ khleb (Comedy). Чужой хлеб (Table PG2)
3420.D5-.D53 Dnevnik lishnego cheloveka (Story). Дневник лишнего человека (Table PG2)
3420.D6-.D63 Dovol′no (Tale). Довольно (Table PG2)
3420.D7-.D73 Dva pomeshchika (Sketch). Два помещика (Table PG2)
3420.D75-.D753 Dva prii͡ateli͡a (Story). Два приятеля (Table PG2)
3420.D8-.D83 Dvori͡anskoe gnezdo (Novel). Дворянское гнездо (Table PG2)
3420.D9-.D93 Dym (Novel). Дым (Table PG2)
3420.E5-.E53 Ėpigrammy. Эпиграммы (Table PG2)
3420.E6-.E63 Ėpilog (Sketch). Эпилог (Table PG2)
3420.E7-.E73 Ermolaĭ i mel′nichikha (Sketch). Ермолай и мельничиха (Table PG2)
3420.F3-.F33 Faust (Tale). Фауст (Table PG2)
(3420.G2) Gamlet i Don Kikhot. Гамлет и Дон Кихот
see PR2807
3420.G3-.G33 Gamlet Shchigrovskogo uezda (Sketch). Гамлет Щигровского уезда (Table PG2)
3420.G4-.G43 Gde tonko, tam i rvetsi͡a (Comedy). Где тонко, там и рвется (Table PG2)
3420.I3-.I33 I͡Akov Pasynkov (Story). Яков Пасынков (Table PG2)
3420.I7-.I73 Istorii͡a leĭtenanta Ergunova (Tale). История лейтенанта Ергунова (Table PG2)

Russian literature
Individual authors and works, 1800-1870
Turgenev, Ivan Sergeevich, 1818-1883. Иван Сергеевич Тургенев
Separate works -- Continued

3420.K3-.K33 Kas͡ťan s Krasivoĭ-Mechi (Sketch). Касьян с Красивой-Мечи (Table PG2)
3420.K4-.K43 Kholost͡iak (Comedy). Холостяк (Table PG2)
3420.K5-.K53 Khor′ i Kalinich (Sketch). Хорь и Калинич (Table PG2)
3420.K6-.K63 Klara Milich (Story). Клара Милич (Table PG2)
3420.K7-.K73 Kone͡ts Chertopkhanova (Sketch). Конец Чертопханова (Table PG2)
3420.K8-.K83 Kontora (Sketch). Контора (Table PG2)
Krepostna͡ia. Крепостная see PG3420.P45+
3420.K9-.K93 Kroket v Vindzore. Крокет в Виндзоре (Table PG2)
3420.L3-.L33 Lebed͡ian′ (Sketch). Лебедянь (Table PG2)
3420.L4-.L43 Les i step′ (Sketch). Лес и степь (Table PG2)
3420.L5-.L53 L′gov (Sketch). Льгов (Table PG2)
3420.M3-.M33 Malinova͡ia voda (Sketch). Малиновая вода (Table PG2)
3420.M4-.M43 Mes͡iat͡s v derevne (Comedy). Месяц в деревне (Table PG2)
3420.M6-.M63 Moĭ sosed Radilov (Sketch). Мой сосед Радилов (Table PG2)
3420.M8-.M83 Mumu (Tale). Муму (Table PG2)
Nakanune (Novel). Накануне
3420.N3 Texts. By date
3420.N32 Criticism
3420.N33-.N333 Nakhlebnik (Comedy). Нахлебник (Table PG2)
3420.N35-.N353 Nashi poslali (Episod). Наши послали (Table PG2)
3420.N38-.N383 Neostorozhnost′ (Comedy). Неосторожность (Table PG2)
3420.N4-.N43 Neschastna͡ia (Tale). Несчастная (Table PG2)
3420.N6-.N63 Nov′ (Novel). Новь (Table PG2)
3420.O3-.O33 Odnodvore͡ts Ovs͡iannikov (Sketch). Однодворец Овсянников (Table PG2)
Otcha͡iannyĭ. Отчаянный see PG3420.O75
3420.O7 Otryvki iz vospominaniĭ svoikh i chuzhikh. Отрывки из воспоминаний своих и чужих
3420.O72 Starye portrety. Старые портреты
3420.O75 Otcha͡iannyĭ. Отчаянный
3420.O8-.O83 O͡ttsy i deti (Novel). Отцы и дети (Table PG2)
3420.P2-.P23 Parasha (Tale in verse). Параша (Table PG2)
3420.P25-.P253 Pegas. Пегас (Table PG2)
3420.P3-.P33 Perepiska (Story). Переписка (Table PG2)
Perva͡ia l͡iubov′ (Story). Первая любовь
3420.P4 Texts. By date

Russian literature
Individual authors and works, 1800-1870
Turgenev, Ivan Sergeevich, 1818-1883. Иван Сергеевич Тургенев
Separate works
Pervai͡a li͡ubov′ (Story). Первая любовь -- Continued

3420.P42 Criticism

3420.P43-.P433 Pesn′ torzhestvui͡ushcheĭ li͡ubvi (Tale). Песнь торжествующей любви (Table PG2)

3420.P45-.P453 Petr Petrovich Karataev (Sketch). Петр Петрович Каратаев (Table PG2)

3420.P5-.P53 Petushkov (Story). Петушков (Table PG2)

3420.P55-.P553 Pevt͡sy (Sketch). Певцы (Table PG2)

3420.P6-.P63 Poezdka v Poles′e (Tale). Поездка в Полесье (Table PG2)

3420.P65-.P653 Pomeshchik (Tale in verse). Помещик (Table PG2)

3420.P7-.P73 Postoi͡alyĭ dvor (Story). Постоялый двор (Table PG2)

3420.P75-.P753 Prizraki (Fantasy). Призраки (Table PG2)

3420.P8-.P83 Provint͡sialka (Comedy). Провинциалка (Table PG2)

3420.P85-.P853 Punin i Baburin (Tale). Пунин и Бабурин (Table PG2)

3420.R3-.R33 Rasskaz ott͡sa Aleksei͡a (Tale). Рассказ отца Алексея (Table PG2)

Rasskaz pomeshchika Karataeva. Рассказ помещика Каратаева see PG3420.P45+

3420.R4-.R43 Razgovor na bol′shoĭ doroge (Dramatic scenes in verse). Разговор на большой дороге (Table PG2)

3420.R8-.R83 Rudin (Novel). Рудин (Table PG2)

3420.S5-.S53 Smert′ (Sketch). Смерть (Table PG2)

3420.S55-.S553 Sobaka (Tale). Собака (Table PG2)

Sobstvennai͡a gospodskai͡a kontora (Fragment of a novel). Собственная господская контора

3420.S6 Texts. By date

3420.S62 Criticism

3420.S63-.S633 Son (Tale). Сон (Table PG2)

Starye portrety. Старые портреты see PG3420.O72

3420.S67-.S673 Stepnoĭ korol′ Lir (Tale). Степной король Лир (Table PG2)

3420.S7-.S73 Stikhotvorenii͡a v proze. Стихотворения в прозе (Table PG2)

3420.S75-.S753 Strannai͡a istorii͡a (Tale). Странная история (Table PG2)

3420.S8-.S83 Stuchit! (Sketch). Стучит! (Table PG2)

3420.S85-.S853 Stuk! Stuk! Stuk! Studii͡a (Tale). Стук! Стук! Стук! Студия (Table PG2)

3420.S9-.S93 Svidan′e (Sketch). Свиданье (Table PG2)

3420.T3-.T33 Tat′i͡ana Borisovna i ee plemi͡annik (Sketch). Татьяна Борисовна и ее племянник (Table PG2)

Russian literature
Individual authors and works, 1800-1870
Turgenev, Ivan Sergeevich, 1818-1883. Иван Сергеевич Тургенев
Separate works -- Continued

3420.T7-.T73 Tri portreta (Story). Три портрета (Table PG2)
3420.T8-.T83 Tri vstrechi (Tale). Три встречи (Table PG2)
3420.U4-.U43 Uezdnyĭ lekar′ (Sketch). Уездный лекарь (Table PG2)
3420.V4-.V43 Vecher v Sorrento (Dramatic scenes). Вечер в Сорренто (Table PG2)
3420.V5-.V53 Veshnie vody (Novel). Вешние воды (Table PG2)
3420.Z3-.Z33 Zapiski okhotnika. Записки охотника (Table PG2)
For separate sketches see the title in PG3420.A3+ e.g. PG3420.B6, Biri͡uk
3420.Z35-.Z353 Zatish′e (Story). Затишье (Table PG2)
3420.Z4-.Z43 Zavtrak u predvoditeli͡a (Comedy). Завтрак у предводителя (Table PG2)
3420.Z5-.Z53 Zhid (Tale). Жид (Table PG2)
3420.Z6-.Z63 Zhivye moshchi (Sketch). Живые мощи (Table PG2)

Translations
English
3421.A1 Collected works. By date
3421.A13 Selected works. By date
3421.A15 Collected novels and tales. By date
3421.A17 Collected essays and miscellaneous works. By date
3421.A19 Collected plays. By date
3421.A2A-.A2Z Selections. By translator or editor, A-Z
3421.A3-Z Separate works. By Russian title, A-Z
French
3422.A1 Collected works. By date
3422.A13 Selected works. By date
3422.A15 Collected novels and tales. By date
3422.A17 Collected essays and miscellaneous works. By date
3422.A19 Collected plays. By date
3422.A2A-.A2Z Selections. By translator or editor, A-Z
3422.A3-Z Separate works. By Russian title, A-Z
German
3423.A1 Collected works. By date
3423.A13 Selected works. By date
3423.A15 Collected novels and tales. By date
3423.A17 Collected essays and miscellaneous works. By date
3423.A19 Collected plays. By date
3423.A2A-.A2Z Selections. By translator or editor, A-Z
3423.A3-Z Separate works. By Russian title, A-Z
Italian
3424.A1 Collected works. By date
3424.A13 Selected works. By date

Russian literature
Individual authors and works, 1800-1870
Turgenev, Ivan Sergeevich, 1818-1883. Иван Сергеевич Тургенев
Translations
Italian -- Continued

3424.A15 Collected novels and tales. By date
3424.A17 Collected essays and miscellaneous works. By date
3424.A19 Collected plays. By date
3424.A2A-.A2Z Selections. By translator or editor, A-Z
3424.A3-Z Separate works. By Russian title, A-Z

Spanish

3425.A1 Collected works. By date
3425.A13 Selected works. By date
3425.A15 Collected novels and tales. By date
3425.A17 Collected essays and miscellaneous works. By date
3425.A19 Collected plays. By date
3425.A2A-.A2Z Selections. By translator or editor, A-Z
3425.A3-Z Separate works. By Russian title, A-Z
3427.A-Z Other languages, A-Z

Subarrange each by Table PG1

3428 Illustrations

Biography and criticism

Bibliography see Z8893.7

3428.5 Periodicals and societies
3429 Dictionaries, indexes, etc.
3430 Autobiography
3431 Journals. Diaries. Memoirs

Correspondence

3432 General. By date of imprint
3433.A-Z Individual correspondents, A-Z
3435 General treatises. Life and works
3436 Early life. Education
3437 Love and marriage. Relations to women
3438 Later life. Death
3439 Relation to contemporaries
3440 Homes and haunts. Local associations
3441 Anniversaries. Celebrations
3441.5 Iconography. Museums. Exhibitions
3442 Authorship
3443 Criticism and interpretation. Appreciation

Characters

3443.2 General
3443.3.A-Z Special, A-Z
3443.3.W6 Women
3444.A-Z Treatment and knowledge of special subjects, A-Z
3444.D4 Democratic ideas

Russian literature
Individual authors and works, 1800-1870
Turgenev, Ivan Sergeevich, 1818-1883. Иван Сергеевич Тургенев
Biography and criticism
Treatment and knowledge of special subjects, A-Z -- Continued

3444.D7 Turgenev as dramatist
3444.G6 Goethe
3444.H8 Humor
3444.J68 Journalism
3444.N3 Nature
3444.O3 Occidentalism
3444.P48 Philosophy
3444.S6 Social problems
3445 Language. Style
3447.A-Z Individual authors, Turgenev - Z
3447.U4 Ulʹi͡anov, Nikolaĭ Dmitrievich, 1816-1856. Николай Дмитриевич Ульянов (Table P-PZ40)
3447.U5 Umanskiĭ, I.V., fl. 1840-1860. И.В. Уманский (Table P-PZ40)
3447.U6 Ushakov, Alekseĭ S., fl. 1850-1870. Алексей С. Ушаков (Table P-PZ40)
3447.U7 Uspenskiĭ, Nikolaĭ Vasilʹevich, 1837-1889. Николай Васильевич Успенский (Table P-PZ40)
3447.U8 Ustri͡alov, Fedor Nikolaevich, 1836-1885. Федор Николаевич Устрялов (Table P-PZ40)
3447.U9 Ustri͡alov, Nikolaĭ Gerasimovich, 1805-1870. Николай Герасимович Устрялов (Table P-PZ40)
3447.V112 Vadbolʹskai͡a, Varvara, kni͡agini͡a, fl. 1850-1860. Варвара Вадбольская (Table P-PZ40)
3447.V115 Vakhnovskai͡a, S., 1829-1891. С. Вахновская (Table P-PZ40)
3447.V23 Vakhrushev, Foma, fl. 1840-1870. Фома Вахрушев (Table P-PZ40)
Vanenko, Ivan. Иван Ваненко see PG3321.B35
3447.V27 Vashchenko-Zakharchenko, Andreĭ Egorovich, f. 1850-1860. Андрей Егорович Ващенко-Захарченко (Table P-PZ40)
3447.V29 Veĭnberg, Pavel Isaevich, 1846-1904. Павел Исаевич Вейнберг (Table P-PZ40)
3447.V3 Velʹi͡ashev-Volynt͡sev, Dmitriĭ Ivanovich, ca. 1770-1818. Дмитрий Иванович Вельяшев-Волынцев (Table P-PZ40)
3447.V33 Velikopolʹskiĭ, Ivan Ermolaevich, 1793-1868. Иван Ермолаевич Великопольский (Table P-PZ40)

Russian literature
Individual authors and works, 1800-1870
Individual authors, Turgenev - Z -- Continued

3447.V36 Vel′tman, Aleksandr Fomich, 1800-1870. Александр Фомич Вельтман (Table P-PZ40)

3447.V38 Vel′tman, Elena Ivanovna (Kube), d. 1868. Елена Ивановна (Кубе) Вельтман (Table P-PZ40)

3447.V4 Venevitinov, Dmitriĭ Vladimirovich, 1805-1827. Дмитрий Владимирович Веневитинов (Table P-PZ40)

3447.V45 Verderevskiĭ, Evgraf Alekseevich, fl. 1850-1860. Евграф Алексеевич Вердеревский (Table P-PZ40)
Sometimes erroneously cited as Evgeniĭ Aleksandrovich Verderevskiĭ (Евгений Александрович Вердеревский)

(3447.V46) Vereshchagin, Vasiliĭ Vasil′evich, 1842-1904. Василий Васильевич Верещагин
see PG3470.V42

3447.V47 Vesen′ev, Ivan. Иван Весеньев (Table P-PZ40)

Vesnin, Semen Avdievich, d. 1853. Семен Авдиевич Веснин see PG3361.S88

3447.V49 V͡iazemskiĭ, K. K. Вяземский (Table P-PZ40)

3447.V497 V͡iazemskiĭ, Pavel Petrovich, kn͡iaz′, 1820-1888. Павелъ Петровичъ Вяземскій (Table P-PZ40)

3447.V5 V͡iazemskiĭ, Petr Andreevich, kn͡iaz′, 1792-1878. Петр Андреевич Вяземский (Table P-PZ40)

3447.V53 Viskonti, Aleksandr, fl. 1860-1870. Александр Висконти (Table P-PZ40)

3447.V55 Vladimirskiĭ, Viktor Aleksandrovich, 1812-1877. Виктор Александрович Владимирский (Table P-PZ40)

Vodovozov, Vasiliĭ Ivanovich. Василий Иванович Водовозов see PG3470.V59

Volgin, I. I. Волгин see PG3447.Z8

3447.V59 Volkonska͡ia, Mari͡ia Vasil′evna, kn͡iagin͡ia. Мария Васильевна Волконская (Table P-PZ40)

3447.V6 Volkonska͡ia, Zinaida Aleksandrovna (Belosel′ska͡ia-Belozerska͡ia), kn͡iagin͡ia, 1792-1862. Зинаида Александровна (Белосельская- Белозерская) Волконская (Table P-PZ40)

3447.V62 Volkov, Aleksandr Abramovich, 1788- . Александр Абрамович Волков (Table P-PZ40)

3447.V64 Volkov, Aleksandr Gavrilovich, 1775-1833. Александр Гаврилович Волков (Table P-PZ40)

3447.V66 Volkov, I͡Uriĭ Aleksandrovich, d. 1862. Юрий Александрович Волков (Table P-PZ40)

3447.V68 Volkova, Anna Alekseevna, 1781-1834. Анна Алексеевна Волкова (Table P-PZ40)

Volzhin, Boris. Борис Волжин see PG3321.B87

Russian literature
Individual authors and works, 1800-1870
Individual authors, Turgenev - Z -- Continued

3447.V7 Vonli͡arli͡arskiĭ, Vasiliĭ Aleksandrovich, 1814-1852. Василий Александрович Вонлярлярский (Table P-PZ40)

Vorob′ev, Dmitriĭ Timofeevich. Дмитрий Тимофеевич Воробьев see PG3337.L3

3447.V77 Voronov, Mikhail Alekseevich, 1840-1873. Михаил Алексеевич Воронов (Table P-PZ40)

3447.V8 Voronova, Elizaveta Petrovna, d. 1881. Елизавета Петровна Воронова (Table P-PZ40)

3447.V84 Voskresenskiĭ, Mikhail Il′ich, d. 1867. Михаил Ильич Воскресенский (Table P-PZ40)

3447.V87 Vostokov, Aleksandr Khristoforovich, 1781-1864. Александр Христофорович Востоков (Table P-PZ40)

3447.V9 Vysota, Aleksandr Pavlovich, fl. 1860-1870. Александр Павлович Высота (Table P-PZ40)

Weltman, Aleksandr Fomich see PG3447.V36

Weltman, Elena Ivanovna see PG3447.V38

3447.Z2 Zagoskin, Mikhail Nikolaevich, 1789-1852. Михаил Николаевич Загоскин (Table P-PZ40)

Zaionchkovska͡ia, Nadezhda Dmitrievna (Khvoshchinska͡ia). Надежда Дмитриевна (Хвощинская) Заиончковская see PG3337.K42

Zaletaeva, Anna Nikanorovna. Анна Никаноровна Залетаева see PG3337.M7

3447.Z23 Zarin, Efim Fedorovich, 1829-1892. Ефим Федорович Зарин (Table P-PZ40)

3447.Z25 Zarubin, Pavel Alekseevich, 1816-1896. Павел Алексеевич Зарубин (Table P-PZ40)

3447.Z28 Zavalishin, Ippolit Irinarkhovich, fl. 1860-1870. Ипполит Иринархович Завалишин (Table P-PZ40)

3447.Z3 Zhadovska͡ia, I͡Uli͡ia Valerianovna, 1824-1883. Юлия Валериановна Жадовская (Table P-PZ40)

3447.Z32 Zhadovskiĭ, Pavel Valerianovich, 1825-1891. Павел Валерианович Жадовский (Table P-PZ40)

3447.Z34 Zhandr, Andreĭ Andreevich, 1789-1873. Андрей Андреевич Жандр (Table P-PZ40)

3447.Z35 Zhandr, Nikolaĭ Pavlovich, 1818-1895. Николай Павлович Жандр (Table P-PZ40)

3447.Z36 Zheleznov, Iosaf Ignat′evich, 1824-1863. Иосаф Игнатьевич Железнов (Table P-PZ40)

Russian literature
Individual authors and works, 1800-1870
Individual authors, Turgenev - Z -- Continued

3447.Z37 Zhemchuzhnikov, Alekseĭ Mikhaĭlovich, 1821-1908. Алексей Михайлович Жемчужников (Table P-PZ40)
Cf. PG3337.P9 Koz′ma Prutkov, collective pseudonym

3447.Z38 Zhemchuzhnikov, Vladimir Mikhaĭlovich, 1830-1884. Владимир Михайлович Жемчужников (Table P-PZ40)
Cf. PG3337.P9 Koz′ma Prutkov, collective pseudonym

3447.Z39 Zhikharev, Stepan Petrovich, 1788-1860. Степан Петрович Жихарев (Table P-PZ40)

3447.Z4 Zhukova, Mariı͡a Semenovna, 1804-1855. Мария Семеновна Жукова (Table P-PZ40)

3447.Z43 Zhukovskiĭ, Aleksandr Kirillovich, 1810-1864. Александр Кириллович Жуковский (Table P-PZ40)

3447.Z45 Zhukovskiĭ, Petr Vladimirovich, 1824-1896. Петр Владимирович Жуковский (Table P-PZ40)

3447.Z5 Zhukovskiĭ, Vasiliĭ Andreevich, 1783-1852. Василий Андреевич Жуковский (Table P-PZ40 modified)

3447.Z5A61-.Z5Z458 Separate works. By title

Agasver, stranstvuı͡ushchiĭ zhid. Агасвер, странствующий жид see PG3447.Z5S8

Agasver, vechnyĭ zhid. Агасвер, вечный жид see PG3447.Z5S8

Ballady. Баллады
see PG3447.Z5A17
For separate ballads see the title in PG3447.Z5A61+

3447.Z5B6 Borodinskai͡a godovshchina (Poem). Бородинская годовщина

3447.Z5D8 Dve byli i eshche odna. Две были и еще одна

3447.Z5D9 Dvenadt͡sat′ spı͡ashchikh dev (Story in verse). Двенадцать спящих дев

3447.Z5G7 Gromoboĭ (Ballad). Громобой

3447.Z5K3 Kamoėns (Dramatic poem). Камоэнс

3447.Z5K4 Kapitan Bopp (Story in verse). Капитан Бопп

3447.Z5K6 Kot v sapogakh (Tale in verse). Кот в сапогах

3447.Z5L5 Lı͡udmila (Ballad). Людмила

3447.Z5N2 Na vzı͡atie Varshavy (Poems). На взятие Варшавы

3447.Z5N3 Nal′ i Damai͡anti (Story in verse). Наль и Дамаянти

3447.Z5O3 Odisseı͡a (Epic poem). Одиссея

3447.Z5O7 Orleanskai͡a deva (Dramatic poem). Орлеанская дева

3447.Z5O8 Ovsı͡anyĭ kisel′ (Poem). Овсяный кисель

Russian literature
Individual authors and works, 1800-1870
Individual authors, Turgenev - Z
Zhukovskiĭ, Vasiliĭ Andreevich, 1783-1852. Василий Андреевич Жуковский
Separate works. By title -- Continued

3447.Z5P3 Pesn′ barda nad grobom slavi͡an pobediteleĭ (Poem). Песнь барда над гробом славян победителей
3447.Z5P35 Pevet͡s na Kremle (Poem). Певец на Кремле
3447.Z5P4 Pevet͡s vo stane russkikh voinov (Poem). Певец во стане русских воинов
3447.Z5P6 Povest′ o Iosife Prekrasnom (Poem). Повесть о Иосифе Прекрасном
3447.Z5P7 Protokol dvadt͡satogo Arzamasskogo zasedanii͡a (in verse). Протокол двадцатого Арзамасского заседания
3447.Z5R8 Russkai͡a slava (Poem). Русская слава
3447.Z5R9 Rustem i Zorab (Poem). Рустем и Зораб
3447.Z5S3 Sel′skoe kladbishche (Elegy). Сельское кладбище
3447.Z5S35 Shil′onskiĭ uznik (Story in verse). Шильонский узник
3447.Z5S4 Skazka o Ivane t͡sareviche i serom volke (Tale in verse). Сказка о Иване царевиче и сером волке
3447.Z5S5 Skazka o spi͡ashcheĭ t͡sarevne (Tale in verse). Сказка о спящей царевне
3447.Z5S55 Skazka o t͡sare Berendee (Tale in verse). Сказка о царе Берендее
3447.Z5S6 Skazki (Tales in verse). Сказки
For separate tales see the title in PG3447.Z5A61+
Spi͡ashchai͡a t͡sarevna. Спящая царевна see PG3447.Z5S5
3447.Z5S8 Stranstvui͡ushchiĭ zhid (Poem). Странствующий жид
3447.Z5S9 Svetlana (Tale in verse). Светлана
3447.Z5U5 Undina, starinnai͡a povest′ (Poem). Ундина, старинная повесть
3447.Z5V6 Voĭna mysheĭ i li͡agushek (Tale in verse). Война мышей и лягушек
3447.Z53 Zhulev, Gavriil Nikolaevich, 1836-1878. Гавриил Николаевич Жулев (Table P-PZ40)
3447.Z55 Zilov, Alekseĭ, fl. 1830-1850. Алексей Зилов (Table P-PZ40)
3447.Z57 Zinov′ev, Fedor Alekseevich, fl. 1860-1870. Федор Алексеевич Зиновьев (Table P-PZ40)
3447.Z574 Zinov′ev, M. (Mikhaĭlo). Михайло Зиновьев (Table P-PZ40)
3447.Z58 Zontag, Anna Petrovna (I͡Ushkova), 1786-1864. Анна Петровна (Юшкова) Зонтаг (Table P-PZ40)

Russian literature
Individual authors and works, 1800-1870
Individual authors, Turgenev - Z -- Continued

3447.Z6 Zotov, Rafail Mikhaĭlovich, 1795-1871. Рафаил Михайлович Зотов (Table P-PZ40)

3447.Z65 Zotov, Vladimir Rafailovich, 1821-1896. Владимир Рафаилович Зотов (Table P-PZ40)

3447.Z7 Zri͡akhov, Nikolaĭ, fl. 1820-1840. Николай Зряхов (Table P-PZ40)

3447.Z8 Zubov, I͡Uliĭ Mikhaĭlovich, 1832- . Юлий Михайлович Зубов (Table P-PZ40)

3447.Z83 Zubov, Platon P., fl. 1830-1850. Платон П. Зубов (Table P-PZ40)

3447.Z87 Zubova, Adelaida Alekseevna, 1830-1893. Аделаида Алексеевна Зубова (Table P-PZ40)

Individual authors and works, 1870-1917

Subarrange each author by Table P-PZ40 unless otherwise specified

3450 Anonymous works (Table P-PZ28 modified)

3450.A1A-.A1Z Works without any indication of author, either by symbol, or initial. By title, A-Z

3450.A1B34 Baletnyĭ mirok. Балетный мирок

3450.A1B58 Bluzhdai͡ushchie ogni. Блуждающие огни

3450.A1D67 Dorogoĭ gost'. Дорогой гость

3450.A1G8 Gubernatorskai͡a revizii͡a. Губернаторская ревизия

3450.A1G85 Gurli (Iz proshloĭ zhenskoĭ zhizni). Гурли (Из прошлой женской жизни)

3450.A1K3 Kallista. Каллиста

3450.A1K47 Khar'kovskie trushchoby i stikhotvorenii͡a. Харьковские трущобы и стихотворения

3450.A1K8 Kupet͡s Igolkin i ego podvig. Купец Иголкин и его подвиг

3450.A1L45 Li͡ubitel'skiĭ spektakl'. Любительский спектакль

3450.A1L5 Li͡ubov' ne pozhar (Comedy). Любовь не пожар

3450.A1M34 Magomet-I͡Akub, ėmir Kashgarskiĭ. Магомет-Якуб, эмир Кашгарский

3450.A1M36 Mat' i machikha. Мать и мачиха

3450.A1M89 Muzh'i͡a odoleli. Мужья одолели

3450.A1N44 Ne gonis' za bol'shim, maloe poteri͡aesh'. Не гонись за большим, малое потеряешь

3450.A1P65 Po Svi͡atoĭ Zemle. По Святой Земле

3450.A1S45 Serdt͡se ne igrushka. Сердце не игрушка

3450.A1S83 Stepnoĭ korol' Lir. Степной король Лир

3450.A1T72 T͡Sar' Ioann IV Groznyĭ v ėpokhu oprichnikov. Царь Иоанн IV Грозный в эпоху опричников

3450.A1T75 T͡Sar' Maksimilian. Царь Максимилиан

3450.A1Z36 Zapiski akusherki. Записки акушерки

Russian literature
Individual authors and works, 1870-1917
Anonymous works
Works without any indication of author, either by symbol, or initial. By title, A-Z -- Continued

3450.A1Z5 Zhizn′, kak ona est′. Жизнь, как она есть
3450.A1Z57 Znaĭ sverchok svoĭ shestok. Знай сверчок свой шесток
3451 Individual authors, A - Andreev, L.
3451.A2 Abaza, Viktor Afanas′evich, 1831?-1898. Виктор Афанасьевич Абаза (Table P-PZ40)
3451.A23 Aboimov, D.V., fl. 1890-1900. Д.В. Абоимов (Table P-PZ40)
3451.A25 Abramov, I͡Akov Vasil′evich, 1858-1906. Яков Васильевич Абрамов (Table P-PZ40 modified)
3451.A25A61-.A25Z458 Separate works. By title
3451.A25B3 Babushka general′sha. Бабушка генеральша
3451.A25B6 Bosai͡a komanda. Босая команда
3451.A25G3 Gamlety - para na grosh. Гамлеты - пара на грош
3451.A25I7 Ishchushchiĭ pravdy (Tale). Ищущий правды
3451.A25I8 Ivan bosyĭ. Иван босый
3451.A25K3 Kak melent′evt͡sy iskali voli. Как мелентьевцы искали воли
3451.A25K6 Korova (Tale). Корова
3451.A25M5 Meshchanskiĭ myslitel′. Мещанский мыслитель
3451.A25S7 Sredi sektantov. Среди сектантов
3451.A25V1 V poiskakh za pravdoĭ. В поисках за правдой
3451.A25V2 V stepi (Tale). В степи
3451.A25V3 Van′ka kli͡ushnik. Ванька клюшник
3451.A26 Abramov, Ivan Spiridonovich, 1874- . Иван Спиридонович Абрамов (Table P-PZ40)
3451.A264 Abramov, Nikolaĭ, fl. 1865-1893. Николай Абрамов (Table P-PZ40)
3451.A27 Abramovich, Mikhail Solomonovich, 1859- . Михаил Соломонович Абрамович (Table P-PZ40)
3451.A28 Abramovich, Vladimir I͡Akovlevich, 1877- . Владимир Яковлевич Абрамович (Table P-PZ40)
3451.A3 Adadurov, Evgraf, d. 1871. Евграф Ададуров (Table P-PZ40)
Admirari, Nil. Нил Адмирари see PG3467.P4
Adodurov, Evgraf. Евграф Адодуров see PG3451.A3
3451.A33 Adol′fin. Адольфин (Table P-PZ40)
3451.A35 Afanas′ev, Leonid Nikolaevich, 1864- . Леонид Николаевич Афанасьев (Table P-PZ40)
3451.A353 Afanas′ev, S.A. (Sergi͡eĭ Aleksandrovich). Сергѣй Александровичъ Афанасьевъ (Table P-PZ40)

Russian literature
Individual authors and works, 1870-1917
Individual authors, A - Andreev, L. -- Continued

3451.A36 Afinogenov, Nikolaĭ Aleksandrovich, 1878- . Николай Александрович Афиногенов (Table P-PZ40)

A--g, Nil, pseud. Нил А--г see PG3460.G24

Agapov, P.B. П.Б. Агапов see PG3467.M32

3451.A37 Agrikov, N.D., fl. 1890-1900. Н.Д. Агриков (Table P-PZ40)

Agrinskiĭ, A. A. Агринский see PG3467.L83

3451.A4 Aĭzman, David I͡Akovlevich, 1869-1922. Давид Яковлевич Айзман (Table P-PZ40 modified)

3451.A4A61-.A4Z458 Separate works. By title

3451.A4B4 Bela͡ia pustosh′. Белая пустошь

3451.A4B5 Bez neba (Story). Без неба

3451.A4B6 Bogema (Story). Богема

3451.A4C4 Chernye dni (Sketches and tales). Черные дни
For separate sketches and tales see the title in PG3451.A4A61+

3451.A4C5 Cheta Krasovit͡skikh (Story). Чета Красовицких

3451.A4D4 Dela semeĭnye (Drama). Дела семейные

3451.A4D5 Deti (Story). Дети

3451.A4D55 Dobroe delo (Tale). Доброе дело

3451.A4D6 Domoĭ (Story). Домой

3451.A4G6 Gore (Story). Горе

3451.A4I7 Istori͡ia odnogo prestupleni͡ia (Story). История одного преступления

3451.A4K6 Konsul Granat (Comedy). Консул Гранат

3451.A4K7 Krovavyĭ razliv (Story). Кровавый разлив

3451.A4L3 Latinskiĭ kvartal (Drama). Латинский квартал

3451.A4L4 Ledokhod (Story). Ледоход

3451.A4L5 Lesnik Zozuli͡a (Story). Лесник Зозуля

3451.A4N3 Nauka (Story). Наука

3451.A4N6 Novobranet͡s Ili͡ushka (Story). Новобранец Илюшка

3451.A4P6 Posle buri (Story). После бури

3451.A4P7 Pravda nebesna͡ia (Drama). Правда небесная

3451.A4R4 Redaktor Solnt͡sev. Редактор Солнцев

3451.A4S4 Serdt͡se byti͡ia (Story). Сердце бытия

3451.A4S6 Soi͡uzniki (Story). Союзники

Stoli͡ar Anchl i ego podruga. Столяр Анчл и его подруга see PG3451.A4U8

3451.A4S8 Svetlyĭ Bog (Story). Светлый Бог

3451.A4T4 Ternovyĭ kust (Tragedy). Терновый куст

3451.A4U3 Udush′e (Story). Удушье

3451.A4U8 Utro Anchla (Story). Утро Анчла
Issued also under title: Stoli͡ar Anchl i ego podruga

3451.A4V2 V chuzhoĭ storone (Story). В чужой стороне

Russian literature
Individual authors and works, 1870-1917
Individual authors, A - Andreev, L.
Aĭzman, David I͡Akovlevich, 1869-1922. Давид Яковлевич Айзман
Separate works. By title -- Continued
3451.A4V28 V uli͡tse Rosier (Story). В улице Rosier
3451.A4V5 Vernostʹ (Story). Верность
3451.A4V7 Vragi (Story). Враги
3451.A4Z4 Zemli͡aki (Story). Земляки
3451.A4Z45 Zheny (Drama). Жены
3451.A416 Akhal-Tekine͡ts. Ахал-Текинец (Table P-PZ40)
3451.A43 Akhmatova, Elizaveta Nikolaevna, 1820-1904. Елизавета Николаевна Ахматова (Table P-PZ40 modified)
3451.A43A61-.A43Z458 Separate works. By title
3451.A43B5 Blistatelʹna͡ia parti͡ia. Блистательная партия
3451.A43K3 Kandidatka na zvanie starykh dev. Кандидатка на звание старых дев
3451.A43M3 Machekha. Мачеха
3451.A43P6 Pomeshchi͡tsa. Помещица
3451.A43P7 Prikli͡ucheni͡ia moeĭ pri͡iatelʹni͡tsy. Приключения моей приятельницы
3451.A43S6 Sovremennyĭ rasskaz. Современный рассказ
3451.A43T7 Tri dni͡a. Три дня
3451.A43V7 Vtora͡ia zhena. Вторая жена
3451.A43Z3 Zamoskovna͡ia letopisʹ. Замосковная летопись
3451.A43Z35 Zaveshchanie. Завещание
3451.A435 Akhsharumov, Dmitriĭ Dmitrievich, 1823-1910. Дмитрий Дмитриевич Ахшарумов (Table P-PZ40)
3451.A44 Akhsharumov, Ivan Dmitrievich, 1831-1903. Иван Дмитриевич Ахшарумов (Table P-PZ40 modified)
3451.A44A61-.A44Z458 Separate works. By title
3451.A44B3 Babushka. Бабушка
3451.A44I7 Irisha. Ириша
3451.A44K3 K chemu? К чему?
3451.A44M3 Maĭor Bessonov. Майор Бессонов
3451.A44P6 Potomok roda Vetrishchevykh. Потомок рода Ветрищевых
3451.A44P7 Prachka. Прачка
3451.A44S5 Semeĭstvo Bryzgalovykh. Семейство Брызгаловых
3451.A45 Akhsharumov, Nikolaĭ Dmitrievich, 1819-1893. Николай Дмитриевич Ахшарумов (Table P-PZ40 modified)
3451.A45A61-.A45Z458 Separate works. By title

Russian literature
Individual authors and works, 1870-1917
Individual authors, A - Andreev, L.
Akhsharumov, Nikolaĭ Dmitrievich, 1819-1893. Николай Дмитриевич Ахшарумов
Separate works. By title -- Continued

3451.A45B5 Bludnyĭ syn. Блудный сын
3451.A45C5 Chuzhoe imi͡a. Чужое имя
3451.A45D8 Dvoĭnik. Двойник
3451.A45G7 Grazhdane lesa. Граждане леса
3451.A45I35 Igrok. Игрок
3451.A45K6 Kont͡sy v vodu. Концы в воду
3451.A45M3 Mandarin. Мандарин
3451.A45M8 Mudrenoe delo. Мудреное дело
3451.A45N3 Naturshchit͡sa. Натурщица
3451.A45N6 Nochnoe. Ночное
3451.A45N67 Novai͡a derevni͡a. Новая деревня
3451.A45O6 Opasnai͡a igra. Опасная игра
3451.A45P6 Pod kolesom. Под колесом
3451.A45R3 Rasskaz chasovogo mastera. Рассказ часового мастера
3451.A45S5 Skazka o Luke Shabashnikove. Сказка о Луке Шабашникове
3451.A45S6 Smert′ Slept͡sova. Смерть Слепцова
3451.A45S7 Starye schety. Старые счеты
3451.A45T5 Temnai͡a karta. Темная карта
3451.A45U9 Uzelok s krasnoĭ metkoĭ. Узелок с красной меткой
3451.A45V3 Vanzamii͡a. Ванзамия
3451.A45V6 Vo chto by ni stalo. Во что бы ни стало
3451.A45V7 Vsesoslovnai͡a sem′i͡a. Всесословная семья
3451.A46 Akhsharumov, Vladimir Dmitrievich, 1824-1911. Владимир Дмитриевич Ахшарумов (Table P-PZ40)
3451.A48 Aksakov, Nikolaĭ Petrovich, 1848-1909. Николай Петрович Аксаков (Table P-PZ40)
Al′binskiĭ, A. A. Альбинский see PG3470.R45
3451.A5 Al′bov, Mikhail Nilovich, 1851-1911. Михаил Нилович Альбов (Table P-PZ40 modified)
3451.A5A61-.A5Z458 Separate works. By title
3451.A5B8 Bubenet͡s. Бубенец
3451.A5D4 Den′ da noch′. День да ночь
Comprises: Book I: Toska; Book II: Sirota; Book III: Glafirina taĭna
For separate books see PG3451.A5T6, PG3451.A5S5, PG3451.A5G5
3451.A5D45 Den′ itoga. День итога
3451.A5D5 Diplomat. Дипломат
3451.A5D6 Do pristani. До пристани

PG

Russian literature
Individual authors and works, 1870-1917
Individual authors, A - Andreev, L.
Al′bov, Mikhail Nilovich, 1851-1911. Михаил Нилович Альбов
Separate works. By title -- Continued

3451.A5F3 Faust i Mefistofel′ (Siluėty). Фауст и Мефистофель
3451.A5F5 Filipp Filippych (Siluėty). Филипп Филиппыч
3451.A5G5 Glafirina taĭna. Глафирина тайна
3451.A5G55 Glava iz nedopisannoĭ povesti. Глава из недописанной повести
3451.A5G6 Golodnyĭ. Голодный
3451.A5K5 Khitryĭ plan Mamaeva. Хитрый план Мамаева
3451.A5K6 Konet͡s Nevedomoĭ ulit͡sy. Конец Неведомой улицы
3451.A5K7 Krestonost͡sy. Крестоносцы
3451.A5N3 Na tochke. На точке
Comprises: Filipp Filippych; O tom, kak goreli drova
For separate works see PG3451.A5F5, PG3451.A5O3
3451.A5N4 Nevedomai͡a ulit͡sa. Неведомая улица
3451.A5O2 O li͡udi͡akh. О людях
3451.A5O3 O tom, kak goreli drova. О том, как горели дрова
3451.A5P7 Pshenit͡syny. Пшеницыны
3451.A5R5 Ri͡asa. Ряса
3451.A5R9 Ryb′i stony. Рыбьи стоны
3451.A5S4 Siluėty. Силуэты
For separate silhouettes see the title in PG3451.A5A61+
3451.A5S5 Sirota. Сирота
3451.A5S6 Sorokovoĭ bes. Сороковой бес
3451.A5T6 Toska. Тоска
Comprises: Sorokovoĭ bes; V tikhikh vodakh
For separate works see PG3451.A5S6, PG3451.A5V27
3451.A5V25 V polden′. В полдень
3451.A5V26 V potemkakh. В потемках
3451.A5V27 V tikhikh vodakh. В тихих водах
3451.A5V28 V tylu armii. В тылу армии
3451.A5V5 Velikiĭ t͡sar′ Petr i Lizeta. Великий царь Петр и Лизета
3451.A55 Aleev, Aleksandr Egorovich, b. 1855. Александр Егорович Алеев (Table P-PZ40)
3451.A57 Aleksandrov, Dmitriĭ Aleksandrovich, fl. 1880-1890. Дмитрий Александрович Александров (Table P-PZ40)
Aleksandrov, L. Л. Александров see PG3470.P56
Aleksandrov, Viktor. Виктор Александров see PG3467.K76

Russian literature
Individual authors and works, 1870-1917
Individual authors, A - Andreev, L. -- Continued

3451.A58 Aleksandrov, Vladimir Aleksandrovich, 1842-1906. Владимир Александрович Александров (Table P-PZ40)

3451.A585 Aleksandrov, Vladimir Aleksandrovich, fl. 1890-1910. Владимир Александрович Александров (Table P-PZ40 modified)

3451.A585A61-.A585Z458 Separate works. By title

3451.A585I7 Iskuplenie (Drama). Искупление

3451.A585I8 Istoriīa odnogo braka (Drama). История одного брака

3451.A585I9 Izlomannye līudi (Drama). Изломанные люди

3451.A585K3 Kaĭsarovy (Drama). Кайсаровы

3451.A585N3 Na zhiznennom piru (Drama). На жизненном пиру

3451.A585P5 Pesn′ gorīa (Drama). Песнь горя

3451.A585P8 Putevodnaīa zvezda (Drama). Путеводная звезда

3451.A585S6 Spornyĭ vopros (Drama). Спорный вопрос

3451.A585U5 Ugolok Moskvy (Drama). Уголок Москвы

3451.A585V2 V neravnoĭ bor′be (Drama). В неравной борьбе

3451.A585V3 V sele Znamenskom (Drama). В селе Знаменском

3451.A59 Alekseev, Nikolaĭ Nikolaevich, 1871-1905. Николай Николаевич Алексеев (Table P-PZ40 modified)

3451.A59A61-.A59Z458 Separate works. By title

3451.A59L9 Lzhet͡sarevich (Novel). Лжецаревич

3451.A59N4 Neschastlivet͡s. Несчастливец

3451.A59O9 Ozhivshie teni (Stories). Ожившие тени

3451.A59P7 Prestupnyĭ put′ (Novel). Преступный путь

3451.A59R3 Raby i vladyki (Novel). Рабы и владыки

3451.A59R6 Rozy i ternii (Novel). Розы и тернии

3451.A59S3 Samozvanet͡s-Osinovik (Story). Самозванец-Осиновик

3451.A59S7 Sredi bed (Novel). Среди бед

3451.A59S8 Sud Bozhiĭ. Суд Божий

3451.A59T3 Tatarskiĭ otprysk (Novel). Татарский отпрыск

3451.A59V6 Volīa sud′by (Novel). Воля судьбы

3451.A59Z3 Zamorskiĭ vykhodet͡s (Novel). Заморский выходец

3451.A6 Alekseev, Sergeĭ Aleksandrovich, 1869-1922. Сергей Александрович Алексеев (Table P-PZ40 modified)

3451.A6A61-.A6Z458 Separate works. By title

3451.A6A8 Avdot′ina zhizn′. Авдотьина жизнь

3451.A6B55 Bludnyĭ syn. Блудный сын

3451.A6B6 Bogatyĭ chelovek. Богатый человек

3451.A6D5 Deti Vanīushina. Дети Ванюшина

Russian literature
Individual authors and works, 1870-1917
Individual authors, A - Andreev, L.
Alekseev, Sergeĭ Aleksandrovich, 1869-1922. Сергей Александрович Алексеев
Separate works. By title -- Continued

3451.A6K5 Khoroshen'kai͡a (Comedy). Хорошенькая
3451.A6N6 No. 13
3451.A6S5 Skuki radi (Drama). Скуки ради
3451.A6S7 Stena. Стена
3451.A615 Aleksin, Sergeĭ Alekseevich, fl. 1900-1920. Сергей Алексеевич Алексин (Table P-PZ40)
Alesha Chudilovich. Алеша Чудилович see PG3453.B83
Al'f, pseud. Альф see PG3467.I35
3451.A62 Alfer'ev, Ieronim Vasil'evich, 1849-1886. Иероним Васильевич Алферьев (Table P-PZ40)
3451.A63 Ali͡ab'ev, Boris Ivanovich, fl. 1890-1900. Борис Иванович Алябьев (Table P-PZ40)
3451.A64 Alin, Nikolaĭ, fl. 1900-1910. Николай Алин (Table P-PZ40)
3451.A65 Alisov, Petr Fedoseevich, 1847- . Петр Федосеевич Алисов (Table P-PZ40)
Allegro, pseud. see PG3470.S73
3451.A66 Almazov, A.P. А.П. Алмазов (Table P-PZ40)
Al'medingen, Ekaterina Alekseevna. Екатерина Алексеевна Альмединген see PG3470.S95
Al'minskiĭ, P. П. Альминский see PG3467.P2
Altaev, Aleksandr. Александр Алтаев see PG3467.I22
Altalena, pseud. see PG3470.Z4
Alymova, Serafima Nikitichna. Серафима Никитична Алымова see PG3453.B36
3451.A7 Amfiteatrov, Aleksandr Valentinovich, 1862-1938. Александр Валентинович Амфитеатров (Table P-PZ40 modified)
Prefer DK for works on Russian history; PG3001, etc. for works on the history and criticism of Russian literature
3451.A7A61-.A7Z458 Separate works. By title
Aglai͡a. Аглая see PG3451.A7P4
3451.A7A75 Akafist' Sergii͡u Kamennoostrovskomu i stikhiry. Акафисть Сергию Каменноостровскому и стихиры
3451.A7A8 Andrea del' Sarto (Drama). Андреа дель Сарто
3451.A7A9 Au! Satiry, rifmy, shutki fel'etony, i stat'i. Ау! Сатиры, рифмы, шутки фельетоны, и статьи
3451.A7B3 Baby i damy (Stories). Бабы и дамы
Subtitle: Mezhdusoslovnye pary
3451.A7B4 Bez serdt͡sa (Novel). Без сердца

Russian literature
Individual authors and works, 1870-1917
Individual authors, A - Andreev, L.
Amfiteatrov, Aleksandr Valentinovich, 1862-1938.
Александр Валентинович Амфитеатров
Separate works

Devi͡atidesi͡atniki. Девятидесятники see PG3451.A7K7

3451.A7D5 Doch′ Viktorii Pavlovny. Дочь Виктории Павловны
A work composed of 3 novels

3451.A7D54 Zlye prizraki. Злые призраки

3451.A7D57 Zakonnyĭ grekh. Законный грех

3451.A7D6 Tovarishch Feni͡a. Товарищ Феня
Comprises:

3451.A7D64 Zvezda zakatnai͡a. Звезда закатная

3451.A7D66 Rubezh. Рубеж

3451.A7D68 Gorodok. Городок

3451.A7D7 Don Zhuan v Neapole (Drama). Дон Жуан в Неаполе

3451.A7D8 Drognuvshai͡a noch′ (Novel). Дрогнувшая ночь

3451.A7D9 Dva chasa v blagorodnom semeĭstve (Drama). Два часа в благородном семействе

3451.A7E4 Ėkho (Essays). Эхо

3451.A7E6 Ėpidemii͡a (Drama). Эпидемия

3451.A7E9 Ėzopov lik (Stories). Эзопов лик

3451.A7F3 Fantasticheskie pravdy (Stories). Фантастические правды

Gnezdo. Гнездо see PG3451.A7S34

Gorodok. Городок see PG3451.A7D68

3451.A7G6 Gospoda Obmanovy (Novel). Господа Обмановы

3451.A7G7 Grezy i teni (Legends). Грезы и тени

3451.A7I2 I cherti i t͡svety. И черти и цветы

Imeniny. Именины see PG3451.A7V5

3451.A7I9 Iz terema na voli͡u (Novel). Из терема на волю

3451.A7K4 Kitaĭskiĭ vopros. Китайский вопрос

3451.A7K5 Kni͡agini͡a Nasti͡a (Drama). Княгиня Настя

3451.A7K55 Kni͡azhna (Novel). Княжна

3451.A7K6 Kont͡sy i nachala. Kronika 1880-1918 g.g. Концы и начала. Кроника 1880-1918 г.г.
Series of novels

3451.A7K61 Series 1. Vos′midesi͡atniki. Восьмидесятники
Comprises:

3451.A7K64 Razrushennye voli. Разрушенные воли

3451.A7K67 Krakh dushi. Крах души

3451.A7K7 Series 2. Devi͡atidesi͡atniki. Девятидесятники
Comprises:

3451.A7K74 Moskovskie oskolki. Московские осколки

Russian literature
Individual authors and works, 1870-1917
Individual authors, A - Andreev, L.
Amfiteatrov, Aleksandr Valentinovich, 1862-1938.
Александр Валентинович Амфитеатров
Separate works. By title
Kont͡sy i nachala. Kronika 1880-1918 g.g. Концы и начала. Кроника 1880-1918 г.г.
Series 2. Devi͡atidesi͡atniki. Девятидесятники -- Continued

3451.A7K76	Podrugi. Подруги
3451.A7K78	Zakat starogo veka. Закат старого века Sequel to Devi͡atidesi͡atniki
	Krakh dushi. Крах души see PG3451.A7K67
3451.A7K8	Krasivye skazki. Красивые сказки
3451.A7K85	Kurgany (Essays). Курганы
3451.A7L5	Lili͡asha (Novel). Лиляша
3451.A7M25	Mandragora (Comedy). Мандрагора Cf. PQ4627.M2 Machiavelli, Niccolò, Mandragola
3451.A7M3	Marʹi͡a Lusʹeva (Novel). Марья Лусьева
3451.A7M4	Mechta (Stories). Мечта
3451.A7M45	Melʹkanie mechty. Мелькание мечты
	Mezhdusoslovnye pary. Междусословные пары see PG3451.A7B3
	Moskovskie oskolki. Московские осколки see PG3451.A7K74
3451.A7N2	Na vsi͡akiĭ zvuk. На всякий звук
3451.A7N3	Na zare i drugie rasskazy. На заре и другие рассказы
	Nasledniki. Наследники see PG3451.A7P35
3451.A7N4	Nedavnie li͡udi. Недавние люди
	Neposeda. Непоседа see PG3451.A7S7
3451.A7O2	Oborvannye struny (Stories). Оборванные струны
3451.A7O3	Oderzhimai͡a Rusʹ. Одержимая Русь
	Oruzhenoset͡s. Оруженосец see PG3451.A7V55
3451.A7O8	Otravlennai͡a sovestʹ (Novel). Отравленная совесть
3451.A7P3	Pautina. Паутина A 1913 edition bore the title Nasledniki, with Pautina as Part 1 A work composed of 3 novels
3451.A7P35	Nasledniki. Наследники
3451.A7P4	Aglai͡a. Аглая
3451.A7P45	Razdel. Раздел

Russian literature
Individual authors and works, 1870-1917
Individual authors, A - Andreev, L.
Amfiteatrov, Aleksandr Valentinovich, 1862-1938. Александр Валентинович Амфитеатров
Separate works. By title -- Continued

3451.A7P5 Pi͡at′ p′es. Пять пьес
Comprises: Polot͡skoe razoren′e; Otravlennai͡a sovest′; Virtus antiqua (Oruzhenoset͡s); Volny (V strane li͡ubvi); Chortushka (Чортушка)
For separate tales see the title in PG3451.A7A61+

3451.A7P6 Pobeg Lizy Basovoĭ. Побег Лизы Басовой

Podrugi. Подруги see PG3451.A7K76

3451.A7P65 Polot͡skoe razoren′e (Drama). Полоцкое разоренье

Primadonna. Примадонна see PG3451.A7S45

3451.A7P7 Pritchi skeptika (Svoe i chuzhoe). Притчи скептика (Свое и чужое)

3451.A7R3 Razbitai͡a armii͡a (Novel). Разбитая армия

Razdel. Раздел see PG3451.A7P45

Razrushennye voli. Разрушенные воли see PG3451.A7K64

Rubezh. Рубеж see PG3451.A7D66

3451.A7S3 Sestry. Сестры
A chronicle composed of 4 novels:

3451.A7S34 Gnezdo. Гнездо

3451.A7S37 Neposeda. Непоседа
Comprises:

3451.A7S38 V debri͡akh. В дебрях

3451.A7S39 V li͡udi͡akh. В людях

3451.A7S4 Suprug. Супруг

3451.A7S45 Primadonna. Примадонна

3451.A7S5 Sibirskie ėti͡udy. Сибирские этюды

3451.A7S52 Skazanii͡a vremeni. Сказания времени

3451.A7S53 Skazka ob odnoĭ golove i ee obladatele. Сказка об одной голове и ее обладателе

3451.A7S54 Skazochnye byli. Сказочные были

3451.A7S55 Sluchaĭnye rasskazy. Случайные рассказы

3451.A7S6 Son i i͡av′ (Stories). Сон и явь

3451.A7S7 Sovremennye skazki. Современные сказки
Comprises: Skazka ob Ivane-muzhike i Petre, zaporozhskom kazake (Сказка об Иване-мужике и Петре, запорожском казаке); Skazka o bogine (Сказка о богине); Skazka o slonakh (Сказка о слонах); Grekhopadenie Minervy (Грехопадение Минервы); Smert′ Ironii (Смерть Иронии)
For separate tales see the title in PG3451.A7A61+

3451.A7S8 Stolichnai͡a bezdna. Столичная бездна

Russian literature
Individual authors and works, 1870-1917
Individual authors, A - Andreev, L.
Amfiteatrov, Aleksandr Valentinovich, 1862-1938. Александр Валентинович Амфитеатров
Separate works. By title -- Continued

3451.A7S85 Sumerki bozhkov. Сумерки божков
Novel in 2 parts: 1. Serebri͡anai͡a fei͡a (Серебряная фея); 2. Krest'i͡anskai͡a voĭna (Крестьянская война)
Suprug. Супруг see PG3451.A7S4
3451.A7S9 Svi͡atochnai͡a knizhka. Святочная книжка
Tovarishch Feni͡a. Товарищ Феня see PG3451.A7D6
V debri͡akh. В дебрях see PG3451.A7S38
V li͡udi͡akh. В людях see PG3451.A7S39
V strane li͡ubvi. В стране любви see PG3451.A7V6
3451.A7V3 Vasiliĭ Buslaev (Drama). Василий Буслаев
3451.A7V4 Vcherashnie predki (Novel). Вчерашние предки
3451.A7V5 Viktorii͡a Pavlovna (Novel). Виктория Павловна
Also published with title: Imeniny
3451.A7V55 Virtus antiqua (Oruzhenoset͡s)
3451.A7V6 Volny (Story). Волны
Vos'midesi͡atniki. Восьмидесятники see PG3451.A7K61
3451.A7Z2 Zabytyĭ smekh. Забытый смех
Satirical collection in 2 parts. 1. Beranzherovt͡sy (Беранжеровцы); 2. Geĭnevt͡sy (Гейневцы)
3451.A7Z3 Zacharovannai͡a step' (Stories). Зачарованная степь
Zakat starogo veka. Закат старого века see PG3451.A7K78
Zakonnyĭ grekh. Законный грех see PG3451.A7D57
3451.A7Z32 Zamety serdt͡sa (Sketches). Заметы сердца
3451.A7Z34 Zhar-t͡svet (Novel). Жар-цвет
3451.A7Z344 Zhenskoe nestroenie. Женское нестроение
3451.A7Z35 Zhiteĭskai͡a nakip'. Житейская накипь
Zlye prizraki. Злые призраки see PG3451.A7D54
Zvezda zakatnai͡a. Звезда закатная see PG3451.A7D64
Amicus, pseud. see PG3470.P235
3451.A75 Amirov, R.M. Р.М. Амиров (Table P-PZ40)
Amori, graf, pseud. Граф Амори see PG3470.R29
3451.A8 Andreev, Aleksandr Nikolaevich, 1830-1891. Александр Николаевич Андреев (Table P-PZ40)
3452 Andreev, Leonid Nikolaevich, 1871-1919. Леонид Николаевич Андреев
Collected works
3452.A1 By date

Russian literature
Individual authors and works, 1870-1917
Andreev, Leonid Nikolaevich, 1871-1919. Леонид Николаевич Андреев
Collected works -- Continued

3452.A11-.A14	By editor
3452.A15	Collected novels, stories, etc.
3452.A19	Collected plays
	Translations (Collected or selected)
3452.A2-.A29	English. By translator
3452.A3-.A39	French. By translator
3452.A4-.A49	German. By translator
3452.A5-.A59	Other. By language (alphabetically)
3452.A6	Selected works. Selections. By date
3452.A7-.Z44	Separate works
3452.A73-.A733	Anatėma (Tragedy). Анатэма (Table P-PZ43)
3452.A75-.A753	Anfisa (Drama). Анфиса (Table P-PZ43)
3452.B4-.B43	Bezdna (Story). Бездна (Table P-PZ43)
3452.C5-.C53	Chernye maski (Drama). Черные маски (Table P-PZ43)
3452.D4-.D43	Den′ gneva (Story). День гнева (Table P-PZ43)
3452.D6-.D63	Dnevnik satany (Novel). Дневник сатаны (Table P-PZ43)
3452.D65-.D653	Dni nasheĭ zhizni (Drama). Дни нашей жизни (Table P-PZ43) Alternative title: Li͡ubov′ studenta
3452.E4-.E43	Ekaterina Ivanovna (Drama). Екатерина Ивановна (Table P-PZ43)
3452.E5-.E53	Eleazar (Story). Елеазар (Table P-PZ43)
3452.G3-.G33	Gaudeamus (Comedy). Гаудеамус (Table P-PZ43)
3452.G8-.G83	Gubernator (Story). Губернатор (Table P-PZ43)
3452.I8-.I83	Iuda Iskariot i drugie. Иуда Искариот и другие (Table P-PZ43)
3452.K2-.K23	K tebe, soldat! К тебе, солдат! (Table P-PZ43)
3452.K25-.K253	K zvezdam (Drama). К звездам (Table P-PZ43)
3452.K3-.K33	Kainova pechat′ (Drama). Каинова печать (Table P-PZ43) Alternative title: Ne ubiĭ
3452.K35-.K353	Kai͡ushchiĭsi͡a (Drama). Кающийся (Table P-PZ43)
3452.K5-.K53	Khristiane (Story). Христиане (Table P-PZ43)
3452.K6-.K63	Korol′, zakon i svoboda. Король, закон и свобода (Table P-PZ43)
3452.K7-.K73	Krasnyĭ smekh (Story). Красный смех (Table P-PZ43)
3452.L5-.L53	Li͡ubov′ k blizhnemu (Drama). Любовь к ближнему (Table P-PZ43)
	Li͡ubov′ studenta. Любовь студента see PG3452.D65+

Russian literature
Individual authors and works, 1870-1917
Andreev, Leonid Nikolaevich, 1871-1919. Леонид Николаевич Андреев
Separate works -- Continued

3452.M5-.M53 Milye prizraki (Drama). Милые призраки (Table P-PZ43)
3452.M6-.M63 Moi zapiski (Story). Мои записки (Table P-PZ43)
3452.M9-.M93 Mysl′ (Tale). Мысль (Table P-PZ43)
3452.N3-.N33 Nadsmertnoe (Tale). Надсмертное (Table P-PZ43)
Ne ubiĭ. Не убий see PG3452.K3+
3452.N5-.N53 Net proshchenii͡a (Story). Нет прощения (Table P-PZ43)
Netlennoe. Нетленное see PG3452.P77+
3452.N6-.N63 Nochnoĭ razgovor (Novel). Ночной разговор (Table P-PZ43)
O semi poveshennykh. О семи повешенных see PG3452.R3+
3452.O5-.O53 Okean (Tragedy). Океан (Table P-PZ43)
3452.O6-.O63 On (Tale). Он (Table P-PZ43)
3452.P5-.P53 Polet (Tales). Полет (Table P-PZ43)
3452.P6-.P63 Popugaĭ (Drama). Попугай (Table P-PZ43)
3452.P7-.P73 Prekrasnye sabini͡anki (Drama). Прекрасные сабинянки (Table P-PZ43)
3452.P74-.P743 Prizraki (Story). Призраки (Table P-PZ43)
3452.P77-.P773 Professor Stori͡tsyn (Drama). Профессор Сторицын (Table P-PZ43)
3452.P8-.P83 Proisshestvie (Drama). Происшествие (Table P-PZ43)
3452.P84-.P843 Prokli͡atie zveri͡a (Story). Проклятие зверя (Table P-PZ43)
3452.R3-.R33 Rasskaz o semi poveshennykh (Story). Рассказ о семи повешенных (Table P-PZ43)
3452.R35-.R353 Rasskaz o Sergee Petroviche (Story). Рассказ о Сергее Петровиче (Table P-PZ43)
3452.S3-.S33 Sashka Zhegulev (Novel). Сашка Жегулев (Table P-PZ43)
3452.S4-.S43 Savva (Drama). Савва (Table P-PZ43)
3452.S5-.S53 Smert′ cheloveka (Drama). Смерть человека (Table P-PZ43)
3452.S55-.S553 Smert′ Senisty (Tale). Смерть Сенисты (Table P-PZ43)
3452.S6-.S63 Sobachiĭ val′s (Drama). Собачий вальс (Table P-PZ43)
3452.S9-.S93 Syn chelovecheskiĭ (Story). Сын человеческий (Table P-PZ43)
3452.T3-.T33 Tak bylo (Tale). Так было (Table P-PZ43)
3452.T6-.T63 T′ma (Tale). Тьма (Table P-PZ43)

Russian literature
Individual authors and works, 1870-1917
Andreev, Leonid Nikolaevich, 1871-1919. Леонид Николаевич Андреев
Separate works -- Continued

3452.T66-.T663 Tot, kto poluchaet poshchechiny (Drama). Тот, кто получает пощечины (Table P-PZ43)
3452.T7-.T73 T͡Sar′ Golod (Drama). Царь Голод (Table P-PZ43)
3452.U2-.U23 U okna (Story). У окна (Table P-PZ43)
3452.V25-.V253 V tumane (Story). В тумане (Table P-PZ43)
3452.V4-.V43 Vesenni͡ia obeshchani͡ia. Весенния обещания (Table P-PZ43)
3452.V6-.V63 Vor (Story). Вор (Table P-PZ43)
3452.V7-.V73 Vozrat (Tale). Возрат (Table P-PZ43)
3452.Z25-.Z253 Zhili-byli (Tale). Жили-были (Table P-PZ43)
3452.Z3-.Z33 Zhizn′ cheloveka (Drama). Жизнь человека (Table P-PZ43)
3452.Z35-.Z353 Zhizn′ Vasili͡ia Fiveĭskogo (Novel). Жизнь Василия Фивейского (Table P-PZ43)

Biography and criticism
3452.Z45 Autobiography
Letters
3452.Z46 Collected. By date of imprint
3452.Z47A-.Z47Z Individual correspondents, A-Z
3452.Z5 General treatises. Life and works
Criticism
3452.Z8 General works
3452.Z9A-.Z9Z Special topics, A-Z

3453 Individual authors, Andreev, L. - Chekhov, Anton
3453.A3 Andreev, Vasiliĭ Nikolaevich, 1843-1888. Василий Николаевич Андреев (Table P-PZ40)
Andreev-Burlak, V.N. В.Н. Андреев-Бурлак see PG3453.A3
Andreeva, E., 1865-1902. Е. Андреева see PG3470.Z427
Andreevich, pseud. Андреевич see PG3470.S685
3453.A4 Andreevskiĭ, Pavel Arkad′evich, 1850-1890. Павел Аркадьевич Андреевский (Table P-PZ40 modified)
3453.A4A61-.A4Z458 Separate works. By title
3453.A4B6 Bolezn′ veka (Drama). Болезнь века
3453.A4I3 Igla. Игла
3453.A4M8 Muzhestvenna͡ia zhenshchina (Farce). Мужественная женщина
3453.A4P7 Prizraki (Comedy). Призраки
3453.A5 Andreevskiĭ, Sergeĭ Arkad′evich, 1848-1919? Сергей Аркадьевич Андреевский (Table P-PZ40)
Andreyev, Leonid see PG3452

Russian literature
Individual authors and works, 1870-1917
Individual authors, Andreev, L. - Chekhov, Anton

3453.A52 Andrievskiĭ, A.M., fl. 1890-1900. А.М. Андриевский (Table P-PZ40)

3453.A53 Andruson, Leonid Ivanovich, 1875- . Леонид Иванович Андрусон (Table P-PZ40)

3453.A54 Anichkova, Anna Mitrofanovna (Avinova), fl. 1900-1910. Анна Митрофановна (Авинова) Аничкова (Table P-PZ40)

3453.A55 Anichkova, Idalii͡a Mechislavovna (Piłsudska), 1843- . Идалия Мечиславовна (Пилсудская) Аничкова (Table P-PZ40)

3453.A56 Anisimov, S.A., fl. 1800-1890. С.А. Анисимов (Table P-PZ40)

Ani͡utin, M. M. Анютин see PG3470.R37

3453.A58 Annenkova-Bernard, Nina Pavlovna. Нина Павловна Анненкова-Бернард (Table P-PZ40 modified)

3453.A58A61-.A58Z458 Separate works. By title

3453.A58B3 Babushkina vnuchka. Бабушкина внучка

3453.A58B5 Beket (Drama). Бекет

3453.A58D6 Doch′ naroda (Drama). Дочь народа

3453.A58G6 Goremychnai͡a (Story). Горемычная

3453.A58I8 I͡Ubileĭ artistki (Story). Юбилей артистки

3453.A58K2 K vysotam (Drama). К высотам

3453.A58K3 Kara (Story). Кара

3453.A58N5 Nezabvennai͡a (Story). Незабвенная

3453.A58O5 Ona. Iz zabroshennykh tetradeĭ. Она. Из заброшенных тетрадей

3453.A58P5 Petli͡a (Story). Петля

3453.A58S6 Sny. Сны

3453.A6 Annenskiĭ, Innokentiĭ Fedorovich, 1855-1909. Иннокентий Федорович Анненский (Table P-PZ40 modified)

3453.A6A61-.A6Z458 Separate works. By title

3453.A6F3 Famira-Kifarėd (Drama). Фамира-Кифарэд

3453.A6K5 Kiparisovyĭ lare͡ts. Кипарисовый ларец

3453.A6K6 Kniga otrazheniĭ. Книга отражений

3453.A6L3 Laodamii͡a (Tragedy). Лаодамия

3453.A6M27 Magdalina (Poem). Магдалина

3453.A6M3 Malanippa-filosof (Tragedy). Маланиппа-философ

3453.A6T5 Tikhie pesni. Тихие песни

3453.A6T7 TSar′ Iksion (Tragedy). Царь Иксион

Annibal, Lidii͡a Dmitrievna Zinov′eva. Лидия Дмитриевна Зиновьева-Аннибал see PG3470.Z5

An-skiĭ, S.A. С.А. Ан-ский see PG3470.R3

Russian literature
Individual authors and works, 1870-1917
Individual authors, Andreev, L. - Chekhov, Anton -- Continued
Antarov, I.V. И.В. Антаров see PG3470.S38
3453.A62 Antonov, K.E., fl. 1900-1920. К.Е. Антонов (Table P-PZ40)
3453.A63 Antonov, S.S., fl. 1890-1900. С.С. Антонов (Table P-PZ40)
3453.A635 Antonov, V.M., fl. 1880-1890. В.М. Антонов (Table P-PZ40)
Antonovich, Ippolit. Ипполит Антонович see PG3470.V47
3453.A64 Antonovich, Maksim Alekseevich, 1835-1918. Максим Алексеевич Антонович (Table P-PZ40)
For Antonovich as a literary critic see PG2947.A3+
3453.A65 Antropov, Luka Nikolaevich, 1843-1884. Лука Николаевич Антропов (Table P-PZ40 modified)
3453.A65A61-.A65Z458 Separate works. By title
3453.A65B5 Bluzhdai͡ushchie ogni (Comedy). Блуждающие огни
3453.A65G6 Gordoe serdt͡se (Comedy). Гордое сердце
3453.A65O2 Ocharovatelʹnyĭ son (Comedy). Очаровательный сон
3453.A65V3 Vanʹka-kli͡uchnik (Dramatic sketch). Ванька-ключник
3453.A653 Antropov, R. (Roman), 1876-1913. Роман Антропов (Table P-PZ40)
3453.A66 Anuchin, Vasiliĭ Ivanovich, 1875- . Василий Иванович Анучин (Table P-PZ40)
Apeka, pseud. Апека see PG3467.K94
Apolinaris, Vikont d'. Виконт д'Аполинарис see PG3453.B4
3453.A67 Apraksin, Aleksandr Dmitrievich, 1851-1913. Александр Дмитриевич Апраксин (Table P-PZ40 modified)
3453.A67A61-.A67Z458 Separate works. By title
15 rasskazov. 15 рассказов see PG3453.A67P5
3453.A67A8 Alzakovy (Novel)
3453.A67B3 Balovni sudʹby (Novel). Баловни судьбы
3453.A67B4 Bezputnai͡a zhiznʹ (Sketch). Безпутная жизнь
3453.A67B6 Bolʹnoe mesto (Novel). Больное место
3453.A67D5 Delo chesti (Novel). Дело чести
3453.A67D6 Dobryĭ geniĭ (Novel). Добрый гений
3453.A67D7 Dorogoi͡u t͡senoi͡u (Novel). Дорогою ценою
3453.A67G6 Gore i radostʹ (Stories). Горе и радость
3453.A67K3 Kain i Avelʹ (Novel). Каин и Авель
3453.A67L6 Lovkachi (Novel). Ловкачи

Russian literature
Individual authors and works, 1870-1917
Individual authors, Andreev, L. - Chekhov, Anton
Apraksin, Aleksandr Dmitrievich, 1851-1913. Александр Дмитриевич Апраксин
Separate works. By title -- Continued

3453.A67M5 Mishura (Story). Мишура
3453.A67N3 Na voloske (Novel). На волоске
3453.A67N4 Nezemnye sozdanii͡a i drugie rasskazy. Неземные создания и другие рассказы
3453.A67O6 Opravdannyĭ (Tale). Оправданный
3453.A67P4 Perovni͡a (Tale). Перовня
3453.A67P5 Pi͡atnadt͡satʹ rasskazov (15 rasskazov). Пятнадцать рассказов
3453.A67P7 Prazdnye li͡udi (Novel). Праздные люди
3453.A67P8 Pustoĭ chelovek (Tale). Пустой человек
3453.A67R3 Razlad (Novel). Разлад
3453.A67S85 Svetlye dni (Novel). Светлые дни
3453.A67S9 Svi͡atai͡a Rusʹ (Novel). Святая Русь
3453.A67T4 Ternistyĭ putʹ (Novel). Тернистый путь
3453.A67T5 Ti͡azhkie milliony (Sketches). Тяжкие миллионы
3453.A67T7 Tri povesti. Три повести
3453.A67V2 V tishi nochnoĭ (Tales, studies, etc.). В тиши ночной
3453.A67V5 Vletel (Dramatic sketch). Влетел

Apreleva, Elena Ivanovna (Blaramberg). Елена Ивановна (Бларамберг) Апрелева see PG3453.B56

3453.A7 Apukhtin, Alekseĭ Nikolaevich, 1841-1893. Алексей Николаевич Апухтин (Table P-PZ40 modified)
3453.A7A61-.A7Z458 Separate works and poems. By title
3453.A7A72 A la pointe (Poem)
3453.A7A75 Arkhiv grafini D** (Story). Архив графини Д**
3453.A7D6 Dnevnik Pavlika Dolʹskogo. Дневник Павлика Дольского
3453.A7G6 God v monastyre (Poem). Год в монастыре
3453.A7I9 Iz bumag prokurora (Poem). Из бумаг прокурора
3453.A7K6 Kni͡azʹ Tavricheskiĭ (Dramatic sketch). Князь Таврический
3453.A7M4 Mezhdu smertʹi͡u i zhiznʹi͡u (Story). Между смертью и жизнью
3453.A7N4 Neokonchennai͡a povestʹ. Неоконченная повесть
3453.A7N5 Niobei͡a. Ниобея
3453.A7S8 Sumasshedshiĭ (Poem). Сумасшедший

Ardov, E.I. Е.И. Ардов see PG3453.B56

3453.A727 Ariman, Zhak d'. Жак д'Ариман (Table P-PZ40)
3453.A73 Arishchenko, Grigoriĭ, fl. 1895-1905. Григорий Арищенко (Table P-PZ40)

Russian literature
Individual authors and works, 1870-1917
Individual authors, Andreev, L. - Chekhov, Anton -- Continued

3453.A75	Arsen′ev, Aleksandr Vasil′evich, 1854-1896. Александр Васильевич Арсеньев (Table P-PZ40 modified)
3453.A75A61-.A75Z458	Separate works. By title
3453.A75A75	Arina boiaryshnia. Арина боярышня
3453.A75A8	Arisha-utochka (Novel). Ариша-уточка
3453.A75B6	Boiarin Nechaĭ-Nogaev (Drama). Боярин Нечай-Ногаев
3453.A75F7	Frantsuzinka (Story). Французинка
3453.A75K6	Kniaz′ Dmitriĭ Ioannovich Donskoĭ (Novel). Князь Дмитрий Иоаннович Донской
3453.A75O8	Otstavnoĭ maĭor Kuritsyn (Story). Отставной майор Курицын
3453.A75P4	Pervaia knizhnaia lavochka v Peterburge pri Petre Velikom (Story). Первая книжная лавочка в Петербурге при Петре Великом
3453.A75S8	Starye byval′shchiny. Старые бывальщины
3453.A75T7	TSarskiĭ sud (Novel). Царский суд
3453.A75Z45	Zhestokoe ispytanie (Novel). Жестокое испытание
3453.A78	Artiushin, P.I., fl. 1890-1900. П.И. Артюшин (Table P-PZ40)
3453.A8	Artsybashev, Mikhail Petrovich, 1878-1927. Михаил Петрович Арцыбашев (Table P-PZ40 modified)
3453.A8A61-.A8Z458	Separate works. By title
3453.A8B7	Brat′ia Arimafeĭskie. Братья Аримафейские
3453.A8B8	Bunt. Бунт
3453.A8C5	Chelovecheskaia volna. Человеческая волна
3453.A8D5	D′iavol (Tragedy). Дьявол
3453.A8D6	Dikie (Story). Дикие
3453.A8I8	Iz dnevnika odnogo pokoĭnika. Из дневника одного покойника
3453.A8I85	Iz podvala. Из подвала
3453.A8I9	Iz zapisok odnogo cheloveka. Из записок одного человека
3453.A8K7	Krov′. Кровь
3453.A8K75	Krovavoe piatno. Кровавое пятно
3453.A8K8	Kupriian. Куприян
3453.A8M5	Milliony (Novel). Миллионы
3453.A8M7	Mstitel′ (Story). Мститель
3453.A8M8	Muzh (Drama). Муж
3453.A8M9	Muzhik i barin. Мужик и барин
	O revnosti. О ревности see PG3453.A8R4
3453.A8O3	Odin den′. Один день

Russian literature
Individual authors and works, 1870-1917
Individual authors, Andreev, L. - Chekhov, Anton
Art͡sybashev, Mikhail Petrovich, 1878-1927. Михаил Петрович Арцыбашев
Separate works. By title -- Continued

3453.A8P3 Palata neizlechimykh. Палата неизлечимых
3453.A8P4 Pasha Tumanov. Паша Туманов
3453.A8P5 Pod soln͡tsem (Stories). Под солнцем
3453.A8P6 Podpraporshchik Gololobov. Подпрапорщик Гололобов
3453.A8P7 Propast′. Пропасть
3453.A8R3 Rabochiĭ Shevyrev (Novel). Рабочий Шевырев
3453.A8R35 Rasskaz o velikom znanii. Рассказ о великом знании
3453.A8R4 Revnost′ (Drama). Ревность
Variant title: O revnosti
3453.A8R5 Revoli͡ut͡sioner. Революционер
3453.A8S3 Sanin (Novel). Санин
3453.A8S5 Skazka starogo prokurora. Сказка старого прокурора
3453.A8S6 Smekh. Смех
3453.A8S7 Smert′ Lande. Смерть Ланде
3453.A8S8 Stara͡ia istori͡ia. Старая история
3453.A8T5 Teni utra. Тени утра
3453.A8U2 U posledneĭ cherty (Novel). У последней черты
3453.A8U9 Uzhas. Ужас
3453.A8V5 Vechnyĭ mirazh. Вечный мираж
3453.A8V6 Voĭna (Drama). Война
3453.A8V7 Vragi (Drama). Враги
3453.A8Z2 Zakon dikari͡a (Drama). Закон дикаря
3453.A8Z3 Zapiski pisateli͡a. Записки писателя
Comprises: I. Voĭna (Война); II. Predateli i renegaty (Предатели и ренегаты); III. Trusy (Трусы)
3453.A8Z4 Zhena. Жена
3453.A8Z45 Zhenshchina sto͡iashcha͡ia posredi (Novel). Женщина стоящая посреди
3453.A83 Asheshov, Nikolaĭ Petrovich, 1866- . Николай Петрович Ашешов (Table P-PZ40)
Astakhov, I. И. Астахов see PG3467.I37
3453.A85 Astyrev, Nikolaĭ Mikhaĭlovich, 1857-1894. Николай Михайлович Астырев (Table P-PZ40)
Atava, Sergeĭ. Сергей Атава see PG3470.T39
3453.A88 Avenarius, Vasiliĭ Petrovich, 1839-1919. Василий Петрович Авенариус (Table P-PZ40)
3453.A9 Averkiev, Dmitriĭ Vasil′evich, 1836-1905. Дмитрий Васильевич Аверкиев (Table P-PZ40 modified)

Russian literature
Individual authors and works, 1870-1917
Individual authors, Andreev, L. - Chekhov, Anton
Averkiev, Dmitriĭ Vasil′evich, 1836-1905. Дмитрий Васильевич Аверкиев -- Continued

3453.A9A61-.A9Z458 Separate works. By title
3453.A9D6 Dogadlivyĭ muzh (Tale). Догадливый муж
3453.A9D8 Dukhovnye pesni. Духовные песни
3453.A9F7 Francheska Riminiĭskai͡a (Tragedy). Франческа Риминийская
3453.A9F8 Frol Skaveev (Comedy). Фрол Скавеев
3453.A9I7 Istorii͡a blednogo molodogo cheloveka (Novel). История бледного молодого человека
3453.A9K3 Kashirskai͡a starina (Drama). Каширская старина
3453.A9K4 Khmelevai͡a noch′ (Novel). Хмелевая ночь
3453.A9K5 Khudozhnik Bezpalov i notarius Podleshchikov (Novel). Художник Безпалов и нотариус Подлещиков
3453.A9K6 Kni͡agini͡a Ul′i͡ana Vi͡azemskai͡a (Drama). Княгиня Ульяна Вяземская
Komedii͡a o rossiĭskom dvori͡anine Frole Skabeeve i stol′nich′ei Nardyn-Nashchokina docheri Annushke. Комедия о российском дворянине Фроле Скабееве и стольничьеи Нардын-Нащокина дочери Аннушке see PG3453.A9F8
3453.A9L4 Leshiĭ (Comedy). Леший
3453.A9L5 Likho (Story). Лихо
3453.A9M3 Mamaevo poboishche (Tales). Мамаево побоище
3453.A9M4 Mest′ (Story). Месть
3453.A9M8 Muzh′i͡a i poklonniki (Comedy). Мужья и поклонники
3453.A9N4 Nepogreshimye (Comedy). Непогрешимые
3453.A9N5 Neumolimo providen′e (Poems). Неумолимо провиденье
3453.A9N6 Novai͡a baryshni͡a (Story). Новая барышня
3453.A9P5 Pesni o starykh bogakh. Песни о старых богах
3453.A9P6 Poslednii͡ prorok (Poems). Последний пророк
3453.A9P65 Povesti iz sovremennogo byta (Stories). Повести из современного быта
For individual stories see the title in PG3453.A9A61+
3453.A9P7 Povesti iz starinnogo byta (Stories). Повести из старинного быта
For individual stories see the title in PG3453.A9A61+
3453.A9R3 Razrushennai͡a nevesta (Drama). Разрушенная невеста
3453.A9S5 Sidorkino delo (Comedy). Сидоркино дело
3453.A9S55 Sloboda Nevoli͡a (Drama). Слобода Неволя
3453.A9S6 Smert′ Messaliny (Drama). Смерть Мессалины

Russian literature
Individual authors and works, 1870-1917
Individual authors, Andreev, L. - Chekhov, Anton
Averkiev, Dmitriĭ Vasil'evich, 1836-1905. Дмитрий Васильевич Аверкиев
Separate works. By title -- Continued

3453.A9S7 Staryĭ liberal i ego pitomit͡sa (Tale). Старый либерал и его питомица
3453.A9S8 Stolichnyĭ sletok (Drama). Столичный слеток
3453.A9T3 Temnyĭ i Shemi͡aka (Tragedy). Темный и Шемяка
3453.A9T4 Teofano (Drama). Теофано
3453.A9T5 Terentiĭ muzh Danil'evich (Comedy). Терентий муж Данильевич
3453.A9T6 Toska po rodine (Poem). Тоска по родине
3453.A9T7 Trogirskiĭ voevoda (Tragedy). Трогирский воевода
3453.A9T8 T͡Sar' Petr i t͡sarevich Alekseĭ (Tragedy). Царь Петр и царевич Алексей
3453.A9T9 T͡Sarevich Alekseĭ (Tragedy). Царевич Алексей
3453.A9V4 Vechu ne byt' (Story). Вечу не быть
3453.A9V5 Viden'e (Poems). Виденье
3453.A92 Avilova, Lidii͡a Alekseevna (Strakhova), 1864-1943. Лидия Алексеевна (Страхова) Авилова (Table P-PZ40 modified)
3453.A92A61-.A92Z458 Separate works. By title
3453.A92K3 Kamardin. Камардин
3453.A92K5 Khristos rozhdaetsi͡a. Христос рождается
3453.A92O2 Obraz chelovecheskiĭ. Образ человеческий
3453.A92O3 Obshchee delo. Общее дело
3453.A92P4 Pervoe gore i drugie rasskazy. Первое горе и другие рассказы
3453.A92P9 Pyshnai͡a zhizn'. Пышная жизнь
3453.A92S3 Schastlivet͡s i drugie rasskazy. Счастливец и другие рассказы
3453.A92S8 Syn. Сын
3453.A92V6 Vlast' i drugie rasskazy. Власть и другие рассказы
Avinova, Anna Mitrofanovna. Анна Митрофановна Авинова see PG3453.A54
3453.A93 Avseenko, Vasiliĭ Grigor'evich, 1842-1913. Василий Григорьевич Авсеенко (Table P-PZ40 modified)
3453.A93A61-.A93Z458 Separate works. By title
3453.A93A8 Andreĭ Mologin (Story). Андрей Мологин
3453.A93B3 Baryshni͡a Susanna (Tale). Барышня Сусанна
3453.A93B5 Blazh' (Tale). Блажь
3453.A93B6 Boi͡arskai͡a pora (Tale). Боярская пора
3453.A93B8 Buri͡a (Story). Буря

Russian literature
Individual authors and works, 1870-1917
Individual authors, Andreev, L. - Chekhov, Anton
Avseenko, Vasiliĭ Grigor′evich, 1842-1913. Василий Григорьевич Авсеенко
Separate works. By title -- Continued

3453.A93C5 Charodeĭ (Tale). Чародей
3453.A93D4 Dela davno minuvshikh dneĭ (Story). Дела давно минувших дней
3453.A93F3 Fantasticheskie rasskazy. Фантастические рассказы
3453.A93G8 Gubernskai͡a Perikola (Tale). Губернская Перикола
3453.A93I7 Ispanskiĭ dvori͡anin (Tale). Испанский дворянин
3453.A93I9 Iz-za blag zemnykh (Novel). Из-за благ земных
3453.A93K3 Kak oni uekhali (Tale). Как они уехали
3453.A93K4 Kar′era Vi͡azigina (Tale). Карьера Вязигина
3453.A93M4 Mgnoven′e (Tale). Мгновенье
3453.A93M5 Mlechnyĭ put′ (Novel). Млечный путь
3453.A93M6 Molodo-zeleno (Story). Молодо-зелено
3453.A93N3 Na rasput′i (Novel). На распутьи
3453.A93O4 Ofelii͡a (Tale). Офелия
3453.A93O5 Okol′nym putem (Story). Окольным путем
Pis′ma o zhenshchinakh. Письма о женщинах see HQ1216
3453.A93P7 Prii͡ateli (Tale). Приятели
3453.A93R4 Rebenok (Tale). Ребенок
3453.A93S5 Skrezhet zubovnyĭ (Novel). Скрежет зубовный
3453.A93S7 Stolknovenie (Tale). Столкновение
3453.A93S8 Svatovstvo (Tale). Сватовство
3453.A93T5 Tishina (Comedy). Тишина
3453.A93U2 U reki (Tale). У реки
3453.A93V2 V ogne (Tale). В огне
3453.A93Z3 Zamuzhestvo Rity (Tale). Замужество Риты
3453.A93Z4 Zloĭ dukh (Novel). Злой дух
3453.B12 Babikov, Aleksandr I͡Akovlevich, 1837-1873. Александр Яковлевич Бабиков (Table P-PZ40)
3453.B125 Babkin, Petr Ivanovich, b. 1842. Петр Иванович Бабкин (Table P-PZ40)
Baĭkova, Nadezhda Aleksandrovna. Надежда Александровна Байкова see PG3467.L8
3453.B13 Baĭlerntov, Vadim, fl. 1880-1890. Вадим Байлернтов (Table P-PZ40)
3453.B14 Bakaleĭnik, P., fl. 1900-1910. П. Бакалейник (Table P-PZ40)
3453.B15 Bakharev, Efim Afanas′evich, 1878- . Ефим Афанасьевич Бахарев (Table P-PZ40)

Russian literature
Individual authors and works, 1870-1917
Individual authors, Andreev, L. - Chekhov, Anton -- Continued

3453.B16 Bakhmetev, Alekseĭ Ivanovich, fl. 1910-1920. Алексей Иванович Бахметев (Table P-PZ40)

3453.B17 Bakhmetev, N.N., fl. 1900-1910. Н.Н. Бахметев (Table P-PZ40)

Balavinskai͡a, Anfisa Petrovna. Анфиса Петровна Балавинская see PG3467.L87

3453.B18 Baldeskul, Aleksandr, fl. 1890-1900. Александр Балдескул (Table P-PZ40)

3453.B2 Bal′mont, Konstantin Dmitrievich, 1867-1943. Константин Дмитриевич Бальмонт (Table P-PZ40 modified)

3453.B2A61-.B2Z458 Separate works. By title

3453.B2B4 Belye zarnit͡sy. Белые зарницы

3453.B2B5 Belyĭ zodchiĭ. Белый зодчий

3453.B2B8 Budem kak solnt͡se. Будем как солнце

3453.B2D3 Dar zemle. Дар земле

3453.B2G3 Gamai͡un. Гамаюн

3453.B2G4 Gde moĭ dom? (Sketches). Где мой дом?

3453.B2G5 Golubai͡a podkova. Голубая подкова

3453.B2G6 Gori͡ashchie zdanii͡a. Горящие здания

3453.B2G7 Gornye vershiny. Горные вершины

3453.B2I2 I͡Asen′. Ясень

Ispanskie narodnye pesni. Испанские народные песни see PG3453.B2L6

3453.B2K5 Khorovod vremeni. Хоровод времени

3453.B2K7 Kraĭ Ozirisa. Край Озириса

3453.B2L5 Liturgii͡a krasoty. Литургия красоты

3453.B2L6 Li͡ubov′ i nenavist′. Любовь и ненависть

3453.B2M3 Marevo. Марево

3453.B2M6 Moe - eĭ. Мое - ей

3453.B2M7 Morskoe svechenie. Морское свечение

3453.B2P4 Persten′. Перстень

3453.B2P44 Pesni mstiteli͡a. Песни мстителя

3453.B2P5 Pesni͡a rabochego molota. Песня рабочего молота

3453.B2P6 Pod novym serpom (Novel). Под новым серпом

3453.B2P65 Pod severnym nebom. Ėlegii, stansy, sonety. Под северным небом. Элегии, стансы, сонеты

3453.B2P7 Poėzii͡a kak volshebstvo. Поэзия как волшебство

3453.B2P8 Ptitsy v vozdukhe. Птитсы в воздухе

3453.B2S4 Sem′ poėm. Семь поэм

3453.B2S5 Severnoe sii͡anie. Северное сияние

3453.B2S6 Solnechnai͡a pri͡azha. Солнечная пряжа

Russian literature
Individual authors and works, 1870-1917
Individual authors, Andreev, L. - Chekhov, Anton
Bal′mont, Konstantin Dmitrievich, 1867-1943. Константин Дмитриевич Бальмонт
Separate works. By title -- Continued

3453.B2S7 Sonety solnt͡sa, meda i luny. Сонеты солнца, меда и луны
3453.B2T5 Tishina. Тишина
3453.B2T6 Tol′ko li͡ubov′. Только любовь
3453.B2T7 Tri rast͡sveta (Drama). Три расцвета
3453.B2V2 V bezbrezhnosti. В безбрежности
Comprises: Za predely (За пределы), Li͡ubov′ i teni (Любовь и тени); Mezhdu noch′i͡u i dnem (Между ночью и днем)
3453.B2V3 V razdvinutoĭ dali. Poėma o Rossii. В раздвинутой дали. Поэма о России
3453.B2V6 Vozdushnyĭ put′. Воздушный путь
3453.B2Z2 Zarevo zor′. Зарево зорь
3453.B2Z25 Zelenyĭ vertograd. Slova pot͡seluĭnye. Зеленый вертоград. Слова поцелуйные
3453.B2Z3 Zhar-ptit͡sa. Svirel′ slavi͡anina. Жар-птица. Свирель славянина
3453.B2Z35 Zlye chary. Kniga zakli͡atiĭ. Злые чары. Книга заклятий
3453.B2Z4 Zovy drevnosti (Hymns, songs, etc.). Зовы древности
3453.B2Z45 Zven′i͡a. Izbrannye stikhi, 1890-1912. Звенья. Избранные стихи, 1890-1912
3453.B22 Balobanova, Ekaterina Vi͡acheslavovna, 1847- . Екатерина Вячеславовна Балобанова (Table P-PZ40)
3453.B23 Baltrušaitis, Jurgis, 1873-1944. Юргис Казимирович Балтрушайтис (Table P-PZ40)
3453.B24 Baranov, Aleksandr Vasil′evich, fl. 1890-1900. Александр Васильевич Баранов (Table P-PZ40)
3453.B25 Barant͡sevich, Kazimir Stanislavovich, 1851-1927. Казимир Станиславович Баранцевич (Table P-PZ40 modified)
3453.B25A61-.B25Z458 Separate works. By title
80 rasskazov. 80 рассказов see PG3453.B25V6
3453.B25B6 Bol′nai͡a krov′. Больная кровь
3453.B25B7 Bort͡sy (Novel). Борцы
3453.B25C6 Chudnye nochi. Чудные ночи
3453.B25D4 Debi͡ut. Дебют
3453.B25D5 Derevenskai͡a idillii͡a. Деревенская идиллия

Russian literature
Individual authors and works, 1870-1917
Individual authors, Andreev, L. - Chekhov, Anton
Barant͡sevich, Kazimir Stanislavovich, 1851-1927.
Казимир Станиславович Баранцевич
Separate works. By title -- Continued

3453.B25D8 Dve zheny (Semeĭnyĭ ochag) (Novel). Две жены
3453.B25F5 Flirt i drugie rasskazy. Флирт и другие рассказы
3453.B25I8 Iz zhizni odinokikh li͡udeĭ. Из жизни одиноких людей
3453.B25I9 Izgar′ (Staroe i novoe). Изгарь (Старое и новое)
3453.B25K2 K chemu prishel Pimen Gerasimovich. К чему пришел Пимен Герасимович
3453.B25K25 K svetu! К свету!
3453.B25K3 Kartinki zhizni. Картинки жизни
3453.B25K5 Kli͡acha. Кляча
3453.B25K7 Krov′ (Novel). Кровь
3453.B25K8 Kukolka (Comedy). Куколка
3453.B25L6 Lit͡so zhizni. Лицо жизни
3453.B25M3 Malen′kie rasskazy. Маленькие рассказы
3453.B25M4 Matushka (Story). Матушка
3453.B25M5 Mechta Atanasa. Мечта Атанаса
3453.B25M8 Mut′. Муть
3453.B25M9 Myshi. Мыши
3453.B25N3 Na severe dikom. На севере диком
3453.B25N6 Novye rasskazy. Новые рассказы
3453.B25O4 Okoldovala. Околдовала
3453.B25O6 Oprichina. Опричина
3453.B25O7 Ot͡sy (Comedy). Отцы
3453.B25P35 Pervyĭ zarabotok i drugie rasskazy. Первый заработок и другие рассказы
3453.B25P4 Peterburgskiĭ sluchaĭ. Петербургский случай
3453.B25P5 Plagiat (Comedy). Плагиат
3453.B25P55 Pobeda. Победа
3453.B25P6 Pod gnetom. Под гнетом
3453.B25P62 Pod krylom. Под крылом
3453.B25P63 Pod molotom. Под молотом
3453.B25P65 Porvannye struny i drugie rasskazy. Порванные струны и другие рассказы
3453.B25P66 Poskonnai͡a zhizn′. Посконная жизнь
3453.B25P67 Poslednii͡a voli͡a. Последняя воля
3453.B25P68 Poslednie list′i͡a. Последние листья
3453.B25P69 Pozharnyĭ prazdnik (Comedy). Пожарный праздник
3453.B25P7 Prakh. Прах
3453.B25P73 Prikli͡uchenie zhenshchiny. Приключение женщины
3453.B25P75 Promashka. Промашка
3453.B25P78 Prostila. Простила
3453.B25P8 Ptit͡sa nebesnai͡a. Птица небесная

Russian literature
Individual authors and works, 1870-1917
Individual authors, Andreev, L. - Chekhov, Anton
Barant͡sevich, Kazimir Stanislavovich, 1851-1927. Казимир Станиславович Баранцевич
Separate works. By title -- Continued

3453.B25R3 Raba (Novel). Раба
3453.B25R6 Rodnye kartinki. Родные картинки
Semeĭnyĭ ochag. Семейный очаг see PG3453.B25D8
3453.B25S5 Simvolicheskie rasskazy. Символические рассказы
3453.B25S55 Skazki zhizni. Сказки жизни
3453.B25S57 Skitanii͡a Egorki. Скитания Егорки
3453.B25S6 Sluchaĭno. Случайно
3453.B25S7 Staroe i novoe. Старое и новое
3453.B25S8 Svobodnye sny i drugie rasskazy. Свободные сны и другие рассказы
3453.B25T5 Tikhoe schast′e i drugie rasskazy. Тихое счастье и другие рассказы
3453.B25U2 U kamel′ka. У камелька
3453.B25U3 Ugolok dushi. Уголок души
3453.B25V2 V chem pravda? В чем правда?
3453.B25V27 V prii͡ute. В приюте
3453.B25V28 V tolpe. В толпе
3453.B25V4 Vechera. Вечера
3453.B25V5 Vesennie skazki. Весенние сказки
3453.B25V55 Vorobyshek (Comedy). Воробышек
3453.B25V6 Vosem′desi͡at rasskazov (80 rasskazov). Восемьдесят рассказов
3453.B25V7 Vospominanie (Ėlegii͡a v proze). Воспоминание (Элегия в прозе)
3453.B25Z3 Zakat. Закат
3453.B25Z4 Zolotye dni. Золотые дни
3453.B25Z45 Zvuki. Звуки
3453.B27 Bari͡atinskiĭ, Vladimir Vladimirovich, kni͡az′, 1874-1941. Владимир Владимирович Барятинский (Table P-PZ40 modified)
3453.B27A61-.B27Z458 Separate works. By title
Ego Prevoskhoditel′stvo. Его Превошодительство see PG3453.B27S47+
Kar′era Nablot͡skogo. Карьера Наблоцкого see PG3453.B27S44+
3453.B27K6 Komedii͡a smerti. Комедия смерти
3453.B27K7 Kontora schast′i͡a. Контора счастья
3453.B27L6 Lolo i Lala. Лоло и Лала
3453.B27M8 Mysli i zametki. Мысли и заметки

Russian literature
Individual authors and works, 1800-1870
Individual authors, Andreev, L. - Chekhov, Anton
Bari͡atinskiĭ, Vladimir Vladimirovich, kni͡az′, 1874-1941. Владимир Владимирович Барятинский
Separate works. By title
Perekaty. Перекаты see PG3453.B27S41+
3453.B27P5 Pli͡aska zhizni. Пляска жизни
3453.B27P6 Posledniĭ Ivanov. Последний Иванов
3453.B27P7 Potomki! (Short stories). Потомки!
3453.B27S4 Sergeĭ Nablot͡skiĭ (Trilogy). Сергей Наблоцкий
3453.B27S41-.B27S43 Perekaty. Перекаты
3453.B27S44-.B27S46 Kar′era Nablot͡skogo. Карьера Наблоцкого
3453.B27S47-.B27S49 Ego Prevoskhoditel′stvo. Его Превошодительство
3453.B27S5 Shelkovichnye chervi. Шелковичные черви
3453.B27S8 Svetlyĭ t͡sar′. Светлый царь
3453.B27V6 Vo dni Petra. Во дни Петра
Baron Galkin; Baron I. Galkin, pseud. Барон Галкин. Барон И. Галкин see PG3460.D57
Baron On dit, pseud. Барон On dit see PG3453.B27
3453.B28 Barykova, Anna Pavlovna (Kamenskai͡a), 1839-1893. Анна Павловна (Каменская) Барыкова (Table P-PZ40 modified)
3453.B28A61-.B28Z458 Separate works. By title
3453.B28D6 Dobroe delo. Доброе дело
3453.B28M3 Mat′ kormilit͡sa (Monolog). Мать кормилица
3453.B28M6 Moim vnukam. Моим внукам
3453.B28N3 Na pami͡at′ vnukam. На память внукам
3453.B28O2 Obrechennai͡a (Monolog). Обреченная
3453.B28S5 Skazka pro to, kak t͡sar′ Akhrei͡an khodil Bogu zhalovat′si͡a. Сказка про то, как царь Ахреян ходил Богу жаловаться
3453.B28S6 Spasennyĭ. Спасенный
Stories in verse. Based on writings of Tennyson
3453.B28V2 V al′bom schastlivit͡se. В альбом счастливице
3453.B29 Baryshev, Efrem Efremovich, d. 1881. Ефрем Ефремович Барышев (Table P-PZ40)
3453.B3 Baryshev, Grigoriĭ, fl. 1865-1875. Григорий Барышев (Table P-PZ40)
3453.B315 Baryshev, Ivan Il′ich, 1854-1911. Иван Ильич Барышев (Table P-PZ40)
Basanin, Mark. Марк Басанин see PG3467.L145

Russian literature
Individual authors and works, 1870-1917
Individual authors, Andreev, L. - Chekhov, Anton -- Continued

3453.B32 Bashkin, Vasiliĭ Vasil′evich, 1880-1909. Василий Васильевич Башкин (Table P-PZ40)

3453.B33 Basov, Sergeĭ Aleksandrovich, 1869-1952. Сергей Александрович Басов (Table P-PZ40)

Basov-Verkhoi͡ant͡sev, S.A. С.А. Басов-Верхоянцев see PG3453.B33

3453.B34 Bazhenov, V.L., fl. 1880-1890. В.Л. Баженов (Table P-PZ40)

3453.B35 Bazhin, Nikolaĭ Fedotovich, 1843-1908. Николай Федотович Бажин (Table P-PZ40 modified)

3453.B35A61-.B35Z458 Separate works. By title

3453.B35D6 Dobrye namerenii͡a. Добрые намерения

3453.B35D7 Domashnie schety. Домашние счеты

3453.B35D8 Drug. Друг

3453.B35G4 Genial′nyĭ plan. Гениальный план

3453.B35G6 G-n Kri͡ukov. Г-н Крюков
Gospodin Kri͡ukov. Господин Крюков

3453.B35I7 Istorii͡a odnogo tovarishchestva (Novel). История одного товарищества

3453.B35I8 Itogi (Novel). Итоги

3453.B35I9 Iz ogni͡a da v polymi͡a. Из огня да в полымя

3453.B35K5 Klad (Novel). Клад

3453.B35K8 Kvartira No. 15. Квартира No. 15

3453.B35L5 Lit͡som k lit͡su (Novel). Лицом к лицу

3453.B35M3 Malysh. Малыш

3453.B35M4 Mani͡a. Маня

3453.B35N6 Noch′ (Novel). Ночь

3453.B35O2 Oblava. Облава

3453.B35O3 Odin. Один

3453.B35O4 Okolo zolota. Около золота

3453.B35P6 Po povodu schast′i͡a. По поводу счастья

3453.B35P63 Poryvami. Порывами

3453.B35P65 Posledni͡ai͡a stavka. Последняя ставка

3453.B35P67 Potok. Поток

3453.B35P7 Prikli͡ucheni͡ia Lavrentii͡a Molodkova. Приключения Лаврентия Молодкова

3453.B35P8 Prizrak. Призрак

3453.B35S5 Skorbnai͡a ėlegii͡a. Скорбная элегия

3453.B35S8 Stepan Rulev. Степан Рулев

3453.B35T7 Tri sem′i. Три семьи

3453.B35T8 Trus (Novel). Трус

3453.B35U9 Uzhas. Ужас

Russian literature
Individual authors and works, 1870-1917
Individual authors, Andreev, L. - Chekhov, Anton
Bazhin, Nikolaĭ Fedotovich, 1843-1908. Николай Федотович Бажин
Separate works. By title -- Continued

3453.B35V2 V lesu. В лесу
3453.B35V25 V nachale zhizni (Novel). В начале жизни
3453.B35Z3 Zhiteĭskai͡a shkola. Житейская школа
3453.B35Z35 Zhizn′ syznova (Novel). Жизнь сызнова
3453.B35Z4 Zloe delo (Novel). Злое дело
3453.B35Z45 "Zovet" (Zapiski Semena Dolgogo). "Зовет" (Записки Семена Долгого)
3453.B35Z5-.B35Z99 Biography and criticism
3453.B36 Bazhina, Serafima Nikitichna (Alymova), 1839-1894. Серафима Никитична (Алымова) Бажина (Table P-PZ40)
3453.B366 Beketova, Ekaterina Andreevna, 1855-1892. Екатерина Андреевна Бекетова (Table P-PZ40)
3453.B368 Bekhti͡eev, Aleksi͡eĭ, 1847-1901. Алексѣй Бехтѣевъ (Table P-PZ40)
3453.B37 Belanovskiĭ, Evgeniĭ Ivanovich, fl. 1880-1890. Евгений Иванович Белановский (Table P-PZ40)
3453.B38 Belet͡skiĭ, I.G., fl. 1890-1900. И.Г. Белецкий (Table P-PZ40)
3453.B385 Belevich, Konstantin Pavlovich, 1825-1890. Константин Павлович Белевич (Table P-PZ40)
3453.B39 Belevskiĭ, Alekseĭ Stanislavovich, 1859-1919. Алексей Станиславович Белевский (Table P-PZ40)
3453.B4 Beli͡aev, I͡Uriĭ Dmitrievich, 1876-1917. Юрий Дмитриевич Беляев (Table P-PZ40 modified)
3453.B4A61-.B4Z458 Separate works. By title
3453.B4B3 Baryshni Shneĭder. Барышни Шнейдер
3453.B4D3 Dama iz Torzhka. Дама из Торжка
3453.B4G6 Gorodok v tabakerke. Городок в табакерке
3453.B4K7 Krasnyĭ Kabachek. Красный Кабачек
3453.B4O7 Otkrytki s voĭny. Открытки с войны
3453.B4P7 Psisha. Псиша
3453.B4P8 Putanit͡sa, ili, 1840 god. Путаница, или, 1840 год
3453.B4S4 Sestry Shneĭder. Сестры Шнейдер
3453.B4T7 T͡Sarevna-li͡agushka. Царевна-лягушка
3453.B4V2 V nekotorom t͡sarstve. В некотором царстве
3453.B4V5 Ved′ma (Novel). Ведьма
3453.B4V6 Vosem′ rasskazov. Восемь рассказов
3453.B413 Beli͡aev, Ivan Stepanovich, 1860-1918. Иван Степанович Беляев (Table P-PZ40)
Belinskiĭ, Maksim. Максим Белинский see PG3467.I3

Russian literature
Individual authors and works, 1870-1917
Individual authors, Andreev, L. - Chekhov, Anton -- Continued

	Bel′mesov, N. H. Бельмесов see PG3470.P65
3453.B42	Belokonskiĭ, Ivan Petrovich, 1855-1931. Иван Петрович Белоконский (Table P-PZ40)
3453.B425	Belomorskiĭ, A.A., fl. 1890-1900. A.A. Беломорский (Table P-PZ40)
	Belorussov, pseud. Белоруссов see PG3453.B39
3453.B43	Belousov, Ivan Alekseevich, 1863-1930. Иван Алексеевич Белоусов (Table P-PZ40)
3453.B432	Belov, Ivan Dmitrievich, d. 1886. Иван Дмитриевич Белов (Table P-PZ40)
3453.B434	Belov, N.N., fl. 1880-1890. Н.Н. Белов (Table P-PZ40)
3453.B437	Belozerskiĭ, Evgeniĭ Mikhaĭlovich, 1853- . Евгений Михайлович Белозерский (Table P-PZ40)
	Belozerskiĭ, N. H. Белозерский see PG3470.P625
	Belyĭ, Andreĭ. Андрей Белый see PG3453.B84
	Benedikt, pseud. Бенедикт see PG3470.V38
	Bengal′skiĭ, graf, pseud. Граф Бенгальский see PG3470.S48
3453.B44	Ber, Boris Vladimirovich, fl. 1890-1910. Борис Владимирович Бер (Table P-PZ40)
3453.B445	Berezin, Vladimir Petrovich, fl. 1880-1890. Владимир Петрович Березин (Table P-PZ40)
3453.B447	Berezkin, Dmitriĭ Mikhaĭlovich, fl. 1900-1910. Дмитрий Михайлович Березкин (Table P-PZ40)
3453.B448	Berezovskiĭ, Feoktist Alekseevich, 1877-1951. Феоктист Алексеевич Березовский (Table P-PZ40)
3453.B45	Berg, Fedor Nikolaevich, 1839-1909. Федор Николаевич Берг (Table P-PZ40 modified)
3453.B45A61-.B45Z458	Separate works. By title
3453.B45K3	Kamennyĭ ostrovok. Каменный островок
3453.B45K4	Kartinki lesnoĭ zhizni. Картинки лесной жизни
3453.B45K5	Khoristy. Хористы
3453.B45M5	Mel′nit͡sa. Мельница
3453.B45N3	Na shli͡uzakh. На шлюзах
3453.B45N5	Neobychaĭnyĭ sluchaĭ. Необычайный случай
3453.B45N6	Nezadacha. Незадача
3453.B45P4	Pervyĭ sneg. Первый снег
3453.B45P5	Pod arestom. Под арестом
3453.B45P6	Pol′ Dzhons. Поль Джонс
3453.B45P7	Proezzhie. Проезжие
3453.B45R6	Rodina i lesnai͡a pustyni͡a. Родина и лесная пустыня
3453.B45S7	Strana gor. Страна гор

Russian literature
Individual authors and works, 1870-1917
Individual authors, Andreev, L. - Chekhov, Anton
Berg, Fedor Nikolaevich, 1839-1909. Федор Николаевич Берг
Separate works. By title -- Continued
3453.B45V2 V chetyrekh stenakh. В четырех стенах
3453.B45V6 Voron. Ворон
3453.B45Z3 Zakoulok (Novel). Закоулок
3453.B45Z33 Zametki iz putevoĭ knizhki. Заметки из путевой книжки
3453.B45Z35 Zaozer′e. Заозерье
3453.B45Z4 Zdes′ zhalkiĭ sbrod shumit. Здесь жалкий сброд шумит
Bernard, Nina Pavlovna Annenkova- . Нина Павловна Анненкова-Бернард see PG3453.A58
3453.B46 Bernov, Mikhail Aleksandrovich, 1864- . Михаил Александрович Бернов (Table P-PZ40)
Bertol′di, pseud. Бертольди see PG3460.G33
Beshent͡sov, A. A. Бешенцов see PG3321.B44
3453.B462 Besp͡iatov, Evgeniĭ Mikhaĭlovich, 1878-1919. Евгений Михайлович Беспятов (Table P-PZ40)
3453.B463 Bessonov, A.I., fl. 1880-1890. А.И. Бессонов (Table P-PZ40)
Bestuzhev, Vl. Вл. Бестужев see PG3460.G49
Bezdol′nyĭ, Ivan. Иван Бездольный see PG3470.P63
Bezhet͡skiĭ, A.N. А.Н. Бежецкий see PG3467.M36
3453.B468 Bezobrazov, N.F., fl. 1880-1900. Н.Ф. Безобразов (Table P-PZ40)
3453.B47 Bezobrazov, Pavel Vladimirovich, 1859-1918. Павел Владимирович Безобразов (Table P-PZ40)
Bezp͡iatov, Evgeniĭ Mikhaĭlovich. Евгений Михайлович Безпятов see PG3453.B462
3453.B475 Bezrodna͡ia, I͡Uli͡ia, 1859-1910. Юлия Безродная (Table P-PZ40)
Bezsonov, A.I. А.И. Безсонов see PG3453.B463
3453.B5 Bibikov, Viktor Ivanovich, 1863-1892. Виктор Иванович Бибиков (Table P-PZ40 modified)
3453.B5A61-.B5Z458 Separate works. By title
3453.B5C5 Chista͡ia l͡iubov′ (Novel). Чистая любовь
3453.B5D4 Deti (Tale). Дети
3453.B5D7 Druz′͡ia pri͡iateli (Novel). Друзья приятели
3453.B5D8 Duėl′ (Story). Дуэль
3453.B5K8 Kumir (Story). Кумир
3453.B5L5 Lgun (Tale). Лгун
3453.B5M3 Marus͡ia (Story). Маруся
3453.B5M6 Mo͡ia mat′ (Novel). Моя мать

Russian literature
Individual authors and works, 1870-1917
Individual authors, Andreev, L. - Chekhov, Anton
Bibikov, Viktor Ivanovich, 1863-1892. Виктор Иванович Бибиков
Separate works. By title -- Continued

3453.B5M8 Mucheniki (Story). Мученики
3453.B5N3 Na poroge k novoĭ zhizni. На пороге к новой жизни
3453.B5P4 Pervai͡a groza (Story). Первая гроза
3453.B5P45 Pervai͡a pobeda (Story). Первая победа
3453.B5P5 Pis′mo (Tale). Письмо
3453.B5R3 Razocharovanie (Tale). Разочарование
3453.B5S6 Slabni͡ak (Story). Слабняк
3453.B5T7 Tri pis′ma. Три письма
3453.B52 Bilibin, Viktor Viktorovich, 1859-1908. Виктор Викторович Билибин (Table P-PZ40 modified)
3453.B52A61-.B52Z458 Separate works. By title
3453.B52B5 Bluzhdai͡ushchai͡a pochka (Comedy). Блуждающая почка
3453.B52C5 Chuchelo (Farce). Чучело
3453.B52D3 Damskai͡a boltovni͡a (Drama). Дамская болтовня
3453.B52D6 Dobrodetel′nyĭ chert (Farce). Добродетельный черт
3453.B52D7 Drakony (Farce). Драконы
3453.B52I5 Interesnai͡a bol′nai͡a (Farce). Интересная больная
3453.B52I7 I͡Umor i fantazii͡a. Юмор и фантазия
3453.B52I8 I͡Umoristicheskie uzory. Юмористические узоры
3453.B52I85 Ivan Ivanovich vinovat! (Comedy). Иван Иванович виноват!
3453.B52I9 Izumitel′nye prevrashchenii͡a (Comedy). Изумительные превращения
3453.B52K3 Kamera obskura (Drama). Камера обскура
3453.B52K4 Kamera-obskura (Vaudeville). Камера-обскура
3453.B52K7 Krugovorot (Drama). Круговорот
3453.B52L5 Li͡ubov′ i smekh (Stories, scenes, etc.). Любовь и смех
3453.B52M5 Milyĭ i͡unosha (Farce). Милый юноша
3453.B52M6 Molchanie (Farce). Молчание
3453.B52M8 Muchenit͡sa (Drama). Мученица
3453.B52P5 Podvigi (Drama). Подвиги
3453.B52P55 Pokhishchenie Sil′fidy (Vaudeville). Похищение Сильфиды
3453.B52P6 Porokh (Farce). Порох
3453.B52P7 Prilichii͡a (Comedy). Приличия
3453.B52R4 Revol′ver (Drama). Револьвер
3453.B52R6 Rokovai͡a skameĭka (Vaudeville). Роковая скамейка
3453.B52S3 Schast′e docheri (Drama). Счастье дочери

Russian literature
Individual authors and works, 1870-1917
Individual authors, Andreev, L. - Chekhov, Anton
Bilibin, Viktor Viktorovich, 1859-1908. Виктор Викторович Билибин
Separate works. By title -- Continued

3453.B52S7 Starichki (Farce). Старички
3453.B52T3 Tant͡sui͡ushchiĭ kavaler (Farce). Танцующий кавалер
3453.B52T75 T͡Sitvarnyĭ rebenok (Vaudeville). Цитварный ребенок
3453.B52V2 V ruki pravosudii͡a (Drama). В руки правосудия
3453.B52Z3 Zloĭ dukh (Comedy). Злой дух
3453.B53 Bilibina, Vera Kornilievna, fl. 1890-1900. Вера Корнилиевна Билибина (Table P-PZ40)
Binoklʹ, pseud. Бинокль see PG3470.V34
3453.B535 Bitner, Vilʹgelʹm Vilʹgelʹmovich, 1865-1921. Вильгельм Вильгельмович Битнер (Table P-PZ40)
Bit͡syn, N. H. Бицын see PG3467.P7
Blager, pseud. Благер see PG3470.S48
3453.B54 Blagodushnai͡a, Sofii͡a, fl. 1900-1910. София Благодушная (Table P-PZ40)
Blagonamerennyĭ grazhdanin, pseud. Благонамеренный гражданин see PG3453.B94
Blagoveshchenskiĭ, Nikolaĭ Aleksandrovich. Николай Александрович Благовещенский see PG3321.B55
3453.B55 Blagovo, Dmitriĭ Dmitrievich, 1827-1897. Дмитрий Дмитриевич Благово
3453.B555 Blank, Nikolaĭ Nikolaevich, fl. 1890-1900. Николай Николаевич Бланк
3453.B56 Blaramberg, Elena Ivanovna, 1846-1923. Елена Ивановна Бларамберг
Blavatskai͡a, Elena Petrovna. Елена Петровна Блаватская see PG3453.B57
3453.B57 Blavatsky, Helene Petrovna (Hahn-Hahn), 1831-1891
For theosophical writings see BP561.A1+
3453.B58 Blinov, Nikolaĭ Nikolaevich, b. 1839. Николай Николаевич Блинов (Table P-PZ40)
3453.B59 Bli͡ummer, Leonid Petrovich, 1840-1888. Леонид Петрович Блюммер (Table P-PZ40)
Blizhnev, E. E. Ближнев see PG3467.L12
3453.B6 Blok, Aleksandr Aleksandrovich, 1880-1921. Александр Александрович Блок (Table P-PZ40 modified)
3453.B6A61-.B6Z458 Separate works. By title
3453.B6B3 Balaganchik (Drama). Балаганчик
3453.B6B4 Belyĭ dom (Drama). Белый дом
3453.B6D4 Deĭstvo o Teofile (Drama). Действо о Теофиле
3453.B6D8 Dvenad͡tsatʹ. Двенадцать
3453.B6I3 I͡Amby. Ямбы

Russian literature
Individual authors and works, 1870-1917
Individual authors, Andreev, L. - Chekhov, Anton
Blok, Aleksandr Aleksandrovich, 1880-1921. Александр Александрович Блок
Separate works. By title -- Continued

3453.B6I8 Ital'ı͡anskie stikhi. Итальянские стихи
3453.B6K6 Korol′ na ploshchadi (Drama). Король на площади
3453.B6N4 Nechaı͡annaı͡a radost′ (Poems). Нечаянная радость
3453.B6N5 Neznakomka (Drama). Незнакомка
3453.B6N6 Nochnye chasy. Ночные часы
3453.B6O2 O lı͡ubvi, poėzii i gosudarstvennoĭ sluzhbe (Dialog). О любви, поэзии и государственной службе
3453.B6O8 Otrocheskie stikhi. Отроческие стихи
3453.B6P4 Pesnı͡a sud′by (Dramatic poem). Песня судьбы
3453.B6P7 Prilozhenii͡a (Poem). Приложения
3453.B6R3 Ramzes (Drama). Рамзес
3453.B6R6 Roza i krest (Drama). Роза и крест
3453.B6R7 Rozhdenie poėta (Story). Рождение поэта
3453.B6S5 Skify (Poem). Скифы
3453.B6S6 Snezhnaı͡a maska (Poem). Снежная маска
3453.B6S7 Solov′inyĭ sad (Poem). Соловьиный сад
3453.B6S8 Stikhi o Prekrasnoĭ Dame. Стихи о Прекрасной Даме
3453.B6S9 Stikhi o Rossii. Стихи о России
3453.B6V6 Vozmezdie (Poem). Возмездие
3453.B6Z3 Za gran′ı͡u proshlykh dneĭ (Poems). За гранью прошлых дней
3453.B6Z4 Zemlı͡a v snegu. Земля в снегу

Blummer, Leonid Petrovich see PG3453.B59
Boborykin, Nikolaĭ Nikolaevich. Николай Николаевич Боборыкин see PG3321.B58

3453.B62 Boborykin, Petr Dmitrievich, 1836-1921. Петр Дмитриевич Боборыкин (Table P-PZ40 modified)
3453.B62A61-.B62Z458 Separate works. By title
3453.B62B4 Bez muzheĭ (Story). Без мужей
3453.B62B5 Bezvestnaı͡a (Story). Безвестная
3453.B62B6 Bol′nye rodinoĭ (Novel). Больные родиной
Bol′shie khoromy. Большие хоромы see PG3453.B62S8
3453.B62B7 Bozh′ı͡a korovka (Comedy). Божья коровка
3453.B62D4 Del′t͡sy (Novel). Дельцы
3453.B62D55 Doktor Moshkov (Comedy). Доктор Мошков
3453.B62D57 Doktor T͡Sybul′ka (Novel). Доктор Цыбулька
3453.B62D6 Dolgo-li? (Story). Долго-ли?
3453.B62D65 Doma (Story). Дома

PG

Russian literature
Individual authors and works, 1870-1917
Individual authors, Andreev, L. - Chekhov, Anton
Boborykin, Petr Dmitrievich, 1836-1921. Петр Дмитриевич Боборыкин
Separate works. By title -- Continued

3453.B62E7 Eretik. Otryvki iz zapisok. Еретик. Отрывки из записок
3453.B62E8 Evropeĭskiĭ roman v XIX-m stoletii (Novel). Европейский роман в XIX-м столетии
3453.B62F3 Faraonchiki (Story). Фараончики
3453.B62F7 Frazery (Drama). Фразеры
3453.B62G6 Goluboĭ lif (Tale). Голубой лиф
3453.B62G7 Gorlenki (Tale). Горленки
3453.B62I7 Ispovedniki (Novel). Исповедники
3453.B62I8 Ivan da Mar'i͡a. Иван да Марья
3453.B62I85 Iz novykh (Novel). Из новых
3453.B62I9 Izgoi (Novel). Изгои
3453.B62I95 Izmennik (Story). Изменник
3453.B62K3 Karty na stol (Novel). Карты на стол
3453.B62K4 Khodok (Novel). Ходок
3453.B62K5 Kitaĭ-gorod (Novel). Китай-город
3453.B62K6 Kleĭmo (Drama). Клеймо
3453.B62K7 Kni͡agini͡a (Novel). Княгиня
3453.B62K8 Kuda itti? (Novel). Куда итти?
3453.B62L5 Likhie bolesti (Novel). Лихие болести
3453.B62M5 Milliony (Story). Миллионы
3453.B62M6 Molodye (Tale). Молодые
3453.B62M7 "Morz" i "I͡Uz" (Tale). "Морз" и "Юз"
3453.B62N2 Na sud (Novel). На суд
3453.B62N25 Na ushcherbe (Novel). На ущербе
3453.B62N27 Na vole (Story). На воле
3453.B62N3 Nakip' (Comedy). Накипь
3453.B62N35 Nashi li͡udi (Story). Наши люди
3453.B62N4 Nashi znakomt͡sy (Comedy). Наши знакомцы
3453.B62N5 Ne u del (Drama). Не у дел
3453.B62N6 Neizlechimye (Story). Неизлечимые
3453.B62O2 Obmirshchenie (Novel). Обмирщение
3453.B62O23 Obnishchalyĭ (Story). Обнищалый
3453.B62O27 Obrechena (Story). Обречена
3453.B62O3 Odna dusha (Tale). Одна душа
3453.B62O36 Odnodvoret͡s (Comedy). Однодворец
3453.B62O37 Odnoĭ porody (Story). Одной породы
3453.B62P4 Pered chem-to (Novel). Перед чем-то
3453.B62P45 Peresililo (Tale). Пересилило
3453.B62P47 Pereval (Novel). Перевал
3453.B62P5 Pi͡at' padeniĭ (Drama). Пять падений

Russian literature
Individual authors and works, 1870-1917
Individual authors, Andreev, L. - Chekhov, Anton
Boborykin, Petr Dmitrievich, 1836-1921. Петр Дмитриевич Боборыкин
Separate works. By title -- Continued

3453.B62P55 Po chuzhim li͡udi͡am (Tale). По чужим людям
3453.B62P6 Po-amerikanski (Story). По-американкси
3453.B62P62 Pobezhdennykh ne sudi͡at (Novel). Побежденных не судят
3453.B62P625 Poddeli! (Story). Поддели!
3453.B62P63 Po-drugomu (Novel). По-другому
3453.B62P635 Polzhizni (Novel). Полжизни
3453.B62P64 Posestrie (Story). Посестрие
3453.B62P645 Poslednii͡ai͡a depesha (Tale). Последняя депеша
3453.B62P65 Poumnel (Story). Поумнел
3453.B62P655 Prezrennyĭ. Zapiski muzha (Story). Презренный. Записки мужа
3453.B62P67 Pristroilsi͡a (Story). Пристроился
3453.B62P675 Proezdom (Story). Проездом
3453.B62P68 Proryv v vechnostʹ (Novel). Прорыв в вечность
3453.B62P685 Prozrela (Story). Прозрела
3453.B62P69 Psarni͡a (Tale). Псарня
3453.B62R3 Rannie vyvodki (Story). Ранние выводки
3453.B62R37 Raspad (Story). Распад
3453.B62R39 Razlad (Novel). Разлад
3453.B62R5 Rebenok (Drama). Ребенок
3453.B62S2 S boi͡u (Comedy). С бою
3453.B62S28 S ubiĭt͡seĭ (Story). С убийцей
3453.B62S3 Sami po sebe (Story). Сами по себе
3453.B62S6 Solidnye dobrodeteli (Novel). Солидные добродетели
3453.B62S8 Staroe zlo (Bolʹshie khoromy) (Drama). Старое зло
3453.B62S85 Svoi͡a ruka vladyka (Drama). Своя рука владыка
3453.B62S9 Sytye (Comedy). Сытые
3453.B62T5 Ti͡aga (Novel). Тяга
3453.B62T7 Tri afishi (Tale). Три афиши
3453.B62T8 Trup (Story). Труп
3453.B62U2 U plity (Tale). У плиты
3453.B62U5 Umeretʹ-usnutʹ (Tale). Умереть-уснуть
3453.B62U7 Uprazdniteli (Novel). Упразднители
3453.B62V2 V bashne (Tale). В башне
3453.B62V23 V chuzhom pole (Novel). В чужом поле
3453.B62V24 V kapkane (Tale). В капкане
3453.B62V25 V mire zhitʹ - mirskoe tvoritʹ (Drama). В мире жить - мирское творить
3453.B62V26 V napersnikakh (Story). В наперсниках

Russian literature
Individual authors and works, 1870-1917
Individual authors, Andreev, L. - Chekhov, Anton
Boborykin, Petr Dmitrievich, 1836-1921. Петр Дмитриевич Боборыкин
Separate works. By title -- Continued

3453.B62V27 V ot′ezd (Tale). В отьезд
3453.B62V28 V put′-dorogu! (Novel). В путь-дорогу!
3453.B62V29 V usad′be i na porîadke (Story). В усадьбе и на порядке
3453.B62V3 Vasiliĭ Terkin (Novel). Василий Теркин
3453.B62V4 Velikaîa razrukha. Semeĭnaîa khronika (Novel). Великая разруха. Семейная хроника
3453.B62V6 Vosem′desîat-shest′ (Tale). Восемьдесят-шесть
3453.B62V7 Vse na kartu (Tale). Все на карту
3453.B62V8 Vtoraîa ot vody (Tale). Вторая от воды
3453.B62V9 Vysshaîa shkola (Story). Высшая школа
3453.B62V95 Vyuchka (Tale). Выучка
3453.B62Z2 Za krasnen′kuîu (Tale). За красненькую
3453.B62Z25 Za rabotu! (Novel). За работу!
3453.B62Z27 Zemskie sily (Novel). Земские силы
3453.B62Z3 Zhertva vecherniaîa (Novel). Жертва вечерняя
3453.B62Z33 Zhestokie (Novel). Жестокие

Bochechkarova, Evgeniîa Ivanovna. Евгения Ивановна Бочечкарова see PG3467.K555

Boev, Nikolaĭ. Николай Боев see PG3453.B45

3453.B623 Bogatyrev, Pavel Ivanovich, 1851-1908. Павел Иванович Богатырев (Table P-PZ40)

Bogdanov, A. A. Богданов see PG3467.M29

3453.B625 Bogdanov, Andreĭ, fl. 1890-1900. Андрей Богданов (Table P-PZ40)

3453.B626 Bogdanov, Ivan Ivanovich, ca. 1840-ca. 1880. Иван Иванович Богданов (Table P-PZ40)

3453.B627 Bogdanov, N. H. Богданов (Table P-PZ40)

Bogemskiĭ, M. M. Богемский see PG3460.C2

3453.B628 Bogolîubov, Nikolaĭ Petrovich, 1820-1898. Николай Петрович Боголюбов (Table P-PZ40 modified)

3453.B628A61-.B628Z458 Separate works. By title

3453.B628N3 Navarinskoe srazhenie (Tale). Наваринское сражение
3453.B628R3 Rasskazy starogo morîaka. Рассказы старого моряка
3453.B628S5 Shapka Ul′rikha (Story). Шапка Ульриха

Bogoras, Waldemar see PG3453.B63

3453.B63 Bogoraz, Vladimir Germanovich, 1865-1936. Владимир Германович Богораз (Table P-PZ40 modified)

Russian literature
Individual authors and works, 1870-1917
Individual authors, Andreev, L. - Chekhov, Anton
Bogoraz, Vladimir Germanovich, 1865-1936. Владимир Германович Богораз -- Continued

3453.B63A61-.B63Z458 Separate works. By title

3453.B63A75 Amerikanskie rasskazy. Американские рассказы
3453.B63A8 Avdot'i͡a i Rivka (Tale). Авдотья и Ривка
3453.B63C4 Chernyĭ student (Tale). Черный студент
3453.B63C5 Chukotskie rasskazy. Чукотские рассказы
3453.B63D6 Dni svobody (Story). Дни свободы
3453.B63G8 Gusi (Sketch). Гуси
3453.B63I7 Iskateli (Sketch). Искатели
3453.B63K5 Khristos na zemle (Fantasy). Христос на земле
3453.B63K6 Kolymskie rasskazy. Колымские рассказы
3453.B63K7 Krasnoe i chernoe. Красное и черное
3453.B63K75 Krivonogiĭ. Кривоногий
3453.B63K8 Kto pervyĭ prolil na zemle krov' (Story). Кто первый пролил на земле кровь
3453.B63L4 Lebedi. Лебеди
3453.B63N3 Na kamennom mysu (Story). На каменном мысу
3453.B63N32 Na kanikulakh (Tale). На каникулах
3453.B63N33 Na krasnom kamne (Tale). На красном камне
3453.B63N34 Na mertvom stoĭbishche (Tale). На мертвом стойбище
3453.B63N35 Na ozere Loche (Story). На озере Лоче
3453.B63N36 Na rastitel'noĭ pishche (Tale). На растительной пище
3453.B63N37 Na rodine (Tales). На родине
3453.B63N38 Na traktu. На тракту
3453.B63N39 Na tundre. На тундре
3453.B63P3 Pashen'kina smert' (Tale). Пашенькина смерть
3453.B63R3 Razvi͡azka (Tale). Развязка
3453.B63S5 Skitanii͡a. Скитания
3453.B63S6 Soi͡uz molodykh (Novel). Союз молодых
3453.B63V2 V doroge (Poem). В дороге
3453.B63V6 Vosem' plemen (Novel). Восемь племен
3453.B63V7 Voskresshee plemi͡a (Novel). Воскресшее племя
3453.B63Z3 Za okeanom (Novel). За океаном
3453.B63Z4 Zhertvy drakona (Novel). Жертвы дракона

3453.B64 Bogoslovskiĭ, Nikolaĭ Gavrilovich, 1824-1892. Николай Гаврилович Богословский (Table P-PZ40)
3453.B643 Bogrov, Grigoriĭ Isaakovich, 1825-1885. Григорий Исаакович Богров (Table P-PZ40)
3453.B645 Boĭchevskiĭ, Ivan Adrianovich, 1860- . Иван Адрианович Бойчевский (Table P-PZ40)

PG

Russian literature
Individual authors and works, 1870-1917
Individual authors, Andreev, L. - Chekhov, Anton -- Continued

Boĭ-kot, pseud. Бой-кот see PG3460.C6

3453.B647 Bolkonskiĭ, D., fl. 1885-1895. Д. Болконский (Table P-PZ40)

Bondarenko, Ostap. Остап Бондаренко see PG3470.S815

3453.B65 Borisovskiĭ, N.F., fl. 1880-1900. Н.Ф. Борисовский (Table P-PZ40)

Borman, Ariadna Vladimirovna. Ариадна Владимировна Борман see PG3470.T98

3453.B657 Borodaevskiĭ, Valerian, 1874?-1923. Валериан Бородаевский (Table P-PZ40)

3453.B66 Borodin, Petr Alekseevich, fl. 1880-1900. Петр Алексеевич Бородин (Table P-PZ40)

3453.B665 Borodzich, Paulin Ivanovich, 1855- . Паулин Иванович Бородзич (Table P-PZ40)

3453.B667 Bostrom, Aleksandra. Александра Бостром (Table P-PZ40)

3453.B67 Bozhich-Savich, V.G., fl. 1850-1870. В.Г. Божич-Савич (Table P-PZ40)

3453.B675 Braĭtsev, ÍA. R., fl. 1880-1890. Я.Р. Брайцев (Table P-PZ40)

3453.B68 Brandt, Nikolaus G., fl. 1910-1920. Николаус Г. Брандт (Table P-PZ40)

3453.B682 Brandt, Roman Fedorovich, 1853-1920. Роман Федорович Брандт (Table P-PZ40)

3453.B684 Brenko, Anna. Анна Бренко (Table P-PZ40)

3453.B685 Breshko-Breshkovskiĭ Nikolaĭ Nikolaevich, 1874-1943. Николай Николаевич Брешко-Брешковский (Table P-PZ40)

3453.B688 Bri͡anchaninov, Anatoliĭ Aleksandrovich, b. 1839. Анатолий Александрович Брянчанинов (Table P-PZ40)

3453.B69 Bri͡anskiĭ, Dmitriĭ, fl. 1890-1900. Дмитрий Брянский (Table P-PZ40)

3453.B695 Bri͡unelli, Pavel Al′fonsovich, 1873-1949. Павел Альфонсович Брюнелли (Table P-PZ40)

3453.B7 Bri͡usov, Valeriĭ I͡Akovlevich, 1873-1924. Валерий Яковлевич Брюсов (Table P-PZ40 modified)

3453.B7A61-.B7Z458 Separate works. By title

3453.B7A75 Altar′ pobedy (Novel). Алтарь победы

(3453.B7A8) Amfitrion. Амфитрион

see Molière, Jean Baptiste Poquelin, Amphitryon PQ1826.A7+

Russian literature
Individual authors and works, 1870-1917
Individual authors, Andreev, L. - Chekhov, Anton
Bri͡usov, Valeriĭ I͡Akovlevich, 1873-1924. Валерий Яковлевич Брюсов
Separate works. By title -- Continued

3453.B7C5 Chefs d'oeuvre (Poems, 1894-1895)
Dalekie i blizkie. Далекие и близкие see PG3051
3453.B7D3 Dali (Poems, 1922). Дали
(3453.B7E4) Elena Spartanskai͡a. Елена Спартанская
see Verhaeren, Emile, Hélène de Sparta PQ2459.V8H4
3453.B7E5 Ėluli, syn Ėluli (Story). Элули, сын Элули
Ėto - i͡a. Это - я see PG3453.B7M4
(3453.B7F7) Francheska da Rimini. Франческа да Римини
see Annunzio, Gabriele d', Francesca da Rimini PQ4803.Z6+
Gradu i miru. Граду и миру see PG3453.B7U7
3453.B7K7 Krugozor (Selected poems, 1893-1922). Кругозор
3453.B7M4 Me eum esse (Poems, 1897)
3453.B7M45 Mea (Poems, 1922-1924)
3453.B7M5 Mig (Poems, 1920-1921). Миг
3453.B7M6 Moi͡a i͡unostʹ (Story). Моя юность
3453.B7N6 Nochi i dni (Stories and dramatic sketches, 1908-1912). Ночи и дни
3453.B7O2 Obruchenie Dashi (Story). Обручение Даши
3453.B7O3 Ognennyĭ angel (Novel). Огненный ангел
(3453.B7P4) Pelleas i Melizanda. Пеллеас и Мелизанда
see Maeterlinck, Maurice, Pelléas et Melisande PQ2625.A5P4
3453.B7P6 Poslednie mechty (Lyric poems, 1917-1919). Последние мечты
3453.B7P7 Protesilaĭ umershiĭ (Tragedy). Протесилай умерший
3453.B7P8 Puti i pereputʹi͡a (Poems, 1892-1908). Пути и перепутья
3453.B7P85 Putnik (Drama). Путник
3453.B7R4 Rei͡a Silʹvii͡a (Story). Рея Сильвия
(3453.B7R6) Romansy bez slov. Романсы без слов
see Verlaine, Paul Marie, Romances sans paroles PQ2463.A61+
3453.B7S4 Semʹ t͡svetov radugi (Poems, 1912-1915). Семь цветов радуги
3453.B7S8 Stephanos (Poems, 1903-1905)
3453.B7T4 Tertia vigilia (Poems, 1897-1900)
Tretʹi͡a strazha. Третья стража see PG3453.B7T4
3453.B7T8 T͡Sepʹ (Poems, 1892-1911). Цепь
3453.B7U7 Urbi et orbi (Poems, 1900-1903)

PG

Russian literature
Individual authors and works, 1870-1917
Individual authors, Andreev, L. - Chekhov, Anton
Bri͡usov, Valeriĭ I͡Akovlevich, 1873-1924. Валерий Яковлевич Брюсов
Separate works. By title -- Continued

3453.B7V2 V takie dni (Poems, 1919-1920). В такие дни
Venok sonetov. Венок сонетов see PG3453.B7S8
3453.B7V7 Vse napevy (Poems, 1906-1909). Все напевы
3453.B7Z3 Zemli͡a (Drama). Земля
3453.B7Z35 Zemnai͡a os′. Земная ось
Stories and dramatic sketches, 1901-1906 (1st ed.); 1901-1907 (2d ed.)
3453.B7Z4 Zerkalo teneĭ (Poems, 1909-1916). Зеркало теней
Bronin, A. A. Бронин see PG3467.K628
3453.B73 Bronskiĭ, Pavel, fl. 1890-1900. Павел Бронский (Table P-PZ40)
3453.B75 Brovt͡syn, Petr Platonovich, fl. 1875-1885. Петр Платонович Бровцын (Table P-PZ40)
3453.B78 Brusi͡anin, Vasiliĭ Vasil′evich, 1867-1919. Василий Васильевич Брусянин (Table P-PZ40 modified)
3453.B78A61-.B78Z458 Separate works. By title
3453.B78B5 Belye nochi (Novel). Белые ночи
3453.B78B6 Bozh′i raby (Tale). Божьи рабы
3453.B78C5 Chas smertnyĭ (Tales). Час смертный
3453.B78D6 Dom na kosti͡akh (Tales). Дом на костях
3453.B78K5 Khristovy brat′i͡a (Stories and tales). Христовы братья
3453.B78K6 Korabl′ mertvykh (Tales). Корабль мертвых
3453.B78M6 Molodezh′ (Novel). Молодежь
3453.B78M8 Muzhchina (Novel). Мужчина
3453.B78N5 Ni zhivye - ni mertvye (Ocherki peterburgskoĭ zhizni). Ни живые - ни мертвые (Очерки петербургской жизни)
3453.B78O6 Opustoshennye dushi (Novel). Опустошенные души
3453.B78P5 Pechal′nai͡a skripka (Tale). Печальная скрипка
3453.B78P6 Posle obeda (Sketch). После обеда
3453.B78T4 Temnyĭ lik (Novel). Темный лик
3453.B78T7 Tragedii͡a Mikhaĭlovskogo zamka (Novel). Трагедия Михайловского замка
3453.B78V2 V bor′be za trud (Story). В борьбе за труд
3453.B78V27 V rabochikh kvartalakh (Tales). В рабочих кварталах
3453.B78V28 V strane ozer (Tales). В стране озер
Brut, Ivan. Иван Брут see PG3470.V62

Russian literature
Individual authors and works, 1870-1917
Individual authors, Andreev, L. - Chekhov, Anton -- Continued

3453.B8 Buchinskai͡a, Nadezhda Aleksandrovna (Lokhvit͡skai͡a), 1872-1952. Надежда Александровна (Лохвицкая) (Table P-PZ40 modified)

3453.B8A61-.B8Z458 Separate works. By title

3453.B8A8 Avanti͡urnyĭ roman. Авантюрный роман

Chelovekoobraznye. Человекообразные see PG3453.B8I8

3453.B8C5 Chernyĭ iris (Dramatic piece). Черный ирис

3453.B8D9 Dym bez ogni͡a (Tales). Дым без огня

3453.B8G6 Gorodok (Tales). Городок

3453.B8I2 I stalo tak. И стало так

3453.B8I8 I͡Umoristicheskie rasskazy. Юмористические рассказы

Title of vol. 2: Chelovekoobraznye

I͡Iun′. Июнь see PG3453.B8K6

3453.B8K3 Karusel′ (Tales). Карусель

3453.B8K6 Kniga I͡Iun′ (Tales). Книга Июнь

3453.B8L4 Leshka vysluzhilsi͡a (Dramatic piece). Лешка выслужился

3453.B8L5 Letniĭ otdykh (Tales). Летний отдых

3453.B8M5 Miniati͡ury i monologi. Миниатюры и монологи

3453.B8N2 Nakazannyĭ zver′ (Dramatic piece). Наказанный зверь

3453.B8N4 Nebol′shoĭ talant (Dramatic piece). Небольшой талант

3453.B8N45 Nezhivoĭ zver′ (Wit and humor). Неживой зверь

3453.B8N5 Nichego podobnogo (Tales). Ничего подобного

3453.B8O2 O nezhnosti (Tales). О нежности

3453.B8P3 Papochka [and other tales]. Папочка

3453.B8P35 Passiflora (Poems)

3453.B8P4 P′esy (Dramatic piece). Пьесы

3453.B8P5 "Pli͡uskeparfe" (Drama). "Плюскепарфе"

3453.B8P7 Prestuplenie (Dramatic piece). Преступление

3453.B8P8 Provorstvo ruk [and other tales]. Проворство рук

3453.B8R8 Russkiĭ izobretatel′ [and other tales]. Русский изобретатель

3453.B8R9 Rys′ (Tales). Рысь

3453.B8S3 Satir Kukin (Dramatic piece). Сатир Кукин

3453.B8S4 Sem′ ogneĭ (Poems). Семь огней

3453.B8S45 Shamram. Шамрам

3453.B8S5 Sharmanka satany (Dramatic piece). Шарманка сатаны

Russian literature
Individual authors and works, 1870-1917
Individual authors, Andreev, L. - Chekhov, Anton
Buchinskai͡a, Nadezhda Aleksandrovna (Lokhvit͡skai͡a), 1872-1952. Надежда Александровна (Лохвицкая)
Separate works. By title -- Continued

3453.B8S6 Sokrovishche zemli [and other tales]. Сокровище земли
3453.B8T2 Tak zhili (Tales). Так жили
3453.B8T3 Tango smerti. Танго смерти
3453.B8T5 Tikhai͡a zavodʹ. Тихая заводь
3453.B8V3 Vchera (Tales). Вчера
3453.B8V4 Vecherniĭ denʹ (Tales). Вечерний день
3453.B8V5 Vedʹma (Tales). Ведьма
3453.B8V6 Vostok [and other tales]. Восток
3453.B8V9 Vzamen politiki [and other tales]. Взамен политики
3453.B8Z3 Zarevo bitvy (Tales). Зарево битвы
3453.B8Z35 Zhitʹe-bytʹe (Tales). Житье-бытье
3453.B8Z4 Zhiznʹ i vorotnik [and other tales]. Жизнь и воротник
3453.B8Z45 Zigzag. Зигзаг
3453.B82 Budchenko, S.S., fl. 1890-1900. С.С. Будченко (Table P-PZ40)
3453.B83 Budishchev, Alekseĭ Nikolaevich, 1867-1916. Алексей Николаевич Будищев (Table P-PZ40 modified)
3453.B83A61-.B83Z458 Separate works. By title
3453.B83B5 Bednyĭ pazh [and other tales]. Бедный паж
3453.B83B8 Bunt sovesti (Novel). Бунт совести
3453.B83C5 Chernyĭ buĭvol (Tales). Черный буйвол
3453.B83D3 Dali tumannye (Tales). Дали туманные
3453.B83D5 Dies irae (Poems)
3453.B83D6 Dikiĭ vsadnik [and other tales]. Дикий всадник
3453.B83I2 I͡A i on (Novel and tales). Я и он
3453.B83I9 Izlomy li͡ubvi [and other tales]. Изломы любви
3453.B83K3 Katastrofa (Drama). Катастрофа
3453.B83K5 Khata s krai͡u (Tales). Хата с краю
3453.B83K7 Krik vo tʹme (Tales). Крик во тьме
3453.B83L5 Lesnye bratʹi͡a (Tales). Лесные братья
3453.B83L6 Li͡ubovʹ - prestuplenie [and other tales]. Любовь - преступление
3453.B83L8 Luchshiĭ drugʹ (Novel). Лучший другь
3453.B83L9 Lunnyĭ svet [and other tales]. Лунный свет
3453.B83M5 Milochki (Sketches and caricatures). Милочки
3453.B83O5 Okhotnit͡sa za skalʹpami [and other tales]. Охотница за скальпами
3453.B83P7 Probuzhdennai͡a sovestʹ [and other tales]. Пробужденная совесть

	Russian literature
	Individual authors and works, 1870-1917
	Individual authors, Andreev, L. - Chekhov, Anton
	Budishchev, Alekseĭ Nikolaevich, 1867-1916. Алексей Николаевич Будищев
	Separate works. By title -- Continued
3453.B83R3	Raspri͡a (Tales). Распря
3453.B83R4	Raznye poni͡atii͡a. Разные понятия
3453.B83S2	S gor voda (Tales). С гор вода
3453.B83S6	Solnechnye dni (Novel). Солнечные дни
3453.B83S7	Step′ grezit (Novel). Степь грезит
3453.B83S75	Stepnye volki (Tales). Степные волки
3453.B83S8	Strannai͡a istorii͡a (Vaudeville). Странная история
3453.B83S9	Strashno zhit′ [and other tales]. Страшно жить
3453.B83T3	Taĭna vremen [and other tales]. Тайна времен
3453.B83T7	T͡Sarevich Maĭ. Царевич Май
3453.B83V9	Vzdornye rasskazy. Вздорные рассказы
	Budzianik, Aleksandra Aleksandrovna Vinit͡skai͡a. Александра Александровна Виницкая Будзианик see PG3470.V55
3453.B84	Bugaev, Boris Nikolaevich, 1880-1934. Борис Николаевич Бугаев (Table P-PZ40 modified)
3453.B84A61-.B84Z458	Separate works. By title
	Dramaticheskai͡a simfonii͡aсимфония see PG3453.B84S55+
3453.B84E6	Ėpopei͡a. Эпопея
	Geroicheskai͡a simfonii͡a. Героическая симфония see PG3453.B84S52+
3453.B84G53	Gibel′ senatora. Гибель сенатора
3453.B84K5	Khristos voskres (Poems). Христос воскрес
3453.B84K6	Korolevna i ryt͡sari (Stories in verse). Королевна рыцари
3453.B84K65	Kotik Letaev (Novel). Котик Летаев
3453.B84K7	Kreshchenyĭ kitaet͡s (Novel). Крещеный китаец
	Kubok meteleĭ. Кубок метелей see PG3453.B84S65+
3453.B84L8	Lug zelenyĭ. Луг зеленый
	Maski. Маски see PG3453.B84M65+
3453.B84M58	Moskva (Drama). Москва
3453.B84M6	Moskva (Novel). Москва
	Comprises:
3453.B84M62-.B84M64	Moskovskiĭ chudak. Московский чудак
3453.B84M65-.B84M67	Moskva pod udarom. Москва под ударом

Russian literature
Individual authors and works, 1870-1917
Individual authors, Andreev, L. - Chekhov, Anton
Bugaev, Boris Nikolaevich, 1880-1934. Борис Николаевич Бугаев
Separate works. By title -- Continued

3453.B84N3 Na perevale (Essays). На перевале
Comprises:
3453.B84N31-.B84N33 Krizis zhizni. Кризис жизни
3453.B84N34-.B84N36 Krizis mysli. Кризис мысли
3453.B84N37-.B84N39 Krizis kulʹtury. Кризис культуры
3453.B84O3 Odna iz obiteleĭ t͡sarstva teneĭ. Одна из обителей царства теней
3453.B84P3 Pepel (Poems). Пепел
3453.B84P4 Pervoe svidanie (Poem). Первое свидание
3453.B84P5 Peterburg (Novel). Петербург
3453.B84P6 Posle razluki (Poems). После разлуки
3453.B84S4 Serebri͡annyĭ golubʹ (Novel). Серебрянный голубь
3453.B84S45 Severnai͡a simfonii͡a. Северная симфония
3453.B84S5 Simfonii͡a. Симфония
Comprises:
3453.B84S52-.B84S54 Geroicheskai͡a. Героическая
3453.B84S55-.B84S57 Dramaticheskai͡a. Драматическая
3453.B84S62-.B84S64 Vozvrat. Возврат
3453.B84S65-.B84S67 Kubok meteleĭ. Кубок метелей
3453.B84S7 Stansy (Poems). Стансы
3453.B84S8 Stikhi o Rossii. Стихи о России
3453.B84U7 Urna (Poems). Урна
3453.B84V6 Vozvrashchenʹe na rodinu (otryvki iz povesti). Возвращенье на родину (отрывки из повести)
Vozvrat. Возврат see PG3453.B84S62+
3453.B84Z2 Zapiski chudaka. Записки чудака
3453.B84Z3 Zoloto v lazuri (Poems). Золото в лазури
3453.B84Z4 Zvezda (Poems). Звезда
3453.B845 Bugaĭskiĭ, P. I͡A., fl 1877-1887. П.Я. Бугайский (Table P-PZ40)
3453.B85 Bukharin, Mikhail Nikolaevich, 1845-1910. Михаил Николаевич Бухарин (Table P-PZ40 modified)
3453.B85A61-.B85Z458 Separate works. By title

Russian literature
Individual authors and works, 1870-1917
Individual authors, Andreev, L. - Chekhov, Anton
Bukharin, Mikhail Nikolaevich, 1845-1910. Михаил Николаевич Бухарин
Separate works. By title -- Continued

3453.B85C5 Chto t͡senít͡ zhenshchiny (Vaudeville). Что ценят женщины
3453.B85I9 Izmail (Drama). Измаил
3453.B85V2 V takui͡u noch′ (Comedy). В такую ночь
3453.B853 Bukharova, Zoi͡a Dmitrievna, 1876-1923. Зоя Дмитриевна Бухарова (Table P-PZ40)
Bukva, pseud. Буква see PG3470.V24
3453.B855 Bulanina, Elena, fl. 1901-1912. Елена Буланина (Table P-PZ40)
3453.B86 Bulat͡sel′, Ivan Mikhaĭlovich, 1846- . Иван Михайлович Булацель (Table P-PZ40 modified)
3453.B86A61-.B86Z458 Separate works. By title
3453.B86E7 Esli zhenshchina reshila (Drama). Если женщина решила
3453.B86G7 Gromootvod (Drama). Громоотвод
3453.B86L5 Lidii͡a (Drama). Лидия
3453.B86P4 Penelopa (Drama). Пенелопа
3453.B86S8 Sud′ba li͡ubvi - igrat′ eĭ v zhmurki (Comedy). Судьба любви - играть ей в жмурки
3453.B86Z5 Zhizn′ za mgnovenie (Drama). Жизнь за мгновение
3453.B87 Bulgakov, Vasiliĭ Konstantinovich, fl. 1890-1900. Василий Константинович Булгаков (Table P-PZ40)
3453.B88 Bulgakovskiĭ, Dmitriĭ Gavrilovich, b. 1845. Дмитрий Гаврилович Булгаковский (Table P-PZ40 modified)
3453.B88A61-.B88Z458 Separate works. By title
3453.B88B5 Blizne͡tsy (Novel). Близнецы
3453.B88B6 Bogatstvo i schast′e (Story). Богатство и счастье
3453.B88N5 Nizhegorodskie legendy. Нижегородские легенды
3453.B88P6 Porazitel′nye sluchai i͡alenii͡a umershikh (Story). Поразительные случаи яления умерших
3453.B88V2 V storone ot zhizni (Story). В стороне от жизни
3453.B89 Bulygin, Petr Pavlovich, b. 1859. Петр Павлович Булыгин (Table P-PZ40 modified)
3453.B89A61-.B89Z458 Separate works. By title
3453.B89K2 K novoĭ zhizni (Story). К новой жизни
3453.B89L5 Li͡ubochkino gore (Story). Любочкино горе
3453.B89N6 Nochnye teni (Story). Ночные тени
3453.B89P6 Po ustavu (Story). По уставу

Russian literature
Individual authors and works, 1870-1917
Individual authors, Andreev, L. - Chekhov, Anton
Bulygin, Petr Pavlovich, b. 1859. Петр Павлович Булыгин
Separate works. By title -- Continued

3453.B89R3 Rasplata (Novel). Расплата
3453.B89S5 Severt͡sev (Story). Северцев
3453.B89V2 V poli͡akh i lesakh (Novel). В полях и лесах
3453.B89V6 Volki (Story). Волки

Bum-Bum, pseud. Бум-Бум see PG3467.M35

3453.B9 Bunin, Ivan Alekseevich, 1870-1953. Иван Алексеевич Бунин (Table P-PZ40 modified)

3453.B9A61-.B9Z458 Separate works. By title
3453.B9A8 Antonovskie i͡abloki. Антоновские яблоки
3453.B9B3 Baĭbaki. Байбаки
3453.B9B4 Bez rodu-plemeni. Без роду-племени
3453.B9B6 Bozh′e drevo (Short stories). Божье древо
3453.B9B7 Brat′i͡a. Братья
3453.B9C5 Chasha zhizni (Stories, 1913-1914). Чаша жизни
3453.B9D4 Delo korneta Elagina. Дело корнета Елагина
3453.B9D5 Derevni͡a (Novel). Деревня
3453.B9D7 Drevniĭ chelovek. Древний человек
3453.B9F3 Fantazer. Фантазер
3453.B9G6 Gospodin iz San-Frant͡sisko. Господин из Сан-Франциско
3453.B9G7 Grammatika li͡ubvi. Грамматика любви
3453.B9I3 Ida. Ида
3453.B9I6 Ioann Rydalet͡s (Tales and poems, 1912-1913). Иоанн Рыдалец
3453.B9I9 Iz zabytoĭ tetradi. Из забытой тетради
3453.B9K3 Kastri͡uk. Кастрюк
3453.B9K4 Khoroshai͡a zhizn′. Хорошая жизнь
3453.B9K5 Khram solnt͡sa. Храм солнца
3453.B9K55 Khudai͡a trava. Худая трава
3453.B9K6 Koster. Костер
3453.B9K7 Krik. Крик
3453.B9L5 Listopad (Poems). Листопад
3453.B9M5 Mitina li͡ubov′. Митина любовь
3453.B9M6 Mordovskiĭ sarafan. Мордовский сарафан
3453.B9N2 Na chuzhoĭ storone. На чужой стороне
3453.B9N25 Na Dont͡se. На Донце
3453.B9N3 Na kraĭ sveta. На край света
3453.B9N4 Nachal′nai͡a li͡ubov′. Начальная любовь
3453.B9N5 Nesrochnai͡a vesna. Несрочная весна
3453.B9N6 Nochnoĭ razgovor. Ночной разговор
3453.B9N65 Novai͡a doroga. Новая дорога

Russian literature
Individual authors and works, 1870-1917
Individual authors, Andreev, L. - Chekhov, Anton
Bunin, Ivan Alekseevich, 1870-1953. Иван Алексеевич Бунин
Separate works. By title -- Continued

3453.B9N7 Novyĭ god. Новый год
3453.B9O4 Okai͡annye dni. Окаянные дни
3453.B9O7 Osenʹi͡u. Осенью
3453.B9P4 Pereval i drugie rasskazy. Перевал и другие рассказы
3453.B9P6 Poslednee svidanie. Последнее свидание
3453.B9P7 Pozdneĭ nochʹi͡u. Поздней ночью
3453.B9R6 Roza Ierikhona. Роза Иерихона
3453.B9R8 Ruda. Руда
3453.B9S3 Schastʹe. Счастье
3453.B9S4 Skit. Скит
3453.B9S5 Smertʹ Moisei͡a. Смерть Моисея
3453.B9S55 Sny Changa. Сны Чанга
3453.B9S6 Solnechnyĭ udar. Солнечный удар
3453.B9S7 Sosny. Сосны
3453.B9S8 Sukhodol (Novel). Суходол
3453.B9S9 Svi͡atai͡a nochʹ. Святая ночь
3453.B9T2 Tanʹka. Танька
3453.B9T3 Tarantella. Тарантелла
3453.B9T4 Temnye allei. Темные аллеи
3453.B9T5 Tenʹ pti͡tsy. Тень птицы
3453.B9T6 Tishina. Тишина
3453.B9T7 T͡Sifry. Цифры
3453.B9T8 Tuman. Туман
3453.B9V2 V avguste. В августе
3453.B9V4 Veseniĭ vecher. Весений вечер
3453.B9V5 Vesti s rodiny. Вести с родины
3453.B9Z2 Zhiznʹ Arsenʹeva (Novel). Жизнь Арсеньева
Comprises: 1. Istoki dneĭ (Истоки дней); 2. Lika (Лика)
3453.B9Z3 Zodiakalʹnyĭ svet. Зодиакальный свет
3453.B9Z4 Zolotoe dno (Tales, 1903-1907). Золотое дно
3453.B94 Burenin, Viktor Petrovich, 1841-1926. Виктор Петрович Буренин (Table P-PZ40 modified)
3453.B94A61-.B94Z458 Separate works. By title
3453.B94B9 Byloe (Poems, 1861-1877). Былое
3453.B94D5 Diana Fornari (Drama). Диана Форнари
(3453.B94D6) Dolores (Drama). Долорес
see Crawford, Francis Marion, In the palace of the king PS1453+
Fʹi͡ammetta. Фьямметта see PG3453.B94S75+

Russian literature
Individual authors and works, 1870-1917
Individual authors, Andreev, L. - Chekhov, Anton
Burenin, Viktor Petrovich, 1841-1926. Виктор Петрович Буренин
Separate works. By title

3453.B94G6 Golubye zvuki i belye poėmy. Голубые звуки и белые поэмы
3453.B94G7 Gore ot gluposti (Dramatic satire). Горе от глупости
3453.B94G8 Graf Filipp Kënigsmark (Drama). Граф Филип Кёнигсмарк
3453.B94I4 Ifgenii͡a (Drama). Ифгения
3453.B94I5 Imperatrit͡sa Vizantii (Drama). Императрица Византии
3453.B94I9 Iz sovremennoĭ zhizni. Fel′etonnye rasskazy. Из современной жизни. Фельетонные рассказы
(3453.B94K3) Kaligula (Tragedy). Калигула
see Dumas, Alexandre, père, Caligula PQ2225.C15
3453.B94K5 Khvost (Poems, parodies). Хвост
3453.B94K6 Komedii͡a o kni͡azhne Zabave Puti͡atishne i boi͡aryne Vasilise Mikulishne. Комедия о княжне Забаве Путятишне и боярыне Василисе Микулишне
Madonna Beatriche. Мадонна Беатриче see PG3453.B94S72+
3453.B94M4 Medei͡a (Drama). Медея
3453.B94M45 Metvai͡a noga (Novel). Мертвая нога
3453.B94M5 Messalina (Drama). Мессалина
(3453.B94N5) Neron (Tragi-comedy). Нерон
see Gutzkow, Karl Ferdinand, Nero PT2282.N4
3453.B94O9 Ozherel′e Afrodity (Drama). Ожерелье Афродиты
3453.B94P4 Pesn′ li͡ubvi i smerti (Drama). Песнь любви и смерти
3453.B94P5 Pipa i Pusi͡a, ili, Gore ot li͡ubvi (Humorous stories and comedies). Пипа и Пуся, или, Горе от любви
3453.B94P6 Plennik Vizantii (Drama). Пленник Византии
(3453.B94P7) Potonuvshiĭ kolokol (Drama). Потонувший колокол
see Hauptmann, Gerhart Johann Robert, Die versunkene Glocke PT2616.Z6+
3453.B94R6 Roman v Kislovodske (Story). Роман в Кисловодске
(3453.B94S4) Serdt͡se print͡sesy Ozry (Comedy). Сердце принцесы Озры
see Hawkins, Anthony Hope, The heart of Princess Osra PR4762
3453.B94S6 Smert′ Agrippiny (Drama). Смерть Агриппины
3453.B94S7 Starye komedii li͡ubvi. Старые комедии любви
Comprises:
3453.B94S72-.B94S74 Madonna Beatriche. Мадонна Беатриче

Russian literature
Individual authors and works, 1870-1917
Individual authors, Andreev, L. - Chekhov, Anton
Burenin, Viktor Petrovich, 1841-1926. Виктор Петрович Буренин
Separate works. By title
Starye komedii li͡ubvi. Старые комедии любви -- Continued

3453.B94S75-.B94S77 F'i͡ammetta. Фьямметта

3453.B94S8 Strely (Poems). Стрелы

3453.B94V2 V vek Ekateriny (Drama). В век Екатерины

3453.B94V7 Vse khorosho, chto khorosho konchilos' (Farce). Все хорошо, что хорошо кончилось

(3453.B94Z3) Zamok smerti (Drama). Замок смерти
see Echegaray y Eizaguirre, José, En el seno de la muerte PQ6516+

(3453.B94Z35) Zhenshchina s kinzhalom (Drama). Женщина с кинжалом
see Schnitzler, Arthur, Die Frau mit dem Dolche PT2638.N5

3453.B94Z4 Zvezda li͡ubvi (Drama). Звезда любви

3453.B945 Burkevich, E., fl. 1890-1900. Е. Буркевич (Table P-PZ40)

Burlak, V.N. Andreev-. В.Н. Андреев-Бурлак see PG3453.A3

Burnashev, Vladimir Petrovich. Владимир Петрович Бурнашев see PG3321.B87

3453.B947 Burt͡sev, M.F., fl. 1880-1890. М.Ф. Бурцев (Table P-PZ40)

3453.B95 Buslavskiĭ, Vsevolod I., fl. 1880-1900. Всеволод И. Буславский (Table P-PZ40)

3453.B96 Butkov, A.I., fl. 1890-1900. А.И. Бутков (Table P-PZ40)

3453.B97 Butovskiĭ, Nikolaĭ Dmitrievich, b. 1850. Николай Дмитриевич Бутовский (Table P-PZ40)

3453.B975 Buturlin, Petr Dmitrievich, graf, 1859-1895. Петр Дмитриевич Бутурлин (Table P-PZ40)

3453.B98 Bykov, Petr Vasil'evich, 1843-1930. Петр Васильевич Быков (Table P-PZ40)

3453.B99 Bystrenin, Vladimir Porfir'evich, 1856- . Владимир Порфирьевич Быстренин (Table P-PZ40 modified)

3453.B99A61-.B99Z458 Separate works. By title

3453.B99B7 Brat'i͡a (Novel). Братья

3453.B99I7 Ishchushchiĭ pravdy (Tale). Ищущий правды

3453.B99L5 Lesnik (Sketch). Лесник

3453.B99M4 Matrena (Tale). Матрена

Russian literature
Individual authors and works, 1870-1917
Individual authors, Andreev, L. - Chekhov, Anton
Bystrenin, Vladimir Porfir′evich, 1856- . Владимир Порфирьевич Быстренин
Separate works. By title -- Continued

3453.B99R3 Razlad. Разлад
3453.B99S5 Skazki zhizni. Сказки жизни
3453.B99S8 Sukhar′ (Tale). Сухарь
3453.B99S85 Svoĭ sud (Tale). Свой суд
3453.B99S9 Syn naroda (Sketch). Сын народа
3453.B99U3 Uchitel′ (Tale). Учитель
3453.B99V2 V poslednīĭ raz (Tale). В последний раз
3453.B99V5 Vernoe sredstvo (Tale). Верное средство
3453.B99Z3 Zhiteĭskie byli; ocherki i rasskazy. Житейские были; очерки и рассказы

Ch...ov, P.V., pseud. П.В. Ч...ов see PG3460.C24
Chaev, I͡Uriĭ. Юрий Чаев see PG3470.P48

3453.C3 Chaev, Nikolaĭ Aleksandrovich, 1824-1914. Николай Александрович Чаев (Table P-PZ40 modified)
3453.C3A61-.C3Z458 Separate works. By title
3453.C3B5 Biri͡uk (Comedy). Бирюк
3453.C3B6 Bogatyri (Novel). Богатыри
3453.C3D5 Dimitriĭ Samozvanet͡s (Drama). Димитрий Самозванец
3453.C3D8 Dupel′ (Comedy). Дупель
3453.C3K5 Kni͡az′ Aleksandr Mikhaĭlovich Tverskoĭ (Drama). Князь Александр Михайлович Тверской
3453.C3M3 Mamaevo poboishche (Drama). Мамаево побоище
3453.C3N3 Nadi͡a (Poem). Надя
3453.C3P6 Podspudnye sily (Novel). Подспудные силы
3453.C3S8 Svat Fadeich. Сват Фадеич
3453.C3S9 Svekrov′ (Tragedy). Свекровь
3453.C3Z3 Znaĭ nashikh (Comedy). Знай наших
3453.C4 Chaĭkovskiĭ, Modest Il′ich, 1850-1916. Модест Ильич Чайковский (Table P-PZ40 modified)
3453.C4A61-.C4Z458 Separate works. By title
3453.C4B6 Boi͡azn′ zhizni (Comedy). Боязнь жизни
3453.C4K5 Kirdzhali (Novel). Кирджали
3453.C4P7 Predrassudki (Comedy). Симфония
3453.C4S5 Simfonii͡a (Comedy). Симфония
3453.C4V3 Vani͡a (Story). Ваня
3453.C5 Chant͡sev, I.A., fl. 1875-1885. И.А. Чанцев
3453.C6 Chaplinskai͡a, M.V., fl. 1890-1900. М.В. Чаплинская
3453.C7 Charskai͡a, Lidii͡a Alekseevna, 1875-1937. Лидия Алексеевна Чарская (Table P-PZ40 modified)
3453.C7A61-.C7Z458 Separate works. By title

Russian literature
Individual authors and works, 1870-1917
Individual authors, Andreev, L. - Chekhov, Anton
Charskai͡a, Lidii͡a Alekseevna, 1875-1937. Лидия Алексеевна Чарская
Separate works. By title -- Continued

3453.C7D8 Durnushka (Story). Дурнушка
3453.C7E8 Evfimii͡a Starit͡skai͡a (Novel). Евфимия Старицкая
3453.C7G3 Gazavat (Story). Газават
3453.C7G5 Gimnazistki (Tales). Гимназистки
3453.C7G7 Groznai͡a druzhina (Story). Грозная дружина
3453.C7I8 I͡Uzhanochka (Story). Южаночка
3453.C7K3 Kak li͡ubi͡at zhenshchiny (Tales). Как любят женщины
3453.C7L5 Lesovichka (Story). Лесовичка
3453.C7M6 Moshkara (Novel). Мошкара
3453.C7N3 Na rassvete (Tales). На рассвете
3453.C7N5 Nekrasivai͡a (Story). Некрасивая
3453.C7O5 Ogonek (Story). Огонек
3453.C7P3 Pazh t͡sesarevny (Story). Паж цесаревны
3453.C7P7 Problemy li͡ubvi (Tales). Проблемы любви
3453.C7P8 Prodannyĭ talant (Story). Проданный талант
3453.C7S4 Semʹi͡a Loranskikh (Story). Семья Лоранских
3453.C7S5 Smelai͡a zhiznʹ (Story). Смелая жизнь
3453.C7S6 Smelye, silʹnye, khrabrye (3 stories). Смелые, сильные, храбрые
3453.C7S8 Svetlyĭ voin (Novel). Светлый воин
3453.C7S9 Svoi, ne boĭtesʹ! i drugie rasskazy. Свои, не бойтесь! и другие рассказы
3453.C7T7 T͡Sarskiĭ gnev (Novel). Царский гнев
3453.C7V5 Vinovna, no . . . (Novel). Виновна, но . . .
3453.C7Z2 Za chto? (Story). За что?
3453.C75 Chaskov, S., fl. 1870-1880. С. Часков (Table P-PZ40)
3453.C8 Chechuev, Modest Ivanovich, fl. 1890-1900. Модест Иванович Чечуев (Table P-PZ40)
Chekhonte, A. A. Чехонте see PG3455+
3453.C9 Chekhov, Aleksandr Pavlovich, 1855-1913. Александр Павлович Чехов (Table P-PZ40)
Chekhov, Anton Pavlovich, 1860-1904. Антон Павлович Чехов
3455.A1 Collected works. By date
3455.A15 Collected novels and tales
Including collections compiled after author's death, even though they have distinctive titles
3455.A16 Essays, miscellanies, notebooks, etc.
3455.A19 Collected plays
3455.A2 Selections

Russian literature
Individual authors and works, 1870-1917
Chekhov, Anton Pavlovich, 1860-1904. Антон Павлович Чехов -- Continued

3455.A3-Z Separate works
For translations see PG3456+

3455.A4-.A43 Agaf'ia (Tale). Агафья (Table PG2)
3455.A7-.A73 Ariadna (Tale). Ариадна (Table PG2)
3455.B2-.B23 Bab'e tsarstvo (Tale). Бабье царство (Table PG2)
3455.B3-.B33 Baby (Tale). Бабы (Table PG2)
3455.B35-.B353 Baryni͡a (Tale). Барыня (Table PG2)
3455.B4-.B43 Beglet͡s (Tale). Беглец (Table PG2)
Chaĭka (Comedy). Чайка
3455.C5 Texts. By date
3455.C52 Criticism
3455.C53-.C533 Chelovek v futli͡are (Tale). Человек в футляре (Table PG2)
3455.C55-.C553 Chernyĭ monakh (Story). Черный монах (Table PG2)
3455.D3-.D33 Dama s sobachkoĭ (Tale). Дама с собачкой (Table PG2)
3455.D4-.D43 Den' za gorodom (Tale). День за городом (Table PG2)
3455.D45-.D453 Detvora (Tale). Детвора (Table PG2)
3455.D5-.D53 Di͡adi͡a Vani͡a (Comedy). Дядя Ваня (Table PG2)
3455.D6-.D63 Dom s mezoninom (Tale). Дом с мезонином (Table PG2)
3455.D7-.D73 Drama na okhote (Drama). Драма на охоте (Table PG2)
3455.D8-.D83 Duėl' (Story). Дуэль (Table PG2)
3455.G6-.G63 Gore (Tale). Горе (Table PG2)
3455.I5-.I53 Imeniny (Tale). Именины (Table PG2)
3455.I6-.I63 Ionych (Tale). Ионыч (Table PG2)
3455.I7-.I73 I͡Ubileĭ (Tale). Юбилей (Table PG2)
I͡Umor. Юмор see PG3455.A15
3455.I8-.I83 Ivanov (Drama). Иванов (Table PG2)
Kalkhas. Калхас see PG3455.L4+
Kashtanka. Каштанка
Texts
see PZ66.3
3455.K33 Criticism
3455.K5-.K53 Khmurye li͡udi (Tales). Хмурые люди (Table PG2)
3455.L4-.L43 Lebedinai͡a pesni͡a (Kalkhas) (Dramatic sketch). Лебединая песня (Table PG2)
3455.L5-.L53 Leshiĭ (Comedy). Леший (Table PG2)
3455.L6-.L63 Lishnie li͡udi (Tale). Лишние люди (Table PG2)
3455.L72-.L723 Loshadinai͡a famili͡a. Лошадиная фамилия (Table PG2)
3455.M4-.M43 Medved' (Comedy). Медведь (Table PG2)

Russian literature
Individual authors and works, 1870-1917
Chekhov, Anton Pavlovich, 1860-1904. Антон Павлович Чехов
Separate works -- Continued

3455.M6-.M63 Moi͡a zhiznʹ (Novel). Моя жизнь (Table PG2)
3455.M8-.M83 Muzhiki (Story). Мужики (Table PG2)
3455.N3-.N33 Na bolʹshoĭ doroge (Drama). На большой дороге (Table PG2)
Nenuzhnai͡a pobeda (Story). Ненужная победа
3455.N4 Texts. By date
3455.N42 Criticism
3455.N43-.N433 Nepri͡iatnostʹ (Tale). Неприятность (Table PG2)
3455.N47-.N473 Nevesta (Tale). Невеста (Table PG2)
3455.N48-.N483 Nevinnye rechi (Tales). Невинные речи (Table PG2)
3455.N5-.N53 Ninochka (Tale). Ниночка (Table PG2)
3455.N6-.N63 Novai͡a dacha (Story). Новая дача (Table PG2)
3455.O2-.O23 O vrede tabaka (Monologue). О вреде табака (Table PG2)
3455.O3-.O33 Ogni (Tale). Огни (Table PG2)
Ostrov Sakhalin. Остров Сахалин see DK771.S2
3455.P3-.P33 Palata No. 6 (Story). Палата No. (Table PG2)
3455.P4-.P43 Perekati-pole (Tale). Перекати-поле (Table PG2)
3455.P45-.P453 Pestrye rasskazy. Пестрые рассказы (Table PG2)
3455.P5-.P53 Poprygunʹi͡a (Story). Попрыгунья (Table PG2)
3455.P6-.P63 Pot͡seluĭ (Tale). Поцелуй (Table PG2)
3455.P7-.P73 Predlozhenie (Comedy). Предложение (Table PG2)
3455.P8-.P83 Pripadok (Tale). Припадок (Table PG2)
Rabʹi dushi. Рабьи души see PG3455.A15
3455.R3-.R33 Rasskaz neizvestnogo cheloveka. Рассказ неизвестного человека (Table PG2)
3455.S38-.S383 Shutochka. Шуточка (Table PG2)
3455.S4-.S43 Shvedskai͡a spichka (Tale). Шведская спичка (Table PG2)
3455.S45-.S453 Skazki Melʹpomeny (6 tales). Сказки Мельпомены (Table PG2)
3455.S5-.S53 Skuchnai͡a istorii͡a (Story). Скучная история (Table PG2)
3455.S6-.S63 Smertʹ chinovnika (Tale). Смерть чиновника (Table PG2)
3455.S7-.S73 Stepʹ (Story). Степь (Table PG2)
Svadʹba (Dramatic piece). Свадьба
3455.S8 Texts. By date
3455.S813 Criticism
3455.S82-.S823 Svadʹba (Tale). Свадьба (Table PG2)
3455.S9-.S93 Svirelʹ (Tale). Свирель (Table PG2)

Russian literature
Individual authors and works, 1870-1917
Chekhov, Anton Pavlovich, 1860-1904. Антон Павлович Чехов
Separate works -- Continued

3455.T3-.T33 Tat'i͡ana Repina (Drama). Татьяна Репина (Table PG2)
3455.T5-.T53 Tina (Tale). Тина (Table PG2)
3455.T6-.T63 Tolstyĭ i tonkiĭ (Tale). Толстый и тонкий (Table PG2)
3455.T7-.T73 Tragik ponevole (Dramatic piece). Трагик поневоле (Table PG2)
3455.T78-.T783 Tri goda (Story). Три года (Table PG2)
3455.T8-.T83 Tri sestry (Drama). Три сестры (Table PG2)
3455.U2-.U23 Ubiĭstvo (Tale). Убийство (Table PG2)
3455.U3-.U33 Uchitel′ slovesnosti (Tale). Учитель словесности (Table PG2)
3455.U5-.U53 Unter Prishibeev (Tale). Унтер Пришибеев (Table PG2)
3455.V2-.V23 V ovrage (Story). В овраге (Table PG2)
3455.V3-.V33 V sumerkakh (Sketches and tales). В сумерках (Table PG2)
3455.V4-.V43 Van′ka (Tale). Ванька (Table PG2)
3455.V5-.V53 Vishnevyĭ sad (Comedy). Вишневый сад (Table PG2)
3455.V6-.V63 Vory (Tale). Воры (Table PG2)
3455.Z4-.Z43 Zhena (Tale). Жена (Table PG2)
3455.Z45-.Z453 Zhivai͡a khronologii͡a (Tale). Живая хронология (Table PG2)
3455.Z5-.Z53 Zhivoĭ tovar (Story). Живой товар (Table PG2)

Translations

3456 English
3456.A1 Collected works. By date
3456.A13 Selected works. By translator or editor
3456.A15 Collected novels and tales. By translator or editor
3456.A16 Collected essays, miscellanies, notebooks, etc.
3456.A19 Collected plays
3456.A3-Z Separate works. By Russian title, A-Z

Subarrange by translator or editor
e. g.

3456.C5 Chaĭka. (The sea gull). Чайка
3456.T8 Tri sestry (The three sisters). Три сестры
3456.V5 Vishnevyĭ sad (The cherry orchard). Вишневый сад
3457.A-Z Other languages, A-Z

Subarrange each language by Table PG1
e. g.

3457.F5 French (Table PG1)
3457.G5 German (Table PG1)

Russian literature
Individual authors and works, 1870-1917
Chekhov, Anton Pavlovich, 1860-1904. Антон Павлович Чехов
Translations
Other languages, A-Z -- Continued
3457.I5 Italian (Table PG1)
3457.S5 Spanish (Table PG1)
Biography and criticism
3458.A1 Collections. By editor
3458.A2-.A5 Autobiography. Journals. Letters
3458.A3 English translations. By translator or editor, A-Z
3458.A33 Other languages, A-Z
3458.A4 Letters (Collected). By date of imprint
3458.A5 Individual correspondents, A-Z
e. g.
3458.A5C5 Ol′ga Leonardovna Knipper Chekhova (Chekhov's wife). Ольга Леонардовна Книппер Чехова
3458.A6-.Z6 General treatises. Life and works
3458.Z7 Iconography. Museums. Exhibitions
3458.Z8 Criticism
3458.Z9 Special topics and subjects, A-Z
3458.Z9A66 Appreciation
3458.Z9C42 Characters
3458.Z9C45 Christianity
3458.Z9D67 Dostoyevsky, Fyodor, 1821-1881. Федор Достоевский
3458.Z9D7 Dramaturgy
3458.Z9E34 Editors
3458.Z9F53 Fictional works
3458.Z9F55 Film adaptations
3458.Z9H65 Homes and haunts
3458.Z9J68 Journalistic career
3458.Z9L35 Language. Style
3458.Z9M43 Medical career
3458.Z9M45 Memory
3458.Z9M87 Music
3458.Z9P48 Philosophy
3458.Z9P64 Political and social views
3458.Z9P83 Publishers
3458.Z9R44 Religion
3458.Z9S8 Stage history
Style see PG3458.Z9L35
3458.Z9T37 Translations (as subject)
3458.Z9W86 Women
3460 Individual authors, Chekhov, Anton - Gorky

PG

Russian literature

Individual authors and works, 1870-1917

Individual authors, Chekhov, Anton - Gorky -- Continued

3460.C2 Chekhov, Mikhail Pavlovich, 1865-1936. Михаил Павлович Чехов (Table P-PZ40 modified)

3460.C2A61-.C2Z458 Separate works. By title

3460.C2S5 Siniĭ chulok (Story). Синий чулок

3460.C2S6 Siroty (Story). Сироты

3460.C2S8 Svirelʹ (Stories). Свирель

3460.Ц24 Цчерепов, П.В., фл. 1880-1890. П.В. Черепов

3460.C26 Cherman, Apollon Nikolaevich, fl. 1890-1900. Аполлон Николаевич Черман

Chermnyĭ, A.N. А.Н. Чермный see PG3460.C26

3460.C28 Cherni͡atin, Konstantin Vasilʹevich, 1878- . Константин Васильевич Чернятин

Chernigovet͡s, F.V. Ф.В. Черниговец see PG3470.V57

3460.C3 Chernov, P., fl. 1890-1900. П. Чернов (Table P-PZ40 modified)

3460.C3A61-.C3Z458 Separate works. By title

3460.C3C5 Chuzhoe dobro (Novel). Чужое добро

3460.C3L5 Li͡ubovʹ. Любовь

3460.C3N3 Na ozere (Story). На озере

3460.C3N4 Na sluzhbe v stolit͡se (Sketch). На службе в столице

3460.C3O2 Ocherki donskogo kazachestva. Очерки донского казачества

3460.C3O4 Ne li͡uba! (Sketch). Не люба!

3460.C3O6 Terpi, kazak (Sketch). Терпи, казак

3460.C3V3 Vagram (Tale). Badpam

3460.C35 Chernyshevskiĭ, Al., fl. 1890-1900. Ал. Чернышевский (Table P-PZ40 modified)

3460.C35A61-.C35Z458 Separate works. By title

3460.C35A75 Antares (Tale). Антарес

3460.C35A8 Arsi i Dina, ili, Serebri͡anoe more (Tale). Арси и Дина, или, Серебряное море

3460.C35F5 "Fiat lux!"

3460.C35O7 Ostrov Orelʹi͡ano. Остров Орельяно

Comprises: I. Fei͡a Mai͡a (Фея Майя); II. "Vspomni obo mne, Mai͡a!" ("Вспомни обо мне, Майя!")

Stikhotvorenii͡a "Fiat lux!". Стихотворения "Fiat lux!" see PG3460.C35F5

3460.Ц3533 Зои͡а Делʹфор. Зоя Дельфор

Chernyshevskiĭ, Nikolaĭ Gavrilovich. Николай Гаврилович Чернышевский see PG3321.C6

3460.C37 Chervinskiĭ, Fedor Alekseevich, 1864- . Федор Алексеевич Червинский (Table P-PZ40)

Russian literature
Individual authors and works, 1870-1917
Individual authors, Chekhov, Anton - Gorky -- Continued

3460.C4 Cheshikhin, Vsevolod Evgrafovich, 1865- . Всеволод Евграфович Чешихин (Table P-PZ40 modified)
3460.C4A61-.C4Z458 Separate works. By title
3460.C4B4 Betkhoven (Poem). Бетховен
3460.C4B5 Blizhnie i dal′nie (Novel). Ближние и дальние
3460.C4C5 Chelovek bez teni (Drama). Человек без тени
3460.C4G3 Gamerling. Гамерлинг
3460.C4G6 Golod (Poems). Голод
3460.C4N3 Napoleon (Drama). Наполеон
3460.C4R8 Rus′ (Prolog in verse). Русь
Chestov, Léon see PG3470.S5
3460.C47 Chikolev, Vladimir Nikolaevich, 1845-1898. Владимир Николаевич Чиколев (Table P-PZ40)
Chinarov, R.Z. Р.З. Чинаров see PG3467.M88
Chinarov, Rubens. Рубенс Чинаров see PG3467.M88
3460.C5 Chirikov, Evgeniĭ Nikolaevich, 1864-1932. Евгений Николаевич Чириков (Table P-PZ40 modified)
3460.C5A61-.C5Z458 Separate works. By title
3460.C5B3 Barin (Tale). Барин
3460.C5B4 Belai͡a vorona (Drama). Белая ворона
3460.C5B5 Bludnyĭ syn (Tale). Блудный сын
3460.C5B7 Brodi͡achiĭ mal′chik (Tale). Бродячий мальчик
3460.C5C5 Chuzhestrant͡sy (Sketch). Чужестранцы
3460.C5D5 Devich′i slezy (Novel). Девичьи слезы
3460.C5D6 Dom Kocherginykh (Drama). Дом Кочергиных
3460.C5D7 Druz′i͡a glasnosti (Drama). Друзья гласности
3460.C5E3 Edinit͡sa (Tale). Единица
3460.C5E4 Ėkho voĭny (Novel). Эхо войны
3460.C5E8 Evrei (Drama). Евреи
3460.C5F3 Faust (Sketch). Фауст
3460.C5G3 Gaudeamus igitur (Tale)
3460.C5G7 Greshnik (Tale). Грешник
3460.C5I5 Imeninnit͡sa (Tale). Именинница
3460.C5I6 Invalidy (Story). Инвалиды
3460.C5I7 Isportilas′ (Tale). Испортилась
3460.C5I8 I͡Unost′ (Novel). Юность
3460.C5I85 Ivan Mironych (Drama). Иван Мироныч
3460.C5I9 Izgnanie (Novel). Изгнание
3460.C5K3 Kak ėto sluchilos′ (Tale). Как это случилось
3460.C5K35 Kaligula (Tale). Калигула
3460.C5K4 Kapituli͡at͡sii͡a (Tale). Капитуляция
3460.C5K5 Khleb vezut (Tale). Хлеб везут
3460.C5K55 Khromoĭ (Tale). Хромой
3460.C5K6 Koldun′i͡a (Drama). Колдунья

Russian literature
Individual authors and works, 1870-1917
Individual authors, Chekhov, Anton - Gorky
Chirikov, Evgeniĭ Nikolaevich, 1864-1932. Евгений Николаевич Чириков
Separate works. By title -- Continued

3460.C5K7 Koli͡a i Kolʹka (Tale). Коля и Колька
3460.C5K8 Krasnye ogni (Drama). Красные огни
3460.C5K9 Krasnyĭ pai͡at͡s (Story). Красный паяц
3460.C5L4 Legenda starogo zamka (Drama). Легенда старого замка
3460.C5L5 Lesnye taĭny (Comedy). Лесные тайны
3460.C5L6 Li͡ubovʹ tovarishcha Muravʹeva (Novel). Любовь товарища Муравьева
3460.C5L7 Loshadka (Tale). Лошадка
3460.C5L8 Lunnai͡a nochʹ (Tale). Лунная ночь
3460.C5M3 Malenʹkiĭ greshnik (Tale). Маленький грешник
3460.C5M35 Marʹi͡a Ivanovna (Comedy). Марья Ивановна
3460.C5M4 Marʹka iz I͡Am (Novel). Марька из Ям
3460.C5M45 Mezhdu nebom i zemleĭ (Novel). Между небом и землей
3460.C5M5 Mi͡atezhniki (Story). Мятежники
3460.C5M6 Mirazh (Tale). Мираж
3460.C5M7 Moĭ roman (Novel). Мой роман
3460.C5M8 Muzh (Tale). Муж
3460.C5M9 Muzhiki (Drama). Мужики
3460.C5N2 Na dvore vo fligele (Comedy). На дворе во флигеле
3460.C5N3 Na poroge zhizni (Tale). На пороге жизни
3460.C5N35 Na porukakh (Tale). На поруках
3460.C5N4 Na stoi͡anke (Tale). На стоянке
3460.C5N5 Nedorod (Tale). Недород
3460.C5O2 Obostrennye otnoshenii͡a (Tale). Обостренные отношения
3460.C5O3 Oduvanchik (Tale). Одуванчик
3460.C5O8 Otchiĭ dom (Story). Отчий дом
3460.C5P7 Predatelʹ (Tale). Предатель
3460.C5P8 Progress (Tale). Прогресс
3460.C5R3 Rannie vskhody (Tale). Ранние вшоды
3460.C5R6 Roman v kletke (Tale). Роман в клетке
3460.C5S2 S nochevoĭ (Tale). С ночевой
3460.C5S4 Semʹi͡a (Novel). Семья
3460.C5S5 Shakaly (Tragicomedy). Шакалы
3460.C5S6 Sobstvennostʹ (Tale). Собственность
3460.C5S7 Sozrel (Tale). Созрел
3460.C5S8 Studenty priekhali (Tale). Студенты приехали
3460.C5S9 Svinʹi͡a (Sketch). Свинья
3460.C5T3 Taĭna (Tale). Тайна

Russian literature
Individual authors and works, 1870-1917
Individual authors, Chekhov, Anton - Gorky
Chirikov, Evgeniĭ Nikolaevich, 1864-1932. Евгений Николаевич Чириков
Separate works. By title -- Continued

3460.C5T4 Tanino schast′e (Tale). Танино счастье
3460.C5T6 Tovarishch (Story). Товарищ
3460.C5T8 T͡Sar′ prirody (Comedy). Царь природы
3460.C5U3 Uchitel′ (Tale). Учитель
3460.C5V2 V lesu (Tale). В лесу
3460.C5V25 V loshchine mezh gor (Tale). В лощине меж гор
3460.C5V27 V otstavku (Tale). В отставку
3460.C5V3 V sugrobakh (Tale). В сугробах
3460.C5V4 Vecherniĭ zvon. Вечерний звон
3460.C5V6 Volshebnik (Tale). Волшебник
3460.C5V7 Vozvrashchenie (Novel). Возвращение
3460.C5Z2 Za slavoĭ (Drama). За славой
3460.C5Z3 Zhizn′ Tarkhanova (Novel). Жизнь Тарханова
3460.C5Z4 Zver′ iz bezdny (Tale). Зверь из бездны
3460.C55 Chist͡iakov, Mikhail Borisovich, 1809-1885. Михаил Борисович Чистяков (Table P-PZ40)
3460.C57 Chist͡iakova, Sof′͡ia Afanas′evna, 1817-1890. Софья Афанасьевна Чистякова (Table P-PZ40)
3460.C6 Ch͡iumina, Ol′ga Nikolaevna, 1863-1909. Ольга Николаевна Чюмина (Table P-PZ40 modified)
3460.C6A61-.C6Z458 Separate works. By title
3460.C6B4 Bez rul͡ia (Drama). Без руля
3460.C6B5 Bez vozvrata (Drama). Без возврата
3460.C6D8 Dumska͡ia vesna. Думская весна
3460.C6F4 Fel′etony v stikhakh. Фельетоны в стихах
3460.C6I7 Iskuplenie (Drama). Искупление
3460.C6M3 Mechta (Drama). Мечта
3460.C6M4 Menestrel′ (Drama). Менестрель
3460.C6N2 Na ogonek rampy (Tales). На огонек рампы
3460.C6N3 Na temy dneĭ svobody. На темы дней свободы
3460.C6N4 Na zhizn′ i na smert′ (Novel). На жизнь и на смерть
3460.C6O7 Osennie vikhri (Poems). Осенние вихри
3460.C6O8 Otche nash. Отче наш
3460.C6P4 Pesni o chetyrekh svobodakh. Песни о четырех свободах
3460.C6R3 Radi kar′ery (Tale). Ради карьеры
3460.C6T5 T′ma (Drama). Тьма
3460.C6U5 Ugassh͡ia iskra (Drama). Угасшая искра
3460.C6V2 V ozhidanii. В ожидании
3460.C6V3 V set͡iakh (Drama). В сетях
3460.C6Z2 Za grekhi ot͡sov (Novel). За грехи отцов

PG

Russian literature
Individual authors and works, 1870-1917
Individual authors, Chekhov, Anton - Gorky -- Continued

3460.C65 Chizhevich, O.O., fl. 1890-1900. О.О. Чижевич (Table P-PZ40)
Chmelov, Ivan. Иван Чмелов see PG3476.S5
3460.C7 Chmyrev, Nikolaĭ Andreevich, 1852-1886. Николай Андреевич Чмырев (Table P-PZ40 modified)
3460.C7A61-.C7Z458 Separate works. By title
3460.C7A75 Aleksandr Nevskiĭ i Novgorodskai͡a vol'ni͡tsa (Novel). Александр Невский и Новгородская вольница
3460.C7A8 Ataman volzhskikh razboĭnikov, Ermak, kni͡az' Sibirskoĭ (Novel). Атаман волжских разбойников, Ермак, князь Сибирской
3460.C7B6 Boi͡arin Petr Basmanov (Novel). Боярин Петр Басманов
Ermak, ataman volzhskikh razboĭnikov. Ермак, атаман волжских разбойников see PG3460.C7A8
3460.C7I8 Ivan Mazepa (Novel). Иван Мазепа
3460.C7P7 Psikhopatka (Novel). Психопатка
3460.C7R3 Raskol'nich'i mucheni͡tsy (Novel). Раскольничьи мученицы
3460.C7R4 Razvenchannai͡a ͡tsarevna v ssylke (Story). Развенчанная царевна в ссылке
3460.C7S9 Sytye i golodnye (Sketches and tales). Сытые и голодные
3460.C7V6 Vo svi͡atoĭ obiteli (Novel). Во святой обители
Chudilovich, Alesha. Алеша Чудилович see PG3453.B83
3460.C75 Chugueve͡ts, Pavel Anastas'evich, fl. 1890-1900. Павел Анастасьевич Чугуевец (Table P-PZ40)
3460.C77 Chukmaldin, Nikolaĭ Martem'i͡anovich, 1836 or 7-1901. Николай Мартемьянович Чукмалдин (Table P-PZ40)
3460.C8 Chulkov, Georgiĭ Ivanovich, 1879-1939. Георгий Иванович Чулков (Table P-PZ40 modified)
3460.C8A61-.C8Z458 Separate works. By title
3460.C8D6 Don Kikhot (Tragicomedy). Дон Кихот
3460.C8K7 Kremnistyĭ put' (Poems). Кремнистый путь
3460.C8L5 Li͡udi v tumane (Tales). Люди в тумане
3460.C8M3 Marii͡a Gamil'ton (Poem). Мария Гамильтон
3460.C8M4 Metel' (Novel). Метель
3460.C8O7 Osennie tumany (Story). Осенние туманы
3460.C8P6 Posramlennye besy (Tales). Посрамленные бесы
3460.C8P7 Prigozhai͡a povarikha (Novel). Пригожая повариха

Russian literature
Individual authors and works, 1870-1917
Individual authors, Chekhov, Anton - Gorky
Chulkov, Georgiĭ Ivanovich, 1879-1939. Георгий Иванович Чулков
Separate works. By title -- Continued

3460.C8S3 Salto mortale, ili, Povest′ o molodom vol′nodumt͡se P′ere Volkhovskom. Salto mortale, или, Повесть о молодом вольнодумце Пьере Волховском
3460.C8S4 Satana (Novel). Сатана
3460.C8S5 Serezha Nestroev (Novel). Сережа Нестроев
3460.C8T3 Taĭga (Drama). Тайга
3460.C8V3 Vchera i segodni͡a (Sketches). Вчера и сегодня
3460.C8V4 Vechernie zori (Tales). Вечерние зори
3460.C8V5 Vesnoi͡u na sever (Poems). Весною на север
3460.C9 Churilin, Tikhon Vasil′evich, 1885-1946. Тихон Васильевич Чурилин (Table P-PZ40)
3460.D2 Daksergof, Lev Georgievich, fl. 1900-1910. Лев Георгиевич Даксергоф (Table P-PZ40)
Dalin, D. Д. Далин see PG3467.L5
Danchenko, Vasiliĭ Ivanovich Nemirovich- . Василий Иванович Немирович-Данченко see PG3467.N4
Danchenko, Vladimir Ivanovich Nemirovich- . Владимир Иванович Немирович-Данченко see PG3467.N5
3460.D22 Dandevil′, Mikhail Viktorovich, fl. 1900-1910. Михаил Викторович Дандевиль (Table P-PZ40)
Danilevskai͡a, Nadezhda Aleksandrovna Lappo- . Надежда Александровна Лаппо-Данилевская see PG3467.L137
Danilevskiĭ, Grigoriĭ Petrovich. Григорий Петрович Данилевский see PG3321.D25
3460.D23 Danilevskiĭ, Mikhail G., fl. 1890-1900. Михаил Г. Данилевский (Table P-PZ40)
3460.D24 Danilin, Ivan Andreevich, 1870- . Иван Андреевич Данилин (Table P-PZ40)
Danin, A. A. Данин see PG3467.K628
3460.D26 Dan′ko, Nikolaĭ, fl. 1900-1910. Николай Данько (Table P-PZ40)
3460.D28 Dar′i͡al, Aleksandra Vasil′evna, fl. 1890-1900. Александра Васильевна Дарьял (Table P-PZ40)
3460.D3 Davidova, M.A., fl. 1890-1900. М.А. Давидова (Table P-PZ40)
Davydov-Gunaropulo, I͡Uriĭ A. Юрий А. Давыдов-Гунаропуло see PG3467.G82
3460.D316 De Gabriak, Cherubina, b. 1887. Черубина де Габриак (Table P-PZ40)

	Russian literature
	Individual authors and works, 1870-1917
	Individual authors, Chekhov, Anton - Gorky -- Continued
3460.D32	Debogoriĭ-Mokrievich, Vladimir Karpovich, 1848-1926. Владимир Карпович Дебогорий-Мокриевич (Table P-PZ40)
	Dedlov, V.L. В.Л. Дедлов see PG3467.K473
	Degaeva, Natalii͡a Petrovna Makleṫsova. Наталия Петровна Маклецова Дегаева see PG3467.M255
3460.D34	Dekhterev, Vladimir, fl. 1900-1910. Владимир Дехтерев (Table P-PZ40)
3460.D36	Delʹvig, Boris Nikolaevich, baron, fl. 1890-1900. Борис Николаевич Дельвиг (Table P-PZ40)
3460.D38	Dementʹev, Ippolit Stepanovich, fl. 1890-1900. Ипполит Степанович Дементьев (Table P-PZ40)
3460.D39	Dementʹev, Petr Alekseevich, 1849-1919. Петр Алексеевич Дементьев (Table P-PZ40)
3460.D4	Denisov, Leonid Ivanovich, fl. 1880-1900. Леонид Иванович Денисов (Table P-PZ40 modified)
3460.D4A61-.D4Z458	Separate works. By title
3460.D4B4	Belosnezhka (Tale). Белоснежка
3460.D4O8	Otkliki Russko-i͡aponskoĭ voĭny (Poems). Отклики Русско-японской войны
3460.D4P5	Pʹi͡anstvo - gibelʹ semʹi (Tale). Пьянство - гибель семьи
3460.D4P6	Podsnezhniki. Idillii͡a v proze. Подснежники. Идиллия в прозе
3460.D4P7	Propovednik-muchenik (Story). Проповедник-мученик
3460.D4R3	Raĭskiĭ t͡svetok (Story). Райский цветок
3460.D4S4	Serafim (Story). Серафим
3460.D4S9	Syny sveta (Stories). Сыны света
3460.D4T7	T͡Senoi͡u very (Novel). Ценою веры
3460.D4V2	V razluke s otchiznoĭ (Tale). В разлуке с отчизной
3460.D4V27	V stranu zhivykh! (Story). В страну живых!
3460.D4V6	Vne vremeni (Tale). Вне времени
3460.D4Z3	Za nebesnye blaga (Story). За небесные блага
3460.D4Z4	Zhiznʹ v khristianskoĭ semʹe (Tales). Жизнь в христианской
3460.D45	Denisova, Lidii͡a, fl. 1900-1910. Лидия Денисова (Table P-PZ40)
3460.D46	D'Ėssar, N. H. Д'Эссар (Table P-PZ40)
3460.D47	Detengof, Aleksandr Karlovich, 1842- . Александр Карлович Детенгоф (Table P-PZ40)
3460.D48	De-Vollan, Grigoriĭ Aleksandrovich, 1847-1916. Григорий Александрович Де-Воллан (Table P-PZ40)
	Di͡adi͡a Pakhom, pseud. Дядя Пахом see PG3467.M87

Russian literature
Individual authors and works, 1870-1917
Individual authors, Chekhov, Anton - Gorky -- Continued

3460.D5 D'i͡akonova, Elizaveta Aleksandrovna, 1874-1902. Елизавета Александровна Дьяконова (Table P-PZ40)

3460.D52 D'i͡akov, Aleksandr Aleksandrovich, 1845-1895. Александр Александрович Дьяков (Table P-PZ40 modified)

3460.D52A61-.D52Z458 Separate works. By title

3460.D52C5 Chuzhai͡a zhena. Чужая жена
3460.D52D4 Denezhnai͡a orgii͡a. Денежная оргия
3460.D52G6 Golovka krasavit͡sy (Tales). Головка красавицы
3460.D52K3 Kartinki i ėti͡udy. Картинки и этюды
3460.D52K5 Klad (Tale in verse). Клад
3460.D52K7 Kruzhkovshchina (Tales). Кружковщина
3460.D52L5 Lesnoĭ t͡sar' (Sketches and tales). Лесной царь
3460.D52O8 Ot sud'by ne uĭdesh' (Tale). От судьбы не уйдешь
3460.D52P7 Prorok (Tale). Пророк
3460.D52R8 Rublevai͡a derevni͡a. Рублевая деревня
3460.D52S8 Susal'nye zvezdy. Сусальные звезды
3460.D52V2 V Belgrade i na pozit͡sii (Tale). В Белграде и на позиции
3460.D52V25 V narod! (Tale). В народ!
3460.D52W4 Weltschmerzer (Tale)

3460.D53 D'i͡akov, Nikita K., fl. 1875-1885. Никита К. Дьяков (Table P-PZ40)

Diogen, pseud. Диоген see PG3453.B52

Dioneo, pseud. Дионео see PG3470.S522

3460.D55 Divavin, M., fl. 1880-1900. M. Дивавин (Table P-PZ40)

3460.D56 Dlusskiĭ, Konstantin Mikhaĭlovich, 1856- . Константин Михайлович Длусский (Table P-PZ40 modified)

3460.D56A61-.D56Z458 Separate works. By title

3460.D56C5 Chasy s kurantami (Tale). Часы с курантами
3460.D56G4 General Onagenko (Fantasy). Генерал Онагенко
3460.D56I8 I͡Ungfrau (Tale). Юнгфрау
3460.D56P6 Posledniĭ tanet͡s (Tale). Последний танец
3460.D56S5 Skaly (Tale). Скалы
3460.D56S6 Sovest' zagovorila (Tale). Совесть заговорила
3460.D56T7 Tri motiva (Tale). Три мотива
3460.D56T8 T͡Svetok oleandra [and other tales]. Цветок олеандра
3460.D56T82 T͡Svetok oleandra (Tale). Цветок олеандра
3460.D56V6 Vne rasscheta (Tale). Вне рассчета

Russian literature
Individual authors and works, 1870-1917
Individual authors, Chekhov, Anton - Gorky -- Continued

3460.D57 Dmitriev, Andreĭ Mikhaĭlovich, d. 1886. Андрей Михайлович Дмитриев (Table P-PZ40 modified)
3460.D57A61-.D57Z458 Separate works. By title
3460.D57E3 Edinstvennai͡a (Comedy). Единственная
3460.D57G4 Geroi birzhi (Comedy). Герои биржи
3460.D57G6 Gospodin Lovelas (Story). Господин Ловелас
3460.D57O8 Ot nechego delat′ (Tales). От нечего делать
3460.D57P3 Padshai͡a (Story). Падшая
3460.D57R3 Raskol′niki i ostrozhniki (Tragedy). Раскольники и острожники
3460.D57R8 Russkai͡a Nana (Novel). Русская Нана
3460.D57S2 S pozvolenii͡a skazat′ (Tale). С позволения сказать
3460.D57V2 V dorogu ... ot skuki. В дорогу ... от скуки
3460.D57V6 Voĭna i mir (Drama). Война и мир
3460.D58 Dmitriev, Dmitriĭ Savvateevich, 1848-1905. Дмитрий Савватеевич Дмитриев (Table P-PZ40 modified)
3460.D58A61-.D58Z458 Separate works. By title
3460.D58A8 Avanti͡uristka (Novel). Авантюристка
3460.D58C5 Chudo-bogatyr′ (Novel). Чудо-богатырь
3460.D58D8 Dva imperatora (Novel). Два императора
3460.D58K3 Kavalerist-devit͡sa. Кавалерист-девица
3460.D58R8 Russkie orly (Story). Русские орлы
3460.D58S3 Samosozhigateli, ili, Za starui͡u veru (Story). Самосожигатели, или, За старую веру
3460.D58V2 V proshlom veke (Story). В прошлом веке
3460.D58Z3 Zachalo Moskvy i boi͡arin Kuchka (Novel). Зачало Москвы и боярин Кучка
3460.D59 Dmitriev, Vasiliĭ Akimovich, fl. 1880-1900. Василий Акимович Дмитриев (Table P-PZ40)
3460.D6 Dmitrieva, Valentina Iovovna, 1859-1948. Валентина Иововна Дмитриева (Table P-PZ40 modified)
3460.D6A61-.D6Z458 Separate works. By title
3460.D6A75 Akhmetkina zhena (Tale). Ахметкина жена
3460.D6A8 Amerikant͡sy (Tale). Американцы
3460.D6B2 Baba-Ivan i ee krestnik (Tale). Баба-Иван и ее крестник
3460.D6B3 Baklan (Tale). Баклан
Published also under the titles: Van′ka; Van′ka-Baklan
3460.D6B4 Belye kryl′i͡a (Tale). Белые крылья
3460.D6B45 Bez Boga zhivogo. Без Бога живого
3460.D6B5 Blizhnie (Tale). Ближние

Russian literature
Individual authors and works, 1870-1917
Individual authors, Chekhov, Anton - Gorky
Dmitrieva, Valentina Iovovna, 1859-1948. Валентина Иововна Дмитриева
Separate works. By title -- Continued

3460.D6B6 Bol′nichnyĭ storozh Khves′ka. Больничный сторож Хвеська
3460.D6B8 Burmistersha (Drama). Бурмистерша
3460.D6C4 Cherez stenu (Tale). Через стену
3460.D6C5 Chervonnyĭ khutor (Novel). Червонный хутор
3460.D6D4 Derevenskie rasskazy. Деревенские рассказы
3460.D6D5 Dimka (Tale). Димка
3460.D6D6 Dobrovolet͡s (Tale). Доброволец
3460.D6D65 Dosvitki (Tale). Досвитки
3460.D6D7 Drug Ksanto (Tale). Друг Ксанто
3460.D6D8 Druz′i͡a detstva (Tale). Друзья детства
3460.D6E4 Eё vse zna͡iut (Tale). Её все знают
3460.D6G6 Gomochka (Story). Гомочка
3460.D6G7 Gorit Rossii͡a (Tale). Горит Россия
3460.D6I7 Iskatel′ krasoty (Tale). Искатель красоты
3460.D6K3 Kak Fili͡ushka v gorode pobyval (Tale). Как Филюшка в городе побывал
3460.D6K4 Kaska (Tale). Каска
3460.D6K7 Krupinka po krupinke (Tale). Крупинка по крупинке
Lipochka-popovna. Липочка-поповна see PG3460.D6M55
3460.D6L5 List′i͡a pada͡iut (Tale). Листья падают
3460.D6L6 L͡iudoedy (Tale). Людоеды
Luga. Луга see PG3460.D6P3
3460.D6M3 Maĭna-vira (Tale). Майна-вира
3460.D6M35 Mama na voĭne (Tale). Мама на войне
Marfutka. Марфутка see PG3460.D6O5
3460.D6M37 Mar′ina berezka (Tale). Марьина березка
3460.D6M4 Mechta (Tale). Мечта
3460.D6M5 Mit͡iukha-uchitel′ (Tale). Митюха-учитель
3460.D6M55 Moloda͡ia zhizn′. Молодая жизнь
Also published with title: Lipochka-popovna
3460.D6M6 Molodn͡iak (Tale). Молодняк
3460.D6M7 M-r Teodor i M-lle Zh͡iul′eta (Tale). M-r Теодор и M-lle Жюльета
3460.D6N3 Na skale (Tale). На скале
3460.D6N4 Ne nasto͡iashchiĭ chelovek (Tale). Не настоящий человек
3460.D6N45 Ne po pravde (Story). Не по правде
3460.D6N5 Neizlechimyĭ (Tale). Неизлечимый
3460.D6N6 Noch′ v Kuchuk-Uzeni (Tale). Ночь в Кучук-Узени

Russian literature
Individual authors and works, 1870-1917
Individual authors, Chekhov, Anton - Gorky
Dmitrieva, Valentina Iovovna, 1859-1948. Валентина Иововна Дмитриева
Separate works. By title -- Continued

3460.D6O5 Ona ne pervai͡a (Tale). Она не первая
Also published under the title: Marfutka
3460.D6O8 Ot sovesti (Tale). От совести
3460.D6P25 Pavil′on amura (Tale). Павильон амура
3460.D6P3 Pchely zhuzhzhat (Tale). Пчелы жужжат
Also published under the titles: Luga; Sarafanovt͡sy
3460.D6P4 Pered lit͡som smerti (Tale). Перед лицом смерти
3460.D6P6 Po derevni͡am. По деревням
3460.D6P63 Po dushe, da ne po razumu (Drama). По душе, да не по разуму
3460.D6P65 Pod solnt͡sem i͡uga (Tale). Под солнцем юга
3460.D6P68 Po-volch′i (Tale). По-волчьи
3460.D6P7 Progulka (Tale). Прогулка
3460.D6R3 Razboĭniki (Tale). Разбойники
Sarafanovt͡sy. Сарафановцы see PG3460.D6P3
3460.D6S5 Smert′ zheny (Tale). Смерть жены
3460.D6S6 Solovushki (Tale). Соловушки
3460.D6S8 Sukhari (Tale). Сухари
3460.D6S9 Svoim sudom (Tale). Своим судом
3460.D6T5 Ti͡ur′ma (Story). Тюрьма
3460.D6T7 T͡Sarstvie nebesnoe (Tale). Царствие небесное
3460.D6T8 Tuchki (Tale). Тучки
3460.D6U2 "Ubivet͡s" (Tale). "Убивец"
3460.D6V27 V raznye storony (Tale). В разные стороны
3460.D6V28 V tikhom omute (Story). В тихом омуте
3460.D6V29 V zai͡ach′em vagone (Tale). В заячьем вагоне
Van′ka. Ванька see PG3460.D6B3
3460.D6V4 Vesennie illi͡uzii (Story). Весенние иллюзии
3460.D6V6 Volki (Tale). Волки
3460.D6V7 Vse li͡udi brat′i͡a (Tale). Все люди братья
3460.D6V8 Vybory (Tale). Выборы
3460.D6V9 "Vzyskui͡ushchiĭ grada" (Tale). "Взыскующий града"
3460.D6Z2 Za veru, t͡sari͡a i otechestvo (Tale). За веру, царя и отечество
3460.D6Z4 Zlai͡a voli͡a (Story). Злая воля
Dneprovskiĭ, A. A. Днепровский see PG3451.A55
3460.D615 Dobri͡anskiĭ, L.V., fl 1890-1900. Л.В. Добрянский (Table P-PZ40)
3460.D617 Dobroli͡ubov, Aleksandr Mikhaĭlovich, 1876-1944? Александр Михайлович Добролюбов (Table P-PZ40)

Russian literature
Individual authors and works, 1870-1917
Individual authors, Chekhov, Anton - Gorky -- Continued

3460.D62 Dobronravov, N.E., fl. 1890-1910. Н.Е. Добронравов (Table P-PZ40 modified)

3460.D62A61-.D62Z458 Separate works. By title

3460.D62B4 Bez deneg gore, pri den′gakh - vdvoe (Story). Без денег горе, при деньгах - вдвое

3460.D62C5 Chernoknizhnik (Tale). Чернокнижник

3460.D62D55 Doch′ palacha (Story). Дочь палача

3460.D62D6 Doktor Stas′ (Tale). Доктор Стась

3460.D62K5 Khristova zapoved′ (Tale). Христова заповедь

3460.D62K6 Koromyslova bashni͡a (Story). Коромыслова башня

3460.D62K7 Krasavit͡sa s togo sveta (Story). Красавица с того света

3460.D62K8 Kuplennyĭ vystrel (Novel). Купленный выстрел

3460.D62M3 Malen′kiĭ oslik (Tale). Маленький ослик

3460.D62M8 Muzheubiĭt͡sa (Story). Мужеубийца

3460.D62N3 Na zare khristianstva (Story). На заре христианства

3460.D62P4 Pervai͡a li͡ubov′ aktera (Story). Первая любовь актера

3460.D62P5 Pervai͡a noch′ novobrachnogo (Novel). Первая ночь новобрачного

3460.D62R8 Ruka krasavit͡sy otechestvo spasla (Story). Рука красавицы отечество спасла

3460.D62S3 Savraskina doli͡a (Story). Савраскина доля

3460.D62S4 Sem′ adskikh pul′, ili, Volshebnyĭ strelok (Tale). Семь адских пуль, или, Волшебный стрелок

3460.D62S9 Syn d′i͡avola, ili, Smertel′nai͡a vetv′ (Tale). Сын дьявола, или, Смертельная ветвь

3460.D62U9 Uzhasy razvrata (Tale). Ужасы разврата

3460.D62V2 V glukhui͡u noch′ (Tale). В глухую ночь

3460.D62V27 V sumasshedshem dome (Sketch). В сумасшедшем доме

3460.D62Z2 Zakoldovannyĭ klad (Story). Заколдованный клад

3460.D62Z4 Zvezdochka (Tale). Звездочка

3460.D625 Dobrotvorskiĭ, Leonid Fedorovich, 1856- . Леонид Федорович Добротворский (Table P-PZ40)

3460.D63 Dobrotvorskiĭ, Petr Ivanovich, 1839-1908. Петр Иванович Добротворский (Table P-PZ40 modified)

3460.D63A61-.D63Z458 Separate works. By title

3460.D63A8 Anna Vasil′evna (Tale). Анна Васильевна

3460.D63B3 Babushka Olena (Tale). Бабушка Олена

3460.D63B6 Bol′shak (Tale). Большак

3460.D63B7 Bozh′e dite (Tale). Божье дите

Russian literature
Individual authors and works, 1870-1917
Individual authors, Chekhov, Anton - Gorky
Dobrotvorskiĭ, Petr Ivanovich, 1839-1908. Петр Иванович Добротворский
Separate works. By title -- Continued

3460.D63B8 Budnichnoe schast′e (Tale). Будничное счастье
3460.D63D4 Devich′i͡a doli͡a (Sketch). Девичья доля
3460.D63D6 Doktor chistoĭ matematiki (Tale). Доктор чистой математики
3460.D63I8 I͡Ukhnovskie zemlekopy (Sketch). Юхновские землекопы
3460.D63M3 Marfa Il′inishna Ri͡abinova (Sketch). Марфа Ильинишна Рябинова
3460.D63P7 Prosta͡ia dusha (Tale). Простая душа
3460.D63S4 Senatorska͡ia revizi͡ia (Sketches). Сенаторская ревизия
3460.D63S6 Smert′ deda (Sketch). Смерть деда
3460.D63T4 Teti͡a Nata (Tale). Тетя Ната
3460.D63T5 Tishka Kochergin (Sketch). Тишка Кочергин
3460.D63V2 V glushi Bashkirii (Tale). В глуши Башкирии
3460.D634 Dobrovo, Mikhail, fl. 1880-1890. Михаил Доброво (Table P-PZ40)

Dobryĭ, Roman, 1876-1913. Роман Добрый see PG3453.A653

3460.D635 Dobryshin, Boris Vasil′evich, fl. 1880-1890. Борис Васильевич Добрышин (Table P-PZ40)
3460.D64 Doganovich, Anna Nikitishna, fl. 1885-1910. Анна Никитишна Доганович (Table P-PZ40 modified)
3460.D64A61-.D64Z458 Separate works. By title
3460.D64D5 Ded Ignat (Tale). Дед Игнат
3460.D64L5 Li͡ubov′ pobedila. Любовь победила
3460.D64P3 Pchelinyĭ domik (Story). Пчелиный домик
3460.D64P4 Pechal′nik zemli russkoĭ (Tale). Печальник земли русской
3460.D64P5 Pesenka ma͡iatinka (Tale). Песенка маятинка
3460.D64S4 Serye geroi (Tale). Серые герои
3460.D64S6 Soldat Li͡uba (Story). Солдат Люба
3460.D64U3 Ugolovnyĭ zashchitnik (Tale). Уголовный защитник

Dolgina, S. C. Долгина see PG3467.M92

3460.D65 Dolgint͡sev, Vasiliĭ, fl. 1890-1900. Василий Долгинцев
3460.D66 Dolgorukov, Vsevolod Alekseevich, d. 1912. Всеволод Алексеевич Долгоруков
3460.D665 Dolgunov, Mikhail S., fl. 1890-1900. Михаил С. Долгунов

Russian literature
Individual authors and works, 1870-1917
Individual authors, Chekhov, Anton - Gorky -- Continued

3460.D667 Dombrovskiĭ, Frant͡s Vikentʹevich, 1857-1909. Франц Викентьевич Домбровский

Domino, pseud. Домино see PG3470.V85

3460.D67 Doroshevich, Vlas Mikhaĭlovich, 1864-1922. Влас Михайлович Дорошевич

3460.D675 Dovgi͡allo, Vladislav Aleksandrovich, d. 1898. Владислав Александрович Довгялло (Table P-PZ40)

3460.D68 Drentelʹn, Vladimir I͡Urʹevich, fl. 1880-1890. Владимир Юрьевич Дрентельн (Table P-PZ40)

3460.D685 Dreving, Aleksandra, fl. 1890-1900. Александра Древинг (Table P-PZ40)

3460.D69 Dri͡akhlov, Vasiliĭ I͡Akovlevich, 1863- . Василий Яковлевич Дряхлов (Table P-PZ40)

3460.D7 Drozhzhin, Spiridon Dmitrievich, 1848-1930. Спиридон Дмитриевич Дрожжин (Table P-PZ40 modified)

3460.D7A61-.D7Z458 Separate works. By title

3460.D7B3 Bai͡an (Poems). Баян

3460.D7I9 Iz mraka k svetu. Из мрака к свету

3460.D7N6 Novye russkie pesni. Новые русские песни

3460.D7P4 Pesni krestʹi͡anina. Песни крестьянина

3460.D7P43 Pesni rabochikh. Песни рабочих

3460.D7P45 Pesni starogo pakhari͡a. Песни старого пахаря

3460.D7P47 Pesni truda i svobody. Песни труда и свободы

3460.D7R6 Rodnai͡a derevni͡a (Poem). Родная деревня

3460.D7S5 Skazki, legendy i byli. Сказки, легенды и были

3460.D7Z3 Zavetnye pesni. Заветные песни

Druzhinina, Nina Pavlovna. Нина Павловна Дружинина see PG3453.A58

Dubelʹt, Elena Aleksandrovna. Елена Александровна Дубельт see PG3470.Z37

3460.D77 Dubov. Дубов (Table P-PZ40)

3460.D79 Dubrovin, Nikolaĭ Fedorovich, 1837-1904. Николай Федорович Дубровин (Table P-PZ40)

3460.D8 Dubrovina, Ekaterina Oskarovna (Deĭkhman), 1840-1913. Екатерина Оскаровна (Дейхман) Дубровина (Table P-PZ40 modified)

3460.D8A61-.D8Z458 Separate works. By title

3460.D8B4 Beskrovnai͡a mestʹ (Novel). Бескровная месть

3460.D8C4 Chem zhitʹ (Story). Чем жить

3460.D8C5 Cherez dvadt͡satʹ let (Novel). Через двадцать лет

3460.D8I9 Iz tʹmy vekov (Novel). Из тьмы веков

3460.D8M4 Mertvet͡sy-mstiteli (Novel). Мертвецы-мстители

3460.D8N3 Na i͡akore (Story). На якоре

3460.D8O6 Opalʹnyĭ (Novel). Опальный

Russian literature
Individual authors and works, 1870-1917
Individual authors, Chekhov, Anton - Gorky
Dubrovina, Ekaterina Oskarovna (Deĭkhman), 1840-1913. Екатерина Оскаровна (Дейхман) Дубровина
Separate works. By title -- Continued

3460.D8O7 Opomnilas′ (Story). Опомнилась
3460.D8P4 Peterburgskai͡a l′vit͡sa (Story). Петербургская львица
3460.D8P5 Pobeda li͡ubvi (Novel). Победа любви
3460.D8P6 Pod kashtanami (Story). Под каштанами
3460.D8P65 Pod natiskom strasti (Novel). Под натиском страсти
3460.D8P7 Pristroilas′ (Story). Пристроилась
3460.D8R8 Rukhnuvshiĭ velikan (Novel). Рухнувший великан
3460.D8S4 Sfinks (Novel). Сфинкс
3460.D8S5 Sila dolga (Novel). Сила долга
3460.D8S6 Sovremennai͡a T͡Sirt͡sei͡a (Story). Современная Цирцея
3460.D8V2 V nochlezhnom prii͡ute (Tale). В ночлежном приюте
3460.D8V25 V tumane zhizni (Novel). В тумане жизни
3460.D8Z2 Zakorenelyĭ (Tale). Закоренелый
3460.D8Z3 Zasluzhennai͡a kara (Novel). Заслуженная кара
3460.D8Z4 Zhertva trekh chestoli͡ubiĭ (Novel). Жертва трех честолюбий

Dukh, pseud. . Дух see PG3453.B98

3460.D83 Dukhovet͡skiĭ, Fedor A., fl. 1890-1900. Федор А. Духовецкий (Table P-PZ40)

3460.D84 Dukhovskai͡a, Varvara Fedorovna (Golit͡syna), 1854- . Варвара Федоровна (Голицына) Духовская (Table P-PZ40)
For her diary see DK188.6

3460.D86 Dunin, Vasiliĭ, fl. 1900-1910. Василий Дунин (Table P-PZ40)

3460.D88 Dvorzhit͡skiĭ, Korneliĭ Adrianovich, 1862- . Корнелий Адрианович Дворжицкий (Table P-PZ40)

3460.D9 Dymow, Ossip, 1878-1959. Осип Дымов (Table P-PZ40 modified)
For his Yiddish works see PJ5129

3460.D9A61-.D9Z458 Separate works. By title
3460.D9B4 Begushchie kresta (Novel). Бегущие креста
3460.D9B8 Buntovshchiki (Tale). Бунтовщики
3460.D9G6 Golos krovi (Drama). Голос крови
3460.D9K3 Kain (Drama). Каин
3460.D9N5 Ni͡u (Tragedy). Ню
3460.D9P5 Pogrom (Tale). Погром
3460.D9P6 Poslednīai͡a li͡ubov′ (Comedy). Последняя любовь

Russian literature
Individual authors and works, 1870-1917
Individual authors, Chekhov, Anton - Gorky
Dymow, Ossip, 1878-1959. Осип Дымов
Separate works. By title -- Continued

3460.D9P7 Prestuplenie protiv nravstvennosti (Tragicomedy). Преступление против нравственности
3460.D9P8 Puti li͡ubvi (Drama). Пути любви
3460.D9S5 Slushaĭ, Izrailʹ! (Drama). Слушай, Израиль!
3460.D9S6 Solnt͡sevorot (Tales). Солнцеворот
3460.D9V4 Vechnyĭ strannik (Drama). Вечный странник
3460.D9V5 Veselai͡a pechalʹ (Tales). Веселая печаль
3460.D9Z4 Zemli͡a t͡svetet (Tales). Земля цветет
3460.D95 Dzhanshiev, Grigoriĭ Avetovich, 1851-1900. Григорий Аветович Джаншиев (Table P-PZ40)
3460.E3 Ėfendi, V.D., fl. 1890-1900. В.Д. Эфенди (Table P-PZ40)
Efimov, A. A. Ефимов see PG3470.Z3
Ėfron, Saveliĭ Konstantinovich. Савелий Константинович Эфрон see PG3467.L535
3460.E35 Egorov, I͡Akov Egorovich, d. 1902. Яков Егорович Егоров (Table P-PZ40)
3460.E37 Ėĭnerling, Glafira Adolʹfovna, 1873-1942. Глафира Адольфовна Эйнерлинг (Table P-PZ40)
Eismann, David see PG3451.A4
Ėk, Ekaterina. Екатерина Эк see PG3467.K83
Elagin, I͡U. Ю. Елагин see PG3467.G35
3460.E4 Eleneva, Serafima Aleksandrovna, fl. 1890-1900. Серафима Александровна Еленева (Table P-PZ40)
Eleonskiĭ, S. C. Елеонский see PG3467.M68
3460.E45 Elet͡s, I͡Uliĭ Lukʹi͡anovich, b. 1862. Юлий Лукьянович Елец (Table P-PZ40)
3460.E453 Ėllis, 1874-1947. Эллис (Table P-PZ40)
3460.E456 Elizarov, Nik. (Nikolaĭ). Николай Елизаров (Table P-PZ40)
3460.E47 Elpatʹevskiĭ, Sergeĭ I͡Akovlevich, 1854-1933. Сергей Яковлевич Елпатьевский (Table P-PZ40)
3460.E48 Ėlʹsner, Anatoliĭ Ottovich. Анатолій Оттовичъ Эльснеръ (Table P-PZ40)
Elʹt͡sova, K. K. Ельцова see PG3467.L59
3460.E5 Emelʹi͡anov-Kokhanskiĭ, Aleksandr Nikolaevich, fl. 1890-1910. Александр Николаевич Емельянов-Коханский (Table P-PZ40)
Ėmze, pseud. Эмзе see PG3470.Z65
3460.E55 Ėngelʹgardt, Nikolaĭ Aleksandrovich, 1866- . Николай Александрович Энгельгардт (Table P-PZ40)

Russian literature
Individual authors and works, 1870-1917
Individual authors, Chekhov, Anton - Gorky -- Continued

3460.E57 Ėngel′meĭer, Aleksandr Klimentovich, 1854- . Александр Климентович Энгельмейер (Table P-PZ40)

Ėnpe, pseud. Энпе see PG3470.P616

3460.E58 Ėnve, graf fon. Граф фон Энве (Table P-PZ40)

3460.E6 Epifanov, S.A., fl. 1900-1910. С.А. Епифанов (Table P-PZ40)

Ėr, A., pseud. А. Эр see PG3460.E72

3460.E7 Eremeev, Nikolaĭ Grigor′evich, 1877- . Николай Григорьевич Еремеев (Table P-PZ40)

3460.E72 Eroshkin, Aleksandr Petrovich, d. 1897. Александр Петрович Ерошкин (Table P-PZ40)

3460.E73 Ershov, M.I., fl. 1870-1880. М.И. Ершов (Table P-PZ40)

3460.E74 Ėrtel, Aleksandr Ivanovich, 1855-1908. Александр Иванович Эртел (Table P-PZ40)

3460.E75 Estifeeva, M.P., fl. 1880-1910. М.П. Естифеева (Table P-PZ40)

3460.E8 Ėval′d, Arkadiĭ Vasil′evich, 1836-1898. Аркадий Васильевич Эвальд (Table P-PZ40)

3460.E85 Evreinov, P.A., fl. 1890-1900. П.А. Евреинов (Table P-PZ40)

3460.E86 Evropeus, Aleksandra Konstantinovna, d. 1895. Александра Константиновна Европеус (Table P-PZ40)

3460.E87 Evstigneev, Misha, fl. 1870-1900. Миша Евстигнеев

3460.E9 Ezhov, Nikolaĭ Mikhaĭlovich, 1862-1941. Николай Михайлович Ежов (Table P-PZ40)

Ėzop, pseud. Эзоп see PG3467.M35

3460.F18 Fal′kevich, M.N. М.Н. Фалькевич (Table P-PZ40)

3460.F2 Fal′kovskiĭ, Fedor Nikolaevich, b. 1874. Федор Николаевич Фальковский (Table P-PZ40)

3460.F3 Faresov, Anatoliĭ Ivanovich, 1852- . Анатолий Иванович Фаресов (Table P-PZ40)

3460.F35 Fausek, Vi͡acheslav Andreevich, fl. 1890-1900. Вячеслав Андреевич Фаусек (Table P-PZ40)

3460.F4 Fedorenko, V.K., fl. 1890-1900. В.К. Федоренко (Table P-PZ40)

3460.F417 Fedorov, Aleksandr. Александр Федоров (Table P-PZ40)

3460.F42 Fedorov, Aleksandr Mitrofanovich, 1868-1949. Александр Митрофанович Федоров (Table P-PZ40)

3460.F44 Fedorov, Innokentiĭ Vasil′evich, 1836-1883. Иннокентий Васильевич Федоров (Table P-PZ40)

3460.F447 Fedorov, M., 1839-1900. М. Федоров (Table P-PZ40)

Russian literature
Individual authors and works, 1870-1917
Individual authors, Chekhov, Anton - Gorky -- Continued
Fedorov-Omulevskiĭ, Innokentiĭ Vasil′evich. Иннокентий Васильевич Федоров-Омулевский see PG3460.F44
3460.F46 Fedorovich, Vladislav Ivanovich, 1845- . Владислав Иванович Федорович (Table P-PZ40)
Fedoseevet͡s, pseud. Федосеевец see PG3451.A25
3460.F47 Fedosova, Irina Andreevna, 1831-1899. Ирина Андреевна Федосова (Table P-PZ40)
3460.F48 Fedotov, Aleksandr Filippovich, 1841-1895. Александр Филиппович Федотов (Table P-PZ40)
3460.F49 Figner, Vera Nikolaevna, 1852-1942. Вера Николаевна Фигнер (Table P-PZ40)
3460.F5 Filimonov, Fedor Fedorovich, 1862-1886. Федор Федорович Филимонов (Table P-PZ40)
3460.F52 Filippov, Mikhail Avraamovich, 1828-1886. Михаил Авраамович Филиппов (Table P-PZ40)
3460.F54 Filippov, Mikhail Mikhaĭlovich, 1858-1903. Михаил Михайлович Филиппов (Table P-PZ40)
3460.F58 Filippov, Sergeĭ Nikitich, 1863-1911. Сергей Никитич Филиппов (Table P-PZ40)
Firsov, V., pseud. В. Фирсов see PG3460.F75
3460.F6 Flekser, Akim L′vovich, 1863-1926. Аким Львович Флексер (Table P-PZ40)
For Flekser as literary critic see PG2947.F5
3460.F7 Fofanov, Konstantin Mikhaĭlovich, 1862-1911. Константин Михайлович Фофанов (Table P-PZ40)
3460.F75 Forselles, Viktor Ėduardovich, fl. 1890-1900. Виктор Эдуардович Форселлес (Table P-PZ40)
3460.F8 Frug, Semen Grigor′evich, 1860-1916. Семен Григорьевич Фруг (Table P-PZ40)
3460.G2 Gabrilovich, G.S., fl. 1880-1890. Г.С. Габрилович (Table P-PZ40)
3460.G213 Gadmer, Elizaveta. Елизавета Гадмер (Table P-PZ40)
3460.G22 Gaĭdeburov, Pavel Aleksandrovich, 1841-1893. Павел Александрович Гайдебуров (Table P-PZ40)
3460.G23 Galibin, A.N., fl. 1880-1900. А.Н. Галибин (Table P-PZ40)
3460.G24 Galin, Petr Nikolaevich, ca. 1836-1908. Петр Николаевич Галин (Table P-PZ40)
Galina, G. Г. Галина see PG3460.E37
3460.G25 Galkin, Alfeĭ Kronidovich, 1858-1896. Алфей Кронидович Галкин (Table P-PZ40)
Galkin, I., baron, pseud. Барон И. Галкин see PG3460.D57
Gamma, pseud. Гамма see PG3467.G43

Russian literature
Individual authors and works, 1870-1917
Individual authors, Chekhov, Anton - Gorky -- Continued
Gan, Vera Petrovna. Вера Петровна Ган see PG3470.Z44
3460.G27 Ganeĭzer, Evgeniĭ Adol′fovich, 1861- Евгений Адольфович Ганейзер (Table P-PZ40)
3460.G29 Garfil′d, Sergeĭ Aleksandrovich, 1873- . Сергей Александрович Гарфильд (Table P-PZ40)
Garin, N.G. Н.Г. Гарин see PG3467.M48
Garin, Sergeĭ. Сергей Гарин see PG3460.G29
3460.G3 Garshin, Vsevolod Mikhaĭlovich, 1855-1888. Всеволод Михайлович Гаршин (Table P-PZ40 modified)
3460.G3A61-.G3Z458 Separate works. By title
3460.G3A7 A͡iasl͡iarskoe delo (Story). Аяслярское дело
Published also under the title: Boevye kartinki
3460.G3A8 Attalea princeps (Fairy tale)
Published also under the titles: Brazil′ska͡ia pal′ma; Gorda͡ia pal′ma
Boevye kartinki. Боевые картинки see PG3460.G3A7
Brazil′ska͡ia pal′ma. Бразильская пальма see PG3460.G3A8
3460.G3C5 Chetyre dn͡ia (Tale). Четыре дня
3460.G3D4 Denshchik i ofit͡ser (Tale). Денщик и офицер
Published also under the title: L͡iudi i voĭna
Gorda͡ia pal′ma. Гордая пальма see PG3460.G3A8
3460.G3I9 Iz vospominaniĭ r͡iadovogo Ivanova (Tale). Из воспоминаний рядового Иванова
Published also under the title: Iz zapisok r͡iadovogo Ivanova o pokhode 1877 goda (Из записок рядового Иванова о походе 1877 года)
Iz zapisok r͡iadovogo Ivanova. Из записок рядового Иванова see PG3460.G3I9
3460.G3K5 Khudozhniki (Tale). Художники
3460.G3K6 Koroten′kiĭ roman (Tale). Коротенький роман
3460.G3K7 Krasnyĭ t͡svetok (Tale). Красный цветок
3460.G3L5 L͡iagushka puteshestvennit͡sa (Tale). Лягушка путешественница
L͡iudi i voĭna. Люди и война see PG3460.G3D4
3460.G3M4 Medvedi (Tale). Медведи
3460.G3N3 Nadezhda Nikolaevna (Story). Надежда Николаевна
3460.G3N6 Noch′ (Tale). Ночь
3460.G3O3 Ochen′ koroten′kiĭ roman (Tale). Очень коротенький роман
3460.G3P7 Proisshestvie (Tale). Происшествие
3460.G3S5 Signal (Tale). Сигнал

Russian literature
Individual authors and works, 1870-1917
Individual authors, Chekhov, Anton - Gorky
Garshin, Vsevolod Mikhaĭlovich, 1855-1888. Всеволод Михайлович Гаршин
Separate works. By title -- Continued

3460.G3S6 Skazanie o gordom Aggee (Tale). Сказание о гордом Аггее
3460.G3T6 To, chego ne bylo (Tale). То, чего не было
3460.G3T7 Trus (Tale). Трус
3460.G3V7 Vstrecha (Tale, fragment). Встреча
3460.G313 Gatovskiĭ, S.O. . С.О. Гатовскiй (Table P-PZ40)
3460.G32 Ge, Grigoriĭ Grigor′evich, 1867- . Григорий Григорьевич Ге (Table P-PZ40)
3460.G33 Ge, Ivan Nikolaevich, 1841-1893. Иван Николаевич Ге (Table P-PZ40)
3460.G35 Gegidze, Boris Mikhaĭlovich, fl. 1890-1900. Борис Михайлович Гегидзе (Table P-PZ40)
3460.G37 Gegidze, Mikhail Egorovich, fl. 1890-1900. Михаил Егорович Гегидзе (Table P-PZ40)
3460.G4 Geĭnt͡se, Nikolaĭ Ėduardovich, 1852-1913. Николай Эдуардович Гейнце (Table P-PZ40)
Gel′man, Lev Grigor′evich. Лев Григорьевич Гельман see PG3470.Z43
3460.G42 Gemmel′man, S. C. Геммельман (Table P-PZ40)
Gendre, Nikolaĭ Pavlovich. Николай Павлович Гендре see PG3331.G35
3460.G43 Genigin, Ivan F., fl. 1900-1915. Иван Ф. Генигин (Table P-PZ40)
Georgievich, N. H. Георгиевич see PG3470.S48
3460.G44 Gerasimenko, Petr Pavlovich, d. 1904. Петр Павлович Герасименко (Table P-PZ40)
3460.G45 Gerbanovskiĭ, Mikhail Mitrofanovich, fl. 1890-1910. Михаил Митрофанович Гербановский (Table P-PZ40)
Gerra, Konstantin. Константин Герра see PG3467.M366
Gershau, Marii͡a Karlovna. Мария Карловна Гершау see PG3470.V22
3460.G462 Gert͡syk, Adelaida, 1874-1925. Аделаида Герцык (Table P-PZ40)
3460.G464 Getling, Nikolaĭ. Николай Гетлинг (Table P-PZ40)
3460.G47 Gili͡arovskiĭ, Vladimir Alekseevich, 1855- . Владимир Алексеевич Гиляровский (Table P-PZ40)
3460.G49 Gippius, Vladimir Vasil′evich, 1876- . Владимир Васильевич Гиппиус (Table P-PZ40)
Gippius, Zinaida Nikolaevna, 1869-1945. Зинаида Николаевна Гиппиус

Russian literature
Individual authors and works, 1870-1917
Individual authors, Chekhov, Anton - Gorky
Gippius, Zinaida Nikolaevna, 1869-1945. Зинаида Николаевна Гиппиус -- Continued

3460.G5	Collected works By date
3460.G5A15	Collected novels and tales. By date Other than those of distinctive title, compiled by the author
3460.G5A16	Collected essays, miscellanies, etc. By date
3460.G5A17	Collected poems. By date
3460.G5A19	Collected plays. By date
	Translations (Collected or selected)
3460.G5A2-.G5A29	English. By translator, if given, or date
3460.G5A3-.G5A39	French. By translator, if given, or date
3460.G5A4-.G5A49	German. By translator, if given, or date
3460.G5A5-.G5A59	Other. By language
3460.G5A6	Selected works. Selections. By date
3460.G5A61-.G5Z458	Separate works. By title
3460.G5A8	Alyĭ mech (Tales). Алый меч
3460.G5B3	Ballada. Баллада
3460.G5B4	Bez talismana (Novel). Без талисмана
3460.G5B5	Blizhe k prirode (Sketch). Ближе к природе
3460.G5B6	Bogini͡a (Tale). Богиня
3460.G5C4	Chernoe po belomu (Tales). Черное по белому
3460.G5C5	Chortova kukla (Novel). Чортова кукла
3460.G5D8	Dva serd͡tsa (Tale). Два сердца
3460.G5K6	Kostino mshchenie (Sketch). Костино мщение
	Literaturnyĭ dnevnik, 1899-1907. Литературный дневник, 1899-1907 see PG3460.G5Z52
3460.G5L5	Li͡udi brat'i͡a (Tale). Люди братья
3460.G5L8	Lunnye murav'i (Tales). Лунные муравьи
3460.G5M3	Makov t͡svet (Drama). Маков цвет
3460.G5M5	Miss Maĭ (Tale). Мисс Май
3460.G5N3	Nebesnye slova i drugie rasskazy. Небесные слова и другие рассказы
3460.G5N4	Nenadolgo (Sketch). Ненадолго
3460.G5N5	Nepri͡iatnoe vospominanie (Tale). Неприятное воспоминание
3460.G5N65	Novye li͡udi (Tales). Новые люди
3460.G5O3	Odinokiĭ (Study). Одинокий
3460.G5R6	Roman-t͡sarevich (Novel). Роман-царевич
3460.G5S5	Si͡iani͡ia (Poems). Сияния
3460.G5S6	Slova ... Slova ... (Tale). Слова ... Слова ...
3460.G5S7	Sredi mertvykh (Tale). Среди мертвых
3460.G5S8	Sumerki dukha (Tale). Сумерки духа
3460.G5S98	Svi͡atai͡a plot' (Tale). Святая плоть

Russian literature
Individual authors and works, 1870-1917
Individual authors, Chekhov, Anton - Gorky
Gippius, Zinaida Nikolaevna, 1869-1945. Зинаида Николаевна Гиппиус
Separate works. By title -- Continued

3460.G5T4 Tet͡ia Liza (Tale). Тетя Лиза
3460.G5V2 V gostinoĭ i li͡udskoĭ (Tale). В гостиной и людской
3460.G5V25 V Moskve (Tale). В Москве
3460.G5V28 V rodnui͡u sem′i͡u (Sketch). В родную семью
3460.G5Z2 Zelenoe kol′t͡so (Drama). Зеленое кольцо
3460.G5Z25 Zerkala (Tales). Зеркала
3460.G5Z3 Zlatot͡svet (Story). Златоцвет
3460.G5Z35 Zloschastnai͡a (Tale). Злосчастная

Biography and criticism
3460.G5Z5 Diaries. Journals
3460.G5Z52 Literaturnyĭ dnevnik, 1899-1907. Литературный дневник, 1899-1907
3460.G5Z53 Sini͡ai͡a kniga; peterburgskiĭ dnevnik, 1914-1918. Синяя книга : петербургский дневник, 1914-1918

Letters
3460.G5Z54 Collected. By date
3460.G5Z55-.G5Z59 Individual correspondents (alphabetically)
3460.G5Z6-.G5Z99 General treatises. Life and works

3460.G52 Girs, Dmitriĭ Konstantinovich, 1836-1886. Дмитрий Константинович Гирс (Table P-PZ40)

Glagol′, S. C. Глаголь see PG3467.G93

3460.G53 Glazunov, Vasiliĭ, fl. 1890-1900. Василий Глазунов (Table P-PZ40)

3460.G54 Glebov, Modest V., fl. 1890-1910. Модест В. Глебов (Table P-PZ40)

3460.G55 Glukharev, Nikolaĭ Polikarpovich, 1869- . Николай Поликарпович Глухарев (Table P-PZ40)

3460.G56 Gmyrev, Alekseĭ Mikhaĭlovich, 1887-1911. Алексей Михайлович Гмырев (Table P-PZ40)

3460.G57 Gnedich, Petr Petrovich, 1855-1927. Петр Петрович Гнедич (Table P-PZ40)

3460.G58 Gofman, Viktor Viktorovich, 1884-1911. Виктор Викторович Гофман (Table P-PZ40)

Gol′debaev, pseud. Гольдебаев see PG3470.S35

3460.G59 Gol′denov, Petr Ivanovich, fl. 1880-1890. Петр Иванович Гольденов (Table P-PZ40)

3460.G6 Gol′dshteĭn, Mark Mikhaĭlovich, fl. 1890-1900. Марк Михайлович Гольдштейн (Table P-PZ40)

3460.G615 Gol′dshteĭn, Moiseĭ Leont′evich. Моисей Леонтьевич Гольдштейн (Table P-PZ40)

Russian literature
Individual authors and works, 1870-1917
Individual authors, Chekhov, Anton - Gorky -- Continued

3460.G62 Golenishchev-Kutuzov, Arseniĭ Arkad′evich, graf, 1848-1913. Арсений Аркадьевич Голенищев-Кутузов (Table P-PZ40)

3460.G63 Golikov, Vladimir Mitrofanovich, 1875- . Владимир Митрофанович Голиков (Table P-PZ40)

3460.G64 Golit͡syn, Dmitriĭ Petrovich, kni͡az′, 1860-1928. Дмитрий Петрович Голицын (Table P-PZ40)

Golit͡syna, Varvara Fedorovna. Варвара Федоровна Голицына see PG3460.D84

3460.G65 Golokhvastov, Pavel Dmitrievich, 1839-1892. Павел Дмитриевич Голохвастов (Table P-PZ40)

3460.G66 Golokhvastova, Ol′ga Andreevna, d. 1894. Ольга Андреевна Голохвастова (Table P-PZ40)

3460.G68 Gololobov, I͡A. E., fl. 1890-1900. Я.Е. Гололобов (Table P-PZ40)

Golovacheva, Evdokii͡a Apollonovna. Евдокия Аполлоновна Головачева see PG3467.N22

3460.G7 Golovachevskiĭ, Sergeĭ Nikolaevich, fl. 1890-1900. Сергей Николаевич Головачевский (Table P-PZ40)

3460.G72 Golovin, Konstantin Fedorovich, 1843-1913. Константин Федорович Головин (Table P-PZ40)

3460.G74 Golovinskai͡a, E.N., fl. 1890-1900. Е.Н. Головинская (Table P-PZ40)

3460.G76 Golovkov, Grigoriĭ Alekseevich, 1868-1892. Григорий Алексеевич Головков (Table P-PZ40)

Golovnin, Orest. Орест Головнин see PG3453.B682

3460.G79 Golubev, A.E., fl. 1890-1900. А.Е. Голубев (Table P-PZ40)

3460.G8 Golubev, Aleksandr Aleksandrovich, 1841-1895. Александр Александрович Голубев (Table P-PZ40)

3460.G814 Golubin, Petr. Петр Голубин (Table P-PZ40)

Goncharov, Ivan Aleksandrovich. Иван Александрович Гончаров see PG3337.G6

3460.G82 Gonet͡skai͡a, M.P., fl. 1900-1910. М.П. Гонецкая (Table P-PZ40)

3460.G84 Gorbunov-Posadov, Ivan Ivanovich, 1864-1940. Иван Иванович Горбунов-Посадов (Table P-PZ40)

3460.G86 Gorchakov, Petr Dmitrievich, kni͡az′, fl. 1890-1910. Петр Дмитриевич Горчаков (Table P-PZ40)

3460.G88 Gord, Boleslav, fl. 1890-1900. Болеслав Горд (Table P-PZ40)

3460.G9 Gordik, Ivan Kallistrovich, fl. 1900-1910. Иван Каллистрович Гордик (Table P-PZ40)

Russian literature
Individual authors and works, 1870-1917
Individual authors, Chekhov, Anton - Gorky -- Continued

3460.G92 Gordin, Vladimir Nikolaevich, 1882- . Владимир Николаевич Гордин (Table P-PZ40)

Goremykin, A. IA. А.Я. Горемыкин see PG3467.M26

3460.G95 Gorin, N.K., fl. 1890-1900. Н.К. Горин (Table P-PZ40)

Gorky, Maksim, 1868-1936. Максим Горький

3462.A1 Collected works. By date

3462.A13 Selected works. By date

3462.A15 Collected novels and stories. By date

3462.A17 Collected essays, miscellanies, etc. By date

3462.A19 Collected plays. By date

3462.A2 Selections. By date

3462.A3-Z Separate works

For translations see PG3463+

9-e ianvaria. 9-е января see PG3462.D53

3462.A4 Aforizmy (Aphorisms). Афоризмы

3462.A5 Anekdot (Tale). Анекдот

3462.B6 Boles′ (Tale). Болесь

3462.B7 Bratskaia pomoshch′ (Tale). Братская помощь

3462.B8 Bukoemov, Karp Ivanovich (Tale). Букоемов, Карп Иванович

3462.B85 Burevestnik (Fantasy). Буревестник

3462.B9 Byk (Tale). Бык

3462.B95 Byvshie liudi (Story). Бывшие люди

3462.C3 Chelkash (Tale). Челкаш

3462.C4 Chelovek (Tale). Человек

3462.C5 Chitatel′ (Tale). Читатель

3462.C6 Chudaki (Comedy). Чудаки

3462.D2 Dachniki (Drama). Дачники

3462.D3 Ded Arkhip i Len′ka (Tale). Дед Архип и Ленька

3462.D4 Delo Artamonovykh (Novel). Дело Артамоновых

3462.D43 Delo s zastezhkami (Tale). Дело с застежками

3462.D47 Deti (Comedy). Дети

3462.D5 Deti solntsa (Comedy). Дети солнца

Detstvo. Децтво see PG3465.A22

3462.D53 Deviatoe ianvaria (9-e ianvaria) (Sketch). Девятое января

3462.D55 Devochka (Tale). Девочка

3462.D57 Devushka i smert′ (Tale in verse). Девушка и смерть

3462.D6 Dostigaev i drugie (Drama). Достигаев и другие

3462.D7 Druzhki (Tale). Дружки

3462.D8 Dvadtsat′ shest′ i odna (Tale in verse). Двадцать шесть и одна

3462.E4 Egor Bulychov i drugie (Drama). Егор Булычов и другие

PG

Russian literature
Individual authors and works, 1870-1917
Gorky, Maksim, 1868-1936. Максим Горький
Separate works -- Continued

3462.E5 Ėkzekut͡sii͡a (Tale). Экзекуция
3462.E6 Ėmblema (Tale). Эмблема
3462.E65 Emelʹi͡an Pili͡aĭ (Tale). Емельян Пиляй
3462.E7 Eralash (Tale). Ералаш
Eshche o chorte. Еще о чорте see PG3462.O24
3462.E8 Evgraf Bukeev (Drama). Евграф Букеев
3462.F3 Falʹshivai͡a moneta (Drama). Фальшивая монета
3462.F6 Foma Gordeev (Novel). Фома Гордеев
3462.G5 Golubai͡a zhiznʹ (Tale). Голубая жизнь
3462.G6 Goremyka Pavel (Story). Горемыка Павел
3462.G7 Gorodok Okurov; khronika (Novel). Городок Окуров; хроника
3462.I3 I͡Akov Bogomolov (Drama). Яков Богомолов
3462.I4 I͡Armarka v Goltve (Tale). Ярмарка в Голтве
3462.I8 Ispovedʹ (Story). Исповедь
3462.K2 Kain i Artem (Tale). Каин и Артем
3462.K25 Kak i͡a uchilsi͡a (Tale). Как я учился
3462.K3 Kak slozhili pesni͡u (Tale). Как сложили песню
3462.K35 Karamora (Tale). Карамора
3462.K4 Khan i ego syn (Fairy tale). Хан и его сын
3462.K45 Khozi͡ain (Tale). Хозяин
3462.K5 Khristofor Bukeev (Drama). Христофор Букеев
3462.K55 Kirilka (Tale). Кирилка
3462.K6 Kladbishche (Tale). Кладбище
3462.K65 Konovalov (Sketch). Коновалов
3462.K7 Krazha (Tale). Кража
3462.K8 Krovʹ skazhetsi͡a (Tale). Кровь скажется
3462.L4 Legkiĭ chelovek (Tale). Легкий человек
3462.L5 Leto (Story). Лето
3462.M2 Makar Chudra (Sketch). Макар Чудра
3462.M25 Malʹva (Story). Мальва
3462.M3 Mamasha Kemskikh (Tale). Мамаша Кемских
3462.M35 Matʹ (Novel). Мать
Matveĭ Kozhemi͡akin. Матвей Кожемякин see PG3462.Z45
3462.M5 Meshchane (Drama). Мещане
3462.M6 Moĭ sputnik (Tale). Мой спутник
Moi universitety. Мои университеты see PG3465.A24
3462.M7 Mordovka (Tale). Мордовка
3462.M8 Mudret͡s (Tale). Мудрец
3462.N23 Na dne (Drama). На дне
3462.N3 Na plotakh (Tale). На плотах
3462.N5 Nilushka (Tale). Нилушка

Russian literature
Individual authors and works, 1870-1917
Gorky, Maksim, 1868-1936. Максим Горький
Separate works -- Continued

3462.O2 O chizhe, kotoryĭ lgal, i o di͡atle - li͡ubitele istiny (Tale). О чиже, который лгал, и о дятле - любителе истины
3462.O23 O chorte (Tale). О чорте
3462.O24 Eshche o chorte (Tale). Еще о чорте
3462.O25 O pervoĭ li͡ubvi (Tale). О первой любви
3462.O26 O pisatele, kotoryĭ zaznalsi͡a (Fantasy). О писателе, который зазнался
3462.O28 O tarakanakh (Tale). О тараканах
3462.O3 Ob izbytke i nedostatkakh (Tale). Об избытке и недостатках
3462.O4 Odnazhdy osenʹi͡u (Tale). Однажды осенью
3462.O7 Orel (Tale). Орел
3462.O75 Oshibka (Tale). Ошибка
3462.O8 Otshelʹnik (Tale). Отшельник
3462.O9 Ozornik (Sketch). Озорник
3462.P3 Pastukh (Tale). Пастух
3462.P35 Pered lit͡som zhizni (Tale). Перед лицом жизни
3462.P4 Pesni͡a o burevestnike (Tale). Песня о буревестнике
3462.P5 Pesni͡a o sokole (Sketch). Песня о соколе
3462.P6 Po Rusi (Sketch). По Руси
3462.P63 Pogrom (Tale). Погром
3462.P67 Pokoĭnik (Drama). Покойник
3462.P7 Poslednie (Drama). Последние
3462.P75 Pozhary (Tale). Пожары
3462.P8 Prokhodimet͡s (Tale). Проходимец
3462.P85 Provodnik (Tale). Проводник
3462.R2 Rasskaz Filippa Vasilʹevicha. Рассказ Филиппа Васильевича
3462.R23 Rasskaz o bezotvetnoĭ li͡ubvi. Рассказ о безответной любви
3462.R24 Rasskaz o geroe. Рассказ о герое
3462.R25 Rasskaz o neobyknovennom (Tale). Рассказ о необыкновенном
3462.R27 Rasskaz ob odnom romane (Tale). Рассказ об одном романе
3462.R3 Rasskazy o geroi͡akh (Tale). Рассказы о героях
3462.R5 Repetit͡sii͡a (Tale). Репетиция
3462.R6 Romantik (Tale). Романтик
3462.R7 Rozhdenie cheloveka (Tale). Рождение человека
3462.R8 Russkie skazki. Русские сказки
3462.S4 Sbornik i pozhar (Tale). Сборник и пожар
3462.S5 Skazki ob Italii. Сказки об Италии

Russian literature
Individual authors and works, 1870-1917
Gorky, Maksim, 1868-1936. Максим Горький
Separate works -- Continued

3462.S6 Skuki radi (Tale). Скуки ради
3462.S65 Sluchaĭ iz zhizni Makara (Tale). Случай из жизни Макара
3462.S68 Soldaty (Sketches). Солдаты
3462.S7 Somov i drugie (Drama). Сомов и другие
3462.S8 Starik (Drama). Старик
3462.S85 Starukha Izergilʹ (Tale). Старуха Изергиль
3462.S9 Storozh (Tale). Сторож
3462.S95 Suprugi Orlovy (Tale). Супруги Орловы
3462.T5 Ti͡urʹma (Tale). Тюрьма
3462.T6 Toska (Tale). Тоска
3462.T65 Tovarishch! (Tale). Товарищ!
3462.T67 Tri dni͡a (Tale). Три дня
3462.T7 Troe (Tale). Трое
3462.T74 Tronulo (Tale). Тронуло
3462.T77 Trubochist (Tale). Трубочист
3462.T8 Tunnelʹ (Tale). Туннель
3462.U2 U russkogo t͡sari͡a (Tale). У русского царя
3462.U3 Ubiit͡sy (Tale). Убийцы
3462.U7 Uri͡adnik Krokhalev (Tale). Урядник Крохалев
3462.V2 V Amerike (Sketches). В Америке
Comprises:
3462.V22 Gorod zheltogo dʹi͡avola. Город желтого дьявола
3462.V23 T͡Sarstvo skuki. Царство скуки
3462.V24 "Mob"
3462.V25 Charli Mėn. Чарли Мэн
3462.V26 V bolʹnom gorode (Sketch). В больном городе
V li͡udi͡akh. В людях see PG3465.A23
3462.V28 V stepi (Tale). В степи
3462.V3 Varenʹka Olesova (Novel). Варенька Олесова
3462.V4 Varvary (Drama). Варвары
3462.V45 Vasʹka Krasnyĭ (Tale). Васька Красный
3462.V5 Vassa Zheleznova (Drama). Васса Железнова
3462.V57 Vesenni͡i͡a melodii (Fantasy). Весенния мелодии
3462.V6 Vezdesushchee (Tale). Вездесущее
3462.V7 Vragi (Drama). Враги
3462.V9 Vyvod (Tale). Вывод
3462.Z2 Zabastovka tramvaĭshchikov (Tale). Забастовка трамвайщиков
3462.Z25 Zazubrina (Tale). Зазубрина
3462.Z3 Zhaloby (Tale). Жалобы
3462.Z4 Zhiznʹ Klima Samgina (Novel). Жизнь Клима Самгина

Russian literature
Individual authors and works, 1870-1917
Gorky, Maksim, 1868-1936. Максим Горький
Separate works -- Continued

3462.Z45 Zhizn′ Matveia͡ Kozhemia͡kina (Tale). Жизнь Матвея Кожемякина
3462.Z5 Zhizn′ nenuzhnogo cheloveka (Novel). Жизнь ненужного человека
3462.Z9 Zykovy (Drama). Зыковы

Translations
For translations of autobiography, letters, etc. see PG3465.A3+

3463 English
3463.A1 Collected works. By date
3463.A15 Collected novels and stories. By date
3463.A16 Collected essays, miscellanies, etc. By date
3463.A19 Collected plays. By date
3463.A3-Z Separate works. By Russian title, A-Z
Subarrange by translator, A-Z
3463.D5 Deti solnt͡sa (Children of the sun). Дети солнца
3463.I8 Ispoved′ (The confession). Исповедь
3463.N2 Na dne (The lower depths; also called, At the bottom, A night's lodging, Submerged, etc.). На дне
3463.S8 Starik (The judge). Старик
3463.V7 Vragi (The enemies). Враги
3464.A-Z Other languages, A-Z
Subarrange each language by Table PG1
e. g.
3464.F5 French (Table PG1)
3464.G5 German (Table PG1)
3464.I5 Italian (Table PG1)
3464.S5 Spanish (Table PG1)

Biography and criticism
Autobiography. Journals. Letters
Russian editions
3465.A2 Collected works. Selected works. Selections. By date
3465.A22 Detstvo. Децтво. By date
3465.A23 V li͡udi͡akh. В людях. By date
3465.A24 Moi universitety. Мои университеты. By date
3465.A25 Zametki iz dnevnika. Заметки из дневника. By date
3465.A27 Vospominanii͡a. Воспоминания. By date
For special persons, see their biography, e.g. PG3385, Tolstoĭ
Letters

Russian literature
Individual authors and works, 1870-1917
Gorky, Maksim, 1868-1936. Максим Горький
Biography and criticism
Autobiography. Journals. Letters
Russian editions
Letters -- Continued

3465.A28 Collected. By date
3465.A29A-.A29Z Individual correspondents, A-Z

Translations
English

3465.A3A-.A3Z Collected works. Selected works. Selections. By translator, A-Z, or date
3465.A32A-.A32Z Detstvo (My childhood). Децтво. By translator, A-Z, or date
3465.A33A-.A33Z V li͡udi͡akh (In the world). В людях. By translator, A-Z, or date
3465.A34A-.A34Z Moi universitety (My university days). Мои университеты. By translator, A-Z, or date
Also called Reminiscences of my youth
3465.A35A-.A35Z Zametki iz dnevnika (Fragments from my diary). Заметки из дневника. By translator, A-Z, or date
3465.A37A-.A37Z Vospominanii͡a (Reminiscences of contemporaries). Воспоминания. By translator, A-Z, or date

Letters

3465.A38 Collected. By date
3465.A39A-.A39Z Individual correspondents, A-Z

French

3465.A4A-.A4Z Collected works. Selected works. Selections. By translator, A-Z, or date
3465.A42A-.A42Z Detstvo. Децтво. By translator, A-Z, or date
3465.A43A-.A43Z V li͡udi͡akh. В людях. By translator, A-Z, or date
3465.A44A-.A44Z Moi universitety. Мои университеты. By translator, A-Z, or date
3465.A45A-.A45Z Zametki iz dnevnika. Заметки из дневника. By translator, A-Z, or date
3465.A47A-.A47Z Vospominanii͡a. Воспоминания. By translator, A-Z, or date

Letters

3465.A48 Collected. By date
3465.A49A-.A49Z Individual correspondents, A-Z

German

3465.A5A-.A5Z Collected works. Selected works. Selections. By translator, A-Z, or date
3465.A52A-.A52Z Detstvo. Децтво. By translator, A-Z, or date

Russian literature
Individual authors and works, 1870-1917
Gorky, Maksim, 1868-1936. Максим Горький
Biography and criticism
Autobiography. Journals. Letters
Translations
German -- Continued

3465.A53A-.A53Z V li͡udi͡akh. В людях. By translator, A-Z, or date
3465.A54A-.A54Z Moi universitety. Мои университеты. By translator, A-Z, or date
3465.A55A-.A55Z Zametki iz dnevnika. Заметки из дневника. By translator, A-Z, or date
3465.A57A-.A57Z Vospominanii͡a. Воспоминания. By translator, A-Z, or date
Letters
3465.A58 Collected. By date
3465.A59A-.A59Z Individual correspondents, A-Z
3465.A6-.A69 Other translations (alphabetically, by language)
3465.A7-.Z5 General treatises. Life and works
3465.Z65 Homes and haunts
3465.Z7 Iconography. Museums. Exhibitions
3465.Z8 Criticism
3465.Z9 Special topics and subjects, A-Z
3465.Z9A3 Aesthetics
3465.Z9A7 Appreciation
3465.Z9A84 Art. Artists
3465.Z9B66 Books and reading
3465.Z9C48 Characters
3465.Z9C6 Contemporaries
3465.Z9D65 Dramatic works
Ethics and religion see PG3465.Z9R37
3465.Z9F52 Film adaptations
3465.Z9G4 Georgian literature
3465.Z9H47 Heroes
3465.Z9I5 Influence
3465.Z9L28 Labor. Working class
3465.Z9L3 Language
3465.Z9L395 Law
3465.Z9L4 Relationship with Lenin
3465.Z9L53 Literature
3465.Z9M53 Middle classes
3465.Z9M96 Mythology
3465.Z9P43 Peasants
3465.Z9P6 Poland
3465.Z9P69 Political and social views
Reading see PG3465.Z9B66
3465.Z9R37 Religion and ethics

Russian literature
Individual authors and works, 1870-1917
Gorky, Maksim, 1868-1936. Максим Горький
Biography and criticism
Special topics and subjects, A-Z -- Continued

3465.Z9S3 Satire

3465.Z9S4 Science

3465.Z9S8 Stage history

Working class see PG3465.Z9L28

3467 Individual authors, Gorky - Per

3467.G15 Gorodet͡skiĭ, M.N., fl. 1890-1900. М.Н. Городецкий (Table P-PZ40)

3467.G2 Gorodet͡skiĭ, Sergeĭ Mitrofanovich, 1884-1967. Сергей Митрофанович Городецкий (Table P-PZ40)

3467.G3 Goslavskiĭ, Evgeniĭ Petrovich, fl. 1890-1900. Евгений Петрович Гославский (Table P-PZ40)

Govorov, K. К. Говоров see PG3467.M372

3467.G35 Govorukha-Otrok, I͡Uriĭ Nikolaevich, 1850-1896. Юрий Николаевич Говоруха-Отрок (Table P-PZ40)

3467.G4 Grabina, Alekseĭ Trofimovich, 1861- . Алексей Трофимович Грабина (Table P-PZ40)

3467.G42 Grachev, A.F., fl. 1890-1910. А.Ф. Грачев (Table P-PZ40)

3467.G43 Gradovskiĭ, Grigoriĭ Konstantinovich, b. 1842. Григорий Константинович Градовский (Table P-PZ40)

Graf Amori, pseud. Граф Амори see PG3470.R29

3467.G438 Granstrem, Ė. (Ėduard), 1844?-1918. Эдуард Гранстрем (Table P-PZ40)

3467.G439 Granstrem, M. (Matilʹda), 1848-1930. Матильда Гранстрем (Table P-PZ40)

3467.G45 Grave, Leonid Grigorʹevich, 1842-1891. Леонид Григорьевич Граве (Table P-PZ40)

Grėk, I. И Грэк see PG3453.B52

3467.G48 Greshner, A.A., fl. 1890-1900. А.А. Грешнер (Table P-PZ40)

3467.G5 Gribovskiĭ, Vi͡acheslav Mikhaĭlovich, 1867-1924. Вячеслав Михайлович Грибовский (Table P-PZ40)

Gridenʹ, pseud. Гридень see PG3467.G5

Gridinskiĭ, pseud. Гридинский see PG3453.B2

3467.G52 Grigorʹev, Alekseĭ Aleksandrovich, fl. 1880-1900. Алексей Александрович Григорьев (Table P-PZ40)

Grigorovich, Dmitriĭ Vasilʹevich. Дмитрий Васильевич Григорович see PG3337.G77

Grinberg, Izabella Lʹvovna. Изабелла Львовна Гринберг see PG3467.L155

3467.G54 Grinev, S.A., fl. 1890-1900. С.А. Гринев (Table P-PZ40)

Grinevich, P.F. П.Ф. Гриневич see PG3467.I2

Russian literature
Individual authors and works, 1870-1917
Individual authors, Gorky - Per -- Continued

3467.G56 Grinevskai͡a, Izabella Arkad′evna, 1854-1942. Изабелла Аркадьевна Гриневская (Table P-PZ40)

3467.G57 Gromov, K., fl. 1890-1900. К. Громов (Table P-PZ40)

3467.G58 Grossul-Tolstoĭ, P.L., fl. 1880-1890. П.Л. Гроссул-Толстой (Table P-PZ40)

3467.G6 Grot, Natal′i͡a Petrovna (Semenova), ca. 1825-1899. Наталья Петровна (Семенова) Грот (Table P-PZ40)

3467.G66 Grum-Grzhimaĭlo, Kondratiĭ Ivanovich, 1794-1874. Кондратій Ивановичъ Грумъ-Гржимайло (Table P-PZ40)

3467.G7 Gruzinskiĭ, Alekseĭ Evgen′evich, 1858-1930. Алексей Евгеньевич Грузинский (Table P-PZ40)

3467.G75 Gruzint͡sov, Aleksandr Nikolaevich, 1779-ca. 1840. Александр Николаевич Грузинцов (Table P-PZ40)

Gulliver, pseud. Гулливер see PG3467.M465

3467.G78 Gumalik, D.I. Д.И. Гумалик (Table P-PZ40)

Gumilev, Nikolaĭ Stepanovich. Николай Степанович Гумилев see PG3476.G85

3467.G82 Gunaropulo-Davydov, I͡Uriĭ A., fl. 1880-1900. Юрий А. Гунаропуло-Давыдов (Table P-PZ40)

3467.G83 Gurevich, I͡Akov I͡Akovlevich, 1869- . Яков Яковлевич Гуревич (Table P-PZ40)

3467.G85 Gurevich, Li͡ubov′ I͡Akovlevna, 1866-1940. Любовь Яковлевна Гуревич (Table P-PZ40)

3467.G9 Guro, Elena, d. 1913. Елена Гуро (Table P-PZ40)

Gusev, Sergeĭ Ivanovich. Сергей Иванович Гусев see PG3467.G94

3467.G93 Gusev, Sergeĭ Sergeevich, 1854- . Сергей Сергеевич Гусев (Table P-PZ40)

3467.G94 Gusev-Orenburgskiĭ, Sergeĭ Ivanovich, 1867-1963. Сергей Иванович Гусев-Оренбургский (Table P-PZ40)

3467.G944 Gusli͡ak, L. Л. Гусляк (Table P-PZ40)

3467.G95 Gutmakher, I.M., fl. 1890-1900. И.М. Гутмахер (Table P-PZ40)

Hahn-Hahn, Helene Petrovna see PG3453.B57

Heintze, Nikolaĭ Ėduardovich. Николай Эдуардович Гейнце see PG3460.G4

Hippius, Zinaida Nikolaevna. Зинаида Николаевна Гиппиус see PG3460.G5+

Hofman, Victor see PG3460.G58

Homo novus, pseud. see PG3467.K78

I Grėk, pseud. И Грэк see PG3453.B52

Russian literature
Individual authors and works, 1870-1917
Individual authors, Gorky - Per -- Continued

IA., P., pseud. П.Я. see PG3467.I2

3467.I12 IAblonovskiĭ, Aleksandr Aleksandrovich, 1870-1934. Александр Александрович Яблоновский (Table P-PZ40)

IAblonovskiĭ, Sergeĭ. Сергей Яблоновский see PG3470.P638

3467.I13 IAdrintsev, Nikolaĭ Mikhaĭlovich, 1842-1894. Николай Михайлович Ядринцев (Table P-PZ40)

3467.I135 IAgodin, A. A. Ягодин (Table P-PZ40)

3467.I14 IAkhontov, Aleksandr Nikolaevich, 1820-1890. Александр Николаевич Яхонтов (Table P-PZ40)

3467.I15 IAkimov, Vasiliĭ, fl. 1900-1910. Василий Якимов (Table P-PZ40)

IAkovlev, I. И. Яковлев see PG3467.P78

IAkovleva, IUliia Ivanovna. Юлия Ивановна Яковлева see PG3453.B475

3467.I17 IAkovleva, Nadezhda Vladimirovna, fl. 1880-1900. Надежда Владимировна Яковлева (Table P-PZ40)

3467.I18 IAkovleva, Zoia IUlianovna, d. 1908. Зоя Юлиановна Яковлева (Table P-PZ40)

3467.I2 IAkubovich, Petr Filippovich, 1860-1911. Петр Филиппович Якубович (Table P-PZ40 modified)

3467.I2A61-.I2Z458 Separate works. By title

3467.I2C4 Chortov iar (Tale). Чортов яр

3467.I2D6 Doroga (Tale). Дорога

3467.I2E6 Ėpilog (Tale). Эпилог

3467.I2F4 Ferganskiĭ orlenok (Sketch). Ферганский орленок

3467.I2I8 Iskorka (Tale). Искорка

3467.I2I9 IUnost′ (Sketch). Юность

3467.I2K6 Kobylka v puti (Tale). Кобылка в пути

3467.I2L5 Liubimtsy katorgi (Tale). Любимцы каторги

3467.I2M3 Malen′kie liudi (Tale). Маленькие люди

3467.I2N2 Na kitaĭskoĭ reke (Tale). На китайской реке

3467.I2O3 Odinochestvo (Tale). Одиночество

3467.I2P3 Pasynki zhizni [and other tales]. Пасынки жизни

3467.I2P4 Pasynki zhizni (Tale). Пасынки жизни

3467.I2S2 S tovarishchami (Tale). С товарищами

3467.I2S4 Shelaevskiĭ rudnik (Tale). Шелаевский рудник

3467.I2S5 Shkola v katorge (Tale). Школа в каторге

3467.I2S7 Sredi sopok (Tale). Среди сопок

3467.I2V2 V mire otverzhennykh (Tales). В мире отверженных

3467.I2V3 V plenu (Tale). В плену

3467.I2V4 V preddverii (Tale). В преддверии

IAkunin, I. И. Якунин see PG3470.Z26

Russian literature
Individual authors and works, 1870-1917
Individual authors, Gorky - Per -- Continued

3467.I22 I͡Amshchikova, Margarita Vladimirovna (Rokotova), 1872-1959. Маргарита Владимировна (Рокотова) Ямщикова (Table P-PZ40)

3467.I23 I͡Anishevskiĭ, Severin, fl. 1890-1900. Северин Янишевский (Table P-PZ40)

3467.I24 I͡Armonkin, Valentin Vasil′evich, fl. 1890-1900. Валентин Васильевич Ярмонкин (Table P-PZ40)

3467.I244 I͡Aron, M.G. М.Г. Ярон (Table P-PZ40)

3467.I26 I͡Aroshevskiĭ, S.O., fl. 1890-1900. С.О. Ярошевский (Table P-PZ40)

3467.I28 I͡Art͡sev, Petr M., fl. 1890-1900. Петр М. Ярцев (Table P-PZ40)

3467.I3 I͡Asinskiĭ, Ieronim Ieronimovich, 1850-1901. Иероним Иеронимович Ясинский (Table P-PZ40)

3467.I32 I͡Askovich, G., 1850-1901. Г. Яскович (Table P-PZ40)

3467.I33 Ierikhonskiĭ, Marala, fl. 1880-1890. Марала Иерихонский (Table P-PZ40)

Igla, pseud. Игла see PG3453.A4

3467.I35 Ignat′ev, E.I., fl. 1900-1910. Е.И. Игнатьев (Table P-PZ40)

Ignat′ev, Ruf Gavrilovich. Руф Гаврилович Игнатьев see PG3337.I45

3467.I36 Ignatov, F.S., fl. 1900-1915. Ф.С. Игнатов (Table P-PZ40)

3467.I37 Ignatov, Il′i͡a Nikolaevich, 1858-1921. Илья Николаевич Игнатов (Table P-PZ40)

Ikhorov, Z. З. Ихоров see PG3467.O85

3467.I385 Ikskul′, V. I͡A. (Vladimir I͡Akovlevich), b. 1860. Владимир Яковлевич Икскуль (Table P-PZ40)

3467.I39 Il′in, A. A. Ильин (Table P-PZ40)

Il′in, Mikhail Andreevich, 1878-1942. Михаил Андреевич Ильин see PG3467.O74

3467.I396 Il′in, Sergeĭ Andreevich, 1867-1914. Сергей Андреевич Ильин (Table P-PZ40)

3467.I4 Il′inskiĭ, I.A., fl. 1870-1880. И.А. Ильинский (Table P-PZ40)

3467.I45 Ili͡ukho, E.P., fl. 1860-1890. Е.П. Илюхо (Table P-PZ40)

3467.I5 Imeretinskiĭ, Nikolaĭ Konstantinovich, kni͡az′, 1830-1894. Николай Константинович Имеретинский (Table P-PZ40)

3467.I53 Inozemt͡seva, Anna Andreevna, 1864- . Анна Андреевна Иноземцева (Table P-PZ40)

3467.I55 Iogel′, M.K., fl. 1880-1900. М.К. Иогель (Table P-PZ40)

3467.I57 Iordan, V.O., fl. 1880-1900. В.О. Иордан (Table P-PZ40)

Russian literature
Individual authors and works, 1870-1917
Individual authors, Gorky - Per -- Continued

3467.I59 Iskeneke-Emelʹi͡anov, N. I͡A. Н.Я. Искенеке-Емельянов (Table P-PZ40)
3467.I595 I͡Unikov, D., fl. 1900-1917. Д. Юников (Table P-PZ40)
3467.I6 I͡Urʹev, Mikhail, fl. 1890-1900. Михаил Юрьев (Table P-PZ40)
I͡Urʹev, Sergeĭ Andreevich. Сергей Андреевич Юрьев see PG3337.I65
I͡Urʹev, Vladimir. Владимир Юрьев see PG3460.D68
I͡Urʹin, N. Н. Юрьин see PG3470.V38
3467.I64 I͡Urevich, Vlad. (Vladimīr). Владимiръ Юревичъ (Table P-PZ40)
3467.I67 I͡Urgenson, S., fl. 1880-1890. С. Юргенсон (Table P-PZ40)
I͡Urko, G. Г. Юрко see PG3467.G35
3467.I7 I͡Ushkevich, Semen Solomonovich, 1868-1927. Семен Соломонович Юшкевич (Table P-PZ40)
3467.I715 I͡Ushkova, O. О. Юшкова (Table P-PZ40)
3467.I72 I͡Utanov, Vladimir Pavlovich, 1876- . Владимир Павлович Ютанов (Table P-PZ40)
3467.I725 I͡Uzefovich, A.D. А.Д. Юзефович (Table P-PZ40)
I͡Uzhin, Aleksandr Ivanovich. Александр Иванович Южин see PG3467.I73
3467.I73 I͡Uzhin-Sumbatov, Aleksandr Ivanovich, 1857-1927. Александр Иванович Южин-Сумбатов (Table P-PZ40)
I͡Uzhnyĭ, A. А. Южный see PG3467.L49
3467.I74 Ivanov, Aleksandr Trofimovich, 1844-1888. Александр Трофимович Иванов (Table P-PZ40)
3467.I75 Ivanov, Alekseĭ Fedorovich, 1841-1894. Алексей Федорович Иванов (Table P-PZ40)
Ivanov, G. Г. Иванов see PG3470.U8
3467.I76 Ivanov, Lev Lʹvovich, fl. 1880-1900. Лев Львович Иванов (Table P-PZ40)
3467.I77 Ivanov, N.G., fl. 1890-1900. Н.Г. Иванов (Table P-PZ40)
3467.I78 Ivanov, Nikolaĭ N., fl. 1860-1890. Николай Н. Иванов (Table P-PZ40)
3467.I789 Ivanov, V.I. (Vasiliĭ Ivanovich), 1865-1912. Василiй Ивановичъ Ивановъ (Table P-PZ40)
3467.I79 Ivanov, Vasiliĭ Ivanovich, 1858- . Василий Иванович Иванов (Table P-PZ40)
3467.I8 Ivanov, Vi͡acheslav Ivanovich, 1866-1949. Вячеслав Иванович Иванов (Table P-PZ40 modified)
3467.I8A61-.I8Z458 Separate works. By title
3467.I8C5 Chelovek (Poems). Человек

Russian literature
Individual authors and works, 1870-1917
Individual authors, Gorky - Per
Ivanov, V͡iacheslav Ivanovich, 1866-1949. Вячеслав Иванович Иванов
Separate works. By title -- Continued

3467.I8C6 Cor ardens (Poems)
3467.I8E7 Ėros (Poems). Эрос
3467.I8K6 Kormchie svezdy (Poems). Кормчие свезды
3467.I8M5 Mladechestvo (Poem). Младечество
3467.I8N4 Nezhnai͡a taĭna (Poems). Нежная тайна
3467.I8P4 Pesni smutnogo vremeni. Песни смутного времени
3467.I8P7 Prometeĭ (Tragedy). Прометей
3467.I8P8 Prozrachnostʹ (Poems). Прозрачность
3467.I8T3 Tantal (Tragedy). Тантал
3467.I8Z3 Zimnie sonety. Зимние сонеты

Ivanov-Klassik, pseud. Иванов-Классик see PG3467.I75

3467.I825 Ivanovich, Ivan, 1842-1901. Иван Иванович (Table P-PZ40)

3467.I83 Ivashkin, V.A., fl. 1900-1910. В.А. Ивашкин (Table P-PZ40)

3467.I85 Ivchenko, Valerian I͡Akovlevich, 1860-1935. Валериан Яковлевич Ивченко (Table P-PZ40)

3467.I87 Ivin, Ivan S., fl. 1880-1900. Иван С. Ивин (Table P-PZ40)

3467.I9 Iz͡iumskiĭ, Ivan Dmitrievich, fl. 1890-1900. Иван Дмитриевич Изюмский (Table P-PZ40)

3467.I93 Izmaĭlov, Aleksandr Alekseevich, 1873-1921. Александр Алексеевич Измайлов (Table P-PZ40)

3467.I95 Izmaĭlov, Ilʹi͡a Nikolaevich, fl. 1880-1890. Илья Николаевич Измайлов (Table P-PZ40)

Izmaĭlov-Smolenskiĭ, A.A. А.А. Измайлов-Смоленский see PG3467.I93

Jabotinsky, Vladimir, 1880-1940 see PG3470.Z4

K.R., pseud. К.Р. see PG3467.K56

3467.K13 Kachurina, S. C. Качурина (Table P-PZ40)

3467.K15 Kakhovskiĭ, Boris V., fl. 1890-1900. Борис В. Каховский (Table P-PZ40)

3467.K18 Kakit͡sati, Mikhail Konstantinovich, fl. 1910-1920. Михаил Константинович Какицати (Table P-PZ40)

Kaktus, pseud. Кактус see PG3467.M35

3467.K22 Kalachev, K.N., fl. 1880-1890. К.Н. Калачев (Table P-PZ40)

3467.K23 Kalenov, Petr Aleksandrovich, 1839-1900. Петр Александрович Каленов (Table P-PZ40)

Kamenskai͡a, Anna Pavlovna. Анна Павловна Каменская see PG3453.B28

Russian literature
Individual authors and works, 1870-1917
Individual authors, Gorky - Per -- Continued

3467.K24 Kamenskiĭ, Anatoliĭ Pavlovich, 1877-1941. Анатолий Павлович Каменский (Table P-PZ40)

3467.K25 Kamenskiĭ, N.D., fl. 1890-1900. Н.Д. Каменский (Table P-PZ40)

3467.K26 Kanaev, Aleksandr Nikolaevich, 1844-1907. Александр Николаевич Канаев (Table P-PZ40)

Kandaurov, Vasiliĭ Alekseevich. Василий Алексеевич Кандауров see PG3337.K23

3467.K27 Kanivet͡skiĭ, N.N., fl. 1890-1900. Н.Н. Канивецкий (Table P-PZ40)

3467.K273 Kantigrov. Кантигров (Table P-PZ40)

3467.K28 Kapnist, Ina Petrovna, grafini͡a, fl. 1890-1900. Ина Петровна Капнист (Table P-PZ40)

3467.K29 Kapnist, Petr Ivanovich, graf, 1830-1898. Петр Иванович Капнист (Table P-PZ40)

3467.K3 Karabchevskiĭ, Nikolaĭ Platonovich, 1851-1925. Николай Платонович Карабчевский (Table P-PZ40)

3467.K313 Karasev, A.A., fl. 1890-1900. А.А. Карасев (Table P-PZ40)

3467.K315 Karashev, A.V., fl. 1890-1900. А.В. Карашев (Table P-PZ40)

3467.K318 Karashev, Aleksandr Fedorovich, 1862- . Александр Федорович Карашев (Table P-PZ40)

3467.K32 Karatygin, Petr Petrovich, 1832-1888. Петр Петрович Каратыгин (Table P-PZ40)

3467.K33 Karazin, Nikolaĭ Nikolaevich, 1842-1908. Николай Николаевич Каразин (Table P-PZ40)

3467.K334 Karelin, K.K., fl. 1880-1900. К.К. Карелин (Table P-PZ40)

Karenin, Vlad. Влад. Каренин see PG3467.K54

Kargina, E. E. Каргина see PG3467.M63

3467.K336 Kargrem, Genrietta R., fl. 1890-1900. Генриетта Р. Каргрем (Table P-PZ40)

Karmasanov, P. П. Кармасанов see PG3460.D63

3467.K338 Karmen, Lazar′ Osipovich, 1876-1920. Лазарь Осипович Кармен (Table P-PZ40)

3467.K339 Karni͡eev, M.V. М.В. Карнѣевъ (Table P-PZ40)

3467.K34 Karnovich, Evgeniĭ Petrovich, 1823-1885. Евгений Петрович Карнович (Table P-PZ40)

Karonin, S. C. Каронин see PG3470.P2

3467.K343 Karpov, Evtikhiĭ Pavlovich, 1857-1926. Евтихий Павлович Карпов (Table P-PZ40)

Karr, S. C. Карр see PG3467.P6

3467.K344 Karskiĭ, M.B. М.Б. Карскiй (Table P-PZ40)

Russian literature
Individual authors and works, 1870-1917
Individual authors, Gorky - Per -- Continued

3467.K345 Kartavov, Mikhail, fl. 1890-1900. Михаил Картавов (Table P-PZ40)

Kartavt͡seva, Marii͡a Vsevolodovna. Мария Всеволодовна Картавцева see PG3467.K73

3467.K347 Kasatkin, Sergi͡eĭ. Сергѣй Касаткинъ (Table P-PZ40)

Kasatkin-Rostovskiĭ, Fedor Nikolaevich. Федор Николаевич Касаткин-Ростовский see PG3467.K6215

3467.K36 Kasatkin-Rostovskiĭ, Sergeĭ Aleksandrovich, fl. 1890-1900. Сергей Александрович Касаткин-Ростовский (Table P-PZ40)

3467.K365 Kastal′skiĭ, Alekseĭ, fl. 1900-1910. Алексей Кастальский (Table P-PZ40)

3467.K367 Katanskiĭ, Efim L′vovich, fl. 1890-1900. Ефим Львович Катанский (Table P-PZ40)

3467.K369 Kazakov, T. T. Казаков (Table P-PZ40)

3467.K37 Kazant͡sev, Nikolaĭ Vladimirovich, 1854-1896. Николай Владимирович Казанцев (Table P-PZ40)

Kazant͡sov, N. H. Казанцов see PG3467.K37

Kazem-Murat, pseud. Казем-Мурат see PG3467.M465

3467.K38 Kazi-Bek, I͡Uriĭ, fl. 1890-1900. Юрий Кази-Бек (Table P-PZ40)

Kazina, Zoi͡a Dmitrievna. Зоя Дмитриевна Казина see PG3453.B853

Khaĭdakov, pseud. Хайдаков see PG3467.K865

3467.K383 Khalatov, Boris. Борис Халатов (Table P-PZ40)

3467.K384 Kharlamov, I͡A. A., fl. 1890-1900. Борис Халатов (Table P-PZ40)

3467.K386 Kharlamov, Ivan Nikolaevich, 1855-1887. Иван Николаевич Харламов (Table P-PZ40)

3467.K388 Kharuzin, Alekseĭ Nikolaevich, 1864-1932. Алексей Николаевич Харузин (Table P-PZ40)

3467.K39 Khashkes, M. I͡A., fl. 1890-1900. М.Я. Хашкес (Table P-PZ40)

3467.K393 Khatunt͡sev, S.M., fl. 1890-1900. С.М. Хатунцев (Table P-PZ40)

3467.K395 Khavskiĭ, Alekseĭ Nikolaevich, 1864-1904. Алексей Николаевич Хавский (Table P-PZ40)

3467.K397 Khetagurov, Konstantin Levanovich, 1859-1906. Константин Леванович Хетагуров (Table P-PZ40)

3467.K4 Khin, Rashel′ Mironovna, 1863-1927. Рашель Мироновна Хин (Table P-PZ40)

3467.K42 Khir′i͡akov, Aleksandr Modestovich, 1863-1940. Александр Модестович Хирьяков (Table P-PZ40)

Russian literature
Individual authors and works, 1870-1917
Individual authors, Gorky - Per -- Continued

3467.K423 Khitrovo, Mikhail Aleksandrovich, 1837-1896. Михаил Александрович Хитрово (Table P-PZ40)

3467.K427 Khlaponina, A.D., fl. 1890-1900. А.Д. Хлапонина (Table P-PZ40)

3467.K428 Khlopov, N. H. Хлопов (Table P-PZ40)

3467.K43 Khmeleva, O.N., fl. 1880-1900. О.Н. Хмелева (Table P-PZ40)

Khmyznikova, Klavdii͡a Vladimirovna. Клавдия Владимировна Хмызникова see PG3467.L7

Khokhri͡akova, Li͡udmilla Khristofovna. Людмилла Христофовна Хохрякова see PG3470.S5716

Kholmin, pseud. Холмин see PG3451.A585

Kholodov, N. H. Холодов see PG3453.B35

Kholostov, V. B. Холостов see PG3453.B52

3467.K435 Khovanskiĭ, M.A., fl. 1880-1890. М.А. Хованский (Table P-PZ40)

Khrenovskai͡a, Olʹga Nesterovna. Ольга Нестеровна Хреновская see PG3467.K639

3467.K44 Khrushchov, Mikhail, fl. 1880-1890. Михаил Хрущов (Table P-PZ40)

3467.K45 Khrushchov-Sokolʹnikov, Gavriil Aleksandrovich, 1845-1890. Гавриил Александрович Хрущов-Сокольников (Table P-PZ40)

3467.K457 Khudekov, Sergeĭ Nikolaevich, 1837-1928. Сергей Николаевич Худеков (Table P-PZ40)

3467.K46 Khvoshchinskai͡a, Praskovʹi͡a Dmitrievna, 1832-1916. Прасковья Дмитриевна Хвощинская (Table P-PZ40)

3467.K464 Khvostov, Nikolaĭ Borisovich, fl. 1870-1900. Николай Борисович Хвостов (Table P-PZ40)

3467.K47 Kicheev, Petr Ivanovich, 1845-1902. Петр Иванович Кичеев (Table P-PZ40)

3467.K473 Kign, Vladimir Li͡udvigovich, 1856-1908. Владимир Людвигович Кигн (Table P-PZ40)

3467.K478 Kinsester, Elena, fl. 1870-1880. Елена Кинсестер (Table P-PZ40)

3467.K48 Kipen, Aleksandr Abramovich, 1870- . Александр Абрамович Кипен (Table P-PZ40)

3467.K485 Kirʹi͡akova, Marii͡a Aleksandrovna, fl. 1870-1890. Мария Александровна Кирьякова (Table P-PZ40)

Kirienko-Voloshin, Maksimilian Aleksandrovich. Максимилиан Александрович Кириенко-Волошин see PG3470.V68

Russian literature
Individual authors and works, 1870-1917
Individual authors, Gorky - Per -- Continued

3467.K488 Kisnemskiĭ, Semen Petrovich, 1859-1906. Семен Петрович Киснемский (Table P-PZ40)

3467.K49 Kivshenko, N.D., fl. 1880-1890. Н.Д. Кившенко (Table P-PZ40)

Klassik, pseud. Классик see PG3467.I75

Klechanov, G. Г. Клечанов see PG3467.K45

3467.K5 Kli͡ushnikov, Viktor Petrovich, 1841-1892. Виктор Петрович Клюшников (Table P-PZ40)

Klopotovskiĭ, Vladimir Vladimirovich. Владимир Владимирович Клопотовский see PG3467.L414

3467.K513 Kni͡azhnin, P.P., fl. 1880-1890. П.П. Княжнин (Table P-PZ40)

Kobylinskiĭ, L.L. Л.Л. Кобылинский see PG3460.E453

3467.K516 Kochergin, Ivan, fl. 1870-1890. Иван Кочергин (Table P-PZ40)

3467.K518 Kocherov, F.M., fl. 1890-1900. Ф.М. Кочеров (Table P-PZ40)

3467.K52 Kochetov, Evgeniĭ L′vovich, fl. 1870-1890. Евгений Львович Кочетов (Table P-PZ40)

Koe-kto, pseud. Кое-кто see PG3470.S84

3467.K522 Kogan, Naum L′vovich, 1863-1893. Наум Львович Коган (Table P-PZ40)

3467.K523 Kogen, A.M., fl. 1890-1910. А.М. Коген (Table P-PZ40)

3467.K525 Koi͡alovich, Mikhail Mikhaĭlovich, fl. 1880-1910. Михаил Михайлович Коялович (Table P-PZ40)

3467.K527 Kokosov, Vladimir I͡Akovlevich, 1845-1911. Владимир Яковлевич Кокосов (Table P-PZ40)

3467.K528 Koksharov, Nikolaĭ Ivanovich, 1818-1893. Николай Иванович Кокшаров (Table P-PZ40)

3467.K53 Kolbasin, Eliseĭ I͡Akovlevich, 1831-1885. Елисей Яковлевич Колбасин (Table P-PZ40)

3467.K532 Kologrivova, L. Л. Кологривова (Table P-PZ40)

3467.K533 Kolomiĭt͡sev, Daniil Vasil′evich, 1866-1915. Даниил Васильевич Коломийцев (Table P-PZ40)

Kolosov, Andreĭ. Андрей Колосов see PG3470.Z3

3467.K535 Koltonovskiĭ, Andreĭ Pavlovich, fl. 1900-1910. Андрей Павлович Колтоновский (Table P-PZ40)

3467.K537 Kolyshko, Iosif Iosifovich, 1862-1938. Иосиф Иосифович Колышко (Table P-PZ40)

3467.K54 Komarova, Varvara Dmitrievna (Stasova), 1862-1943. Варвара Дмитриевна (Стасова) Комарова (Table P-PZ40)

3467.K542 Komarovskiĭ, Vasiliĭ Alekseevich, 1881-1914. Василий Алексеевич Комаровский (Table P-PZ40)

Russian literature
Individual authors and works, 1870-1917
Individual authors, Gorky - Per -- Continued

3467.K544 Kon, Feliks I͡Akovlevich, 1864-1941. Феликс Яковлевич Кон (Table P-PZ40)

3467.K546 Konchakovskai͡a, Anna, fl. 1890-1900. Анна Кончаковская (Table P-PZ40)

3467.K547 Kondratʹev, Aleksandr Alekseevich, 1876-1967. Александр Алексеевич Кондратьев (Table P-PZ40)

3467.K548 Kondratʹev, Ivan Kuzʹmich, fl. 1870-1900. Иван Кузьмич Кондратьев (Table P-PZ40)

3467.K55 Kondratova, Li͡udmila, fl. 1870-1890. Людмила Кондратова (Table P-PZ40)

3467.K553 Kondurushkin, Stepan Semenovich, 1874-1919. Степан Семенович Кондурушкин (Table P-PZ40)

Konevskoĭ, Ivan. Иван Коневской see PG3467.O6

3467.K554 Konovnit͡sin, Stefan Gerasimovich, b. 1862. Стефан Герасимович Коновницин (Table P-PZ40)

3467.K555 Konradi, Evgenii͡a Ivanovna (Bochechkarova), 1838-1898. Евгения Ивановна (Бочечкарова) Конради (Table P-PZ40)

3467.K558 Konshin, V.V., fl. 1880-1900. В.В. Коншин (Table P-PZ40)

3467.K56 Konstantin Konstantinovich, Grand Duke of Russia, 1858-1915. Константин Константинович (Table P-PZ40)

Konstantinov, M.K. М.К. Константинов see PG3467.K18

Konstantinovich, D. Д. Константинович see PG3460.G52

3467.K57 Korchagin, Ilʹi͡a Gavrilovich, fl. 1890-1900. Илья Гаврилович Корчагин (Table P-PZ40)

3467.K573 Korchemnyĭ, Veniamin Matveevich, b. 1884. Вениамин Матвеевич Корчемный (Table P-PZ40)

Korenman, Lazarʹ Osipovich, 1876-1920. Лазарь Осипович Коренман see PG3467.K338

3467.K58 Korinfskiĭ, Apollon Apollonovich, 1868-1937. Аполлон Аполлонович Коринфский (Table P-PZ40)

3467.K5817 Kornatovskiĭ, Dm. (Dmitriĭ). Дмитрій Корнатовскій (Table P-PZ40)

Kornelieva, V. B. Корнелиева see PG3453.B53

3467.K585 Korobov, I͡Akov Evdokimovich, 1874-1928 (Table P-PZ40)

3467.K59 Korolenko, Lavr Grigorʹevich, 1821 or 2-1886. Лавр Григорьевич Короленко (Table P-PZ40)

Korolenko, Vladimir Galaktionovich, 1853-1921. Владимир Галактионович Короленко

3467.K6 Collected works. By date

Russian literature
Individual authors and works, 1870-1917
Individual authors, Gorky - Per
Korolenko, Vladimir Galaktionovich, 1853-1921. Владимир Галактионович Короленко -- Continued

3467.K6A15 Collected tales, sketches, etc. By date
Translations (Collected or selected)
3467.K6A2-.K6A29 English. By translator, if given, or date
3467.K6A3-.K6A39 French. By translator, if given, or date
3467.K6A4-.K6A49 German. By translator, if given, or date
3467.K6A5-.K6A59 Other. By language
3467.K6A6 Selected works. Selections. By date
3467.K6A61-.K6Z458 Separate works. By title
3467.K6A8 At-Davan (Tale). Ат-Даван
3467.K6B4 Bez i͡azyka (Tale). Без языка
3467.K6B6 Bozhiĭ gorodok (Sketch). Божий городок
3467.K6C4 Cherkes (Sketch). Черкес
Published also under the title: Iz zapisnoĭ knizhki
3467.K6C5 Chudnai͡a. Чудная
Published also under the title: Komandirovka
Deti podzemelʹi͡a. Дети подземелья see PG3467.K6V3
3467.K6D6 Dom No. 13-yĭ (Sketch). Дом No. 13-ый
3467.K6D7 Draka v dome (Sketch). Драка в доме
Dva malʹchika. Два мальчика see PG3467.K6N4
3467.K6F4 Fedor Bespriiutnyĭ; iz rasskazov o brodi͡agakh (Sketch). Федор Бесприютный; из рассказов о бродягах
3467.K6F5 Feodaly (Tale). Феодалы
3467.K6G6 Gosudarevy i͡amshchiki (Tale). Государевы ямщики
3467.K6I3 I͡Ashka (Tale). Яшка
Iom-Kipur. Иом-Кипур see PG3467.K6S8
Iskateli. Искатели see PG3467.K6V24
3467.K6I7 Iskushenie (Sketch). Искушение
Istorii͡a moego sovremennika. История моего современника see PG3467.K6Z52
Iz zapisnoĭ knizhki. Из записной книжки see PG3467.K6C4
Komandirovka. Командировка see PG3467.K6C5
3467.K6K8 Kuplennye malʹchiki (Tale). Купленные мальчики
3467.K6L4 Les shumit (Legend). Лес шумит
3467.K6M3 Marusina zaimka (Sketch). Марусина заимка
3467.K6M5 Mgnovenie (Tale). Мгновение
3467.K6M6 Moroz (Tale). Мороз
3467.K6N2 Na Volge (Sketch). На Волге
3467.K6N3 Na zatmenii (Sketch). На затмении

Russian literature
Individual authors and works, 1870-1917
Individual authors, Gorky - Per
Korolenko, Vladimir Galaktionovich, 1853-1921. Владимир Галактионович Короленко
Separate works. By title -- Continued

3467.K6N4 Na zavode (Tale). На заводе
Published also under title: Dva mal'chika

Nad limanom. Над лиманом see PG3467.K6V22

Nashi na Dunae. Наши на Дуна see PG3467.K6V26

3467.K6N45 Ne strashnoe. Не страшное

Nekrasovskiĭ koren'. Некрасовский корень see PG3467.K6V23

3467.K6N5 Neobkhodimost' (Tale). Необходимость

Nevol'nyĭ ubiĭt͡sa. Невольный убийца see PG3467.K6U2

Nirvana. Нирвана see PG3467.K6V28

Noch' pod svetlyĭ prazdnik. Ночь под светлый праздник see PG3467.K6V6

3467.K6N6 Nochʹi͡u (Sketch). Ночью

3467.K6O3 Ocherki sibirskogo turista (Sketches). Очерки сибирского туриста
For separate sketches see the title in PG3467.K6A61+

3467.K6O5 Ogon'ki (Tale). Огоньки

3467.K6P3 Paradoks (Sketch). Парадокс

3467.K6P5 Po puti (Tale). По пути

3467.K6P6 Posledniĭ luch (Tale). Последний луч

3467.K6P7 Priemysh (Tale). Приемыш

3467.K6P75 Prokhor i studenty (Story). Прохор и студенты

3467.K6P8 Ptit͡sy nebesnye (Tale). Птицы небесные

(3467.K6P9) Puteshestvie v Ameriku (Sketches, tales, observations, etc.). Путешествие в Америку
see E168

3467.K6R4 Reka igraet (Tale). Река играет

3467.K6S2 S dvukh storon (Tale). С двух сторон

3467.K6S3 Skazanie o Flore, Agrippe i Menakheme syne Ierudy (Tale). Сказание о Флоре, Агриппе и Менахеме сыне Иеруды

3467.K6S4 Slepoĭ muzykant (Psychological study). Слепой музыкант

3467.K6S5 Smirennye (Sketch). Смиренные

3467.K6S6 Sokolinet͡s (Tale). Соколинец

3467.K6S65 Son Makara (Tale). Сон Макара

3467.K6S7 Staryĭ zvonar' (Tale). Старый звонарь

3467.K6S75 Stoĭ, solnt͡se, i ne dvizhis' luna (Tale). Стой, солнце, и не движись луна

Russian literature
Individual authors and works, 1870-1917
Individual authors, Gorky - Per
Korolenko, Vladimir Galaktionovich, 1853-1921. Владимир Галактионович Короленко
Separate works. By title -- Continued

	Strastnai͡a subbota. Страстная суббота see PG3467.K6V6
3467.K6S8	Sudnyĭ den′ (Iom-Kipur) (Tale). Судный день
3467.K6T4	Teni (Fantasy). Тени
	Turchin i my. Турчин и мы see PG3467.K6V27
3467.K6U2	Ubivet͡s (Tale). Убивец Published also under the title: Nevol′nyĭ ubiĭt͡sa
3467.K6V2	V Dobrudzhe (Tales). В Добрудже Comprises:
3467.K6V22	Nad limanom. Над лиманом
3467.K6V23	Nekrasovskiĭ koren′. Некрасовский корень
3467.K6V24	Iskateli. Искатели
3467.K6V26	Nashi na Dunae. Наши на Дунае
3467.K6V27	Turchin i my. Турчин и мы
3467.K6V28	Nirvana. Нирвана
3467.K6V3	V durnom obshchestve (Sketch). В дурном обществе Published also under the title: Deti podzemel′i͡a
3467.K6V4	V golodnyĭ god. В голодный год
3467.K6V5	V Krymu (Sketch). В Крыму
3467.K6V6	V noch′ pod svetlyĭ prazdnik (Tale). В ночь под светлый праздник Published also under the title: Strastnai͡a subbota
3467.K6V7	V oblachnyĭ den′ (Sketch). В облачный день
3467.K6V8	V podsledstvennom otdelenii (Tale). В подследственном отделении
3467.K6V9	V pustynnykh mestakh (Sketches). В пустынных местах For separate sketches see the title in PG3467.K6A61+
3467.K6Z3	Za ikonoĭ (Tale). За иконой
	Biography and criticism
	Journals. Reminiscences. Letters
3467.K6Z52	Istorii͡a moego sovremennika. История моего современника Comprises:
3467.K6Z53	Rannee detstvo i gody uchenii͡a. Раннее детство и годы учения
3467.K6Z54	Studencheskie gody i ssyl′nye skitanii͡a Студенческие годы и ссыльные скитания
3467.K6Z55	Zapisnai͡a knizhka: 1879. Записная книжка: 1879

	Russian literature
	Individual authors and works, 1870-1917
	Individual authors, Gorky - Per
	Korolenko, Vladimir Galaktionovich, 1853-1921. Владимир Галактионович Короленко
	Biography and criticism
	Journals. Reminiscences. Letters -- Continued
3467.K6Z56	Zapisnai͡a knizhka: 1880-1900. Записная книжка: 1880-1900
	Letters
3467.K6Z57	Collected. By date
3467.K6Z58-.K6Z59	Individual correspondents (alphabetically)
3467.K6Z6-.K6Z99	General treatises. Life and works
	Korolivna, L. Л. Короливна see PG3467.M25
	Koronin, S. C. Коронин see PG3470.P2
3467.K612	Koropchevskiĭ, Dmitriĭ Andreevich, 1842-1903. Дмитрий Андреевич Коропчевский (Table P-PZ40)
3467.K613	Koropt͡sov, Petr Prokofʹevich, fl. 1870-1880. Петр Прокофьевич Коропцов (Table P-PZ40)
3467.K614	Korostovet͡s, Ivan I͡Akovlevich, fl. 1890- . Иван Яковлевич Коростовец (Table P-PZ40)
3467.K616	Korotkov, F.E., fl. 1870-1880. Ф.Е. Коротков (Table P-PZ40)
3467.K618	Korvin-Krukovskiĭ, Petr, 1850-1899. Петр Корвин-Круковский (Table P-PZ40)
3467.K62	Korzhet͡s, Vladimir, fl. 1890-1900. Владимир Коржец (Table P-PZ40)
3467.K6215	Kosatkin-Rostovskiĭ, Fedor Nikolaevich, kni͡azʹ, 1875-1940. Федор Николаевич Косаткин-Ростовский (Table P-PZ40)
3467.K622	Koshkarov, Sergeĭ N., d. 1920. Сергей Н. Кошкаров (Table P-PZ40)
	Kosmatyĭ lirik, pseud. Косматый лирик see PG3453.B98
3467.K623	Kosorotov, Aleksandr Ivanovich, 1868-1912. Александр Иванович Косоротов (Table P-PZ40)
	Kʺosta, 1859-1906. Къоста see PG3467.K397
	Kostin, M. M. Костин see PG3470.S75
3467.K624	Kostomarova, Aleksandra, fl. 1900-1910. Александра Костомарова (Table P-PZ40)
3467.K625	Kostrit͡skiĭ, Mikhail Dmitrievich, b. 1887. Михаил Дмитриевич Кострицкий (Table P-PZ40)
3467.K626	Kosunovich, Lev Ivanovich, b. 1864. Лев Иванович Косунович (Table P-PZ40)
3467.K6264	Kotelʹva, Alekseĭ, fl. 1890-1900. Алексей Котельва (Table P-PZ40)
3467.K627	Kotin, Andreĭ, fl. 1880-1890. Андрей Котин (Table P-PZ40)

Russian literature
Individual authors and works, 1870-1917
Individual authors, Gorky - Per -- Continued

Kot-Murlyka, pseud. Кот-Мурлыка see PG3470.V2

3467.K628 Kot͡s, Arkadiĭ I͡Akovlevich, 1872-1943. Аркадий Яковлевич Коц (Table P-PZ40)

3467.K63 Kotyleva, Olʹga Ėmmanuilovna (Rozenfelʹd), 1875- . Ольга Эммануиловна (Розенфельд) Котылева (Table P-PZ40)

3467.K637 Kovalevskai͡a, Sofʹi͡a Vasilʹevna, 1850-1891. Софья Васильевна Ковалевская (Table P-PZ40)

Kovalevskiĭ, Pavel Mikhaĭlovich. Павел Михайлович Ковалевский see PG3337.K65

3467.K639 Kovalʹskai͡a, Olʹga Nesterovna (Khrenovskai͡a), 1876- . Ольга Нестеровна (Хреновская) Ковальская (Table P-PZ40)

3467.K64 Kovalʹskiĭ, Kazimir Adolʹfovich, b. 1878. Казимир Адольфович Ковальский (Table P-PZ40)

3467.K644 Kovrigin, Ivan K., fl. 1890-1900. Иван К. Ковригин (Table P-PZ40)

Kovshov, pseud. Ковшов see PG3467.K783

3467.K65 Kozhevnikov, Petr Alekseevich, 1872- . Петр Алексеевич Кожевников (Table P-PZ40)

3467.K652 Kozhevnikov, Valentin Alekseevich, 1867-1902. Валентин Алексеевич Кожевников (Table P-PZ40)

3467.K654 Kozlov, Pavel Alekseevich, 1841-1891. Павел Алексеевич Козлов (Table P-PZ40)

3467.K656 Kozlov, Vladimir I., fl. 1880-1890. Владимир И. Козлов (Table P-PZ40)

3467.K6575 Kozʹmin-Pervago, P.K. (Petr Konstantinovich). Петр Константинович Козьмин-Перваго (Table P-PZ40)

3467.K658 Kozochkin, A.P., fl. 1900-1910. А.П. Козочкин (Table P-PZ40)

3467.K66 Kozyrev, Matveĭ Alekseevich, 1852-1912. Матвей Алексеевич Козырев (Table P-PZ40)

3467.K67 Krachkovskiĭ, Dmitriĭ Nikolaevich, 1882-1934. Дмитрий Николаевич Крачковский (Table P-PZ40)

3467.K675 Kraevskiĭ, Aleksandr, fl. 1890-1900. Александр Краевский (Table P-PZ40)

Kraĭniĭ, Anton. Антон Крайний see PG3460.G5+

3467.K68 Krandievskai͡a, Anastasii͡a Romanovna (Tarkhova), 1865- . Анастасия Романовна (Тархова) Крандиевская (Table P-PZ40)

3467.K69 Krasheninnikov, Nikolaĭ Aleksandrovich, 1878-1941. Николай Александрович Крашенинников (Table P-PZ40)

Russian literature
Individual authors and works, 1870-1917
Individual authors, Gorky - Per -- Continued

3467.K693 Krasil′nikova, E.A., fl. 1890-1900. Е.А. Красильникова (Table P-PZ40)

3467.K695 Kraskovskiĭ, Ippolit Feofilovich, d. 1899. Ипполит Феофилович Красковский (Table P-PZ40)

3467.K697 Krasnit͡skiĭ, Aleksandr Ivanovich, 1866-1917. Александр Иванович Красницкий (Table P-PZ40)

3467.K698 Krasnoramenskiĭ, M., fl. 1890-1900. М. Краснораменскій (Table P-PZ40)

3467.K7 Krasnov, Petr Nikolaevich, 1869-1947. Петр Николаевич Краснов (Table P-PZ40)

Krasnova, Ekaterina Andreevna (Beketova). Екатерина Андреевна (Бекетова) Краснова see PG3453.B366

Krasov, M.I. М.И. Красов see PG3467.O2

3467.K715 Krasovskiĭ, N. Ivanovich, fl. 1890-1900. Н. Иванович Красовский (Table P-PZ40)

3467.K717 Krauze, Vl. (Vladimir), 1858-1901. Владимир Краузе (Table P-PZ40)

3467.K72 Kravchinskiĭ, Sergeĭ Mikhaĭlovich, 1852-1895. Сергей Михайлович Кравчинский (Table P-PZ40)

Krechetov, Sergeĭ. Сергей Кречетов see PG3470.S676

3467.K725 Kremlev, Anatoliĭ Nikolaevich, 1859-1919. Анатолий Николаевич Кремлев (Table P-PZ40)

3467.K73 Krestovskai͡a, Marii͡a Vsevolodovna, 1862-1910. Мария Всеволодовна Крестовская (Table P-PZ40)

3467.K74 Krestovskiĭ, Vsevolod Vladimirovich, 1840-1895. Всеволод Владимирович Крестовский (Table P-PZ40)

Krinit͡skiĭ, Mark. Марк Криницкий see PG3470.S27

Krinit͡skiĭ, N. Н. Криницкий see PG3470.T53

3467.K742 Kristi, E.K., fl. 1900-1910. Е.К. Кристи (Table P-PZ40)

3467.K743 Kri͡ukov, Fedor Dmitrievich, 1870-1920. Федор Дмитриевич Крюков (Table P-PZ40)

Kri͡ukovskiĭ, I͡A. Я. Крюковский see PG3467.G83

3467.K744 Kri͡ukovskoĭ, Arkadiĭ Fedorovich, 1840-1911. Аркадий Федорович Крюковской (Table P-PZ40)

For Kri͡ukovskoĭ's Polish works see PG7158.K775+

3467.K745 Krivenko, Vasiliĭ Silovich, 1854-1931. Василий Силович Кривенко (Table P-PZ40)

3467.K7457 Krongel′m av Khakunge, V.A. В.А. Кронгельм ав Хакунге (Table P-PZ40)

3467.K746 Kropotkin, A., kni͡az′. А. Кропоткин (Table P-PZ40)

3467.K747 Krotkov. Кротков (Table P-PZ40)

3467.K748 Krotkov, Valeriĭ Stepanovich, 1846- . Валерий Степанович Кротков (Table P-PZ40)

Russian literature
Individual authors and works, 1870-1917
Individual authors, Gorky - Per -- Continued

3467.K75 Kruglov, Aleksandr Vasil′evich, 1853-1915. Александр Васильевич Круглов (Table P-PZ40)

3467.K755 Krupnov, A.E., fl. 1890-1900. А.Е. Крупнов (Table P-PZ40)

3467.K758 Krushevan, Pavel Aleksandrovich, 1860-1909. Павел Александрович Крушеван (Table P-PZ40)

3467.K76 Krylov, Viktor Aleksandrovich, 1838-1906. Виктор Александрович Крылов (Table P-PZ40)

3467.K77 Kryzhanovskai͡a, Vera Ivanovna. Вера Ивановна Крыжановская (Table P-PZ40)

3467.K775 Ksenin, Iosif, fl. 1900-1910. Иосиф Ксенин (Table P-PZ40)

3467.K778 Kudinov, I.F., fl. 1880-1900. И.Ф. Кудинов (Table P-PZ40)

3467.K78 Kugel′, Aleksandr Rafailovich, 1864-1928. Александр Рафаилович Кугель (Table P-PZ40)

3467.K782 Kugushev, A.P., kni͡az′, fl. 1890-1900. А.П. Кугушев (Table P-PZ40)

3467.K783 Kugushev, Flor Vasil′evich, kni͡az′, 1851-1881. Флор Васильевич Кугушев (Table P-PZ40)

3467.K784 Kukolevskiĭ, Nikolaĭ Sergeevich, 1842-1889. Николай Сергеевич Куколевский (Table P-PZ40)

3467.K7843 Kulebi͡akin, A.P. А.П. Кулебякин (Table P-PZ40)

3467.K7845 Kuleshov, Mikhail, fl. 1880-1890. Михаил Кулешов (Table P-PZ40)

Kulikov, Nikolaĭ Ivanovich. Николай Иванович Куликов see PG3337.K8

3467.K785 Kulikov, Pavel Petrovich, 1838-1905. Павел Петрович Куликов (Table P-PZ40)

3467.K786 Kulin, Vasiliĭ Petrovich, 1822-1900. Василий Петрович Кулин (Table P-PZ40)

Kungurt͡sev, Nikolaĭ Nikolaevich. Николай Николаевич Кунгурцев see PG3451.A59

3467.K788 Kupchinskiĭ, Filipp Petrovich, fl. 1900-1910. Филипп Петрович Купчинский (Table P-PZ40)

3467.K79 Kupchinskiĭ, Ivan Aleksandrovich, fl. 1880-1900. Иван Александрович Купчинский (Table P-PZ40)

3467.K795 Kuprei͡anova, A.N., fl. 1880-1890. А.Н. Купреянова (Table P-PZ40)

Variant of surname: Kuprii͡anova

3467.K8 Kuprin, Aleksandr Ivanovich, 1870-1938. Александр Иванович Куприн (Table P-PZ40 modified)

3467.K8A61-.K8Z458 Separate works. By title

3467.K8A8 Anafema (Tale). Анафема

Russian literature
Individual authors and works, 1870-1917
Individual authors, Gorky - Per
Kuprin, Aleksandr Ivanovich, 1870-1938. Александр Иванович Куприн
Separate works. By title -- Continued

3467.K8B3	Beglet͡sy (Tale). Беглецы
3467.K8B6	Boloto (Tale). Болото
3467.K8B7	Bred (Tale). Бред
3467.K8C4	Chernai͡a molnii͡a (Tale). Черная молния
3467.K8C45	Chernyĭ tuman (Tale). Черный туман
3467.K8D4	Demir-Kai͡a. Демир-Кая
3467.K8D6	Doznanie (Tale). Дознание
3467.K8E4	Elan′ (Tales). Елань
3467.K8G3	Gambrinus (Tale). Гамбринус
3467.K8G6	Gospodni͡a ryba (Tale). Господня рыба
3467.K8G7	Granatovyĭ braslet (Tale). Гранатовый браслет
3467.K8G8	Gruni͡a (Tale). Груня
3467.K8I3	I͡Ama (Novel). Яма
3467.K8I7	Iskusstvo (Tale). Искусство
3467.K8I8	I͡Unkera (Novel). Юнкера
3467.K8I9	Izumrud (Tale). Изумруд
3467.K8K4	Kazhdoe zhelanie (Tale). Каждое желание
3467.K8K6	Koleso vremeni (Novel). Колесо времени
3467.K8K7	Kor′ (Tale). Корь
3467.K8K8	Kupol sv. Isaakii͡a Dalmatskogo (Tale). Купол св. Исаакия Далматского
3467.K8L3	Lazurnye berega (Tales). Лазурные берега
3467.K8L45	Lesnai͡a glush′ (Tale). Лесная глушь
3467.K8L5	Lidochka (Tale). Лидочка
3467.K8L6	Limonnai͡a korka (Tale). Лимонная корка
3467.K8L8	Lunnoĭ noch′i͡u (Tale). Лунной ночью
3467.K8M4	Meli͡uzga (Tale). Мелюзга
3467.K8M5	Miniati͡ury (Sketches and tales). Миниатюры
3467.K8M6	Molokh (Tale). Молох
3467.K8M7	Morskai͡a bolezn′ (Tale). Морская болезнь
3467.K8M8	Muchenik mody (Tale). Мученик моды
3467.K8N25	Na glukhareĭ (Tale). На глухарей
3467.K8N3	Na perelome (Tale). На переломе
3467.K8N35	Na pokoe (Drama). На покое
3467.K8N4	Natal′i͡a Davydovna (Tale). Наталья Давыдовна
3467.K8N6	Nochnai͡a smena (Tale). Ночная смена
3467.K8O4	Olesi͡a (Story). Олеся
3467.K8O7	Osennie t͡svety (Tale). Осенние цветы
3467.K8P3	Parizh domashniĭ (Tale). Париж домашний
3467.K8P5	Po tu storonu (Tale). По ту сторону
3467.K8P6	Poedinok (Novel). Поединок

Russian literature
Individual authors and works, 1870-1917
Individual authors, Gorky - Per
Kuprin, Aleksandr Ivanovich, 1870-1938. Александр Иванович Куприн
Separate works. By title -- Continued

3467.K8P65 Pokhod (Tale). Поход
3467.K8P7 Praporshchik armeĭskiĭ i drugie rasskazy. Прапорщик армейский и другие рассказы
3467.K8R4 Reka zhizni (Tale). Река жизни
3467.K8S2 S ulit͡sy (Tale). С улицы
3467.K8S3 Sashka i I͡Ashka (Tale). Сашка и Яшка
3467.K8S35 Schast′e (Tale). Счастье
3467.K8S4 Sentimental′nyĭ roman (Tale). Сентиментальный роман
3467.K8S5 Shtabs-kapitan Rybnikov (Tale). Штабс-капитан Рыбников
3467.K8S8 Sulamif′ (Tale). Суламифь
3467.K8S9 Svad′ba (Tale). Свадьба
3467.K8T7 Trus (Tale). Трус
3467.K8T8 T͡Sarskiĭ pisar′ (Tale). Царский писарь
3467.K8U3 Uchenik (Tale). Ученик
3467.K8V2 V t͡sirke (Tale). В цирке
3467.K8V4 Vecherniĭ gost′ (Tale). Вечерний гость
3467.K8V6 Vpot′makh (Story). Впотьмах
3467.K8Z2 Zhaneta (Novel). Жанета
3467.K8Z25 Zhidkoe soln͡tse (Tale). Жидкое солнце
3467.K8Z3 Zhidovka (Tale). Жидовка
3467.K8Z45 Zvezda Solomona (Tale). Звезда Соломона

Kurbanovska͡ia, Ekaterina Mikhaĭlovna. Екатерина Михайловна Курбановская see PG3467.K83

3467.K82 Kurbskiĭ, A.S., fl. 1870-1880. А.С. Курбский (Table P-PZ40)

3467.K83 Kurch, Ekaterina Mikhaĭlovna (Kurbanovska͡ia), 1861- . Екатерина Михайловна (Курбановская) Курч (Table P-PZ40)

3467.K84 Kurkin, N.I., fl. 1880-1890. Н.И. Куркин (Table P-PZ40)

3467.K85 Kurlov, Evgeniĭ Evgrafovich, 1876- Евгений Евграфович Курлов (Table P-PZ40)

Kurochkin, Nikolaĭ Stepanovich. Николай Степанович Курочкин see PG3337.K85

3467.K86 Kursinskiĭ, Aleksandr, fl. 1890-1900. Александр Курсинский (Table P-PZ40)

Kurskiĭ, I. И. Курский see PG3467.K79

3467.K865 Kushchevskiĭ, Ivan Afanas′evich, 1847-1876. Иван Афанасьевич Кущевский (Table P-PZ40)

Russian literature
Individual authors and works, 1870-1917
Individual authors, Gorky - Per -- Continued

Kushnerev, Ivan Nikolaevich. Иван Николаевич Кушнерев see PG3337.K89

3467.K87 Kuskov, Platon Aleksandrovich, 1834-1909. Платон Александрович Кусков (Table P-PZ40)

3467.K88 Kutcher, Genrikh Ferdinandovich, fl. 1890-1900. Генрих Фердинандович Кутчер (Table P-PZ40)

Kutuzov, Arseniĭ Arkad′evich Golenishchev- Арсений Аркадьевич Голенищев-Кутузов see PG3460.G62

3467.K89 Kutuzov, Petr, graf, b. 1845. Петр Кутузов (Table P-PZ40)

3467.K9 Kuz′michev, Egor Kuz′mich, 1867- . Егор Кузьмич Кузьмичев (Table P-PZ40)

3467.K92 Kuz′min, Dmitriĭ A., fl. 1880-1890. Дмитрий А. Кузьмин (Table P-PZ40)

3467.K93 Kuzmin, Mikhail Alekseevich, 1872-1936. Михаил Алексеевич Кузмин (Table P-PZ40)

3467.K94 Kuz′mina, Anna Pavlovna, fl. 1870-1880. Анна Павловна Кузьмина (Table P-PZ40)

3467.K95 Kuzminskiĭ, P.P., fl. 1890-1910. П.П. Кузминский (Table P-PZ40)

3467.K956 Kuznet͡sov, E.V. (Evgeniĭ Vasil′evich), 1848-1900. Евгеній Васильевичъ Кузнецовъ (Table P-PZ40)

3467.K96 Kuznet͡sov, N.P., fl. 1890-1910. Н.П. Кузнецов (Table P-PZ40)

3467.K97 Kvashnin, Nikolaĭ Aleksandrovich. Николай Александрович Квашнин (Table P-PZ40)

3467.L12 Lachinova, Praskov′i͡a Aleksandrovna, 1829-1892. Прасковья Александровна Лачинова (Table P-PZ40)

Ladyzhenskiĭ, Ivan Nikolaevich. Иван Николаевич Ладыженский see PG3467.L56

3467.L125 Ladyzhenskiĭ, Vladimir Nikolaevich, 1859-1932. Владимир Николаевич Ладыженский (Table P-PZ40)

Lakidė, A. A. Лакидэ see PG3467.L455

Lamanchskiĭ, D.K. Д.К. Ламанчский see PG3460.E9

3467.L127 Lang, Aleksandr Aleksandrovich, fl. 1900-1910. Александр Александрович Ланг (Table P-PZ40)

Lanskai͡a, N. H. Ланская see PG3467.I17

3467.L13 Lapidus, Vladimir Semenovich, 1869-1914. Владимир Семенович Лапидус (Table P-PZ40)

3467.L135 Lappo, D.E., fl. 1890-1900. Д.Е. Лаппо (Table P-PZ40)

Russian literature
Individual authors and works, 1870-1917
Individual authors, Gorky - Per -- Continued

3467.L137 Lappo-Danilevskaīa, Nadezhda Aleksandrovna (Līutkevich), b. 1876. Надежда Александровна (Люткевич) Лаппо-Данилевская (Table P-PZ40)

3467.L14 Laptev, V.V., fl. 1890-1900. В.В. Лаптев (Table P-PZ40)

3467.L143 Las, Nadezhda, fl. 1890-1900. Надежда Лас (Table P-PZ40)

3467.L145 Lasheeva, Lidiīa Alekseevna, fl. 1890-1900. Лидия Алексеевна Лашеева (Table P-PZ40)

3467.L15 Lashkov, Vasiliĭ Lukich, fl. 1880-1900. Василий Лукич Лашков (Table P-PZ40)

3467.L155 Laskos, Izabella L′vovna (Grinberg), d. 1877. Изабелла Львовна (Гринберг) Ласкос (Table P-PZ40)

3467.L16 Latkin, Nikolaĭ Vasil′evich, 1833-1904. Николай Васильевич Латкин (Table P-PZ40)

Lavintsev, A. (Aleksandr), b. 1866. Александр Лавинцев see PG3467.K697

3467.L165 Lavrent′eva, S.I., fl. 1880-1900. С.И. Лаврентьева (Table P-PZ40)

Lavretskiĭ, M. M. Лаврецкий see PG3467.L53

3467.L17 Lavrichenko, Kondrat Gavrilovich, fl. 1875- . Кондрат Гаврилович Лавриченко (Table P-PZ40)

3467.L18 Lavrov, A.I., fl. 1900-1910. А.И. Лавров (Table P-PZ40)

3467.L183 Lavrov, A.N., fl. 1900-1910. А.Н. Лавров (Table P-PZ40)

3467.L185 Lavrov, Aleksandr Dmitrievich, fl. 1880-1900. Александр Дмитриевич Лавров (Table P-PZ40)

3467.L19 Lavrov, Mitrofan Ivanovich, 1840-1907. Митрофан Иванович Лавров (Table P-PZ40)

Lavskiĭ, V.I. В.И. Лавский see PG3453.B95

3467.L195 Lazarev, Mikhail Naumovich, 1850-1912. Михаил Наумович Лазарев (Table P-PZ40)

Lazarev, Nikolaĭ Artem′evich, 1863-1910. Николай Артемьевич Лазарев see PG3470.T374

3467.L22 Lazarevskiĭ, Boris Aleksandrovich, 1871-1936. Борис Александрович Лазаревский (Table P-PZ40)

3467.L23 Lazovskiĭ, Viktor Stanislavovich, 1858-1893. Виктор Станиславович Лазовский (Table P-PZ40)

3467.L24 L′dov, Konstantin Nikolaevich, 1862-1937. Константин Николаевич Льдов (Table P-PZ40)

3467.L25 Lebedev, Ivan Ivanovich, 1859- . Иван Иванович Лебедев (Table P-PZ40)

3467.L255 Lebedev, K.A. fl. 1870-1890. К.А. Лебедев (Table P-PZ40)

Lebedev, Nikolaĭ Konstantinovich. Николай Константинович Лебедев see PG3467.M854

Russian literature
Individual authors and works, 1870-1917
Individual authors, Gorky - Per -- Continued

3467.L27 Lebedev, Vladimir Petrovich, 1869-1939. Владимир Петрович Лебедев (Table P-PZ40)

3467.L275 Lebedeva, E.A., fl. 1900-1910. Е.А. Лебедева (Table P-PZ40)

3467.L28 Lebedeva, Lidii͡a, fl. 1900-1910. Лидия Лебедева (Table P-PZ40)

3467.L29 Lebedinskiĭ, P.A., fl. 1890-1900. П.А. Лебединский (Table P-PZ40)

3467.L3 Leĭkin, Nikolaĭ Aleksandrovich, 1841-1906. Николай Александрович Лейкин (Table P-PZ40)

Leĭla, pseud. Лейла see PG3451.A43

Leĭtenant S., pseud. Лейтенант С. see PG3470.S59

3467.L32 Leleva, M.P., fl. 1870-1880. М.П. Лелева (Table P-PZ40)

3467.L33 Leli͡akov, Rodion Efimovich, fl. 1890-1900. Родион Ефимович Леляков (Table P-PZ40)

3467.L34 Leman, Anatoliĭ Ivanovich, 1859-1913. Анатолий Иванович Леман (Table P-PZ40)

Leman, Lidii͡a Alekseevna. Лидия Алексеевна Леман see PG3467.L145

3467.L35 Lender, Nikolaĭ Nikolaevich, b. 1864. Николай Николаевич Лендер (Table P-PZ40)

Lenskiĭ, Vladimir. Владимир Ленский see PG3451.A28

3467.L36 Lenskiĭ-Raĭskiĭ, M., fl. 1870-1880. М. Ленский-Райский (Table P-PZ40)

3467.L37 Lentovskiĭ, Mikhail Valentinovich, d. 1906. Михаил Валентинович Лентовский (Table P-PZ40)

Lent͡sevich, Alekseĭ. Алексей Ленцевич see PG3467.K395

3467.L38 Leonov, Maksim Leonovich, 1872-1929. Максим Леонович Леонов (Table P-PZ40)

3467.L39 Leont′ev, Ivan Leont′evich, 1856-1911. Иван Леонтьевич Леонтьев (Table P-PZ40)

3467.L4 Leont′ev, Konstantin Nikolaevich, 1831-1891. Константин Николаевич Леонтьев (Table P-PZ40 modified)

3467.L4A61-.L4Z458 Separate works. By title

3467.L4A75 Aĭ-Burun (Story). Ай-Бурун

3467.L4A8 Aspazii͡a Lampridi (Story). Аспазия Ламприди

3467.L4D5 Diti͡a dushi (Story). Дитя души

3467.L4E3 Egipetskiĭ golub′ (Novel). Египетский голубь

3467.L4I2 I͡Ades (Tale). Ядес

Russian literature
Individual authors and works, 1870-1917
Individual authors, Gorky - Per
Leont′ev, Konstantin Nikolaevich, 1831-1891. Константин Николаевич Леонтьев
Separate works. By title -- Continued

3467.L4I9 Iz zhizni khristian v Turt͡sii. Из жизни христиан в Турции
For separate stories and tales see the title in PG3467.L4A61+
3467.L4K3 Kapitan Il′i͡a (Tale). Капитан Илья
3467.L4K4 Khamid i Manoli (Tale). Хамид и Маноли
3467.L4K5 Khrizo (Story). Хризо
3467.L4P4 Pembe (Story). Пембе
3467.L4P6 Podlipki (Novel). Подлипки
3467.L4P7 Polikarp Kostaki (Tale). Поликарп Костаки
3467.L4S4 Sfakiot (Tale). Сфакиот
3467.L4V2 V svoem krai͡u (Novel). В своем краю
3467.L4V8 Vtoroĭ brak (Story). Второй брак

Biography and criticism
For treatises on Leont′ev as a mystic see B4249.L4+
For treatises on Leont'ev as a literary critic see PG2947

3467.L4Z5-.L4Z999 General treatises. Life and works
3467.L414 Leri. Лери
3467.L417 Leshchinskiĭ, Viktor Egorovich. Викторъ Егоровичъ Лещинскій (Table P-PZ40)
Leskov, Nikolaĭ Semenovich. Николай Семенович Лесков see PG3337.L5+
3467.L419 Leśmian, Bolesław, pseud. (Table P-PZ40)
3467.L42 Lesnit͡skai͡a, V., fl. 1890-1910. В. Лесницкая (Table P-PZ40)
Lesnit͡skiĭ, В. Б. Лесницкий see PG3467.M327
3467.L43 Letkova, Ekaterina Pavlovna, 1856- . Екатерина Павловна Леткова (Table P-PZ40)
Letnev, P. П. Летнев see PG3467.L12
3467.L435 Levanda, Lev Osipovich, 1835-1888. Лев Осипович Леванда (Table P-PZ40)
Levin, N. H. Левин see PG3467.N3
3467.L437 Levinskiĭ. Левинскій (Table P-PZ40)
3467.L44 Levit͡skiĭ, Ivan Semenovich, 1838-1918. Иван Семенович Левицкий (Table P-PZ40)
3467.L443 Levit͡skiĭ, Mikhail, fl. 1900-1910. Михаил Левицкий (Table P-PZ40)
3467.L445 Levit͡skiĭ, Mikhail Alekseevich, fl. 1880-1900. Михаил Алексеевич Левицкий (Table P-PZ40)

Russian literature
Individual authors and works, 1870-1917
Individual authors, Gorky - Per -- Continued

	Li, Maks, pseud. Макс Ли see PG3467.K639
3467.L45	L͡iakhov, D.N., fl. 1880-1890. Д.Н. Ляхов (Table P-PZ40)
3467.L455	L͡iakidė, Ananiĭ Gavrilovich, 1855-1895. Ананий Гаврилович Лякидэ (Table P-PZ40)
	L͡iashchenko, Nikolaĭ Nikolaevich. Николай Николаевич Лященко see PG3476.L55
3467.L457	L͡iashenko, M.M. М.М. Ляшенко (Table P-PZ40)
3467.L46	Libakov, I.M., fl. 1890-1900. И.М. Либаков (Table P-PZ40)
3467.L465	Librovich, Sigizmund Feliksovich, 1855-1918. Сигизмунд Феликсович Либрович (Table P-PZ40)
3467.L47	Lidov, A.F., fl. 1890-1900. А.Ф. Лидов (Table P-PZ40)
3467.L48	Likhachev, Vladimir Sergeevich, 1849-1910. Владимир Сергеевич Лихачев (Table P-PZ40)
3467.L484	Likharev, N. Н. Лихарев (Table P-PZ40)
3467.L49	Likhterman, A.N., fl. 1890-1900. А.Н. Лихтерман (Table P-PZ40)
3467.L5	Linev, Dmitriĭ Aleksandrovich, 1853-1920. Дмитрий Александрович Линев (Table P-PZ40)
3467.L52	Linovskiĭ, Nikolaĭ Osipovich, 1846- . Николай Осипович Линовский (Table P-PZ40)
	Linovskiĭ-Trofimov, N. Н. Линовский-Трофимов see PG3467.L52
	Lionel′, pseud. Лионель see PG3453.B2
3467.L523	Lip͡iazhanin. Липяжанин (Table P-PZ40)
3467.L524	Lipkin. Липкин (Table P-PZ40)
3467.L525	Lipkin, M.K., fl. 1880-1890. М.К. Липкин (Table P-PZ40)
	Lirik, pseud. Лирик see PG3453.B98
	Lisenko, Natal′i͡a I͡Ul′evna Zhukovskai͡a- Наталья Юльевна Жуковская-Лисенко see PG3470.Z47
3467.L53	Lisit͡syn, Mikhail Mikhaĭlovich, 1862-1913. Михаил Михайлович Лисицын (Table P-PZ40)
3467.L535	Litvin, S.K. С.К. Литвин (Table P-PZ40)
3467.L54	L͡iubich-Koshurov, I.A., fl. 1900-1910. И.А. Любич-Кошуров (Table P-PZ40)
	L͡iubin, Ivan. Иван Любин see PG3470.P56
3467.L545	L͡iutov, S.V., fl. 1890-1900. С.В. Лютов (Table P-PZ40)
	Lizander, Dmitriĭ Karlovich fon. Дмитрий Карлович фон Лизандер see PG3337.L68
3467.L549	Lobachevskiĭ, A. A. Лобачевскій (Table P-PZ40)
3467.L55	Lobanov, Dmitriĭ Ivanovich, fl. 1870-1890. Дмитрий Иванович Лобанов (Table P-PZ40)
3467.L56	Lodyzhenskiĭ, Ivan Nikolaevich, 1848- . Иван Николаевич Лодыженский (Table P-PZ40)

Russian literature
Individual authors and works, 1870-1917
Individual authors, Gorky - Per -- Continued

Lodyzhenskiĭ, Vladimir Nikolaevich. Владимир Николаевич Лодыженский see PG3467.L125

3467.L57 Lokhvit͡skai͡a, Mirra Aleksandrovna, 1869-1905. Мирра Александровна Лохвицкая (Table P-PZ40)
Variant of forename: Marii͡a (Мария)

Lokhvit͡skai͡a, Nadezhda Aleksandrovna. Надежда Александровна Лохвицкая see PG3453.B8

Lolo, pseud. Лоло see PG3467.M94

3467.L58 Lomachevskiĭ, Dmitriĭ Platonovich, ca. 1830-1877? Дмитрий Платонович Ломачевский (Table P-PZ40)

3467.L585 Lomakin, Nikolaĭ, fl. 1890-1910. Николай Ломакин (Table P-PZ40)

3467.L59 Lopatina, Ekaterina Mikhaĭlovna, 1865-1935. Екатерина Михайловна Лопатина (Table P-PZ40)

Lorer, N. N. Лорер see PG3467.K45

3467.L6 Lourié, Ossip, 1868- (Table P-PZ40)

Lugovoĭ, A. A. Луговой see PG3470.T5

3467.L7 Lukashevich-Khmyznikova, Klavdii͡a Vladimirovna (Miret͡s-Imshenet͡skai͡a), 1859-1937. Клавдия Владимировна (Мирец-Имшенецкая) Лукашевич-Хмызникова (Table P-PZ40)

3467.L8 Lukhmanova, Nadezhda Aleksandrovna (Baĭkova), 1840-1907. Надежда Александровна (Байкова) Лухманова (Table P-PZ40)

3467.L82 Luk′i͡anov, Aleksandr Aleksandrovich, 1871- . Александр Александрович Лукьянов (Table P-PZ40)

Luk′i͡anov, L. Л. Лукьянов see PG3470.P56

3467.L83 Lunin, Alekseĭ Alekseevich, 1839- . Алексей Алексеевич Лунин (Table P-PZ40)

Lur′e, Osip Davydovich. Осип Давыдович Лурье see PG3467.L6

3467.L84 L′vov, Arkadiĭ, fl. 1900-1910. Аркадий Львов (Table P-PZ40)

L′vov, Evgeniĭ. Евгений Львов see PG3467.K52

3467.L85 L′vov, Tikhon Nikolaevich, fl. 1890-1900. Тихон Николаевич Львов (Table P-PZ40)

3467.L86 L′vova, Aleksandra Dmitrievna, 1849-1932. Александра Дмитриевна Львова (Table P-PZ40)

3467.L87 L′vova, Anfisa Petrovna (Balavinskai͡a), 1829-1891. Анфиса Петровна (Балавинская) Львова (Table P-PZ40)

3467.L88 L′vova, Elizaveta Vasil′evna, fl. 1890-1900. Елизавета Васильевна Львова (Table P-PZ40)

Russian literature
Individual authors and works, 1870-1917
Individual authors, Gorky - Per -- Continued

3467.L882 L′vova, Elizaveta Vladimirovna. Елизавета Владимировна Львова (Table P-PZ40)

3467.L885 L′vova, Nadezhda Grigor′evna (Poltorat͡skai͡a), 1891-1913. Надежда Григорьевна (Полторацкая) Львова (Table P-PZ40)

3467.L89 L′vovich, Andreĭ, fl. 1880-1890. Андрей Львович (Table P-PZ40)

3467.L9 Lykoshin, Nil Sergeevich, fl. 1890-1900. Нил Сергеевич Лыкошин (Table P-PZ40)

3467.L94 Lytkina, E.A., fl. 1890-1900. Е.А. Лыткина (Table P-PZ40)

3467.M2 Machtet, Grigoriĭ Aleksandrovich, 1852-1901. Григорий Александрович Мачтет (Table P-PZ40)

3467.M215 Mai͡a. Маия (Table P-PZ40)

Maĭkov, Apollon Nikolaevich. Аполлон Николаевич Майков see PG3337.M2

3467.M22 Maĭkov, Mikhail Grigor′evich, d. 1905. Михаил Григорьевич Майков (Table P-PZ40)

3467.M23 Maĭkova, Ekaterina Pavlovna, 1836- . Екатерина Павловна Майкова (Table P-PZ40)

Maĭor Burbonov, pseud. Майор Бурбонов see PG3467.M7

Maĭskai͡a, Tat′i͡ana. Татьяна Майская see PG3467.M24

3467.M24 Maĭzel, Tat′i͡ana Aleksandrovna. Татьяна Александровна Майзел (Table P-PZ40)

3467.M245 Makedonskiĭ, D.N., fl. 1980-1900. Д.Н. Македонский (Table P-PZ40)

3467.M25 Maklakova, Lidii͡a Filippovna, 1851-1936. Лидия Филипповна Маклакова (Table P-PZ40)

3467.M255 Maklet͡sova-Degaeva, Natalii͡a Petrovna, fl. 1890-1900. Наталия Петровна Маклецова-Дегаева (Table P-PZ40)

3467.M26 Maksimov, Aleksandr I͡Akovlevich, 1851-1896. Александр Яковлевич Максимов (Table P-PZ40)

3467.M27 Maksimov, Konstantin Afanas′evich, 1848- . Константин Афанасьевич Максимов (Table P-PZ40)

3467.M275 Maksimov, Nikolaĭ Vasil′evich, 1848-1900. Николай Васильевич Максимов (Table P-PZ40)

Maleonskiĭ, M. M. Малеонский see PG3453.B947

3467.M28 Mali͡arevskiĭ, Ivan Vasil′evich, 1846-1915. Иван Васильевич Маляревский (Table P-PZ40)

3467.M29 Malinovskiĭ, Aleksandr Aleksandrovich, 1873-1928. Александр Александрович Малиновский (Table P-PZ40)

Russian literature
Individual authors and works, 1870-1917
Individual authors, Gorky - Per -- Continued

3467.M294 Mal′mgren, A.Ė. А.Э. Мальмгрен (Table P-PZ40)
3467.M3 Mamin, Dmitriĭ Narkisovich, 1852-1912. Дмитрий Наркисович Мамин (Table P-PZ40 modified)
3467.M3A61-.M3Z458 Separate works. By title
3467.M3A8 Annushka (Tale). Аннушка
3467.M3B3 Bashka (Tale). Башка
3467.M3B4 Beloe zoloto (Story). Белое золото
3467.M3B5 Bez nazvanii͡a (Novel). Без названия
3467.M3B55 Bogach i Eremka (Tale). Богач и Еремка
3467.M3B6 Boĭt͡sy (Tale). Бойцы
3467.M3B7 Brat′i͡a Gordeevy (Story). Братья Гордеевы
3467.M3B75 Bui͡anka (Story). Буянка
3467.M3B8 Burnyĭ potok (Novel). Бурный поток
3467.M3C4 Chelovek s proshlym i drugie rasskazy. Человек с прошлым и другие рассказы
3467.M3C5 Cherty iz zhizni Pepko (Novel). Черты из жизни Пепко
3467.M3D4 Dedushkino zoloto (Tale). Дедушкино золото
3467.M3D5 Dikoe schast′e (Novel). Дикое счастье
3467.M3D6 Dorogoĭ kamen′ (Tale). Дорогой камень
3467.M3D7 Dorogoĭ khleb nauki (Tale). Дорогой хлеб науки
3467.M3G6 Gornoe gnezdo (Novel). Горное гнездо
3467.M3I5 Imeninnik (Novel). Именинник
3467.M3I7 Ispoved′ (Tale). Исповедь
3467.M3I9 Iz ural′skoĭ stariny (Tales). Из уральской старины
3467.M3K3 Kara-Khanym (Tale). Кара-Ханым
3467.M3K4 Khleb (Novel). Хлеб
3467.M3K5 Kiseĭnai͡a baryshni͡a (Story). Кисейная барышня
3467.M3K6 Kon′ "Razboĭnik" (Sketch). Конь "Разбойник"
3467.M3K63 Konet͡s voĭne (Tale). Конец войне
3467.M3K67 Kormilet͡s (Tale). Кормилец
3467.M3K7 Krasnai͡a shapochka (Tale). Красная шапочка
3467.M3K75 Krasnoe i͡aichko (Tale). Красное яичко
3467.M3K8 Kukol′nyĭ magazin (Tale). Кукольный магазин
3467.M3L4 Lëtnye (Tale). Лётные
3467.M3M3 Maksim Beneli͡avdov (Story). Максим Бенелявдов
3467.M3M35 Malinovye gory (Tale). Малиновые горы
3467.M3M4 Medvedit͡sa (Tale). Медведица
3467.M3M5 Million i drugie rasskazy. Миллион и другие рассказы
3467.M3M6 Mizgir′ (Tale). Мизгирь
3467.M3N2 Na reke Chusovoĭ (Sketches). На реке Чусовой
3467.M3N24 Na shestom nomere (Story). На шестом номере

Russian literature
Individual authors and works, 1870-1917
Individual authors, Gorky - Per
Mamin, Dmitriĭ Narkisovich, 1852-1912. Дмитрий Наркисович Мамин
Separate works. By title -- Continued

3467.M3N27 Na ulit͡se (Novel). На улице
3467.M3N3 Na vol′nom vozdukhe (Tale). На вольном воздухе
3467.M3N33 Na zaimke (Tale). На заимке
3467.M3N4 Ne to (Story). Не то
3467.M3N8 Nuzhno pooshchri͡at′ iskusstvo (Story). Нужно поощрять искусство
3467.M3O2 Obshchiĭ li͡ubimet͡s publiki (Novel). Общий любимец публики
3467.M3O35 Okhoniny brovi (Story). Охонины брови
3467.M3O4 Okolo gospod (Sketches). Около господ
3467.M3O7 Osennie list′i͡a (Sketches and tales). Осенние листья
3467.M3O75 Osip Ivanovich (Tale). Осип Иванович
3467.M3O8 Ot″ezd (Sketch). Отъезд
3467.M3O9 Ozornik (Tale). Озорник
3467.M3P3 Padai͡ushchie zvezdy (Novel). Падающие звезды
3467.M3P4 Perevodchit͡sa na priiskakh (Tale). Переводчица на приисках
3467.M3P45 Pesni͡a mistera Kal′ (Tale). Песня мистера Каль
3467.M3P5 Po novomu puti (Novel). По новому пути
3467.M3P55 Po Uralu (Tales and sketches). По Уралу
3467.M3P6 Poslednii͡ai͡a treba (Tale). Последняя треба
3467.M3P7 Prestupniki (Tales and stories). Преступники
3467.M3P75 Privalovskie milliony (Novel). Приваловские миллионы
3467.M3R3 Rannie vskhody (Novel). Ранние всходы
3467.M3R6 Rozhdestvenskie ogni (Stories and tales). Рождественские огни
3467.M3S3 Savka (Tale). Савка
3467.M3S4 Sharlatan (Tale). Шарлатан
3467.M3S5 Sibirskie rasskazy. Сибирские рассказы
3467.M3S6 Slava Bogu (Tale). Слава Богу
3467.M3S8 Svi͡atochnye rasskazy. Святочные рассказы
3467.M3T7 Tri druga (Tale). Три друга
3467.M3T8 Tri kont͡sa (Novel). Три конца
3467.M3U2 U svi͡atykh mogilok (Sketch). У святых могилок
3467.M3U7 Ural′skie rasskazy. Уральские рассказы
3467.M3V14 V doroge (Sketches and tales). В дороге
3467.M3V17 V glushi (Stories and tales). В глуши
3467.M3V2 V kamennom kolodt͡se (Tales). В каменном колодце
3467.M3V23 V khudykh dushakh [i drugie rasskazy]. В худых душах [и другие рассказы]

Russian literature
Individual authors and works, 1870-1917
Individual authors, Gorky - Per
Mamin, Dmitriĭ Narkisovich, 1852-1912. Дмитрий Наркисович Мамин
Separate works. By title -- Continued

3467.M3V25 V khudykh dushakh (Tale). В худых душах
3467.M3V3 V uchen'i (Tale). В ученьи
3467.M3V4 Velikiĭ greshnik (Tale). Великий грешник
3467.M3V43 Vernyĭ rab (Story). Верный раб
3467.M3V47 Vertel (Tale). Вертел
3467.M3V5 Vesennie grozy (Novel). Весенние грозы
3467.M3V55 Vkrug rakitova kusta i drugie rasskazy. Вкруг ракитова куста и другие рассказы
3467.M3V57 Vkrug rakitova kusta (Tale). Вкруг ракитова куста
3467.M3V6 Volshebnik (Tale). Волшебник
3467.M3V8 Vstrechi (Tale). Встречи
3467.M3Z12 Za dragot͡sennymi kamni͡ami (Story). За драгоценными камнями
3467.M3Z14 Zarnit͡sy (Tales). Зарницы
3467.M3Z18 Zelenye gory (Tale). Зеленые горы
3467.M3Z2 Zhid (Tale). Жид
3467.M3Z23 Zhivai͡a voda [i drugie rasskazy]. Живая вода [и другие рассказы]
3467.M3Z25 Zhivai͡a voda (Tale). Живая вода
3467.M3Z3 Zimov'e na Studenoĭ (Tale). Зимовье на Студеной
3467.M3Z35 Zolotai͡a likhoradka (Sketches and tales). Золотая лихорадка
3467.M3Z37 Zolotai͡a mukha i drugie rasskazy. Золотая муха и другие рассказы
3467.M3Z38 Zolotai͡a mukha (Tale). Золотая муха
3467.M3Z4 Zoloto (Novel). Золото
3467.M3Z42 Zolotopromyshlenniki (Drama). Золотопромышленники

Mamin-Sibiri͡ak, pseud. Мамин-Сибиряк see PG3467.M3

3467.M315 Mamontov, Sergeĭ Savvich, 1867-1915. Сергей Саввич Мамонтов (Table P-PZ40)
3467.M317 Mandel'shtam, Iosif Emel'i͡anovich, 1846-1911. Иосиф Емельянович Мандельштам (Table P-PZ40)
3467.M32 Mann, Ippolit Aleksandrovich, 1823-1894. Ипполит Александрович Манн (Table P-PZ40)
3467.M323 Mansfel'd, Dmitriĭ Avgustovich, 1851-1909. Дмитрий Августович Мансфельд (Table P-PZ40)
3467.M324 Mansfel'd, Evgeniĭ, fl. 1890-1900. Евгеній Мансфельдъ (Table P-PZ40)

Mantasheva, Kapitolina Valer'i͡anovna. Капитолина Валерьяновна Манташева see PG3467.N3

Russian literature
Individual authors and works, 1870-1917
Individual authors, Gorky - Per -- Continued

3467.M325 Manzhura, Ivan Ivanovich, 1851-1893. Иван Иванович Манжура (Table P-PZ40)

3467.M326 Mar, N., fl. 1890-1900. Н. Мар (Table P-PZ40)

Maralo Īerikhonskiĭ, 1841-1891. Марало Іерихонскій see PG3467.I33

3467.M3264 Maraskin, fl. 1870-1880. Мараскин (Table P-PZ40)

Marchenko, Anastasii͡a I͡Akovlevna. Анастасия Яковлевна Марченко see PG3337.M32

Marivė, K., pseud. К. Маривэ see PG3470.V63

3467.M327 Markevich, Boleslav Mikhaĭlovich, 1822-1884. Болеслав Михайлович Маркевич (Table P-PZ40)

Marko Vovchok, pseud. Марко Вовчок see PG3467.M34

3467.M328 Markov, Alekseĭ Alekseevich, 1847-1893. Алексей Алексеевич Марков (Table P-PZ40)

3467.M33 Markov, Evgeniĭ L′vovich, 1835-1903. Евгений Львович Марков (Table P-PZ40)

3467.M333 Markov, Rostislav L′vovich, fl. 1880-1900. Ростислав Львович Марков (Table P-PZ40)

3467.M334 Markov, Vasiliĭ Vasil′evich, 1834-1883. Василий Васильевич Марков (Table P-PZ40)

3467.M335 Markov, Vladislav L′vovich, 1832- . Владислав Львович Марков (Table P-PZ40)

3467.M338 Markovich, Dmitriĭ Vasil′evich, 1848-1920. Дмитрий Васильевич Маркович (Table P-PZ40)

Markovich, Marii͡a Aleksandrovna (Vilinskai͡a). Мария Александровна (Вилинская) Маркович see PG3467.M34

3467.M34 Markovych, Marii͡a Oleksandrivna (Vilins′ka), 1834-1907. Марія Олександрівна (Вілінська) Маркович (Table P-PZ40)

3467.M347 Martakov, Aleksandr, fl. 1880-1890. Александр Мартаков (Table P-PZ40)

3467.M35 Mart′i͡anov, Petr Kuz′mich, 1827-1899. Петр Кузьмич Мартьянов (Table P-PZ40)

Martov, V. B. Мартов see PG3467.M47

3467.M353 Martynov, Ivan Andreevich, 1845-1901. Иван Андреевич Мартынов (Table P-PZ40)

3467.M355 Marusenko, E.A., fl. 1880-1890. Е.А. Марусенко (Table P-PZ40)

Masaĭ, pseud. Масай see PG3470.Z2

3467.M358 Mashkin, N.P., fl. 1890-1900. Н.П. Машкин (Table P-PZ40)

3467.M36 Maslov, Alekseĭ Nikolaevich, 1853- . Алексей Николаевич Маслов (Table P-PZ40)

Russian literature
Individual authors and works, 1870-1917
Individual authors, Gorky - Per -- Continued

3467.M362 Maslov, Nikolaĭ Dmitrievich, 1833-1892. Николай Дмитриевич Маслов (Table P-PZ40)

3467.M363 Maslovich, Nikolaĭ Vasil′evich, 1832- . Николай Васильевич Маслович (Table P-PZ40)

Mastityĭ belletrist, pseud. Маститый беллетрист see PG3453.B94

3467.M364 Matern, Ėmiliĭ Ėmilievich, 1854- . Эмилий Эмилиевич Матерн (Table P-PZ40)
Variant of surname: Mattern (Маттерн)

3467.M365 Mazepin, Evgeniĭ Konstantinovich, 1872-1911. Евгений Константинович Мазепин (Table P-PZ40)

3467.M366 Mazurin, Konstantin Mitrofanovich, 1866-1927. Константин Митрофанович Мазурин (Table P-PZ40)

3467.M367 Mazurkevich, Vladimir Aleksandrovich, 1871-1942. Владимир Александрович Мазуркевич (Table P-PZ40)

3467.M369 Medem,I.M., baronessa, fl. 1890-1900. И.М. Медем (Table P-PZ40)

3467.M37 Medvedev, Lev Mikhaĭlovich, 1865-1904. Лев Михайлович Медведев (Table P-PZ40)

3467.M372 Medvedskiĭ, Konstantin Petrovich, 1867- . Константин Петрович Медведский (Table P-PZ40)

3467.M375 Meĭsner, Aleksandr Fedorovich, 1865-1922. Александр Федорович Мейснер (Table P-PZ40)

3467.M378 Meklenburg, A.N., fl. 1880-1890. А.Н. Мекленбург (Table P-PZ40)

3467.M38 Mel′nikova, Aleksandra Nikolaevna (Ustinovich), 1848 or 9-1902. Александра Николаевна (Устинович) Мельникова (Table P-PZ40)

3467.M385 Mel′nit͡skai͡a, An. V., fl. 1890-1900. Ан. В. Мельницкая (Table P-PZ40)

Mel′shin, L. Л. Мельшин see PG3467.I2

3467.M39 Mendelevich, Rodion Abramovich, fl. 1890-1920. Родион Абрамович Менделевич (Table P-PZ40)

3467.M393 Men′shikov, Mikhail Osipovich, 1859-1918. Михаил Осипович Меньшиков (Table P-PZ40)

Men′shikova, Varvara Nikolaevna. Варвара Николаевна Меньшикова see PG3470.T782

3467.M395 Merder, Nadezhda Ivanovna (Svechina), 1839-1906. Надежда Ивановна (Свечина) Мердер (Table P-PZ40)

PG

Russian literature
Individual authors and works, 1870-1917
Individual authors, Gorky - Per -- Continued
Merezhkovskai͡a, Zinaida Nikolaevna (Gippius). Зинаида Николаевна (Гиппиус) Мережковская see PG3460.G5+
3467.M4 Merezhkovskiĭ, Dmitriĭ Sergeevich, 1865-1941. Дмитрий Сергеевич Мережковский (Table P-PZ40 modified)
3467.M4A61-.M4Z458 Separate works. By title
14 dekabri͡a. 14 декабря see PG3467.M4C5
3467.M4A75 Aleksandr I (Novel). Александр I
3467.M4A8 Angel (Novel). Ангел
Antikhrist. Антихрист see PG3467.M4K5
3467.M4B6 Bog (Poem). Бог
3467.M4B8 Budet radost′ (Drama). Будет радость
3467.M4C5 Chetyrnadt͡satoe dekabri͡a (14 dekabri͡a) (Novel). Четырнадцатое декабря
Dafnis i Khloi͡a. Дафнис и Хлоя see PA4229.L8
3467.M4F7 Frant͡sisk Assizskiĭ (Legend in verse). Франциск Ассизский
3467.M4G8 Groza (Dramatic piece). Гроза
3467.M4I5 Imogena (Legend). Имогена
3467.M4I6 Iov (Poem). Иов
3467.M4I8 Ital′i͡anskie novelly. Итальянские новеллы
Comprises: Li͡ubov′ sil′nee smerti, etc.
For separate tales see the title in PG3467.M4A61+
I͡Ulian Otstupnik. Юлиан Отступник see PG3467.M4K3
3467.M4K2-.M4K5 Khristos i antikhrist (Trilogy) (Novels). Христос и антихрист
Comprises:
3467.M4K3 Smert′ bogov. I͡Ulian Otstupnik. Смерть богов. Юлиан Отступник
Also published under the title: Otverzhennyi
3467.M4K4 Voskresshie bogi. Leonardo da Vinchi. Воскресшие боги. Леонардо да Винчи
Also published under the title: Vozrozhdenie
3467.M4K5 Antikhrist. Petr i Alekseĭ. Антихрист. Петр и Алексей
3467.M4K6 Konet͡s veka (Poem). Конец века
Leonardo da Vinchi. Леонардо да Винчи see PG3467.M4K4
3467.M4L5 Li͡ubov′ sil′nee smerti (Tale). Любовь сильнее смерти
3467.M4M3 Makov t͡svet (Drama). Маков цвет

Russian literature
Individual authors and works, 1870-1917
Individual authors, Gorky - Per
Merezhkovskiĭ, Dmitriĭ Sergeevich, 1865-1941. Дмитрий Сергеевич Мережковский
Separate works. By title -- Continued

3467.M4M34 Malen'kaia Tereza. Маленькая Тереза
3467.M4M4 Messiia (Novel). Мессия
3467.M4M5 Mikel' Anzhelo (Novel). Микель Анжело
3467.M4N3 Nauka liubvi (Tale). Наука любви
Otverzhennyĭ. Отверженный see PG3467.M4K3
3467.M4P3 Pavel I (Drama). Павел I
3467.M4R5 Romantika (Drama). Романтика
3467.M4R6 Rozhdenie bogov: Tutankamon na Krite (Novel). Рождение богов: Тутанкамон на Крите
3467.M4S4 Sil'vio (Fantasy). Сильвио
3467.M4S5 Simvoly (Songs and poems). Символы
3467.M4S55 Smert' (Poem). Смерть
Smert' bogov. Смерть богов see PG3467.M4K3
3467.M4S7 Starinnye oktavy (Poem). Старинные октавы
3467.M4S8 Sviatoĭ Satir (Legend). Святой Сатир
3467.M4T3 Taĭna trekh. Egipet i Vavilon. Тайна трех. Египет и Вавилон
3467.M4T7 TSarevich Alekseĭ (Tragedy). Царевич Алексей
Vechnye sputniki. Вечные спутники see PN517
3467.M4V5 Vera (Story in verse). Вера
Voskresshie bogi. Воскресшие боги see PG3467.M4K4
Vozrozhdenie. Возрождение see PG3467.M4K4
3467.M4V6 Vozvrashchenie k prirode (Drama). Возвращение к природе

3467.M413 Merezhkovskiĭ, K.S. (Konstantin Sergeevich), 1854-1921. Константин Сергеевич Мережковский (Table P-PZ40)
Meshcherkaia, Ol'ga Pavlovna. Ольга Павловна Мещеркая see PG3470.R86
3467.M42 Meshcherskiĭ, Aleksandr Vasil'evich, kniaz', d. 1900. Александр Васильевич Мещерский (Table P-PZ40)
3467.M427 Meshcherskiĭ, P.P. (Petr Platonovich), kniaz'. Петр Платонович Мещерский (Table P-PZ40)
3467.M43 Meshcherskiĭ, Vladimir Petrovich, kniaz', 1839-1914. Владимир Петрович Мещерский (Table P-PZ40)
Miasnitskiĭ, I.I. И.И. Мясницкий see PG3453.B315
3467.M44 Miasoedov, Aleksandr Dmitrievich, fl. 1880-1900. Александр Дмитриевич Мясоедов (Table P-PZ40)
3467.M45 Miatlev, Vladimir Ivanovich, d. 1900. Владимир Иванович Мятлев (Table P-PZ40)

Russian literature
Individual authors and works, 1870-1917
Individual authors, Gorky - Per -- Continued

3467.M46 Mi͡atlev, Vladimir Petrovich, 1868- . Владимир Петрович Мятлев (Table P-PZ40)

Mikhaĭlov, A. A. Михайлов see PG3470.S486

3467.M465 Mikhaĭlov, Konstantin Arsen′evich, 1868-1919. Константин Арсеньевич Михайлов (Table P-PZ40)

3467.M47 Mikhaĭlov, Vladimir Petrovich, 1855-1901. Владимир Петрович Михайлов (Table P-PZ40)

Mikhaĭlova, Ol′ga Nikolaevna (Chi͡umina). Ольга Николаевна (Чюмина) Михайлова see PG3460.C6

3467.M48 Mikhaĭlovskiĭ, Nikolaĭ Georgievich, 1852-1906. Николай Георгиевич Михайловский (Table P-PZ40 modified)

3467.M48A61-.M48Z458 Separate works. By title

3467.M48A75 Adochka (Tale). Адочка

3467.M48B3 Babushka (Tale). Бабушка

3467.M48B8 Burlaki (Tale). Бурлаки

3467.M48D4 Derevenskie panoramy (Tales). Деревенские панорамы

For separate tales see the title in PG3467.M48A61+

Detstvo Tëmy. ДетствоТёмы see PG3467.M48I93

3467.M48D5 Dikiĭ chelovek (Sketch). Дикий человек

3467.M48D8 Dvoret͡s dima (Tale). Дворец дима

3467.M48E8 Evreĭskiĭ pogrom (Tale). Еврейский погром

3467.M48G4 Geniĭ (Tale). Гений

Gimnazisty. Гимназисты see PG3467.M48I95

3467.M48I5 Inzhenery (Novel). Инженеры

3467.M48I7 Ispoved′ ot͡sa (Tale). Исповедь отца

3467.M48I8 It͡ska i Davydka (Tale). Ицка и Давыдка

3467.M48I9 Iz semeĭnoĭ khroniki (Trilogy). Из семейной хроники

Comprises:

3467.M48I93 Detstvo Tëmy. Детство Тёмы

3467.M48I95 Gimnazisty. Гимназисты

3467.M48I97 Studenty. Студенты

3467.M48K5 Khudozhnik (Tale). Художник

3467.M48K6 Klotil′da (Story). Клотильда

3467.M48K7 Koroten′ki͡a zhizn′ (Tale). Коротенькая жизнь

3467.M48N15 Na khodu (Tale). На ходу

3467.M48N2 Na nochlege (Tale). На ночлеге

3467.M48N23 Na praktike (Sketch). На практике

3467.M48N27 Na stant͡sii (Sketch). На станции

3467.M48N3 Natasha (Tale). Наташа

3467.M48N4 Nemal′t͡sev (Tale). Немальцев

3467.M48N5 Neskol′ko let v derevne (Tale). Несколько лет в деревне

Russian literature
Individual authors and works, 1870-1917
Individual authors, Gorky - Per
Mikhaĭlovskiĭ, Nikolaĭ Georgievich, 1852-1906. Николай Георгиевич Михайловский
Separate works. By title -- Continued

3467.M48O7 Orkhidei͡a (Drama). Орхидея
3467.M48P5 Pod vecher (Sketch). Под вечер
3467.M48P6 Podrostki (Drama). Подростки
3467.M48P7 Pravda (Tale). Правда
3467.M48S6 Sochel′nik v russkoĭ derevne (Tale). Сочельник в русской деревне
3467.M48S7 Staryĭ evreĭ (Tale). Старый еврей
Studenty. Студенты see PG3467.M48I97
3467.M48S8 Sumerki (Sketch). Сумерки
3467.M48V2 V usad′be pomeshchit͡sy I͡Aryshchevoĭ (Tale). В усадьбе помещицы Ярыщевой
3467.M48V3 Variant (Tale). Вариант
3467.M48V7 Vstrecha (Tale). Встреча
3467.M48Z3 Zora (Prolog). Зора
3467.M49 Mikhaĭlovskiĭ, Nikolaĭ Konstantinovich, 1842-1904. Николай Константинович Михайловский (Table P-PZ40)
Chiefly a literary critic and sociologist
For his biography and work as a critic see PG2947.M5
Mikhalovskiĭ, Dmitriĭ Lavrent′evich. Дмитрий Лаврентьевич Михаловский see PG3337.M53
3467.M5 Mikheev, Vasiliĭ Mikhaĭlovich, 1859-1908. Василий Михайлович Михеев (Table P-PZ40)
3467.M55 Mikhnevich, Aleksandr Petrovich, 1853-1912. Александр Петрович Михневич (Table P-PZ40)
3467.M6 Mikhnevich, Vladimir Osipovich, 1841-1899. Владимир Осипович Михневич (Table P-PZ40)
Mikulich, V. B. Микулич see PG3470.V49
3467.M62 Mili͡aev, Vasiliĭ Evgen′evich, 1873- . Василий Евгеньевич Миляев (Table P-PZ40)
3467.M623 Milich, Ch. Ч. Милич (Table P-PZ40)
3467.M63 Milit͡syna, E. (Elena), 1874-1930. Елена Милицына (Table P-PZ40)
Mili͡ukov, Aleksandr Petrovich. Александр Петрович Милюков see PG3337.M54
3467.M65 Miller, Georgiĭ, fl. 1890-1900. Георгий Миллер (Table P-PZ40)
3467.M66 Miller, N.K., fl. 1880-1890. Н.К. Миллер (Table P-PZ40)
3467.M68 Milovskiĭ, Sergeĭ Nikolaevich, 1861-1911. Сергей Николаевич Миловский (Table P-PZ40)

Russian literature
Individual authors and works, 1870-1917
Individual authors, Gorky - Per -- Continued

3467.M7 Minaev, Dmitriĭ Dmitrievich, 1835-1889. Дмитрий Дмитриевич Минаев (Table P-PZ40)

Minskiĭ, N. H. Минский see PG3470.V525

3467.M72 Mint͡slov, Sergeĭ Rudolʹfovich, 1870-1933. Сергей Рудольфович Минцлов (Table P-PZ40)

Miret͡s-Imshenet͡skai͡a, Klavdii͡a Vladimirovna. Клавдия Владимировна Мирец-Имшенецкая see PG3467.L7

Miropolʹskiĭ, A. A. Миропольский see PG3467.L127

Mirtov, O. O. Миртов see PG3467.K63

3467.M724 Mishla, 1847-1884. Мишла (Table P-PZ40)

3467.M728 Mochalova, A. A. Мочалова (Table P-PZ40)

3467.M73 Mokrinskiĭ, Georgiĭ, fl. 1880-1900. Георгий Мокринский (Table P-PZ40)

3467.M74 Molchanov, Aleksandr Nikolaevich, 1847- . Александр Николаевич Молчанов (Table P-PZ40)

Molotov, Aleksandr. Александр Молотов see PG3460.D47

Monteverde, Petr Avgustinovich, 1839-1919. Петр Августинович Монтеверде see PG3470.P235

3467.M76 Montvid, Aleksandra Stanislavovna, 1845- . Александра Станиславовна Монтвид (Table P-PZ40)

Moravskai͡a, Marii͡a Li͡udvigovna. Мария Людвиговна Моравская see PG3467.M78

3467.M78 Moravsky, Maria, 1889-1947 (Table P-PZ40)

Morawska, Marja see PG3467.M78

3467.M8 Mordovt͡sev, Daniil Lukich, 1830-1905. Даниил Лукич Мордовцев (Table P-PZ40)

3467.M82 Mordvin-Shchodro, A.O., fl. 1890-1900. A.O. Мордвин-Щодро (Table P-PZ40)

3467.M84 Morozov, Evgeniĭ, fl. 1890-1900. Евгений Морозов (Table P-PZ40)

3467.M85 Morozov, Nikolaĭ Aleksandrovich, 1854-1946. Николай Александрович Морозов (Table P-PZ40)

3467.M854 Morskoĭ, N., 1846-1888. Н. Морской (Table P-PZ40)

3467.M86 Moshin, Alekseĭ Nikolaevich, 1870- . Алексей Николаевич Мошин (Table P-PZ40)

Moskovskiĭ, Gavriil. Гавриил Московский see PG3467.K45

3467.M87 Mozhaĭskiĭ, Ivan Pavlovich, 1830-1893. Иван Павлович Можайский (Table P-PZ40)

Mozharov, pseud. Можаров see PG3467.L37

3467.M88 Mserian͡ts, Rubens Zarmaĭrovich, 1869- . Рубенс Зармайрович Мсерианц (Table P-PZ40)

Russian literature
Individual authors and works, 1870-1917
Individual authors, Gorky - Per -- Continued

3467.M9 Mundt, Fedor, fl. 1890-1900. Федор Мундт (Table P-PZ40)

3467.M92 Mundt, Sofii͡a Nikolaevna, 1848- . София Николаевна Мундт (Table P-PZ40)

3467.M94 Munshteĭn, Leonid Grigor′evich, 1868-1947. Леонид Григорьевич Мунштейн (Table P-PZ40)

Muravlin, D. Д. Муравлин see PG3460.G64

3467.M96 Murinov, Vladimir I͡Akovlevich, 1863- . Владимир Яковлевич Муринов (Table P-PZ40)

3467.M97 Mushinskiĭ, N.I., fl. 1870-1900. Н.И. Мушинский (Table P-PZ40)

My, pseud. Мы see PG3470.S48

3467.N17 Nadinskiĭ, A. A. Надинский (Table P-PZ40)

3467.N2 Nadson, Semen I͡Akovlevich, 1862-1887. Семен Яковлевич Надсон (Table P-PZ40 modified)

3467.N2A61-.N2Z458 Separate works. By title

3467.N2D7 Drug moĭ, brat moĭ, stradai͡ushchiĭ brat (Poem). Друг мой, брат мой, страдающий брат

3467.N2G7 Grezy (Poem). Грезы

3467.N2I8 Iuda (Poem). Иуда

3467.N2I9 Iz t′my vremen (Poem). Из тьмы времен

3467.N2M4 Mechty korolevy (Poem). Мечты королевы

3467.N2N3 Na zare (Poem). На заре

3467.N2N4 Net, legche mne dumat′, chto ty umerla (Poem). Нет, легче мне думать, что ты умерла

3467.N2T6 Tomi͡as′ i stradai͡a vo mrake nenast′i͡a (Poem). Томясь и страдая во мраке ненастья

3467.N2T7 T͡Sarevna Sof′i͡a (Tragedy, fragment). Царевна Софья

3467.N22 Nagrodskai͡a, Evdokii͡a Apollonovna (Golovacheva), 1866-1930. Евдокия Аполлоновна (Головачева) Нагродская (Table P-PZ40)

Naidenov, S. C. Наиденов see PG3451.A6

3467.N23 Nakrokhin, Prokofiĭ Egorovich, 1850-1903. Прокофий Егорович Накрохин (Table P-PZ40)

Narovchatskiĭ, N. H. Наровчатский see PG3451.A36

3467.N25 Nart͡sov, A.N., fl. 1900-1910. А.Н. Нарцов (Table P-PZ40)

3467.N26 Naumov, Nikolaĭ Ivanovich, 1838-1903. Николай Иванович Наумов (Table P-PZ40)

3467.N27 Naumovych, I.H., 1826-1891. Іван Григорович Наумович (Table P-PZ40)

Russian form: Ioann Grigor′evich Naumovich (Иоанн Григорьевич Наумович)

Russian literature
Individual authors and works, 1870-1917
Individual authors, Gorky - Per -- Continued
Nauta, pseud. Наута see PG3460.D625
3467.N28 Navrot͡skiĭ, Aleksandr Aleksandrovich, 1839-1914. Александр Александрович Навроцкий (Table P-PZ40)
3467.N29 Nazar′ev, Valerian Nikanorovich, 1830-1902. Валериан Никанорович Назарьев (Table P-PZ40)
3467.N3 Nazar′eva, Kapitolina Valer′i͡anovna (Mantasheva), 1847-1900. Капитолина Валерьяновна (Манташева) Назарьева (Table P-PZ40)
3467.N32 Nazarov, Egor Ivanovich, 1884-1900. Егор Иванович Назаров (Table P-PZ40)
Nazhivin, Ivan Fedorovich. Иван Федорович Наживин see PG3476.N4
Ne-Bukva, pseud. Не-Буква see PG3470.V23
3467.N33 Nechaev, Egor Efimovich, 1859-1925. Егор Ефимович Нечаев (Table P-PZ40)
Nechuĭ, I. И. Нечуй see PG3467.L44
3467.N332 Nedetovskiĭ, Grigoriĭ Ivanovich, 1846-1922. Григорий Иванович Недетовский (Table P-PZ40)
3467.N335 Nedobrovo, Nikolaĭ Vladimirovich, 1883-1919. Николай Владимирович Недоброво (Table P-PZ40)
3467.N34 Nedolin, M.A., fl. 1870-1880. M.A. Недолин (Table P-PZ40)
3467.N35 Nedolin, Sergeĭ Aleksandrovich, 1880-1954. Сергей Александрович Недолин (Table P-PZ40)
3467.N36 Nefedov, Filipp Diomidovich, 1838-1902. Филипп Диомидович Нефедов (Table P-PZ40)
3467.N37 Neglukhovskiĭ, F.K., fl. 1880-1890. Ф.К. Неглуховский (Table P-PZ40)
3467.N38 Nekrasov, Nikita, fl. 1870-1880. Никита Некрасов (Table P-PZ40)
Neledinskiĭ, Vl. Вл. Нелединский see PG3460.G49
3467.N39 Nelidova, Ekaterina, fl. 1880-1900. Екатерина Нелидова (Table P-PZ40)
Nelidova, L. Л. Нелидова see PG3467.M25
3467.N395 Nemirov, Grigoriĭ Aleksandrovich, 1847-1905. Григорий Александрович Немиров (Table P-PZ40)
3467.N4 Nemirovich-Danchenko, Vasiliĭ Ivanovich, 1845-1936. Василий Иванович Немирович-Данченко (Table P-PZ40)
3467.N5 Nemirovich-Danchenko, Vladimir Ivanovich, 1858-1943. Владимир Иванович Немирович-Данченко (Table P-PZ40)

Russian literature
Individual authors and works, 1870-1917
Individual authors, Gorky - Per -- Continued
Nemirovskai͡a, Anna Abramovna. Анна Абрамовна Немировская see PG3470.S18
3467.N52 Nemirovskiĭ, A.O., fl. 1890-1900. А.О. Немировский (Table P-PZ40)
3467.N57 Nesterov, Sergeĭ Markovich, fl. 1890-1900. Сергей Маркович Нестеров (Table P-PZ40)
3467.N6 Nevezhin, Petr Mikhaĭlovich, 1841-1919. Петр Михайлович Невежин (Table P-PZ40)
Cf. PG3337.O8B55 Blazh′, joint author Ostrovskiĭ
3467.N63 Nezhata, Nikolaĭ, fl. 1880-1890. Николай Нежата (Table P-PZ40)
Nezlobin, A. A. Незлобин see PG3460.D52
Nezlobivyĭ poėt, pseud. Незлобивый поэт see PG3453.B98
Nik T--o, pseud. Ник Т--о see PG3453.A6
3467.N66 Nikiforov, Nikolaĭ Konstantinovich, 1856- . Николай Константинович Никифоров (Table P-PZ40)
3467.N68 Nikitin, Aleksandr, fl. 1900-1910. Александр Никитин (Table P-PZ40)
3467.N69 Nikitin, N.V., fl. 1900-1910. Н.В. Никитин (Table P-PZ40)
3467.N7 Nikitin, Viktor Nikitich, 1839-1908. Виктор Никитич Никитин (Table P-PZ40)
Nikolaev, I͡U. Ю. Николаев see PG3467.G35
3467.N72 Nikolaev, Nikolaĭ, fl. 1890-1900. Николай Николаев (Table P-PZ40)
3467.N73 Nikolaeva, E., fl. 1880-1890. Е. Николаева (Table P-PZ40)
Nikolaeva, M. M. Николаева see PG3470.T77
3467.N75 Nikol′skiĭ, Boris Vladimirovich, 1870-1919. Борис Владимирович Никольский (Table P-PZ40)
3467.N76 Nikol′skiĭ, Mikhail Ėrastovich, 1878- . Михаил Эрастович Никольский (Table P-PZ40)
3467.N78 Nikonov, Boris Pavlovich, fl. 1910-1920. Борис Павлович Никонов (Table P-PZ40)
Nil Admirari, pseud. Нил Адмирари see PG3467.P4
Nivin, A. A. Нивин see PG3470.Z45
Normanskiĭ, S. C. Норманский see PG3470.S9
3467.N8 Nort͡sov, Alekseĭ Nikolaevich, 1859-1922. Алексей Николаевич Норцов (Table P-PZ40)
3467.N82 Nosilov, Konstantin Dmitrievich, 1858-1923. Константин Дмитриевич Носилов (Table P-PZ40)
Nosorogov, Vonifatiĭ. Вонифатий Носорогов see PG3467.M363

PG

Russian literature
Individual authors and works, 1870-1917
Individual authors, Gorky - Per -- Continued

Notenberg, Eleonora. Элеонора Генриховна фон Нотенберг see PG3467.G9

3467.N84 Notovich, Osip Konstantinovich, 1849-1914. Осип Константинович Нотович (Table P-PZ40)

3467.N86 Novikov, Aleksandr Ivanovich, 1861-1913. Александр Иванович Новиков (Table P-PZ40)

3467.N88 Novikova-Zarina, E.I., 1835-1940. Е.И. Новикова-Зарина (Table P-PZ40)

3467.N9 Novodvorskiĭ, Andreĭ Osipovich, 1853-1882. Андрей Осипович Новодворский (Table P-PZ40)

3467.N95 Novosil′t͡seva, Ekaterina Vladimirovna, d. 1885. Екатерина Владимировна Новосильцева (Table P-PZ40)

Oblichitel′nyĭ poėt, pseud. Обличительный поэт see PG3467.M7

3467.O2 Obolenskiĭ, Leonid Egorovich, 1845-1906. Леонид Егорович Оболенский (Table P-PZ40)

3467.O3 Obol′i͡aninov, Vladimir Adol′fovich, 1850- . Владимир Адольфович Обольянинов (Table P-PZ40)

3467.O4 Okreĭt͡s, Stanislav Stanislavovich, ca. 1834- . Станислав Станиславович Окрейц (Table P-PZ40)

Old gentleman, pseud. see PG3451.A7

3467.O43 Olenin, K.L., fl. 1890-1910. К.Л. Оленин (Table P-PZ40)

3467.O44 Oliger, Nikolaĭ Fridrikhovich, 1882-ca. 1919. Николай Фридрихович Олигер (Table P-PZ40)

3467.O45 Ol′khin, Aleksandr Aleksandrovich, 1839-1897. Александр Александрович Ольхин (Table P-PZ40)

Ol′nem, O. O. Ольнем see PG3470.T782

3467.O47 Ol′shanin, Dmitriĭ M., fl. 1880-1900. Дмитрий М. Ольшанин (Table P-PZ40)

Omulevskiĭ, I.V. И.В. Омулевский see PG3460.F44

On dit, baron, pseud. Барон On dit see PG3453.B27

3467.O5 Opochinin, Evgeniĭ Nikolaevich, fl. 1880-1910. Евгений Николаевич Опочинин (Table P-PZ40)

Optimist, pseud. Оптимист see PG3460.C6

Ordynt͡sev, M. M. Ордынцев see PG3467.K625

Orenburgskiĭ, Sergeĭ Ivanovich Gusev-. Сергей Иванович Гусев-Оренбургский see PG3467.G94

3467.O6 Oreus, Ivan Ivanovich, 1877-1901. Иван Иванович Ореус (Table P-PZ40)

3467.O62 Oreus, V.F., fl. 1880-1890. В.Ф. Ореус (Table P-PZ40)

Orfanov, Mikhail Ivanovich. Михаил Иванович Орфанов see PG3467.M724

Orlit͡skiĭ, S. C. Орлицкий see PG3467.O4

Russian literature
Individual authors and works, 1870-1917
Individual authors, Gorky - Per -- Continued
Orlovskiĭ, K. K. Орловский see PG3460.G72
3467.O67 Ornatskiĭ, Ivan Vasil′evich. Иван Васильевич Орнатский (Table P-PZ40)
3467.O71 Osetrov, Zakhar Borisovich, fl. 1890-1910. Захар Борисович Осетров (Table P-PZ40)
3467.O72 Osipov, Andreĭ Andreevich, 1867-1908. Андрей Андреевич Осипов (Table P-PZ40)
Osipova, E.A. Е.А. Осипова see PG3467.P76
Osipovich, A. A. Осипович see PG3467.N9
3467.O73 Osipovich, Naum Markovich, 1870- . Наум Маркович Осипович (Table P-PZ40)
3467.O74 Osorgin, Mikhail Andreevich, 1878-1942. Михаил Андреевич Осоргин (Table P-PZ40)
Ossip-Lourié see PG3467.L6
3467.O75 Ostashev, Leonid Ivanovich, fl. 1890-1900. Леонид Иванович Осташев (Table P-PZ40)
Otradin, Vasiliĭ. Василий Отрадин see PG3470.S56
Otrok, I͡Uriĭ Nikolaevich Govorukha-. Юрий Николаевич Говоруха-Отрок see PG3467.G35
3467.O8 Ovsi͡aniko-Kulikovskiĭ, Dmitriĭ Nikolaevich, 1853-1920. Дмитрий Николаевич Овсянико-Куликовский (Table P-PZ40)
For Ovsi͡aniko-Kulikovskiĭ as a literary critic see PG2947.O8
3467.O85 Ozerov, Ivan Khristoforovich, 1869-1942. Иван Христофорович Озеров (Table P-PZ40)
3467.O86 Ozhegov, Matveĭ Ivanovich, 1860- . Матвей Иванович Ожегов (Table P-PZ40)
3467.O87 Ozhigina, L͡iudmila Aleksandrovna, 1837-1899. Людмила Александровна Ожигина (Table P-PZ40)
Ozmidova, Zinaida Konstantinovna. Зинаида Константиновна Озмидова see PG3470.Z393
P. I͡A., pseud. П.Я. see PG3467.I2
3467.P15 Paĭvel, S.A., fl. 1900-1910. С.А. Пайвел (Table P-PZ40)
3467.P2 Pal′m, Aleksandr Ivanovich, 1822-1885. Александр Иванович Пальм (Table P-PZ40)
3467.P3 Pal′min, Liodor Ivanovich, 1841-1891. Лиодор Иванович Пальмин (Table P-PZ40)
Forename is sometimes written "Iliodor"
3467.P35 Panchulidzev, D.A., fl. 1890-1900. Д.А. Панчулидзев (Table P-PZ40)
3467.P4 Pani͡utin, Lev Konstantinovich, 1831-1882. Лев Константинович Панютин (Table P-PZ40)

Russian literature
Individual authors and works, 1870-1917
Individual authors, Gorky - Per -- Continued

3467.P5 Panov, Nikolaĭ Andreevich, 1861-1906. Николай Андреевич Панов (Table P-PZ40)

3467.P52 Panov, S.N., fl. 1870-1880. С.Н. Панов (Table P-PZ40)

3467.P55 Panteleev, Longin Fedorovich, 1840-1919. Лонгин Федорович Пантелеев (Table P-PZ40)

3467.P58 Parenago, M.N., fl. 1890-1900. М.Н. Паренаго (Table P-PZ40)

3467.P6 Pataraki, Sergeĭ Aleksandrovich, fl. 1890-1900. Сергей Александрович Патараки (Table P-PZ40)

3467.P63 Pavlov, Aleksandr, fl. 1890-1900. Александр Павлов (Table P-PZ40)

3467.P65 Pavlov, Anatoliĭ, fl. 1900-1910. Анатолий Павлов (Table P-PZ40)

3467.P67 Pavlov, Nikolaĭ D., fl. 1890-1900. Николай Д. Павлов (Table P-PZ40)

3467.P7 Pavlov, Nikolaĭ Mikhaĭlovich, fl. 1860-1890. Николай Михайлович Павлов (Table P-PZ40)

3467.P72 Pavlova, Natalʹi͡a I., fl. 1890-1900. Наталья И. Павлова (Table P-PZ40)

3467.P74 Pavlovich, Feodor Aleksandrovich, 1832-1905. Феодор Александрович Павлович (Table P-PZ40)

3467.P76 Pavlovskai͡a, E.A. (Osipova), fl. 1890-1900. Е.А. (Осипова) Павловская (Table P-PZ40)

3467.P78 Pavlovskiĭ, Isaak I͡Akovlevich, 1853-1924. Исаак Яковлевич Павловский (Table P-PZ40)

3467.P8 Pazukhin, Alekseĭ Mikhaĭlovich, 1851-1919. Алексей Михайлович Пазухин (Table P-PZ40)

3467.P82 Pazukhin, Nikolaĭ Mikhaĭlovich, 1858-1898. Николай Михайлович Пазухин (Table P-PZ40)

Peėmpe, pseud. Пэмпе see PG3470.P618

Pʹer-Nevskiĭ, pseud. Пьер-Невский see PG3467.K618

Perelʹman, Osip Isidorovich. Осип Исидорович Перельман see PG3460.D9

3467.P85 Perelygin, Nikolaĭ Ivanovich, 1835- . Николай Иванович Перелыгин (Table P-PZ40)

3467.P88 Persii͡aninova, Natalʹi͡a Lʹvovna, fl. 1890-1900. Наталья Львовна Персиянинова (Table P-PZ40)

3467.P9 Pert͡sov, Nikolaĭ Vladimirovich, d. 1912. Николай Владимирович Перцов (Table P-PZ40)

3467.P95 Pervukhin, Mikhail Konstantinovich, 1870-1928. Михаил Константинович Первухин (Table P-PZ40)

3470 Individual authors, Pes - Z

Peshkov, Alekseĭ Maksimovich. Алексей Максимович Пешков see PG3462+

Russian literature
Individual authors and works, 1870-1917
Individual authors, Pes - Z -- Continued

3470.P15 Peskovskiĭ, Matveĭ Leont′evich, 1843-1903. Матвей Леонтьевич Песковский (Table P-PZ40)

3470.P16 Peterson, Ol′ga Mikhaĭlovna, 1857- . Ольга Михайловна Петерсон (Table P-PZ40)

3470.P18 Petrishchev, Afanasiĭ Borisovich, 1872- . Афанасий Борисович Петрищев (Table P-PZ40)

3470.P19 Petrokov, I͡Uriĭ, fl. 1900-1910. Юрий Петроков (Table P-PZ40)

3470.P2 Petropavlovskiĭ, Nikolaĭ Elpidiforovich, 1853-1892. Николай Елпидифорович Петропавловский (Table P-PZ40)

3470.P23 Petrov, Grigoriĭ Spiridonovich, 1867-1927. Григорий Спиридонович Петров (Table P-PZ40)

3470.P235 Petrov, Petr, 1839-1916. Петр Петров (Table P-PZ40)

3470.P24 Petrov, Petr Nikolaevich, 1827-1891. Петр Николаевич Петров (Table P-PZ40)

3470.P25 Petrov, Stepan Gavrilovich, 1869-1941. Степан Гаврилович Петров (Table P-PZ40)

Petrovich, I. И. Петрович see PG3453.B42

3470.P26 Petrovskiĭ, Petr Nikolaevich, 1864- . Петр Николаевич Петровский (Table P-PZ40)

Piłsudska, Idalii͡a Mechislavovna. Идалия Мечиславовна Пилсудская see PG3453.A55

3470.P27 Pimenova, Ėmilii͡a Kirillovna, 1855- . Эмилия Кирилловна Пименова (Table P-PZ40)

3470.P28 Pisarev, Dmitriĭ Ivanovich, 1840-1868. Дмитрий Иванович Писарев (Table P-PZ40)
For Pisarev as a literary critic see PG2947.P5

3470.P283 Piven′, Aleksandr, 1872-1962. Александр Пивень (Table P-PZ40)

3470.P285 Plaksin, Sergeĭ Ivanovich, fl. 1880-1900. Сергей Иванович Плаксин (Table P-PZ40)

3470.P29 Platon, Ivan Stepanovich, 1870- . Иван Степанович Платон (Table P-PZ40)

3470.P3 Pleshcheev, Aleksandr Alekseevich, 1858- . Алексей Николаевич Плещеев (Table P-PZ40)

Pleshcheev, Alekseĭ Nikolaevich. Алексей Николаевич Плещеев see PG3337.P54

3470.P33 Pletnev, Alekseĭ Petrovich, b. 1854. Алексей Петрович Плетнев (Table P-PZ40)

3470.P35 Pod″i͡achev, Semen Pavlovich, 1866-1934. Семен Павлович Подъячев (Table P-PZ40)

Podkalyvatel′, pseud. Подкалыватель see PG3470.S48

Pogorelov, A. A. Погорелов see PG3470.S568

Russian literature
Individual authors and works, 1870-1917
Individual authors, Pes - Z
Pogozheva, Lidii͡a Nikolaevna. Лидия Николаевна Погожева see PG3467.M215
3470.P37 Pokrovskiĭ, Alekseĭ Ivanovich, b. 1851. Алексей Иванович Покровский (Table P-PZ40)
3470.P38 Pokrovskiĭ, Nikolaĭ Nikolaevich, fl. 1890-1910. Николай Николаевич Покровский (Table P-PZ40)
3470.P39 Polevoĭ, Petr Nikolaevich, 1839-1902. Петр Николаевич Полевой
3470.P4 Polezhaev, Petr Vasilʹevich, fl. 1880-1890. Петр Васильевич Полежаев (Table P-PZ40)
3470.P45 Poli͡akov, D.S., fl. 1880-1890. Д.С. Поляков (Table P-PZ40)
3470.P48 Polilov, Georgiĭ Tikhonovich, 1859-1915. Георгий Тихонович Полилов (Table P-PZ40)
3470.P5 Polinovskiĭ, M.B., fl. 1890-1900. М.Б. Полиновский (Table P-PZ40)
3470.P52 Politkovskai͡a, M.E., fl. 1870-1880. М.Е. Политковская (Table P-PZ40)
3470.P53 Polivanov, P. (Petr), 1859-1903. Петр Поливанов (Table P-PZ40)
3470.P54 Polivanov, Sergeĭ Petrovich, 1835-1889. Сергей Петрович Поливанов (Table P-PZ40)
Polochanin, V.A. В.А. Полочанин see PG3460.D59
3470.P56 Polonskiĭ, Leonid Aleksandrovich, 1833- . Леонид Александрович Полонский (Table P-PZ40)
Poltorat͡skai͡a, Nadezhda Grigorʹevna. Надежда Григорьевна Полторацкая see PG3467.L885
3470.P58 Ponomarev, Ivan Nikolaevich, d. 1904. Иван Николаевич Пономарев (Table P-PZ40)
3470.P6 Popov, Aleksandr Serafimovich, 1863-1949. Александр Серафимович Попов (Table P-PZ40)
3470.P612 Popov, B.N., fl. 1880-1890. Б.Н. Попов (Table P-PZ40)
3470.P613 Popov, Grigoriĭ Polikarpovich, d. 1921. Григорий Поликарпович Попов (Table P-PZ40)
3470.P614 Popov, N.A., fl. 1880-1900. Н.А. Попов (Table P-PZ40)
3470.P616 Popov, N.E., fl. 1900-1910. Н.Е. Попов (Table P-PZ40)
3470.P618 Popov, P.M., fl. 1890-1900. П.М. Попов (Table P-PZ40)
3470.P619 Popova, Olʹga Nikolaevna, fl. 1900-1910. Ольга Николаевна Попова (Table P-PZ40)
3470.P62 Porfirov, Petr Fedorovich, 1870-1903. Петр Федорович Порфиров (Table P-PZ40)
Poroshilov, V. B. Порошилов see PG3453.A93
3470.P625 Poroshin, Ivan Aleksandrovich, fl. 1890-1910. Иван Александрович Порошин (Table P-PZ40)

Russian literature
Individual authors and works, 1870-1917
Individual authors, Pes - Z -- Continued
Posadov, Ivan Ivanovich Gorbunov-. Иван Иванович Горбунов-Посадов see PG3460.G84

3470.P627	Posenit͡skiĭ, V.V., fl. 1890-1910. В.В. Посеницкий (Table P-PZ40)
3470.P63	Potapenko, Ignatiĭ Nikolaevich, 1856-1929. Игнатий Николаевич Потапенко (Table P-PZ40 modified)
3470.P63A61-.P63Z458	Separate works. By title
3470.P63A9	Azorka (Story). Азорка
3470.P63B3	Bez boi͡u (Story). Без бою
3470.P63B4	Bez promakha (Tale). Без промаха
3470.P63B5	Bludnyĭ syn (Sketch). Блудный сын
3470.P63B6	Brat Andreĭ (Tale). Брат Андрей
3470.P63B7	Brat′i͡a (Tale). Братья
3470.P63B8	Buket (Comedy). Букет
3470.P63C3	Chelovek iz prorubi. Человек из проруби
3470.P63C4	Cherez li͡ubov′ (Novel). Через любовь
3470.P63C5	Chestnai͡a kompanii͡a (Tale). Честная компания
3470.P63C6	Chuzhie (Drama). Чужие
3470.P63D4	Derevenskiĭ roman (Tale). Деревенский роман
3470.P63D5	Do i posle (Tale). До и после
3470.P63D6	Dobrye li͡udi (Tale). Добрые люди
3470.P63D65	Doktor Kochnev (Story). Доктор Кочнев
3470.P63D7	Domashniĭ sud (Tale). Домашний суд
3470.P63D8	Dva schast′i͡a (Novel). Два счастья
3470.P63D9	Dve polosy (Episode). Две полосы
3470.P63G3	Gastroler (Sketch). Гастролер
3470.P63G4	General′skai͡a doch′ (Story). Генеральская дочь
3470.P63G5	Gore-bogatyr′ (Tale). Горе-богатырь
3470.P63G6	Gore-devit͡sa (Tale). Горе-девица
3470.P63G65	Gori͡achai͡a stat′i͡a (Sketch). Горячая статья
3470.P63G7	Grekhi (Tale). Грехи
3470.P63I7	Iskuplenie (Drama). Искупление
3470.P63I8	Ispolnitel′nyĭ organ (Story). Исполнительный орган
3470.P63K3	Kamennyĭ vek (Dramatic piece). Каменный век
3470.P63K4	Kanun (Tale). Канун
3470.P63K5	Klavdii͡a Mikhaĭlovna (Story). Клавдия Михайловна
3470.P63K7	Krylatoe slovo (Sketch). Крылатое слово
3470.P63L4	Lepta vdovit͡sy (Tale). Лепта вдовицы
3470.P63L5	Lishennyĭ prav (Drama). Лишенный прав
3470.P63L6	Li͡ubov′ (Drama). Любовь
3470.P63L7	Li͡ubov′ (Novel). Любовь
3470.P63M3	Malen′kai͡a igra (Story). Маленькая игра
3470.P63M4	Mat′ i doch′ (Tale). Мать и дочь

PG

Russian literature
Individual authors and works, 1870-1917
Individual authors, Pes - Z
Potapenko, Ignatiĭ Nikolaevich, 1856-1929. Игнатий Николаевич Потапенко
Separate works. By title -- Continued

3470.P63M5 Mishuris (Tale). Мишурис
3470.P63M8 Muzh chesti (Tale). Муж чести
3470.P63N2 Na deĭstvitel'noĭ sluzhbe (Story). На действительной службе
3470.P63N25 Na lone prirody (Farce). На лоне природы
3470.P63N3 Na pensii͡u (Story). На пенсию
3470.P63N35 Nadvornyĭ sovetnik (Tale). Надворный советник
3470.P63N4 Ne geroĭ (Novel). Не герой
3470.P63N5 Nebyvaloe delo (Tale). Небывалое дело
3470.P63N7 Novyĭ (Tale). Новый
3470.P63O3 Odin (Novel). Один
3470.P63O4 Oksana i drugie rasskazy. Оксана и другие рассказы
3470.P63O5 Oktava (Sketch). Октава
3470.P63O6 On i ona (Novel). Он и она
3470.P63O7 Ostroumno (Tale). Остроумно
3470.P63O8 Otechestvo v opasnosti (Tale). Отечество в опасности
3470.P63P3 Peshkom za slavoĭ (Tale). Пешком за славой
3470.P63P4 Peterburgska͡ia istorii͡a (Tale). Петербургская история
3470.P63P5 Pis'mo (Tale). Письмо
3470.P63P55 Platforma (Drama). Платформа
3470.P63P6 Pobeda (Story). Победа
3470.P63P65 Podval'nyĭ ėtazh (Story). Подвальный этаж
3470.P63P7 Poteshna͡ia istorii͡a (Tale). Потешная история
3470.P63P73 Povozka (Tale). Повозка
3470.P63P75 Prokli͡ata͡ia slava (Tale). Проклятая слава
3470.P63P8 Prosta͡ia sluchaĭnost' (Tale). Простая случайность
3470.P63R3 Radi khozi͡aĭstva (Tale). Ради хозяйства
3470.P63R4 Rechnye li͡udi (Tale). Речные люди
3470.P63R45 Redkiĭ prazdnik (Sketch). Редкий праздник
3470.P63R5 Reshils͡ia (Sketch). Решился
3470.P63R6 Ri͡asa (Drama). Ряса
3470.P63S15 Samorodok (Story). Самородок
3470.P63S2 Schast'e ponevole (Novel). Счастье поневоле
3470.P63S25 Schastlivyĭ (Tale). Счастливый
3470.P63S3 Sekretar' ego prevoskhoditel'stva (Sketch). Секретарь его превосходительства
3470.P63S35 Semeĭka (Sketch). Семейка
3470.P63S4 Semeĭna͡ia istorii͡a (Story). Семейная история

Russian literature
Individual authors and works, 1870-1917
Individual authors, Pes - Z
Potapenko, Ignatiĭ Nikolaevich, 1856-1929. Игнатий Николаевич Потапенко
Separate works. By title -- Continued

3470.P63S45 Shestero (Tale). Шестеро
3470.P63S5 Sil′fida (Novel). Сильфида
3470.P63S55 Slovo i delo (Novel). Слово и дело
3470.P63S6 Smertnyĭ boĭ (Novel). Смертный бой
3470.P63S65 Smysl zhizni (Tale). Смысл жизни
3470.P63S7 Staroe i i͡unoe (Story). Старое и юное
3470.P63S8 Staryĭ khozi͡ain (Drama). Старый хозяин
3470.P63S9 Svetlyĭ luch (Novel). Светлый луч
3470.P63S95 Svi͡atoe iskusstvo (Story). Святое искусство
3470.P63T3 Taĭna (Sketch). Тайна
3470.P63T6 Tozhe zhizn′ (Sketch). Тоже жизнь
3470.P63U9 Uzhas schast′i͡a (Story). Ужас счастья
3470.P63V2 V derevne (Sketches and tales). В деревне
For separate titles see the title in PG3470.P63A61+
3470.P63V4 Velikoe v malom (Tale). Великое в малом
3470.P63V6 Volshebnai͡a skazka (Drama). Волшебная сказка
3470.P63V8 Vstrecha (Novel). Встреча
3470.P63V9 Vysshai͡a shkola (Drama). Высшая школа
3470.P63Z13 Zabytyĭ ponomar′ (Story). Забытый пономарь
3470.P63Z15 Zadacha (Tale). Задача
3470.P63Z2 Zapiski molodogo cheloveka (Novel). Записки молодого человека
3470.P63Z23 Zapiski starogo studenta. Записки старого студента
3470.P63Z25 Zdravye poni͡atii͡a (Novel). Здравые понятия
3470.P63Z28 Zemli͡a (Story). Земля
3470.P63Z3 Zhertva (Tale). Жертва
3470.P63Z32 Zhestokoe schast′e (Story). Жестокое счастье
3470.P63Z34 Zhit′ mozhno (Comedy). Жить можно
3470.P63Z36 Zhivai͡a zhizn′ (Novel). Живая жизнь
3470.P63Z38 Zhizn′ (Drama). Жизнь
3470.P63Z45 Zvezda (Novel). Звезда

3470.P633 Potapov, Ivan, fl. 1900-1910. Иван Потапов (Table P-PZ40)

Potekhin, Alekseĭ Antipovich. Алексей Антипович Потехин see PG3337.P8

Potekhin, Nikolaĭ Antipovich. Николай Антипович Потехин see PG3337.P82

3470.P635 Potekhin, Pavel Borisovich, 1852-1910. Павел Борисович Потехин (Table P-PZ40)

3470.P638 Potresov, Sergeĭ Viktorovich, 1870-1953. Сергей Викторович Потресов (Table P-PZ40)

Russian literature
Individual authors and works, 1870-1917
Individual authors, Pes - Z -- Continued

3470.P64 Poznīak, Dmitriĭ Mikhaĭlovich, 1842-1896. Дмитрий Михайлович Позняк (Table P-PZ40)

3470.P65 Poznīakov, Nikolaĭ Ivanovich, 1856-1910. Николай Иванович Позняков (Table P-PZ40)

3470.P66 Praskunin, Mikhail Vasil′evich, 1874- . Михаил Васильевич Праскунин (Table P-PZ40)

3470.P67 Premirov, Mikhail, 1878- . Михаил Премиров (Table P-PZ40)

3470.P68 Press, Arkadiĭ Germanovich, fl. 1890-1900. Аркадий Германович Пресс (Table P-PZ40)

3470.P7 Prishvin, Mikhail Mikhaĭlovich, 1873-1954. Михаил Михайлович Пришвин (Table P-PZ40)

3470.P75 Protopopov, Viktor Viktorovich, 1866- . Виктор Викторович Протопопов (Table P-PZ40)

Pruzhanskiĭ, N. H. Пружанский see PG3467.L52

3470.P78 Purishkevich, Vladimir Mitrofanovich, 1870-1920. Владимир Митрофанович Пуришкевич (Table P-PZ40)

3470.P8 Pushkarev, Nikolaĭ Lukich, 1841-1906. Николай Лукич Пушкарев (Table P-PZ40)

3470.P85 Putilin, Ivan Dmitrievich, 1830-1893. Иван Дмитриевич Путилин (Table P-PZ40)

Putnik, pseud. Путник see PG3467.L35

3470.P9 Pylīaev, Mikhail Ivanovich, 1842-1899. Михаил Иванович Пыляев (Table P-PZ40)

R., K. К.Р. see PG3467.K56

R., N., pseud. Н.Р. see PG3470.T77

3470.R13 Radchenko, A.F, fl. 1900-1910. А.Ф. Радченко (Table P-PZ40)

Radda-Baĭ, pseud. Радда-Бай see PG3453.B57

3470.R15 Radich, Vasiliĭ Andreevich, d. 1904. Василий Андреевич Радич (Table P-PZ40)

3470.R18 Raevskiĭ, Petr Ivanovich, 1847-1886. Петр Иванович Раевский (Table P-PZ40)

3470.R2 Rafalovich, Sergeĭ L′vovich, b. 1875. Сергей Львович Рафалович (Table P-PZ40)

3470.R27 Rakshanin, N.O., fl. 1890-1900. Н.О. Ракшанин (Table P-PZ40)

Ramshev, Matveĭ. Матвей Рамшев see PG3467.I2

3470.R29 Rapgof, Ippolit Pavlovich, fl. 1910-1920. Ипполит Павлович Рапгоф (Table P-PZ40)

3470.R3 Rappoport, Semen Akimovich, 1863-1920. Семен Акимович Раппопорт (Table P-PZ40)
Variant of surname: Rapoport (Рапопорт)

Russian literature
Individual authors and works, 1870-1917
Individual authors, Pes - Z -- Continued

3470.R32 Rasteri͡aev, Grigoriĭ Grigor′evich, 1861-1892. Григорий Григорьевич Растеряев (Table P-PZ40)

3470.R34 Ratgauz, Daniil Maksimovich, 1868-1937. Даниил Максимович Ратгауз (Table P-PZ40)

Ratishchev, M. M. Ратищев see PG3470.V34

3470.R35 Ratomskiĭ, N.A., fl. 1890-1910. Н.А. Ратомский (Table P-PZ40)

3470.R3515 Razorenov, A.E. (Aleksi͡eĭ Ermilovich), 1819-1891. Алексѣй Ермиловичъ Разореновъ (Table P-PZ40)

3470.R352 Rebikov, Vladimir Ivanovich, 1866-1920. Владимир Иванович Ребиков (Table P-PZ40)

Reĭkh, Marii͡a Zakrevskai͡a. Мария Закревская Рейх see PG3470.Z27

3470.R37 Remezov, Mitrofan Nilovich, 1835-1901. Митрофан Нилович Ремезов (Table P-PZ40)

3470.R38 Remezova, Marii͡a Ksenofontovna, fl. 1890-1900. Мария Ксенофонтовна Ремезова (Table P-PZ40)

3470.R4 Remizov, Alekseĭ Mikhaĭlovich, 1877- . Алексей Михайлович Ремизов (Table P-PZ40 modified)

3470.R4A61-.R4Z458 Separate works. By title

3470.R4A8 Akhru (Story). Ахру

3470.R4B4 Besovskoe deĭstvo (Drama). Бесовское действо

Bespri͡i͡utnai͡a. Бесприютная see PG3470.R4S8

3470.R4B5 Biser malyĭ. Бисер малый

3470.R4C3 Chakkhchygys-Taasu (Tale). Чакхчыгыс-Таасу

3470.R4C35 Chasy (Novel). Часы

3470.R4C4 Chertykhanet͡s (Tale). Чертыханец

3470.R4C45 Chortik (Tale). Чортик

3470.R4C5 Chortov log i Polunoshchnoe solnt͡se (Tales and poems). Чортов лог и Полунощное солнце

3470.R4C55 Chto est′ tabak (Tale). Что есть табак

3470.R4D4 Deĭstvo o Georgii Khrabrom (Drama). Действо о Георгии Храбром

3470.R4D6 Dokuka i balagur′e. Докука и балагурье

3470.R4E2 Ë (Tibetan tale)

3470.R4E4 Ėlektron (Poem). Электрон

3470.R4E5 Ėmalion′ (Tale). Эмалионь

3470.R4G3 Galstuk (Tale). Галстук

3470.R4G7 Grad obrechennyĭ (Tale). Град обреченный

3470.R4K3 Kamennye prudy (Tale). Каменные пруды

3470.R4K35 Kavkazskiĭ churek (Tale). Кавказский чурек

3470.R4K4 Kazennai͡a dacha (Tale). Казенная дача

3470.R4K5 Kitaĭ (Tale). Китай

3470.R4K6 Kori͡avka (Story). Корявка

PG

Russian literature
Individual authors and works, 1870-1917
Individual authors, Pes - Z
Remizov, Alekseĭ Mikhaĭlovich, 1877- . Алексей Михайлович Ремизов
Separate works. By title -- Continued

3470.R4K7 Krashennye ryla. Крашенные рыла
3470.R4K8 Krestovye sestry (Novel). Крестовые сестры
Kukkha, Rozanovy pis′ma. Кукха, Розановы письма see PG2947
3470.R4L3 Lalazar (Tale). Лалазар
Limonar′. Лимонарь see PG3470.R4L8
3470.R4L8 Lug dukhovnyĭ (Apocrypha). Луг духовный
Cover title: Limonar′, sirech: Lug dukhovnyĭ (Лимонарь, сиречь, Луг духовный)
3470.R4M2 Maka. Мака
3470.R4M3 Mara (Tales). Мара
3470.R4M4 Mara (Tale). Мара
3470.R4M6 Morshchinka (Tale). Морщинка
3470.R4M7 Moskovskie l͡iubimye legendy. Tri serpa. Московские любимые легенды. Три серпа
Neuëmnyĭ buben. Неуёмный бубен see PG3470.R4P7
3470.R4N4 Nikoliny pritchi (Parables). Николины притчи
3470.R4N5 Nikolaĭ Milostivyĭ. Николай Милостивый
3470.R4N6 Novyĭ god (Tale). Новый год
3470.R4O2 O sud′be ognennoĭ (Poems). О судьбе огненной
3470.R4O3 Ognenn͡ai͡a Rossii͡a. Огненная Россия
3470.R4O5 Ol͡ia. Оля
3470.R4O6 Opera (Tale). Опера
3470.R4P3 Paralipomenon (Story). Паралипоменон
3470.R4P35 Pavlin′im perom. Павлиньим пером
3470.R4P4 Perchatki (Tale). Перчатки
3470.R4P45 Petushok (Tale). Петушок
3470.R4P5 P͡iatai͡a i͡azva (Story). Пятая язва
3470.R4P53 Pl͡ias Prodiady (Tale). Пляс Продиады
3470.R4P55 Po karnizam (Novel). По карнизам
3470.R4P56 Podorozhie (Tales). Подорожие
3470.R4P58 Pokrovenn͡ai͡a (Tale). Покровенная
3470.R4P6 Posolon′ (Tale). Посолонь
3470.R4P7 Povest′ ob Ivane Semenoviche Stratilatove - neuëmnyĭ buben (Story). Повесть об Иване Семеновиче Стратилатове - неуёмный бубен
3470.R4P74 Pozhar (Tale). Пожар
3470.R4P78 Pridvornyĭ i͡uvelir (Tale). Придворный ювелир
3470.R4P8 Prud (Novel). Пруд
3470.R4R6 Rossii͡a v pis′menakh. Россия в письменах

Russian literature
Individual authors and works, 1870-1917
Individual authors, Pes - Z
Remizov, Alekseĭ Mikhaĭlovich, 1877- . Алексей Михайлович Ремизов
Separate works. By title -- Continued

3470.R4R7 Rusalii͡a. Русалия
3470.R4R8 Rusalʹnye deĭstva (Drama). Русальные действа
3470.R4R9 Russkie zhenshchiny (Folk tales). Русские женщины
3470.R4S3 Serebri͡anye lozhki (Tale). Серебряные ложки
3470.R4S4 Shumy goroda (Tales). Шумы города
3470.R4S5 Sibirskiĭ pri͡anik (Folk tales). Сибирский пряник
3470.R4S55 Skazki russkogo naroda. Сказки русского народа
3470.R4S57 Slonenok (Tale). Слоненок
3470.R4S6 Sobachʹi͡a doli͡a (Tales). Собачья доля
3470.R4S7 Sredi murʹi͡a (Tales). Среди мурья
3470.R4S8 Strannit͡sa (Story). Странница
Also published under the title: Bespriiu͡tnai͡a (Бесприютная)
3470.R4S85 Sud Bozhiĭ (Tale). Суд Божий
3470.R4S9 Svi͡atoĭ vecher (Tale). Святой вечер
3470.R4T3 Tatʹ i pautina (Tale). Тать и паутина
3470.R4T5 Tibetskie skazki. Тибетские сказки
3470.R4T7 Tragedii͡a o Iude, print͡se Iskariotskom (Drama). Трагедия о Иуде, принце Искариотском
3470.R4T73 Trava-murava (Legends). Трава-мурава
Tri serpa. Три серпа see PG3470.R4M7
3470.R4T8 T͡Sarʹ Maksimilian (Comedy). Царь Максимилиан
3470.R4T85 T͡Sarevna Mymra (Tale). Царевна Мымра
3470.R4U25 Uchitelʹ muzyki. Учитель музыки
3470.R4U4 Ukrepa. Укрепа
3470.R4V2 V plenu (Tale). В плену
3470.R4V3 V pole blakitnom. В поле блакитном
3470.R4V4 Vesennee poroshʹe (Tales). Весеннее порошье
3470.R4V9 Vzvikhrennai͡a Rusʹ. Взвихренная Русь
3470.R4Z2 Za svi͡atui͡u Rusʹ (Tales). За святую Русь
3470.R4Z23 Zanofa (Tale). Занофа
3470.R4Z25 Zavetnye skazy (Tales). Заветные сказы
3470.R4Z3 Zga (Tales). Зга
3470.R4Z35 Zhertva (Tale). Жертва
3470.R4Z4 Zvenigorod oklikannyĭ (St. Nicholas parables). Звенигород окликанный
3470.R4Z45 Zvezda nadzvezdnai͡a (Legends in verse). Звезда надзвездная
3470.R45 Rikhter, K.A., fl. 1890-1900. К.А. Рихтер (Table P-PZ40)
Rin, Z.A. З.А. Рин see PG3470.Z3
Rinev, N. H. Ринев see PG3467.L35

Russian literature
Individual authors and works, 1870-1917
Individual authors, Pes - Z -- Continued

3470.R47 Ritter, A.A. von, fl. 1890-1900. А.А. фон Риттер (Table P-PZ40)

3470.R5 Rival′, V.A., fl. 1880-1900. В.А. Риваль (Table P-PZ40)

Roberti-Laserda, Mariīa Valentinovna de. Мария Валентиновна де Роберти-Ласерда see PG3470.V28

Rochester, Vera Ivanovna. Вера Ивановна Рочестер see PG3467.K77

Rodislavskiĭ, Vladimir Ivanovich. Владимир Иванович Родиславский see PG3360.R53

3470.R54 Rogalevich, G.A., fl. 1890-1900. Г.А. Рогалевич (Table P-PZ40)

3470.R55 Rogova, O.I., fl. 1900-1910. О.И. Рогова (Table P-PZ40)

3470.R57 Rokotkov, Aleksandr, fl. 1900-1910. Александр Рокотков (Table P-PZ40)

Rokotova, Margarita Vladimirovna. Маргарита Владимировна Рокотова see PG3467.I22

3470.R58 Romanov, Fedor Petrovich, fl. 1890-1900. Федор Петрович Романов (Table P-PZ40)

Romanov, Konstantin Konstantinovich, velikiĭ knīaz′. Константин Константинович Романов see PG3467.K56

3470.R59 Romanov, Vadim Vladimirovich, 1841-1890. Вадим Владимирович Романов (Table P-PZ40)

3470.R6 Romer, Fedor Ėmil′evich, 1838-1901. Федор Эмильевич Ромер (Table P-PZ40)

3470.R62 Romias, Sergeĭ, fl. 1890-1900. Сергей Ромиас (Table P-PZ40)

Ropshin, V. B. Ропшин see PG3470.S3

Rosenberg, Petr. see PG3470.R78

Rosenblum, Konstantin (Konstantin-Vitol′d; Vitol′d-Konstantin) Nikolaevich see PG3467.L24

Rosenfeld, Ol′ga Ėmmanuilovna see PG3467.K63

Rosenheim, Mikhail Pavlovich see PG3360.R74

3470.R67 Roshchinin, Fedor Antipovich, 1841-1905. Федор Антипович Рощинин (Table P-PZ40)

3470.R7 Roslavlev, Aleksandr Stepanovich, 1883-1920. Александр Степанович Рославлев (Table P-PZ40)

3470.R73 Rossiev, Pavel A., fl. 1900-1910. Павел А. Россиев (Table P-PZ40)

Rostovskiĭ, Fedor Nikolaevich Kasatkin-. Федор Николаевич Касаткин-Ростовский see PG3467.K6215

Russian literature
Individual authors and works, 1870-1917
Individual authors, Pes - Z -- Continued
Rostovskiĭ, Sergeĭ Aleksandrovich Kasatkin-. Сергей Александрович Касаткин-Ростовский see PG3467.K36
3470.R77 Rozanov, Vasiliĭ Vasil′evich, 1856-1919. Василий Васильевич Розанов (Table P-PZ40)
For Rozanov as a literary critic see PG2947.R6
Rozenberg, Elena Vasil′evna. Елена Васильевна Розенберг see PG3470.V9
3470.R78 Rozenberg, Petr, fl. 1880-1890. Петр Розенберг (Table P-PZ40)
Rozenbli͡um, Konstantin (Konstantin-Vitol′d; Vitol′d-Konstantin) Nikolaevich. Константин (Константин-Витольд; Витольд-Константин) Николаевич Розенблюм see PG3467.L24
Rozenfel′d, Ol′ga Ėmmanuilovna. Ольга Эммануиловна Розенфельд see PG3467.K63
Rozengeĭm, Mikhail Pavlovich. Михаил Павлович Розенгейм see PG3360.R74
Rozov, V. B. Розов see PG3467.L24
3470.R8 Rubakin, Nikolaĭ Aleksandrovich, 1862-1946. Николай Александрович Рубакин (Table P-PZ40)
3470.R815 Rubashkin, K.P. К.П. Рубашкин (Table P-PZ40)
3470.R82 Rudich, Vera Ivanovna, 1872- . Вера Ивановна Рудич (Table P-PZ40)
3470.R84 Rukavishnikov, Ivan Sergeevich, 1877-1930. Иван Сергеевич Рукавишников (Table P-PZ40)
3470.R86 Runova, Ol′ga Pavlovna (Meshcherska͡ia), 1864- . Ольга Павловна (Мещерская) Рунова (Table P-PZ40)
Rusak, pseud. Русак see PG3467.L465
Rusakov, Viktor. Виктор Русаков see PG3467.L465
3470.R88 Rusov, Nikolaĭ Nikolaevich, 1894- . Николай Николаевич Русов (Table P-PZ40)
3470.R89 Rutkovskiĭ, Faddeĭ Viktorovich, fl. 1890-1910. Фаддей Викторович Рутковский (Table P-PZ40)
3470.R9 Ryba͡tskiĭ, Nikolaĭ Ivanovich, 1880-1920. Николай Иванович Рыбацкий (Table P-PZ40)
3470.R93 Ryshkov, Viktor Aleksandrovich, fl. 1890-1910. Виктор Александрович Рышков (Table P-PZ40)
3470.R95 Ryskin, S.F., d. 1895. С.Ф. Рыскин (Table P-PZ40)
3470.S13 Saburova, E.A., fl. 1890-1900. E.A. Сабурова (Table P-PZ40)
3470.S14 Sadovnikov, Dmitriĭ Nikolaevich, 1846-1883. Дмитрий Николаевич Садовников (Table P-PZ40)

PG

Russian literature
Individual authors and works, 1870-1917
Individual authors, Pes - Z -- Continued

3470.S15 Sadovskiĭ, Mikhail Provych, 1847-1910. Михаил Провыч Садовский (Table P-PZ40)

3470.S16 Sadovskoĭ, Boris Aleksandrovich, 1881-1952. Борис Александрович Садовской (Table P-PZ40)

3470.S17 Safonov, Sergeĭ Aleksandrovich, 1867-1904. Сергей Александрович Сафонов (Table P-PZ40)

Sakmarov, A. A. Сакмаров see PG3467.K42

3470.S18 Saksaganskai͡a, Anna Abramovna (Nemirovskai͡a), 1876- . Анна Абрамовна (Немировская) Саксаганская (Table P-PZ40)

3470.S19 Salʹi͡anova, Elena, fl. 1890-1900. Елена Сальянова (Table P-PZ40)

3470.S2 Salias de Turnemir, Evgeniĭ Andreevich, graf, 1840-1908. Евгений Андреевич Салиас де Турнемир (Table P-PZ40)

3470.S22 Salʹkov, V.P., fl. 1900-1910. В.П. Сальков (Table P-PZ40)

3470.S23 Salmanov, Petr Alekseevich, 1817-1882. Петр Алексеевич Салманов (Table P-PZ40)

3470.S24 Salʹnikov, A.N., fl. 1900-1910. А.Н. Сальников (Table P-PZ40)

3470.S25 Salov, Ilʹi͡a Aleksandrovich, 1834-1902. Илья Александрович Салов (Table P-PZ40)

Saltykov, Mikhail Evgrafovich. Михаил Евграфович Салтыков see PG3361.S3

3470.S26 Samoĭlov, Mark, fl. 1880-1890. Марк Самойлов (Table P-PZ40)

Samoĭlovich, V. B. Самойлович see PG3470.S64

3470.S27 Samygin, Mikhail Vladimirovich, 1874-1952. Михаил Владимирович Самыгин (Table P-PZ40)

Saratovet͡s. Саратовец see PG3453.A78

Sarmat, pseud. Сармат see PG3453.B25

3470.S29 Satin, Nikolaĭ Mikhaĭlovich, 1814-1873. Николай Михайлович Сатин (Table P-PZ40)

Savenkova, S.A. С.А. Савенкова see PG3470.S315

Savikhin, V. B. Савихин see PG3467.I79

3470.S3 Savinkov, Boris Viktorovich, 1879-1925. Борис Викторович Савинков (Table P-PZ40)

3470.S315 Savinkova, Sofʹi͡a Aleksandrovna, 1852?-1923. Софья Александровна Савинкова (Table P-PZ40)

3470.S32 Savinov, Feodosiĭ P., fl. 1880-1900. Феодосий П. Савинов (Table P-PZ40)

3470.S325 Savodnik, Vladimir Fedorovich, 1874-1940. Владимир Федорович Саводник (Table P-PZ40)

Russian literature
Individual authors and works, 1870-1917
Individual authors, Pes - Z -- Continued

Sazonova, Sofʹi͡a Ivanovna. Софья Ивановна Сазонова see PG3470.S62

Schwarzmann, Lev Isaakovich see PG3470.S5

3470.S33 Sebri͡akova, Aleksandra Vasilʹevna, fl. 1880-1890. Александра Васильевна Себрякова (Table P-PZ40)

3470.S335 Sedelʹnikov, Nikolaĭ Mikhaĭlovich, d. 1887. Николай Михайлович Седельников (Table P-PZ40)

Sedoĭ, A. A. Седой see PG3453.C9

3470.S34 Selivanov, Alekseĭ Nikolaevich, ca. 1850-1906. Алексей Николаевич Селиванов (Table P-PZ40)

3470.S35 Semenov, Aleksandr Kondratʹevich, 1863-1924. Александр Кондратьевич Семенов (Table P-PZ40)

3470.S36 Semenov, Leonid, fl. 1900-1910. Леонид Семенов (Table P-PZ40)

3470.S37 Semenov, Sergeĭ Terentʹevich, 1868-1922. Сергей Терентьевич Семенов (Table P-PZ40)

3470.S372 Semenov, Stepan Stepanovich, 1878- . Степан Степанович Семенов (Table P-PZ40)

3470.S375 Semenov, Vladimir Ivanovich, 1867-1910. Владимир Иванович Семенов (Table P-PZ40)

Semenova, Natalʹi͡a Petrovna. Наталья Петровна Семенова see PG3467.G6

3470.S38 Sementkovskiĭ, Rostislav Ivanovich, 1846-1918. Ростислав Иванович Сементковский (Table P-PZ40)

3470.S382 Semiganovskiĭ, Nikolaĭ, fl. 1880-1890. Николай Семигановский (Table P-PZ40)

Semipalatinskiĭ, pseud. Семипалатинскiй see PG3467.K7845

3470.S384 Serafimov, M.S., fl. 1880-1900. М.С. Серафимов (Table P-PZ40)

Serafimovich, A. A. Серафимович see PG3470.P6

3470.S386 Serebri͡akov, V.E., fl. 1880-1900. В.Е. Серебряков (Table P-PZ40)

3470.S388 Sereda, V.N., fl. 1890-1900. В.Н. Середа (Table P-PZ40)

3470.S39 Sergeenko, Petr Alekseevich, 1854-1930. Петр Алексеевич Сергеенко (Table P-PZ40)

3470.S4 Sergeev-T͡Senskiĭ, Sergeĭ Nikolaevich, 1875-1958. Сергей Николаевич Сергеев-Ценский (Table P-PZ40 modified)

3470.S4A61-.S4Z458 Separate works. By title

3470.S4A8 Arakush (Tale). Аракуш

Russian literature
Individual authors and works, 1870-1917
Individual authors, Pes - Z
Sergeev-TSenskiĭ, Sergeĭ Nikolaevich, 1875-1958.
Сергей Николаевич Сергеев-Ценский
Separate works. By title -- Continued

3470.S4B3 Babaev (Novel). Бабаев
3470.S4B35 Baten′ka (Sketch). Батенька
3470.S4B4 Beregovoe (Tales). Береговое
3470.S4B5 Blistatel′nai͡a zhizn′(Tale). Блистательная жизнь
3470.S4B6 Blizhniĭ (Tale). Ближний
3470.S4B67 Bred (Tale). Бред
3470.S4B7 Brusilovskiĭ proryv (Novel). Брусиловский прорыв
Comprises:
3470.S4B73 Burnai͡a vesna. Бурная весна
3470.S4B76 Gori͡achee leto. Горячее лето
Burnai͡a vesna. Бурная весна see PG3470.S4B73
3470.S4C5 Chudo (Tale). Чудо
3470.S4D5 Difterit (Tale). Дифтерит
3470.S4D7 Drofy (Tale). Дрофы
3470.S4D8 Dumy i grezy (Poems). Думы и грезы
3470.S4D85 Dvizhenie [i drugie rasskazy]. Движение [и другие рассказы]
3470.S4D9 Dvizhenie (Tale). Движение
3470.S4G6 Gogol′ ukhodit v noch′ (Story). Гоголь уходит в ночь
Gori͡achee leto. Горячее лето see PG3470.S4B76
3470.S4G8 Grobnit͡sa Tamerlana (Tale). Гробница Тамерлана
3470.S4K5 Khitrai͡a devchonka (Tale). Хитрая девчонка
3470.S4K6 Kost′ v golove (Tale). Кость в голове
3470.S4K8 Kukushka (Tale). Кукушка
3470.S4L4 Lesnai͡a top′ (Tale). Лесная топь
3470.S4L5 Liza Vinogradova (Tale). Лиза Виноградова
3470.S4L8 L′vy i solnt͡se (Tale). Львы и солнце
3470.S4M2 Mai͡ak v tumane (Tales). Маяк в тумане
3470.S4M3 Maska [i drugie rasskazy]. Маска [и другие рассказы]
3470.S4M33 Maska (Tale). Маска
3470.S4M35 Massy, mashiny, stikhii (Novel). Массы, машины, стихии
3470.S4M4 Meduza (Tale). Медуза
3470.S4M45 Medvezhonok (Tale). Медвежонок
3470.S4M5 Mishel′ Lermontov (Novel). Мишель Лермонтов
Comprises:
3470.S4M53 Poėt i poėt. Поэт и поэт
3470.S4M55 Poėt i poėtessa. Поэт и поэтесса
3470.S4M57 Poėt i chern′. Поэт и чернь
3470.S4M6 Molchal′niki (Tales). Молчальники

Russian literature
Individual authors and works, 1870-1917
Individual authors, Pes - Z
Sergeev-TSenskiĭ, Sergeĭ Nikolaevich, 1876-
Separate works. By title
Muzhestvo i doblestʹ. Мужество и доблесть see PG3470.S4S4

3470.S4N25 Naklonnai͡a Elena (Novel). Наклонная Елена
3470.S4N3 Nastoi͡ashchie li͡udi (Tales). Настоящие люди
3470.S4N4 Nebo (Tale). Небо
3470.S4N43 Nedra [i drugie rasskazy]. Недра [и другие рассказы]
3470.S4N45 Nedra (Tale). Недра
3470.S4N47 Netoroplivoe solnt͡se [i drugie rasskazy]. Неторопливое солнце [и другие рассказы]
3470.S4N48 Netoroplivoe solnt͡se (Tale). Неторопливое солнце
3470.S4N5 Nevesta Pushkina (Novel). Невеста Пушкина

Obrechennye na gibelʹ. Обреченные на гибель see PG3470.S4P75

3470.S4O4 Okolo mori͡a (Tales). Около моря
3470.S4P3 Pami͡atʹ serdt͡sa (Tale). Память сердца
3470.S4P4 Pechalʹ poleĭ (Tale). Печаль полей

Poėt i chernʹ. Поэт и чернь see PG3470.S4M57

Poėt i poėt. Поэт и поэт see PG3470.S4M53

Poėt i poėtessa. Поэт и поэтесса see PG3470.S4M55

3470.S4P6 Pogost (Tale). Погост
3470.S4P7 Preobrazhenie (Novel). Преображение
Comprises:
3470.S4P73 Vali͡a. Валя
3470.S4P75 Obrechennye na gibelʹ. Обреченные на гибель
3470.S4P77 Pushki vydvigai͡ut. Пушки выдвигают
3470.S4P8 Pristav Deri͡abin (Tale). Пристав Дерябин

Pushki vydvigai͡ut. Пушки выдвигают see PG3470.S4P77

3470.S4R3 Rasskaz professora. Рассказ профессора
3470.S4S3 Sad (Story). Сад
3470.S4S35 Schastlivit͡sa (Tale). Счастливица

Sevastopolʹskai͡a oborona, 1854-1855. Севастопольская оборона, 1854-1855 see DK215.7

3470.S4S4 Sevastopolʹskai͡a strada (Novel). Севастопольская страда
3470.S4S45 Simferopolʹ (Tale). Симферополь
3470.S4S5 Sinopskiĭ boĭ. Синопский бой
3470.S4S53 Skuka (Tale). Скука

Russian literature
Individual authors and works, 1870-1917
Individual authors, Pes - Z
Sergeev-T͡Senskiĭ, Sergeĭ Nikolaevich, 1875-1958. Сергей Николаевич Сергеев-Ценский
Separate works. By title -- Continued

3470.S4S55 Slivy, vishni, chereshni (Tale). Сливы, вишни, черешни
3470.S4S6 Smert′ (Drama). Смерть
3470.S4S8 Sumerki (Tale). Сумерки
3470.S4T8 Tundra (Tale). Тундра
3470.S4U2 Ubiĭstvo (Tale). Убийство
3470.S4U3 Ugolok (Tale). Уголок
3470.S4U4 Ulybki (Tale). Улыбки
3470.S4V2 V grozu (Tales). В грозу
Vali͡a. Валя see PG3470.S4P73
3470.S4Z2 Zabyl (Tale). Забыл
3470.S4Z25 Zauri͡ad-polk (Novel). Зауряд-полк
3470.S4Z3 Zhestokost′ (Story). Жестокость
3470.S4Z35 Zhivai͡a voda (Tale). Живая вода
3470.S43 Sergievskiĭ, N. (Nikolaĭ), 1875-1955. Николай Сергиевский (Table P-PZ40)
Seroshevskiĭ, Vat͡slav Leopol′dovich. Вацлав Леопольдович Серошевский see PG3470.S565
Seryĭ, pseud. Серый see PG3453.B35
Severin, N.I. Н.И. Северин see PG3467.M395
3470.S435 Severnai͡a, Mar′i͡a, fl. 1880-1900. Марья Северная (Table P-PZ40)
3470.S437 Severova, N.B., fl. 1900-1910. Н.Б. Северова
Severt͡sev, G. Г. Северцев see PG3470.P48
Shabel′skai͡a, A. A. Шабельская see PG3467.M76
3470.S44 Shakh-Paronian͡ts, Leon Mikhaĭlovich, fl. 1890-1920. Леон Михайлович Шах-Паронианц (Table P-PZ40)
3470.S445 Shakhovskai͡a, Li͡udmila, kni͡azhna, fl. 1880-1910. Людмила Шаховская (Table P-PZ40)
3470.S45 Shapir, Ol′ga Andreevna, 1850-1916. Ольга Андреевна Шапир (Table P-PZ40)
3470.S453 Sharapov, Sergeĭ Fedorovich, 1855-1911. Сергей Федорович Шарапов (Table P-PZ40)
For collected works see AC65
Sharchenko, N. H. Шарченко see PG3460.F52
Shatov, A. A. Шатов see PG3467.K628
Shcheglov, Ivan. Иван Щеглов see PG3467.L39
3470.S455 Shcheglovitov, A.T., fl. 1890-1900. А.Т. Щегловитов (Table P-PZ40)

Russian literature
Individual authors and works, 1870-1917
Individual authors, Pes - Z -- Continued

3470.S458 Shchepkina, Aleksandra Vladimirovna, fl. 1890-1915. Александра Владимировна Щепкина (Table P-PZ40)

3470.S46 Shchepkina-Kupernik, Tat′i͡ana L′vovna, 1874-1952. Татьяна Львовна Щепкина-Куперник (Table P-PZ40)

3470.S465 Shcherbachev, Grigoriĭ Dmitrievich, 1823-1900. Григорий Дмитриевич Щербачев (Table P-PZ40)

3470.S47 Shcherbachev, S.G., fl. 1890-1900. С.Г. Щербачев (Table P-PZ40)

3470.S472 Shcherbinskiĭ, K.O., fl. 1890-1900. К.О. Щербинский (Table P-PZ40)

3470.S475 Shcheshinskiĭ, Ė.I., fl. 1880-1890. Э.И. Щешинский (Table P-PZ40)

3470.S477 Shchetinin, B.A., kni͡az′, fl. 1890-1900. Б.А. Щетинин (Table P-PZ40)

3470.S48 Shebuev, Nikolaĭ Georgievich, 1874-1937. Николай Георгиевич Шебуев (Table P-PZ40)

3470.S484 Shelkar′, Grigoriĭ Markovich, fl. 1880-1890. Григорий Маркович Шелкарь (Table P-PZ40)

3470.S486 Sheller, Aleksandr Konstantinovich, 1838-1900. Александр Константинович Шеллер (Table P-PZ40)

3470.S49 Shelonskiĭ, N.N., fl. 1890-1900. Н.Н. Шелонский (Table P-PZ40)

3470.S493 Shemshurin, Andreĭ, fl. 1900-1910. Андрей Шемшурин (Table P-PZ40)

3470.S496 Sheremetev, Sergeĭ Dmitrievich, graf, 1844-1918. Сергей Дмитриевич Шереметев (Table P-PZ40)

3470.S498 Shestakov, D.P., fl. 1890-1900. Д.П. Шестаков (Table P-PZ40)

3470.S499 Shestakov, K. K. Шестаков (Table P-PZ40)

3470.S5 Shestov, Lev, 1866-1938. Лев Шестов (Table P-PZ40)

3470.S513 Shevli͡akov, Mikhail Viktorovich, fl. 1890-1900. Михаил Викторович Шевляков (Table P-PZ40)

Shigaleev, N. H. Шигалеев see PG3470.S48

3470.S515 Shigarin, N.D., fl. 1860-1880. Н.Д. Шигарин (Table P-PZ40)

3470.S518 Shishlo, Konstantin. Константин Шишло (Table P-PZ40)

3470.S52 Shkli͡arevskiĭ, Aleksandr Andreevich, 1837-1883. Александр Андреевич Шкляревский (Table P-PZ40)

3470.S522 Shklovskiĭ, Isaak Vladimirovich, 1865-1935. Исаак Владимирович Шкловский (Table P-PZ40)

Russian literature
Individual authors and works, 1870-1917
Individual authors, Pes - Z -- Continued

3470.S525 Shkulev, Filipp Stepanovich, 1868-1930. Филипп Степанович Шкулев (Table P-PZ40)

Shmelev, Ivan Sergeevich. Иван Сергеевич Шмелев see PG3476.S5

3470.S54 Shpazhinskiĭ, Ippolit Vasil′evich, 1844-1917. Ипполит Васильевич Шпажинский (Table P-PZ40)

3470.S544 Shreknik, Evgeniĭ Fedorovich, fl. 1890-1900. Евгений Федорович Шрекник (Table P-PZ40)

3470.S548 Shubinskiĭ, Sergeĭ Nikolaevich, 1834-1913. Сергей Николаевич Шубинский (Table P-PZ40)

3470.S55 Shuf, Vladimir Aleksandrovich, 1865-1913. Владимир Александрович Шуф (Table P-PZ40)

3470.S555 Shustikov, A.A., fl. 1890-1900. А.А. Шустиков (Table P-PZ40)

Shuvalov, V. B. Шувалов see PG3453.B52

Shvart͡sman, Lev Isaakovich. Лев Исаакович Шварцман see PG3470.S5

3470.S5557 Shvedov, I.G. И.Г. Шведов (Table P-PZ40)

Sibiri͡ak, Mamin-, pseud. Мамин-Сибиряк see PG3467.M3

Sibirskiĭ, Vsevolod. Всеволод Сибирский see PG3460.D66

3470.S56 Sidorov, Vasiliĭ, fl. 1890-1900. Василий Сидоров (Table P-PZ40)

3470.S565 Sieroszewski, Wacław, 1858-1945 (Table P-PZ40)

Sigma, S.N. С.Н. Сигма see PG3470.S9

3470.S568 Sigov, Alekseĭ Sergeevich, 1850- . Алексей Сергеевич Сигов (Table P-PZ40)

3470.S569 Sikevic, V.M. (Table P-PZ40)

3470.S57 Simborskiĭ, Nikolaĭ Vasil′evich, 1851-1881. Николай Васильевич Симборский (Table P-PZ40)

3470.S5716 Simonova, L. Л. Симонова (Table P-PZ40)

3470.S572 Sinegub, Sergeĭ Silovich, 1851-1907. Сергей Силович Синегуб (Table P-PZ40)

3470.S574 Sirik, Ivan Avramovich, fl. 1880-1890. Иван Аврамович Сирик (Table P-PZ40)

Sirko Wacław, pseud. see PG3470.S565

3470.S575 Sirotinin, S.V., fl. 1900-1910. С.В. Сиротинин (Table P-PZ40)

3470.S576 Sivachev, Mikhail Gordeevich, 1877-1937. Михаил Гордеевич Сивачев (Table P-PZ40)

3470.S577 Sizova, A.K., fl. 1900-1910. А.К. Сизова (Table P-PZ40)

Russian literature
Individual authors and works, 1870-1917
Individual authors, Pes - Z -- Continued

3470.S579 Skabichevskiĭ, Aleksandr Mikhaĭlovich, 1838-1910. Александр Михайлович Скабичевский (Table P-PZ40)

3470.S58 Skal'kovskiĭ, Konstantin Apollonovich, 1843-1905. Константин Аполлонович Скальковский (Table P-PZ40)

Skitalet͡s, pseud. Скиталец see PG3470.P25

3470.S582 Skli͡adnev, I.V., fl. 1880-1890. И.В. Скляднев (Table P-PZ40)

3470.S583 Skorbilin, M.M., fl. 1890-1900. М.М. Скорбилин (Table P-PZ40)

3470.S584 Skovronskai͡a, Marii͡a S., fl. 1890-1900. Мария С. Сковронская (Table P-PZ40)

3470.S585 Skripit͡syn, V.A., fl. 1890-1900. В.А. Скрипицын (Table P-PZ40)

3470.S586 Slanskai͡a, Ekaterina Vissarionovna, fl. 1900-1910. Екатерина Виссарионовна Сланская (Table P-PZ40)

3470.S587 Slavin, I. I͡A, fl. 1900-1910. И.Я. Славин (Table P-PZ40)

Slavit͡skiĭ, Alekseĭ Mikhaĭlovich. Алексей Михайлович Славицкий see PG3467.K6264

Slavutinskiĭ, Stepan Timofeevich. Степан Тимофеевич Славутинский see PG3361.S55

3470.S588 Slept͡sov, Aleksandr Aleksandrovich, 1835-1906. Александр Александрович Слепцов (Table P-PZ40)

Slivit͡skiĭ, Alekseĭ Mikhaĭlovich, fl. 1890-1900. Алексей Михайлович Сливицкий see PG3467.K6264

Slovo-glagol', pseud. Слово-глаголь see PG3467.G93

Slovskiĭ, E. E. Словский see PG3453.B64

3470.S59 Sluchevskiĭ, Konstantin Konstantinovich, 1837-1904. Константин Константинович Случевский (Table P-PZ40)

3470.S6 Smidovich, Vikentiĭ Vikent'evich, 1867-1945. Викентий Викентьевич Смидович (Table P-PZ40 modified)

3470.S6A61-.S6Z458 Separate works. By title

3470.S6B4 Bez dorogi (Story). Без дороги

Chestnym putem. Честным путем see PG3470.S6D9

3470.S6D8 Dva kont͡sa (Story). Два конца

Comprises:

3470.S6D85 Konet͡s Andrei͡a Ivanovicha. Конец Андрея Ивановича

PG

Russian literature
Individual authors and works, 1870-1917
Individual authors, Pes - Z
Smidovich, Vikentiĭ Vikent′evich, 1867-1945. Викентий Викентьевич Смидович
Separate works. By title
Dva kont͡sa (Story). Два конца -- Continued

3470.S6D9 Konet͡s Aleksandry Mikhaĭlovny. Конец Александры Михайловны
Subtitle: Chestnym putem

3470.S6I8 Ispravilas′ (Tale). Исправилась
3470.S6I9 Iz obetovannoĭ zemli (Tale). Из обетованной земли
3470.S6K2 K spekhu (Tale). К спеху
3470.S6K3 K zhizni (Story). К жизни
Konet͡s Aleksandry Mikhaĭlovny. Конец Александры Михайловны see PG3470.S6D9
Konet͡s Andrei͡a Ivanovicha. Конец Андрея Ивановича see PG3470.S6D85
3470.S6L5 Lizar (Tale). Лизар
3470.S6N2 Na mertvoĭ doroge (Tale). На мертвой дороге
3470.S6N25 Na povorote (Story). На повороте
Na voĭne. На войне see DS517.9
3470.S6N3 Na vysote (Tale). На высоте
3470.S6O2 Ob odnom dome (Tale). Об одном доме
3470.S6P3 Pautina (Tale). Паутина
3470.S6P6 Poryv (Tales). Порыв
3470.S6P65 Povetrie (Tale). Поветрие
3470.S6P7 Prekrasnai͡a Elena (Tale). Прекрасная Елена
3470.S6S4 Sestry (Novel). Сестры
3470.S6T6 Tovarishchi (Tale). Товарищи
3470.S6V2 V stepi (Tale). В степи
3470.S6V25 V sukhom tumane (Tale). В сухом тумане
3470.S6V28 V tupike (Novel). В тупике
3470.S6V3 Van′ka (Tale). Ванька
3470.S6Z2 Za prava (Tale). За права
3470.S615 Smirnov, D.F., fl. 1890-1900. Д.Ф. Смирнов (Table P-PZ40)
3470.S617 Smirnov, Il′i͡a Dmitrievich, fl. 1900-1910. Илья Дмитриевич Смирнов (Table P-PZ40)
3470.S618 Smirnov, Nikolaĭ Ivanovich. Николай Иванович Смирнов (Table P-PZ40)
3470.S62 Smirnova, Sof′i͡a Ivanovna, 1852-1921. Софья Ивановна Смирнова (Table P-PZ40)
3470.S63 Snezhina, O.K., fl. 1880-1890. О.К. Снежина (Table P-PZ40)
3470.S633 Sobolev, Aleksandr Sergeevich. Александр Сергеевич Соболев (Table P-PZ40)

Russian literature
Individual authors and works, 1870-1917
Individual authors, Pes - Z -- Continued

3470.S64 Soboleva, Sof͡ia Pavlovna, 1840-1884. Софья Павловна Соболева (Table P-PZ40)

3470.S65 Sobolevskiĭ, P.O., fl. 1890-1900. П.О. Соболевский (Table P-PZ40)

3470.S66 Soĭmonov, Mikhail Nikolaevich, 1851-1888. Михаил Николаевич Соймонов (Table P-PZ40)

Sokhanskai͡a, Nadezhda Stepanovna. Надежда Степановна Соханская see PG3361.S67

Sokol′nikov, Gavriil Aleksandrovich Khrushchov-. Гавриил Александрович Хрущов-Сокольников see PG3467.K45

3470.S67 Sokolov, Aleksandr Alekseevich, 1840- . Александр Алексеевич Соколов (Table P-PZ40)

3470.S672 Sokolov, Avdiĭ Ivanovich, 1824-1893. Авдий Иванович Соколов (Table P-PZ40)

3470.S673 Sokolov, Nikolaĭ Matveevich, 1860-1908. Николай Матвеевич Соколов (Table P-PZ40)

3470.S674 Sokolov, Pavel Zakharovich, fl. 1890-1900. Павел Захарович Соколов (Table P-PZ40)

3470.S676 Sokolov, Sergeĭ Alekseevich, 1878-1936. Сергей Алексеевич Соколов (Table P-PZ40)

3470.S678 Sokolovskiĭ, A.Z., fl. 1880-1890. А.З. Соколовский (Table P-PZ40)

3470.S68 Sollogub, Aleksandr Vladimirovich, graf, 1845- . Александр Владимирович Соллогуб (Table P-PZ40)

Sologub, Fedor. Федор Сологуб see PG3470.T4

3470.S685 Solov′ev, Evgeniĭ Andreevich, 1863-1905. Евгений Андреевич Соловьев (Table P-PZ40)

For Solov′ev as a literary critic see PG2947.S6

3470.S69 Solov′ev, Nikolaĭ I͡Akovlevich, 1845-1899. Николай Яковлевич Соловьев (Table P-PZ40)

For works jointly authored with A. N. Ostrovskiĭ see PG3337.O8A7+

Solov′ev, Vladimir Sergeevich, 1853-1900. Владимир Сергеевич Соловьев

For works in ethics, religion, etc., see BJ, BL-BX, etc.

For biography, collected works, and philosophical works see B4260+

3470.S7A17 Collected poems

Translations (Collected or selected)

3470.S7A2-.S7A29 English. By translator, if given, or date

3470.S7A3-.S7A39 French. By translator, if given, or date

3470.S7A4-.S7A49 German. By translator, if given, or date

Russian literature
Individual authors and works, 1870-1917
Individual authors, Pes - Z
Solov′ev, Vladimir Sergeevich, 1853-1900. Владимир Сергеевич Соловьев
Translations (Collected or selected) -- Continued
3470.S7A5-.S7A59 Other. By language
Separate literary works. By title
3470.S7B4 Belye kolokol′chiki (Poem). Белые колокольчики
3470.S7E9 Ex oriente lux (Poem)
3470.S7K6 Kollum-kamen′ (Poem). Коллум-камень
3470.S7K7 Kratkai͡a povest′ ob Antikhriste. Краткая повесть об Антихристе
3470.S7M5 Milyĭ drug, il′ ty ne vidish′ (Poem). Милый друг, иль ты не видишь
3470.S7N2 Na poezde utrom (Poem). На поезде утром
3470.S7N3 Na tom zhe meste (Poem). На том же месте
3470.S7R6 Rodina russkoĭ poėzii (Poem). Родина русской поэзии
3470.S7S5 Shutochnye p′esy. Шуточные пьесы
3470.S7S6 Son nai͡avu (Poem). Сон наяву
3470.S7T7 Tri svidanii͡a (Poem). Три свидания
3470.S7Z4 Zemli͡a-vladychit͡sa (Poem). Земля-владычица
3470.S7Z4581-.S7Z999 Criticism of literary works
3470.S72 Solov′ev, Vsevolod Sergeevich, 1849-1903. Всеволод Сергеевич Соловьев (Table P-PZ40)
3470.S725 Solov′ev-Nesmelov, Nikolaĭ Aleksandrovich, 1849-1901. Николай Александрович Соловьев-Несмелов (Table P-PZ40)
3470.S73 Solov′eva, Poliksena Sergeevna, 1867-1924. Поликсена Сергеевна Соловьева (Table P-PZ40)
Solugub, Fedor see PG3470.T4
Spit͡syna, Ekaterina Andreevna, 1865-1902. Екатерина Андреевна Спицына see PG3470.Z427
3470.S74 Stakheev, Dmitriĭ Ivanovich, 1840-1918. Дмитрий Иванович Стахеев (Table P-PZ40)
3470.S745 Stakhevich, N.P., fl. 1880-1900. Н.П. Стахевич (Table P-PZ40)
3470.S75 Stani͡ukovich, Konstantin Mikhaĭlovich, 1843-1903. Константин Михайлович Станюкович (Table P-PZ40)
3470.S754 Starostin, I͡Akov, fl. 1870-1800. Яков Старостин (Table P-PZ40)
3470.S756 Starostin, Vasiliĭ Grigor′evich, 1840-1902. Василий Григорьевич Старостин (Table P-PZ40)

Russian literature
Individual authors and works, 1870-1917
Individual authors, Pes - Z -- Continued

Staryĭ ėmigrant, pseud. Старый эмигрант see PG3460.D39

Staryĭ mali͡ar, pseud. Старый маляр see PG3453.B35

Starynkevich, E. E. Старынкевич see PG3470.S19

Stasova, Varvara Dmitrievna. Варвара Дмитриевна Стасова see PG3467.K54

3470.S759 Stavrovskiĭ-Popradov, I͡Uliĭ Ivanovich. Юлий Иванович Ставровский-Попрадов (Table P-PZ40)

3470.S76 Stepanov, Nikolaĭ V., fl. 1890-1900. Николай В. Степанов (Table P-PZ40)

3470.S765 Stepanov, P.A., fl. 1880-1890. П.А. Степанов (Table P-PZ40)

Stepni͡ak, Sergeĭ. Сергей Степняк see PG3467.K72

Stepnoĭ, N. H. Степной see PG3451.A36

3470.S769 Stern, A.V., 1843- . А.В. Стерн (Table P-PZ40)

Stoi͡anov, Mark. Марк Стоянов see PG3467.N3

3470.S775 Stolit͡sa, Li͡ubov′, fl. 1910-1920. Любовь Столица (Table P-PZ40)

Strakhov, Nikolaĭ Nikolaevich. Николай Николаевич Страхов see PG3361.S775

Strakhova, Lidii͡a Alekseevna. Лидия Алексеевна Страхова see PG3453.A92

Strannik, Ivan. Иван Странник see PG3453.A54

3470.S78 Strazhev, Viktor Ivanovich, 1879-1950. Виктор Иванович Стражев (Table P-PZ40)

3470.S785 Stremoukhov, N.P., fl. 1880-1890. Н.П. Стремоухов (Table P-PZ40)

3470.S8 Struve, Aleksandr Filippovich, 1874- . Александр Филиппович Струве (Table P-PZ40)

Struzhkin, N. H. Стружкин see PG3467.K784

3470.S813 Stulli, Fedor Stepanovich, 1834- . Федор Степанович Стулли (Table P-PZ40)

3470.S815 Sukhomlinov, Vladimir Aleksandrovich, 1848-1926. Владимир Александрович Сухомлинов (Table P-PZ40)

Sukhonin, Petr Petrovich. Петр Петрович Сухонин see PG3361.S795

3470.S818 Sulkovskiĭ, Vladimir. Владимир Сулковский (Table P-PZ40)

Sultanova, Ekaterina Pavlovna. Екатерина Павловна Султанова see PG3467.L43

Sumbatov, Aleksandr Ivanovich I͡Uzhin-. Александр Иванович Южин-Сумбатов see PG3467.I73

PG

Russian literature
Individual authors and works, 1870-1917
Individual authors, Pes - Z -- Continued

3470.S82 Surikov, Ivan Zakharovich, 1841-1880. Иван Захарович Суриков (Table P-PZ40)

3470.S83 Suvorin, Alekseĭ Sergeevich, 1834-1912. Алексей Сергеевич Суворин (Table P-PZ40)

3470.S84 Suvorin, Mikhail Alekseevich, fl. 1880-1900. Михаил Алексеевич Суворин (Table P-PZ40)

3470.S85 Suvorov, Petr Pavlovich, 1839-1901. Петр Павлович Суворов (Table P-PZ40)

Svechina, Nadezhda Ivanovna. Надежда Ивановна Свечина see PG3467.M395

Svedent͡sov, Ivan Ivanovich, 1842-1901. Иван Иванович Сведенцов see PG3467.I825

Svetlov, Valerian. Валериан Светлов see PG3467.I85

3470.S87 Svirskiĭ, Alekseĭ Ivanovich, 1865-1942. Алексей Иванович Свирский (Table P-PZ40)

3470.S88 Svoekhotov, Dmitriĭ, fl. 1870-1890. Дмитрий Своехотов (Table P-PZ40)

3470.S9 Syromi͡atnikov, Sergeĭ Nikolaevich, 1864-1933. Сергей Николаевич Сыромятников (Table P-PZ40)

3470.S93 Sysoev, Valeriĭ, fl. 1880-1900. Валерий Сысоев (Table P-PZ40)

3470.S95 Sysoeva, Ekaterina Alekseevna (Alʹmedingen), 1829-1893. Екатерина Алексеевна (Альмединген) Сысоева (Table P-PZ40)

T--o, Nik, pseud. Ник Т--о see PG3453.A6

Tambovskiĭ, A.P. А.П. Тамбовский see PG3467.M55

Tan, V.G. В.Г. Тан see PG3453.B63

3470.T27 Tani͡eev, S.V. С.В. Танѣевъ (Table P-PZ40)

3470.T3 Taranovskiĭ, N.G., fl. 1880-1900. Н.Г. Тарановский (Table P-PZ40)

Taranskiĭ, G. Г. Таранский see PG3467.K612

3470.T32 Tarasov, Evgeniĭ Mikhaĭlovich, 1882-1944. Евгений Михайлович Тарасов (Table P-PZ40)

Tarkhova, Anastasii͡a Romanovna. Анастасия Романовна Тархова see PG3467.K68

Tarnovskiĭ, Konstantin Avgustovich. Константин Августович Тарновский see PG3361.T25

3470.T34 Tarutin, Aleksandr, fl. 1890-1900. Александр Тарутин (Table P-PZ40)

3470.T356 Tatarin, Petr. Петр Татарин (Table P-PZ40)

3470.T36 Tatishchev, Sergeĭ Spiridonovich, 1846-1906. Сергей Спиридонович Татищев (Table P-PZ40)

Tėffi, N.A. Н.А. Тэффи see PG3453.B8

Russian literature
Individual authors and works, 1870-1917
Individual authors, Pes - Z -- Continued

3470.T37 Teleshov, Nikolaĭ Dmitrievich, 1867-1957. Николай Дмитриевич Телешов (Table P-PZ40)

3470.T374 Temnyĭ, N. H. Темный (Table P-PZ40)

Temnyĭ chelovek, pseud. Темный человек see PG3467.M7

3470.T38 Teodorovich, G.A., fl. 1890-1900. Г.А. Теодорович (Table P-PZ40)

3470.T385 Teplov, V.V., fl. 1880-1900. В.В. Теплов (Table P-PZ40)

3470.T39 Terpigorev, Sergeĭ Nikolaevich, 1841-1895. Сергей Николаевич Терпигорев (Table P-PZ40)

3470.T4 Teternikov, Fedor Kuz′mich, 1863-1927. Федор Кузьмич Тетерников (Table P-PZ40 modified)

3470.T4A61-.T4Z458 Separate works. By title

3470.T4A65 Alai͡a lenta (Tale). Алая лента

3470.T4A69 Alchushchiĭ i zhazhdushchiĭ (Tale). Алчущий и жаждущий

3470.T4A7 Alyĭ mak (Poems). Алый мак

3470.T4B3 Baranchik (Tale). Баранчик

3470.T4B4 Baryshni͡a Liza (Story). Барышня Лиза

3470.T4C4 Charodeĭnai͡a chasha (Poems). Чародейная чаша

3470.T4C5 Chervi͡ak (Tale). Червяк

3470.T4D3 Dar mudrykh pchel (Tragedy). Дни печали

3470.T4D6 Dni pechali (Tales). Два Готика

3470.T4D8 Dva Gotika (Tale). Два Готика

Dym i pepel. Дым и пепел see PG3470.T4N38

3470.T4E4 Elkich (Tale). Елкич

3470.T4F5 Fimiamy (Poems). Фимиамы

3470.T4I2 I͡Aryĭ god (Tales). Ярый год

3470.T4I7 Istlevai͡ushchie lichiny (Tales). Истлевающие личины

3470.T4K2 K zvezdam (Tale). К звездам

3470.T4K3 Kamen′ broshennyĭ v vodu (Drama). Камень брошенный в воду

Kapli krovi. Капли крови see PG3470.T4N34

3470.T4K5 Kniga ocharovaniĭ (Stories and legends). Книга очарований

3470.T4K52 Kniga prevrashcheniĭ (Tales). Книга превращений

3470.T4K54 Kniga razluk (Tales). Книга разлук

3470.T4K56 Kniga skazok. Книга сказок

3470.T4K58 Kniga stremleniĭ (Tales). Книга стремлений

Koroleva Ortruda. Королева Ортруда see PG3470.T4N36

3470.T4K6 Koster dorozhnyĭ (Poems). Костер дорожный

3470.T4K7 Krasnogubai͡a gost′i͡a (Tale). Красногубая гостья

Russian literature
Individual authors and works, 1870-1917
Individual authors, Pes - Z
Teternikov, Fedor Kuz′mich, 1863-1927. Федор Кузьмич Тетерников
Separate works. By title -- Continued

3470.T4K75 Krasota (Tale). Красота
3470.T4L3 Lazurnye gory (Poems). Лазурные горы
3470.T4L5 Liturgii͡a mne, misterii͡a. Литургия мне, мистерия
3470.T4L6 Li͡ubov′ nad bezdnami (Drama). Любовь над безднами
3470.T4L65 Li͡ubvi (Drama). Любви
3470.T4M3 Malen′kiĭ chelovek (Tale). Маленький человек
3470.T4M4 Melkiĭ bes (Novel). Мелкий бес
3470.T4M5 Melkiĭ bes (Drama). Мелкий бес
3470.T4N2 Naivnye vstrechi (Tale). Наивные встречи
3470.T4N3 Nav′i chary (Novel). Навьи чары
Comprises:
3470.T4N32 Tvorimai͡a legenda (Novel). Творимая легенда
3470.T4N34 Kapli krovi (Novel). Капли крови
3470.T4N36 Koroleva Ortruda (Novel). Королева Ортруда
3470.T4N38 Dym i pepel (Novel). Дым и пепел
3470.T4N4 Nebo goluboe. Небо голубое
3470.T4N45 Nedobrai͡a gospozha (Tales). Недобрая госпожа
3470.T4N5 Neutolimoe (Tale). Неутолимое
3470.T4N6 Nochnye pli͡aski (Drama). Ночные пляски
3470.T4O2 Obruch (Tale). Обруч
3470.T4O25 Ocharovanie zemli (Poems). Очарование земли
3470.T4O3 Odna li͡ubov′ (Poems). Одна любовь
3470.T4O6 Opechalennai͡a nevesta (Tale). Опечаленная невеста
3470.T4O7 Otrok Lin (Tale). Отрок Лин
3470.T4P55 Plamennyĭ krug (Poems). Пламенный круг
3470.T4P6 Pobeda smerti (Tragedy). Победа смерти
3470.T4P65 Politicheskie skazochki. Политические сказочки
3470.T4P67 Pomnish′, ne zabudesh′ (Tale). Помнишь, не забудешь
3470.T4P7 Pretvorivshai͡a vodu v vino (Tale). Претворившая воду в вино
3470.T4P75 Provody (Drama). Проводы
3470.T4P8 Put′ v Ėmmaus (Tale). Путь в Эммаус
3470.T4R6 Rodine (Poems). Родине
3470.T4S5 Slashche i͡ada (Novel). Слаще яда
3470.T4S55 Zheni͡a i Shani͡a (Tale). Женя и Шаня
3470.T4S57 Slepai͡a babochka (Tales). Слепая бабочка
3470.T4S58 Smert′ po ob″i͡avlenii͡u (Tale). Смерть по объявлению

Russian literature
Individual authors and works, 1870-1917
Individual authors, Pes - Z
Teternikov, Fedor Kuz′mich, 1863-1927. Федор Кузьмич Тетерников
Separate works. By title -- Continued

3470.T4S59 Snegurochka (Tale). Снегурочка
3470.T4S6 Sobornyĭ blagovest (Poems). Соборный благовест
3470.T4S63 Sochtennye dni [i drugie rasskazy]. Сочтенные дни [и другие рассказы]
3470.T4S65 Sochtennye dni (Tale). Сочтенные дни
3470.T4S7 Strazh velikogo t͡sari͡a (Drama). Страж великого царя
3470.T4S8 Svet′ i teni (Tale). Светь и тени
3470.T4S85 Svirel′, russkie berzherety (Poems). Свирель, русские бержереты
3470.T4T4 Teni (Tale). Тени
3470.T4T5 Ti͡azhelye sny (Novel). Тяжелые сны
3470.T4T6 Zador (Tale). Задор
3470.T4T7 TSarit͡sa pot͡seluev. Царица поцелуев
Tvorimai͡a legenda. Творимая легенда see PG3470.T4N32
3470.T4U8 Uteshenie (Tale). Утешение
3470.T4V2 V plenu (Tale). В плену
3470.T4V25 V tolpe. В толпе
3470.T4V3 Van′ka-kli͡uchnik i pazh Zhean (Drama). Ванька-ключник и паж Жеан
3470.T4V4 Velikiĭ blagovest (Poems). Великий благовест
3470.T4V6 Voĭna (Poems). Война
Zador. Задор see PG3470.T4T6
3470.T4Z15 Zaklinatel′nit͡sa smeĭ (Novel). Заклинательница смей
3470.T4Z17 Zalozhniki zhizni (Drama). Заложники жизни
3470.T4Z2 Zemle zemnoe (Tales). Земле земное
3470.T4Z23 Zemli͡a rodnai͡a (Poems). Земля родная
3470.T4Z25 Zemnoĭ raĭ (Tale). Земной рай
3470.T4Z27 Zemnye deti (Tales). Земные дети
3470.T4Z3 Zhalo smerti [and other tales]. Жало смерти [и другие рассказы]
3470.T4Z33 Zhalo smerti (Tale). Жало смерти
3470.T4Z36 Zhemchuzhnye svetila (Poems). Жемчужные светила
Zheni͡a i Shani͡a (Poems). Женя и Шаня see PG3470.T4S55
3470.T4Z4 Zmeinye ochi (Poems). Змеиные очи
3470.T4Z45 Zmiĭ (Poems). Змий
Ti͡apkin, S. C. Тяпкин see PG3451.A615

Russian literature
Individual authors and works, 1870-1917
Individual authors, Pes - Z -- Continued

3470.T43 T͡iazhelov, N.V. Н.В. Тяжелов (Table P-PZ40)

3470.T5 Tikhonov, Alekseĭ Alekseevich, 1853-1914. Алексей Алексеевич Тихонов (Table P-PZ40)

3470.T52 Tikhonov, Vladimir Alekseevich, 1857-1914. Владимир Алексеевич Тихонов (Table P-PZ40)

3470.T53 Timkovskiĭ, Nikolaĭ Ivanovich, 1863-1922. Николай Иванович Тимковский (Table P-PZ40)

3470.T54 Timofeev, N.P., fl. 1870-1890. Н.П. Тимофеев (Table P-PZ40)

3470.T55 Titov, Andreĭ Aleksandrovich, 1845-1911. Андрей Александрович Титов (Table P-PZ40)

3470.T555 T͡iumenev, Il′i͡a Fedorovich, b. 1855. Илья Федорович Тюменев (Table P-PZ40)

3470.T56 T͡iutchev, Fedor Fedorovich, fl. 1890-1910. Федор Федорович Тютчев (Table P-PZ40)

3470.T57 Tkhorzhevskiĭ, Ivan Feliksovich, fl. 1870-1880. Иван Феликсович Тхоржевский (Table P-PZ40)

3470.T58 Tkhorzhevskiĭ, Korneliĭ Vladislavovich, 1858-1896. Корнелий Владиславович Тхоржевский (Table P-PZ40)

Tolsta͡ia, Aleksandra L′vovna, grafini͡a, fl. 1880-1920. Александра Львовна Толстая see PG3453.B667

3470.T65 Tolstoĭ, Lev L′vovich, graf, 1869-1945. Лев Львович Толстой (Table P-PZ40)

Tolstoĭ, Lev Nikolaevich. Лев Николаевич Толстой see PG3365+

Tolycheva, T. T. Толычева see PG3467.N95

3470.T67 Tomashevska͡ia, Vera Ivanovna, (T͡Svetkova), fl. 1890-1910. Вера Ивановна (Цветкова) Томашевская (Table P-PZ40)

3470.T7 Trakhtenberg, Vladimir Osipovich, 1861-1914. Владимир Осипович Трахтенберг (Table P-PZ40)

3470.T73 Trefolev, Leonid Nikolaevich, 1839-1905. Леонид Николаевич Трефолев (Table P-PZ40)

3470.T74 Trigorskiĭ, Aleksandr, 19th cent. Александр Тригорский (Table P-PZ40)

3470.T75 Trizna, Dmitriĭ S., fl. 1880-1900. Дмитрий С. Тризна (Table P-PZ40)

Trofimov, A. A. Трофимов see PG3467.I74

Trofimov, N. H. Трофимов see PG3467.L52

3470.T76 Trofimovskiĭ, Ieronim, fl. 1880-1890. Иероним Трофимовский (Table P-PZ40)

3470.T768 T͡Sagolov, Georgiĭ, 1871-1939. Георгий Цаголов (Table P-PZ40)

Russian literature
Individual authors and works, 1870-1917
Individual authors, Pes - Z -- Continued

3470.T77 TSebrikova, Mariīa Konstantinovna, 1835-1917. Мария Константиновна Цебрикова (Table P-PZ40)

3470.T775 TSeĭner, M.A., fl. 1890-1910. М.А. Цейнер (Table P-PZ40)

3470.T78 TSekhanovich, Aleksandr Nikolaevich, 1862-1897. Александр Николаевич Цеханович (Table P-PZ40)

3470.T782 TSekhovskaīa, Varvara Nikolaevna (Men′shikova), 1872- . Варвара Николаевна (Меньшикова) Цеховская (Table P-PZ40)

3470.T784 TSenzor, Dmitriĭ Mikhaĭlovich, 1879- . Дмитрий Михайлович Цензор (Table P-PZ40)

3470.T785 TSertelev, Dmitriĭ Nikolaevich, kniaz′, 1852-1911. Дмитрий Николаевич Цертелев (Table P-PZ40)

TSvetkova, Vera Ivanovna. Вера Ивановна Цветкова see PG3470.T67

3470.T9 Tugan-Baranovskaīa, Lidiīa Karlovna, 1869-1900. Лидия Карловна Туган-Барановская (Table P-PZ40)

3470.T92 Tugan-Baranovskaīa, Taisiīa Petrovna, 1831- . Таисия Петровна Туган-Барановская (Table P-PZ40)

3470.T95 Tunoshenskiĭ, Vladimir Vladimirovich, 1865-1910. Владимир Владимирович Туношенский (Table P-PZ40)

Tverskoĭ, P.A. П.А. Тверской see PG3460.D39

3470.T98 Tyrkova, Ariadna Vladimirovna, 1869-1962. Ариадна Владимировна Тыркова (Table P-PZ40)

3470.U3 Ukhach-Ogorovich, N.A., fl. 1890-1900. Н.А. Ухач-Огорович (Table P-PZ40)

3470.U4 Ukhtomskiĭ, Ėsper Ėsperovich, kniaz′, 1861-1921. Эспер Эсперович Ухтомский (Table P-PZ40)

3470.U5 Umanets, Sergeĭ Ignat′evich, fl. 1890-1900. Сергей Игнатьевич Уманец (Table P-PZ40)

3470.U6 Umanov-Kaplunovskiĭ, Vladimir Vasil′evich, 1865- . Владимир Васильевич Уманов-Каплуновский (Table P-PZ40)

3470.U7 Urusov, Nikolaĭ Pavlovich, kniaz′, fl. 1880-1890. Николай Павлович Урусов (Table P-PZ40)

3470.U73 Urvantsov, Lev Nikolaevich, 1865-1929. Лев Николаевич Урванцов (Table P-PZ40)

3470.U75 Ushak, Ivan, fl. 1890-1900. Иван Ушак (Table P-PZ40)

3470.U8 Uspenskiĭ, Gleb Ivanovich, 1843-1902. Глеб Иванович Успенский (Table P-PZ40)

Uspenskiĭ, Nikolaĭ Vasil′evich. Николай Васильевич Успенский see PG3447.U7

Ustalyĭ, pseud. Усталый see PG3470.V78

PG

Russian literature
Individual authors and works, 1870-1917
Individual authors, Pes - Z -- Continued

Ustinovich, Aleksandra Nikolaevna. Александра Николаевна Устинович see PG3467.M38

Ustri͡alov, Fedor Nikolaevich. Федор Николаевич Устрялов see PG3447.U8

3470.V2 Vagner, Nikolaĭ Petrovich, 1829-1907. Николай Петрович Вагнер (Table P-PZ40)

3470.V215 Valuev, Petr Aleksandrovich, graf, 1814-1890. Петр Александрович Валуев (Table P-PZ40)

Vampirov, Ėndimion. Эндимион Вампиров see PG3453.B98

Vasilʹeva, Elizaveta Ivanovna, 1887-1928. Елизавета Ивановна Васильева see PG3460.D316

3470.V22 Vasilʹeva, Marii͡a Karlovna, fl. 1870-1880. Мария Карловна Васильева (Table P-PZ40)

3470.V23 Vasilevskiĭ, Ilʹi͡a Markovich, 1882-1938. Илья Маркович Василевский (Table P-PZ40)

3470.V24 Vasilevskiĭ, Ippolit Fedorovich, 1850- . Ипполит Федорович Василевский (Table P-PZ40)

3470.V25 Vasilevskiĭ, Lev Markovich, 1876-1936. Лев Маркович Василевский (Table P-PZ40)

3470.V26 Vasi͡ukov, Semen Ivanovich, 1854-1908. Семен Иванович Васюков (Table P-PZ40)

3470.V28 Vatson, Marii͡a Valentinovna (de Roberti-Laserda), 1848-1932. Мария Валентиновна (де Роберти-Ласерда) Ватсон (Table P-PZ40)

3470.V3 Veĭnberg, Pavel Pavlovich, 1874-1908. Павел Павлович Вейнберг (Table P-PZ40)

3470.V32 Veĭnberg, Petr Isaevich, 1830-1908. Петр Исаевич Вейнберг (Table P-PZ40)

3470.V34 Velichko, Vasiliĭ Lʹvovich, 1860-1904. Василий Львович Величко (Table P-PZ40)

Velinskai͡a, Marʹi͡a Aleksandrovna. Марья Александровна Велинская see PG3467.M34

Venkstern, Aleksandra Alekseevna. Александра Алексеевна Венкстерн see PG3470.S769

3470.V38 Vent͡selʹ, Nikolaĭ Nikolaevich, 1855-1920. Николай Николаевич Вентцель (Table P-PZ40)

3470.V4 Verbit͡skai͡a, Anastasii͡a Alekseevna (Zi͡ablova), 1861-1928. Анастасия Алексеевна (Зяблова) Вербицкая (Table P-PZ40)

Verbovchanin, pseud. Вербовчанин see PG3470.S572

Veresaev, V.V. В.В. Вересаев see PG3470.S6

3470.V416 Vereshchagin, A. V. (Aleksandr Vasilʹevich), 1850-1909. Александр Васильевич Верещагин (Table P-PZ40)

Russian literature
Individual authors and works, 1870-1917
Individual authors, Pes - Z -- Continued

3470.V417 Vereshchagin, G.E. (Grigoriĭ Egorovich), 1851-1930. Григорий Егорович Верещагин (Table P-PZ40)

3470.V418 Vereshchagin, Sergeĭ, fl. 1890-1900. Сергей Верещагин (Table P-PZ40)

3470.V42 Vereshchagin, Vasiliĭ Vasilʹevich, 1842-1904. Василий Васильевич Верещагин (Table P-PZ40)
For general biography and criticism of his works as an artist see ND699.V5

Vergezhskiĭ, A. A. Вергежский see PG3470.T98

Verkhoi͡ant͡sev, S. C. Верхоянцев see PG3453.B33

3470.V45 Verkhoustinskiĭ, Boris Alekseevich, 1888-1921. Борис Алексеевич Верхоустинский (Table P-PZ40)

3470.V46 Verner, Alekseĭ Antonovich, 1868- . Алексей Антонович Вернер (Table P-PZ40)

3470.V47 Verner, Ippolit Antonovich, 1852-1927. Ипполит Антонович Вернер (Table P-PZ40)

Vershinin, Alekseĭ Platonovich. Алексей Платонович Вершинин see PG3451.A66

3470.V49 Veselit͡skai͡a, Lidii͡a Ivanovna, 1857- . Лидия Ивановна Веселицкая (Table P-PZ40)

3470.V494 Veselkova-Kilʹshtet, M. M. Веселкова-Кильштет (Table P-PZ40)

Vezovskiĭ, Iv. Ив. Везовский see PG3470.S54

Vikont d'Apolinaris, pseud. Виконт д'Аполинарис see PG3453.B4

Viktorov, pseud. Викторов see PG3453.B5

3470.V5 Vilʹde, Nikolaĭ Evstafievich, 1832-1896. Николай Евстафиевич Вильде (Table P-PZ40)

3470.V52 Vilʹde, Nikolaĭ Nikolaevich, d. 1918. Николай Николаевич Вильде (Table P-PZ40)

3470.V525 Vilenkin, Nikolaĭ Maksimovich, 1855-1937. Николай Максимович Виленкин (Table P-PZ40)

Vilenkina, Li͡udmila Nikolaevna. Людмила Николаевна Виленкина see PG3470.V53

Vilinsʹka, Marii͡a Oleksandrivna. Марія Олександрівна Вілінська see PG3467.M34

Vilinskai͡a, Marii͡a OleksandrivnaAleksandrovna. Мария Александровна Вилинская see PG3467.M34

3470.V53 Vilʹkina, Li͡udmila Nikolaevna, 1873-1920. Людмила Николаевна Вилькина (Table P-PZ40)

Villamov, Vladimir Aleksandrovich, 1837-1889. Владимир Александрович Вилламов see PG3470.S818

Russian literature
Individual authors and works, 1870-1917
Individual authors, Pes - Z -- Continued

3470.V54 Villiam, Georgiĭ I͡Akovlevich, 1874- . Георгий Яковлевич Виллиам (Table P-PZ40)

3470.V55 Vinit͡skai͡a, Aleksandra Aleksandrovna, 1847-1914. Александра Александровна Виницкая (Table P-PZ40)

3470.V56 Vinogradov, Leontiĭ Nikitich, fl. 1890-1900. Леонтий Никитич Виноградов (Table P-PZ40)

3470.V57 Vishnevskiĭ, Fedor Vladimirovich, 1838- . Федор Владимирович Вишневский (Table P-PZ40)

Vitte, Sergeĭ I͡Ulʹevich. Сергей Юльевич Витте see PG3470.W56

Vladimirov, S. C. Владимиров see PG3467.L13

Vladimirov, V.D. В.Д. Владимиров see PG3470.V6

Vladimirova, A.K. А.К. Владимирова see PG3460.E86

3470.V58 Vladykin, Mikhail Nikolaevich, 1830-1887. Михаил Николаевич Владыкин (Table P-PZ40)

3470.V585 Vlasov, Vsevolod Vasilʹevich, fl. 1890-1900. Всеволод Васильевич Власов (Table P-PZ40)

Vodevilʹ, pseud. Водевиль see PG3453.B4

3470.V59 Vodovozov, Vasiliĭ Ivanovich, 1825-1886. Василий Иванович Водовозов

3470.V6 Volʹfson, Vladimir Dmitrievich, fl. 1890-1900. Владимир Дмитриевич Вольфсон (Table P-PZ40)

3470.V62 Volkhovskiĭ, Feliks Vadimovich, 1846-1914. Феликс Вадимович Волховский (Table P-PZ40)

3470.V63 Volkonskai͡a, Marii͡a Vasilʹevna, kni͡aginі͡a, fl. 1890-1910. Мария Васильевна Волконская (Table P-PZ40)

3470.V64 Volkonskiĭ, Mikhail Nikolaevich, kni͡azʹ, 1860-1917. Михаил Николаевич Волконский (Table P-PZ40)

3470.V65 Volkov, Leonid Petrovich, 1870-1900. Леонид Петрович Волков (Table P-PZ40)

Vollan, Grigoriĭ Aleksandrovich de-. Григорий Александрович Де-Воллан see PG3460.D48

Volʹnyĭ, Ivan. Иван Вольный see PG3460.D6

Volodin, V.V. В.В. Володин see PG3453.B27

Vologdin, P. П. Вологдин see PG3470.Z34

3470.V68 Voloshin, Maksimilian Aleksandrovich, 1877-1932. Максимилиан Александрович Волошин (Table P-PZ40)

Volynskiĭ, A. A. Волынский see PG3460.F6

3470.V69 Volynskiĭ, Nikolaĭ Pavlovich, 1878- Николай Павлович Волынский (Table P-PZ40)

Volzhskiĭ, pseud. Волжский see PG3470.S372

Russian literature
Individual authors and works, 1870-1917
Individual authors, Pes - Z -- Continued

	Vonifatiĭ Nosorogov, pseud. Вонифатий Носорогов see PG3467.M363
	Voronet͡skiĭ, V. B. Воронецкий see PG3470.V34
3470.V7	Voronin, Ivan Grigor′evich, 1840-1883. Иван Григорьевич Воронин (Table P-PZ40)
3470.V74	Voronova, E.A., fl. 1900-1910. E.A. Воронова (Table P-PZ40)
	Vovchok, Marko. Марко Вовчок see PG3467.M34
3470.V78	Voznesenskiĭ, Aleksandr Nikolaevich, 1879- . Александр Николаевич Вознесенский (Table P-PZ40)
	Vrot͡skiĭ, N. H. Вроцкий see PG3467.N28
3470.V8	Vsevolodskai͡a, O.V., fl. 1890-1900. O.B. Всеволодская (Table P-PZ40)
3470.V85	Vuchetich, Nikolaĭ Gavrilovich, 1845- . Николай Гаврилович Вучетич (Table P-PZ40)
3470.V9	Vvedenskai͡a, Elena Vasil′evna (Rozenberg), ca. 1850-1911. Елена Васильевна (Розенберг) Введенская (Table P-PZ40)
	Wagner, Nikolaĭ Petrovich see PG3470.V2
	Watson, Marii͡a Valentinovna see PG3470.V28
	Weinberg, Pavel Pavlovich see PG3470.V3
	Weinberg, Petr Isaevich see PG3470.V32
	Wenkstern, Aleksandra Alekseevna see PG3470.S769
	Wentzel, Nikolaĭ Nikolaevich see PG3470.V38
	Werkhoustinskiĭ, Boris Alekseevich see PG3470.V45
	Werner, Alekseĭ Antonovich see PG3470.V46
	Werner, Ippolit Antonovich see PG3470.V47
	Wilde, Nikolaĭ Estafievich see PG3470.V5
	Wilde, Nikolaĭ Nikolaevich see PG3470.V52
3470.W56	Witte, Sergeĭ I͡Ul′evich, graf, 1849-1915 (Table P-PZ40)
	Wolfson, Vladimir Dmitrievich see PG3470.V6
3470.Z2	Zabelin, Nikolaĭ Nikolaevich, d. 1913. Николай Николаевич Забелин (Table P-PZ40)
	Zabytyĭ, O. O. Забытый see PG3467.N332
3470.Z22	Zaguli͡aev, Mikhail Andreevich, 1834-1900. Михаил Андреевич Загуляев (Table P-PZ40)
3470.Z23	Zaĭt͡sev, Boris Konstantinovich, 1881-1972. Борис Константинович Зайцев (Table P-PZ40)
3470.Z24	Zaĭt͡sev, Petr Egorovich, 1873- . Петр Егорович Зайцев (Table P-PZ40)
3470.Z25	Zakharchenko, Iosif Ivanovich, 1837-1894. Иосиф Иванович Захарченко (Table P-PZ40)
3470.Z26	Zakhar′in, Ivan Nikolaevich, 1839-1906. Иван Николаевич Захарьин (Table P-PZ40)

Russian literature
Individual authors and works, 1870-1917
Individual authors, Pes - Z -- Continued

3470.Z27 Zakrevskai͡a, Marii͡a, fl. 1890-1910. Мария Закревская (Table P-PZ40)

3470.Z28 Zamyslov, A.N., fl. 1880-1890. А.Н. Замыслов (Table P-PZ40)

3470.Z3 Zarin, Andreĭ Efimovich, 1862-1929. Андрей Ефимович Зарин (Table P-PZ40)

3470.Z32 Zarin, Fedor Efimovich, fl. 1890-1920. Федор Ефимович Зарин (Table P-PZ40)

3470.Z33 Zashchuk, Lidii͡a Vasilʹevna, fl. 1900-1920. Лидия Васильевна Защук (Table P-PZ40)

3470.Z34 Zasodimskiĭ, Pavel Vladimirovich, 1843-1912. Павел Владимирович Засодимский (Table P-PZ40)

3470.Z35 Zaviset͡skiĭ, I͡Uriĭ Gennadievich, d. 1901. Юрий Геннадиевич Зависецкий (Table P-PZ40)

Zavrazhnyĭ, G. Г. Завражный see PG3470.P613

3470.Z36 Zazulin, Ivan Petrovich, d. 1893. Иван Петрович Зазулин (Table P-PZ40)

Zeland, E. E. Зеланд see PG3470.Z37

3470.Z37 Zeland-Dubelʹt, Elena Aleksandrovna, b. 1863. Елена Александровна Зеланд-Дубельт (Table P-PZ40)

3470.Z38 Zemskiĭ, Aleksandr Mikhaĭlovich, fl. 1870-1900. Александр Михайлович Земский (Table P-PZ40)

3470.Z39 Zenger, Anatoliĭ, fl. 1890-1900. Анатолий Зенгер (Table P-PZ40)

3470.Z393 Zèo, 1851-1899. Зèо (Table P-PZ40)

3470.Z4 Zhabotinskiĭ, Vladimir Evgenʹevich, 1880-1940. Владимир Евгеньевич Жаботинский (Table P-PZ40)

Zhadovskai͡a, I͡Ulii͡a Valerianovna. Юлия Валериановна Жадовская see PG3447.Z3

3470.Z42 Zhakov, Kallistrat, 1866-1926. Каллистрат Жаков (Table P-PZ40)

Zhasminov, Aleksis, graf. Алексис Жасминов see PG3453.B94

3470.Z427 Zhdan, Ekaterina Andreevna, 1865-1902. Екатерина Андреевна Ждан (Table P-PZ40)

3470.Z43 Zhdanov, Lev, b. 1854. Лев Жданов (Table P-PZ40)

3470.Z435 Zhedilov. Жедилов (Table P-PZ40)

3470.Z44 Zhelikhovskai͡a, Vera Petrovna (Gan), 1835-1896. Вера Петровна (Ган) Желиховская (Table P-PZ40)

Zhiber, Mirra Aleksandrovna. Мирра Александровна Жибер see PG3467.L57

3470.Z447 Zhilin, M.M. (Mikhail Mikhaĭlovich). Михаил Михайлович Жилин (Table P-PZ40)

Russian literature
Individual authors and works, 1870-1917
Individual authors, Pes - Z -- Continued

3470.Z45 Zhirkevich, Aleksandr Vladimirovich, 1857-1927. Александр Владимирович Жиркевич (Table P-PZ40)

Zhitel′, pseud. Житель see PG3460.D52

3470.Z46 Zhukov, Ivan Aleksandrovich, d. 1891. Иван Александрович Жуков (Table P-PZ40)

3470.Z47 Zhukovskai͡a, Natal′i͡a I͡Ul′evna, fl. 1900-1910. Наталья Юльевна Жуковская (Table P-PZ40)

3470.Z48 Zhukovskiĭ, Vladimir Grigor′evich, fl. 1890-1910. Владимир Григорьевич Жуковский (Table P-PZ40)

Zi͡ablova, Anastasii͡a Alekseevna. Анастасия Алексеевна Зяблова see PG3470.V4

Zimarova, S. C. Зимарова see PG3467.K46

Zinin, M. M. Зинин see PG3470.S453

3470.Z5 Zinov′eva-Annibal, Lidii͡a Dmitrievna, d. 1907. Лидия Дмитриевна Зиновьева-Аннибал (Table P-PZ40)

3470.Z55 Zlatkovskiĭ, Mikhail Leont′evich, 1836-1904. Михаил Леонтьевич Златковский (Table P-PZ40)

3470.Z6 Zlatovratskiĭ, Nikolaĭ Nikolaevich, 1845-1911. Николай Николаевич Златовратский (Table P-PZ40)

Zlobin, Petr. Петр Злобин see PG3453.B98

3470.Z65 Zmienko, Mikhail Efimovich, 1858-1898. Михаил Ефимович Змиенко (Table P-PZ40)

3470.Z7 Znamenskiĭ, Mikhail S., fl. 1890-1900. Михаил С. Знаменский (Table P-PZ40)

3470.Z75 Zotov, Mikhail, fl. 1900-1920. Михаил Зотов (Table P-PZ40)

3470.Z8 Zvonarev, Aleksandr A., fl. 1860-1890. Александр А. Звонарев (Table P-PZ40)

3470.Z85 Zvorykin, Ivan Fedorovich, 1863-1893. Иван Федорович Зворыкин (Table P-PZ40)

Individual authors and works, 1917-1960

Subarrange each author by Table P-PZ40 unless otherwise specified

Authors born after 1885, beginning to publish about 1910 and flourishing after 1917 are usually classified in this group

3475 Anonymous works (Table P-PZ28)

3476.A-Z Individual authors, A-Z

3476.A2 Abramov, Aleksandr Vasil′evich, 1887-1924. Александр Васильевич Абрамов (Table P-PZ40)

Adalis, A. A. Адалис see PG3476.E4

3476.A248 Adamovich, Ales′, 1927-1994. Алесь Адамович (Table P-PZ40)

Russian literature
Individual authors and works, 1917-1960
Individual authors, A-Z -- Continued

3476.A25 Adamovich, Georgiĭ Viktorovich, 1892-1972. Георгий Викторович Адамович (Table P-PZ40)

3476.A3 Afinogenov, Aleksandr Nikolaevich, 1904-1941. Александр Николаевич Афиногенов (Table P-PZ40)

3476.A318 Agnivt͡sev, Nikolaĭ I͡Akovlevich, 1888-1932. Николай Яковлевич Агнивцев (Table P-PZ40)

3476.A324 Akhmatova, Anna Andreevna, 1889-1966. Анна Андреевна Ахматова (Table P-PZ40)

Aksen-Achkasov, pseud. Аксен-Ачкасов see PG3476.S23

Akulʹshin, Rodion Mikhaĭlovich. Родион Михайлович Акульшин see PG3476.B443

Aldan-Semenov, A.I. А.И. Алдан-Семенов see PG3476.S424

3476.A327 Aldanov, Mark Aleksandrovich, 1886-1957. Марк Александрович Алданов (Table P-PZ40)

3476.A34 Aleksandrovskiĭ, Vasiliĭ Dmitrievich, 1897-1934. Василий Дмитриевич Александровский (Table P-PZ40)

3476.A35 Alekseev, Gleb Vasilʹevich, 1892-1938. Глеб Васильевич Алексеев (Table P-PZ40)

3476.A36 Alekseev, Mikhail, 1895- . Михаил Алексеев (Table P-PZ40)

Alʹf, pseud. Альф see PG3476.B57

3476.A37 Aliger, Margarita Iosifovna, 1915-1992. Маргарита Иосифовна Алигер (Table P-PZ40)

3476.A39 Altauzen, Dzhek, Moiseevich, 1907-1942. Джек Моисеевич Алтаузен (Table P-PZ40)

3476.A4 Alymov, Sergeĭ I͡Akovlevich. Сергей Яковлевич Алымов (Table P-PZ40)

3476.A5 Amur-Sanan, Anton Mudrenovich, 1888-1940. Антон Мудренович Амур-Санан (Table P-PZ40)

3476.A52 Andreev, Vasiliĭ. Василий Андреев (Table P-PZ40)

Andreevskai͡a, Marii͡a Mikhaĭlovna. Мария Михайловна Андреевская see PG3476.S484

3476.A53 Anisimov, I͡Ulian Pavlovich, 1886-1940. Юлиан Павлович Анисимов (Table P-PZ40)

Ani͡utin, pseud. Анютин see PG3476.L8

3476.A54 Anov, Nikolaĭ Ivanovich. Николай Иванович Анов (Table P-PZ40)

3476.A55 Antokolʹskiĭ, Pavel Grigorʹevich, 1896-1978. Павел Григорьевич Антокольский (Table P-PZ40)

3476.A633 Arbuzov, Alekseĭ Nikolaevich. Алексей Николаевич Арбузов (Table P-PZ40)

Russian literature
Individual authors and works, 1917-1960
Individual authors, A-Z -- Continued

3476.A66 Argutinskai͡a, Li͡usi͡a Aleksandrovna. Люся Александровна Аргутинская (Table P-PZ40)

3476.A67 Arkhangelʹskiĭ, Aleksandr Grigorʹevich, 1889-1934. Александр Григорьевич Архангельский (Table P-PZ40)

Arkhip, pseud. Архип see PG3476.A67

3476.A68 Arkhipov, Nikolaĭ Arkhipovich, 1880-1942. Николай Архипович Архипов (Table P-PZ40)

3476.A7 Arosev, Aleksandr I͡Akovlevich, 1890-1938. Александр Яковлевич Аросев (Table P-PZ40)

3476.A716 Arskiĭ, Pavel Aleksandrovich, 1886-1967. Павел Александрович Арский (Table P-PZ40)

3476.A72 Artamonov, Mikhail Dmitrievich, 1888-1958. Михаил Дмитриевич Артамонов (Table P-PZ40)

3476.A73 Asanov, Nikolaĭ. Николай Асанов (Table P-PZ40)

3476.A74 Aseev, Nikolaĭ Nikolaevich, 1889-1963. Николай Николаевич Асеев (Table P-PZ40)

3476.A745 Ashukin, Nikolaĭ Sergeevich, 1890-1972. Николай Сергеевич Ашукин (Table P-PZ40)

3476.A88 Auslender, Sergeĭ Abramovich, 1886-1937. Сергей Абрамович Ауслендер (Table P-PZ40)

3476.A89 Avdeenko, Aleksandr Ostapovich, 1908-1996. Александр Остапович Авдеенко (Table P-PZ40)

3476.A92 Averchenko, Arkadiĭ Timofeevich, 1881-1925. Аркадий Тимофеевич Аверченко (Table P-PZ40)

3476.A94 Avramenko, Ilʹi͡a K. Илья К. Авраменко (Table P-PZ40)

3476.B2 Babelʹ, Isaak Ėmmanuilovich, 1894-1941. Исаак Эммануилович Бабель (Table P-PZ40)

3476.B23 Bagrit͡skiĭ, Ėduard Georgievich, 1895-1934. Эдуард Георгиевич Багрицкий (Table P-PZ40)

3476.B258 Bakhmetʹev, Vladimir Matveevich, 1885-1963. Владимир Матвеевич Бахметьев (Table P-PZ40)

Bakhrakh, Isaak Abramovich. Исаак Абрамович Бахрах see PG3476.I77

3476.B286 Bakhterev, I. И. Бахтерев (Table P-PZ40)

3476.B287 Barkova, Anna Aleksandrovna, 1901-1976. Анна Александровна Баркова (Table P-PZ40)

3476.B288 Barshev, Nikolaĭ Valerianovich, 1888-1938. Николай Валерианович Баршев (Table P-PZ40)

3476.B3 Barto, Agnii͡a Lʹvovna, 1906-1981. Агния Львовна Барто (Table P-PZ40)

3476.B336 Baumwoll, Rokhl, 1914-2000 (Table P-PZ40)
For Baumwolls' Yiddish works see PJ5129.B34

Russian literature
Individual authors and works, 1917-1960
Individual authors, A-Z -- Continued

3476.B34 Bazhov, Pavel Petrovich, 1879-1950. Павел Петрович (Table P-PZ40)

3476.B36 Bebutova, Olʹga Georgievna, kni͡agini͡a. Ольга Георгиевна Бебутова (Table P-PZ40)

3476.B37 Bednyĭ, Demʹi͡an, 1883-1945. Демьян Бедный (Table P-PZ40)

3476.B38 Bek, Aleksandr, 1903-1972. Александр Бек (Table P-PZ40)

3476.B415 Belenson, Aleksandr Ėmmanuilovich. Александр Эммануилович Беленсон (Table P-PZ40)

3476.B423 Beli͡aev, Sergeĭ Mikhaĭlovich, 1883-1953. Сергей Михайлович Беляев (Table P-PZ40)

Belyĭ, Andreĭ. Андрей Белый see PG3453.B84

Benshteĭn, Nikolaĭ Arkhipovich. Николай Архипович Бенштейн see PG3476.A68

3476.B43 Berdnikov, I͡Akov P., 1889-1940. Яков П. Бердников (Table P-PZ40)

The patronymic is Pavlovich (Павлович) or Petrovich (Петрович)

3476.B435 Berendgof, Nikolaĭ Sergeevich, 1900-1990. Николай Сергеевич Берендгоф (Table P-PZ40)

3476.B443 Berezov, Rodion Mikhaĭlovich, 1896-1988. Родион Михайлович Березов (Table P-PZ40)

3476.B45 Berggolʹt͡s, Olʹga, 1910-1975. Ольга Берггольц (Table P-PZ40)

3476.B455 Berzin, I͡Uliĭ Solomonovich, 1904-1938. Юлий Соломонович Берзин (Table P-PZ40)

3476.B458 Bessalʹko, Pavel Karpovich, 1887-1920. Павел Карпович Бессалько (Table P-PZ40)

3476.B46 Bezymenskiĭ, Aleksandr Ilʹich, 1898-1973. Александр Ильич Безыменский (Table P-PZ40)

3476.B47 Bianki, Vitaliĭ Valentinovich, 1894-1959. Виталий Валентинович Бианки (Table P-PZ40)

3476.B48 Bibik, Alekseĭ Pavlovich, 1877-1976. Алексей Павлович Бибик (Table P-PZ40)

3476.B5 Billʹ-Belot͡serkovskiĭ, Vladimir Naumovich, 1885-1970. Владимир Наумович Билль-Белоцерковский (Table P-PZ40)

Blok, Aleksandr Aleksandrovich. Александр Александрович Блок see PG3453.B6

3476.B55 Bobrov, Sergeĭ Pavlovich, 1889-1971. Сергей Павлович Бобров (Table P-PZ40)

3476.B553 Bobrov, V.A. (Vladimir Antonovich), 1921-1977. Владимир Антонович Бобров (Table P-PZ40)

Russian literature
Individual authors and works, 1917-1960
Individual authors, A-Z -- Continued

3476.B57 Bogdanov, Aleksandr Alekseevich, 1874-1939. Александр Алексеевич Богданов (Table P-PZ40)

3476.B58 Bogdanov, Nikolaĭ Ivanovich, 1898- . Николай Иванович Богданов (Table P-PZ40)

3476.B6 Bogdanovich, Tat'i͡ana Aleksandrovna (Tkacheva). Татьяна Александровна (Ткачева) Богданович (Table P-PZ40)

Boris Chuzhoĭ, pseud. Борис Чужой see PG3476.S69

3476.B646 Boranenkov, Nikolaĭ. Николай Бораненков (Table P-PZ40)

3476.B647 Borisoglebskiĭ, Mikhail Vasil'evich, 1896-1942. Михаил Васильевич Борисоглебский (Table P-PZ40)

3476.B65 Borisov, Leonid Il'ich, 1897-1972. Леонид Ильич Борисов (Table P-PZ40)

3476.B66 Borisov, Nikolaĭ. Николай Борисов (Table P-PZ40)

Boymvol, Rachel, 1914-2000 see PG3476.B336

3476.B74 Brik, Osip Maksimovich, 1888-1945. Осип Максимович Брик (Table P-PZ40)

3476.B76 Brykin, Nikolaĭ Aleksandrovich, 1895-1979. Николай Александрович Брыкин (Table P-PZ40)

Bryzdnikov, Mikhail. Михаил Брыздников see PG3476.A36

3476.B77 Budant͡sev, Sergeĭ Fedorovich, 1896-1940. Сергей Федорович Буданцев (Table P-PZ40)

Budant͡seva, Vera Vasil'evna. Вера Васильевна Буданцева see PG3476.I462

Bugaev, Boris Nikolaevich, 1880-1934. Борис Николаевич Бугаев see PG3453.B84

3476.B78 Bulgakov, Mikhail Afanas'evich, 1891-1940. Михаил Афанасьевич Булгаков (Table P-PZ40)

3476.B8 Burd-Voskhodov, Aleksandr Pavlovich, b. 1876. Александр Павлович Бурд-Вошодов (Table P-PZ40)

3476.B83 Burli͡uk, David Davidovich, 1882-1967. Давид Давидович Бурлюк (Table P-PZ40)

Burov, Aleksandr. Александр Буров see PG3476.B8

3476.B9 Buti͡agina, Varvara Aleksandrovna, 1901- . Варвара Александровна Бутягина (Table P-PZ40)

3476.C3 Chachikov, Aleksandr Mikhaĭlovich, 1894- . Александр Михайлович Чачиков (Table P-PZ40)

Chaĭnikov, Kuz'ma Pavlovich. Кузьма Павлович Чайников see PG3476.G447

3476.C35 Chapygin, Alekseĭ Pavlovich, 1870-1937. Алексей Павлович Чапыгин (Table P-PZ40)

Russian literature

Individual authors and works, 1917-1960

Individual authors, A-Z -- Continued

Chernyĭ, Sasha. Саша Черный see PG3476.G545

Chernysheva, Marii͡a Davydovna. Мария Давыдовна Чернышева see PG3476.M3718

3476.C45 Chetverikov, Dmitriĭ Borisovich, 1896-1981. Дмитрий Борисович Четвериков (Table P-PZ40)

3476.C475 Chizhevskiĭ, Dmitriĭ Fedotovich, 1885-1951. Дмитрий Федотович Чижевский (Table P-PZ40)

Chornyĭ, Sasha. Саша Чорный see PG3476.G545

Chudakov, Gerasim. Герасим Чудаков see PG3476.T55

3476.C485 Chukovskai͡a, Lidii͡a Korneevna. Лидия Корнеевна Чуковская (Table P-PZ40)

3476.C49 Chukovskiĭ, Korneĭ, 1882-1969. Корней Чуковский (Table P-PZ40)

3476.C493 Chukovskiĭ, Nikolaĭ Korneevich. Николай Корнеевич Чуковский (Table P-PZ40)

Chulkov, Georgiĭ Ivanovich. Георгий Иванович Чулков see PG3460.C8

3476.C5 Churkin, Vladimir Mikhaĭlovich. Владимир Михайлович Чуркин (Table P-PZ40)

Chuzhoĭ, Boris. Борис Чужой see PG3476.S59

3476.D3 Dalet͡skiĭ, Pavel Leonidovich. Павел Леонидович Далецкий (Table P-PZ40)

3476.D32 Dandurova, Aleksandra Ivanovna. Александра Ивановна Дандурова (Table P-PZ40)

3476.D35 Deev-Khomi͡akovskiĭ, Grigoriĭ Dmitrievich, 1888-1946. Григорий Дмитриевич Деев-Хомяковский (Table P-PZ40)

Delarm, Zhorzh. Жорж Деларм see PG3476.S564

3476.D38 Dement'ev, Nikolaĭ Ivanovich, 1907-1935. Николай Иванович Дементьев (Table P-PZ40)

3476.D4 Demidov, Alekseĭ Alekseevich, 1883-1934. Алексей Алексеевич Демидов (Table P-PZ40)

Diėz, pseud. Диэз see PG3476.D58

3476.D5 Dikovskiĭ, Sergeĭ Vladimirovich. Сергей Владимирович Диковский (Table P-PZ40)

Di͡uri͡agina, Galina. Галина Дюрягина see PG3476.H6

3476.D55 Dmitriev, Timofeĭ Pavlovich. Тимофей Павлович Дмитриев (Table P-PZ40)

3476.D58 Dobrzhinskiĭ, Gavriil Valer'i͡anovich, 1883-1946. Гавриил Валерьянович Добржинский (Table P-PZ40)

Dollar, Dzhim. Джим Доллар see PG3476.S437

3476.D6 Dolmatovskiĭ, Evgeniĭ Aronovich, 1915-1994. Евгений Аронович Долматовский (Table P-PZ40)

Russian literature
Individual authors and works, 1917-1960
Individual authors, A-Z -- Continued

3476.D613 Dombrovskiĭ, I͡Uriĭ Osipovich. Юрий Осипович Домбровский (Table P-PZ40)
3476.D63 Dorogoĭchenko, Alekseĭ I͡Akovlevich, 1894-1947. Алексей Яковлевич Дорогойченко (Table P-PZ40)
3476.D65 Dorokhov, Pavel Nikolaevich, 1886-1942. Павел Николаевич Дорохов (Table P-PZ40)
3476.D67 Doronin, Ivan Ivanovich, 1900-1978. Иван Иванович Доронин (Table P-PZ40)
Dozorov, I. И. Дозоров see PG3476.G37
3476.D7 Drozdov, Aleksandr Mikhaĭlovich, 1896-1963. Александр Михайлович Дроздов (Table P-PZ40)
3476.D75 Druzhinin, Pavel Davydovich, 1890-1965. Павел Давыдович Дружинин (Table P-PZ40)
3476.D8 Dudin, Mikhail. Михаил Дудин (Table P-PZ40)
3476.D85 Dudorov, Matveĭ Semenovich, 1891-1956. Матвей Семенович Дудоров (Table P-PZ40)
Dzi͡ubin, Ėduard Georgievich. Эдуард Георгиевич Дзюбин see PG3476.B23
3476.E4 Ėfron, Adelina Efimovna, 1902-1969. Аделина Ефимовна Эфрон (Table P-PZ40)
Ėfron, Marina Ivanovna. Марина Ивановна Эфрон see PG3476.T75
3476.E44 Ėfron, Sergeĭ, 1893-1941. Сергей Эфрон (Table P-PZ40)
3476.E45 Ėgart, Mark. Марк Эгарт (Table P-PZ40)
3476.E5 Ehrenburg, Il'i͡a Grigor'evich, 1891-1867 (Table P-PZ40)
Ėnskiĭ, Nikolaĭ. Николай Энский see PG3476.Z32
3476.E66 Ėpshteĭn, Mikhail Semenovich, 1903-1949. Михаил Семенович Эпштейн (Table P-PZ40)
Epstein, Mikhail Semenovich see PG3476.E66
3476.E7 Ėrdman, N. H. Эрдман (Table P-PZ40)
Ėrenburg, Il'i͡a, 1891-1967 see PG3476.E5
3476.E75 Eroshin, Ivan Evdokimovich. Иван Евдокимович Ерошин (Table P-PZ40)
3476.E8 Esenin, Sergeĭ Aleksandrovich, 1895-1925. Сергей Александрович Есенин (Table P-PZ40)
3476.E9 Evdokimov, Ivan Vasil'evich, 1887-1941. Иван Васильевич Евдокимов (Table P-PZ40)
3476.E95 Evreinov, Nikolaĭ Nikolaevich, 1879-1953. Николай Николаевич Евреинов (Table P-PZ40)
3476.E96 Evtushenko, Evgeniĭ. Евгений Евтушенко (Table P-PZ40)
3476.F2 Fadeev, Aleksandr Aleksandrovich, 1901-1956. Александр Александрович Фадеев (Table P-PZ40)

Russian literature
Individual authors and works, 1917-1960
Individual authors, A-Z -- Continued

3476.F3 Faĭko, Alekseĭ Mikhaĭlovich, 1893-1978. Алексей Михайлович Файко (Table P-PZ40)

3476.F4 Fedin, Konstantin Aleksandrovich, 1892-1977. Константин Александрович Федин (Table P-PZ40)

3476.F42 Fedorchenko, Sof'i͡a Zakharovna, 1880-1959. Софья Захаровна Федорченко (Table P-PZ40)

3476.F43 Fedorov, Evgeniĭ A. Евгений А. Федоров (Table P-PZ40)

3476.F435 Fedorovich, Vitaliĭ Fedorovich. Виталий Федорович Федорович (Table P-PZ40)

3476.F44 Fibikh, Daniil Vladimirovich. Даниил Владимирович Фибих (Table P-PZ40)

3476.F45 Filipchenko, Ivan Gur'evich, 1887-1939. Иван Гурьевич Филипченко (Table P-PZ40)

3476.F47 Fink, Viktor Grigor'evich. Виктор Григорьевич Финк (Table P-PZ40)

Finn, Konstantin. Константин Финн see PG3476.K456

3476.F52 Fish, Gennadiĭ Semenovich, 1903-1971. Геннадий Семенович Фиш (Table P-PZ40)

3476.F55 Flit, Aleksandr Matveevich. Александр Матвеевич Флит (Table P-PZ40)

3476.F6 Fomin, Semen Dmitrievich, 1881-1958. Семен Дмитриевич Фомин (Table P-PZ40)

Forsch, Ol'ga Dmitrievna, 1873-1961 see PG3476.F65

3476.F65 Forsh, Ol'ga Dmitrievna, 1873-1961. Ольга Дмитриевна Форш (Table P-PZ40)

3476.F67 Fraerman, R. (Ruvim), 1891-1972. Рувим Фраерман (Table P-PZ40)

3476.F7 Frenkel', Il'i͡a L'vovich. Илья Львович Френкель (Table P-PZ40)

3476.F76 Frolov, Aleksandr Sergeevich, b. 1880. Александр Сергеевич Фролов (Table P-PZ40)

3476.F79 Furmanov, Dmitriĭ Andreevich, 1891-1926. Дмитрий Андреевич Фурманов (Table P-PZ40)

3476.F8 Furmanova, Anna Nikolaevna. Анна Николаевна Фурманова (Table P-PZ40)

3476.G3 Gabrilovich, Evgeniĭ Osipovich. Евгений Осипович Габрилович (Table P-PZ40)

Gaĭ, I͡Ulius Markovich. Юлиус Маркович Гай see PG3476.H3

3476.G33 Gaĭdar, Arkadiĭ Petrovich, 1904-1941. Аркадий Петрович Гайдар (Table P-PZ40)

3476.G333 Gaĭdovskiĭ, Georgiĭ Nikolaevich, 1902-1962. Георгий Николаевич Гайдовский (Table P-PZ40)

Russian literature
Individual authors and works, 1917-1960
Individual authors, A-Z -- Continued

3476.G34 Galich, Aleksandr, 1918-1977. Александр Галич (Table P-PZ40)

3476.G344 Galich, IUriĭ, 1877-1940. Юрйи Галич (Table P-PZ40)

3476.G354 Gal′perin, Mikhail Petrovich, 1882-1944. Михаил Петрович Гальперин (Table P-PZ40)

3476.G36 Gandurin, Konstantin Dmitrievich, 1884-1953. Константин Дмитриевич Гандурин (Table P-PZ40)

3476.G37 Gastev, Alekseĭ Kapitonovich, 1882-1941. Алексей Капитонович Гастев (Table P-PZ40)

3476.G43 Gerasimov, Mikhail Prokof′evich, 1889-1939. Михаил Прокофьевич Герасимов (Table P-PZ40)

3476.G44 Gerasimov, Sergeĭ A. Сергей А. Герасимов (Table P-PZ40)

3476.G447 Gerd, Kuzebaĭ, 1898-1941. Кузебай Герд (Table P-PZ40)

3476.G458 German, Ėmmanuil IAkovlevich, 1892-1963. Эммануил Яковлевич Герман (Table P-PZ40)

3476.G46 German, IUriĭ Pavlovich, 1910-1967. Юрий Павлович Герман (Table P-PZ40)

3476.G47 GiliarovskaIa, Nadezhda Vladimirovna, b. 1886. Надежда Владимировна Гиляровская (Table P-PZ40)

GiliarovskaIa-Lobanova, Nadezhda Vladimirovna. Надежда Владимировна Гиляровская-Лобанова see PG3476.G47

3476.G48 Gitovich, Aleksandr Il′ich. Александр Ильич Гитович (Table P-PZ40)

3476.G53 Gladkov, Fedor Vasil′evich, 1883-1958. Федор Васильевич Гладков (Table P-PZ40)

3476.G543 Glebov, Anatoliĭ Glebovich, 1899-1964. Анатолий Глебович Глебов (Table P-PZ40)

3476.G545 Glikberg, Aleksandr Mikhaĭlovich, 1880-1932. Александр Михайлович Гликберг (Table P-PZ40)

Glikman, Viktor IAkovlevich. Виктор Яковлевич Гликман see PG3476.I7

3476.G55 Globa, Andreĭ Pavlovich, 1888-1964. Андрей Павлович Глоба (Table P-PZ40)

Gofman, Modest Liudvigovich. Модест Людвигович Гофман see PG3476.H55

3476.G563 Gol′dberg, Isaak Grigor′evich, 1884-1939. Исаак Григорьевич Гольдберг (Table P-PZ40)

3476.G565 Golichnikov, Viacheslav Andreevich, 1899-1955. Вячеслав Андреевич Голичников (Table P-PZ40)

Golodnyĭ, Mikhail. Михаил Голодный see PG3476.E66

Russian literature
Individual authors and works, 1917-1960
Individual authors, A-Z -- Continued

3476.G6 Golubov, Sergeĭ Nikolaevich. Сергей Николаевич Голубов (Table P-PZ40)

Gomberg, Vladimir Germanovich. Владимир Германович Гомберг see PG3476.L56

3476.G62 Goncharov, Viktor Alekseevich. Виктор Алексеевич Гончаров (Table P-PZ40)

3476.G622 Goncharova-Viktorova, Natalii͡a Petrovna, 1898- . Наталия Петровна Гончарова-Викторова (Table P-PZ40)

3476.G63 Gor, Gennadiĭ Samoĭlovich, 1907-1981. Геннадий Самойлович Гор (Table P-PZ40)

3476.G64 Gorbatov, Boris Leont′evich, 1908-1954. Борис Леонтьевич Горбатов (Table P-PZ40)

Gorenko, Anna Andreevna. Анна Андреевна Горенко see PG3476.A324

3476.G65 Gorin-Gori͡aĭnov, Boris Anatol′evich, 1883-1944. Борис Анатольевич Горин-Горяйнов (Table P-PZ40)

Gorky, Maksim see PG3462+

Gorodet͡skiĭ, Sergeĭ Mitrofanovich. Сергей Митрофанович Городецкий see PG3467.G2

Gorshkov, Vasiliĭ Grigor′evich. Василий Григорьевич Горшков see PG3476.R53

3476.G6545 Grabar′, Leonid I͡Ur′evich. Леонид Юрьевич Грабарь (Table P-PZ40)

3476.G655 Gradov, Grigoriĭ I͡Akovlevich. Григорий Яковлевич Градов (Table P-PZ40)

3476.G67 Grigor′ev, Sergeĭ Timofeevich, 1875-1953. Сергей Тимофеевич Григорьев (Table P-PZ40)

Grin, Aleksandr. Александр Грин see PG3476.G68

3476.G68 Grinevskiĭ, Aleksandr Stepanovich, 1880-1932. Александр Степанович Гриневский (Table P-PZ40)

3476.G685 Gromov, Moiseĭ Georgievich, 1896- . Моисей Георгиевич Громов (Table P-PZ40)

3476.G689 Grossman, Leonid Petrovich, 1888-1965. Леонид Петрович Гроссман (Table P-PZ40)

3476.G7 Grossman, Vasiliĭ Semenovich. Василий Семенович Гроссман (Table P-PZ40)

3476.G74 Grushko, Natalii͡a Vasil′evna, 1891-1974. Наталия Васильевна Грушко (Table P-PZ40)

3476.G76 Gruzdev, Il′i͡a Aleksandrovich, 1892-1960. Илья Александрович Груздев (Table P-PZ40)

3476.G77 Gruzinov, Ivan Vasil′evich. Иван Васильевич Грузинов (Table P-PZ40)

Russian literature
Individual authors and works, 1917-1960
Individual authors, A-Z -- Continued

3476.G78 Guber, Boris Andreevich, 1903-1937. Борис Андреевич Губер (Table P-PZ40)

3476.G825 Gul′, Roman Borisovich. Роман Борисович Гуль (Table P-PZ40)

3476.G85 Gumilev, Nikolaĭ Stepanovich, 1886-1921. Николай Степанович Гумилев (Table P-PZ40)

Gumileva, Anna Andreevna (Gorenko). Анна Андреевна (Горенко) Гумилева see PG3476.A324

3476.G86 Gumilevskiĭ, Lev Ivanovich, 1890-1976. Лев Иванович Гумилевский (Table P-PZ40)

3476.G9 Gusev, Viktor Mikhaĭlovich, 1909-1944. Виктор Михайлович Гусев (Table P-PZ40)

Gusev-Orenburgskiĭ, Sergeĭ Ivanovich. Сергей Иванович Гусев-Оренбургский see PG3467.G94

3476.H3 Háy, Gyula (Table P-PZ40)

Cf. PH3241 Hungarian

Cf. PT2617 German

Herman, I͡Uriĭ Pavlovich see PG3476.G46

3476.H55 Hofmann, Modeste, 1887-1959 (Table P-PZ40)

3476.H6 Hoyer, Galina (Di͡uri͡agina) von, 1898-1991 (Table P-PZ40)

3476.I17 I͡Akovlev, Aleksandr Stepanovich, 1886-1953. Александр Степанович Яковлев (Table P-PZ40)

3476.I175 I͡Akubovskiĭ, Georgiĭ Vasil′evich, 1891-1930. Георгий Васильевич Якубовский (Table P-PZ40)

3476.I2 I͡An, Vasiliĭ G. Василий Г. Ян (Table P-PZ40)

3476.I217 I͡Anovskiĭ, Aleksandr Markovich, 19031945. Александр Маркович Яновский (Table P-PZ40)

3476.I229 I͡Arovoĭ, Pavel, 1887-1951. Павел Яровой (Table P-PZ40)

I͡Asenskiĭ, Bruno, 1901-1939. Бруно Ясенский see PG3476.J3

I͡Asnyĭ, A. A. Ясный see PG3476.I217

3476.I245 I͡Avich, Avgust Efimovich, 1900-1979. Август Ефимович Явич (Table P-PZ40)

3476.I25 I͡Azvit͡skiĭ, Valeriĭ Ioilovich, 1884-1957. Валерий Иоилович Язвицкий (Table P-PZ40)

Igor′-Severi͡anin. Игорь-Северянин see PG3476.S4352

3476.I4 Il′enkov, Vasiliĭ Pavlovich. Василий Павлович Ильенков (Table P-PZ40)

3476.I44 Il′f, Il′i͡a Arnol′dovich, 1897-1937. Илья Арнольдович Ильф (Table P-PZ40)

Il′in, Fedor Fedorovich. Федор Федорович Ильин see PG3476.R36

Russian literature
Individual authors and works, 1917-1960
Individual authors, A-Z -- Continued

3476.I458 Il′in, I͡Akov, Il′ich. Яков Ильич Ильин (Table P-PZ40)
Il′ina, Aleksandra. Александра Ильина see PG3476.S38
3476.I462 Il′ina, Vera Vasil′evna, 1894-1966. Вера Васильевна Ильина (Table P-PZ40)
3476.I47 Il′inskiĭ, Fedor Vladimirovich, 1889-1944. Федор Владимирович Ильинский (Table P-PZ40)
3476.I55 Inber, Vera Mikhaĭlovna, 1890-1972. Вера Михайловна Инбер (Table P-PZ40)
Inokov, pseud. Иноков see PG3476.O33
3476.I6 Ionov, Il′i͡a Ionovich, 1887-1942. Илья Ионович Ионов (Table P-PZ40)
3476.I7 Ire͡tskiĭ, Viktor I͡Akovlevich, 1882-1936. Виктор Яковлевич Ирецкий (Table P-PZ40)
3476.I75 Isakovskiĭ, Mikhail Vasil′evich, 1900-1973. Михаил Васильевич Исаковский (Table P-PZ40)
3476.I77 Isbakh, Aleksandr, 1904-1977. Александр Исбах (Table P-PZ40)
Isbakh, I.A. И.А. Исбах see PG3476.I77
3476.I8 Itin, Vivian Azar′evich, 1893-1945. Вивиан Азарьевич Итин (Table P-PZ40)
3476.I83 I͡Ufit, Matil′da I. Матильда И. Юфит (Table P-PZ40)
3476.I84 I͡Ugov, Alekseĭ Kuz′mich. Алексей Кузьмич Югов (Table P-PZ40)
3476.I853 I͡Ur′in, I͡Uriĭ Nikolaevich, 1889-1927. Юрий Николаевич Юрьин (Table P-PZ40)
3476.I857 Ivanoff, Iraida, 1895-1990 (Table P-PZ40)
3476.I858 Ivanov, Georgiĭ Vladimirovich, 1894-1958. Георгий Владимирович Иванов (Table P-PZ40)
3476.I859 Ivanov, Petr Anisimovich, 1884-1949. Петр Анисимович Иванов (Table P-PZ40)
3476.I868 Ivanov, Valentin. Валентин Иванов (Table P-PZ40)
3476.I9 Ivanov, Vsevolod Vi͡acheslavovich, 1895-1963. Всеволод Вячеславович Иванов (Table P-PZ40)
Ivnev, Ri͡urik. Рюрик Ивнев see PG3476.K652
3476.J3 Jasieński, Bruno, 1901-1939
For biography and criticism (General) see PG7158.J35+
3476.K3 Kallinikov, Iosif Fedorovich, 1890-1934. Иосиф Федорович Каллиников (Table P-PZ40)
Kalmanson, Labori Gilelevich. Лабори Гилелевич Калмансон see PG3476.L47
3476.K32 Kamanin, Fedor Georgievich, 1897-1979. Федор Георгиевич Каманин (Table P-PZ40)

Russian literature
Individual authors and works, 1917-1960
Individual authors, A-Z -- Continued

3476.K33 Kamenskiĭ, Vasiliĭ Vasil′evich, 1884-1961. Василий Васильевич Каменский (Table P-PZ40)

3476.K36 Kantorovich, Lev Vladimirovich, 1911-1941. Лев Владимирович Канторович (Table P-PZ40)

3476.K365 Kapler, Alekseĭ I͡Akovlevich. Алексей Яковлевич Каплер (Table P-PZ40)

3476.K38 Karavaeva, Anna Aleksandrovna, 1893-1979. Анна Александровна Караваева (Table P-PZ40)

3476.K385 Karpov, Mikhail, 1898- . Михаил Карпов (Table P-PZ40)

3476.K386 Karpov, Nikolaĭ Alekseevich, 1887-1945. Николай Алексеевич Карпов (Table P-PZ40)

3476.K387 Karpov, Pimen Ivanovich, 1884-1963. Пимен Иванович Карпов (Table P-PZ40)

3476.K388 Kasatkin, Ivan Mikhaĭlovich, 1880-1938. Иван Михайлович Касаткин (Table P-PZ40)

3476.K39 Kassil′, Lev Abramovich, 1905-1970. Лев Абрамович Кассиль (Table P-PZ40)

Kataev, Evgeniĭ Petrovich. Евгений Петрович Катаев see PG3476.P435

3476.K398 Kataev, Ivan Ivanovich, 1902-1939. Иван Иванович Катаев (Table P-PZ40)

3476.K4 Kataev, Valentin Petrovich, 1897-1986. Валентин Петрович Катаев (Table P-PZ40)

3476.K43 Kaverin, Veniamin Aleksandrovich, 1902-1989. Вениамин Александрович Каверин (Table P-PZ40)

3476.K435 Kazin, Vasiliĭ Vasil′evich, 1898-1981. Василий Васильевич Казин (Table P-PZ40)

Keen, Victor see PG3476.K5

Khabias, Nina. Нина Хабиас see PG3476.O13

3476.K45 Khait, David Markovich, 1899-1979. Давид Маркович Хаит (Table P-PZ40)

3476.K456 Khal′fin, Konstantin I͡Akovlevich, 1904-1975. Константин Яковлевич Хальфин (Table P-PZ40)

3476.K485 Khlebnikov, Velemir, 1885-1922. Велемир Хлебников (Table P-PZ40)

Khlebnikov, Viktor Vladimirovich. Виктор Владимирович Хлебников see PG3476.K485

3476.K488 Khodasevich, Vladislav Feli͡tsianovich, 1886-1939. Владислав Фелицианович Ходасевич (Table P-PZ40)

3476.K5 Kin, Viktor Pavlovich, 1903-1937. Виктор Павлович Кин (Table P-PZ40)

3476.K52 Kirillov, Vladimir Timofeevich, 1890-1943. Владимир Тимофеевич Кириллов (Table P-PZ40)

PG

Russian literature

Individual authors and works, 1917-1960

Individual authors, A-Z -- Continued

3476.K53 Kirsanov, Semen Isaakovich, 1906-1972. Семен Исаакович Кирсанов (Table P-PZ40)

3476.K54 Kirshon, Vladimir Mikhaĭlovich, 1902-1938. Владимир Михайлович Киршон (Table P-PZ40)

3476.K542 Kisin, Veniamin Moiseevich, 1897-1922. Вениамин Моисеевич Кисин (Table P-PZ40)

3476.K544 Kli͡uev, Nikolaĭ Alekseevich, 1887-1937. Николай Алексеевич Клюев (Table P-PZ40)

3476.K546 Klychkov, Sergeĭ Antonovich, 1889-1937. Сергей Антонович Клычков (Table P-PZ40)

3476.K554 Kni͡azev, Vasiliĭ Vasil′evich, 1887-1937? Василий Васильевич Князев (Table P-PZ40)

Kochkurov, Nikolaĭ Ivanovich. Николай Иванович Кочкуров see PG3476.V42

3476.K568 Kogan, Feĭga Izrailevna, 1892-1974. Фейга Израилевна Коган (Table P-PZ40)

3476.K58 Kollontaĭ, Aleksandra Mikhaĭlovna, 1872-1952. Александра Михайловна Коллонтай (Table P-PZ40)

3476.K584 Kolokolov, Nikolaĭ Ivanovich, 1897-1933. Николай Иванович Колоколов (Table P-PZ40)

3476.K586 Kolomeĭt͡sev, Anatoliĭ Samuĭlovich. Анатолий Самуйлович Коломейцев (Table P-PZ40)

3476.K59 Kolosov, Mark Borisovich, 1904-1989. Марк Борисович Колосов (Table P-PZ40)

3476.K6 Kol′t͡sov, Mikhail Efimovich, 1898-1942. Михаил Ефимович Кольцов (Table P-PZ40)

Komarov, Fedot Ėmel′i͡anovich. Федот Эмельянович Комаров see PG3476.I229

3476.K63 Kononov, Aleksandr Terent′evich. Александр Терентьевич Кононов (Table P-PZ40)

3476.K632 Konovalov, Grigoriĭ Ivanovich. Григорий Иванович Коновалов (Table P-PZ40)

3476.K636 Kostarev, Nikolaĭ Konstantinovich, 1893-1941? Николай Константинович Костарев (Table P-PZ40)

3476.K638 Kosterin, Alekseĭ Evgrafovich, 1896-1968. Алексей Евграфович Костерин (Table P-PZ40)

3476.K64 Kostylev, Valentin Ivanovich. Валентин Иванович Костылев (Table P-PZ40)

3476.K652 Kovalev, Mikhail Aleksandrovich, 1891-1981. Михаил Александрович Ковалев (Table P-PZ40)

3476.K654 Kovalevskiĭ, Vi͡acheslav. Вячеслав Ковалевский (Table P-PZ40)

Russian literature
Individual authors and works, 1917-1960
Individual authors, A-Z -- Continued

3476.K66 Kozakov, Mikhail Ėmmanuilovich, 1897-1954. Михаил Эммануилович Козаков (Table P-PZ40)

3476.K668 Kozhevnikov, Alekseĭ Venediktovich, 1891-1980. Алексей Венедиктович Кожевников (Table P-PZ40)

3476.K67 Kozhevnikov, Vadim Mikhaĭlovich, 1909-1984. Вадим Михайлович Кожевников (Table P-PZ40)

3476.K686 Kozyrev, Mikhail I͡Akovlevich, b. 1892. Михаил Яковлевич Козырев (Table P-PZ40)

3476.K688 Kraĭskiĭ, Alekseĭ Petrovich, 1891?-1941. Алексей Петрович Крайский (Table P-PZ40)

3476.K689 Krandievskai͡a, Natalʹi͡a Vasilʹevna, 1888-1963. Наталья Васильевна Крандиевская (Table P-PZ40)

3476.K72 Kremlev, Ilʹi͡a Lʹvovich, 1897-1971. Илья Львович Кремлев (Table P-PZ40)

3476.K725 Krepti͡ukov, Daniil Aleksandrovich, 1888-1957. Даниил Александрович Крептюков (Table P-PZ40)

3476.K74 Krivit͡skiĭ, Aleksandr. Александр Кривицкий (Table P-PZ40)

3476.K75 Kron, Aleksandr. Александр Крон (Table P-PZ40)

3476.K76 Kruchenykh, Alekseĭ Eliseevich, 1886-1969? Алексей Елисеевич Крученых (Table P-PZ40)

3476.K775 Krutikov, Dmitriĭ Ivanovich, 1893-1932. Дмитрий Иванович Крутиков (Table P-PZ40)

3476.K78 Krymov, Vladimir Pimenovich, 1878-1968. Владимир Пименович Крымов (Table P-PZ40)

3476.K782 Krzhizhanovskiĭ, Sigizmund, 1881-1950. Сигизмунд Кржижановский (Table P-PZ40)

Kumach, V. B. Кумач see PG3476.L45

3476.K84 Kushner, Boris Anisimovich, 1888-1937. Борис Анисимович Кушнер (Table P-PZ40)

3476.K86 Kusikov, Aleksandr Borisovich, 1896-1977. Александр Борисович Кусиков (Table P-PZ40)

Kuzʹmin, Alekseĭ Petrovich. Алексей Петрович Кузьмин see PG3476.K688

3476.K94 Kuznet͡sov, Nikolaĭ Adrianovich, 1904-1924. Николай Адрианович Кузнецов (Table P-PZ40)

Landau, Mark Aleksandrovich. Марк Александрович Ландау see PG3476.A327

3476.L353 Lapin, Boris Matveevich. Борис Матвеевич Лапин (Table P-PZ40)

3476.L4 Lavrenev, Boris Andreevich, 1891-1959. Борис Андреевич Лавренев (Table P-PZ40)

3476.L43 Lebedenko, Aleksandr Gervasʹevich. Александр Гервасьевич Лебеденко (Table P-PZ40)

Russian literature
Individual authors and works, 1917-1960
Individual authors, A-Z -- Continued

3476.L45 Lebedev-Kumach, Vasiliĭ Ivanovich, 1898-1949. Василий Иванович Лебедев-Кумач (Table P-PZ40)

Lelevich, G. Г. Лелевич see PG3476.L47

3476.L47 Lelevich, Labori Gilelevich, 1901-1945. Лабори Гилелевич Лелевич (Table P-PZ40)

3476.L5 Leonov, Leonid Maksimovich, 1899-1994. Леонид Максимович Леонов (Table P-PZ40)

3476.L512 Leonov, Mikhail Petrovich. Михаил Петрович Леонов (Table P-PZ40)

3476.L515 Lerner, Nikolaĭ Nikitich, 1884-1946. Николай Никитич Лернер (Table P-PZ40)

3476.L517 Leshchinskiĭ, Naum Efremovich, 1879-1961. Наум Ефремович Лещинский (Table P-PZ40)

Leshenkov, Sergeĭ Antonovich. Сергей Антонович Лешенков see PG3476.K546

3476.L52 Levakovskai͡a, Evgenii͡a. Евгения Леваковская (Table P-PZ40)

3476.L527 Levidov, Mikhail I͡Ul′evich, 1891-1942. Михаил Юльевич Левидов (Table P-PZ40)

3476.L529 Levin, Boris Mikhaĭlovich. Борис Михайлович Левин (Table P-PZ40)

Levyĭ, Anton. Антон Левый see PG3476.L8

3476.L54 Lezhnev, Isaak Grigor′evich, 1891-1955. Исаак Григорьевич Лежнев (Table P-PZ40)

3476.L55 Li͡ashchenko, Nikolaĭ Nikolaevich, 1884-1953. Николай Николаевич Лященко (Table P-PZ40)

Li͡ashko, N. H. Ляшко see PG3476.L55

3476.L554 Libedinskiĭ, I͡Uriĭ Nikolaevich, 1898-1959. Юрий Николаевич Либединский (Table P-PZ40)

3476.L56 Lidin, Vladimir Germanovich, 1894-1979. Владимир Германович Лидин (Table P-PZ40)

3476.L57 Lifshit͡s, Vladimir. Владимир Лифшиц (Table P-PZ40)

Linovskiĭ, Aleksandr Nikolaevich. Александр Николаевич Линовский see PG3476.P63

3476.L6 Lipskerov, Konstantin Abramovich, 1889-1954. Константин Абрамович Липскеров (Table P-PZ40)

3476.L63 Litovskiĭ, Osaf Semenovich. Осаф Семенович Литовский (Table P-PZ40)

Litovt͡sev, Solomon L′vovich Poli͡akov-. Соломон Львович Поляков-Литовцев see PG3476.P6

3476.L66 Loginov, Ivan, 1891-1942. Иван Логинов (Table P-PZ40)

3476.L663 Loginov-Lesni͡ak, Pavel Semenovich, 1891-1938. Павел Семенович Логинов-Лесняк (Table P-PZ40)

Russian literature
Individual authors and works, 1917-1960
Individual authors, A-Z -- Continued
Lotarev, Igor′ Vasil′evich. Игорь Васильевич Лотарев see PG3476.S4352

3476.L73 Lozinskiĭ, Mikhail Leonidovich, 1886-1955. Михаил Леонидович Лозинский (Table P-PZ40)

3476.L75 Lugovskoĭ, Vladimir Aleksandrovich, 1901-1957. Владимир Александрович Луговской (Table P-PZ40)

3476.L76 Lukash, Ivan Sozontovich, 1892-1940. Иван Созонтович Лукаш (Table P-PZ40)

3476.L763 Lukashin, Il′i͡a Denisovich, 1894- . Илья Денисович Лукашин (Table P-PZ40)

3476.L77 Lukhmanov, Dmitriĭ Afanas′evich. Дмитрий Афанасьевич Лухманов (Table P-PZ40)

3476.L78 Lukni͡tskiĭ, Pavel Nikolaevich. Павел Николаевич Лукницкий (Table P-PZ40)

3476.L8 Lunacharskiĭ, Anatoliĭ Vasil′evich, 1875-1933. Анатолий Васильевич Луначарский (Table P-PZ40)

3476.L85 Lundberg, Evgeniĭ Germanovich, 1883-1965. Евгений Германович Лундберг (Table P-PZ40)

3476.L9 Lun͡ts, Lev Natanovich, 1901-1924. Лев Натанович Лунц (Table P-PZ40)

3476.L95 Luzgin, Mikhail Vasil′evich, 1899-1942. Михаил Васильевич Лузгин (Table P-PZ40)

3476.M3-.M312 Mai͡akovskiĭ, Vladimir Vladimirovich, 1894-1930. Владимир Владимирович Маяковский

3476.M3 Collected works. By date

3476.M3A7-.M3Z4 Separate works

3476.M312 Biography and criticism

3476.M34 Makarenko, Anton Semenovich, 1888-1939. Антон Семенович Макаренко (Table P-PZ40)

3476.M342 Makar′ev, Leonid Fedorovich, 1892-1975. Леонид Федорович Макарьев (Table P-PZ40)

3476.M343 Makarov, Aleksandr Antonovich, 1898- . Александр Антонович Макаров (Table P-PZ40)

3476.M345 Malakhov, Sergeĭ Arsen′evich, 1902-1973. Сергей Арсеньевич Малахов (Table P-PZ40)

3476.M347 Malashkin, Sergeĭ Ivanovich, 1888-1988. Сергей Иванович Малашкин (Table P-PZ40)

3476.M35 Malyshkin, Aleksandr Georgievich, 1890-1938. Александр Георгиевич Малышкин (Table P-PZ40)

3476.M355 Mandel′shtam, Osip Ėmil′evich, 1891-1938. Осип Эмильевич Мандельштам (Table P-PZ40)

3476.M3715 Mar′i͡anova, Mal′vina, 1896-1972. Мальвина Марьянова (Table P-PZ40)

Russian literature
Individual authors and works, 1917-1960
Individual authors, A-Z -- Continued

3476.M3718 Marich, M. M. Марич (Table P-PZ40)
3476.M372 Mariengof, Anatoliĭ Borisovich, 1897-1962. Анатолий Борисович Мариенгоф (Table P-PZ40)
3476.M3725 Marshak, Samuil I͡Akovlevich, 1887-1964. Самуил Яковлевич Маршак (Table P-PZ40)
3476.M3728 Mashirov, Alekseĭ Ivanovich, 1884-1943. Алексей Иванович Маширов (Table P-PZ40)
Maslovskiĭ-Mstislavskiĭ, Sergeĭ Dmitrievich. Сергей Дмитриевич Масловский-Мстиславский see PG3476.M73
3476.M3734 Mass, Vladimir Zakharovich. Владимир Захарович Масс (Table P-PZ40)
3476.M44 Men′shikov, Ivan N. Иван Н. Меньшиков (Table P-PZ40)
Mėnskiĭ, Nikolaĭ Nikolaevich Zakharov-. Николай Николаевич Захаров-Мэнский see PG3476.Z32
Mikitov, Ivan Sergeevich Sokolov-. Иван Сергеевич Соколов-Микитов see PG3476.S62
Mogilevskiĭ, L. Л. Могилевский see PG3476.L47
3476.M57 Molchanov, Ivan Nikanorovich, 1903-1984. Иван Никанорович Молчанов (Table P-PZ40)
3476.M6 Morozov, Aleksandr. Александр Морозов (Table P-PZ40)
3476.M62 Morozov, Ivan Ignat′evich, 1883-1942. Иван Игнатьевич Морозов (Table P-PZ40)
Morozov, K.I. К.И. Морозов see PG3476.S69
Moskvin, Nikolaĭ. Николай Москвин see PG3476.V653
3476.M73 Mstislavskiĭ, Sergeĭ Dmitrievich, 1876-1943. Сергей Дмитриевич Мстиславский (Table P-PZ40)
3476.M77 Muguev, Khadzhi-Murat. Хаджи-Мурат Мугуев (Table P-PZ40)
Muguev, Murat. Мурат Мугуев see PG3476.M77
3476.M78 Muĭzhel′, Viktor Vasil′evich, 1880-1924. Виктор Васильевич Муйжель (Table P-PZ40)
3476.M8 Muratov, Pavel Pavlovich, 1881-1950. Павел Павлович Муратов (Table P-PZ40)
Murinskiĭ, L. Л. Муринский see PG3476.L85
3476.N3 Nabokov, Vladimir Vladimirovich, 1899-1977. Владимир Владимирович Набоков (Table P-PZ40)
3476.N34 Nagibin, I͡Uriĭ. Юрий Нагибин (Table P-PZ40)
3476.N365 Narbut, Vladimir Ivanovich, 1888-1938. Владимир Иванович Нарбут (Table P-PZ40)
3476.N37 Nasedkin, Vasiliĭ Fedorovich, 1895-1937. Василий Федорович Наседкин (Table P-PZ40)

Russian literature
Individual authors and works, 1917-1960
Individual authors, A-Z -- Continued

3476.N374 Nasimovich, Aleksandr Fedorovich, 1880-1947. Александр Федорович Насимович (Table P-PZ40)

3476.N4 Nazhivin, Ivan Fedorovich, 1874-1940. Иван Федорович Наживин (Table P-PZ40)

3476.N48 Nel′dikhen, Sergeĭ Evgen′evich, 1891-1942. Сергей Евгеньевич Нельдихен (Table P-PZ40)

Neverov, A. A. Неверов see PG3476.S543

3476.N5 Nikandrov, Nikolaĭ Nikandrovich, 1878-1964. Николай Никандрович Никандров (Table P-PZ40)

3476.N52 Nikiforov, Georgiĭ Konstantinovich, 1884-1937? Георгий Константинович Никифоров (Table P-PZ40)

3476.N527 Nikitin, Ivan Fedorovich, 1891- . Иван Федорович Никитин (Table P-PZ40)

3476.N53 Nikitin, Mikhail Aleksandrovich, 1903- . Михаил Александрович Никитин (Table P-PZ40)

3476.N54 Nikitin, Nikolaĭ Nikolaevich, 1895-1963. Николай Николаевич Никитин (Table P-PZ40)

3476.N55 Nikulin, Lev Veniaminovich, 1891-1967. Лев Вениаминович Никулин (Table P-PZ40)

3476.N57 Nilin, Pavel, 1908-1981. Павел Нилин (Table P-PZ40)

Nizovoĭ, P. П. Низовой see PG3476.T8

3476.N65 Novikov, Alekseĭ . Алексей Новиков (Table P-PZ40)

3476.N66 Novikov, Ivan Alekseevich, 1877-1959. Иван Алексеевич Новиков (Table P-PZ40)

3476.N67 Novikov-Priboĭ, Alekseĭ Silych, 1877-1944. Алексей Силыч Новиков-Прибой (Table P-PZ40)

3476.N675 Novokshenov, Ivan Mikhaĭlovich, 1895-1945. Иван Михайлович Новокшенов (Table P-PZ40)

3476.N69 Nozdrin, Avenir, 1862-1938. Авенир Ноздрин (Table P-PZ40)

3476.O13 Obolenskaia͡, Nina, 1892-1943. Нина Оболенская (Table P-PZ40)

3476.O15 Obradovich, Sergeĭ Aleksandrovich, 1892-1956. Сергей Александрович Обрадович

Odinokiĭ, pseud. Одинокий see PG3476.T55

Odoevt͡seva, Irina. Ирина Одоевцева see PG3476.I857

Ognev, Nikolaĭ. Николай Огнев see PG3476.R76

3476.O25 Ogurt͡sov, Serafim Ivanovich, 1904-1934. Серафим Иванович Огурцов (Table P-PZ40)

3476.O3 Okhotnikova, Dionisii͡a Ignat′evna. Дионисия Игнатьевна Охотникова (Table P-PZ40)

3476.O33 Oksenov, Innokentiĭ Aleksandrovich, 1897-1942. Иннокентий Александрович Оксенов (Table P-PZ40)

Russian literature
Individual authors and works, 1917-1960
Individual authors, A-Z -- Continued

3476.O34 Okulov, Alekseĭ Ivanovich, 1880-1939. Алексей Иванович Окулов (Table P-PZ40)

3476.O35 Okunev, I͡Akov Markovich, 1882-1922. Яков Маркович Окунев (Table P-PZ40)

3476.O37 Olesha, I͡Uriĭ Karlovich, 1899-1960. Юрий Карлович Олеша (Table P-PZ40)

Orenburgskiĭ, Sergeĭ Ivanovich Gusev-. Сергей Иванович Гусев-Оренбургский see PG3467.G94

3476.O7 Oreshin, Petr Vasil′evich, 1887-1938. Петр Васильевич Орешин (Table P-PZ40)

3476.O78 Ostroumov, Lev Evgen′evich, 1892-1955. Лев Евгеньевич Остроумов (Table P-PZ40)

3476.O79 Ostrover, Leon Isaakovich, 1890-1962. Леон Исаакович Островер (Table P-PZ40)

3476.O8 Ostrovskiĭ, Nikolaĭ Alekseevich, 1904-1936. Николай Алексеевич Островский (Table P-PZ40)

3476.P2 Paderin, Ivan Grigor′evich, 1918- . Иван Григорьевич Падерин (Table P-PZ40)

3476.P219 Panev, Georgiĭ Ioakimovich, 1901- . Георгий Иоакимович Панев (Table P-PZ40)

3476.P22 Panferov, Fedor Ivanovich, 1896-1960. Федор Иванович Панферов (Table P-PZ40)

3476.P23 Panfilov, Evgeniĭ Ivanovich. Евгений Иванович Панфилов (Table P-PZ40)

3476.P25 Panov, Nikolaĭ Nikolaevich, 1903-1973. Николай Николаевич Панов (Table P-PZ40)

3476.P255 Panova, Vera Fedorovna, 1905-1973. Вера Федоровна Панова (Table P-PZ40)

Panskiĭ, pseud. Панский see PG3476.S68

3476.P26 Parnakh, Valentin I͡Akovlevich. Валентин Яковлевич Парнах (Table P-PZ40)

3476.P264 Parnok, Sof′i͡a I͡Akovlevna, 1885-1933. Софья Яковлевна Парнок (Table P-PZ40)

3476.P27 Pasternak, Boris Leonidovich, 1890-1960. Борис Леонидович Пастернак (Table P-PZ40)

3476.P28 Pasynkov, Lev Pavlovich, 1886-1956. Лев Павлович Пасынков (Table P-PZ40)

Patrashkin, Sergeĭ Timofeevich. Сергей Тимофеевич Патрашкин see PG3476.G67

3476.P29 Paustovskiĭ, Konstantin Georgievich, 1892-1968. Константин Георгиевич Паустовский (Table P-PZ40)

3476.P3 Pavlenko, Petr Andreevich, 1899-1951. Петр Андреевич Павленко (Table P-PZ40)

Russian literature
Individual authors and works, 1917-1960
Individual authors, A-Z -- Continued

3476.P33 Pavlov, Georgiĭ. Георгий Павлов (Table P-PZ40)
3476.P35 Pavlov, Vladimir Konstantinovich. Владимир Константинович Павлов (Table P-PZ40)
3476.P4 Peregudov, Aleksandr Vladimirovich, 1894-1989. Александр Владимирович Перегудов (Table P-PZ40)
3476.P414 Pereleshin, Platon. Платон Перелешин (Table P-PZ40)
3476.P42 Permi͡ak, Evgeniĭ Andreevich. Евгений Андреевич Пермяк (Table P-PZ40)
3476.P422 Permitin, Efim Nikolaevich, 1896-1971. Ефим Николаевич Пермитин (Table P-PZ40)
3476.P424 Perven͡tsev, Arkadiĭ Alekseevich, 1905-1981. Аркадий Алексеевич Первенцев (Table P-PZ40)
3476.P425 Petnikov, Grigoriĭ Nikolaevich, 1894-1971. Григорий Николаевич Петников (Table P-PZ40)
3476.P426 Petrashkevich, Nikolaĭ Aleksandrovich. Николай Александрович Петрашкевич (Table P-PZ40)
3476.P435 Petrov, Evgeniĭ, 1903-1942. Евгений Петров (Table P-PZ40)
3476.P45 Petrovskiĭ, Dmitriĭ Vasil′evich, 1892-1955. Дмитрий Васильевич Петровский (Table P-PZ40)
3476.P46 Pi͡ast, Vladimir Alekseevich, 1886-1940. Владимир Алексеевич Пяст (Table P-PZ40)
Pilni͡ak, Boris. Борис Пилняк see PG3476.V6
3476.P47 Pil′skiĭ, Petr Moiseevich. Петр Моисеевич Пильский (Table P-PZ40)
3476.P48 Piotrovskiĭ, Adrian Ivanovich. Адриан Иванович Пиотровский (Table P-PZ40)
3476.P5 Pis′mennyĭ, Aleksandr Grigor′evich. Александр Григорьевич Письменный (Table P-PZ40)
Platon, Ivan Stepanovich. Иван Степанович Платон see PG3470.P29
Platonov, Alekseĭ. Алексей Платонов see PG3476.R715
3476.P543 Platonov, Andreĭ Platonovich, 1899-1951. Андрей Платонович Платонов (Table P-PZ40)
3476.P545 Platonych, N. H. Платоныч (Table P-PZ40)
3476.P547 Platoshkin, Mikhail Nikolaevich, 1904-1958. Михаил Николаевич Платошкин (Table P-PZ40)
3476.P55 Pletnev, Valerian Fedorovich, 1886-1942. Валериан Федорович Плетнев (Table P-PZ40)
3476.P57 Pogodin, Nikolaĭ Fedorovich, 1900-1962. Николай Федорович Погодин (Table P-PZ40)
3476.P575 Poletaev, Nikolaĭ Gavrilovich, 1889-1935. Николай Гаврилович Полетаев (Table P-PZ40)

PG

Russian literature
Individual authors and works, 1917-1960
Individual authors, A-Z -- Continued

3476.P578 Polevoĭ, Boris Nikolaevich. Борис Николаевич Полевой (Table P-PZ40)

3476.P6 Poli͡akov, Solomon L′vovich, 1875-1945. Соломон Львович Поляков (Table P-PZ40)

3476.P614 Polivanov, Sergeĭ. Сергей Поливанов (Table P-PZ40)

3476.P617 Polonskai͡a, Elizaveta Grigor′evna, 1890-1969. Елизавета Григорьевна Полонская (Table P-PZ40)

3476.P63 Pomorskiĭ, Aleksandr Nikolaevich, 1891-1977. Александр Николаевич Поморский (Table P-PZ40)

3476.P66 Potapenko, Natalii͡a Ignat′evna. Наталия Игнатьевна Потапенко (Table P-PZ40)

3476.P675 Pozner, Vladimir, 1905-1992. Владимир Познер (Table P-PZ40)

3476.P68 Pravdukhin, Valerian Pavlovich, 1892-1939. Валериан Павлович Правдухин (Table P-PZ40)

Priboĭ, Alekseĭ Silych Novikov-. Алексей Силыч Новиков-Прибой see PG3476.N67

Pridvorov, Efim Alekseevich. Ефим Алексеевич Придворов see PG3476.B37

3476.P69 Prikhodchenko, Evgeniĭ Semenovich. Евгений Семенович Приходченко (Table P-PZ40)

3476.P75 Prokof′ev, Aleksandr Andreevich, 1900-1971. Александр Андреевич Прокофьев (Table P-PZ40)

3476.P78 Prudkovskiĭ, Petr Nikolaevich. Петр Николаевич Прудковский (Table P-PZ40)

3476.P8 Prut, Iosif Leonidovich. Иосиф Леонидович Прут (Table P-PZ40)

3476.P88 Pushkov, Valeriĭ Dmitrievich, 1896- . Валерий Дмитриевич Пушков (Table P-PZ40)

Rachmanowa, Alexandra see PG3476.H6

3476.R15 Radimov, Pavel Aleksandrovich, 1887-1967. Павел Александрович Радимов (Table P-PZ40)

3476.R18 Radlova, Anna Dmitrievna, 1891-1949. Анна Дмитриевна Радлова (Table P-PZ40)

3476.R3 Rakhillo, Ivan Spiridonovich, 1904-1979. Иван Спиридонович Рахилло (Table P-PZ40)

3476.R32 Rakhmanov, Leonid. Леонид Рахманов (Table P-PZ40)

3476.R34 Rakovskiĭ, Leontiĭ Osipovich. Леонтий Осипович Раковский (Table P-PZ40)

3476.R36 Raskol′nikov, Fedor Fedorovich, 1892-1939. Федор Федорович Раскольников (Table P-PZ40)

3476.R38 Ravich, Nikolaĭ Aleksandrovich. Николай Александрович Равич (Table P-PZ40)

Russian literature
Individual authors and works, 1917-1960
Individual authors, A-Z -- Continued

3476.R39 Razumovskiĭ, I͡Uriĭ Georgievich. Юрий Георгиевич Разумовский (Table P-PZ40)

3476.R4 Reĭsner, Larissa Mikhaĭlovna, 1895-1926. Лариса Михайловна Рейснер (Table P-PZ40)

Rennikov, A. A. Ренников see PG3476.S415

Rerikh, Nikolaĭ Konstantinovich. Николай Константинович Рерих see PG3476.R6

3476.R46 Reshetov, Aleksandr Efimovich, 1909-1971. Александр Ефимович Решетов (Table P-PZ40)

3476.R5 Ri͡akhovskiĭ, Vasiliĭ Dmitrievich, 1897-1951. Василий Дмитриевич Ряховский (Table P-PZ40)

3476.R53 Ri͡azant͡sev, Vsevolod, 1869-1942. Всеволод Рязанцев (Table P-PZ40)

3476.R55 Rikhter, Zinaida Vladimirovna, 1890-1967. Зинаида Владимировна Рихтер (Table P-PZ40)

Rodionov, Aleksandr Ignat′evich Tarasov-. Александр Игнатьевич Тарасов-Родионов see PG3476.T3

3476.R58 Rodov, Semen Abramovich, 1893-1968. Семен Абрамович Родов (Table P-PZ40)

3476.R6 Roerich, Nikolaĭ Konstantinovich, 1874-1947 (Table P-PZ40)

3476.R62 Rogi, Mikhail Pavlovich. Михаил Павлович Роги (Table P-PZ40)

3476.R64 Roĭzman, Matveĭ Davidovich, 1896-1973. Матвей Давидович Ройзман (Table P-PZ40)

3476.R7 Romanov, Panteleĭmon Sergeevich, 1884-1938. Пантелеймон Сергеевич Романов (Table P-PZ40)

3476.R715 Romanov, Petr Alekseevich, 1900- . Петр Алексеевич Романов (Table P-PZ40)

3476.R72 Romashov, Boris Sergeevich, 1895-1958. Борис Сергеевич Ромашов (Table P-PZ40)

Roshchin, E. E. Рощин see PG3476.L85

Rovinska͡ia, Ekaterina Dmitrievna. Екатерина Дмитриевна Ровинская see PG3476.V63

3476.R76 Rozanov, Mikhail Grigor′evich, 1888-1938. Михаил Григорьевич Розанов (Table P-PZ40)

3476.R77 Rozhdestvenskiĭ, Vsevolod Aleksandrovich, 1895-1977. Всеволод Александрович Рождественский (Table P-PZ40)

3476.R8 Rumi͡ant͡sev, Timofeĭ Zakharovich, 1886- . Тимофей Захарович Румянцев (Table P-PZ40)

3476.R85 Russat, Evgenii͡a R. Евгения Р. Руссат (Table P-PZ40)

3476.R87 Rybakov, Anatoliĭ Naumovich. Анатолий Наумович Рыбаков (Table P-PZ40)

Russian literature
Individual authors and works, 1917-1960
Individual authors, A-Z -- Continued

3476.R9 Rylenkov, Nikolaĭ Ivanovich. Николай Иванович Рыленков (Table P-PZ40)

3476.S23 Sadof'ev, Il'i͡a Ivanovich, 1889-1965. Илья Иванович Садофьев

3476.S27 Sai͡anov, Vissarion Mikhaĭlovich, 1903-1959. Виссарион Михайлович Саянов (Table P-PZ40)

3476.S3 Sakharov, Konstantin Vi͡acheslavovich, 1881-1941. Константин Вячеславович Сахаров (Table P-PZ40)

Samobytnik, pseud. Самобытник see PG3476.M3728

Sanan, Anton Mudrenovich Amur-. Антон Мудренович Амур-Санан see PG3476.A5

3476.S33 Sannikov, Grigoriĭ Aleksandrovich, 1899-1969. Григорий Александрович Санников (Table P-PZ40)

Sant-Ėlli, pseud. Сант-Элли see PG3476.D32

3476.S35 Savich, Ovadiĭ. Овадий Савич (Table P-PZ40)

Savvatiĭ, pseud. Савватий see PG3476.O3

Sedykh, Andreĭ. Андрей Седых see PG3476.Z96

3476.S38 Seferi͡ant͡s, Aleksandra Ivanova, 1890- . Александра Иванова Сеферянц (Table P-PZ40)

3476.S4 Seĭfullina, Lidii͡a Nikolaevna, 1889-1954. Лидия Николаевна Сейфуллина (Table P-PZ40)

3476.S415 Selitrennikov, Andreĭ Mitrofanovich. Андрей Митрофанович Селитренников (Table P-PZ40)

3476.S42 Sel'vinskiĭ, Il'i͡a L'vovich, 1899-1968. Илья Львович Сельвинский (Table P-PZ40)

3476.S424 Semenov, Andrei Ignat'evich, 1908-1985. Андреи Игнатьевич Семенов (Table P-PZ40)

3476.S43 Semenov, Sergeĭ Aleksandrovich, 1893-1942. Сергей Александрович Семенов (Table P-PZ40)

3476.S432 Semenovskiĭ, Dmitriĭ Nikolaevich, 1894-1960. Дмитрий Николаевич Семеновский (Table P-PZ40)

3476.S4346 Serebri͡akova, Galina Iosifovna. Галина Иосифовна Серебрякова (Table P-PZ40)

Sergeev-T͡Senskiĭ, Sergeĭ Nikolaevich. Сергей Николаевич Сергеев-Ценский see PG3470.S4

3476.S4352 Severi͡anin, Igor'. Игорь Северянин (Table P-PZ40)

3476.S436 Shadrin, Ilariĭ Grigor'evich. Иларий Григорьевич Шадрин (Table P-PZ40)

3476.S437 Shagini͡an, Mariėtta Sergeevna, 1888-1982. Мариэтта Сергеевна Шагинян (Table P-PZ40)

3476.S4375 Shapovalenko, Nikolaĭ Nikolaevich. Николай Николаевич Шаповаленко (Table P-PZ40)

3476.S456 Shcheglov, Dmitriĭ Alekseevich, 1896-1963. Дмитрий Алексеевич Щеглов (Table P-PZ40)

Russian literature
Individual authors and works, 1917-1960
Individual authors, A-Z -- Continued

3476.S46 Shchipachev, Stepan Petrovich, 1899-1980. Степан Петрович Щипачев (Table P-PZ40)

3476.S468 Shengeli, Georgiĭ Arkad′evich, 1894-1956. Георгий Аркадьевич Шенгели (Table P-PZ40)

3476.S472 Shershenevich, Vadim Gabriėlevich, 1893-1942. Вадим Габриэлевич Шершеневич (Table P-PZ40)

3476.S473 Shestakov, Nikolaĭ I͡Akovlevich. Николай Яковлевич Шестаков (Table P-PZ40)

3476.S474 Shil′dkret, Konstantin Georgievich, 1886-1965. Константин Георгиевич Шильдкрет (Table P-PZ40)

Shileĭko, Anna Andreevna (Gorenko). Анна Андреевна (Горенко) Шилейко see PG3476.A324

3476.S475 Shiri͡aev, Petr Alekseevich, 1888-1935. Петр Алексеевич Ширяев (Table P-PZ40)

Shiri͡aevet͡s, pseud. . Ширяевец see PG3476.A2

3476.S4755 Shirman, Grigoriĭ. Григорий Ширман (Table P-PZ40)

3476.S476 Shishko, Anatoliĭ Valer′i͡anovich, 1899-1956. Анатолий Валерьянович Шишко (Table P-PZ40)

3476.S48 Shishkov, Vi͡acheslav I͡Akovlevich, 1873-1945. Вячеслав Яковлевич Шишков (Table P-PZ40)

3476.S482 Shishova, Zinaida. Зинаида Шишова (Table P-PZ40)

3476.S484 Shkapskai͡a, Marii͡a Mikhaĭlovna (Andreevskai͡a), 1891-1952. Мария Михайловна (Андреевская) Шкапская

3476.S488 Shklovskiĭ, Viktor Borisovich, 1893-1984. Виктор Борисович Шкловский (Table P-PZ40)

3476.S49 Shkvarkin, Vasiliĭ Vasil′evich, 1894-1967. Василий Васильевич Шкваркин (Table P-PZ40)

3476.S5 Shmelev, Ivan Sergeevich, 1873-1950. Иван Сергеевич Шмелев (Table P-PZ40)

3476.S514 Shmerel′son, Grigoriĭ Benediktovich, 1901-1943. Григорий Бенедиктович Шмерельсон (Table P-PZ40)

3476.S52 Sholokhov, Mikhail Aleksandrovich, 1905-1984. Михаил Александрович Шолохов (Table P-PZ40)

3476.S5215 Sholokhov-Sini͡avskiĭ, Georgiĭ Filippovich. Георгий Филиппович Шолохов-Синявский (Table P-PZ40)

3476.S522 Shoshin, Mikhail Dmitrievich. Михаил Дмитриевич Шошин (Table P-PZ40)

3476.S523 Shpanov, Nikolaĭ Nikolaevich. Николай Николаевич Шпанов (Table P-PZ40)

3476.S5238 Shubin, Georgiĭ Petrovich. Георгий Петрович Шубин (Table P-PZ40)

3476.S5243 Shul′gin, Adrian Gavrilovich, 1896-1940. Адриан Гаврилович Шульгин (Table P-PZ40)

Russian literature
Individual authors and works, 1917-1960
Individual authors, A-Z -- Continued

3476.S5248 Shvedov, I͡Akov Zakharovich, 1905-1985. Яков Захарович Шведов (Table P-PZ40)
3476.S525 Shvet͡sov, Sergeĭ Aleksandrovich. Сергей Александрович Швецов (Table P-PZ40)
3476.S53 Simonov, Konstantin Mikhaĭlovich, 1915-1979. Константин Михайлович Симонов (Table P-PZ40)
Singer, Maks Ėmmanuilovich see PG3476.Z56
3476.S539 Sini͡avskiĭ, Andreĭ Donatovich, 1925-1997. Андрей Донатович Синявский (Table P-PZ40)
Sirin, Vl. Вл. Сирин see PG3476.N3
3476.S543 Skobelev, Aleksandr Sergeevich, 1886-1923. Александр Сергеевич Скобелев (Table P-PZ40)
Skorbnyĭ, Andreĭ. Андрей Скорбный see PG3476.S573
3476.S545 Skorinko, Ivan Vladimirovich. Иван Владимирович Скоринко (Table P-PZ40)
3476.S55 Skosyrev, Petr Georgievich, 1900-1960. Петр Георгиевич Скосырев (Table P-PZ40)
3476.S56 Slavin, Lev Isaevich, 1896-1984. Лев Исаевич Славин (Table P-PZ40)
3476.S564 Slezkin, I͡Uriĭ L′vovich, 1887-1947. Юрий Львович Слезкин (Table P-PZ40)
3476.S57 Slonimskiĭ, Mikhail Leonidovich, 1897-1972. Михаил Леонидович Слонимский (Table P-PZ40)
3476.S572 Smirenskiĭ, Boris Viktorovich. Борис Викторович Смиренский (Table P-PZ40)
3476.S573 Smirenskiĭ, Vladimir Viktorovich, 1902-1977. Владимир Викторович Смиренский (Table P-PZ40)
3476.S575 Smirnova, Nina. Нина Смирнова (Table P-PZ40)
3476.S576 Smolin, Dmitriĭ Petrovich. Дмитрий Петрович Смолин (Table P-PZ40)
3476.S577 Sobol′, Andreĭ Mikhaĭlovich, 1888-1926. Андрей Михайлович Соболь (Table P-PZ40)
3476.S58 Sobolev, Leonid Sergeevich, 1898-1971. Леонид Сергеевич Соболев (Table P-PZ40)
3476.S584 Sofronov, Anatoliĭ Vladimirovich. Анатолий Владимирович Софронов (Table P-PZ40)
3476.S586 Sokol, Evgeniĭ Grigor′evich, 1892- . Евгений Григорьевич Сокол (Table P-PZ40)
3476.S59 Sokoloff, Boris, 1893- (Table P-PZ40)
Sokolov, Boris Fedorovich. Борис Федорович Соколов see PG3476.S59
3476.S6 Sokolov, Vasiliĭ Nikolaevich, 1874-1959. Василий Николаевич Соколов (Table P-PZ40)

Russian literature
Individual authors and works, 1917-1960
Individual authors, A-Z -- Continued

3476.S62 Sokolov-Mikitov, Ivan Sergeevich, 1892-1975. Иван Сергеевич Соколов-Микитов (Table P-PZ40)
3476.S624 Sokolovskiĭ, Mikhail Vladimirovich. Михаил Владимирович Соколовский (Table P-PZ40)
3476.S63 Solov′ev, Boris I. Борис И. Соловьев. (Table P-PZ40)
3476.S65 Solov′ev, Leonid V. Леонид В. Соловьев (Table P-PZ40)
3476.S66 Solov′ev, Sergeĭ Mikhaĭlovich, 1885-1942. Сергей Михайлович Соловьев (Table P-PZ40)
3476.S68 Sol′skiĭ, Vat͡slav Aleksandrovich. Вацлав Александрович Сольский (Table P-PZ40)
3476.S69 Sol′skiĭ, Vladimir. Владимир Сольский (Table P-PZ40)
Sorgenfrei, Vil′gel′m Aleksandrovich see PG3476.Z65
3476.S78 Stavskiĭ, Vladimir Petrovich, 1900-1943. Владимир Петрович Ставский (Table P-PZ40)
3476.S786 Stonov, Dmitriĭ Mironovich, 1898-1962. Дмитрий Миронович Стонов (Table P-PZ40)
3476.S788 Stradnyĭ, Sergeĭ, 1901-1921. Сергей Страдный (Table P-PZ40)
Stukalov, Nikolaĭ Fedorovich. Николай Федорович Стукалов see PG3476.P57
3476.S79 Subbotin, Leonid Arsen′evich. Леонид Арсеньевич Субботин (Table P-PZ40)
3476.S795 Sukhotin, Pavel Sergeevich, 1884-1935. Павел Сергеевич Сухотин (Table P-PZ40)
3476.S8 Surguchev, Il′i͡a Dmitrievich, 1881-1956. Илья Дмитриевич Сургучев (Table P-PZ40)
3476.S83 Surkov, Alekseĭ Aleksandrovich, 1899-1983. Алексей Александрович Сурков (Table P-PZ40)
Surovikin, Viktor Pavlovich. Виктор Павлович Суровикин see PG3476.K5
3476.S844 Surozhskiĭ, Pavel Nikolaevich, 1872- . Павел Николаевич Сурожский (Table P-PZ40)
Svėn, I. И. Свэн see PG3476.K72
3476.S85 Sverchkov, Dmitriĭ Fedorovich, 1882-1938. Дмитрий Федорович Сверчков (Table P-PZ40)
3476.S86 Svetlov, Mikhail Arkad′evich, 1903-1964. Михаил Аркадьевич Светлов (Table P-PZ40)
3476.S9 Sytin, Aleksandr Pavlovich, 1894- . Александр Павлович Сытин (Table P-PZ40)
3476.T2 Tarasenko, Boris Dmitrievich. Борис Дмитриевич Тарасенко (Table P-PZ40)

Russian literature
Individual authors and works, 1917-1960
Individual authors, A-Z -- Continued

3476.T3 Tarasov-Rodionov, Aleksandr Ignat′evich,1885-1938. Александр Игнатьевич Тарасов-Родионов (Table P-PZ40)

Terts, Abram. Абрам Терц see PG3476.S539

3476.T48 Tikhomirov, Nikifor Semenovich, 1888-1945. Никифор Семенович Тихомиров (Table P-PZ40)

3476.T5 Tikhonov, Nikolaĭ Semenovich, 1896-1979. Николай Семенович Тихонов (Table P-PZ40)

3476.T55 Tiniakov, Aleksandr Ivanovich. Александр Иванович Тиняков (Table P-PZ40)

Tkacheva, Tat′iana Aleksandrovna. Татьяна Александровна Ткачева see PG3476.B6

Tolstaia, Natal′ia Vasil′evna. Наталья Васильевна Толстая see PG3476.K689

3476.T6 Tolstoĭ, Alekseĭ Nikolaevich, graf, 1882-1945. Алексей Николаевич Толстой (Table P-PZ40)

3476.T67 Trenev, Konstantin Andreevich, 1876-1945. Константин Андреевич Тренев (Table P-PZ40)

3476.T7 Tret′iakov, Sergeĭ Mikhaĭlovich, 1892-1939. Сергей Михайлович Третьяков (Table P-PZ40)

3476.T72 Triger, Maks IAkovlevich. Макс Яковлевич Тригер (Table P-PZ40)

3476.T73 Triole, Ėl′za IUr′evna, 1896-1970. Эльза Юрьевна Триоле (Table P-PZ40)

3476.T749 TSvetaeva, Anastasiia, 1894-1993. Анастасия Цветаева (Table P-PZ40)

3476.T75 TSvetaeva, Marina Ivanovna, (Ėfron), 1892-1941. Марина Ивановна (Эфрон) Цветаева (Table P-PZ40)

TSvibak, IAkov Moiseevich. Яков Моисеевич Цвибак see PG3476.Z96

Tumannyĭ, D. Д. Туманный see PG3476.P25

3476.T8 Tupikov, Pavel Georgievich, 1882-1940. Павел Георгиевич Тупиков (Table P-PZ40)

3476.T85 Tvardovskiĭ, Aleksandr Trifonovich, 1910-1971. Александр Трифонович Твардовский (Table P-PZ40)

3476.T87 Tveriak, Alekseĭ Artem′evich, 1900-1937. Алексей Артемьевич Тверяк (Table P-PZ40)

3476.T88 Tverskoĭ, Nikita. Никита Тверской (Table P-PZ40)

3476.T9 Tynianov, IUriĭ Nikolaevich, 1894-1943. Юрий Николаевич Тынянов (Table P-PZ40)

3476.U3 Ul′ianskiĭ, Anton Grigor′evich, 1887-1935. Антон Григорьевич Ульянский (Table P-PZ40)

Russian literature
Individual authors and works, 1917-1960
Individual authors, A-Z -- Continued

3476.U4 Unkovskiĭ, V. B. Унковский (Table P-PZ40)
3476.U5 Urin, Dmitriĭ Ėrikhovich. Дмитрий Эрихович Урин (Table P-PZ40)
3476.U6 Ushakov, Nikolaĭ Nikolaevich, 1899-1973. Николай Николаевич Ушаков (Table P-PZ40)
3476.U65 Uspenskiĭ, Andreĭ Vasil′evich. Андрей Васильевич Успенский (Table P-PZ40)
3476.U67 Uspenskiĭ, L.V. (Lev Vasil′evich). Лев Васильевич Успенский (Table P-PZ40)
3476.U7 Ustinov, Georgiĭ. Георгий Устинов (Table P-PZ40)
3476.U8 Utkin, Iosif Pavlovich, 1903-1944. Иосиф Павлович Уткин (Table P-PZ40)
3476.U9 Uzhgin, Semen Semenovich, 1883-1956. Семен Семенович Ужгин (Table P-PZ40)
3476.V28 Vagin, Petr. Петр Вагин (Table P-PZ40)
3476.V285 Vaginov, Konstantin Konstantinovich, 1899-1934. Константин Константинович Вагинов (Table P-PZ40)
3476.V3 Vagramov, Fedor Arkad′evich, 1899-1967. Федор Аркадьевич Ваграмов (Table P-PZ40)
3476.V334 Vashent︡sev, Sergeĭ Ivanovich, 1898-1970. Сергей Иванович Вашенцев (Table P-PZ40)
3476.V336 Vasil′chenko, Semen Filippovich, 1884-1937. Семен Филиппович Васильченко (Table P-PZ40)
3476.V337 Vasilenko, Vladimir Martynovich, 1892-1941. Владимир Мартынович Василенко (Table P-PZ40)
3476.V339 Vasil′ev, Ivan. Иван Васильев (Table P-PZ40)
3476.V34 Vasil′ev, Sergeĭ. Сергей Васильев (Table P-PZ40)
3476.V35 Veĭngrov, Moiseĭ Pavlovich, 1894-1962. Моисей Павлович Вейнгров (Table P-PZ40)
Vengrov, Natan. Натан Венгров see PG3476.V35
3476.V36 Venkstern, Natalii︠a︡ Alekseevna, 1893-1957. Наталия Алексеевна Венкстерн (Table P-PZ40)
3476.V37 Verevkin, Vladimir Vsevolodovich, 1904-1938. Владимир Всеволодович Веревкин (Table P-PZ40)
3476.V375 Vergasov, Il′i︠a︡. Илья Вергасов (Table P-PZ40)
3476.V38 Vergun, Dmitriĭ Nikolaevich. Дмитрий Николаевич Вергун (Table P-PZ40)
3476.V4 Verkhovskiĭ, I︠U︡riĭ Nikandrovich, 1878-1956. Юрий Никандрович Верховский (Table P-PZ40)
3476.V42 Veselyĭ, Artem, 1899-1939. Артем Веселый (Table P-PZ40)
3476.V43 Veshnev, Vladimir Georgievich, 1881-1932. Владимир Георгиевич Вешнев (Table P-PZ40)

Russian literature
Individual authors and works, 1917-1960
Individual authors, A-Z -- Continued

3476.V44 Vesnina, Anna. Анна Веснина (Table P-PZ40)
3476.V445 Vetrov, D. Д. Ветров (Table P-PZ40)
3476.V45 V͡iatkin, Georgiĭ Andreevich, 1885-1938. Георгий Андреевич Вяткин (Table P-PZ40)
Viktorova, Natalii͡a Petrovna Goncharova-. Наталия Петровна Гончарова-Викторова see PG3476.G622
3476.V5 Vilenskiĭ, Ėzra Samoĭlovich. Эзра Самойлович Виленский (Table P-PZ40)
3476.V53 Vinogradov, Anatoliĭ Kornelievich, 1888-1946. Анатолий Корнелиевич Виноградов (Table P-PZ40)
3476.V54 Virta, Nikolaĭ Evgen′evich, 1906-1976. Николай Евгеньевич Вирта (Table P-PZ40)
3476.V545 Vishnevskiĭ, Vsevolod Vital′evich, 1900-1951. Всеволод Витальевич Вишневский (Table P-PZ40)
3476.V55 Vladimirskiĭ, Nikolaĭ Sergeevich, 1905- . Николай Сергеевич Владимирский (Table P-PZ40)
3476.V552 Vladimirskiĭ, Vladimir Konstantinovich, 1901- . Владимир Константинович Владимирский (Table P-PZ40)
3476.V56 Vlasov-Okskiĭ, Nikolaĭ Stepanovich, 1888-1947. Николай Степанович Власов-Окский (Table P-PZ40)
3476.V57 Vodop′i͡anov, Mikhail Vasil′evich, 1899-1980. Михаил Васильевич Водопьянов (Table P-PZ40)
3476.V6 Vogau, Boris Andreevich, 1894-1937. Борис Андреевич Вогау (Table P-PZ40)
Volinov, pseud. Волинов see PG3476.L8
3476.V62 Voinov, Vladimir Vasil′evich. Владимир Васильевич Воинов (Table P-PZ40)
Voinova, A.I. А.И. Воинова see PG3476.D32
3476.V63 Volchanet͡skai͡a, Ekaterina Dmitrievna (Rovinskai͡a). Екатерина Дмитриевна (Ровинская) Волчанецкая (Table P-PZ40)
Volgin, A. A. Волгин see PG3476.B57
3476.V635 Vol′kenshteĭn, Vladimir Mikhaĭlovich, 1883-1974. Владимир Михайлович Волькенштейн (Table P-PZ40)
3476.V64 Volkov, Mikhail Ivanovich, 1886-1946. Михаил Иванович Волков (Table P-PZ40)
3476.V644 Vol′nov, Ivan Egorovich, 1885-1931. Иван Егорович Вольнов (Table P-PZ40)
Vol′nyĭ, Ivan. Иван Вольный see PG3476.V644
3476.V646 Volokhov, Mark. Марк Волохов (Table P-PZ40)
Volzhskiĭ, A.A. А.А. Волжский see PG3476.B57
3476.V65 Volzhskiĭ, Alekseĭ Pavlovich, 1889- . Алексей Павлович Волжский (Table P-PZ40)

Russian literature
Individual authors and works, 1917-1960
Individual authors, A-Z -- Continued

3476.V653 Vorob'ev, Nikolaĭ IAkovlevich, 1900-1968. Николай Яковлевич Воробьев (Table P-PZ40)
3476.V8 Vsevolozhskiĭ, Igor'. Игорь Всеволожский (Table P-PZ40)
Vysotskiĭ, A. A. Высоцкий see PG3476.W54
3476.W54 Wisotsky, Abraham L. (Table P-PZ40)
Wolkenstein, Vladimir Mikhaĭlovich see PG3476.V635
Yevtushenko, Yevgeny see PG3476.E96
3476.Z2 Zabolotskiĭ, Nikolaĭ Alekseevich. Николай Алексеевич Заболоцкий (Table P-PZ40)
3476.Z22 Zaiaitskiĭ, Sergeĭ Sergeevich, 1893-1930. Сергей Сергеевич Заяицкий (Table P-PZ40)
Zaitsev, Boris Konstantinovich. Борис Константинович Зайцев see PG3470.Z23
3476.Z273 Zaitsev, Petr Nikanorovich, 1889-1970. Петр Никанорович Зайцев (Table P-PZ40)
3476.Z32 Zakharov-Mėnskiĭ, Nikolaĭ Nikolaevich, 1895-1942. Николай Николаевич Захаров-Мэнский (Table P-PZ40)
3476.Z34 Zamiatin, Evgeniĭ Ivanovich, 1884-1937. Евгений Иванович Замятин (Table P-PZ40)
3476.Z36 Zamoĭskiĭ, Petr Ivanovich, 1896-1958. Петр Иванович Замойский ((Table P-PZ40)
3476.Z37 Zarudin, Nikolaĭ Nikolaevich, 1899-1937. Николай Николаевич Зарудин (Table P-PZ40)
3476.Z38 Zavadovskiĭ, Leonid, b. 1888. Леонид Завадовский (Table P-PZ40)
3476.Z385 Zavalishin, Aleksandr Ivanovich, 1891-1939. Александр Иванович Завалишин (Table P-PZ40)
3476.Z39 Zazubrin, Vladimir IAkovlevich, 1895-1938. Владимир Яковлевич Зазубрин (Table P-PZ40)
3476.Z4 Zenkevich, Mikhail Aleksandrovich, 1886-1973. Михаил Александрович Зенкевич (Table P-PZ40)
3476.Z47 Zharov, Aleksandr Alekseevich, 1904-1984. Александр Алексеевич Жаров (Table P-PZ40)
3476.Z5 Zhdanov, Nikolaĭ. Николай Жданов (Table P-PZ40)
3476.Z535 Zhitkov, Boris Stepanovich, 1882-1938. Борис Степанович Житков (Table P-PZ40)
3476.Z54 Zhizhmor, Maks IAkovlevich, 1888-1936. Макс Яковлевич Жижмор (Table P-PZ40)
3476.Z55 Zilov, Lev Nikolaevich, 1883-1937. Лев Николаевич Зилов (Table P-PZ40)
3476.Z56 Zinger, Maks Ėmmanuilovich. Макс Эммануилович Зингер (Table P-PZ40)

Russian literature
Individual authors and works, 1917-1960
Individual authors, A-Z -- Continued

3476.Z6 Zolin, Aleksandr Samuĭlovich. Александр Самуйлович Золин (Table P-PZ40)

3476.Z65 Zorgenfreĭ, Vil′gel′m Aleksandrovich, 1882-1938. Вильгельм Александрович Зоргенфрей (Table P-PZ40)

3476.Z66 Zorich, A., 1900- . А. Зорич (Table P-PZ40)

3476.Z7 Zoshchenko, Mikhail Mikhaĭlovich, 1895-1958. Михаил Михайлович Зощенко (Table P-PZ40)

Zozuli͡a, Alekseĭ Pavlovich. Алексей Павлович Зозуля see PG3476.V65

3476.Z78 Zozuli͡a, Efim Davidovich, 1891-1941. Ефим Давидович Зозуля (Table P-PZ40)

3476.Z8 Zuev, Aleksandr Nikolaevich, 1895- . Александр Николаевич Зуев (Table P-PZ40)

3476.Z9 Zurov, Leonid. Леонид Зуров (Table P-PZ40)

3476.Z945 Zverev, Nikolaĭ Vasil′evich. Николай Васильевич Зверев (Table P-PZ40)

3476.Z95 Zvi͡agint͡seva, Vera Klavdievna, 1894-1972. Вера Клавдиевна Звягинцева (Table P-PZ40)

3476.Z96 Zwibak, Jacques, 1902-1994 (Table P-PZ40)

3476.Z98 Zyri͡anov, Venedikt Ermilovich. Венедикт Ермилович Зырянов (Table P-PZ40)

Zysman, Wiktor B., 1901-1939 see PG3476.J3

Individual authors, 1961-2000

Subarrange each author by Table P-PZ40 unless otherwise specified

Here are usually to be classified authors beginning to publish about 1950, flourishing after 1960

3477 Anonymous works (Table P-PZ28)

3478 A

The author number is determined by the second letter of the name

3478.L4265 Alekseev, Sergeĭ, 1952- . Сергей Алексеев (Table P-PZ40)

3478.N34 Anatoliĭ, A., 1929-1979. А. Анатолий (Table P-PZ40)

Andreev, Aleksandr. Александр Андреев see PG3478.N415

3478.N415 Andreev, Vasiliĭ Dmitrievich, 1915-1975. Василий Дмитриевич Андреев (Table P-PZ40)

Asfatullin, Salavat. Салават Асфатуллин see PG3485.8.L56

Ashurko Vladimir Nikolaevich. Владимир Николаевич Ашурко see PG3485.L3877

Astakhova, Ol′ga. Ольга Астахова see PG3482.7.R42

Russian literature
Individual authors, 1961-2000 -- Continued

3479 Ba
The author number is determined by the third letter of the name

3479.I8 Baĭukanskiĭ, Anatoliĭ Borisovich. Анатолий Борисович Баюканский (Table P-PZ40)

3479.3 Be
The author number is determined by the third letter of the name

3479.4 Bf - Bz
The author number is determined by the second letter of the name

3479.4.L35 Blagova, Elena, 1956- . Елена Благова (Table P-PZ40)

Bogatykh, Ė. Э Богатых see PG3485.5.A42

3479.4.O463 Bokser, O.ĬA. (Oskar ĬAkovlevich). Оскар Яковлевич Боксер (Table P-PZ40)

3479.5 C
The author number is determined by the second letter of the name

3479.6 D
The author number is determined by the second letter of the name

Daniliuk, S.A. (Sergeĭ Aleksandrovich). Сергей Александрович Данилюк see PG3479.6.A48

3479.6.A48 Danilov, Vsevolod. Всеволод Данилов (Table P-PZ40)

3479.6.E98 Dezhnev, Nikolaĭ, 1946- . Николай Дежнев (Table P-PZ40)

3479.7 E
The author number is determined by the second letter of the name

3479.7.F49 Efimov, Igorʹ Markovich. Игорь Маркович Ефимов (Table P-PZ40)

3479.7.V82 Evsevʹev, Vladimir. Владимир Евсевьев (Table P-PZ40)
Cf. PG3489.3.I48 VIN

3480 F
The author number is determined by the second letter of the name

3481 G - Gn
The author number is determined by the second letter of the name

3481.2 Go
The author number is determined by the third letter of the name

3481.4 Gr
The author number is determined by the third letter of the name

PG

Russian literature
Individual authors, 1961- 2000

3481.6 Gs - Gz
The author number is determined by the second letter of the name
Gushchina, Irina. Ирина Гущина see PG3482.R35

3481.8 H
The author number is determined by the second letter of the name

3482 Ia - Ivam
The author number is determined by the second letter of the name
I͡An. Ян see PG3487.A5993
I͡An, Sh. Ш. Ян see PG3487.A5993
I͡An, Viktor Aleksandrovich. Виктор Александрович Ян see PG3487.A5993

3482.A93 I͡Avrumi͡an, Aram. Арам Яврумян (Table P-PZ40)
Inozemt͡sev, Ėduard. Эдуард Иноземцев see PG3482.A93

3482.R35 Irbis, Irina. Ирина Ирбис (Table P-PZ40)

3482.2 Ivan
The author number is determined by the fifth letter of the name

3482.3 Ivao - Iz
The author number is determined by the second letter of the name
Ivashchenko, Sergeĭ, I͡Ur′evich. Сергей Юрьевич Иващенко see PG3485.7.Z56

3482.4 J
The author number is determined by the second letter of the name

3482.5 Ka
The author number is determined by the third letter of the name

3482.6 Kb - Kn
The author number is determined by the second letter of the name
Kent, Dzhek. Джек Кент see PG3489.2.L46

3482.7 Ko
The author number is determined by the third letter of the name

3482.7.R42 Koreneva, Ol′ga. Ольга Коренева (Table P-PZ40)
Kozenkov, I͡Uriĭ. Юрий Козенков see PG3485.6.S668

3482.8 Kp - Kz
The author number is determined by the second letter of the name

Russian literature
Individual authors, 1961-2000
Kp - Kz -- Continued
Kri͡ukova, Elena, 1956- . Елена Крюкова see PG3479.4.L35
(3482.8.U894) Kuznet͡sov, Anatoliĭ, 1929-1979. Анатолий Кузнецов see PG3478.N34
3483 L
The author number is determined by the second letter of the name
3483.E78 Levashov, Viktor. Виктор Левашов (Table P-PZ40)
3483.I15 Li͡agachev, Oleg, 1939- . Олег Лягачев (Table P-PZ40)
Luknit͡skiĭ, Sergeĭ. Сергей Лукницкий see PG3485.A8685
Luzhin, Khelʹgi, 1939- . Хельги Лужин see PG3483.I15
3483.2 Ma
The author number is determined by the third letter of the name
3483.3 Mb - Mz
The author number is determined by the second letter of the name
Melentʹev, Vasiliĭ. Василий Мелентьев see PG3485.3.R78
Moskovit, Andreĭ. Андрей Московит see PG3479.7.F49
3484 N
The author number is determined by the second letter of the name
3484.I454 Nikonova, Rea, 1942- (Table P-PZ40)
Nikonova, Ry, 1942- . Ры Никонова see PG3484.I454
3484.2 O
The author number is determined by the second letter of the name
3484.2.L33 Oldi, Genri Laĭon. Генри Лайон Олди (Table P-PZ40)
Collective pseudonym for: Gromov, Dmitriĭ Evgenʹevich (Дмитрий Евгеньевич Громов); Ladyzhenskiĭ, Oleg Semenovich (Олег Семенович Ладыженский)
Oleg XXX, pseud. Олег XXX see PG3489.I876
3485 Pa - Pn
The author number is determined by the second letter of the name
3485.A774 Pashut, Adam. Адам Пашут (Table P-PZ40)
3485.A8685 Pavlov, Kirill, 1954- . Кирилл Павлов (Table P-PZ40)
3485.L3877 Plėĭs, Filmor. Филмор Плэйс (Table P-PZ40)
3485.2 Po
The author number is determined by the third letter of the name

Russian literature
Individual authors, 1961-2000
Po -- Continued
Popov, Nikolaĭ (Nikolaĭ Borisovich), 1946- . Николай Борисович Попов see PG3479.6.E98

3485.3 Pq - Pz
The author number is determined by the second letter of the name

3485.3.R78 Pravdivyĭ, Ivan. Иван Правдивый (Table P-PZ40)

3485.4 Q
The author number is determined by the second letter of the name

3485.5 Ra - Rn
The author number is determined by the second letter of the name

3485.5.A42 Rakitskai͡a, Ėvelina, 1960- . Эвелина Ракитская (Table P-PZ40)

3485.6 Ro
The author number is determined by the third letter of the name

3485.6.S668 Rossich, Svi͡atoslav. Святослав Россич (Table P-PZ40)

Rozin, Mikhail Zalmonovich. Михаил Залмонович Розин see PG3485.A774

3485.7 Rp - Rz
The author number is determined by the second letter of the name

3485.7.Y136 Rybakov, Vi͡acheslav. Вячеслав Рыбаков (Table P-PZ40)

3485.7.Z56 Rzhevskiĭ, S. (Serzh). Серж Ржевский (Table P-PZ40)

3485.8 Sa
The author number is determined by the third letter of the name

3485.8.L56 Salavat. Салават (Table P-PZ40)

3486 Sb - Sg
The author number is determined by the second letter of the name

3487 Sh
The author number is determined by the third letter of the name

3487.A5993 Shanli, I͡An. Ян Шанли (Table P-PZ40)

3488 Si - Sz
The author number is determined by the second letter of the name

3488.T732 Strugat͡skiĭ, Boris Natanovich. Борис Натанович Стругацкий (Table P-PZ40)

Russian literature
Individual authors, 1961-2000 -- Continued
3489 T
The author number is determined by the second letter of the name
Tamant͡sev, Andreĭ. Андрей Таманцев see PG3483.E78
Tarshis, Anna, 1942- . Анна Таршис see PG3484.I454
Tert͡s, Abram, 1925-1997. Абрам Терц see PG3476.S539
3489.I876 Ti͡ul′kin, Oleg, 1970- . Олег Тюлькин (Table P-PZ40)
3489.2 U
The author number is determined by the second letter of the name
3489.2.L46 Ul′ev, Sergeĭ. Сергей Ульев (Table P-PZ40)
3489.3 Va - Vn
The author number is determined by the second letter of the name
Verner, I͡Akov. Яков Вернер see PG3479.4.O463
Vesta, A., 1952- . А. Веста see PG3478.L4265
3489.3.I48 VIN. ВИН (Table P-PZ40)
Cf. PG3479.7.V82 Evsev′ev, Vladimir
Vitit͡skiĭ, S. C. Витицкий see PG3488.T732
3489.4 Vo
The author number is determined by the third letter of the name
3489.5 Vp - Vz
The author number is determined by the second letter of the name
3489.6 W
The author number is determined by the second letter of the name
3489.7 X
The author number is determined by the second letter of the name
3489.8 Y
The author number is determined by the second letter of the name
3489.9 Za
The author number is determined by the third letter of the name
Zaĭchik, Khol′m van. Хольм ван Зайчик see PG3485.7.Y136
3490 Zb - Zz
The author number is determined by the second letter of the name
Individual authors, 2001-
Subarrange each author by Table P-PZ40

Russian literature
Individual authors, 2001- -- Continued

3491.2 Anonymous works (Table P-PZ28)

3491.3 A
The author number is determined by the second letter of the name

3491.42 Ba
The author number is determined by the third letter of the name

3491.44 Be
The author number is determined by the third letter of the name

3491.46 Bf - Bz
The author number is determined by the second letter of the name

Brunov, Vladimir. Владимир Брунов see PG3492.84.E85

Burdavit͡syna, Ėlla. Элла Бурдавицына see PG3491.7.L35

3491.5 C
The author number is determined by the second letter of the name

3491.5.H46 Cherkasov, Dmitriĭ. Дмитрий Черкасов (Table P-PZ40)

3491.6 D
The author number is determined by the second letter of the name

3491.7 E
The author number is determined by the second letter of the name

3491.7.L35 Ėlana. Элана (Table P-PZ40)

3491.8 F
The author number is determined by the second letter of the name

3491.94 G - Gn
The author number is determined by the second letter of the name

Gasanova, Lala. Лала Гасанова see PG3493.5.I89

3491.96 Go
The author number is determined by the third letter of the name

3491.97 Gr
The author number is determined by the third letter of the name

Grin′ko, Alisa Arkad′evna. Алиса Аркадьевна Гринько see PG3492.6.I883

Russian literature
Individual authors, 2001- -- Continued

3491.98 Gs - Gz
The author number is determined by the second letter of the name

3492.2 H
The author number is determined by the second letter of the name

Ḣăsănova, Lală. Лалə Һəсəнова see PG3493.5.I89

3492.34 Ia - Ivam
The author number is determined by the second letter of the name

3492.37 Ivan
The author number is determined by the fifth letter of the name

3492.38 Ivao - Iz
The author number is determined by the second letter of the name

3492.4 J
The author number is determined by the second letter of the name

3492.52 Ka
The author number is determined by the third letter of the name

3492.54 Kb - Kn
The author number is determined by the second letter of the name

3492.56 Ko
The author number is determined by the third letter of the name

3492.58 Kp - Kz
The author number is determined by the second letter of the name

3492.6 L
The author number is determined by the second letter of the name

3492.6.A66 Laptev, Anton. Антон Лаптев (Table P-PZ40)

3492.6.I883 L︠i︡ubimova, Olʹga. Ольга Любимова (Table P-PZ40)

3492.72 Ma
The author number is determined by the third letter of the name

Magomet, Sergeĭ. Сергей Магомет see PG3492.76.O67

Mat︠i︡ukhina, A. A. Матюхина see PG3492.72.T84

3492.72.T84 Matt, Anna. Анна Матт (Table P-PZ40)

3492.76 Mb - Mz
The author number is determined by the second letter of the name

Russian literature
Individual authors, 2001-
Mb-Mz -- Continued

3492.76.O67 Morozov, Sergeĭ. Сергей Морозов (Table P-PZ40)

3492.84 N
The author number is determined by the second letter of the name

3492.84.E85 Neskazhu, V. B. Нескажу (Table P-PZ40)

Nova, Uli͡a. Уля Нова see PG3493.6.L53

3492.87 O
The author number is determined by the second letter of the name

3492.94 Pa - Pn
The author number is determined by the second letter of the name

3492.96 Po
The author number is determined by the third letter of the name

3492.98 Pq - Pz
The author number is determined by the second letter of the name

3493.2 Q
The author number is determined by the second letter of the name

3493.34 Ra - Rn
The author number is determined by the second letter of the name

3493.36 Ro
The author number is determined by the third letter of the name

3493.38 Rp - Rz
The author number is determined by the second letter of the name

3493.42 Sa
The author number is determined by the third letter of the name

3493.44 Sb - Sg
The author number is determined by the second letter of the name

Serebri͡akov, Dmitriĭ. Дмитрий Серебряков see PG3491.5.H46

3493.46 Sh
The author number is determined by the third letter of the name

3493.48 Si - Sz
The author number is determined by the second letter of the name

Russian literature

Individual authors, 2001- -- Continued

3493.5 T

The author number is determined by the second letter of the name

3493.5.I89 T︠i︡udor, Ėlizabet. Элизабет Тюдор

Topchiĭ, I︠U︡riĭ, 1961- . Юрий Топчий see PG3493.76.D54

Tunii︠a︡nt︠s︡, Tigran. Тигран Туниянц see PG3493.5.U76

3493.5.U76 Tuti. Тути (Table P-PZ40)

3493.6 U

The author number is determined by the second letter of the name

Ulʹrikh, Anton. Антон Ульрих see PG3492.6.A66

3493.6.L53 Uli︠a︡nova, Masha. Маша Улянова (Table P-PZ40)

3493.74 Va - Vn

The author number is determined by the second letter of the name

3493.74.A43 Valfar. Валфар (Table P-PZ40)

Valiullin, Farkhad Rafkatovich. Фархад Рафкатович Валиуллин see PG3493.74.A43

3493.76 Vo

The author number is determined by the third letter of the name

3493.76.D54 Vodichka, Gustav, 1961- . Густав Водичка (Table P-PZ40)

3493.76.L45 Volʹf, D. Д. Вольф. (Table P-PZ40)

3493.78 Vp - Vz

The author number is determined by the second letter of the name

3493.83 W

The author number is determined by the second letter of the name

3493.85 X

The author number is determined by the second letter of the name

3493.87 Y

The author number is determined by the second letter of the name

3493.92 Za

The author number is determined by the third letter of the name

3493.96 Zb - Zz

The author number is determined by the second letter of the name

Zhitnikov, Dmitriĭ Lʹvovich. Дмитрий Львович Житников see PG3493.76.L45

Russian literature -- Continued
Russian literature, provincial, local, etc.
Class here literary history, biography, criticism and collections of the literature of republics, provinces, regions, islands and other places within the Russian Federation
For works, biography and criticism of individual authors, see PG3300+
Cf. PG2700+ Russian dialects and their literatures
By republic, province, region, etc.
History
3500 General
3501.A-Z Individual republics, provinces, regions, etc., A-Z
Collections
3503 General
3504.A-Z Individual republics, provinces, regions, etc., A-Z
e. g.
3504.A7 Archangel (Province)
3504.T8 Tver (Government)
3504.U7 Ural (Province)
3505.A-Z By city, town, etc., A-Z
Subarrange individual cities, towns, etc., by Table P-PZ26 unless otherwise specified
e. g.
Gor'kiĭ. Nizhniĭ Novgorod
3505.G6 History
3505.G7 Collections
3505.I74-.I742 Irkutsk (Table P-PZ26)
Leningrad. Saint Petersburg
3505.L4 History
3505.L5 Collections
Moscow
3505.M6 History
3505.M7 Collections
Nizhniĭ Novgorod see PG3505.G6+
Saint Petersburg see PG3505.L4+
3505.V6-.V62 Vologda (Table P-PZ26)
Russian literature outside the Russian Federation
For works, biography and criticism of individual authors, except those from the United States and Canada, see PG3300+
General
3515 History
3516 Collections
Special
3520.A-Z European countries, A-Z
Subarrange individual countries by Table P-PZ26
e. g.
3520.F7-.F72 France (Table P-PZ26)

Russian literature
Russian literature outside the Russian Federation
Special -- Continued
3522 Russian literature outside of Europe
3525 America
United States. Canada
History
3530 Periodicals. Societies. Collections
3531 General works. Compends
3532 Special aspects
3533 Collected essays
3534 Biography (Collective)
By period
3535 To 1900
3536 20th-21st centuries
Local see PG3547+
By form
3537 Poetry
3538 Drama
3539 Other
Collections
3540 General
3541 Translations
3542 Poetry
3543 Translations
3544 Drama
3546.A-Z Other, A-Z
Local
3547.A-Z By state, region, A-Z
3548.A-Z By city, town, A-Z
3549.A-Z Individual authors, A-Z
Subarrange each author by Table P-PZ40 unless otherwise specified
e. g.
3549.A6 Antonova, Elena Anatol′evna, 1904- . Елена Анатольевна Антонова (Table P-PZ40)
Erusalimchik, Mainna Ivanovna. Маинна Ивановна Ерусалимчик see PG3549.S34
Fialko, Natan Moiseevich. Натан Моисеевич Фиалко see PG3549.F5
3549.F5 Fialko, Nathan, 1881- (Table P-PZ40)
Fiveĭskai͡a, Lidii͡a I͡Akovlevna. Лидия Яковлевна Фивейская see PG3549.N4
3549.G6 Golokhvastov, Georgiĭ Vladimirovich. Георгий Владимирович Голохвастов (Table P-PZ40)

Russian literature
Russian literature outside the Russian Federation
Special
Russian literature outside of Europe
America
United States. Canada
Individual authors, A-Z -- Continued

3549.G7 Grebenshchikov, Georgiĭ Dmitrievich, 1882-1964. Георгий Дмитриевич Гребенщиков (Table P-PZ40)

3549.L6 Loshak, Israel Moses, 1883- . И. Лошак (Table P-PZ40)

Nelidova, Lidii͡a I͡Akovlevna. Лидия Яковлевна Нелидова see PG3549.N4

3549.N4 Nelidova-Fiveĭskai͡a, Lidii͡a I͡Akovlevna (Zadirakina). Лидия Яковлевна (Задиракина) Нелидова-Фивейская (Table P-PZ40)

3549.O3 Oginskiĭ, Maksim Aleksandrovich, 1892- . Максим Александрович Огинский (Table P-PZ40)

3549.S34 Sanina, Inna. Инна Санина (Table P-PZ40)

Sibiri͡ak, pseud. Сибиряк see PG3549.G7

3549.S8 Sto͡tskiĭ, Maksim Kirillovich, 1891-1945. Максим Кириллович Стоцкий (Table P-PZ40)

T͡S′orokh, Il′i͡a Ivanovich. Илья Иванович Цьорох see PG3549.T9

3549.T9 Tziorogh, Elias I., 1880-1942 (Table P-PZ40)

Zadirakina, Lidii͡a I͡Akovlevna. Лидия Яковлевна Задиракина see PG3549.N4

3550.A-Z Other regions or countries, A-Z

Subarrange each by Table P-PZ26

Subjects other than Russian literature

At the Library of Congress Russian books on special subjects are classified in Classes A-Z according to the subject treated

<3651> Polygraphy
<3652> Philosophy
<3653> Religion
History
<3654> Chronology. Diplomatics. Numismatics
<3655> Biography. Genealogy
<3656> General history
<3657> Ancient history
<3658> Medieval history
Modern history see PG3656
<3659> Russia
<3660> Great Britain

Russian literature
Subjects other than Russian literature
History -- Continued
<3661> France
<3662> Germany
<3665.A-Z> Other European, A-Z
<3666> Asia
<3667> Africa
<3670> Australia and Oceania
<3671> United States
<3672> British America
<3673> Other American
<3674> Geography. Anthropology
<3675> Folklore, etc.
<3676> Social sciences
<3677> Economics
<3678> Sociology
<3679> Political science
<3680> Law
<3681> Education
<3682> Music
<3683> Fine arts
<3684> Language (General philology, linguistics and languages other than Russian)
Prefer PG2001-2850 for the Russian language
<3685> Literature (Literary history: General and special)
<3685.5> Science (General)
<3686> Mathematics. Astronomy. Physics. Chemistry
<3687> Geology. Natural history. Botany. Zoology. Human anatomy. Physiology. Bacteriology
<3688> Medicine
<3689> Agriculture
<3690> Technology. Manufactures. Trades
<3691> Engineering. Building
<3692> Mineral industries. Chemical technology
<3693> Photography
<3694> Domestic science. Home economics
<3695> Military science
<3696> Naval science
<3698> Bibliography
Ukrainian
Malo-Russian; Little Russian; Ruthenian
3801-3813 Philology (Table P-PZ4a modified)
History of philology
Cf. PG3815 History of the language
3807 General works
Biography, memoirs, etc.

Ukrainian
Philology
History of philology
Biography, memoirs, etc. -- Continued
3809.A2 Collective
3809.A5-Z Individual, A-Z
Subarrange each by Table P-PZ50
3814-3899.5 Language (Table P-PZ4b modified)
Add number in table to PG3800
3817 Script
Cf. PG89+ Slavic alphabet
Grammar
Readers
3825 Primers. Primary grade readers
Readers on special subjects
see PG3827.15
Readers for special classes of students
see PG3826.5
3826.A-Z Intermediate level readers. Advanced readers.
Subarrange by main entry
3826.5.A-Z Manuals for special classes of students, A-Z
3826.5.C6 Commercial. Business
3826.5.S3 Science and technology
Style. Composition. Rhetoric
For study and teaching see PG3811
3875 General works
3878 Choice of words. Vocabulary, etc.
Etymology
3883.5 Dictionaries (exclusively etymological)
Lexicography
For biography of lexicographers see PG3809.A2+
3887 Treatises
Dictionaries
3888 Ukrainian only
Interlingual
Classify with language less known
3889 Polyglot
Cf. PG2635 Russian first
(3890) Ukrainian-Greek (Ancient)
see PA445
Ukrainian-Greek (Modern) see PA1139.A+
Ukrainian-Latin see PA2365.A+
3891 Ukrainian-English; English-Ukrainian
3892 Ukrainian-French [German, etc.]
(3892.8) Ukrainian-Romanian
see PC781
3893.A-Z Ukrainian-Slavic. By language, A-Z

Ukrainian
Language
Lexicography
Dictionaries
Interlingual
Ukrainian-Slavic -- Continued
Belarusian see PG2834
(3893.B8) Bulgarian
see PG982.U4
3893.C9 Czech
3893.R8 Russian
3893.S4 Serbo-Croatian
(3894) Oriental languages
see PJ-PL
3895 Other special lists
For etymological dictionaries see PG3883.5
Linguistic geography. Dialects, etc.
3896.A1 Linguistic geography
Dialects, provincialisms, etc.
3896.A2-.A29 Periodicals. Collections
3896.A3 Collections of texts. Specimens, etc.
3896.A5-.Z3 General works. Grammar
3897 Dictionaries
(3898.A1) Atlases. Maps
see class G
3898.A5-Z Local. By region, place, A-Z
3899 Slang. Argot
3899.5 Old Ukrainian (Table P-PZ15)
Literature
3900 Periodicals. Societies. Serials
3900.4 Congresses
3900.5 Museums. Exhibitions
3901 Collections: Monographs. Studies, etc.
3901.5 Encyclopedias and dictionaries
3902.5 History of Ukrainian literary history and criticism
3903 Study and teaching
Biography of teachers, critics, and historians
3904.5 Collective
3904.52.A-Z Individual, A-Z
Subarrange each by Table P-PZ50
History
3905 General works. Compends
3906.A-Z Special subjects, A-Z
3906.A85 Atheism
3906.B56 Biography (as a literary form)
3906.C45 Censorship
3906.C53 Classical influences

PG

Ukrainian
Literature
History
Special subjects, A-Z -- Continued

3906.C65 Communists. Communism
3906.C68 Country life
3906.C75 Crimea
3906.F64 Folklore and literature
3906.F87 Futurism
3906.I6 Internationalism
3906.J49 Jews
3906.K54 Kiev (Ukraine)
3906.L3 Labor. Working class
3906.L44 Lenin, Vladimir Il′ich, 1870-1924
3906.M64 Modernism
3906.N3 Nationalism
3906.P48 Petli͡ura, Symon Vasyl′ovych, 1879-1926
3906.P54 Pilate, Pontius, 1st cent.
3906.P64 Politics
3906.R36 Realism
3906.R4 Religion
3906.R42 Renaissance
3906.R44 Revolutions. Revolutionaries
3906.R65 Romanticism
3906.S6 Social problems
3906.U4 Ukraine
3906.W66 World War II
3907 Collected essays
Relation to other literatures
3908.A1 General works
3908.A2-Z Individual literatures, A-Z
3909 Translations (as subject)
3913 Biography (Collective)
3913.5 Literary landmarks. Homes and haunts of authors
(3914) Bibliography
see Z2519.64.L5
Origins. Early period to 1800
Cf. PG701+ Church Slavic literature
3915 General works
3915.5.A-Z Special topics, A-Z
3915.5.C47 Chronicles
3916 19th century
3916.2 20th century
3916.3 21st century
Poetry
3917 General works
3917.5.A-Z Special forms or topics, A-Z

Ukrainian
Literature
History
Poetry
Special forms or topics, A-Z -- Continued

3917.5.B52 Bible
3917.5.B8 Burlesque
3917.5.E44 Elegiac poetry
3917.5.F87 Futurism
3917.5.M64 Modernism
3917.5.R44 Religious poetry
3917.5.R65 Romanticism
3917.5.W66 World War I
3921 Drama
3924.A-Z Other forms, A-Z
3924.B56 Biographical fiction
3924.C55 Children's stories
3924.D54 Diaries
3924.E88 Essays
3924.F3 Fables
3924.F5 Fiction
3924.H5 Historical fiction
3924.P3 Parodies
3924.P7 Prose literature
3924.S3 Satire

Folk literature

For general works on and collections of folk literature see GR203.8+

(3925.A1-.A6) Periodicals. Societies

History and criticism

(3925.A7-Z) General works

Folk poetry. Folk songs

3925.4 General works
3925.5.A-Z Special forms, A-Z
3925.5.B34 Ballads
3925.5.C48 Children's poetry
3925.6 Folk drama

Collections of texts

(3926.A3-.A39) General
3926.A7-.Z3 Poetry
3926.Z5 Drama

Fables, proverbs, riddles see PN

(3927) Legends. Fairy tales
(3928.A-Z) By region, province, etc., A-Z
(3929.A-Z) Translations. By language, A-Z

Ukrainian
Literature
History -- Continued
3930 Juvenile literature (General)
For special genres, see the genre
Collections
3931 General
3932 Selections. Anthologies
3932.5.A-Z Special classes or authors, A-Z
3932.5.C55 Children
3932.5.C64 College students
3932.5.J48 Jews
3932.5.W65 Women
3933.A-Z Special topics, A-Z
3933.C44 Chernobyl Nuclear Accident
3933.C47 Christianity
3933.C5 Christmas
(3933.C6) College verse and prose
see PG3932.5.C64
3933.C63 Communism
3933.E2 Easter
3933.F36 Famine
3933.H5 History of Ukraine
(3933.J48) Jewish authors
see PG3932.5.J48
3933.K45 Kherson
3933.K55 Kiev (Ukraine)
3933.K57 Kievan Rus
3933.L68 Love
3933.N3 Nationalism
3933.P35 Patriotic literature
3933.R4 Religion
3933.S45 Shevchenko, Taras Hryhorovych, 1814-1861
3933.S7 Stalin, Joseph, 1879-1953
3933.W3 War
(3933.W65) Women authors
see PG3932.5.W65
Poetry
3934 General works
3934.4.A-Z By subject, A-Z
3934.4.B35 Baikal-Amur Railroad
3934.4.B36 Bandera, Stepan
3934.4.K5 Kiev (Ukraine)
3934.4.L46 Lesi͡a Ukraïnka
3934.4.L68 Love
3934.4.P38 Patriotic poetry
3934.4.P6 Political poetry

Ukrainian
Literature
Collections
Poetry
By subject, A-Z -- Continued

3934.4.R44 Religious poetry
3934.4.R86 Russia. Soviet Union
3934.4.R88 Russian Revolution
3934.4.S43 Sea poetry
Soviet Union see PG3934.4.R86
3934.4.U4 Ukraine
3934.4.V5 Viburnum
3934.4.V56 Visual poetry
3934.4.W37 War
3934.4.W6 Work
3934.4.Z34 Zakarpats'ka oblast' (Ukraine)
3937 Drama
Prose (General and miscellaneous)
3939 General works
3940 Fiction
3941 Other
Individual authors and works
3948.A-Z To 1960, A-Z
Subarrange individual authors by Table P-PZ40 except where otherwise indicated
Subarrange individual works by Table P-PZ43
3948.B245 Bal'men, I͡Akiv de, 1813-1845. Яків де Бальмен (Table P-PZ40)
3948.B265 Barvinok, Vasyl', 1850-1883. Василь Барвінок (Table P-PZ40)
3948.B49 Bilet͡s'kyĭ-Nosenko, P. (Pavlo), 1774-1856. Павло Білецький-Носенко (Table P-PZ40)
3948.B575 Bokhensk'a, I͡Evheniı͡a, 1867-1944. Євгенія Бохенскьа (Table P-PZ40)
3948.B577 Bordulı͡ak, Tymofiĭ, 1863-1936. Тимофій Бордуляк (Table P-PZ40)
3948.B58 Borovykovs'kyĭ, Levko Ivanovych, 1808-1889. Левко Іванович Боровиковський (Table P-PZ40)
3948.B82 Burhardt, Osval'd, 1891-1947. Освальд Бургардт (Table P-PZ40)
3948.C45 Chaĭkovs'kyĭ, Andriĭ, 1857-1935. Андрій Чайковський (Table P-PZ40)
3948.C473 Charnet͡s'kyĭ, Stepan, 1881-1944. Степан Чарнецький (Table P-PZ40)
3948.C48 Cheremshyna, Marko, 1874-1927. Марко Черемшина (Table P-PZ40)

Ukrainian
Literature
Individual authors and works
To 1960, A-Z -- Continued

Dniprova Chaĭka, 1861-1927. Дніпрова Чайка see PG3948.V34

Domontovych, Viktor, 1894-1969. Віктор Домонтович see PG3948.P42

3948.D85 Dukhnovych, O.V. (Oleksandr Vasylʹovych), 1803-1865. Олександр Васильович Духнович (Table P-PZ40)

Ėvarnit͡skiĭ, D.I. (Dmitriĭ Ivanovich), 1855-1940. Дмитрий Иванович Эварницкий see PG3948.I345

3948.F4 Fedʹkovych, I͡Uriĭ, 1834-1888. Юрій Федькович (Table P-PZ40)

3948.F7-.F72 Franko, Ivan, 1856-1916. Іван Франко (Table P-PZ44)

3948.F89 Fylypchak, Ivan. Іван Филипчак (Table P-PZ40)

Grendz͡ha-Donsʹkyĭ, Vasylʹ, 1897-1974. Василь Ґренджа-Донський see PG3948.H6943

3948.H48-.H482 Hlibov, Leonid Ivanovych, 1827-1893. Леонід Іванович Глібов (Table P-PZ44)

3948.H656 Horbanʹ, Mykola, 1899-1973. Микола Горбань (Table P-PZ40)

3948.H66 Hordii͡enko, Kostʹ, 1899- . Кость Гордієнко (Table P-PZ40)

3948.H67 Hordynsʹkyĭ, Svi͡atoslav, 1906- . Святослав Гординський (Table P-PZ40)

Horobet͡sʹ, Tyberiĭ, 1881-1944. Тиберій Горобець see PG3948.C473

3948.H69 Hrabovsʹkyĭ, Pavlo Arsenovych, 1864-1902. Павло Арсенович Грабовський (Table P-PZ40)

3948.H694 Hrebinka, I͡Evhen Pavlovych, 1812-1848. Євген Павлович Гребінка (Table P-PZ40)
Including biography and criticism (General)
For Hrebinka's Russian works, including criticism see PG3337.H7

3948.H6943 Hrendz͡ha-Donsʹkyĭ, Vasylʹ, 1897-1974. Василь Гренджа-Донський (Table P-PZ40)

3948.H6947 Hrinchenko, Borys, 1863-1910. Борис Грінченко (Table P-PZ40)

3948.H6948 Hrinchenko, Marii͡a, 1863-1928. Марія Грінченко (Table P-PZ40)

3948.H698 Hrushevsʹkyĭ, Mykhaĭlo, 1866-1934. Михайло Грушевський (Table P-PZ40)

3948.H699 Hryhorenko, Hryt͡sʹko, 1867-1924. Грицько Григоренко (Table P-PZ40)

Ukrainian
Literature
Individual authors and works
To 1960, A-Z -- Continued

3948.H72 Hrynevycheva, Katri͡a, 1875-1947. Катря Гриневичева (Table P-PZ40)

3948.I25 I͡Anovs′ka, Li͡ubov, 1861-1933. Любов Яновська (Table P-PZ40)

3948.I3 I͡Anovs′kyĭ, I͡Uriĭ, 1902-1954. Юрій Яновський (Table P-PZ40)

3948.I345 I͡Avornyt͡s′kyĭ, Dmytro Ivanovych, 1855-1940. Дмитро Іванович Яворницький (Table P-PZ40)

Karpenko-Karyĭ, I., 1845-1907. Іван Карпенко-Карий see PG3948.T6

3948.K49 Khvyl′ovyĭ, Mykola. Микола Хвильовий (Table P-PZ40)

Klen, I͡Uriĭ, 1891-1947. Юрій Клен see PG3948.B82

3948.K515 Klymentiĭ Zynoviïv syn, ca. 1650-ca. 1712. Климентій Зиновіїв син (Table P-PZ40)

3948.K53 Kobryns′ka, Natalii͡a, 1855-1920. Наталія Кобринська (Table P-PZ40)

3948.K55-.K552 Kobyli͡ans′ka, Ol′ha, 1863-1942. Ольга Кобилянська (Table P-PZ44)

3948.K5862 Kononenko, Musiĭ, 1864-1922. Мусій Кононенко (Table P-PZ40)

3948.K598 Kotli͡arevs′kyĭ, Ivan Petrovych, 1769-1838. Іван Петрович Котляревський (Table P-PZ40)

3948.K6-.K612 Kot͡si͡ubyns′kyĭ, Mykhaĭlo, 1864-1913. Михайло Коцюбинський (Table P-PZ44a)

3948.K64 Kozachyns′kyĭ, Mykhaĭlo, 1699-1755. Михайло Козачинський (Table P-PZ40)

3948.K693 Kravchenko, Uli͡ana, 1860-1947. Уляна Кравченко (Table P-PZ40)

3948.K73 Kropyvnyt͡s′kyĭ, Marko Lukych, 1840-1910. Марко Лукич Кропивницький (Table P-PZ40)

3948.K788 Krymskiĭ, A.E. (Agafangel Efimovich), 1871-1942. Агафангел Ефимович Крымский (Агатангел Юхимович Кримський) (Table P-PZ40)

3948.K856-.K8562 Kulish, Panteleĭmon Oleksandrovych, 1819-1897. Пантелеймон Олександрович Куліш (Table P-PZ44)

3948.K87 Kvitka-Osnov′i͡anenko, H.F., 1778-1843. Григорій Федорович Квітка-Основ'яненко (Table P-PZ40)

3948.K89 Kyrchiv, Bohdar, 1856-1900. Богдар Кирчів (Table P-PZ40)

3948.L45 Lepkyĭ, Bohdan, 1872-1941. Богдан Лепкий (Table P-PZ40)

Ukrainian
Literature
Individual authors and works
To 1960, A-Z -- Continued

3948.L47 Levyts'kyĭ, Ivan, 1837-1918. Іван Левицький (Table P-PZ40)

3948.M84 Myrnyĭ, Panas, 1849-1920. Панас Мирний (Table P-PZ40)

Nechuĭ-Levyts'kyĭ, I.S., 1837-1918. Іван Семенович Нечуй-Левицький see PG3948.L47

3948.P34 Pavlovych, Oleksandr, 1819-1900. Олександр Павлович (Table P-PZ40)

3948.P35 Pavlyk, Mykhaĭlo, 1853-1915. Михайло Павлик (Table P-PZ40)

3948.P42 Petrov, V. (Viktor), 1894-1969. Віктор Петров (Table P-PZ40)

3948.R33 Radyvylovs'kyĭ, Antoniĭ, d. 1668. Антоній Радивиловський (Table P-PZ40)

3948.R78 Rudans'kyĭ, Stepan, 1833-1873. Степан Руданський (Table P-PZ40)

3948.S37 Savchyns'kyĭ, Hryhoriĭ. Григорій Савчинський (Table P-PZ40)

3948.S448 Shashkevych, Markiian, 1811-1843. Маркіян Шашкевич (Table P-PZ40)

3948.S449 Shashkevych, Volodymir, 1839-1885. Володимір Шашкевич (Table P-PZ40)

Shevchenko, Taras Hryhorovych, 1814-1861. Тарас Григорович Шевченко
For Shevchenko as a painter see ND699.S48
For Russian works see PG3361.S42

Collected works
3948.S5 By date
3948.S5A11-.S5A13 By editor, if given
3948.S5A16 Collected essays. By date
3948.S5A17 Collected poems. By date

Translations (Collected or selected)
3948.S5A2-.S5A29 English. By translator, if given, or date
3948.S5A3-.S5A39 French. By translator, if given, or date
3948.S5A4-.S5A49 German. By translator, if given, or date
3948.S5A5-.S5A59 Other. By language

3948.S5A6 Selections. By date
3948.S5A61-.S5Z4 Separate works. By title
(3948.S5Z5-.S5Z999) Biography and criticism
see PG3948.S51A+

Biography and criticism
3948.S51A1-.S51A19 Periodicals. Societies. Serials
3948.S51A2 Dictionaries, indexes, etc. By date

Ukrainian
Literature
Individual authors and works
To 1960, A-Z
Shevchenko, Taras Hryhorovych, 1814-1861. Тарас Григорович Шевченко
Biography and criticism -- Continued

3948.S51A31-.S51A39 Autobiography, journals, memoirs. By title

3948.S51A4 Letters (Collections). By date

3948.S51A41-.S51A49 Letters to and from particular individuals. By correspondent (alphabetically)

3948.S51A5-.S51Z General works

3948.S532 Skovoroda, Hryhoriĭ Savych, 1722-1794. Григорій Савич Сковорода (Table P-PZ40)
For general biography and criticism see B4218.S47+
For Skovoroda's Russian literary works see PG3317.S56

3948.S75 Staryt͡sʹkyĭ, M.P., 1840-1904. Михайло Петрович Старицький (Table P-PZ40)

3948.S76 Stavrovsʹkyĭ-Popradov, I͡Uliĭ Ivanovych, 1850-1899. Юлій Іванович Ставровський-Попрадов (Table P-PZ40)

3948.S78 Stefanyk, Vasylʹ Semenovych, 1871-1936. Василь Семенович Стефаник (Table P-PZ40)

3948.S8 Stelʹmakh, Mykhaĭlo Panasovych. Михайло Панасович Стельмах (Table P-PZ40)

Sudovshchykova, Oleksandra I͡Evhenivna. Олександра Євгенівна Судовщикова see PG3948.H699

3948.S9 Svydnyt͡sʹkyĭ, Anatolʹ, 1834-1871. Анатоль Свидницький (Table P-PZ40)

3948.T6 Tobilevych, I.K. (Ivan Karpovych), 1845-1907. Іван Карпович Тобілевич (Table P-PZ40)

3948.U4-.U42 Ukraïnka, Lesi͡a, 1871-1913. Леся Українка (Table P-PZ44)

3948.U75 Ustyi͡anovych, Mykola, 1811-1885. Микола Устиянович (Table P-PZ40)

3948.V34 Vasylevsʹka, Li͡udmyla Oleksiïvna, 1861-1927. Людмила Олексіївна Василевська (Table P-PZ40)

3948.V66 Vovchok, Marko, 1834-1907. Марко Вовчок (Table P-PZ40)

Zahirni͡a, Marii͡a, 1863-1928. Марія Загірня see PG3948.H6948

Ukrainian
Literature
Individual authors and works
To 1960, A-Z -- Continued
3948.Z46 Z͡Huravnyt͡sʹkyĭ, Ivan Markovych, 1525?-1589. Іван Маркович Журавницький (Table P-PZ40)
3948.Z475 Zinʹkivsʹkyĭ, Trokhym, 1861-1891. Трохим Зіньківський (Table P-PZ40)
3949-3949.36 1961-2000 (Table P-PZ29 modified)
3949.23 M
Mishchenko, Oleksandr. Олександр Міщенко see PG3949.32.O38
3949.32 V
3949.32.O38 Voli͡a, Olesʹ. Олесь Воля (Table P-PZ40)
3950-3950.36 2001- (Table P-PZ29)
Local
For works, biography and criticism of individual local authors, except North American see PG3948+
3956.A-Z By region, province, etc., A-Z
Including Poland, Hungary, etc.
3957.A-Z By city, town, etc., A-Z
Outside Ukraine
General
3958 History
3959 Collections
3960-3969 United States (Table P-PZ24)
3970-3979 Canada (Table P-PZ24)
3980 Spanish America
3981.A-Z Other countries, A-Z
3986-3987 Translations from Ukrainian into foreign languages (Table P-PZ30)
3990-3990.95 Carpatho-Rusyn (Table P-PZ15a)
Czech
4001-4840 Philology. Language (Table P-PZ1 modified)
Periodicals. Serials
4004 Czech
Societies
4014 Czech
History of philology
Biography, memoirs, etc.
4063 Collective
4064.A-Z Individual, A-Z
Subarrange each by Table P-PZ50
Etymology
4580 Dictionaries (exclusively etymological)
4582.A-Z Special elements. By language, A-Z

Czech
Philology. Language
Etymology
Special elements. By language, A-Z -- Continued
4582.A3 Foreign elements (General)
Cf. PG4670 Dictionaries
Lexicography
4601 Collections (of studies, etc.)
4611 General works. Treatises. History
Biography of lexicographers see PG4063+
4617 Criticism, etc., of particular dictionaries
Dictionaries
Czech only
4625 General works
4628 Minor, abridged, school dictionaries
4629 Picture dictionaries
4630 Supplementary dictionaries. Dictionaries of new words
Interlingual
(4633) Early glossaries
see PG4728
4635 Polyglot
Cf. PG2635 Russian first
Cf. PG4647.A2 Czech-Slavic
4637 Classical (Greek and Latin)
For Czech-Greek; Greek-Czech see PA445.A+
For Czech-Latin; Latin-Czech see PA2365.A+
For early Czech-Latin glossaries see PG4728
4640 Czech-English; English-Czech
4645.A-Z Other Germanic, Romance, etc. By language, A-Z
e. g.
4645.D8 Czech-Dutch
4645.F5 Czech-French
4645.G5 Czech-German
4647.A-Z Czech-Slavic. By language, A-Z
4647.A2 Polyglot. By date
Cf. PG2635 Russian first
(4647.B7) Czech-Bulgarian; Bulgarian-Czech
see PG982.C9
4647.P7 Czech-Polish; Polish-Czech
4647.R8 Czech-Russian; Russian-Czech
(4647.S4) Czech-Serbo-Croatian; Serbo-Croatian-Czech
see PG1378
Czech-Slovak; Slovak-Czech see PG5382.A+
Czech-Slovenian; Slovenian-Czech see PG1893.C9
Czech-Ukrainian; Ukrainian-Czech see PG3893.C9

Czech
Philology. Language
Lexicography
Dictionaries
Interlingual -- Continued
(4653) Czech-Oriental
see subclasses PJ-PL
(4654) Czech-American (Aboriginal languages)
see subclass PM
Czech-Artificial languages see PM8001+
Special dictionaries
Dictionaries exclusively etymological see PG4580
(4655) Dictionaries of particular authors
see the author in classes PA-PT
4660 Dictionaries of names
Cf. CS2300+ Personal and family names
Cf. PG4673 Foreign names
4667 Dictionaries of obsolete or archaic words
Dictionaries of foreign words
4670 General
4673 Names
Special. By language see PG4582.A+
Rhyming dictionaries
see PG4519
Special lists
4680 Miscellaneous
(4683.A-Z) By subject, A-Z
see the subject in classes A-N, Q-Z
4689 Dictionaries of terms and phrases
4691 Word frequency lists
4692 Reverse indexes
4693 Abbreviations, Lists of
Linguistic geography. Dialects, etc.
4700 Linguistic geography
Dialects. Provincialisms, etc.
4701 Periodicals. Societies. Yearbooks
Collections
4702.A1-.A6 Texts (Specimens, etc.)
4702.A7-Z Treatises. Studies, etc.
4703 General works
4704 History
Grammar
4705 General works
4706 Special
4707 Etymology
4708 Dictionaries

	Czech
	Philology. Language
	Linguistic geography. Dialects, etc.
	Dialects. Provincialisms, etc. -- Continued
(4709)	Atlases. Maps
	see class G
	Old Czech (to ca. 1400-1500)
4721	Periodicals. Societies. Yearbooks
	Collections
4722.A1-.A6	Texts (Specimens, etc.)
4722.A7-Z	Treatises. Studies, etc.
4723	General works
4724	History
	Grammar
4725	General works
4726	Special
4727	Etymology
4728	Dictionaries
(4729)	Atlases. Maps
	see class G
	Local: By region, province, place
4741-4745	Bohemia (Table P-PZ9)
4751-4755	Moravia. Silesia (Table P-PZ9)
4756	Slovakia
4771.A-Z	By place, A-Z
	Slang. Argot
4800	Collections
4810	General works
4815	Dictionaries. Lists
4820	Texts
4830.A-Z	Special topics, A-Z
4830.R3	Railroad language
4840.A-Z	Special local, A-Z
	Czech literature
	History and criticism
5000	Periodicals. Societies. Serials
5000.15	Congresses
5000.16	Museums. Exhibitions
	Subarrange by author
	Collected works (nonserial)
5000.17	Several authors
5000.18	Individual authors
5000.2	Encyclopedias. Dictionaries
5000.3	Study and teaching
	Biography of critics, historians, etc.
5000.4	Collective

Czech
Czech literature
History and criticism
Biography of critics, historians, etc. -- Continued

5000.5.A-Z Individual, A-Z
Subarrange each by Table P-PZ50
5001 General works. Compends
5002 General special
5002.5.A-Z Relation to other literatures, A-Z
5003 Collected essays
5003.2.A-Z Treatment of special subjects, A-Z
5003.2.B3 Baroque literature
Betlémská kaple (Prague) see PG5003.2.P7
5003.2.B85 Bulgaria
5003.2.C4 České Budéjovic
5003.2.C6 Comenius, Johann Amos
5003.2.F7 Franciscans
5003.2.I5 Indonesia
5003.2.J4 Jews. Judaism
5003.2.L4 Lenin, Vladimir Il'ich, 1870-1924
5003.2.M9 Mythology
5003.2.N36 Nationalism. Patriotism
Patriotism see PG5003.2.N36
5003.2.P64 Popular literature
5003.2.P7 Prague. Betlémská kaple
5003.2.R6 Rome
5003.2.T7 Travel
5003.2.T77 Truth
5003.2.V5 Vienna
5003.2.W33 Warsaw
5003.2.Y8 Yugoslavia
5004 Biography (Collective)
5004.5 Literary landmarks. Homes and haunts of authors
5004.8.A-Z Special classes of authors, A-Z
5004.8.L3 Laboring class authors. Working class authors
5004.8.W65 Women
(5004.9) Bibliography. Bio-bibliography
see Z2138.L5
Origins. Early to 1800
5005 General works
5005.5.A-Z Special topics, A-Z
5005.5.P37 Parodies
5005.5.S62 Social aspects
19th century
5006 General works
5006.3.A-Z Special topics, A-Z
5006.3.A48 Antisemitism

Czech
Literature
History
19th century
Special topics, A-Z -- Continued

5006.3.D42 Decadence
5006.3.G46 Gender identity
5006.3.J83 Judaism
5006.3.M63 Modernism
5006.3.P36 Pastoral literature
5006.3.P64 Popular literature
5006.3.R4 Realism
5006.3.R64 Romanticism
5006.3.S44 Semiotics
5006.3.S77 Spirituality
5006.3.S87 Structuralism

20th century

5007 General works
5007.2.A-Z Special topics, A-Z
5007.2.E85 Experimental literature
5007.2.E87 Expressionism
5007.2.P65 Popular literature
5007.2.U53 Underground literature
5007.2.Z35 Zakarpats'ka oblast' (Ukraine)

21st century

5007.4 General works
5007.5.A-Z Special topics, A-Z

Poetry

5008 General works

By period

5008.2 Early to 1800
5008.3 19th century
5008.4 20th century
5008.45 21st century
5008.5.A-Z Special topics, A-Z
5008.5.C45 Children's poetry
5008.5.P54 Philosophy
5008.5.S87 Surrealism
5009 Drama

Prose

5010 General works

By period

5010.2 Early to 1800
5010.3 19th century
5010.4 20th century
5010.5 21st century
5011 Fiction

Czech
Literature
History
Prose -- Continued
5012 Other
Folk literature
For general works on and collections of folk literature, see GR
(5013) History and criticism
Collections of texts
(5014) General
5015 Folk songs
(5017) Prose, tales, etc.
(5018.A-Z) By locality, region, etc., A-Z
(5019.A-Z) Translations. By language, A-Z
5019.5 Juvenile literature (General)
For specific genres, see the genre
Collections
5020 General works
5020.3.A-Z Special classes of authors, A-Z
5020.3.A34 Aged. Older people
5020.3.C38 Catholic authors
5020.3.C54 Children
5020.3.J48 Jewish authors
Older people see PG5020.3.A34
5020.4.A-Z Special topics, A-Z
5020.4.C68 Coup d'état, 1948
5020.4.P56 Písek
5020.4.P73 Prague
By period
5021 Early to 1600
5021.4 17th-18th centuries
19th century
5021.5 General works
Královédvorský rukopis and Zelenohorský rukopis
Forgeries by V. Hanka and others
Texts
5022.A1 Collections (General)
Královédvorský rukopis
5022.A2 Editions. By date
5022.A2A-.A2Z Translations. By language and date
Zelenohorský rukopis (Libušin soud)
5022.A3 Editions. By date
5022.A3A-.A3Z Translations. By language and date
Treatises
5022.A7-.Z3 General works
5022.Z5 Language: Grammar, etc. By author

Czech
Literature
Collections
By period
19th century
Královédvorský rukopis and Zelenohorský rukopis
Treatises -- Continued
5022.Z8 Glossaries. By date
5023 20th century
5024 21st century
Poetry
Cf. PG5015 Folk songs
5025 General
By period
5025.2 Early to 1800
5025.3 19th century
5025.4 20th century
5025.5 21st century
Drama
5027 Drama
5027 General collections
By period
5027.4 Early to 1800
5027.5 19th-20th centuries
5027.6 21st century
Prose
5029 General collections
By period
5029.4 Early to 1800
5029.5 19th-20th centuries
5029.6 21st century
Fiction
5031 General collections
5031.4 Short stories
5031.6.A-Z Special. By form or subject, A-Z
5031.6.D47 Detective and mystery stories
5031.6.L44 Legal stories
5031.6.L68 Love stories
5031.6.S34 Science fiction
5032 Other
Individual authors and works
5036.A-Z To 1600, A-Z
Subarrange each author by Table P-PZ40 unless otherwise indicated
5036.A1A-.A1Z Anonymous works. By title, A-Z
5036.A1T6 Tkadleček
5036.L65 Lomnický, Šimon, 1552-ca. 1622 (Table P-PZ40)

PG

Czech
Literature
Individual authors and works -- Continued
5037.A-Z 17th-18th centuries, A-Z
Subarrange each author by Table P-PZ40 unless otherwise indicated
5037.A1A-.A1Z Anonymous works. By title, A-Z
5037.B68 Božan, Jan Josef, 1644-1716 (Table P-PZ40)
5037.B7 Bridel, Bedřich, 1619-1680 (Table P-PZ40)
5037.C6 Comenius, Johann Amos, 1592-1670 (Table P-PZ40)
For general works on Comenius see LB475.C59+
5037.M5 Michna z Otradovic, Adam, ca. 1600-1676 (Table P-PZ40)
5037.M68 Mouřenín, Tobiáš, d. ca. 1625 (Table P-PZ40)
5037.R33 Račín, Karel, ca. 1660-1711 (Table P-PZ40)
5037.V38 Vavák, František, 1741-1816 (Table P-PZ40)
5038.A-Z 1800-1960, A-Z
Subarrange each author by Table P-PZ40 unless otherwise indicated
e.g.
5038.A1A-.A1Z Anonymous works. By title, A-Z
5038.A7 Arbes, Jakub, 1840-1914 (Table P-PZ40)
5038.B2 Baar, Jindřich Šimon, 1869-1925 (Table P-PZ40)
5038.B43 Beneš-Třebízský, Václav, 1849-1884 (Table P-PZ40)
5038.B45 Benešová, Božena Zapletalová (Table P-PZ40)
Bezruč, Petr, 1867-1958 see PG5038.V35
Březina, Otokar, 1868-1929 see PG5038.J4
5038.B95 Bystřina, Otakar, 1861-1931 (Table P-PZ40)
5038.C24 Cajthaml, F. (František), 1868-1936 (Table P-PZ40)
5038.C3 Čapek, Karel, 1890-1938 (Table P-PZ40)
Čapek, Karel Matěj see PG5038.C32
5038.C32 Čapek-Chod, K.M. (Karel Matěj), 1860-1927 (Table P-PZ40)
5038.C45 Čech, Svatopluk, 1846-1908 (Table P-PZ40)
5038.C47 Čelakovský, František Ladislav, 1799-1852 (Table P-PZ40)
5038.C483 Červinková-Riegrová, Marie (Table P-PZ40)
5038.C75 Crha, Václav Antonín, 1836-1905 (Table P-PZ40)
5038.D2 Dagan, Avigdor, 1912- (Table P-PZ40)
5038.D819 Dvořák, Xaver, 1858-1939 (Table P-PZ40)
5038.E7 Erben, Karel Jaromír, 1811-1870 (Table P-PZ40)
Fischl, Viktor, 1912- see PG5038.D2
5038.F8 Frída, Emil Bohuslav, 1853-1912 (Table P-PZ38)
5038.F88 Furch, Vincenc, 1817-1864 (Table P-PZ40)
5038.G4 Gellner, František, 1881-1914? (Table P-PZ40)
5038.H28 Hašek, Jaroslav, 1883-1923 (Table P-PZ40)
5038.H33 Havlíček-Borovský, Karel, 1821-1856 (Table P-PZ40)

Czech
Literature
Individual authors and works
1800-1960, A-Z -- Continued

5038.H363 Hek, František Vladislav, 1769-1847 (Table P-PZ40)
5038.H4 Herites, František, 1851-1929 (Table P-PZ40)
5038.H45 Herrmann, Ignát, 1854-1935 (Table P-PZ40)
5038.H48 Heyduk, Adolf, 1835-1923 (Table P-PZ40)
5038.H53 Hlaváček, Karel, 1874-1898 (Table P-PZ40)
5038.H56 Hněvkovský, Šebastián, 1770-1847 (Table P-PZ40)
5038.H57 Hodža, Michal Miloslav, 1811-1870 (Table P-PZ40)
5038.H615 Hofmeister, Rudolf Richard, 1868-1934 (Table P-PZ40)
5038.H63 Holeček, Josef, 1853-1929 (Table P-PZ40)
5038.J3 Jahn, Metoděj, 1865-1942 (Table P-PZ40)
5038.J4 Jebavý, Václav, 1868-1929 (Table P-PZ40)
5038.J424 Jeřábek, František Věnceslav, 1836-1893 (Table P-PZ40)
5038.J43 Jeřábek, V.K. (Viktor Kamil), b. 1859 (Table P-PZ40)
5038.J45 Jesenská, Růžena, 1863-1940 (Table P-PZ40)
5038.J5 Jirásek, Alois, 1851-1930 (Table P-PZ40)
John, Jaromír, 1882-1952 see PG5038.M379
5038.K277 Kamarýt, Josef Vlastimil, 1797-1833 (Table P-PZ40)
5038.K417 Karásek ze Lvovic, Jiří, 1871-1951 (Table P-PZ40)
Kaván, Josef, 1903-1986 see PG5038.N58
5038.K48 Klášterský, Antonín, 1866-1938 (Table P-PZ40)
5038.K56 Klicpera, Václav Kliment, 1792-1859 (Table P-PZ40)
5038.K58 Klostermann, Karel, 1848-1923 (Table P-PZ40)
5038.K647 Kolár, Josef Jiří, 1812-1896 (Table P-PZ40)
5038.K7 Kollár, Ján, 1793-1852 (Table P-PZ40)
For general biography and criticism see PG5438.K57
5038.K774 Kosmák, Václav, 1843-1898 (Table P-PZ40)
5038.K7745 Kosterka, Hugo, 1867-1956 (Table P-PZ40)
5038.K7749 Koubek, Jan Pravoslav, 1805-1854 (Table P-PZ40)
5038.K7774 Krapka-Náchodský, Josef, 1862-1909 (Table P-PZ40)
5038.K7775 Krásnohorská, Eliška, 1847-1926 (Table P-PZ40)
5038.K847 Kubín, Josef Štefan, 1864-1965 (Table P-PZ40)
5038.K8623 Kučera, Karel, 1854-1915 (Table P-PZ40)
5038.M27 Macek, Antonín, 1872-1923 (Table P-PZ40)
5038.M28 Mácha, Karel Hynek, 1810-1836 (Table P-PZ40)
5038.M3 Machar, Josef Svatopluk, 1864-1942 (Table P-PZ40)
5038.M3753 Marek, Antonín, 1785-1877 (Table P-PZ40)
5038.M379 Markalous, Bohumil, 1882-1952 (Table P-PZ40)
5038.M38 Martínek, Vojtěch, 1887-1960 (Table P-PZ40)
5038.M385 Mašínová, Leontina, 1882- (Table P-PZ40)
5038.M3914 Mayer, Rudolf, 1837-1865 (Table P-PZ40)
5038.M68 Mrštík, Alois, 1861-1925 (Table P-PZ40)

Czech
Literature
Individual authors and works
1800-1960, A-Z -- Continued

5038.M7 Mrštík, Vilém, 1863-1912 (Table P-PZ40)
5038.M8 Mužáková, Johana Rottová, 1830-1899 (Table P-PZ40)
5038.N4 Němcová, Božena, 1820-1862 (Table P-PZ40)
5038.N45 Neruda, Jan, 1834-1891 (Table P-PZ40)
5038.N46 Neumann, Stanislav Kostka, 1875-1947 (Table P-PZ40)
5038.N58 Nor, A.C., 1903-1986 (Table P-PZ40)
5038.O4 Ohrenstein, Jiří, 1919-1941 (Table P-PZ40)
Olbracht, Ivan see PG5038.Z35
Orten, Jiří, 1919-1941 see PG5038.O4
5038.P277 Pammrová, Anna, 1860-1945 (Table P-PZ40)
Pechová-Krásnohorská, Eliška, 1847-1926 see PG5038.K7775
5038.P6 Podlipská, Sofie, 1833-1897 (Table P-PZ40)
5038.P753 Procházka, František Serafinský, 1861-1939 (Table P-PZ40)
5038.R3 Rais, Karel Václav, 1859-1926 (Table P-PZ40)
5038.R32 Rakous, Vojtěch, 1862-1935 (Table P-PZ40)
5038.R375 Rettigová, Magdalena Dobromila, 1785-1845 (Table P-PZ40)
5038.R8 Rubeš, František Jaromír, 1814-1853 (Table P-PZ40)
5038.S14 Sabina, Karel, 1813-1877 (Table P-PZ40)
5038.S25 Šalda, František Xaver, 1867-1937 (Table P-PZ40)
5038.S436 Sedlák, Jan Vojtěch, 1889-1941 (Table P-PZ40)
5038.S5233 Šír, Josef, 1859-1920 (Table P-PZ40)
5038.S53 Sládek, Josef Václav, 1845-1912 (Table P-PZ40)
5038.S6 Sova, Antonín, 1864-1928 (Table P-PZ40)
5038.S7 Šrámek, Fráňa, 1877-1952 (Table P-PZ40)
5038.S824 Stroupežnický, Ladislav, 1850-1892 (Table P-PZ40)
Světlá, Karolína see PG5038.M8
5038.S88 Svobodová, Růžena Čápová, 1868-1920 (Table P-PZ40)
5038.S9 Sychra, Matěj Josef, 1776-1830 (Table P-PZ40)
5038.T2 Táborský, František, 1858-1940 (Table P-PZ40)
5038.T85 Turnovský, Josef Ladislav, 1837-1901 (Table P-PZ40)
5038.T9 Tyl, Josef Kajetán, 1808-1856 (Table P-PZ40)
5038.V35 Vašek, Vladimír, 1867-1958 (Table P-PZ40)
5038.V6 Vocel, Jan Erazim, 1803-1871 (Table P-PZ40)
Vrchlický, Jaroslav see PG5038.F8
5038.W55 Winter, Zikmund, 1846-1912 (Table P-PZ40)
5038.Z22 Zahradník-Brodský, Bohumil, 1862-1939 (Table P-PZ40)
5038.Z35 Zeman, Kamil, 1882-1952 (Table P-PZ40)

Czech
Literature
Individual authors and works
1800-1960, A-Z -- Continued
5038.Z4 Zeyer, Julius, 1841-1901 (Table P-PZ40)
5039-5039.36 1961-2000 (Table P-PZ29 modified)
5039.1 A
Alenský, Jan see PG5039.32.O54
5039.23 M
Matulová, Nina, 1935- see PG5039.29.I44
5039.29 S
5039.29.I44 Šiklová, Jiřina, 1935- (Table P-PZ40)
5039.32 V
5039.32.O54 Vondruška, Vlastimil (Table P-PZ40)
5040-5040.36 2001- (Table P-PZ29)
Local
For works, biography, criticism of individual local authors, except North American, see PG5036+
5041.A-Z By region, province, etc., A-Z
5045.A-Z By place, A-Z
Outside of the Czech Republic
General
5047 History
5048 Collections
America
5050-5069 United States and Canada (Table P-PZ23 modified)
Local
5067.A-Z By state, region, etc., A-Z
5068.A-Z By place, A-Z
5070 Spanish America
5080 Brazil
5090 Other
5145-5146 Translations from Czech literature into foreign languages (Table P-PZ30)
Slovak
5201-5223 Philology (Table P-PZ3a modified)
History of philology
Cf. PG5225 History of the language
5215 General works
Biography, memoirs, etc.
5217.A2 Collective
5217.A5-Z Individual, A-Z
Subarrange each by Table P-PZ50
Language
5224 General. Relation to other languages
5225 History
Grammar

Slovak
Language
Grammar -- Continued
5231 General works
5235 Textbooks. Exercises
Readers. Chrestomathies
5236 Series
5237 Primary
5238 Intermediate. Advanced
5238.5.A-Z Manuals for special classes of students, A-Z
5238.5.T43 Technical students
5239 Conversation. Phrase books
Phonology
Including phonemics
Cf. PG5251 Alphabet
5240 General works
Phonetics
5241 General works
5242 Palatalization
5243 Pronunciation
5244 Accent
5244.3 Clitics
5244.5 Intonation
5244.7 Prosodic analysis
5244.9 Phonetics of the sentence (Sandhi)
5245 Orthography. Spelling
5251 Alphabet. Vowels, etc.
Morphology. Inflection. Accidence
5259 General works
5261 Word formation. Derivation. Suffixes, etc.
Noun. Verb, etc. see PG5270+
5269 Tables. Paradigms
Parts of speech (Morphology and syntax)
5270 General works
5271 Noun
5277 Adjective. Adverb. Comparison
5283 Pronoun
Verb
5285 General works
5287 Person
5288 Number
5289 Voice
5291 Mood
5295 Tense
5295.5 Aspects of verbal action
5296 Infinitive and participle
Including gerund

Slovak
Language
Grammar
Parts of speech (Morphology and syntax)
Verb -- Continued
5297.A-Z Special classes of verbs, A-Z
5298.A-Z Particular verbs, A-Z
5299 Other. Miscellaneous
Particle
5301 General works
5303 Adverb
5305 Preposition
5306 Postposition
5307 Conjunction
5309 Interjection
5311.A-Z Other special, A-Z
5311.C54 Clitics
5311.N4 Negatives
Syntax
General
5313 General works
5315 Outlines
5317 General special
Sentences
5319 General arrangement, etc.
5321 Order of words
5323 Order of clauses
5325 Clauses
5327 Other special
5329.A-Z Other aspects, A-Z
For list of Cutter numbers, see Table P-PZ1 398.A+
5335 Style. Composition. Rhetoric
5349 Letter writing
5353 Prosody. Metrics. Rhythmics
Etymology
5361 Treatises
5361.5 Popular works
5362 Names (General)
For personal names see CS2300+ ; for place names, see G104+ (General) or classes D-F for names of specific continents or countries
5363 Dictionaries (exclusively etymological)
5364.A-Z Special elements. By language, A-Z
5364.A3 Foreign elements (General)
5364.3 Other special
5364.5 Folk etymology
5365 Semantics

Slovak
Language
Etymology -- Continued
5367 Synonyms. Antonyms. Paronyms. Homonyms
5368 Onomatopoeic words
5369.A-Z Particular words, A-Z
5374 Lexicography
For biography of lexicographers see PG5217.A2+
Dictionaries
For dictionaries exclusively etymological see PG5363
5375 Slovak only
5378 Polyglot (three or more languages)
Cf. PG2635 Russian first
5379 Slovak-English; English-Slovak
5381.A-Z Slovak-French [-German, etc]; French [German, etc.]-Slovak, A-Z
5382.A-Z Slovak-Slavic (Czech, Polish, Russian, etc.), A-Z
(5383) Slovak-Oriental
see subclasses PJ-PL
5384 Special. Technical, etc.
Linguistic geography. Dialects, etc.
5387 Linguistic geography
Dialects. Provincialisms, etc.
5388 Treatises. Monographs. Studies
5389 Grammar
5391 Dictionaries
(5392) Atlases. Maps
see class G
5393.A-Z Special, by region, A-Z
Literature
5400 Periodicals. Societies. Collections
5400.2 Congresses
5400.3 Museums. Exhibitions
5400.4 Encyclopedias. Dictionaries
5400.5 Study and teaching
5400.6 History of Slovak literary history and criticism
Biography of teachers, critics, and historians
5400.7.A2 Collective
5400.7.A3-Z Individual, A-Z
Subarrange each by Table P-PZ50
History
5401 General works. Compends
5402 General special. Minor
5402.5.A-Z Relation to other literatures, A-Z
5403 Collected essays
5403.2.A-Z Treatment of special subjects, A-Z
5403.2.B3 Baroque literature

Slovak
Literature
History
Treatment of special subjects, A-Z -- Continued

5403.2.B85 Bulgaria
5403.2.C4 České Budějovice
5403.2.C6 Comenius, Johann Amos
5403.2.F7 Franciscans
5403.2.I5 Indonesia
5403.2.J4 Jews. Judaism
5403.2.L4 Lenin, Vladimir Il'ich, 1870-1924
5403.2.M9 Mythology
5403.2.N36 Nationalism. Patriotism
Patriotism see PG5403.2.N36
5403.2.P64 Popular literature
5403.2.P7 Prague. Betlémská kaple
5403.2.R6 Rome
5403.2.T7 Travel
5403.2.W33 Warsaw
5403.2.Y8 Yugoslavia
5404 Biography (Collective)
5404.5 Literary landmarks. Homes and haunts of authors
5404.8.A-Z Special classes of authors, A-Z
5404.8.L3 Laboring class authors. Working class authors
5404.8.W65 Women
(5404.9) Bibliography. Bio-bibliography
see Z2158.L5
5405 Origins. Early to 1800
19th century
5406 General works
5406.3.A-Z Special topics, A-Z
5406.3.J34 Jánošík, Juraj, 1688-1713
5406.3.R65 Romanticism
20th century
5407 General works
5407.3.A-Z Special topics, A-Z
5407.3.C65 Communism
5407.3.M64 Modernism
5407.3.S56 Slovak Uprising, 1944
21st century
5407.5 General works
5407.7.A-Z Special topics, A-Z
Poetry
5408 General works
5408.5.A-Z Special topics, A-Z
5408.5.C45 Children's poetry
Drama

Slovak
Literature
History
Drama -- Continued
5409 General works
5409.5.A-Z Special topics, A-Z
5409.5.F64 Folk drama
Prose
5410 General works
5411 Fiction
5412 Other prose forms
5412.5.A-Z Special topics, A-Z
5412.5.N38 Naturalism
Folk literature
For general works on and collections of folk literature, see GR
For folk drama see PG5409.5.F64
(5413) History and criticism
Collections of texts
(5414) General
5415 Folk songs
(5417) Prose, tales, etc.
(5418.A-Z) By locality, region, etc., A-Z
(5419.A-Z) Translations. By language, A-Z
5419.5 Juvenile literature (General)
For specific genres, see the genre
Collections
5420 General works
5420.3.A-Z Special classes of authors, A-Z
5420.3.W65 Women
5420.4.A-Z Special topics, A-Z
5420.4.B73 Bratislava
By period
5421 Early through 1800
5422 19th century
5423 20th century
5424 21st century
5425 Poetry
5427 Drama
Prose
5428 General collections
Fiction
5428.5 General collections
5429 Short stories
5430 Other
Individual authors

Slovak
Literature
Individual authors and works -- Continued

5436.A-Z To 1600, A-Z
Subarrange each author by Table P-PZ40
5436.A1A-.A1Z Anonymous works. By title, A-Z
5437.A-Z 17th-19th centuries, A-Z
Subarrange each author by Table P-PZ40
5437.A1A-.A1Z Anonymous works. By title, A-Z
5437.B3 Bajza, Jozef Ignác, 1755-1836 (Table P-PZ40)
5437.G3 Gavlovič, Hugolín, 1712-1787 (Table P-PZ40)
5438.A-Z 1800-1960, A-Z
Subarrange each author by Table P-PZ40 unless otherwise indicated
e. g.
5438.B4 Bencúr, Matej, 1860-1928 (Table P-PZ40)
5438.B7 Botto, Ján, 1829-1881 (Table P-PZ40)
5438.B71 Botto, Ján, 1876-1958 (Table P-PZ40)
5438.C323 Čajak, Janko, 1830-1867 (Table P-PZ40)
5438.C5 Cíger-Hronský, Jozef, 1896-1962 (Table P-PZ40)
5438.D6 Dobšinský, Pavol, 1828-1885 (Table P-PZ40)
5438.D65 Dohnány, Mikuláš, 1824-1852 (Table P-PZ40)
5438.D8 Dvořáková, Ludmila, 1900-1984 (Table P-PZ40)
5438.F67 Francisci-Rimavský, Janko, 1822-1905 (Table P-PZ40)
5438.G68 Graichman, Jakub, 1822-1897 (Table P-PZ40)
5438.G7 Gregor-Tajovský, Jozef, 1874-1940 (Table P-PZ40)
5438.H28 Halaša, Ondrej, 1852-1913 (Table P-PZ40)
5438.H615 Hollý, Ján, 1785-1845 (Table P-PZ40)
5438.H695 Hrebenda, Matej, 1796-1880 (Table P-PZ40)
5438.H697 Hroboň, Samo Bohdan (Table P-PZ40)
Hronský, Jozef Cíger see PG5438.C5
5438.H75 Hurban, Jozef Miloslav, 1817-1888 (Table P-PZ40)
5438.H8 Hurban Vajanský, Svetozár, 1847-1916 (Table P-PZ40)
Hviezdoslav, 1849-1921 see PG5438.O7
Jégé, 1866-1940 see PG5438.N3
5438.J4 Jesenský, Janko, 1874-1945 (Table P-PZ40)
5438.K27 Kalinčiak, Jan (Table P-PZ40)
5438.K36 Kellner-Hostinský, Peter, 1823-1873 (Table P-PZ40)
5438.K57 Kollár, Ján, 1793-1852 (Table P-PZ40)
For criticism of Kollár's literary works see PG5038.K7
5438.K75 Kráľ, Janko, 1822-1876 (Table P-PZ40)
Krasko, Ivan, 1876-1958 see PG5438.B71
5438.K799 Kubáni, Ľudovít, 1830-1869 (Table P-PZ40)
Kukučín, Martin, 1860-1928 see PG5438.B4
5438.K83 Kuzmány, Pavol, 1835-1900 (Table P-PZ40)
5438.L5 Lichard, Daniel G., 1812-1882 (Table P-PZ40)

Slovak
Literature
Individual authors and works
1800-1960, A-Z -- Continued
Martinský, Janko, 1874-1945 see PG5438.J4
5438.M36 Matúška, Janko, 1821-1877 (Table P-PZ40)
Mistrík, Ľudovít see PG5438.O6
5438.N3 Nádaši, Ladislav, 1866-1940 (Table P-PZ40)
5438.N55 Nosák-Nezabudov, Bohuš, 1818-1877 (Table P-PZ40)
5438.O6 Ondrejov, Ľudo (Table P-PZ40)
5438.O7 Országh, Pavol, 1849-1921 (Table P-PZ40)
5438.P35 Pauliny-Tóth, Viliam, 1826-1877 (Table P-PZ40)
5438.R3 Rázus, Martin, 1888-1937 (Table P-PZ40)
5438.S6 Sládkovič, Andrej, 1820-1872 (Table P-PZ40)
Slančiková, Božena, 1867-1951 see PG5438.T5
5438.S685 Šparnensis, Eugen Vrahobor, 1827-ca. 1853 (Table P-PZ40)
5438.T26 Tablic, Bohuslav, 1769-1832 (Table P-PZ40)
5438.T5 Timrava, 1867-1951 (Table P-PZ40)
5438.U65 Uram Podtatranský, Rehor, 1846-1924 (Table P-PZ40)
5438.V3 Vansová, Terézia, 1857-1942 (Table P-PZ40)
5438.Z2 Záborský, Jonáš, 1812-1876 (Table P-PZ40)
5438.Z29 Zechenter-Laskomerský, Gustáv Kazimír, 1824-1908 (Table P-PZ40)
Zguriška, Zuzka, 1900-1984 see PG5438.D8
5439-5439.36 1961-2000 (Table P-PZ29)
5440-5440.36 2001- (Table P-PZ29)
Local
For works, biography, and criticism of individual local authors, except North American, see PG5436+
5441.A-Z By region, province, etc., A-Z
5445.A-Z By place, A-Z
America
5450-5469 United States and Canada (Table P-PZ23 modified)
Local
5467.A-Z By state, region, etc., A-Z
5468.A-Z By place, A-Z
5470 Spanish America
5480 Brazil
5490 Other
5545-5546 Translations from Slovak into foreign languages (Table P-PZ30)
Sorbian (Wendic)
Languages
5631 Periodicals. Societies. Collections
Biography of philologists
5634 Collective

Sorbian (Wendic)
Languages
Biography of philologists -- Continued
5634.2.A-Z Individual, A-Z
Subarrange each by Table P-PZ50
5635 Study and teaching
5636 General works
5637 History of the language
Grammar
5639 General works
5639.5 Textbooks for foreign speakers
5639.7 Conversation and phrase books
5640 Readers
5641 Phonology. Phonetics. Orthography
5643 Morphology. Inflection. Parts of speech
5645 Syntax
5651 Etymology
5653.A-Z Dictionaries. By author, A-Z
Linguistic geography. Dialects, etc.
5656.8 Linguistic geography
5657 Dialects (General only)
Lower Sorbian
5658.A1-.A5 Collections
5658.A51-.Z3 General works
5658.Z5 Miscellaneous works
5658.2 Grammar
5658.25 Etymology. Lexicology
5658.3 Dictionaries
Dialects
5658.4 General
5658.42.A-Z Local, A-Z
Upper Sorbian
5659.A1-.A5 Collections
5659.A51-.Z3 General works
5659.Z5 Miscellaneous works
5659.2 Grammar
5659.25 Etymology. Lexicology
5659.3 Dictionaries
Dialects
5659.4 General
5659.42.A-Z Local, A-Z
Literature
History
5661 Collections
5663 General works
5665 Biography of authors (Collective)
5669 Special subjects

Sorbian (Wendic)
Literature -- Continued
Collections
5673 General
5675 Poetry
5676 Drama
5679 Prose
5681.A-Z Individual authors and works, A-Z
Subarrange each author by Table P-PZ40 unless otherwise specified
5681.B3 Bart-Ćišinski, Jakub, 1856-1909 (Table P-PZ40)
5681.C4 Ćěsla, Jan, 1840-1915 (Table P-PZ40)
5681.D67 Domaškojc, Marjana, 1872-1946 (Table P-PZ40)
5681.K67 Kosyk, Mato, 1853-1940 (Table P-PZ40)
5681.L64 Lorenc-Zalěski, Jakub, 1874-1939 (Table P-PZ40)
Radyserb-Wjela, Jan, 1822-1907 see PG5681.W53
5681.T5 Tharaeus, Andreas, ca. 1570-ca. 1639 (Table P-PZ40)
5681.W43 Wićaz, Ota, 1874-1952 (Table P-PZ40)
5681.W53 Wjela, Jan, 1822-1907 (Table P-PZ40)
5681.Z4 Zejler, Handrij, 1804-1872 (Table P-PZ40)
Local
For works, biography, and criticism of individual local authors, including those outside the Sorbian national area, see PG5681.A+
5683 Lower Lusatia
5684 Upper Lusatia
5685.A-Z Other, A-Z
5688-5689 Translations from Sorbian into foreign languages (Table P-PZ30)
Polish
6001-6840 Philology. Language (Table P-PZ1 modified)
Periodicals
6004 Polish
History of philology
Biography, memoirs, etc.
6063 Collective
6064.A-Z Individual, A-Z
Subarrange each by Table P-PZ50
Grammar
Readers
6117.5 Readers for Poles in the U.S.
Etymology
6580 Dictionaries (exclusively etymological)
6582.A-Z Special elements. By language, A-Z
6582.A3 Foreign elements (General)
Cf. PG6670 Dictionaries
Lexicography

Polish
Philology. Language
Lexicography -- Continued
6601 Periodicals. Societies. Serials. Collections (nonserial)
6611 General works
Biography of lexicographers see PG6063+
6617 Criticism, etc., of particular dictionaries
Dictionaries
Polish only
6625 General works
6628 Minor, abridged, school dictionaries
6629 Picture dictionaries
6630 Supplementary dictionaries. Dictionaries of new words
6635 Polyglot
Bilingual
Classify with language less known
(6637) Polish-Greek (Ancient)
see PA445
6638 Polish-Celtic
6640 Polish-English; English-Polish
6645.A-Z Polish-French [-German, etc.]; French [German, etc.]-Polish, A-Z
6647 Polish-Slavic
For Czech see PG4647.P7
For Slovak see PG5382.A+
(6649) Minor (European) languages
see the language
(6653) Polish-Oriental
see subclasses PJ-PL
(6654) Polish-American (aboriginal languages)
see subclass PM
Polish-Artificial languages see PM8060+
Special dictionaries
Dictionaries exclusively etymological see PG6580
(6655) Dictionaries of particular authors
see the author in classes PA-PT
6660 Dictionaries of names
Cf. CS2300+ Personal and family names
Cf. PG6673 Foreign names
6667 Dictionaries of obsolete or archaic words
Local provincialisms see PG6740+
Dictionaries of foreign words
6670 General
6673 Names
Special. By language see PG6582.A+

Polish
Philology. Language
Lexicography
Dictionaries
Special dictionaries -- Continued
Rhyming dictionaries
see PG6519
Special lists
6680 Miscellaneous
(6683.A-Z) By subject, A-Z
see the subject in classes A-N, Q-Z
6689 Dictionaries of terms and phrases
6691 Word frequency lists
6692 Reverse indexes
6693 Abbreviations, Lists of
Linguistic geography. Dialects, etc.
6700 Linguistic geography
Dialects
6700.A1-.A5 Periodicals. Societies. Collections
6700.A7-Z Collections of texts
6703 General works
6704 General special. Minor
6705 History
Grammar
6706 General works
6707 Special. Phonology. Orthography, etc.
6708 Etymology
6709 Dictionaries
(6710) Atlases. Maps
see class G
Early Polish (to ca. 1500)
6721.A1-.A5 Periodicals. Societies. Collections
6721.A7-Z Collections of texts
Cf. PG7134.A2 Old Polish literature
Cf. PG7136.A3+ Old Polish poetry
6723 General works
6724 General special. Minor
6725 History
Grammar
6726 General works
6727 Special. Phonology. Orthography, etc.
6728 Etymology
6729 Dictionaries
(6730) Atlases. Maps
see class G
Local: By region, province, etc.
6740 Wielkopolska (Table P-PZ15)

Polish
Philology. Language
Linguistic geography. Dialects, etc.
Dialects
Local: By region, province, etc. -- Continued
6750 Małopolska (Table P-PZ15)
6760 Masovia. Mazury (Table P-PZ15)
6765 Chełmno. Kociewie. Warmia (Table P-PZ15)
6770 Lithuania (Table P-PZ15)
6780 Silesia (Table P-PZ15)
6790 Other (not A-Z)
Arrange by author
Slang. Argot
6800 Collections
6810 General works
6815 Dictionaries. Lists
6820 Texts
6830.A-Z Special topics, A-Z
For list of Cutter numbers, see Table P-PZ2 421.A+
6840.A-Z Special local, A-Z
Literature
7001 Periodicals
(7002) Yearbooks
see PG7001
7003 Societies
7004 Congresses
7004.5 Museums. Exhibitions
Collections
7005 Series. Monographs by various authors
7006 Individual authors (Collected works, studies, etc.)
7007 Encyclopedias. Dictionaries
7008 History of Polish literary history and criticism
7009 Study and teaching
Biography of teachers, critics, and historians
7011.A2 Collective
7011.A3-Z Individual, A-Z
Subarrange each by Table P-PZ50
History
7012 General works
7013 Compends
7014 Outlines. Syllabi, etc.
7015 Collected essays
7017 Lectures, addresses, pamphlets
7019 Relations to history, civilization, culture, etc.
7020.A-Z Relations to other literatures, A-Z
7021 Translations (as subject)
Treatment of special subjects, classes, etc.

Polish
Literature
History
Treatment of special subjects, classes, etc. -- Continued

7023.A-Z Subjects, A-Z
7023.A44 Alienation. Isolation
7023.A54 Animals
7023.A86 Authorship
7023.B37 Baroque
7023.B53 Bible
7023.C45 Censorship
7023.C49 Children. Childhood
7023.C55 Classicism
7023.C93 Czarniecki, Stefan, 1599-1665
7023.D36 Dance
7023.D43 Death
7023.D48 Devil
7023.E36 Egypt
7023.E85 Europe
7023.E87 Europe, Eastern. Kresy Wschodnie
7023.H43 Health
Isolation see PG7023.A44
7023.J47 Jesus Christ
Kresy Wschodnie see PG7023.E87
7023.L42 Lech (Legendary character)
7023.L53 Libraries
7023.M5 Military history
7023.M68 Mountains
7023.N37 Nature
7023.O3 Oder River
7023.P38 Pastoral literature
7023.P46 Plants
7023.P56 Podhale
7023.Q86 Quotations
7023.S3 Science
7023.S4 Sea
7023.S83 Sudeten
7023.S85 Suffering
7023.S87 Swedish-Polish War, 1655-1660
7023.T36 Tannenberg, Battle of, Poland, 1410
7023.T37 Tatra Mountains
7023.T73 Tragic, The
7023.T74 Trees
7023.W3 Wanda (Mythical queen)
7024.A-Z Classes and ethnic groups, A-Z
7024.B7 Brigands and robbers
7024.C6 Cossacks

Polish
Literature
History
Treatment of special subjects, classes, etc.
Classes and ethnic groups, A-Z -- Continued

7024.J4 Jews
7024.P4 Peasants
7024.S6 Slavs
7024.T42 Teachers
(7026) Bibliography. Bio-bibliography
see Z2528.L5
Awards, prizes
7027 General works
7027.2.A-Z Special, A-Z
7027.2.S63 Śląski Wawrzyn Literacki
Biography
7028 Collective
Individual see PG7157+
7030 Memoirs. Letters, etc.
7032 Literary landmarks. Homes and haunts of authors
7034 Women authors. Literary relations of women
7035.A-Z Special classes of authors, A-Z
7035.C38 Catholic
7035.C45 Children
7035.J48 Jewish
7035.L88 Lutheran
7035.P43 Peasants
7035.P52 Piarists
7035.P75 Prisoners
7035.S34 Sailors
7035.S64 Soldiers
7035.T73 Travelers
By period
Origins. Early to 1800
7036 General works
7038.A-Z Special topics, A-Z
7038.A44 Alexander, the Great, 356-323 B.C.
7038.A94 Authorship
7038.B37 Baroque
7038.B52 Bible
7038.B62 Body, Human
7038.C48 Christianity
7038.C55 Classicism
7038.C66 Conspiracies
7038.C68 Country life
7038.C74 Criticism, History of
7038.D43 Death

Polish
Literature
History
By period
Origins. Early to 1800
Special topics, A-Z -- Continued

7038.E4 Emblem books
7038.E43 Enlightenment
7038.E83 Eschatology
7038.E95 Exoticism
7038.F43 Fear
7038.F66 Forecasting
7038.F67 Fortuna (Roman deity)
7038.G64 Golden age (Mythology)
Human body see PG7038.B62
7038.H85 Human beings
7038.J47 Jesuits
7038.J49 Jews
7038.J64 John, the Baptist, Saint
7038.K64 Konstytucja (1791)
7038.K73 Kraków (Poland)
7038.L35 Landscape
7038.L38 Laughter
7038.L68 Love poetry
7038.N37 Narration
7038.P47 Personification
7038.P62 Politics and literature
7038.P64 Poniatowski, Józef Antoni, książę, 1763-1813
7038.P65 Popular literature. Sowizdrzal literature
7038.R45 Renaissance
7038.R65 Rome (Italy)
7038.S28 Satire
7038.S35 Sea
Sowizdrzal literature see PG7038.P65
7038.S85 Stoics
7038.U76 Utopias

19th-20th centuries

7051 General works
7053.A-Z Special topics, A-Z
7053.A44 Allusions
7053.A73 Arcadia
7053.A78 Art
7053.A85 Austria
7053.A88 Authentism
7053.A89 Authorship
7053.A9 Autobiography
7053.B3 Baltic Sea Region

Polish
Literature
History
By period
19th-20th centuries
Special topics, A-Z -- Continued

7053.B35 Barska konfederacja
7053.B52 Bible
7053.B64 Body, Human
7053.B67 Borderlands
7053.B68 Boundaries
7053.B73 Brazil
7053.C28 Cathedrals
(7053.C3) Catholic authors
see PG7035.C38
7053.C46 Characters and characteristics
7053.C47 Children
7053.C48 Christianity
7053.C56 Cities and towns
7053.C58 Civilization, Occidental
7053.C63 Classical civilization
7053.C64 Classicism
7053.C66 Concentration camps
7053.C67 Constructivism
7053.C68 Country life
7053.C85 Culture
7053.C93 Cycles
7053.D35 Death
7053.D4 Decadence
7053.D95 Dystopias
7053.E54 Enemies
7053.E76 Ethics
7053.E84 Europe, Eastern. Kresy Wschodnie
7053.E85 Existentialism
7053.E86 Exoticism
7053.E89 Experimental literature
7053.F38 Fate and fatalism
Folklore see PG7053.L58
7053.G46 Geology
7053.G48 German influences
7053.G63 God
7053.G75 Grotesque
7053.H34 Hamlet
7053.H47 Heroes
7053.H56 History and literature. History in literature
For historical fiction see PG7099.5.H57
7053.H63 Holocaust, Jewish (1939-1945)

Polish
Literature
History
By period
19th-20th centuries
Special topics, A-Z -- Continued

7053.H64 Holy, The
7053.H65 Home
Human body see PG7053.B64
7053.H87 Hutsulshchyna (Ukraine)
7053.I33 Identity (Philosophical concept)
7053.I53 India
7053.I55 Intimacy
7053.I73 Italy
7053.J46 Jewish women
7053.J47 Jews
Kresy Wschodnie see PG7053.E84
7053.L33 Labor. Working class
7053.L44 Legiony Polskie
7053.L58 Literature and folklore
7053.L68 Love
7053.M3 Masovia
7053.M45 Mentally ill
7053.M47 Metaphysics
7053.M52 Middle class
7053.M55 Młoda Polska
7053.M6 Modernism
7053.M68 Mountains
7053.M86 Myth
7053.M88 Mythology, Slavic
7053.N25 Names
7053.N27 Nationalism
7053.N3 Naturalism
7053.N68 Nowa Fala
7053.O24 Object (Philosophy)
7053.O43 Old age
7053.O75 Oriental influences
7053.O84 Other (Philosophy)
7053.P4 Peasants
7053.P5 Philosophy
7053.P54 Piłsudski, Józef, 1867-1935
7053.P56 Point of view
7053.P58 Poland
7053.P582 Polemics
7053.P584 Polish Americans
7053.P585 Politics and literature
7053.P59 Popular literature

Polish
Literature
History
By period
19th-20th centuries
Special topics, A-Z -- Continued

7053.P6 Positivism
7053.P63 Postmodernism
7053.R4 Realism
7053.R414 Reality
7053.R42 Regionalism
7053.R44 Religion
7053.R48 Revolution (General)
7053.R482 Revolution, 1830-1832
7053.R483 Revolution, 1846
7053.R484 Revolution, 1848-1849
7053.R486 Revolution, 1863-1864
7053.R6 Romanticism
7053.S24 Sadness
7053.S3 Satire
7053.S35 Scandals
7053.S4 Sentimentalism
7053.S48 Silence
7053.S55 Skamander (Group of writers)
7053.S57 Sleep
7053.S65 Socialist realism
7053.S73 Stereotype (Psychology)
7053.S9 Surrealism
7053.S94 Świętokrzyskie Mountains
7053.S97 Symbolism
7053.T26 Tales (Literary)
7053.T3 Tatra Mountains
7053.T7 Traugutt, Romuald, 1826-1864
7053.T73 Travel
7053.U3 Ukraine
7053.U53 Underground literature
7053.U74 Urbanization
7053.U86 Utopias
7053.V34 Values
7053.V45 Venice (Italy)
7053.W29 War
7053.W32 Warmia (Poland)
7053.W33 Warsaw
7053.W34 Warsaw Uprising, 1944
7053.W4 Weddings
7053.W46 Wernyhora
7053.W6 Women

Polish
Literature
History
By period
19th-20th centuries
Special topics, A-Z -- Continued
Working class see PG7053.L33
7053.W64 World War I
7053.W65 World War II
7053.Z54 Ziewonia (Group of writers)
21st century
7055 General works
7056.A-Z Special topics, A-Z
Poetry
7062 General works
By period
7068 16th-18th centuries
7070 19th-20th centuries
7072 21st century
Special forms and topics
7078 Epic
7080 Lyric
(7082) Other forms
see PG7083
7083.A-Z Other forms or topics, A-Z
7083.A44 Allegory
7083.A9 Authentism
7083.A92 Autobiography
7083.A94 Avant-garde
7083.B37 Baroque
7083.B53 Bible
7083.C36 Catastrophism
7083.C44 Censorship
7083.C48 Children's poetry
7083.C5 Chopin, Frédéric, 1810-1849
7083.C54 Christian poetry
7083.C55 Classicism
7083.C97 Cycles
7083.D36 Dance
7083.D42 Death
Cf. PG7083.L35 Laments
7083.D53 Didactic poetry
7083.E37 Elegiac poetry
7083.E43 Emblem books
7083.E62 Epigrams
7083.E64 Epistolary poetry
7083.E65 Epitaphs

Polish
Literature
History
Poetry
Special forms or topics
Other forms or topics, A-Z -- Continued

7083.E66 Epithalamia
7083.E76 Erotic poetry
7083.F35 Family
7083.F43 Fear
7083.F55 Flowers
7083.F77 Funeral rites and ceremonies
7083.F8 Futurism
7083.G76 Grotesque
7083.H65 Holy, The
7083.H66 Home
7083.H86 Hunting
7083.J47 Jesuits
7083.L35 Laments
Cf. PG7083.D42 Death
7083.L57 Lithuania
7083.L67 Lot's wife (Biblical figure)
7083.L68 Love poetry
7083.M34 Manors
7083.M37 Martial law
7083.M46 Metaphor
7083.M48 Metaphysical poetry
7083.M63 Mock-heroic poetry
7083.M636 Modernism
7083.M87 Muses (Greek deities)
7083.N36 Naples (Italy)
7083.N37 Narrative poetry
7083.N53 Night
7083.P33 Parnassianism
7083.P336 Pastoral poetry
7083.P34 Patriotic poetry
7083.P56 Philosophical anthropologyy
7083.P58 Piarists
7083.P6 Politics
7083.P75 Pride
7083.P77 Prose poems
7083.R44 Religious poetry
7083.R48 Revolutionary poetry
7083.R52 Rhetoric
7083.R64 Romanticism
7083.S27 Satire
7083.S43 Sea

Polish
Literature
History
Poetry
Special forms or topics
Other forms or topics, A-Z -- Continued

7083.S47 Senses and sensation
7083.S49 Shakespeare, William, 1564-1616
7083.S52 Skamander (Group of writers)
7083.S63 Socialist realism
7083.S68 Soviet Union
7083.S73 Stanisław II August, King of Poland, 1732-1798
7083.S76 Stoics
7083.S9 Symbolism
7083.T56 Time
Travels see PG7083.V68
7083.V68 Voyages and travels
7083.W37 Warsaw Uprising, 1944
7083.W66 World War I
7083.W67 World War II
7083.W75 Wspólność (Organization)
Drama
7084 General works
By period
7087 Early through 1800
7088 19th-20th centuries
7089 21st century
7090.A-Z Special types of drama, A-Z
7090.C54 Children's plays
7090.C64 Comedy
7090.O54 One-act plays
7090.T7 Tragedy
7092.A-Z Special topics, A-Z
7092.A27 Absurd
7092.B52 Bible
7092.C57 Christian drama
7092.D48 Devil
7092.E86 Expressionism
7092.H57 Historical drama
7092.I57 Intertextuality
7092.J47 Jesuit drama
7092.J84 Judas Iscariot
7092.K67 Kościuszko, Tadeusz, 1746-1817
7092.M56 Młoda Polska
7092.M95 Mysteries and miracle plays
7092.P37 Patriotism
7092.P43 Peasants

Polish
Literature
History
Drama
Special topics, A-Z -- Continued

7092.P6 Power
7092.R65 Romanticism
7092.S44 Self

Prose
7098 General works
By period
7098.3 Early through 1800
7098.4 19th-20th centuries
7098.5 21st century
Fiction
7099 General works
By period
7099.2 Early through 1800
7099.25 19th century
7099.3 20th century
7099.4 21st century
7099.5.A-7099.5Z Special types of fiction, A-Z
7099.5.A87 Autobiographical fiction
7099.5.C57 Children's stories
7099.5.D54 Didactic fiction
7099.5.E94 Experimental fiction
7099.5.F35 Fantastic fiction
7099.5.H57 Historical fiction
7099.5.H67 Horror tales
7099.5.K85 Künstlerromane
7099.5.P37 Pastoral fiction
7099.5.P65 Political fiction
7099.5.P89 Psychological fiction
7099.5.S35 Science fiction
7099.5.S47 Serialized fiction
7099.5.T34 Tales (Literary)
7100 Other
7102.A-Z Special topics, A-Z
7102.A43 Alcoholism
7102.A87 Autobiography
7102.B56 Biographical technique. Biography
7102.C44 Censorship
7102.C46 Characters and characteristics
7102.C47 Christian prose
7102.C65 Concentration camps
7102.C66 Confession
7102.C92 Cycles

Polish
Literature
History
Prose
Special topics, A-Z -- Continued

7102.E47 Empathy
7102.F35 Family
7102.G34 Galicia (Poland and Ukraine)
7102.G45 Gender identity
7102.H47 Heroes
7102.H57 History in literature
7102.I73 Italy
7102.J48 Jews
7102.L32 Labyrinths
7102.M37 Maturation (Psychology)
7102.M46 Młoda Polska
7102.M95 Mysticism
7102.N37 Naturalism
7102.N38 Nature
7102.N66 Nostalgia
7102.P4 Peasants
7102.P67 Positivism
7102.P68 Postmodernism
7102.R42 Realism
7102.R44 Religion
7102.R48 Revolution, 1905-1907
7102.R65 Romanticism
7102.S4 Seafaring life. Sea
7102.S44 Self-consciousness (Awareness)
7102.S45 Sentimentalism
7102.S53 Skamander (Group of writers)
7102.S58 Socialist realism
7102.S62 Space and time
7102.T73 Travel
7102.U37 Ukraine
7102.W65 Women
7102.W67 World War II

Folk literature
For general works on and collections of folk literature see GR195+

(7121) Periodicals. Societies. Collections

History and criticism

(7122) General works
(7123) Addresses, essays, lectures
7123.5.A-Z Special forms, A-Z
7123.5.B35 Ballads
7123.5.C54 Christmas carols

Polish
Literature
History
Folk literature
History and criticism
Special forms, A-Z -- Continued
7123.5.L68 Love poetry
Collections of texts
(7124) General
By form
Folk songs and poetry. Ballads
7125 General
7125.5.A-Z Special forms and topics, A-Z
7125.5.C45 Christmas carols
7125.5.W43 Weddings
7127 Drama
Fables, proverbs, riddles
see PN
Tales, legends, etc. see GR195+
(7128.A-Z) By locality, region, etc., A-Z
(7129.A-Z) Translations. By language, A-Z
7130 Juvenile literature (General)
For special genres, see the genre
Collections
7132 General
7133 Selections. Anthologies
7133.5.A-Z Special classes of authors, A-Z
7133.5.C55 Children
7133.5.J48 Jews
7133.5.P46 People with disabilities
7133.5.S64 Soldiers
By period
7134.A2 Early to 1500
Cf. PG6721.A7+ Old Polish texts
7134.A5-Z 16th-18th centuries
7135 19th-20th centuries
7135.15 21st century
7135.2.A-Z Special topics, A-Z
7135.2.B3 Barska konfederacja
7135.2.B53 Białystok Region
7135.2.B94 Bydgoszcz (Poland)
7135.2.C47 Christianity
7135.2.C57 Cmentarz Powązkowski (Warsaw, Poland)
7135.2.F35 Fantastic literature
7135.2.F65 Food
7135.2.F67 Forests and forestry
7135.2.G38 Gawędy

PG

Polish
Literature
Collections
Special topics, A-Z -- Continued

7135.2.H64 Holocaust, Jewish (1939-1945)
7135.2.J48 Jews
7135.2.K37 Katyn Forest Massacre, 1940
7135.2.K66 Kościuszko, Tadeusz, 1746-1817
7135.2.K87 Kurpiowska Forest
7135.2.L57 Lithuania
7135.2.M45 Mental illness
7135.2.N37 Nature
Ocean see PG7135.2.S42
7135.2.O48 Olympics
7135.2.P4 Peasants
7135.2.P6 Poland
7135.2.P62 Poland. Wojska Lotnicze
7135.2.R8 Russia
7135.2.R83 Russian Revolution, 1917-1921
7135.2.S37 Satire
7135.2.S42 Sea. Ocean
7135.2.S47 Siberia
7135.2.S52 Slavs
7135.2.S65 Sports
7135.2.T38 Tatra Mountains
7135.2.W3 Warsaw
7135.2.W54 Wielkopolska Uprising, 1918-1919
7135.2.W55 Wielkopolska Uprisings, 1846-1848
7135.2.W65 Women
7135.2.W67 World War II

Poetry
7136.A2 General
7136.A25A-.A25Z Special classes of authors, A-Z
7136.A25C45 Children
7136.A25P74 Prisoners
7136.A25W64 Women
By period
7136.A3-Z Early to 1500
Cf. PG6721.A7+ Old Polish texts
7137.A2 16th-18th centuries
7137.A5-Z 19th-20th centuries
7138 21st century
Special forms or topics
7139 Ballads
For folk songs see PG7125+
7139.3 Epic

Polish
Literature
Collections
Poetry
Special forms or topics -- Continued

(7140) Other forms
see PG7141

7141.A-Z Other forms or topics, A-Z
7141.A53 Anders, Władysław, 1892-1970
7141.A87 Auschwitz (Concentration camp)
7141.B38 Bawdy poetry
7141.B86 Broniewski, Władysław, 1897-1962
7141.C48 Children's poetry
7141.C49 Christian poetry
7141.C59 Conrad, Joseph, 1857-1924
7141.C6 Copernicus, Nicolaus, 1473-1543
7141.C64 Cossack-Polish War, 1648-1657
7141.D74 Drinking customs
7141.E64 Epigrams
7141.E76 Erotic poetry
7141.E95 Experimental poetry
7141.H34 Haiku
7141.H59 Historical poetry
7141.J63 John Paul II, Pope, 1920-
7141.K63 Kochanowski, Jan, 1530-1584
7141.K72 Kraków (Poland)
7141.K86 Kunegunda, Queen, consort of Bolesław V, 1234-1292
7141.L3 Labor. Working class
7141.L6 Love poetry
7141.M35 Mary, Blessed Virgin, Saint
7141.M38 Masovia
7141.M67 Morskie Oko
7141.M68 Mothers
7141.M69 Motion pictures
7141.N57 Nisko (Poland)
7141.N67 Norwid, Cyprian, 1821-1883
7141.O86 Our Lady of Vilnius (Icon)
7141.P28 Parachute troops
7141.P29 Pastoral poetry
7141.P3 Patriotic poetry
7141.P64 Poland
7141.P67 Political poetry
7141.R4 Religious poetry
7141.R45 Revolutionary poetry
7141.S3 Satire
7141.S4 Sea. Ocean

Polish
Literature
Collections
Poetry
Special forms or topics
Other forms or topics, A-Z -- Continued
7141.S43 Seasons
7141.S6 Soldiers
7141.S62 Songs
7141.S64 Soviet Union
7141.S86 Suwałki Region
7141.S96 Szymanowski, Karol, 1882-1937
7141.T38 Tatra Mountains
7141.V54 Vilnius (Lithuania)
7141.W26 War poetry
7141.W29 Wars of 1918-1921
7141.W3 Warsaw
7141.W32 Warsaw Uprising, 1944
7141.W45 Wielkopolska (Poland)
7141.W57 Women
7141.W6 World War II
Working class see PG7141.L3
7141.W76 Wrocław (Poland)
7141.Z43 Żeleński, Tadeusz, 1874-1941
Drama
7141.5 General works
By period
7142 Early through 1800
7143 19th-20th centuries
7143.5 21st century
7144.A-Z Special types or topics, A-Z
7144.C54 Children's plays
7144.C55 Christian drama
7144.C56 Christmas plays
7144.C6 Comedy
7144.J47 Jesuit drama
7144.P38 Pastoral drama
7144.T72 Tragedy
Prose
7145 General prose collections
By period
Early to 1500 see PG6721.A7+
7146 16th-18th centuries
7147 19th-20th centuries
7147.5 21st century
7148.A-Z Special. By form or subject, A-Z
7148.A36 AIDS (Disease)

Polish
Literature
Collections
Prose
Special. By form or subject, A-Z -- Continued

7148.A76 Apocryphal literature
7148.C47 Christmas
7148.C65 Concentration camps
7148.C75 Crime
7148.D48 Detective and mystery stories
7148.F35 Fantastic fiction
7148.F87 Future
7148.J48 Jews
7148.M47 Metaphysics
7148.P73 Prayer
7148.S35 Science. Science fiction
7148.W65 Women

Fiction
7149 General collections
7150 Short stories
Special. By form or subject see PG7148.A+
7153 Oratory
7153.3 Diaries
7153.5 Letters
7154 Essays
7155 Wit and humor
7156 Miscellany

Individual authors and works
Early through 1800
7157.A1A-.A1Z Anonymous. By title, A-Z
7157.A1B64 Bogurodzica
7157.A1O34 Obleżenie Jasnej Góry Częstochowskiej
7157.A1P65 Postepek prawa czartowskiego przeciw narodowi ludzkiemu
7157.A1R68 Rozmowa mistrza Polikarpa ze śmiercią
7157.A1S75 Straszliwe widzenie Piotra Pęgowskiego
7157.A2A-.A2Z Early through 1500, A-Z
7157.A5-Z 16th-18th centuries, A-Z
Subarrange individual authors by Table P-PZ44 unless otherwise specified
7157.B24-.B242 Baka, Józef, 1707-1780 (Table P-PZ44)
7157.B45-.B452 Benisławska, Konstancja, 1747-1806 (Table P-PZ44)
7157.B54-.B542 Bielawski, Tomasz (Table P-PZ44)
7157.B55-.B552 Biernat, z Lublina, ca. 1465-ca. 1529 (Table P-PZ44)
7157.B58-.B582 Bogusławski, Wojciech, 1757-1829 (Table P-PZ44)
7157.B6-.B62 Bohomolec, Franciszek, 1720-1784 (Table P-PZ44)
7157.B63-.B632 Bolesławiusz, Klemens, 1625-1689 (Table P-PZ44)

PG

Polish
Literature
Individual authors and works
Early through 1800
16th-18th centuries, A-Z -- Continued

7157.C55-.C552 Chmielowski, Joachim Benedykt, 1700-1763 (Table P-PZ44)
7157.C57-.C572 Chrościński, Wojciech Stanislaw, ca. 1660-1717 (Table P-PZ44)
7157.D78-.D782 Drużbacka, Elżbieta, 1698 or 9-1765 (Table P-PZ44)
7157.G36-.G362 Gawiński, Jan, ca. 1622-ca. 1684 (Table P-PZ44)
7157.G5-.G52 Głuchowski, Jan, 16th cent. (Table P-PZ44)
7157.G6-.G62 Górnicki, Łukasz, 1527-1603 (Table P-PZ44)
7157.G65-.G652 Gosławski, Stanisław, 16th cent. (Table P-PZ44)
7157.G7-.G72 Grabowiecki, Sebastian, 1543?-1607 (Table P-PZ44)
7157.G76-.G762 Grochowski, Stanisław, 1540-1612 (Table P-PZ44)
7157.G87-.G872 Gutkowski, Wojciech, 1775-1826 (Table P-PZ44)
7157.J29-.J292 Jarzębski, Adam, ca. 1590-ca. 1649 (Table P-PZ44)
7157.J49-.J492 Jezierski, Franciszek Salezy, 1740-1791 (Table P-PZ44)
7157.J8-.J82 Jurkowski, Jan (Table P-PZ44)
7157.J83-.J832 Jurkowski, Michał, 1682-1758 (Table P-PZ44)
7157.K3-.K32 Karpiński, Franciszek, 1741-1825 (Table P-PZ44)
7157.K54-.K542 Klonowicz, Sebastian Fabian, ca. 1545-1602 (Table P-PZ44)
7157.K58-.K582 Kniaźnin, Franciszek Dionizy, 1750-1807 (Table P-PZ44)
7157.K6-.K612 Kochanowski, Jan, 1530-1584 (Table P-PZ44a)
For Kochanowski's Latin works see PA8540.K6
7157.K613-.K6132 Kochanowski, Mikołaj, 1533-1582 (Table P-PZ44)
7157.K615-.K6152 Kochanowski, Piotr, 1566-1620 (Table P-PZ44)
7157.K63-.K632 Kochowski, Wespazjan, 1633-1700 (Table P-PZ44)
7157.K643-.K6432 Kołłątaj, Hugo, 1750-1812 (Table P-PZ44)
For historical biography and criticism see DK4348.K6
7157.K65-.K652 Korczyński, Adam (Table P-PZ44)
7157.K66-.K662 Krajewski, Michał Dymitr, 1746-1817 (Table P-PZ44)
7157.K7-.K72 Krasicki, Ignacy, 1735-1801 (Table P-PZ44)
7157.K74-.K742 Krasiński, Gabriel, ca. 1620-1674 (Table P-PZ44)
7157.K82-.K822 Kunicki, Wacław, 16th/17th cent. (Table P-PZ44)
7157.K85-.K852 Kwiatkowski, Marcin, 16th cent. (Table P-PZ44)
7157.L34-.L342 Lacki, Aleksander Teodor, ca. 1614-ca. 1683 (Table P-PZ44)
7157.L44-.L442 Leszczyński, Samuel, 1637-1676 (Table P-PZ44)
7157.L77-.L772 Lubelczyk, Jakub, 16th cent. (Table P-PZ44)
7157.L8-.L82 Lubomirski, Stanisław Herakliusz, 1642-1702 (Table P-PZ44)

Polish
Literature
Individual authors and works
Early through 1800
16th-18th centuries, A-Z -- Continued

7157.M5-.M52 Miaskowski, Kasper, ca. 1549-1622 (Table P-PZ44)
7157.M53-.M532 Mier, Wojciech, 1759-1831 (Table P-PZ44)
7157.M57-.M572 Morsztyn, Hieronim, 1581-ca. 1623 (Table P-PZ44)
7157.M58-.M582 Morsztyn, Jan Andrzej, 1613?-1693 (Table P-PZ44)
7157.M6-.M62 Morsztyn, Zbigniew, ca. 1628-1689 (Table P-PZ44)
7157.M87-.M872 Murzynowski, Stanisław, ca. 1528-1553 (Table P-PZ44)
7157.N25-.N252 Naborowski, Daniel, 1573-1640 (Table P-PZ44)
7157.N3-.N32 Naruszewicz, Adam, 1733-1796 (Table P-PZ44)
7157.O67-.O672 Opaliński, Krzysztof, 1610?-1655 or 6 (Table P-PZ44)
7157.O85-.O852 Otwinowski, Erazm, ca. 1526-1614 (Table P-PZ44)
7157.P26-.P262 Paprocki, Bartosz, 1540?-1614 (Table P-PZ44)
7157.P47-.P472 Pisarzowski, Adam Jacek, ca. 1658-1696 (Table P-PZ44)
7157.P58-.P582 Potocki, Stanisław Kostka, 1755-1821 (Table P-PZ44)
7157.P6-.P62 Potocki, Wacław, 1621-1696 (Table P-PZ44)
7157.P76-.P762 Protasowicz, Jan, fl. ca. 1600 (Table P-PZ44)
7157.R3-.R32 Radziwiłłowa, Franciszka Urszula, księżna, 1705-1753 (Table P-PZ44)
7157.R4-.R42 Rej, Mikołaj, 1505-1569 (Table P-PZ44)
7157.R65-.R652 Roździeński, Walenty, ca. 1560-ca. 1622 (Table P-PZ44)
7157.R67-.R672 Rożniatowski, Abraham, d. 1665 (Table P-PZ44)
7157.R83-.R832 Rudnicki, Dominik, 1676-1739 (Table P-PZ44)
7157.R9-.R92 Rzewuski, Wacław, 1706-1779 (Table P-PZ44)
7157.S53-.S532 Skarga, Piotr, 1536-1612 (Table P-PZ44)
7157.S73-.S732 Stanisławska, Anna, ca. 1651-1700 or 1 (Table P-PZ44)
7157.S743-.S7432 Starzeński, Melchior, ca. 1722-ca. 1788 (Table P-PZ44)
7157.S76-.S762 Strumieński, Olbrycht, fl. 1555-1600 (Table P-PZ44)
7157.S77-.S772 Stryjkowski, Maciej, 1547-ca. 1582 (Table P-PZ44)
7157.S9-.S92 Szarzyński Sęp, Mikołaj, 1550?-1581 (Table P-PZ44)
7157.S95-.S952 Szymonowicz, Szymon, 1558-1629 (Table P-PZ44)
For Szymonowicz's Latin works see PA8585.S95
7157.T7-.T72 Trembecki, Stanisław, ca. 1733-1812 (Table P-PZ44)
7157.T88-.T882 Twardowski, Kasper, ca. 1593-1641 (Table P-PZ44)
7157.T9-.T92 Twardowski, Samuel, ca. 1600-1660 (Table P-PZ44)
7157.W33-.W332 Węgierski, Kajetan, 1756-1787 (Table P-PZ44)
7157.W38-.W382 Wereszczyński, Józef, Bishop of Kiev, ca. 1530-ca. 1599 (Table P-PZ44)

Polish
Literature
Individual authors and works
Early through 1800
16th-18th centuries, A-Z -- Continued

7157.W48-.W482 Wieszczycki, Adrian (Table P-PZ44)
7157.Z16-.Z162 Zabłocki, Franciszek, 1752-1821 (Table P-PZ44)
7157.Z35-.Z352 Załuski, Józef Jędrzej, 1701 or 2-1774 (Table P-PZ44)
7157.Z55-.Z552 Zimorowic, Bartłomiej, 1597-1677 (Table P-PZ44)
7157.Z65-.Z652 Żółkiewski, Stanisław, 1547?-1620 (Table P-PZ44)
For general works on Żółkiewski see DK4302.Z6
7158.A-Z 1801-1960, A-Z
Subarrange individual authors by Table P-PZ44 unless otherwise specified
e. g.
7158.A1A-.A1Z Anonymous works. By title, A-Z
7158.A9-.A92 Asnyk, Adam, 1838-1897 (Table P-PZ44)
7158.B326-.B3262 Bałucki, Michał, 1837-1901 (Table P-PZ44)
7158.B386-.B3862 Bełcikowski, Adam, 1839-1909 (Table P-PZ44)
7158.B39-.B392 Bełza, Władysław, 1847-1913 (Table P-PZ44)
7158.B4-.B42 Berent, Wacław, 1873-1940 (Table P-PZ44)
7158.B444-.B4442 Berwiński, Ryszard, 1819-1879 (Table P-PZ44)
7158.B56-.B562 Bliziński, Józef, 1827-1893 (Table P-PZ44)
7158.B594-.B5942 Bonczyk, Norbert, 1837-1893 (Table P-PZ44)
7158.B614-.B6142 Borowy, Piotr, 1858-1932 (Table P-PZ44)
7158.B73-.B732 Brodziński, Kazimierz, 1791-1835 (Table P-PZ44)
7158.B775-.B7752 Brzechwa, Jan, 1898- (Table P-PZ44)
7158.C39-.C392 Chodźko, Ignacy, 1794-1861 (Table P-PZ44)
7158.C75-.C752 Czajkowski, Michał, 1804-1896 (Table P-PZ44)
7158.C8214-.C82142 Czartoryski, Adam Jerzy, książę, 1770-1861 (Table P-PZ44)
Cf. DK4355.C9 Polish history
7158.C823-.C8232 Czeczot, Jan, 1796-1847 (Table P-PZ44)
7158.C9-.C92 Czyński, Jan, 1801-1867 (Table P-PZ44)
Dołęga-Mostowicz, Tadeusz see PG7158.M6+
7158.D9-.D912 Dygasiński, Adolf, 1839-1902 (Table P-PZ44a)
7158.D95-.D952 Dziekoński, Józef Bohdan, 1816-1855 (Table P-PZ44)
Dziryt, Jan, 1856-1929 see PG7158.P68+
Eiger, Stefan Marek, 1899-1940 see PG7158.N35+
7158.F27-.F272 Faleński, Felicjan, 1825-1910 (Table P-PZ44)
7158.F353-.F3532 Feliński, Alojzy, 1771-1820 (Table P-PZ44)
7158.F42-.F4212 Ficowski, Jerzy (Table P-PZ44a)
7158.F7-.F72 Fredro, Aleksander, hrabia, 1793-1876 (Table P-PZ44)
Gabryella, 1819-1876 see PG7158.Z58+
7158.G3-.G32 Gałecki, Tadeusz, 1871?-1937 (Table P-PZ44)
7158.G36-.G362 Garczyński, Stefan, 1805-1833 (Table P-PZ44)

Polish
Literature
Individual authors and works
1801-1960, A-Z -- Continued

7158.G373-.G3732	Gąsiorowski, Wacław, 1869-1939 (Table P-PZ44)
7158.G375-.G3752	Gaszyński, Konstanty, 1808-1866 (Table P-PZ44)
7158.G513-.G5132	Giller, Stefan, 1833 or 4-1918 (Table P-PZ44)
7158.G55-.G552	Gliński, Kazimierz, 1850-1920 (Table P-PZ44)
7158.G57-.G572	Gliszczyński, Artur, 1869-1910 (Table P-PZ44)
7158.G6-.G62	Głowacki, Aleksander, 1847-1912 (Table P-PZ44)
7158.G66-.G662	Goldszmit, Henryk, 1878-1942 (Table P-PZ44) For Goldszmit as an educator see LB775.A+
7158.G67-.G672	Gomulicki, Wiktor Teofil, 1850-1919 (Table P-PZ44)
7158.G677-.G6772	Gorczyczewski, Jan, 1751-1823 (Table P-PZ44)
7158.G69-.G692	Górski, Artur, 1870-1959 (Table P-PZ44)
7158.G693-.G6932	Górski, Konstanty Maria (Table P-PZ44)
7158.G695-.G6952	Gosławski, Maurycy, 1802-1834 (Table P-PZ44)
7158.G7-.G712	Goszczyński, Seweryn, 1801-1876 (Table P-PZ44a)
7158.G7283-.G72832	Grabowski, Bronisław, 1841-1900 (Table P-PZ44)
7158.G7285-.G72852	Grabowski, Tadeusz, 1871-1960 (Table P-PZ44)
7158.G8-.G82	Gruszecki, Artur, 1853-1929 (Table P-PZ44)
7158.G846-.G8462	Guldenstern (Table P-PZ44)
7158.H27-.H272	Hâjdeu, Tadeu, 1769-1835 (Table P-PZ44)
	Halina, 1856-1929 see PG7158.P68+
7158.H45-.H452	Hertz, Benedykt, 1872-1952 (Table P-PZ44)
7158.H6-.H62	Hofmanowa, Klementyna (Tańska), 1798-1845 (Table P-PZ44)
7158.I7-.I72	Irzykowski, Karol, 1873-1944 (Table P-PZ44)
7158.J217-.J2172	Jabłonowski, Ludwik Grzymała, 1810-1887 (Table P-PZ44)
7158.J23-.J232	Jachowicz, Stanisław, 1796-1857 (Table P-PZ44)
7158.J32-.J322	Jasieńczyk, Janusz (Table P-PZ44)
7158.J35-.J352	Jasieński, Bruno, 1901-1939 (Table P-PZ44) For Jasieński's Russian works see PG3476.J3
7158.J357-.J3572	Jaxa-Ronikier, Bogdan, 1873-1956 (Table P-PZ44)
7158.J49-.J492	Jeż, Teodor Tomasz, 1824-1915 (Table P-PZ44)
7158.K24-.K242	Kajka, Michał, 1858-1940 (Table P-PZ44)
7158.K245-.K2452	Kajsiewicz, Hieronim, 1812-1873 (Table P-PZ44)
7158.K3-.K32	Kasprowicz, Jan, 1860-1926 (Table P-PZ44)
7158.K57-.K572	Kondratowicz, Ludwik, 1823-1862 (Table P-PZ44)
7158.K6-.K62	Konopnicka, Maria, 1842-1910 (Table P-PZ44)
	Korczak, Janusz, 1878-1942 see PG7158.G66+
7158.K652-.K6522	Korzeniowski, Józef, 1797-1863 (Table P-PZ44)
7158.K6527-.K65272	Kosiakiewicz, Wincenty, 1860-1918 (Table P-PZ44)
7158.K65428-.K654282	Koźmian, Kajetan, 1771-1856 (Table P-PZ44)
7158.K7-.K72	Krasiński, Zygmunt, 1812-1859 (Table P-PZ44)

PG

Polish
Literature
Individual authors and works
1801-1960, A-Z -- Continued

7158.K75-.K752 Kraszewski, Józef Ignacy, 1812-1887 (Table P-PZ44)
7158.K76-.K762 Kraszewski, Kajetan, 1827-1896 (Table P-PZ44)
7158.K775-.K7752 Krïukovskoĭ, A. (Arkadiĭ) (Table P-PZ44)
For Krïukovskoĭ's Russian works see PG3467.K744
7158.K7783-.K77832 Krysińska, Marie, 1857-1908 (Table P-PZ44)
7158.K7788-.K77882 Krzeptowski Biały, Stanisław, 1860-1932 (Table P-PZ44)
7158.K834-.K8342 Kulikowska, Marcelina, 1872-1910 (Table P-PZ44)
7158.L23-.L232 Łada-Zabłocki, Tadeusz, 1813-1847 (Table P-PZ44)
7158.L24-.L242 Lam, Jan (Table P-PZ44)
7158.L25-.L252 Lange, Antoni, 1861-1929 (Table P-PZ44)
Lechoń, Jan, 1899-1956 see PG7158.S36+
7158.L394-.L3942 Lemański, Jan, 1866-1933 (Table P-PZ44)
7158.L4-.L42 Lenartowicz, Teofil, 1822-1893 (Table P-PZ44)
Lesman, Jan, 1898- see PG7158.B775+
7158.L5-.L512 Liebert, Jerzy, 1905-1931 (Table P-PZ44a)
7158.L65-.L652 Łoziński, Walery, 1837-1861 (Table P-PZ44)
7158.M15-.M152 Maciejowski, Ignacy, 1835-1901 (Table P-PZ44)
7158.M175-.M1752 Magnuszewski, Dominik (Table P-PZ44)
7158.M3-.M312 Malczewski, Antoni, 1793-1826 (Table P-PZ44a)
7158.M39-.M392 Mediceus, A. (Table P-PZ44)
7158.M48-.M482 Miciński, Tadeusz, 1873-1918 (Table P-PZ44)
Mickiewicz, Adam, 1798-1855
Collected works
7158.M5 By date
7158.M5A11-.A13 By editor, if given
7158.M5A15 Collected fiction. By date
7158.M5A16 Collected essays. By date
7158.M5A17 Collected poems. By date
Translations (Collected or selected)
7158.M5A2-.M5A29 English. By translator, if given, or date
7158.M5A3-.M5A39 French. By translator, if given, or date
7158.M5A4-.M5A49 German. By translator, if given, or date
7158.M5A5-.M5A59 Other. By language
7158.M5A6 Selections. By date
7158.M5A61-.M5Z95 Separate works. By title
Biography and criticism
7158.M51A1-.M51A19 Periodicals. Societies. Serials
7158.M51A2 Dictionaries, indexes, etc. By date
7158.M51A31-.M51A39 Autobiography, journals, memoirs. By title
7158.M51A4 Letters (Collections). By date

Polish
Literature
Individual authors and works
1801-1960, A-Z
Mickiewicz, Adam, 1798-1855
Biography and criticism -- Continued

7158.M51A41-.M51A49 Letters to and from particular individuals. By correspondent (alphabetically)
7158.M51A5-.M51Z General works
7158.M55-.M552 Miłkowski, Zygmunt, 1824-1915 (Table P-PZ44)
7158.M56-.M562 Mniszek, Helena, 1878-1943 (Table P-PZ44)
7158.M574-.M5742 Morawska, Zuzanna, 1848-1922 (Table P-PZ44)
7158.M576-.M5762 Morawski, Stanisław, 1802-1853 (Table P-PZ44)
7158.M578-.M5782 Morgenbesser, Aleksander, 1816-1893 (Table P-PZ44)
7158.M6-.M62 Mostowicz, Tadeusz Dołęga (Table P-PZ44)
7158.N35-.N352 Napierski, Stefan, 1899-1940 (Table P-PZ44)
7158.N5-.N512 Niemcewicz, Julian Ursyn, 1758-1841 (Table P-PZ44a)
7158.N517-.N5172 Nienacki, Zbignew (Table P-PZ44)
7158.N57-.N572 Norwid, Cyprian, 1821-1883 (Table P-PZ44)
Nowicki, Zbignew Tomasz see PG7158.N517+
7158.N6-.N612 Nowaczyński, Adolf, 1876-1944 (Table P-PZ44a)
7158.O3-.O32 Odyniec, Antoni Edward, 1804-1885 (Table P-PZ44)
7158.O68-.O682 Orkan, Władysław (Table P-PZ44)
7158.O7-.O72 Orzeszkowa, Eliza, 1842-1910 (Table P-PZ44)
7158.P458-.P4582 Pisarz Poematu Rolnictwo, 1749-1825 (Table P-PZ44)
7158.P55-.P552 Pol, Wincenty, 1807-1872 (Table P-PZ44)
Poray-Biernacki, Janusz, 1907- see PG7158.J32+
7158.P573-.P5732 Potocka, Anna, 1846-1926 (Table P-PZ44)
Prus, Bolesław, 1847-1912 see PG7158.G6+
Przerwa-Tetmajer, Kazimierz, 1865-1940 see PG7158.T4+
7158.P65-.P652 Przybyszewski, Stanisław, 1868-1925 (Table P-PZ44)
7158.P68-.P682 Przyjemska, Władysława, 1856-1929 (Table P-PZ44)
7158.R375-.R3752 Reklewski, Wincenty (Table P-PZ44)
7158.R4-.R42 Reymont, Władysław Stanisław, 1867-1925 (Table P-PZ44)
7158.R55-.R552 Rodziewiczówna, Maria, 1863-1944 (Table P-PZ44)
7158.R585-.R5852 Romanowski, Mieczysław, 1834-1863 (Table P-PZ44)
7158.R8-.R82 Rydel, Lucjan, 1870-1960 (Table P-PZ44)
7158.R9-.R92 Rzewuski, Henryk, 1791-1866 (Table P-PZ44)
Sadyk Pasza, 1804-1896 see PG7158.C75+
7158.S223-.S2232 Samulowski, Andrzej, 1840-1928 (Table P-PZ44)
7158.S36-.S362 Serafinowicz, Leszek Józef, 1899-1956 (Table P-PZ44)
Sewer, 1835-1901 see PG7158.M15+
7158.S4-.S42 Sienkiewicz, Henryk, 1846-1916 (Table P-PZ44)
7158.S54-.S5412 Sieroszewski, Wacław, 1858-1945 (Table P-PZ44a)

Polish
Literature
Individual authors and works
1801-1960, A-Z -- Continued

7158.S5427-.S54272	Skarbek, Fryderyk Florian, hrabia, 1792-1866 (Table P-PZ44)
7158.S56-.S562	Słoński, Edward, 1872-1926 (Table P-PZ44)
7158.S6-.S62	Słowacki, Juliusz, 1809-1849 (Table P-PZ44)
7158.S667-.S6672	Spitznagel, Ludwik, 1807-1827 (Table P-PZ44)
7158.S669-.S6692	Stabik, Antoni, 1807-1887 (Table P-PZ44)
7158.S67-.S672	Stablewska, Irena, 1864-1939 (Table P-PZ44)
7158.S7158-.S71582	Starzeński, Leopold, 1835-1904 (Table P-PZ44)
7158.S718-.S7182	Stateczny, Franciszek Euzebiusz, 1864-1921 (Table P-PZ44)
	Strug, Andrzej, 1871?-1937 see PG7158.G3+
7158.S7362-.S73622	Strzelnicki, Władysław, ca. 1820-1846 (Table P-PZ44)
7158.S75-.S752	Świętochowski, Aleksander, 1849-1938 (Table P-PZ44)
	Syrokomla, Władysław, 1823-1862 see PG7158.K57+
7158.S775-.S7752	Sygietyński, Antoni (Table P-PZ44)
7158.S776-.S7762	Szajnocha, Karol, 1818-1868 (Table P-PZ44)
7158.S81163-.S811632	Szczepański, Ludwik, 1872-1954 (Table P-PZ44)
7158.S878-.S8782	Sztyrmer, Ludwik, 1809-1886 (Table P-PZ44)
7158.S884-.S8842	Szukiewicz, Maciej (Table P-PZ44)
7158.T4-.T412	Tetmajer, Kazimierz, 1865-1940 (Table P-PZ44a)
7158.T42-.T422	Tetmajer, Włodzimierz, 1862-1923 (Table P-PZ44)
7158.T87-.T872	Tymowski, Kantorbery Tomasz, 1790-1854 (Table P-PZ44)
7158.U4-.U42	Ujejski, Kornel, 1823-1897 (Table P-PZ44)
7158.W4-.W412	Weyssenhoff, Józef, 1860-1932 (Table P-PZ44a)
7158.W4124-.W41242	Wężyk, Franciszek, 1785-1862 (Table P-PZ44)
	Wiech, 1896- see PG7158.W415+
7158.W415-.W4152	Wiechecki, Stefan, 1896- (Table P-PZ44)
7158.W473-.W4732	Wirtemberska, Maria, księżna, 1768-1854 (Table P-PZ44)
7158.W5-.W512	Witkiewicz, Stanisław, 1851-1915 (Table P-PZ44a)
7158.W576-.W5762	Witwicki, Stefan, 1801-1847 (Table P-PZ44)
7158.W59-.W592	Wójcicki, Kazimierz Władysław, 1807-1879 (Table P-PZ44)
7158.W688-.W6882	Wolska, Maryla, 1873-1930 (Table P-PZ44)
7158.W7144-.W71442	Woronicz, Jan Paweł, 1757-1829 (Table P-PZ44)
7158.W8-.W82	Wyspiański, Stanisław, 1869-1907 (Table P-PZ44)
7158.Z33-.Z332	Zalewski, Kazimierz, 1849-1919 (Table P-PZ44)
7158.Z35-.Z352	Zapolska, Gabriela, 1857-1921 (Table P-PZ44)
7158.Z376-.Z3762	Zaruski, Mariusz, 1867-1943 (Table P-PZ44)

Polish
Literature
Individual authors and works
1801-1960, A-Z -- Continued
7158.Z396-.Z3962 Żeleński, Tadeusz, 1874-1941 (Table P-PZ44)
7158.Z4-.Z42 Żeromski, Stefan, 1864-1925 (Table P-PZ44)
7158.Z58-.Z582 Żmichowska, Narcyza, 1819-1876 (Table P-PZ44)
7158.Z8-.Z82 Żuławski, Jerzy, 1874-1915 (Table P-PZ44)
Zysman, Wiktor B., 1901-1939 see PG7158.J35+
1961-2000
Here are usually to be classified authors beginning to publish about 1950, flourishing after 1960.
7159 Anonymous works (Table P-PZ28)
7160 A
The author number is determined by the second letter of the name
Subarrange each author by Table P-PZ40 unless otherwise indicated
7161 B
The author number is determined by the second letter of the name
Subarrange each author by Table P-PZ40 unless otherwise indicated
Baldhead, Valdemar, 1944- see PG7171.Y86
7162 C
The author number is determined by the second letter of the name
Subarrange each author by Table P-PZ40 unless otherwise indicated
7163 D
The author number is determined by the second letter of the name
Subarrange each author by Table P-PZ40 unless otherwise indicated
7164 E
The author number is determined by the second letter of the name
Subarrange each author by Table P-PZ40 unless otherwise indicated
7165 F
The author number is determined by the second letter of the name
Subarrange each author by Table P-PZ40 unless otherwise indicated

Polish
Literature
Individual authors and works
1961-2000 -- Continued

7166 G

The author number is determined by the second letter of the name

Subarrange each author by Table P-PZ40 unless otherwise indicated

7167 H

The author number is determined by the second letter of the name

Subarrange each author by Table P-PZ40 unless otherwise indicated

7168 I

The author number is determined by the second letter of the name

Subarrange each author by Table P-PZ40 unless otherwise indicated

7169 J

The author number is determined by the second letter of the name

Subarrange each author by Table P-PZ40 unless otherwise indicated

7170 K

The author number is determined by the second letter of the name

Subarrange each author by Table P-PZ40 unless otherwise indicated

7171 L

The author number is determined by the second letter of the name

Subarrange each author by Table P-PZ40 unless otherwise indicated

7171.Y86 Łysiak, Waldemar, 1944- (Table P-PZ40)

7172 M

The author number is determined by the second letter of the name

Subarrange each author by Table P-PZ40 unless otherwise indicated

7173 N

The author number is determined by the second letter of the name

Subarrange each author by Table P-PZ40 unless otherwise indicated

Polish
Literature
Individual authors and works
1961-2000 -- Continued

7174 O
The author number is determined by the second letter of the name
Subarrange each author by Table P-PZ40 unless otherwise indicated

7175 P
The author number is determined by the second letter of the name
Subarrange each author by Table P-PZ40 unless otherwise indicated

7175.I39 Piepka, Jan, 1926-2001 (Table P-PZ40)
For Piepka's Kashubian works see PG7904.P54

7176 Q
The author number is determined by the second letter of the name
Subarrange each author by Table P-PZ40 unless otherwise indicated

7177 R
The author number is determined by the second letter of the name
Subarrange each author by Table P-PZ40 unless otherwise indicated

7178 S
The author number is determined by the second letter of the name
Subarrange each author by Table P-PZ40 unless otherwise indicated

Staszków Jan, 1926-2001 see PG7175.I39

7179 T
The author number is determined by the second letter of the name
Subarrange each author by Table P-PZ40 unless otherwise indicated

7180 U
The author number is determined by the second letter of the name
Subarrange each author by Table P-PZ40 unless otherwise indicated

7181 V
The author number is determined by the second letter of the name
Subarrange each author by Table P-PZ40 unless otherwise indicated

Polish
Literature
Individual authors and works
1961-2000 -- Continued

7182 W
The author number is determined by the second letter of the name
Subarrange each author by Table P-PZ40 unless otherwise indicated

7183 X
The author number is determined by the second letter of the name
Subarrange each author by Table P-PZ40 unless otherwise indicated

7184 Y
The author number is determined by the second letter of the name
Subarrange each author by Table P-PZ40 unless otherwise indicated

7185 Z
The author number is determined by the second letter of the name
Subarrange each author by Table P-PZ40 unless otherwise indicated

2001-

7200 Anonymous works (Table P-PZ28)

7201 A
The author number is determined by the second letter of the name
Subarrange each author by Table P-PZ40

7202 B
The author number is determined by the second letter of the name
Subarrange each author by Table P-PZ40

7203 C
The author number is determined by the second letter of the name
Subarrange each author by Table P-PZ40

7204 D
The author number is determined by the second letter of the name
Subarrange each author by Table P-PZ40

7205 E
The author number is determined by the second letter of the name
Subarrange each author by Table P-PZ40

Polish
Literature
Individual authors and works
2001- -- Continued

7206 F
The author number is determined by the second letter of the name
Subarrange each author by Table P-PZ40

7207 G
The author number is determined by the second letter of the name
Subarrange each author by Table P-PZ40

7208 H
The author number is determined by the second letter of the name
Subarrange each author by Table P-PZ40

7209 I
The author number is determined by the second letter of the name
Subarrange each author by Table P-PZ40

7210 J
The author number is determined by the second letter of the name
Subarrange each author by Table P-PZ40

7211 K
The author number is determined by the second letter of the name
Subarrange each author by Table P-PZ40

7212 L
The author number is determined by the second letter of the name
Subarrange each author by Table P-PZ40

7213 M
The author number is determined by the second letter of the name
Subarrange each author by Table P-PZ40

7214 N
The author number is determined by the second letter of the name
Subarrange each author by Table P-PZ40

7215 O
The author number is determined by the second letter of the name
Subarrange each author by Table P-PZ40

Polish
Literature
Individual authors and works
2001- -- Continued

7216 P
The author number is determined by the second letter of the name
Subarrange each author by Table P-PZ40

7217 Q
The author number is determined by the second letter of the name
Subarrange each author by Table P-PZ40

7218 R
The author number is determined by the second letter of the name
Subarrange each author by Table P-PZ40

7219 S
The author number is determined by the second letter of the name
Subarrange each author by Table P-PZ40

7220 T
The author number is determined by the second letter of the name
Subarrange each author by Table P-PZ40

7221 U
The author number is determined by the second letter of the name
Subarrange each author by Table P-PZ40

7222 V
The author number is determined by the second letter of the name
Subarrange each author by Table P-PZ40

7223 W
The author number is determined by the second letter of the name
Subarrange each author by Table P-PZ40

7224 X
The author number is determined by the second letter of the name
Subarrange each author by Table P-PZ40

7225 Y
The author number is determined by the second letter of the name
Subarrange each author by Table P-PZ40

Polish
Literature
Individual authors and works
2001- -- Continued
7226 Z
The author number is determined by the second letter of the name
Subarrange each author by Table P-PZ40
Local
For works, biography, and criticism of individual local authors, except North American see PG7157+
By region, province, county, etc.
Including regions, formerly provinces of Russia, Austria, and Prussia, respectively, e.g. Posen; Galicia
7362.A-Z History. By region, province, etc., A-Z
7364.A-Z Collections. By region, province, etc., A-Z
7365.A-Z By city, A-Z
Outside Poland
General
7367 History
7368 Collections
7369 Austria. Hungary
7371 Germany
7375.A-Z Other, A-Z
America
7380-7399 United States. Canada (Table P-PZ23)
7399.A-Z Individual authors or work, A-Z
Subarrange individual authors by Table P-PZ40
Subarrange individual works by Table P-PZ43
Chełchowski, T. (Telesfor), 1883-1917 see PG7399.S85
7399.S85 Szczypawka, 1883-1917 (Table P-PZ40)
7401 Spanish America
7405 Brazil
7445-7446 Translations from Polish into foreign languages (Table P-PZ30)
For individual authors see PG7157+
Lechitic languages and dialects
Except Polish
Cf. PG471+ Western Slavic (General)
7900 General
7901-7904 Kashubian (Table P-PZ11 modified)
Literature
7904.A3-.Z5 Individual authors or works, A-Z
Subarrange individual authors by Table P-PZ40
Subarrange individual works by Table P-PZ43
7904.B83 Budzisz, Alojzy, 1874-1934 (Table P-PZ40)

Lechitic languages and dialects
Kashubian
Literature
Individual authors or works, A-Z -- Continued
7904.D47 Derdowski, Hieronim, 1852-1902 (Table P-PZ40)
7904.P54 Piepka, Jan, 1926-2001 (Table P-PZ40)
For Piepka's Polish works see PG7175.I39
Staszków Jan, 1926-2001 see PG7904.P54
7911-7915 Polabian (Table P-PZ9)
7921-7925 Slovincian (Table P-PZ9)
Baltic philology and languages
8001-8099 Baltic languages (General) (Table P-PZ4)
Baltic literature (General)
History
8101 General works
8102 Poetry
8103 Drama
8104 Other
Collections
8105 General
8106 Poetry
8107 Drama
8108 Other
8111-8112 Translations (Table P-PZ30)
Old Prussian
8201 Collections
8202 General works
8204 Grammar
8205 Etymology
8206 Dictionaries
8208 Texts
Lithuanian
8501-8523 Philology (Table P-PZ3a modified)
History of philology
Cf. PG8525 History of the language
8515 General works
Biography, memoirs, etc.
8517.A2 Collective
8517.A5-Z Individual, A-Z
Subarrange each by Table P-PZ50
8524-8693 Language (Table P-PZ3b modified)
Add number in table to PG8500
Grammar
8531 General works
8533 Historical grammar
Style. Composition. Rhetoric
For study and teaching see PG8519+

Baltic philology and languages
Lithuanian
Language
Style. Composition. Rhetoric -- Continued
8635 General works
Etymology
8663 Dictionaries (exclusively etymological)
8674 Lexicography
For biography of lexicographers see PG8517.A2+
Dictionaries
Lithuanian only
8675 General
8676 Picture dictionaries
8677 Supplementary dictionaries. Dictionaries of new words
8678 Polyglot (three or more languages)
Cf. PG2635 Russian first
8679 Lithuanian-English; English-Lithuanian
8681.A-Z Lithuanian-French [-German, etc]; French [German, etc.]-Lithuanian, A-Z
8682.A-Z Lithuanian-Slavic (Czech, Polish, Russian, etc.), A-Z
Lithuanian-Oriental
see subclasses PJ-PL
Dictionaries exclusively etymological see PG8663
8683 Dictionaries of names
Cf. CS2300+ Genealogy
Rhyming dictionaries
see PG8658
8684 Special. Technical, etc.
8685 Other special lists
Including glossaries, dictionaries of terms and phrases, word frequency lists, reverse indexes, and lists of abbreviations
Linguistic geography. Dialects, etc.
8687 Linguistic geography
Dialects. Provincialisms, etc.
8688 Treatises. Monographs. Studies
8689 Grammar
8691 Dictionaries
(8692) Atlases. Maps
see class G
8693.A-Z Special, by region, A-Z
Literature
Biography of critics, historians, etc.
8700 Collective
8700.2.A-Z Individual, A-Z
Subarrange each by Table P-PZ50

PG

Baltic philology and languages
Lithuanian
Literature -- Continued
History

8701	Periodicals. Societies. Collections
8703	Treatises
(8709)	Special subjects see PG8710
8710.A-8710.Z	Special topics, A-Z
8710.M68	Mothers
8711	Biography (Collective)
	By period
8711.3	Early to 1800
8711.4	19th century
8711.5	20th century
8711.6	21st century
8712	Poetry
8712.2	Drama
8712.3	Other
	Collections
8713	General and miscellaneous
8713.5.A-Z	By subject, A-Z
8713.5.P38	Patriotic literature
8713.5.R45	Religious literature
8715	Poetry. Folk-songs
8717	Drama
8719	Prose. Tales, etc.
	Individual authors
8721.A-Z	To 1960, A-Z Subarrange each author by Table P-PZ40 unless otherwise specified e. g.
8721.B3	Baltrušaitis, Jurgis, 1873-1944 (Table P-PZ40)
8721.B325	Baranauskas, Antanas, 1835-1902 (Table P-PZ40)
8721.D7	Donelaitis, Kristijonas, 1714-1780 (Table P-PZ40)
8721.G48	Gimžauskas, Silvestras, 1845-1897 (Table P-PZ40)
8721.K8	Kudirka, Vincas, 1858-1899 (Table P-PZ40)
8721.L48	Lindė-Dobilas, Julijonas, 1872-1934 (Table P-PZ40)
8721.M3	Maironis, 1862-1932 (Table P-PZ40)
8721.M364	Mašiotas, Pranas, 1863-1940 (Table P-PZ40)
8721.P4	Pečkauskaitė, Marija, 1877-1930 (Table P-PZ40)
8721.P5	Pietaris, Vincas, 1850-1902 (Table P-PZ40)
	Šatrijos Ragana, 1877-1930 see PG8721.P4
8721.T77	Tumas, Juozas, 1869-1933 (Table P-PZ40)
	Vaižgantas, 1869-1933 see PG8721.T77
	Žemaitė, 1845-1921 see PG8721.Z9

Baltic philology and languages
Lithuanian
Literature
Individual authors
To 1960, A-Z -- Continued
8721.Z9 Žymantienė, Julija Beniuševičiūtė, 1845-1921 (Table P-PZ40)
8722-8722.36 1961-2000 (Table P-PZ29)
8723-8723.36 2001- (Table P-PZ29)
Local
For works, biography, and criticism of individual local authors, except North American see PG8721+
By region, province, county, etc.
8732.A-Z History. By region, province, etc., A-Z
8734.A-Z Collections. By region, province, etc., A-Z
8735.A-Z By city, A-Z
Outside Lithuania
8737 General
8738.A-Z European countries, A-Z
8740-8749 United States and Canada (Table P-PZ24)
8750.A-Z Other, A-Z
8771-8772 Translations from Lithuanian into foreign languages (Table P-PZ30)
Latvian
8801-8823 Philology (Table P-PZ3a modified)
History of philology
Cf. PG8825 History of the language
8815 General works
Biography, memoirs, etc.
8817.A2 Collective
8817.A5-Z Individual, A-Z
Subarrange each by Table P-PZ50
8824-8993 Language (Table P-PZ3b modified)
Add number in table to PG8800
Grammar
8831 General works
8833 Historical grammar
Style. Composition. Rhetoric
For study and teaching see PG8819+
8935 General works
Etymology
8963 Dictionaries (exclusively etymological)
8974 Lexicography
For biography of lexicographers see PG8817.A2+
Dictionaries
Latvian only
8975 General

PG

Baltic philology and languages
Latvian
Language
Dictionaries
Latvian only -- Continued
8976 Picture dictionaries
8977 Supplementary dictionaries. Dictionaries of new words
8978 Polyglot (three or more languages)
Cf. PG2635 Russian first
8979 Latvian-English; English-Latvian
8981.A-Z Latvian-French [-German, etc]; French [German, etc.]-Latvian, A-Z
8982.A-Z Latvian-Slavic (Czech, Polish, Russian, etc.), A-Z
Latvian-Oriental
see subclasses PJ-PL
Dictionaries exclusively etymological see PG8963
8983 Dictionaries of names
Cf. CS2300+ Genealogy
Rhyming dictionaries
see PG8958
8984 Special. Technical, etc.
8985 Other special lists
Including glossaries, dictionaries of terms and phrases, word frequency lists, reverse indexes, and lists of abbreviations
Linguistic geography. Dialects, etc.
8987 Linguistic geography
Dialects. Provincialisms, etc.
8988 Treatises. Monographs. Studies
8989 Grammar
8991 Dictionaries
(8992) Atlases. Maps
see class G
8993.A-Z Special, by region, A-Z
Slang. Argot
8995 General
8996.A-Z Special topics, A-Z
For list of Cutter numbers, see Table P-PZ2 421.A+
8997.A-Z Local, A-Z
Literature
8998 Periodicals. Societies. Serials
8998.15 Congresses
8998.2 Encyclopedias. Dictionaries
8998.3 Study and teaching
Biography of critics, historians, etc.
8998.5 Collective

Baltic philology and languages
Latvian
Literature
Biography of critics, historians, etc. -- Continued
8998.52.A-Z Individual, A-Z
Subarrange each by Table P-PZ50
History
9000 Periodicals. Societies. Serials
9005 General works. Compends
9006 General special
9006.5.A-Z Treatment of special subjects, A-Z
9006.5.M95 Mythology
9007 Biography (Collective)
9007.5.A-Z Special classes of authors, A-Z
9007.5.W65 Women
9007.5.Y68 Youth
By period
9008 Early to 1800
9008.2 19th century
9008.3 20th century
9008.4 21st century
9009 Poetry
Cf. PG9013.5 Folk poetry
9010 Drama
9011 Prose. Fiction
9012 Other
Folk literature
For general works on and collections of folk literature see GR204.5
History and criticism
(9013) General works
9013.5 Folk songs. Folk poetry
Collections of texts
(9014) General
9015 Folk songs
(9017) Prose, tales, etc.
(9019) Translations
9020 Juvenile literature (General)
For special genres see the genre
Collections
9031 General and miscellaneous
9031.5.A-Z By subject, A-Z
9031.5.J64 John the Baptist's Day
9031.5.M67 Mothers
Poetry
Cf. PG9015 Folk songs
9034 General works

Baltic philology and languages
Latvian
Literature
Collections
Poetry -- Continued
By period
9034.4 To 1800
9034.5 19th-20th centuries
9034.6 21st century
9035.A-Z Special. By form or subject, A-Z
9035.C35 Candles
9035.C48 Children's poetry
9035.C518 Christian poetry
9035.C52 Christmas
9035.E74 Epigrams
9035.E77 Erotic poetry
9035.F35 Family
9035.H34 Haiku
9035.L35 Latgale (Latvia)
9035.L37 Latvia
9035.L68 Love poetry
9035.M67 Mothers
9035.P37 Patriotic poetry
9035.R53 Rīga (Latvia)
9035.S34 Schools
9035.W45 Weddings
9035.W56 Winter
9037 Drama
Prose
9038 General collections
By period
9038.4 Early to 1800
9038.5 19th-20th centuries
9038.6 21st century
Fiction
9038.8 General collections
9039 Short stories
9042.A-Z Special. By form or subject, A-Z
9042.H83 Humorous stories
9042.H85 Hunting stories
9045 Other
Individual authors
9048.A-Z To 1960, A-Z
Subarrange each author by Table P-PZ40 unless otherwise specified
e. g.
9048.A63 Alunāns, Adolfs, 1848-1912 (Table P-PZ40)

Baltic philology and languages
Latvian
Literature
Individual authors
To 1960, A-Z -- Continued

	Apsīšu Jēkabs, 1858-1929 see PG9048.J33
	Aspazija, 1868-1943 see PG9048.P47
9048.A86	Auseklis, 1850-1879 (Table P-PZ40)
	Augenbergs, Kārlis, 1869-1923 see PG9048.E818
9048.B37	Barons, Krišjānis, 1835-1923 (Table P-PZ40)
9048.B45	Bērziņš, Ludis, 1870-1965 (Table P-PZ40)
9048.B5	Birznieks-Upītis, E. (Ernsts), 1871-1960 (Table P-PZ40)
9048.B6	Blaumanis, Rūdolfs, 1863-1908 (Table P-PZ40)
9048.B7	Brigadere, Anna, 1861-1933 (Table P-PZ40)
9048.D25	Dagda, Anna, 1915-1996 (Table P-PZ40)
9048.E48	Egle, Kārlis (Table P-PZ40)
9048.E818	Ezerietis, 1869-1923 (Table P-PZ40)
9048.F6	Folmanis, Žanis, 1910- (Table P-PZ40)
	Frīdis-Mīlbergs, Skuju, b. 1887 see PG9048.S59
	Grīva, Žanis, 1910- see PG9048.F6
	Gulbis, Fricis Jānis, 1908-1940 see PG9048.V45
9048.J3	Jaunsudrabiņš, Jānis, 1877-1962 (Table P-PZ40)
9048.J33	Jaunzemis, Jānis, 1858-1929 (Table P-PZ40)
9048.J87	Jūrdžs, Andrivs, 1845-1925 (Table P-PZ40)
9048.K26	Kārkliņš, Jānis, 1891-1975 (Table P-PZ40)
9048.K3	Kaudzīte, Reinis, 1839-1920 (Table P-PZ40)
9048.K44	Ķeniņš, Atis, 1874-1961 (Table P-PZ40)
9048.K486	Ķikuļa, Jēkabs, 1740-1777? (Table P-PZ40)
	Krogzemis, Miķelis, 1850-1879 see PG9048.A86
	Liekna, Jēkabs Eduards, 1883-1940 see PG9048.V54
	Ludbōržs, Jōņs, 1913-1975 see PG9048.M23
9048.M23	Madsolas Jōņs, 1913-1975 (Table P-PZ40)
	Māters, Juris, 1845-1885 see PG9048.M28
9048.M28	Māteru Juris, 1845-1885 (Table P-PZ40)
9048.M47	Michelsons, Arveds, 1886-1961 (Table P-PZ40)
	Mīlbergs, Gotfrīds, b. 1887 see PG9048.S59
9048.N35	Neredzīgais Indriķs, 1783-1828
9048.N4	Niedra, Andrievs, 1871-1942 (Table P-PZ40)
9048.P47	Pliekšāne, Elza Rozenberga, 1868-1943 (Table P-PZ40)
9048.P5	Pliekšāns, Jānis, 1865-1929 (Table P-PZ40)
9048.P7	Poruks, Janis, 1871-1911 (Table P-PZ40)
9048.P9	Pumpurs, Andrejs, 1841-1902 (Table P-PZ40)
9048.P95	Purapuķe, Jānis, 1864-1902 (Table P-PZ40)
	Rainis, Jānis, 1865-1929 see PG9048.P5

Baltic philology and languages
Latvian
Literature
Individual authors
To 1960, A-Z -- Continued

	Rutku tēvs, 1886-1961 see PG9048.M47
9048.S3	Sakse, Anna, 1905- (Table P-PZ40)
9048.S59	Skuju Frīdis, b. 1887 (Table P-PZ40)
9048.S72	Steiks, Jānis, 1855-1932 (Table P-PZ40)
9048.S73	Stenders, Gothard Frīdrichs, 1714-1796 (Table P-PZ40)
	Taube, Olga Veronika, 1915-1996 see PG9048.D25
	Trimda, Jānis, 1908-1940 see PG9048.V45
9048.U7	Upīts, Andrejs, 1877-1970 (Table P-PZ40)
9048.V45	Veldre, Vilis, 1908-1940 (Table P-PZ40)
9048.V54	Virza, Edvarts, 1883-1940 (Table P-PZ40)
9048.Z37	Zeibolts, Jēkabs, 1867-1924 (Table P-PZ40)
9048.Z39	Zeltmatis, 1868-1961 (Table P-PZ40)
9049-9049.36	1961-2000 (Table P-PZ29 modified)
9049.1	A
9049.1.P7	Apsītis, Jānis, 1905- (Table P-PZ40)
	Auziņš, Imants, 1957-1987 see PG9049.19.M33
9049.12	B
9049.12.I7	Birze, Miervaldis (Table P-PZ40)
9049.14	D
	Dikele, Alma, 1914- see PG9049.25.S4
9049.15	E
9049.15.Z4	Ezera, Regīna, 1930- (Table P-PZ40)
9049.19	I
9049.19.M33	Imants, 1959-1987 (Table P-PZ40)
	Indrāne, Ilze, 1927- see PG9049.2.A72
9049.2	J
9049.2.A72	Jātniece, Undina, 1927- (Table P-PZ40)
9049.21	K
9049.21.A52	Kalniņš, Viktors (Table P-PZ40)
	Kuraž Krišs, 1921- see PG9049.36.V395
	Kurbads, Kārlis, 1921- see PG9049.36.V395
9049.22	L
9049.22.A25	Lācis, Ēvalds, 1923-1976 (Table P-PZ40)
9049.25	O
9049.25.S4	Ose, Alīda, 1914- (Table P-PZ40)
9049.29	S
	Sārts, Jānis, 1905- see PG9049.1.P7
9049.29.K84	Skujiņš, Zigmunds, 1926- (Table P-PZ40)
9049.32	V
9049.32.A25	Vācietis, Ojārs (Table P-PZ40)
	Viks see PG9049.21.A52

Baltic philology and languages
Latvian
Literature
Individual authors
1961-2000
V -- Continued
Vilks, Ēvalds, 1923-1976 see PG9049.22.A25
9049.36 Z
9049.36.I4 Ziedonis, Imants, 1933- (Table P-PZ40)
9049.36.V395 Zvejnieks, Kārlis, 1921- (Table P-PZ40)
9050-9050.36 2001- (Table P-PZ29)
9050.14 D
9050.14.Z54 Dzīle, Laimdota, 1925- (Table P-PZ40)
9050.15 E
Eglīte, Mirdza, 1925- see PG9050.14.Z54
9050.15.L57 Eliss (Table P-PZ40)
9050.17 G
9050.17.R38 Grava, Otvars, 1959- (Table P-PZ40)
9050.21 K
Ķlaviņš, Aivars see PG9050.15.L57
9050.29 S
Silnieks, Pāvils, 1959- see PG9050.17.R38
Local
For works, biography, and criticism of individual local authors, except North American see PG9048+
By region, place, etc.
9102.A-Z History. By region, province, etc., A-Z
9104.A-Z Collections. By region, province, etc., A-Z
9105.A-Z By city, A-Z
Outside of Latvia
9108 General works
9109.A-Z European countries, A-Z
9110-9119 United States and Canada (Table P-PZ24)
9120.A-Z Other, A-Z
9145-9146 Translations from Latvian literature into foreign languages (Table P-PZ30)
Albanian philology and languages
9501-9513 Philology (Table P-PZ4a modified)
History of philology
Cf. PG9515 History of the language
9507 General works
Biography, memoirs, etc.
9509.A2 Collective
9509.A5-Z Individual, A-Z
Subarrange each by Table P-PZ50
9514-9586.9 Language (Table P-PZ4b modified)
Add number in table to PG9500

PG

Albanian philology and languages
Language -- Continued
Style. Composition. Rhetoric
For study and teaching see PG9511
9575 General works
Etymology
9583.5 Dictionaries (exclusively etymological)
Lexicography
For biography of lexicographers see PG9509.A2+
9587 General works
Dictionaries
9589 Albanian only
9591 Albanian-English; English-Albanian
9593.A-Z Other. By author, A-Z
9595 Other special lists
For etymological dictionaries see PG9583.5
Linguistic geography. Dialects, etc.
9596.A1 Periodicals. Societies. Serials
9596.A3 Collections of texts. Specimens, etc.
(9596.A4) Atlases. Maps
see class G
9596.A5-Z General works
9597 Dictionaries
9598.A-Z Special dialects. By region, place, dialect group, etc., A-Z
e. g.
9598.G5 Gheg (Latin alphabet)
9598.T7 Tosk (Greek alphabet)
9599 Slang. Argot
Literature
9601 Periodicals. Societies. Serials
9602 Encyclopedias. Dictionaries
9602.2 Study and teaching
Biography of critics, historians, etc.
9602.5 Collective
9602.52.A-Z Individual, A-Z
Subarrange each by Table P-PZ50
History
9603 General works
9603.2 General special
9603.3 Collected essays
9603.4.A-Z Relation to other literatures, A-Z
9604 Biography of authors (Collective)
9604.5.A-Z Special classes of authors, A-Z
9604.5.M86 Muslim
By period
9605 Origins. Through 1800
19th-20th centuries

Albanian philology and languages
Literature
History
By period
19th-20th centuries -- Continued
9606 General works
9606.2.A-Z Special topics, A-Z
9606.2.E54 Enlightenment
9606.2.M64 Modernism
9606.2.P64 Politics and literature
9606.2.R65 Romanticism
9606.2.S6 Socialist realism
9606.4 21st century
Poetry
9607 General works
9607.5.A-Z Special topics, A-Z
9607.5.C47 Children's poetry
9607.5.C55 Classical influences
9607.5.S66 Sonnets
9608 Drama
9609 Other
Folk literature
For general works on and collections of folk literature see GR251
History and criticism
(9610) General
Folk songs. Folk poetry
9610.3 General works
9610.5.A-Z Special forms, A-Z
9610.5.E64 Epic poetry
Collections of texts
(9611) General
9612 Folk songs and poetry. Ballads
Drama see PG9617
Fables, proverbs, riddles, etc. see PN
Tales, legends, etc. see GR251
(9612.5.A-Z) By locality, region, etc., A-Z
(9612.6.A-Z) Translations. By language, A-Z
9612.8 Juvenile literature (General)
For specific genres, see the genre
Collections
9613 General
9613.5.A-Z Special classes of authors, A-Z
9613.5.P49 Physicians
9614.A-Z Special topics, A-Z
9614.P37 Partia e Punës së Shqipërisë

Albanian philology and languages
Literature
Collections
Special topics, A-Z -- Continued
9614.S27 Scanderbeg, 1405?-1468
9614.W65 Women
Poetry
9615 General
9615.5.A-Z Special topics, A-Z
9615.5.M54 Migjeni, 1911-1938
9617 Drama
9619 Other
9621.A-Z Individual authors, A-Z
Subarrange each author by Table P-PZ40 unless otherwise specified
9621.A35 Agolli, Dritëro, 1931- (Table P-PZ40)
Asdren, 1872-1947 see PG9621.D7
9621.B27 Bageri, Josif, 1870-1915 (Table P-PZ40)
9621.B79 Budi, Pjetër, 1566-1622 (Table P-PZ40)
Çajupi, Andon Zako, 1866-1930 see PG9621.Z3
Çomaga, Bamkë, 1931- see PG9621.A35
9621.D46 De Rada, Girolamo, 1814-1903 (Table P-PZ40)
9621.D7 Drenova, Aleksandër Stavre, 1872-1947 (Table P-PZ40)
9621.F5 Fishta, Gjergj, 1871-1940 (Table P-PZ40)
9621.F74 Frashëri, Naim, 1846-1900 (Table P-PZ40)
9621.G49 Gjeçov, Shtjefën, 1874-1929 (Table P-PZ40)
Goliku, Sazan, 1942- see PG9621.K5
9621.K5 Koçi, Pandeli, 1942- (Table P-PZ40)
9621.K646 Korça, Hafiz Ali, 1874-1957 (Table P-PZ40)
9621.M47 Migjeni, 1911-1938 (Table P-PZ40)
9621.M56 Mjedja, Ndre, 1866-1937 (Table P-PZ40)
9621.N47 Nikaj, Ndoc, 1864-1945 (Table P-PZ40)
Nikolla, Millosh Gjergj, 1911-1938 see PG9621.M47
9621.Q53 Qiriazi, Gjerasim, 1858-1894 (Table P-PZ40)
9621.S34 Şemseddin Sâmî, 1850-1904 (Table P-PZ40)
For Şemseddin's Turkish works see PL248.S359
9621.S48 Shiroka, Filip, 1859-1935 (Table P-PZ40)
9621.S593 Skiroi, Zef, 1865-1927 (Table P-PZ40)
9621.T75 Troukēs, Mētros, 1815-1898 (Table P-PZ40)
9621.V32 Variboba, Jul, 1724 or 5-1788 (Table P-PZ40)
9621.V34 Vasa, Pashko, 1825-1892 (Table P-PZ40)
9621.Z3 Zako, Andon, 1866-1930 (Table P-PZ40)
Local
For works, biography, and criticism of individual local authors, except North American see PG9621.A+
9631.A-Z By region, district, etc., A-Z

Albanian philology and languages
Literature
Local -- Continued
9634.A-Z By city, A-Z
Outside of Albania
9636 General works
9638.A-Z European countries, A-Z
9640-9649 United States and Canada (Table P-PZ24)
9650.A-Z Other, A-Z
Translations
(9661) From foreign languages into Albanian
see the original language
9665.A-Z From Albanian into foreign languages, A-Z

Uralic. Basque
Cf. PL1+ Ural-Altaic languages
Uralic. Finno-Ugric
Class here works dealing with the Uralic languages in general, as well as works dealing with both the Finnic and the Ugric languages.
For the Samoyedic languages see PH3801+
Philology
1 Periodicals. Societies. Serials
1.5 Congresses
Collected works (nonserial)
2 Sets of monographic works by various authors
2.Z5A-.Z5Z Studies in honor of a particular person or institution. Festschriften. By honoree, A-Z
3 Collected works of individual authors
4 Encyclopedias. Dictionaries
5 Philosophy. Theory. Methodology
7 History of philology
Biography
9.A2 Collective
9.A5-Z Individual, A-Z
Subarrange each by Table P-PZ50
Study and teaching
11 General works
12.A-Z By region or country, A-Z
13 General works
Languages
14 Treatises
15 History
16 Proto-Uralic language
17 Outlines, syllabi, etc.
18 Addresses, essays, lectures
Grammar
21 Historical. Comparative. Descriptive
23 Phonology. Phonetics
27 Morphology. Inflection. Accidence
31 Word formation. Suffixes, etc.
33 Noun. Adjective. Pronoun. Article. Numerals
35 Verb
41 Syntax
61 Prosody. Metrics. Rhythmics
65 Etymology. Lexicology
71 Dictionaries
79 Dialects
Literature
81 History and criticism

Uralic. Finno-Ugric
Literature -- Continued
(83) Folk literature
see GR93.5
85 Collections
87.A-Z Translations. By language, A-Z
Finnic. Baltic-Finnic
Class here works on the Finnic branch of the Finno-Ugric languages in general or on several of the Finnic languages treated collectively
91.A1-.A5 Collections
91.A6-Z General works
92 General special
93 Grammar. Treatises. Textbooks
96 Etymology. Lexicology
97 Dictionaries. Glossaries, etc.
Literature
98 History and criticism
(98.3) Folk literature
see GR
98.5 Collections
Finnish
101-123 Philology (Table P-PZ3a modified)
History of philology
Cf. PH125 History of the language
Biography, memoirs, etc.
117.A2 Collective
117.A5-Z Individual, A-Z
Subarrange each by Table P-PZ50
124-299 Language (Table P-PZ3b modified)
Add number in table to PH100
Grammar
Readers
136 Primary
137 Intermediate. Advanced
Style. Composition. Rhetoric
For study and teaching see PH119+
235 General works
Etymology
263 Dictionaries (exclusively etymological)
264.A-Z Special elements. By language, A-Z
264.A3 Foreign elements (General)
Cf. PH284 Dictionaries
Lexicography
271 Periodicals. Societies. Serials. Collections (nonserial)
273 General works
Biography of lexicographers see PH117.A2+

Finnish
Language
Lexicography -- Continued
273.5 Criticism, etc., of particular dictionaries
Dictionaries
Finnish (only)
275 General
276 Picture dictionaries
277 Supplementary dictionaries. Dictionaries of new words
278 Polyglot (Definitions in two or more languages)
279 Finnish-English; English-Finnish
281.A-Z Other Western European languages, A-Z
282.A-Z Finnish-Slavic; Slavic-Finnish. By Slavic language, A-Z
Dictionaries exclusively etymological see PH263
283 Dictionaries of names
Cf. CS2300+ Genealogy
284 Dictionaries of foreign words
For special languages see PH264.A+
Rhyming dictionaries
see PH258
285 Other special lists
Including glossaries, dictionaries of terms and phrases, word frequency lists, reverse indexes, and lists of abbreviations
Linguistic geography. Dialects, etc.
287 Linguistic geography
Dialects. Provincialisms, etc.
288 Treatises. Monographs. Studies
289 Grammar
291 Dictionaries
(292) Atlases. Maps
see class G
293.A-Z Special (local) dialects, A-Z
Slang. Argot
295 Collections
296 General works
297 Dictionaries. Lists
297.5 Texts
298.A-Z Special topics, A-Z
For list of Cutter numbers, see Table P-PZ2 421.A+
299.A-Z Special local, A-Z
Literature
History
300 Periodicals. Societies. Serials
Biography of critics, historians, etc.
300.5 Collective

Finnish
Literature
History
Biography of critics, historians, etc. -- Continued
300.52.A-Z Individual, A-Z
Subarrange each by Table P-PZ50
301 General works
302 General special
303 Collected essays
303.4.A-Z Relations to other literatures, A-Z
304 Biography (Collective)
306 Early to 1800
308 1800-
310 Poetry
311 Drama
312 Prose. Fiction, etc.
Folk literature
For general works on and collections of folk literature see GR200+
History and criticism
(315.A1-.A5) Periodicals. Societies. Serials
(315.A6-Z) Treatises
(316) Addresses, essays, lectures
Texts
(317) General
Poetry
319 General
Kalevala
323.A1 Editions. By date
323.A15 Early versions. Fragments. By editor
323.A2 Selections. By editor
323.A3 Special parts
Including Kullervon runot
324.A-Z Translations. By language, A-Z
Criticism
325 General works
326 Special topics
327.A-.Z3 Language. Metrics, etc.
327.Z5 Dictionaries, indexes, etc. By date
329 Kanteletar (Table P-PZ41)
330.A-Z Ballads, etc., A-Z
(335) Legends. Tales
(337.A-Z) Local. By region, place, etc., A-Z
(339.A-Z) Translations. By language, A-Z
340 Children's literature
Collections
341 General

Finnish
Literature
Collections -- Continued
342 Anthologies, etc.
By period
343 To 1800
344 1800-
Poetry
345 General
346 Anthologies, etc.
347 Drama
Prose
349 General
351 Fiction
Individual authors or works
353.A-Z Through 1800, A-Z
Subarrange individual authors by Table P-PZ40
Subarrange individual works by Table P-PZ43
355.A-Z 1801-2000, A-Z
Subarrange individual authors by Table P-PZ40
Subarrange individual works by Table P-PZ43
e. g.
355.A4 Ahlqvist, August, 1826-1889 (Table P-PZ40)
355.A42 Aho, Juhani, 1861-1921 (Table P-PZ40)
Brofeldt, Juhani, 1861-1921 see PH355.A42
355.C3 Canth, Minna (Table P-PZ40)
355.F5 Finne, Jalmari, 1874-1938 (Table P-PZ40)
355.I8 Ivalo, Santeri, 1866-1937 (Table P-PZ40)
355.J27 Järnefelt, Arvid,1861-1932 (Table P-PZ40)
355.K5 Kianto, Ilmari, 1874-1970 (Table P-PZ40)
355.K52 Kilpi, Volter, 1874-1939 (Table P-PZ40)
355.K548 Kivi, Aleksis, 1834-1872 (Table P-PZ40)
355.K5937 Korpela, Kaarlo (Table P-PZ40)
355.L32 Lassila, Maiju, 1868-1918 (Table P-PZ40)
355.L4898 Linder, Marie, 1840-1870 (Table P-PZ40)
355.P33 Pakkala, Teuvo, 1862-1925 (Table P-PZ40)
356.A-Z 2001- , A-Z
Subarrange individual authors by Table P-PZ40
Subarrange individual works by Table P-PZ43
Local
By region, province, or place
362.A-Z History. By region, province, or place, A-Z
364.A-Z Collections. By region, province, or place, A-Z
Outside of Finland
365 Soviet Union. Russia
366 Sweden
America

Finnish
Literature
Local
Outside of Finland
America -- Continued
History
381 General works
382 Special
Collections
383 General
384 Special
385 Individual authors
Translations
From foreign languages into Finnish
see the original language
From Finnish into foreign languages
Including translations of Finnish literature composed outside of Finland. Class translations of individual authors with the author
English
401.E1 General
401.E3 Poetry
401.E5 Drama
401.E8 Prose. Prose fiction
French
401.F1 General
401.F3 Poetry
401.F5 Drama
401.F8 Prose. Prose fiction
German
401.G1 General
401.G3 Poetry
401.G5 Drama
401.G8 Prose. Prose fiction
Russian
401.R1 General
401.R3 Poetry
401.R5 Drama
401.R8 Prose. Prose fiction
405.A-Z Other languages, A-Z
Karelian
Cf. PH327.A+ Language of Kalevala
Other Finnic languages and dialects
501.A1-.A5 Periodicals. Societies. Serials
501.A6-Z General works
502 General special
503 Grammar. Treatises. Textbooks

Other Finnic languages and dialects
Karelian -- Continued
505 Prosody. Metrics. Rhythmics
506 Etymology. Lexicology
507 Dictionaries. Glossaries, etc.
Dialects
507.4 General works
507.5.A-Z Special. By name or place, A-Z
Literature
508 History and criticism
(508.4) Folk literature
see GR
508.5 Collections
508.9.A-Z Individual authors or works, A-Z
Subarrange each author by Table P-PZ40
Subarrange each individual work by Table P-PZ43
509.A-Z Translations. By language, A-Z
Olonets
521.A1-.A5 Periodicals. Societies. Serials
521.A6-Z General works
522 General special
523 Grammar. Treatises. Textbooks
526 Etymology. Lexicology
527 Dictionaries. Glossaries, etc.
Dialects
527.4 General works
527.5.A-Z Special. By name or place, A-Z
Literature
528 History and criticism
(528.4) Folk literature
see GR
528.5 Collections
528.9.A-Z Individual authors or works, A-Z
Subarrange each author by Table P-PZ40
Subarrange each individual work by Table P-PZ43
529.A-Z Translations. By language, A-Z
Ludic
531.A1-.A5 Periodicals. Societies. Serials
531.A6-Z General works
532 General special
533 Grammar. Treatises. Textbooks
536 Etymology. Lexicology
537 Dictionaries. Glossaries, etc.
Dialects
537.4 General works
537.5.A-Z Special. By name or place, A-Z
Literature

Other Finnic languages and dialects
Ludic
Literature -- Continued
538 History and criticism
(538.4) Folk literature
see GR
538.5 Collections
538.9.A-Z Individual authors or works, A-Z
Subarrange each author by Table P-PZ40
Subarrange each individual work by Table P-PZ43
539.A-Z Translations. By language, A-Z
Veps
541.A1-.A5 Periodicals. Societies. Serials
541.A6-Z General works
542 General special
543 Grammar. Treatises. Textbooks
546 Etymology. Lexicology
547 Dictionaries. Glossaries, etc.
Dialects
547.4 General works
547.5.A-Z Special. By name or place, A-Z
Literature
548 History and criticism
(548.4) Folk literature
see GR
548.5 Collections
548.9.A-Z Individual authors or works, A-Z
Subarrange each author by Table P-PZ40
Subarrange each individual work by Table P-PZ43
549.A-Z Translations. By language, A-Z
Ingrian
551.A1-.A5 Periodicals. Societies. Serials
551.A6-Z General works
552 General special
553 Grammar. Treatises. Textbooks
556 Etymology. Lexicology
557 Dictionaries. Glossaries, etc.
Dialects
557.4 General works
557.5.A-Z Special. By name or place, A-Z
Literature
558 History and criticism
(558.4) Folk literature
see GR
558.5 Collections

Other Finnic languages and dialects
Ingrian
Literature -- Continued
558.9.A-Z Individual authors or works, A-Z
Subarrange each author by Table P-PZ40
Subarrange each individual work by Table P-PZ43
559.A-Z Translations. By language, A-Z
Votic
561.A1-.A5 Periodicals. Societies. Serials
561.A6-Z General works
562 General special
563 Grammar. Treatises. Textbooks
566 Etymology. Lexicology
567 Dictionaries. Glossaries, etc.
Dialects
567.4 General works
567.5.A-Z Special. By name or place, A-Z
Literature
568 History and criticism
(568.4) Folk literature
see GR
568.5 Collections
568.9.A-Z Individual authors or works, A-Z
Subarrange each author by Table P-PZ40
Subarrange each individual work by Table P-PZ43
569.A-Z Translations. By language, A-Z
Livonian
581.A1-.A5 Periodicals. Societies. Serials
581.A6-Z General works
582 General special
583 Grammar. Treatises. Textbooks
586 Etymology. Lexicology
587 Dictionaries. Glossaries, etc.
Dialects
587.4 General works
587.5.A-Z Special. By name or place, A-Z
Literature
588 History and criticism
(588.4) Folk literature
see GR
588.5 Collections
588.9.A-Z Individual authors or works, A-Z
Subarrange each author by Table P-PZ40
Subarrange each individual work by Table P-PZ43
589.A-Z Translations. By language, A-Z
Estonian
601-629 Language (Table P-PZ6 modified)

Other Finnic languages and dialects
Estonian
Language -- Continued
Grammar
610 Textbooks. Exercises. Conversation
611 Readers
612 Phonology. Phonetics
612.5 Transliteration
Literature
History
630 Periodicals. Societies. Serials
630.2 Encyclopedias. Dictionaries
Biography of critics, historians, etc.
630.5 Collective
630.52.A-Z Individual, A-Z
Subarrange each by Table P-PZ50
631 General works
632 General special
633 Biography (Collective)
By period
633.5 Early to 1800
633.6 19th century
633.7 20th century
633.8 21st century
635 Poetry
637 Drama
639 Prose. Fiction
Folk literature
For general works on and collections of folk literature see subclass GR
History
(641.A1-.A5) Periodicals. Societies. Serials
(641.A6-Z) Treatises
642 Folk songs. Folk poetry
Collections of texts
(643) General
645 Poetry
(655) Legends. Tales
(656.A-Z) Local. By region, province, etc., A-Z
(659.A-Z) Translations. By language, A-Z
660 Juvenile literature (General)
For special genres, see the genre
Collections
661 General
662 Poetry
663 Drama
664 Prose

Other Finnic languages and dialects
Estonian
Literature -- Continued
Individual authors or works
665.A-Z Through 1960, A-Z
Subarrange each author by Table P-PZ40 unless otherwise specified
e. g.
665.A78 Aspe, Elizabeth, 1860-1927 (Table P-PZ40)
665.B3 Barbarus, Johannes, 1890-1946 (Table P-PZ40)
665.J32 Jakobson, Carl Robert, 1841-1882 (Table P-PZ40)
665.K28 Kalmus, Ain (Table P-PZ40)
665.K47 Kitzberg, August, 1855-1927 (Table P-PZ40)
665.K6 Koidula, Lydia, 1843-1886 (Table P-PZ40)
665.K68 Kreutzwald, Friedrich Reinhold, 1803-1882 (Table P-PZ40)
665.L47 Liiv, Juhan, 1864-1913 (Table P-PZ40)
Mand, Ewald see PH665.K28
665.M32 Mändmets, Jakob, 1871-1930 (Table P-PZ40)
665.P33 Pärn, J., 1843-1916 (Table P-PZ40)
665.S19 Saal, Andres (Table P-PZ40)
665.T3 Tamm, Jakob, 1861-1907 (Table P-PZ40)
665.T58 Tõnisson, Mats, 1853-1915 (Table P-PZ40)
Vares-Barbarus, Johannes see PH665.B3
665.V48 Vilde, Eduard, 1865-1933 (Table P-PZ40)
666-666.36 1961-2000 (Table P-PZ29 modified)
666.25 O
Õnnepalu, Tõnu, 1962- see PH666.3.O33
666.3 T
666.3.O33 Tode, Emil, 1962- (Table P-PZ40)
667-667.36 2001- (Table P-PZ29)
669.A-Z Local. By region, province, etc., A-Z
669.5.A-Z Local. By city, A-Z
Outside of Estonia
670 General works
670.5.A-Z Individual countries, A-Z
671.A-Z Translations. By language, A-Z
Sami
701-729 Language (Table P-PZ6 modified)
Grammar
710 Textbooks. Exercises. Conversation
711 Readers
712 Phonology. Phonetics
712.5 Transliteration
Linguistic geography. Dialects
727 General works
728.A-Z Special dialects, A-Z

Other Finnic languages and dialects
Sami
Language
Linguistic geography. Dialects
Special dialects, A-Z -- Continued

728.A74 Arjeplog
728.I52 Inari
728.K54 Kildin
728.L84 Lule
728.S57 Skolt
728.S68 Southern Sami

Literature
731 History and criticism
(732) Folk literature
see GR
733 Collections
734.A-Z Individual authors or works, A-Z
Subarrange each author by Table P-PZ40 unless otherwise specified
735.A-Z Translations. By language, A-Z

Mordvin
751-779 Language (Table P-PZ6 modified)
Grammar
760 Textbooks. Exercises. Conversation
761 Readers
762 Phonology. Phonetics
762.2 Orthography. Spelling
762.5 Transliteration
Linguistic geography. Dialects
777 General works
778.A-Z Special dialects, A-Z
778.E8-.E895 Erzya (Table P-PZ16a)
778.M6-.M695 Moksha (Table P-PZ16a)

Literature
781 History and criticism
(782) Folk literature
see GR
783 Collections
784.A-Z Individual authors or works, A-Z
Subarrange each author by Table P-PZ40
Subarrange each individual work by Table P-PZ43
785.A-Z Translations. By language, A-Z

790 Merya

Mari
Language
801.A2 Periodicals. Serials
801.A3 Societies

Other Finnic languages and dialects
Mari
Language -- Continued
801.A4-.A5 Collected works (nonserial)
801.A6-Z General works
802 General special
Includes Script. Transliteration
803 Grammar. Treatises. Textbooks
806 Etymology. Lexicology
807 Dictionaries. Glossaries, etc.
Dialects
807.4 General works
807.5.A-Z Special. By name or place, A-Z
Literature
History
811 General works
812 General special
Folk literature
see GR
(814) History
Texts
(815) General works
see GR
816 Poetry. Folk songs
(819.A-Z) Translations. By language, A-Z
Collections
821 General
824 Poetry
825 Drama
826 Prose
827.A-Z Individual authors or works, A-Z
Subarrange each author by Table P-PZ40
Subarrange each individual work by Table P-PZ43
Translations
From foreign language into Mari
see the original language
835-836 From Mari into foreign languages (Table P-PZ30)
Permic
1001-1004 General works (Table P-PZ14)
Komi
1051.A1-.A5 Periodicals. Societies. Serials
1051.A6-Z General works
1052 General special
1053 Grammar. Treatises. Textbooks
1056 Etymology. Lexicology
1057 Dictionaries. Glossaries, etc.
Dialects

Other Finnic languages and dialects
Permic
Komi
Dialects -- Continued
1057.4 General works
1057.5.A-Z Special. By name or place, A-Z
Literature
1058 History and criticism
(1058.4) Folk literature
see GR
1058.5 Collections
1058.9.A-Z Individual authors or works, A-Z
Subarrange each author by Table P-PZ40
Subarrange each individual work by Table P-PZ43
e.g.
1058.9.K85 Kuratov, Ivan Alekseevich, 1839-1875 (Table P-PZ40)
1059.A-Z Translations. By language, A-Z
Komi-Permyak
1071.A1-.A5 Periodicals. Societies. Serials
1071.A6-Z General works
1072 General special
1073 Grammar. Treatises. Textbooks
1076 Etymology. Lexicology
1077 Dictionaries. Glossaries, etc.
Dialects
1077.4 General works
1077.5.A-Z Special. By name or place, A-Z
Literature
1078 History and criticism
(1078.4) Folk literature
see GR
1078.5 Collections
1078.9.A-Z Individual authors or works, A-Z
Subarrange individual authors by Table P-PZ40
Subarrange individual works by Table P-PZ43
1079.A-Z Translations. By language, A-Z
Udmurt
1101.A1-.A5 Periodicals. Societies. Serials
1101.A6-Z General works
1102 General special
1103 Grammar. Treatises. Textbooks
1106 Etymology. Lexicology
1107 Dictionaries. Glossaries, etc.
Dialects
1107.4 General works
1107.5.A-Z Special. By name or place, A-Z

Other Finnic languages and dialects
Permic
Udmurt -- Continued
Literature
1108 History and criticism
(1108.4) Folk literature
see GR
1108.5 Collections
1108.9.A-Z Individual authors or works, A-Z
Subarrange individual authors by Table P-PZ40
Subarrange individual works by Table P-PZ43
1109.A-Z Translations. By language, A-Z
Ugric languages
Class here works on Mansi, Khanty, and Hungarian treated collectively
1201-1229 General (Table P-PZ6 modified)
Grammar
1210 Textbooks. Exercises. Conversation
1211 Readers
1212 Phonology. Phonetics
1212.5 Transliteration
Ob-Ugric
1251-1254 General (Table P-PZ14)
Mansi
1301.A1-.A5 Periodicals. Societies. Serials
1301.A6-Z General works
1302 General special
1303 Grammar. Treatises. Textbooks
1306 Etymology. Lexicology
1307 Dictionaries. Glossaries, etc.
Dialects
1307.4 General works
1307.5.A-Z Special. By name or place, A-Z
Literature
1308 History and criticism
(1308.4) Folk literature
see GR
1308.5 Collections
1308.9.A-Z Individual authors or works, A-Z
Subarrange individual authors by Table P-PZ40
Subarrange individual works by Table P-PZ43
1309.A-Z Translations. By language, A-Z
Khanty
1401.A1-.A5 Periodicals. Societies. Serials
1401.A6-Z General works
1402 General special
1403 Grammar. Treatises. Textbooks

	Ugric languages
	Ob-Ugric
	Khanty -- Continued
1406	Etymology. Lexicology
1407	Dictionaries. Glossaries, etc.
	Dialects
1407.4	General works
1407.5.A-Z	Special. By name or place, A-Z
	Literature
1408	History and criticism
(1408.4)	Folk literature see GR
1408.5	Collections
1408.9.A-Z	Individual authors or works, A-Z Subarrange each author by Table P-PZ40 Subarrange each individual work by Table P-PZ43
1409.A-Z	Translations. By language, A-Z
	Hungarian
2001-2071	Philology (Table P-PZ1a modified)
	History of philology Cf. PH2075+ History of the language
	Biography, memoirs, etc.
2063	Collective
2064.A-Z	Individual, A-Z Subarrange each by Table P-PZ50
	Study and teaching. Research
2065	General works
	By period For period of study, teaching, or research see PH2053+ For period of history of the language see PH2077+
2073-2830	Language (Table P-PZ1b modified) Add number in table to PH2000
2097	Script Including Old Hungarian runic script
	Grammar
	General works
2103	Early through 1850
2105	1851-
	Textbooks
2109	Early through 1850
2111	1851-2000
2112	2001-
	Alphabet
	Vowels
2155	General works
2156	Vowel harmony

Hungarian
Language -- Continued
Style. Composition. Rhetoric
For study and teaching see PH2065+
2410 General works
Etymology
2580 Dictionaries (exclusively etymological)
2582.A-Z Special elements. By language, A-Z
2582.A3 Foreign elements (General)
Cf. PH2670 Dictionaries
Lexicography
2601 Collections (of studies, etc.)
2611 General works. Treatises. History
Biography of lexicographers see PH2063+
Dictionaries
Hungarian (only)
2625 General
2628 Minor, abridged, school dictionaries
2629 Picture dictionaries
Supplementary dictionaries. Dictionaries of new words
2630 Treatises
2631 Dictionaries. Glossaries
Interlingual
2635 Polyglot (Definitions in two or more languages)
Bilingual
Classify with language less known
Hungarian-Latin; Latin-Hungarian
2637.A2 Early to 1500 (Glossaries)
2637.A5-Z 1500-
2640 Hungarian-English; English-Hungarian
2645.A-Z Other Western European languages. By language, A-Z
2647.A-Z Hungarian-Slavic; Slavic-Hungarian. By Slavic language, A-Z
Special dictionaries
Dictionaries exclusively etymological see PH2580
(2655) Dictionaries of particular authors
see the author in PH3194+
2660 Dictionaries of names
Cf. CS2300+ Personal and family names
Cf. PH2673 Foreign names
2667 Dictionaries, etc., of obsolete or archaic words
Dictionaries of foreign words
2670 General works
2673 Names
Special. By language see PH2582.A+

Hungarian
Language
Lexicography
Dictionaries
Special dictionaries -- Continued
Rhyming dictionaries
see PH2519
Special lists. Terms and phrases
2680 Miscellaneous
(2683.A-Z) By subject
see the subject in classes A-N, Q-Z
2691 Other
2693 Abbreviations, Lists of
Linguistic geography. Dialects
2700 Linguistic geography
Dialects. Provincialisms, etc.
2701 Periodicals. Societies. Serials
2707 Collections of texts
2711 General works
Grammar
2713 General works
2715 Phonology. Phonetics
2717 Morphology. Inflection. Accidence
2731 Syntax
2735 Other
2740 Dictionaries
(2745) Atlases. Maps
see class G
Special dialects
2751-2755 Szeklers (Table P-PZ9)
2761.A-Z Other. By region, province, etc., A-Z
Slang. Argot
2800 General works
2830.A-Z Special topics, A-Z
2830.O27 Obscene words
2830.S64 Soldiers' language
Literature
3001 Periodicals. Serials
(3002) Yearbooks
see PH3001
3003 Societies
Collected works (nonserial)
3005 Series. Monographs by various authors
3006 Individual authors (Collected works, studies, etc.)
3007 Encyclopedias. Dictionaries
3009 Study and teaching
3009.Z9 Audiovisual materials

Hungarian
Literature -- Continued
Biography of scholars, teachers, etc.
3010.4 Collective
3010.5.A-Z Individual, A-Z
Subarrange each by Table P-PZ50
History
3012 General works
3013 Outlines, syllabi, etc.
3015 Collected essays
3017 Addresses, essays, lectures
3019 Relation to history, civilization, culture, etc.
Relation to other literatures
3020 General
3021 Translations (as subject)
Treatment of special subjects, classes, etc.
3023.A-Z Subjects, A-Z
3023.C48 Christianity
3023.E34 Eastern Europe
3023.E5 Enlightenment
3023.M53 Middle class
3023.P64 Poland
3023.R3 Realism
3023.S94 Symbolism
3023.S97 Szántód-fürdötelep
3024.A-Z Classes and ethnic groups, A-Z
3024.G47 German
3024.J4 Jews
3024.P7 Priests
3024.P8 Puritans
3024.W65 Women
3025.A-Z Special characters, persons, etc., A-Z
Biography
3028 Collective
Individual see PH3194+
3030 Memoirs. Letters, etc.
3032 Literary landmarks. Homes and haunts of authors
3034 Women authors. Literary relations of women
By period
3036 Origins. Early to 1800
19th and 20th centuries
3042 General works
3053.A-Z Special topics, A-Z
3053.D69 Dózsa, György, ca. 1470-ca. 1514
3053.E64 Epic literature
3053.E88 Experimental literature
3053.E9 Expressionism

Hungarian
Literature
History
By period
19th and 20th centuries
Special topics, A-Z -- Continued

3053.N3 Nationalism
3053.P64 Politics
3053.R4 Realism
3053.R7 Romanticism
3053.S6 Socialism
3053.S64 Soldiers
3053.S9 Surrealism
3053.W67 World War I

21st century

3055 General works
3056.A-Z Special topics, A-Z

Poetry

3062 General works
3068 16th-18th centuries
3070 19th-20th centuries
3072 21st century
3078 Epic
3080 Lyric
3082 Other

3084 Drama

Prose. Fiction

3098 General
3100 Early to 1800
3102 19th century
3104 20th century
3106 21st century

3116 Wit and humor

Folk literature

For general works on and collections of folk literature see GR154.5+

History

(3122.A1-.A5) Periodicals. Societies. Serials
(3122.A6-Z) General works
(3123) Addresses, essays, lectures

Collections of texts

(3124) General
3125 Folk songs
(3126) Legends. Tales
(3128.A-Z) Local. By region, etc., A-Z
(3129.A-Z) Translations. By language, A-Z

Hungarian
Literature
History -- Continued
3130 Juvenile literature (General)
For special genres, see the genre
Collections
3132 General
3136 Selections. Anthologies
3138.A-Z Special classes of authors, A-Z
3138.J48 Jews
By period
3141 Early to ca. 1800
3144 1800-2000
3145 2001-
Poetry
3151 General
3152 Selections. Anthologies
By period
3156 Early to ca. 1800
3158 1801-
Special
Epic
3160 General
3161 Ballads. Kurucz poetry
Cf. PH3125 Folk songs
3162 Lyric
3163 Other
3164.A-Z By subject or form, A-Z
3164.B33 Babits, Mihály, 1883-1941
3164.B37 Bartók, Béla, 1881-1945
3164.C48 Children's poetry
3164.E75 Erotic poetry
3164.H5 Historical, political, patriotic poetry
3164.K38 Kazinczy, Ferenc, 1759-1831
3164.L32 Labor. Working class
3164.L6 Love
3164.M6 Mothers
3164.M8 Music
3164.N37 Nature
3164.O3 Occasional verse
3164.R3 Radnóti, Miklós, 1909-1944
3164.R4 Religious poetry
3164.V58 Visual poetry
3164.W37 War
Working class see PH3164.L32
Drama
3165 General

Hungarian
Literature
Collections
Drama -- Continued
3166 Selections. Anthologies
3167 Early to 1800
(3169) 1800-
see PH3165
3171.A-Z Special types or topics, A-Z
3171.O53 One-act plays
3171.R33 Radio plays
3171.T44 Television plays
Prose
3172 General
3173 Selections. Anthologies
3174 Early to 1800
(3175) 1800-
see PH3172
Fiction
3176 General
3177 Short stories
3180 Oratory
3182 Letters
3185 Essays
3186 Wit and humor
3188 Miscellany
Individual authors or works
3194.A-Z Early to ca. 1800, A-Z
Subarrange each author by Table P-PZ40 unless otherwise specified
e.g.
3194.A46 Amade, Antal, várkonyi, báró, 1676-1737 (Table P-PZ40)
3194.A47 Amade, László, 1704-1764 (Table P-PZ40)
3194.A5 Ányos, Pál, 1756-1784 (Table P-PZ40)
3194.B3 Balassa, Bálint, báro, 1551-1594 (Table P-PZ40)
3194.B33 Bároczi, Sándor (Table P-PZ40)
3194.B4 Bessenyei, György, 1747-1811 (Table P-PZ40)
3194.B43 Bethlen, Miklós, 1642-1716 (Table P-PZ40)
3194.B6 Bornemisza, Péter, 1535-1584 (Table P-PZ40)
3194.C7 Csáktornyai, Mátyás, 16th cent. (Table P-PZ40)
3194.C8 Csokonai Vitéz, Mihály, 1773-1805 (Table P-PZ40)
3194.F3 Faludi, Ferenc, 1704-1779 (Table P-PZ40)
3194.G8 Gvadányi, József, gróf, 1725-1801 (Table P-PZ40)
3194.H2-.H3 Halotti Beszéd és Könyörgés (Table P-PZ43a)
3194.H45 Hermányi Dienes, József, 1699-1763 (Table P-PZ40)
3194.K27 Kalmár, György, b. 1726 (Table P-PZ40)

Hungarian
Literature
Individual authors or works
Early to ca. 1800, A-Z -- Continued

3194.K64 Kónyi, János (Table P-PZ40)
3194.M28 Marosvásárhelyi Sorok (Table P-PZ40)
3194.M5 Mikes, Kelemen, 1690-1761 (Table P-PZ40)
3194.M55 Miskolczi, Gáspár, b. 1628 (Table P-PZ40)
3194.O42-.O423 Ómagyar Mária-siralom (Table P-PZ43)
3194.P23 Pálóczi Horváth, Ádám, 1760-1820 (Table P-PZ40)
3194.P24 Pápai Páriz, Ferenc, 1649-1716 (Table P-PZ40)
3194.T55 Tinódi, Sebestyén, d. 1556 (Table P-PZ40)
3194.T68 Tóth, István, 1710?-1772 (Table P-PZ40)
3194.V52 Virág, Benedek (Table P-PZ40)
3194.W37 Wathay, Ferenc, 1568-1606 (Table P-PZ40)
3194.Z8 Zrínyi, Miklós, gróf, 1620-1664 (Table P-PZ40)

1801-2000

3201.A-Z Anonymous works, A-Z
Subarrange each work by Table P-PZ43
3202 A - Arany
Subarrange individual authors by Table P-PZ40
e. g.
3202.A5 Ambrus, Zoltán, 1861-1932 (Table P-PZ40)

Arany, János, 1817-1882
Editions. By date
3205.A1 Collected and selected works
3205.A2 Epic poems
3205.A3 Minor epic poems, ballads
3205.A4 Lyric poems
(3205.Z5) Translations of foreign works
see PN6065.H8 or author
3206.A-Z Single works, A-Z
3207.A-Z Translations. By language, A-Z
Biography. Criticism, etc.
3208 General ("Life and works")
3209 Criticism
3213 Arany - Eötvös, J.
Subarrange individual authors by Table P-PZ40
e. g.
3213.B2 Bajza, József (Table P-PZ40)
3213.B24 Bánffy, Miklós, 1874-1950 (Table P-PZ40)
3213.B2936 Barcsa, János, 1871-1910 (Table P-PZ40)
3213.B3597 Benedek, Elek, 1859-1929 (Table P-PZ40)
3213.B4 Berzsenyi, Dániel, 1776-1836 (Table P-PZ40)
3213.B7 Bródy, Sándor, 1863-1924 (Table P-PZ40)
3213.C84 Czóbel, Minka, 1854-1947 (Table P-PZ40)
3213.C85 Czuczor, Gergely, 1800-1866 (Table P-PZ40)

Hungarian
Literature
Individual authors or works
1801-2000 -- Continued
Eötvös, József, báró, 1813-1871
Editions. By date
3220.A1 Collected works (Comprehensive)
3220.A2 Literary works (Collected)
3220.A3 Fiction
3220.A4 Other prose works. Orations
For specific subjects see the subject
3220.A5 Poems
(3220.A6) Translations of foreign literature
see PN6065.H8 or author
3221.A-Z Single works, A-Z
3222.A-Z Translations. By language, A-Z
Biography. Criticism, etc.
3223 General ("Life and works")
3224 Criticism
3241 Eötvös, J. - Jókai
Subarrange individual authors by Table P-PZ40
e. g.
3241.E6 Eötvös, Károly, 1842-1916 (Table P-PZ40)
3241.E619 Erdélyi, János, 1814-1868 (Table P-PZ40)
3241.F3 Fáy, András, 1786-1864 (Table P-PZ40)
3241.F343 Fazekas, Mihály, 1766-1828 (Table P-PZ40)
3241.G3 Garay, János, 1812-1853 (Table P-PZ40)
3241.G4 Gárodnyi, Géza, 1863-1922 (Table P-PZ40)
3241.G67 Gozsdu, Elek, 1849-1919 (Table P-PZ40)
3241.H35 Heltai, Jenő, 1871-1957 (Table P-PZ40)
3241.H4 Herczeg, Ferenc, 1863-1954 (Table P-PZ40)
3241.J256 Jámbor, Pál, 1821-1897 (Table P-PZ40)
Jókai, Mór, 1825-1904
Editions. By date
3260.A1 Collected works
Including collected novels
3260.A2 Selected works or novels
3260.A3 Selections. Anthologies
3260.A5 Plays
3260.A6 Poems
3260.A7 Prose (other than novels)
For political treatises, see subclass DB
3261.A-Z Single works, A-Z
3270.A-Z Translations. By language, A-Z
Biography. Criticism, etc.
3273 General ("Life and works")
3274 Criticism

Hungarian
Literature
Individual authors or works
1801-2000 -- Continued

3281 Jókai - Molnár, F.
Subarrange individual authors by Table P-PZ40
e. g.
3281.J8 Justh, Zsigmond, 1863-1894 (Table P-PZ40)
3281.K235445 Karay, Ilona, 1866-1881 (Table P-PZ40)
3281.K245 Katona, József, 1792-1830 (Table P-PZ40)
3281.K25 Kazinczy, Ferencz, 1759-1831 (Table P-PZ40)
3281.K3 Kemény, Zsigmond, báró, 1814-1875 (Table P-PZ40)
3281.K4 Kisfaludy, Károly, 1788-1830 (Table P-PZ40)
3281.K5 Kisfaludy, Sándor, 1772-1844 (Table P-PZ40)
3281.K6 Kiss, József, 1843-1921 (Table P-PZ40)
3281.K68 Kölcsey, Antónia, 1821-1876 (Table P-PZ40)
3281.K7 Kölcsey, Ferenc, 1790-1838 (Table P-PZ40)
3281.K888 Kriza, János, 1811-1875 (Table P-PZ40)
3281.L67 Lévay, József, 1825-1918 (Table P-PZ40)
3281.M15 Madách, Imre, 1823-1864 (Table P-PZ40)
3281.M6 Mikszáth, Kálmán, 1847-1910 (Table P-PZ40)
Molnár, Eva, 1956- see PH3351.V355
Molnár, Ferenc, 1878-1952
3285.A1 Collected works. By date
3285.A6-Z Translations. By language, A-Z
3286 Selections. By date
3287.A-Z Separate works, A-Z
3288 Biography and criticism
3291 Molnár, F. - Petőfi, S.
Subarrange individual authors by Table P-PZ40
e. g.
3291.M486 Móricz, Pál, 1870-1936 (Table P-PZ40)
3291.N326 Nagy, Iván, 1824-1898 (Table P-PZ40)
3291.P28317 Papp, Dániel, 1865-1900 (Table P-PZ40)
3291.P465 Petelei, István, 1852-1910 (Table P-PZ40)
3291.P47 Péterfy, Jenő, 1850-1899 (Table P-PZ40)
3291.P49 Petőfi, István, 1825-1880 (Table P-PZ40)
Petőfi, Sándor, 1823-1849
Editions. By date
3300.A1 Collected works
3300.A2 Collected poems (Összes költeményei)
For collections of poems published by the author with specific titles see PH3304.A+
3300.A3 Selections. Anthologies

Hungarian
Literature
Individual authors or works
1801-2000
Petőfi, Sándor, 1823-1849
Editions. By date -- Continued

3301 Particular groups of poems
Including Narative poems (Elbeszélő költeményei); Patriotic and revolutionary poems (Hazafías költeményei); Unedited poems

3302 Fiction

3303 Miscellaneous works (Vegyes művek)

(3303.2) Translations of foreign literature
see PN6065.H8 or author

3304.A-Z Single works, A-Z

Translations

3305 English

3306.A-Z Other. By language, A-Z

Biography. Criticism, etc.

3307 General ("Life and works")

3308 Criticism

3310 Dictionaries, indexes, etc.

3321 Petőfi, S. - R
Subarrange individual authors by Table P-PZ40
e. g.

3321.P6 Podmaniczky, Frigyes, báró, 1824-1907 (Table P-PZ40)

3321.P8 Pulszky, Ferencz Aurelius, 1814-1897 (Table P-PZ40)

3321.R38 Ráth Végh, István, 1870-1959 (Table P-PZ40)

3351 S - Vörösmarty
Subarrange individual authors by Table P-PZ40
e. g.

3351.S6 Széchenyi, István, gróf, 1791-1860 (Table P-PZ40)

3351.S863 Szigligeti, Ede, 1814-1878 (Table P-PZ40)

3351.S96 Szomory, Dezső, 1869-1944 (Table P-PZ40)

3351.T496 Thury, Zoltán, 1870-1906 (Table P-PZ40)

3351.T54 Tömörkény, István, 1866-1917 (Table P-PZ40)

3351.T59 Tompa, Mihály, 1817-1868 (Table P-PZ40)

3351.T8 Tóth, Kálmán, 1831-1881 (Table P-PZ40)

3351.U39 Ujvári, Péter, 1869-1931 (Table P-PZ40)

3351.V22 Vajda, János, 1827-1897 (Table P-PZ40)

3351.V222 Vajda, Péter, 1808-1846 (Table P-PZ40)

3351.V324 Vasvári, Pál, 1826-1849 (Table P-PZ40)

3351.V355 Vavyan, Fable, 1956- (Table P-PZ40)

3351.V758 Vörös, Mihály, 1758-1830 (Table P-PZ40)

Vörösmarty, Mihály, 1800-1855

Hungarian
Literature
Individual authors or works
1801-2000
Vörösmarty, Mihály, 1800-1855 -- Continued
Editions. By date
3360.A1 Collected works
3360.A15 Selected works
Poems
3360.A2 Lyric
3360.A3 Epic
3360.A4 Dramas
3360.A5 Novels. Tales
(3360.A6) Translations from foreign literature
see PN6065.H8 or author
3361.A-Z Single works, A-Z
3362.A-Z Translations. By language, A-Z
Biography. Criticism, etc.
3363 General ("Life and works")
3364 Criticism
3381 Vörösmarty - Z
Subarrange individual authors by Table P-PZ40
3382-3382.36 2001- (Table P-PZ29)
Local
By region, province, or place
Including regions separated from Hungary in 1919
3402.A-Z History. By region, province, or place, A-Z
e. g.
3402.B8 Budapest
3402.S5 Slovakia
3402.T7 Transylvania
3402.V6 Vojvodina
3404.A-Z Collections. By region, province, or place, A-Z
Outside of Hungary
General
3407 History
3408 Collections
3409 Europe
America
History
3415 General works
3416 Special
Collections
3417 General
3418 Special
3419.A-Z Individual authors, A-Z
Subarrange each by Table P-PZ40

Hungarian
Literature
Local
Outside of Hungary -- Continued
3420 Asia
3425 Australia
3426 New Zealand
Translations
From foreign languages into Hungarian
see the original language
3441-3442 From Hungarian into foreign languages (Table P-PZ30)
Class translations of individual authors with the author
Samoyedic languages
3801-3809.5 General works (Table P-PZ8a)
Special languages
3812-3812.95 Enets (Table P-PZ15a)
3814-3814.95 Kamassin (Table P-PZ15a)
3815-3815.95 Mator (Table P-PZ15a)
3816-3816.95 Nenets (Table P-PZ15a)
3818-3818.95 Nganasan (Table P-PZ15a)
3820-3820.95 Selkup (Table P-PZ15a)
Basque
Philology
5001 Periodicals. Serials
5003 Societies. Congresses
Collected works (nonserial)
5005 Texts. Sources, etc.
Cf. PH5187.A3 Dialects
Monographs. Studies
5007 Various authors
5008.A-Z Studies in honor of a particular person or institution, A-Z
5009 Individual authors
5015 History of philology
Cf. PH5019 Study and teaching
Cf. PH5024 History of the language
Biography
5016 Collective
5017.A-Z Individual, A-Z
Subarrange each by Table P-PZ50
5019 Study and teaching
5022 General works
Language
5023 General. Relation to other languages
5024 History
5024.73 Political aspects
5024.75 Social aspects

Basque
Language -- Continued
Grammar
5031 Comprehensive works. Compends (Advanced)
5035 Textbooks. Exercises
5039 Readers
5039.17 Conversation and phrase books
Textbooks for foreign speakers
5039.3 General
5039.5.A-Z By language, A-Z
Phonology
5040 General works
Phonetics
5041 General works
5042 Palatalization
5044 Accent
Orthography. Spelling
5045 General works
5049 Spelling reform
5051 Alphabet. Vowels, consonants, etc.
Morphology. Inflection. Accidence
5059 General works
5061 Word formation. Derivation. Suffixes, etc.
Parts of speech (Morphology and syntax)
5070 General works
5071 Noun
5077 Adjective. Adverb. Comparison
5083 Pronoun
5085 Verb
5101 Particle
Syntax
5113 General works
5119 Sentences
5125 Clauses
Style. Composition. Rhetoric
For study and teaching see PH5019
5135 General works
5141 Vocabulary
5150 Translating
5153 Prosody. Metrics. Rhythmics
Etymology
5161 General works
5162 Names
For personal names see CS2300+ ; for place names, see G104+ (General) or classes D-F for names of specific continents or countries
5163 Dictionaries (exclusively etymological)

Basque
Language
Etymology -- Continued
5164.A-Z Special elements. By language, A-Z
5164.A3 Foreign elements (General)
5165 Semantics
5167 Synonyms. Antonyms. Paronyms. Homonyms
5169.A-.A Particular words, A-Z
Lexicography
5171 Collections (of studies)
5173 Treatises
Biography of lexicographers see PH5016+
Dictionaries
5175 Basque (only)
5177.A-Z Interlingual. By language, A-Z
5177.A1 Polyglot
5179 Special
For etymological dictionaries see PH5163
Linguistic geography. Dialects
5187.A1 Linguistic geography
Dialects. Provincialisms, etc.
5187.A3 Collections of texts
5187.A7-Z General works
(5188) Grammar
see PH5031+
(5191) Dictionaries
see PH5175+
(5192) Atlases. Maps
see class G
5193.A-Z Local. By region, place, etc., A-Z
Particular dialects
Biscayan
5201 Collections
5203 General works
5205 Grammar
5207 Dictionaries
5209 Other
Other
Guipúzcoan
5211 Collections
5213 General works
5215 Grammar
5217 Dictionaries
5219 Other
Labourdin
5221 Collections
5223 General works

Basque
Language
Linguistic geography. Dialects
Dialects. Provincialisms, etc.
Particular dialects
Other
Labourdin -- Continued
5225 Grammar
5227 Dictionaries
5229 Other
Navarrese
5231 Collections
5233 General works
5235 Grammar
5237 Dictionaries
5239 Other
Low Navarrese
5241 Collections
5243 General works
5245 Grammar
5247 Dictionaries
5249 Other
Souletin
5251 Collections
5253 General works
5255 Grammar
5257 Dictionaries
5259 Other
Literature
History
5280 Periodicals. Societies. Serials
5281 General works
5282 General special
5284 Biography (Collective)
By period
5286 Early to 1800
5287 1801-
5290 Poetry
5291 Drama
5292.A-Z Other, A-Z
5292.F5 Fiction
Folk literature
see GR137.3
(5295) History
(5296) Collections
5298 Children's literature
Collections

Basque
Literature
Collections -- Continued
5301 General
5303.A-Z Special classes of authors, A-Z
5303.C45 Children
5311 Poetry
5321 Drama
5331 Prose
5339 Individual authors or works, A-Z
Subarrange individual authors by Table P-PZ40
Subarrange individual works by Table P-PZ43
e. g.
5339.A6 Apaolaza, Antero, 1845-1908 (Table P-PZ40)
5339.A79 Ataño (Table P-PZ40)
5339.A917 Azkue, Resurrección María de, 1864-1951 (Table P-PZ40)
5339.B35 Barrutia, Pedro, 1682-1759 (Table P-PZ40)
5339.B46 Bengoechea, Fernando, 1764-1823 (Table P-PZ40)
Bustinza, Ebaristo see PH5339.K55
5339.D4 Dechepare, Bernat (Table P-PZ40)
5339.E58 Elicegui, Pedro José, 1840-1919 (Table P-PZ40)
5339.E59 Elissamburu, Jean Baptiste, 1828-1891 (Table P-PZ40)
5339.E67 Erauskin, Patxi, 1874-1945 (Table P-PZ40)
5339.E72 Errikotxia, 1855-1932 (Table P-PZ40)
5339.E85 Etxeita, Jose Manuel, 1842-1915 (Table P-PZ40)
5339.H57 Hiribarren, J. M. , 1810-1866 (Table P-PZ40)
5339.I47 Imaz, Alzo, 1811-1895 (Table P-PZ40)
5339.I6 Iparraguirre y Valerdi, José María de, 1820-1881 (Table P-PZ40)
5339.I66 Iraola Aristiguieta, Bitoriano, 1841-1919 (Table P-PZ40)
5339.I83 Iturriaga, Agustin Paskual, 1778-1851 (Table P-PZ40)
5339.K55 Kirikiño, 1866-1929 (Table P-PZ40)
5339.M57 Moguel y Urquiza, Juan Antonio de, 1745-1804 (Table P-PZ40)
5339.P47 Peñaflorida, Francisco Javier María de Munibe e Idiáquez, conde de, 1723-1785 (Table P-PZ40)
5339.T6 Topet-Etchahun, Pierre, 1786-1862 (Table P-PZ40)
5339.T84 Txirrita, 1860-1936 (Table P-PZ40)
5339.U5 Ulibarri y Galindez, José Paulo, 1775-1847 (Table P-PZ40)
5339.U7 Urruzuno Salegi, Pedro Migel, 1844-1923 (Table P-PZ40)
5339.Z27 Zabala, Alfonso Mária, 1847-1919 (Table P-PZ40)
Zapirain, Salbador see PH5339.A79
5339.Z78 Zubizarreta, Juan Maria, 1855-1905 (Table P-PZ40)
Translations

Basque
Literature
Translations -- Continued
From foreign languages into Basque
see the original language
5397-5398 From Basque into foreign languages (Table P-PZ30)
Local
5401.A-Z By region, province, county, A-Z
5431.A-Z By city, A-Z
America
5450-5469 United States and Canada (Table P-PZ23 modified)
Local
5467.A-Z By state, region, etc., A-Z
5468.A-Z By place, A-Z
5470 Spanish America
5480 Brazil
5490 Other

.xA1	Collected works. By date
(.xA13)	Selected works For selected works see PG1 .xA2
.xA15	Collected novels and stories. Collected tales. By date
.xA16	Collected essays, miscellanies, etc. By date
.xA17	Collected poems. By date
.xA19	Collected plays. By date
.xA2	Selected works. Selections. By date
.xA3-.xZ	Separate works. By Russian title, A-Z Subarrange by date

.x date	Texts. By date
.x2	Selections. By date
.x3	Criticism

A

C

INDEX

INDEX

H

I

INDEX

J

INDEX

S

Y

INDEX

U.S. GOVERNMENT PRINTING OFFICE: 2009–357–380/60038